PRAISE FOR THE FIRST

"Brilliant overview... A superbly argued book which presents all the facts... will intrigue fans of horror movies as well as social historians."

★★★★★

Film Review

"Exhaustive and very, very cool."

★★★★★

Kerrang!

"Comprehensive and informed... the authors deserve high praise."

Shivers

"Particularly interesting and relevant."

★★★★★★★★★★

Fortean Times

"Impressively researched and highly readable... a compelling piece of social history."

Video Watchdog

"Absorbing, excellently written and researched... definitive."

The Dark Side

"A disturbing and fascinating look at the peculiarity of Little England and the knee-jerk idiocy of our moral guardians."

★★★★★

SFX

"Several books have been devoted to this phenomenon, but this is the most intelligent, thoroughly researched and longest."

Psychotronic

"Intelligently and clearly written... likely to stand as the last word on the nasties brouhaha." [*Empire*'s pick of books of the last three months]

★★★★★

Empire

"A 'turn the page fast' slice of history that must nestle on any film watchers shelf."

BBC Radio

"A fascinating read... Excellent."

Dutch Courier

DAVID KEREKES & DAVID SLATER

CANNIBAL ERROR

ANTI-FILM PROPAGANDA AND THE 'VIDEO NASTIES' PANIC OF THE 1980s

HEADPRESS

A HEADPRESS BOOK
This edition published by Headpress in 2024, Oxford, United Kingdom.
Originally published in different form as *See No Evil: Banned Films and Video Controversy* in 2000 (reprinted 2001).
headoffice@headpress.com

CANNIBAL ERROR
Anti-Film Propaganda and the 'Video Nasties' Panic of the 1980s

Cover design and book layout: MARK CRITCHELL <mark.critchell@gmail.com>
The Publisher wishes to thank Gareth Wilson and Jennifer Wallis

10 9 8 7 6 5 4 3 2 1

A CIP catalogue record for this book is available from the British Library

ISBN 978-1-909394-95-7 paperback
ISBN 978-1-909394-96-4 ebook
ISBN NO-ISBN hardback

HEADPRESS. POP AND UNPOP CULTURE.

Exclusive NO-ISBN special editions and other items of interest are available at
HEADPRESS.COM

Also by David Kerekes & David Slater from Headpress:

Last Orgy by the Cemetery: A 'Video Nasties' Synopsis, Film By Shocking Film!
978-1-909394-97-1 (digital only)

Killing for Culture: From Edison to ISIS, A New History of Death on Film
978-1-909394-34-6 (paperback) / 978-1-909394-35-3 (digital)

Contents

Preface

THIS BOOK ISN'T an encyclopaedia of contentious films or an attempt to discuss every video that has had a run-in with the law or the British Board of Film Classification (BBFC). *Cannibal Error* is primarily a chronicle of video culture in Britain, and of political anti-film propaganda from the late seventies through to the end of the millennium. A substantial part deals with the Video Recordings Act 1984 and the so-called 'video nasties'. It was during this turbulent era – to paraphrase the little boy in one 'banned' film, *Shogun Assassin* – that everything changed forever.

The original edition was published as *See No Evil: Banned Films and Video Controversy* (Headpress, 2000). It concluded with the retirement of BBFC director James Ferman, a figure unpopular with filmmakers (he kept cutting their films) and later out of sorts with members of the British government and arguably the Board itself. In revising the book, the authors have stuck with the original framework and not diffused what, in hindsight, is a solid time-capsule of a key period of film and socio-political culture in Britain. Without Ferman the narrative changes and the 'video nasties' become another story. However, the inclusion of new material,

Bold statements and bold haircuts: *Shogun Assassin*.

notably the appendix, offers an insight into the Board today and a timely reflection on attitudes towards this volatile era.

A NOTE ON FILM TITLES

Titles commonly attributed to the 'video nasties' are not always the same titles that appear on the prints themselves, i.e. packaging might say *Late Night Trains* but the print says *Night Train Murders*. For clarity and uniformity, films appear under the titles they are best known by – the ones on video boxes and which were used by the Director of Public Prosecutions (DPP) when compiling their list of films liable to be prosecuted under the Obscene Publications Act 1959.

ACKNOWLEDGEMENTS

As per the original edition, extended thanks and gratitude go to Stefan Jaworzyn for the loan of illustrations, support and help, and to David Kenny for access to his interview with James Ferman, later the backbone of his documentary *Fear, Panic & Censorship* (A ShashMedia Production for Channel 4). For contributions to the text and speaking about their experiences, we thank William Black, Mikita Brottman, Steve Ellison, Carl Daft (Exploited), Richard King (Screen Edge), Christopher Glazebrook and Julian Upton. Julian kindly supplied interviews he had conducted with Steve Webber (VCL Video Services) and Iain Muspratt (Guild Home Video), which appear in this edition for the first time. Other new additions appear in the appendix: INTERVIEWS WITH THE BBFC, thank you David Hyman, Catherine Anderson, David Austin; ANATOMY OF A RAID, thank you David Flint; and 'VIDEO NASTIES' – WHERE ARE THEY NOW? thank you David Hinds.

We are also grateful to the following for assistance, newspaper clippings, assorted ephemera and information: Gerard Alexander, Douglas Baptie, Bruce Barnard, David Barraclough, KA Beer, Anton Black, Ray Brady, Paul Brown, Tim Buggie, Simon Collins, Jonathan Davies, David Greenall, David Gregory, Marie-Luce Giordani, Adrian Horrocks, David Huxley, David Hyman, Martin Jones, Paul Kevern, Chris Mikul, David Monaghan, Carl Nolan, Sun Paige, Steve Puchalski, Roger Sabin, Salvation Films (Chris Charlston, Marc Morris, Louise Ross), Mark Slater, David Lass, Shaun Kimber, Tristan Thompson, and Johnny Walker.

Many others deserve thanks but wish to remain anonymous. Some can be found under pseudonyms in the chapter BLACK MARKET AND PIRATES.

WHY 'CANNIBAL ERROR'?

The cannibal film as a genre was repeatedly presented by watchdogs and the media as a typical example of what constituted a 'video nasty', in that the subject matter was perceived as unsavoury and the gore often highly visible on the screen. The cannibalism in these films is fabricated and much of the supposedly accurate rituals are crass exaggeration, but a scene in Umberto Lenzi's 1981 *Cannibal Ferox* might be considered as a metaphor for the era covered in this book. Actor John Morghen has the top of his head removed and his brains consumed. New Guinea cannibals once held the belief that devouring the brains of the deceased would imbue them with that person's attributes – personality traits, skills and knowledge. In truth it was a potentially lethal practice. Ingesting prion proteins held within the brain matter could pass on a fatal spongiform encephalopathy called kuru. Anyone contaminated by kuru would slowly lose their mind before dying. In the mid 1980s, at the height of the 'video nasty' moral panic, there existed a widely held conviction that certain films may well pass on attributes to the persona of the viewer. The viewer, it was surmised, might absorb the personality traits of whatever villainous character was portrayed in the film. As one outraged mother declared, "These films have helped destroy my son's life. They must be banned before another boy's mind is infected by them." (See UNEASE). Cannibalism is no longer practised in New Guinea but this sense of the 'cannibal error' is a widely held belief even today.

John Morghen loses his mind in *Cannnibal Ferox*.

"The more you try to ban it the more it grows."

James Ferman, director of the BBFC 1975–1998

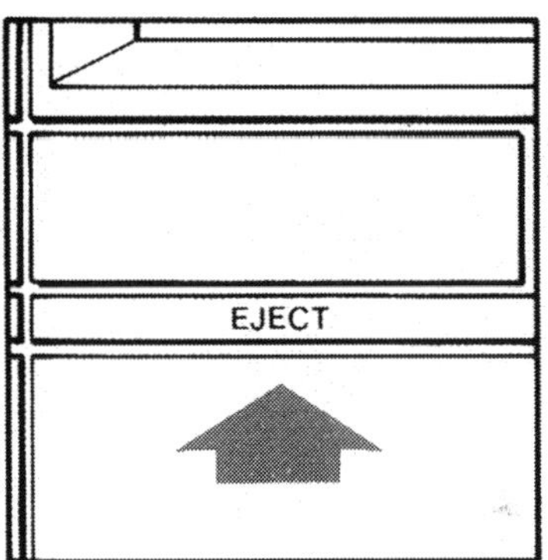

"Something huge, like an elephant."

James C. Wasson's *Night of the Demon* (1980)

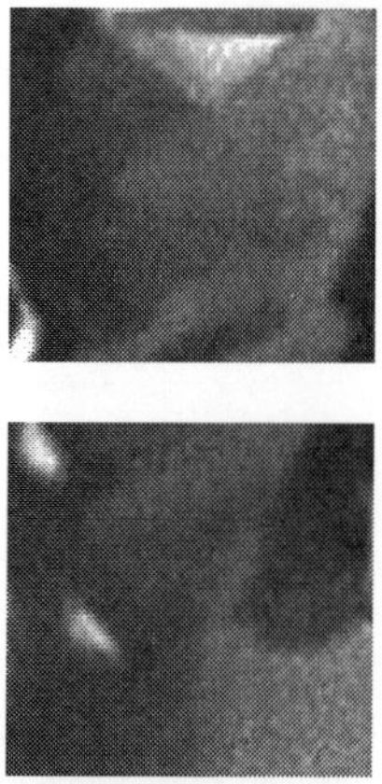

Beginnings

'TIME MARCHES ON!'

Beginnings

'TIME MARCHES ON!'

"Time marches on!"

TIME MARCHES ON! – this was a pronouncement made by the *International Film Guide* of 1982 in relation to the rapid encroachment of video in the film collector's marketplace, once the bastion of Super 8 and, to a lesser extent, 16mm. So swift was its encroachment that by the time the article appeared many cine specialists had folded or already switched to a dedicated video dealership. The reasons for this transition are numerous. On the face of it, escalating increases in the price of raw stock and labour intensive laboratory costs meant that Super 8 was unable to compete financially with pre-recorded videocassettes.[1] Video better domesticated home entertainment, with complete films in a single manageable cartridge as opposed to the 'digest' versions of movies or 'extracts' generally offered for Super 8 consumption.[2] The new technology was more user-friendly too, eliminating the necessity for darkened rooms, projectors and screens for viewing.

As interest rose dramatically through the early eighties, video ceased to be the reserve of film buffs. By 1983, close on six million video machines had found their way into homes across Britain. Fresh distribution outlets for films appeared with unerring regularity. Major film studios struggled to keep pace as upstart independents with little to lose and a lot to gain took the initiative and forced the market to expand. With film and distribution companies barely able to meet the demand for new product, all manner

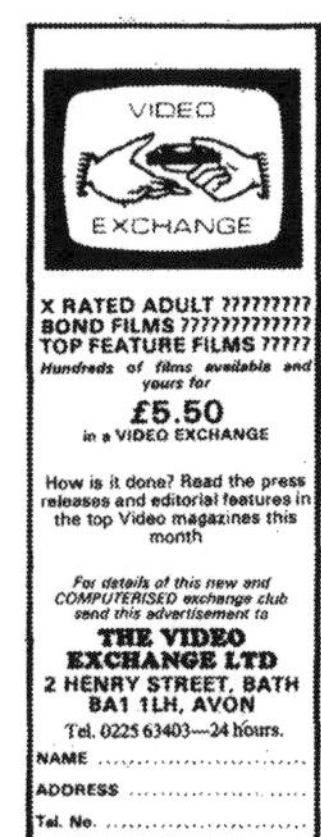

of diverse material found its way onto magnetic tape. It seemed that any topic, no matter how esoteric or specialist, was guaranteed a sizeable audience amongst video viewers. Documentaries on surrealist painters (*Monsieur Rene Magritte*), experimental graphics set to music (*Music-Image Odyssey*), home help guides (*Bar-B-Q*) and tutorials for everyone from Rubik's Cube enthusiasts (*You Too Can Do the Cube*) to budding guitarists, were promoted as major acquisitions in early video catalogues. Even *The Entertaining Electron*, an insight into the way television programmes were made and broadcast, and the 156-minute *The Mighty Micro*, had commercial potential thanks to video. British Home Video was a company specialising in teach-yourself home courses, with a selection of three-hour-long videocassettes devoted to subjects as diverse as motor mechanics, kung fu, medical advice and even video maintenance (which answered questions like "What is a tracking fault?"). Following the announcement in February 1981 of Prince Charles' marriage to Lady Diana Spencer,[3] video wasn't absent from the souvenir cash-ins of a country gripped by royal wedding fever. Michael Barratt Home Video Programmes offered "exclusive new sequences and intimate glimpses" in *Princess*,[4] while its companion release *The Story of Prince Charles and Lady Diana* traced the couple's "parallel life stories from birth up to the day of their engagement." *The Glittering Crowns* was The Electronic Publishing Company's first production for videocassette and featured the story of the monarchy in the twentieth century. Another company, World of Video, simply offered consumers of their thirty-minute guide to London landmarks an optional second sleeve that depicted the royal couple.

The demand for video meant that even promotional films – 'infomercials' by

another name – could be sold to the public, as in the case of Pedigree Petfood's *All You Need To Know About Dogs* and practical painting advice with *The Dulux Videoguide To Colouring Your Home*. Narration by TV favourites Edward Fox, Sir Huw Wheldon, Leslie Judd, and Johnny Ball gave many tapes a familiar, friendly feel.

Another addition to the video market came in the guise of the video magazine programme, a compilation of material in the manner of a television variety show, albeit more 'alternative' in keeping with the modern, cutting-edge medium on which it now existed. Indeed one of the first, a one-hour programme entitled *The Mad Tape* – containing a juggler of meat, a Wild West shootout, and a singing jukebox – was made primarily for TV but never broadcast. Another one-hour video magazine programme, *Red Tape*, hosted by "zany" comedian Keith Allen, promoted itself as "alternative television for the eighties." Within its line-up was an X-rated cartoon, a look at hang-gliding, *Star Trek* bloopers, and a bevy of topless girls. Along the same lines was *Rewind*, which Catalyst Video purported hit sales of almost 40,000. Quick to follow was *Rewind 2*, a one-hour programme on a three-hour tape, the incentive being that the purchaser would not only be entertained for an hour but also receive precious blank tape to use as they pleased. The fact the programme's running time was taken up with trailers for EMI movies lasting almost twenty minutes couldn't have impressed many viewers, however.

Disc jockey and popular entertainer Kenny Everett was the host and star of *The Kenny Everett Naughty Joke Box*, a live show recorded exclusively for release on video, whose content – famous comedians telling blue jokes, with some scantily clad ladies running about – was promoted by VideoSpace as going beyond the limit of broadcast television acceptability. Everett found success in television (reaching the audience that eluded his earlier small screen ventures) when he launched *The Kenny Everett Video Show* in 1978. Not only did it utilise state of the art video effects to bring the comedian's many grotesque characters to life, it also piqued interest with a title that incorporated the new buzz word: video.

With *Electric Blue*, the Electric Video company developed and specialised what it billed as "the world's first and original men's magazine on a videocassette." This "Electronic Sex for the eighties" was a series of highly successful video programmes[5] – which included nude wives, centrefolds, film clips (several starring Traci Lords) and sporting mishaps.[6] In spite of a slowmotion replay of Erica Rowe streaking across a Twickenham rugby pitch, and women riding a mechanical bull in the nude, the highlight of *Electric Blue* volume eight was "The World's First 3-D Centrefold." Coming with a free pair of 3-D glasses, this special seven-minute segment – filmed in Los Angeles and utilising new technology – was described by *Continental Film and Video Review*[7] as working "quite effectively at the press launch."[8]

The *Electric Blue* tapes inspired imitators, notably *Mirage* and *Shades of Blue*, "the

'All-American Video Magazine' aimed at the man who still likes his fruit ripe!" Following the Miss Nude Europe pageant held in Paris, a British model agent hit on the idea for *Miss Nude UK* – a series of video tapes of one-hour duration, each of which depicted four girls going about their daily routines, their pastimes and, of course, stripping off for the camera. Viewers were invited to vote for a girl from each tape and ultimately select Miss Nude UK.

Crest Films had a different tack with *Stag & Hen Night*, which attempted to redress the bias of the "girlie video magazines," and reach an audience of both sexes with the crossover implied in its title. Shot live (with psychedelic effects) and featuring two male strippers, two female strippers, a female impersonator and a comedian, *Stag & Hen Night* encouraged the home viewer to "find out what the other half gets up to"...

Aerobicise–The Beautiful Workout, the first original production from CIC Video and one that established a trend for glamorous aerobic workout tapes for years to come, promised to be desirable to the passive hot-blooded male viewer as well as the keep-fit enthusiast.[9] Unlike *Aerobicise*, many video tie-ins fell from public view as swiftly as they had materialised. Interactive video games were a fad resurrected on several occasions but always met with public indifference. Waddington turned their famous detective board game Cluedo into a not-so-famous video game (which required players to gather facts from scenes on the tape), while Tevele tried their luck with *Travel Bug* and *The Great Australian Horse Racing Game*. Using Fast Forward and Rewind, players of the former were required to complete a journey by air – courtesy of playing cards, a score sheet and video footage especially shot by a wildlife photographer; the latter required players to randomly stop the video tape on one of a number of pre-recorded horse races, placing a bet and then running the race to determine the winner.

Later, Scotch videocassettes ran a promotion in which they gave away a free £1 Ladbrokes betting voucher on selected blank tapes. "It costs the consumer nothing extra," said a spokesperson for Scotch, "and it provides a chance to have a bit of fun and – who knows? – win back the price of the cassette and a bit more besides." Other companies, notably those in tobacco and alcohol, saw an opportunity in video no longer open to them elsewhere. Given the ban on commercials for cigarettes and alcohol, video was for a time the only way these manufacturers could get their products on domestic TV screens. Holiday Video Brochures – a concept developed by Pebblebond International on behalf of the leading holiday tour operators – were the first tapes in the UK to feature such commercials. Stocked by travel agents and available to potential holiday goers on a free-of-charge rental basis, the overheads for Video Brochures were met with outside advertising. Not a fact lost on Viewpoint Ltd, a new company that announced to the press in late 1982 its plan to introduce advertising spots on pre-recorded cassettes, located before or after the tape's main feature.[10] Such a move was seen as an opportunity to keep rental costs down for consumers and help suppliers generate revenue for more and better films.[11]

Music and video were a natural combination, given that pop musicians were turning to ever more elaborate and controversial 'featurettes' in which to promote their releases (or, in the case of Buggles and Video Killed The Radio Star, lamenting the fact). *Making Michael Jackson's Thriller* was one of video's first success stories, selling 800,000 copies in the first two months of sale. But not all music/video pairings were harmonious: the world wasn't quite ready to switch vinyl for the 'video single', for instance, nor particularly interested in simultaneous LP and video releases, as in the case of Toni Basil's *Word of Mouth* album, priced at £29.95 on video and £3.99 on vinyl. The fad of the video jukebox served to distract patrons in pubs and clubs with a sometimes esoteric selection of audio-visual material. Manufactured by Thorn EMI, the video jukebox played clips from a videodisc (supplied by Albion Leisure Services in the UK). The unit was available originally in a standalone design, and later as a wall box with a 'hideaway' unit. Steve Webber, before he became Marketing Director of VCL Video Services, worked for Trans Vision Leasing, whose speciality was discotheques:

> The whole idea was you sold the whole thing to the discotheque – the TV set, the video player (U-matic at that time) and then you leased them the tapes. They got a new video tape every month. The musician's union hated us. But there were no rules. The tapes were pop promos that we put together to make one-hour programmes. The record company sent us master tapes. The only other company doing this was Intervision. We all went out to the discos and we were competing. That effectively was the business. We were charging hundreds of pounds and it wasn't easy.[12]

One author of this book recalls a video jukebox in a northern pub he frequented, and customers crowding around it, drinks in hands. Alas, the Camelot song-and-dance sketch from *Monty Python and the Holy Grail* couldn't sustain interest indefinitely and, despite its high profile, the plug was pulled on the 'VJB.'

At least one vicar in Britain considered that video films might help church services and turn around the steady decline in attendances. But families stayed away, no doubt glued to the home movies they had recently converted to video tape, an inspiration derived in part from *Middle Age Crazy*, a Canadian movie starring Ann-Margret as a woman who presents her husband with a video-biography of his life. Its screening on ITV in 1981 prompted one critic to comment: "Video is now starting to infiltrate even the traditional arts" – a viewpoint perhaps more suited to the idea of selling videocassettes of stage shows to theatre audiences, which Carnaby Video had proposed to the Apollo chain of theatres earlier in the year. In principle, each show's performance would be recorded, and the video then offered for sale in the foyer. The negotiations between the two companies came to nothing, but the concept found favour with the New Theatre in Oxford, who wouldn't offer original recordings as such but existing theatrical productions on video, comprising shows in their repertoire (such as *Oh Calcutta*, *The Mikado* and *HMS Pinafore*). Competitors in the 1982 Gillette London Marathon had the opportunity to buy the BBC's rush video release – which incorporated highlights from the previous year's race – at a discounted price. The idea met with greater success when cinemas offered patrons movies on videocassette – albeit not those movies currently playing. Alongside the soft drinks machines, the Odeon group installed dispensers in its foyers from which video tapes could be obtained. With a capacity to hold 270 videocassettes these dispensers from The UK Video Vending Corporation, directed at the "places where the public regularly visit," were operated via a special charge card. Although such machines weren't that common and only circulated for a brief period, the sale of videos in cinemas prompted at least one Odeon cinema (in central Manchester) to refurbish the foyer to accommodate a dedicated video store.

How much of an impact video would have on cinema attendance remained a concern.[13] But as early as 1981 – four years after the first domestic recorders had gone on sale in Britain – the threat that 'legitimate' cinema might be

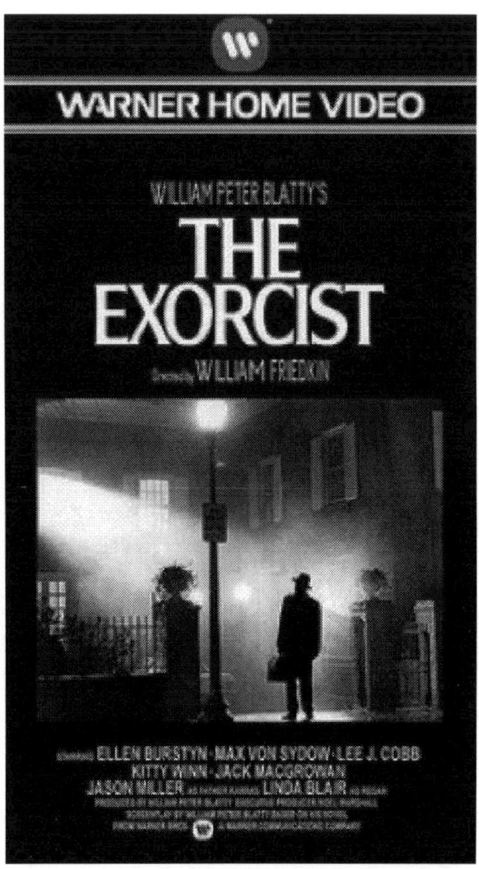

effectively wiped out was no longer an issue. Cinema attendance varied across Europe, fluctuating as it always did, with West Germany seeing a slump in 1981, while France enjoyed something of a boom. A survey carried out in Britain suggested that the availability on video of films like *The Exorcist* and *Every Which Way But Loose* had no adverse effect on audience attendance when the same films played the cinemas. Studios started to consider video a means to augment a film's revenue beyond its theatrical life, sometimes making up for poor box office returns. It was cost-effective, given that the audience for a film on video was pre-sold on publicity from theatrical advertising campaigns.

Iain Muspratt, former Managing Director of Guild Home Video reflects on the transition period:

> The studios were slow in responding to video, they were fixated, and probably still are, on 'theatrical'. They thought video was going to take the theatrical audience away. But what happened was the opposite. A lot of distributors bought the video rights to films and in order to create a platform, released them theatrically. So theatrical volumes actually went up, as well as attendance. There are a whole series of films that went to the cinema that never would have gone to the cinema if it wasn't for home video One film had been made by a Hollywood property developer, *The Stunt Man*. Fox had this on their shelves, they had distributed it theatrically and it hadn't done very well. So we bought the UK rights. It was very successful, and it went back onto the cinema circuits afterwards and became successful there too. We put money into *Scandalous*. *Irreconcilable Differences*. Both those we released theatrically as well, we had them on in Leicester Square for a week, at vast expense.[14]

TV advertisements for video releases started to appear in the spring of 1981.

As proprietor of Phoenix Home Leisure in the north of England – formerly Phoenix Film Services, one of the biggest 8mm libraries in the country – Steve Ellison recalls the formative years of video.

Published by Virgin in 1981, *The Complete Video Guide* offered consumers an introduction to the new home entertainment medium – hardware, software and also the illegal business. Author Tim Smith prophesied that 'future generations, in the home and in the classroom, will be brought up on video'.

> We were an established Super 8 library and did a lot of mail order and rental. What happened was that Intervision — who were distributors of Super 8 movies, and our suppliers — started renting videos through some of their retail outlets in London. Then they spread their wings throughout the country, going first to all the 8mm film libraries. I think I may have been the first video library in the country outside London because my Intervision account number was '001.'
>
> Other Super 8 suppliers got on the bandwagon, like Mountain Films, Derann and Iver.
>
> A lot of the stuff that they had rights for on Super 8, they transferred to video. There was a bit of a grey area about the rights, the films were vaguely public domain stuff, but that was what happened.
>
> And it sort of caught on with people who were hiring films on Super 8, and it kind of caught on a little bit with people who were buying equipment at the hardware places. But it was a few years before it really caught on big. Most people weren't in the habit of renting a film to watch at home. It was a whole new concept for movies — people watched television at home. It was probably 1979 or 1980 before it really started taking off. And then of course the whole thing exploded. Then we were very busy.[15]

Although the idea of a technological revolution had been anticipated some

TOP RENTAL

1. BLACK DEEP THROAT
2. THE REAL BRUCE LEE
3. UPS AND DOWNS OF A HANDYMAN
4. HARDWARE
5. CONFESSIONS OF A SEX KITTEN
6. MAID IN SWEDEN
7. NORTHVILLE CEMETRAY MASSACRE
8. TAKE TIME TO SMELL THE FLOWERS
9. PETS
10. SUPERKNIGHT
11. No. 1. OF THE SECRET SERVICE
12. FALL OF THE ROMAN EMPIRE
13. EL CID
14. HARDCORE
15. EXPOSE
16. LETS GET LAID
17. LOVE BUTCHER
18. DEVIL x FIVE
19. HAPPY HOOKER
20. 55 DAYS TO PEKING

Intervision's Top 20 charts are compiled from dealers returns for rental and retail each month.

years before the boom of the eighties, video itself has a lineage dating back to 1956, when the Ampex corporation in the USA developed the forerunner of the domestic video recorder ('VTR' – Video Tape Recorder – was originally a trademark). The system was a complex and costly piece of hardware directed primarily at television networks. Ampex were quick to realise the potential that a cheaper and more compact system might have on the consumer market, as did manufacturers in Europe and Japan, eager to capitalise on a successor to the lucrative colour TV market[16] – which, in the 1960s, showed little signs of waning.

The result of all these different manufacturers working independently to one another was a series of different, incompatible recording formats. When the much-vaunted videocassette revolution seemed imminent in 1970, American backers sunk money into what was heralded as the system leader in the projected marketplace. Unfortunately, the system thought most-likely-to-succeed was Cartrivision, a cumbersome machine with an integral TV set. Endorsed by Columbia film studios, Cartrivision carried a certain prestige. But with poor picture quality, cartridges that quickly perished, and predicted sales figures that failed to materialise, backers pulled out.

Cartrivision was by no means the only system to suffer and, come 1973, the videocassette revolution was being dismissed as "The Great Videocassette Fiasco." The fortunes that had been invested and lost in those few short years

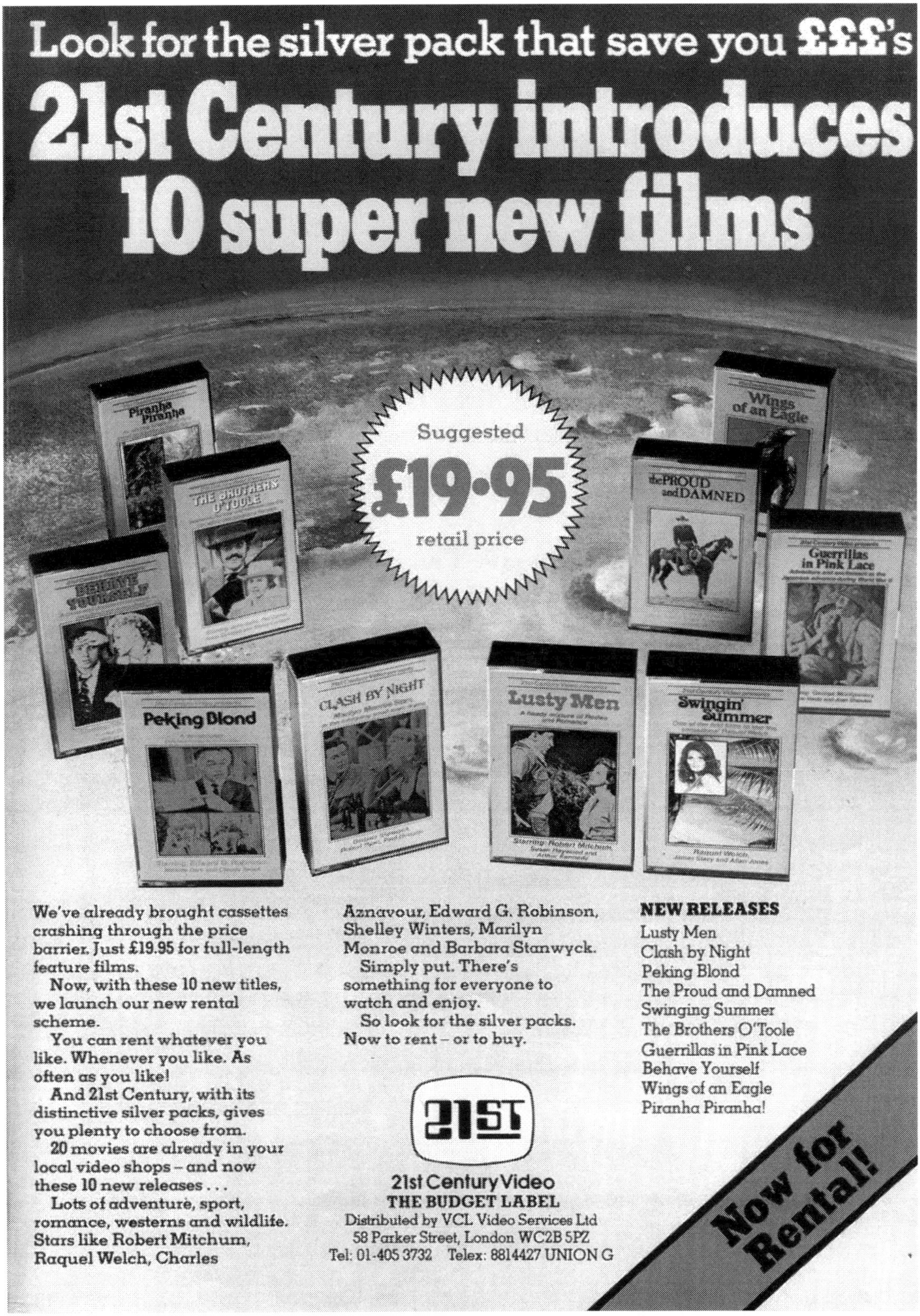

Look for the silver pack that save you £££'s

21st Century introduces 10 super new films

Suggested
£19·95
retail price

We've already brought cassettes crashing through the price barrier. Just £19.95 for full-length feature films.

Now, with these 10 new titles, we launch our new rental scheme.

You can rent whatever you like. Whenever you like. As often as you like!

And 21st Century, with its distinctive silver packs, gives you plenty to choose from.

20 movies are already in your local video shops – and now these 10 new releases . . .

Lots of adventure, sport, romance, westerns and wildlife. Stars like Robert Mitchum, Raquel Welch, Charles Aznavour, Edward G. Robinson, Shelley Winters, Marilyn Monroe and Barbara Stanwyck.

Simply put. There's something for everyone to watch and enjoy.

So look for the silver packs. Now to rent – or to buy.

21st Century Video
THE BUDGET LABEL
Distributed by VCL Video Services Ltd
58 Parker Street, London WC2B 5PZ
Tel: 01-405 3732 Telex: 8814427 UNION G

NEW RELEASES

Lusty Men
Clash by Night
Peking Blond
The Proud and Damned
Swinging Summer
The Brothers O'Toole
Guerrillas in Pink Lace
Behave Yourself
Wings of an Eagle
Piranha Piranha!

Now for Rental!

didn't deter all manufacturers however, and while many companies abandoned video development, many more persevered, adamant that a multibillion-pound industry lay within reach.

By the mid seventies, technology had overcome the practical problems that hitherto prevented mass production of video recorders, and the second video wave got underway. The consumer now had a choice between several fresh and reliable systems, notably Sony's Betamax format (launched in 1975) and Japan Victor Company's (JVC) Video Home System (VHS; launched the following year, and again a trade name which has been assimilated as a common term). Other formats, which included Video 2000, Micro Video and CED, found a market but lacked the commercial support to make much of a lasting impact and soon fell by the wayside – as ultimately would Betamax, leaving the arguably inferior VHS to dominate by the latter half of the 1980s.[17]

If technological advances brought renewed interest to video, it was the volatile political climate that helped crystallise its success in the late seventies. The world was in the midst of a new economic recession. In Britain, the Conservatives had come to power with Margaret Thatcher as the country's first female Prime Minister. Strikes were common as workers fought for better pay and working conditions, and their jobs. The process of economic deregulation championed by Thatcher, President Reagan in the US, and other western leaders had begun to change the powers of big business, trade unions and even the established church.

As cinema had done in America during the Great Depression in the 1930s, video was an escape valve for troubled times. And, for families and groups of friends, hiring a videocassette offered a cheaper alternative to paying for cinema seats.

Another factor that helped to elevate interest in video was hardcore pornography, which couldn't be accessed via conventional broadcast media in the United States and was banned outright in Britain. Courtesy of a network of underground suppliers (with exotic sounding names like Emerald Nederland and J Svenson) typically accessed via a Dutch postal address, hardcore movies in the Super 8 format had been available illegally for years in the UK. The alternative was the members-only film club and, in the US, adult XXX theatres, neither of which was safe from impromptu visits by the local vice squad. As noted at the beginning of this chapter, cumbersome Super 8 was rendered obsolete virtually overnight by the arrival of video – so why risk a film club or theatre when the same films could be seen in the privacy of one's own home, not only feature-length (complete with sound and in colour), but 'interactive' as well (thanks to Fast Forward, Rewind and Pause facilities)? None of this was lost on the commercial sectors, who had bought the video rights to blue movies virtually ad hoc back in the early seventies, transferring in the region of 10,000 films to video by the mid eighties.

Indeed, European porn giant Rodox Trading, manufacturers of the Color Climax line, met some of the cost of their sophisticated video editing and copying facilities in Denmark by reproducing under licence Hollywood blockbusters like *First Blood*, *Police Academy* and – shifting 80,000 videocassettes in just five weeks in the UK alone – *Raiders of the Lost Ark*.

The fact that an estimated sixty per cent of all pre-recorded videocassettes

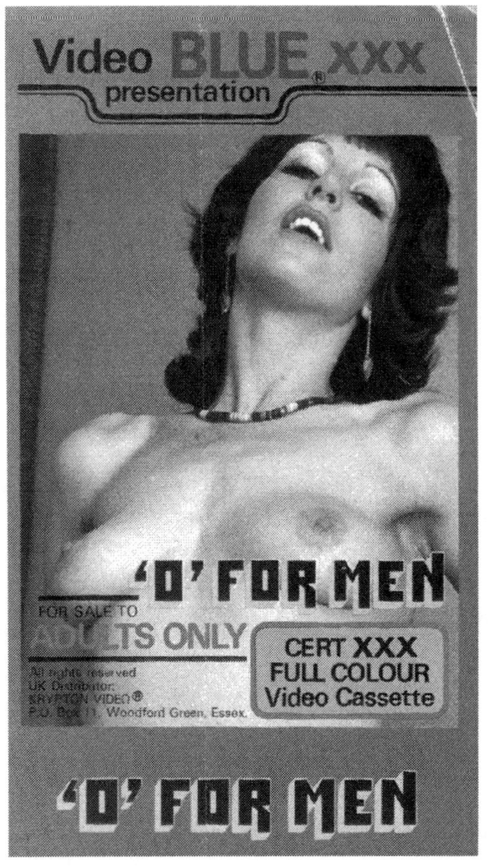

sold in 1978 were pornographic wasn't necessarily because this material was favoured by the public; other types of product were scarce. This imbalance was gradually redressed in Britain, courtesy of film companies Rank and EMI and the publishing group IPC, who had started to issue sport and documentary features through their newly formed video auxiliary.

The video software of this time didn't consist of any notable movie releases. Even Rank and EMI's video catalogue excluded their own best product, concentrating instead on early feature films already available to TV companies.

At a time when most video releases were cartoon programmes for children, music or documentary related ("special interest" being the favoured expression), companies starved of anything fresh tried desperately to make old movies sound new and exciting. Take, for instance, *The Big Cat*, a 1949 thriller that was advertised by Krypton Video as being

> More terrifying than *Jaws*!!! Great entertainment for all the family. Made among the stunning canyons and landscapes of Utah. This film is a story similar to *Jaws* except that instead of a shark the actors are terrorised by a deadly mountain lion, preying on people and cattle. It is even more terrifying than *Jaws*. This film will keep you on the edge of your seat.

Kingston Video of London offered two creaky b&w movies for the price of a single pre-recorded videocassette (£39.95), when they relaunched the 'double-bill' using "the latest video technology." The ingenious idea was to recreate in the home the glory days of cinema-going, when a main feature was preceded by a B-picture, news bulletins and perhaps even a cartoon. A sampling of their double-bill tapes include *Second Chance* and *Great Day in the Morning*, *The Sky's the Limit* and *Step Lively*, and *Berlin Express* and *Isle of the Dead* – films dating back to the 1940s for the most part.

Says Steve Ellison:

> There wasn't a lot of top stuff available. It was a bit like, "My God, there's a feature film!" A lot of the stuff was what you'd regard as run of the mill, mostly B-movies. Or very bad movies that someone had bought rights for very cheaply. You've got to remember that the film companies were a little bit wary of video. They didn't really want their product getting into people's homes that easily.[18]

This state of affairs enabled the film arm of Brent Walker to score a huge hit with two decidedly average – but *recent* – movies, releasing both *The Bitch* and *The Stud* to video hot on the heels of their theatrical run. "Popular by default," as Ellison puts it, because they were two of the few big movies available. And popular enough to make something of a video superstar out of actress Joan Collins, described affectionately as a "heavy video user" in one industry newsletter. "When I get home from a performance at the Cambridge Theatre," Joan is quoted, "there is nothing I like better than sitting down before a warm fire with my video recorder."

Iain Muspratt explains Guild Home Video's move into the home rental market:

> I worked for a merchant bank; the merchant bank ended up owning Guild because they thought that something was going to happen in this market. We did promotional films for companies like ICI and also management training films, us and Video Arts. We were also a huge educational programmes distributor, for example, Open University programmes, distributing them on 16mm and U-matic, and a couple of other institutional formats. We also ran a television service via U-matic cassettes for

V80

STRAW DOGS
ANIMAL HOUSE
JAWS I & II
KOTCH
ELVIS IN HAWAII
BABYFACE
VILLAIN
GREASE
SCANNERS
COMMANDOS
SMOKEY AND THE BANDIT
DEEP THROAT

RENT FILMS LIKE THESE
FROM AS LITTLE AS £3-27
OVER 400 TITLES. ALL CATAGORIES

JOIN VIDEO 80 CLUB NOW AND RENT FULL LENGTH MOVIES, THE LOWEST PRICES AROUND OR BUY AT SPECIAL MEMBERSHIP DISCOUNTS. ALL FILMS ARE FIRST GENERATION TOP QUALITY.
SEND TODAY FOR OUR FREE LIST AND DESCRIPTIVE BROCHURE. PLEASE ENCLOSE LARGE S.A.E.

TO VIDEO 80 CLUB DEPT TEL: 01-435 9426
324a WEST END LANE, HAMPSTEAD, LONDON NW6
PLEASE SEND ME YOUR DESCRIPTIVE BROCHURE
(I AM OVER 18 YEARS OF AGE) VR3

NAME..
ADDRESS..
SIGNATURE.....................................

VIDEO 80

PRERECORDED VIDEO FILMS ALL AT GREAT DISCOUNTS
POST AND PACK FREE

THE SECRET POLICEMANS BALL	£35.95
THE EAGLE HAS LANDED	,,
STRAW DOGS	,,
STAR TREK THE MOVIE	,,
AIRPORT 77	,,
THE WARRIORS	,,
ANIMAL HOUSE	,,
ALIEN	,,
THE EXORCIST	,,
THE ROSE	,,
JAWS	,,
JAWS II	,,
THE OMEN	,,
JUST A GIGOLO	,,
THE DEER HUNTER	,,
THE STUD	,,
THE BITCH	,,
SCUM	,,
CONVOY	,,
EAGLES WING	,,
THE WILD GEESE	,,
RISING DAMP	£26.95
ESCAPE TO ATHENA	,,
THE MUPPET MOVIE	,,
PORRIDGE	,,
SATURN 3	,,
FAREWELL MY LOVELY	,,
SCANNERS	,,

PLEASE SEND ME THE
FOLLOWING FILMS

TITLE	PRICE
1	
2	
3	
4	
5	
VHS ★ BETA ★ TOTAL	

ALLOW 28 DAYS DELIVERY

NAME
ADDRESS

SIGNATURE

VIDEO 80
324a West End Lane, Hampstead, London, NW6. Tel: 01 435 9426

expatriates working overseas, people like British Aerospace in Saudi Arabia. We also supplied the universities in those relatively new parts of the world in Africa and Europe with Open University programmes. And then home video did start to take off. I remember having a discussion with a couple [of] leading lights of the industry one evening and they were saying nobody's ever going to buy these things, but I said, I don't know, I think one day there might be a rental market. So we decided that might be an opportunity. So we stopped doing management training films and went into home video, which meant going out and licensing programmes. We had a presence, the Americans were very aware of us, but at least they felt we were relatively honest. We went out to see producers in Hollywood. We didn't pay very much. The biggest deal we ever did was buy a library from Lorimar, which included films like *The Postman Always Rings Twice*. We also bought a lot of pictures from ABC. I think both those deals were in the region of half a million dollars each. We were lucky because we had that capital; we didn't have to raise it.[19]

A video explosion was imminent, but the long-term effects on an entertainment industry grounded in traditional media was open to conjecture. When Magnetic Video – later to become Twentieth Century-Fox Video – began to distribute film classics and recent Hollywood blockbusters, other companies were forced to sit up and acknowledge that video might not merely be a slight return of the fad of the early seventies. The prospect of being left behind didn't appeal to anyone, but at the same time the major studios were hesitant to make a decision that might adverse ly effect their product.

Gulf & Western – the parent company of Paramount Motion Pictures – employed a marketing research and consulting firm to determine whether they should diversify into video. Ultimately they did, with a reserved announcement to the press.

> By being a part of potential threats, Paramount will not only be protecting itself against an uncertain future, but could be getting itself involved in a lucrative industry. Video is likely to be as popular in the next decade as television was in the fifties.

The future of the movie industry was seen as unpredictable because of video, but there was no way around it. With the acquiescence of Paramount, together with other major studios United Artists, Universal, and Warner Brothers, and the launch of Lord Grade's ITC, video entered a period of sudden and rapid growth.

At the end of 1980 a modest 600 pre-recorded videocassette titles were available in Britain, sales of which notched £15 million. By 1981 the choice had more than doubled, creating sales of £36 million[20] – more when revenue generated by rental is taken into consideration.

Some of the trepidation was shared by other parties and manifested in high videocassette prices, as well as conflicting and unnecessary restrictions placed on the consumer, who had no choice but to rent tapes.

Obtaining videogram clearing rights was a nightmare for film companies, as nobody wanted to miss out on profits that had not been anticipated a year-or-so earlier. Film directors, producers, actors, music publishers, distributors and studios hammered it out, one result being that Thorn EMI was taken to court over a dispute pertaining to royalties on six films they released to video – including *Stardust* and *That'll Be The Day* – which they were forced to withdraw. Matters like this also caused consternation for the TV networks, particularly the BBC whose launch into video was delayed for a year pending a satisfactory agreement with the various unions. Despite a back catalogue renowned as being the largest of any broadcasting organisation, BBC Video wasn't launched until the latter months of 1981 and for a long time comprised a tentative eighteen titles (*Play Golf*, *Toyah at the Rainbow* and *The Story of English Furniture* among them).

As with the film companies, video dealers were advancing into uncharted territory. There were no guidelines or rules as such, and anyone with a little collateral who was prepared to take a chance stood to make money. Video clubs were predominantly mail order to begin with. Notching up a self-proclaimed 500 new members a week, the biggest of these was perhaps Video Club, which sold its membership kits in selected high street TV rental and department stores, as well as through magazine advertisements and leisure centres.[21] Mail order generally offered the consumer a wider selection of titles than could be found in high street rental outlets, where a stock of 100 different tapes was considered expansive. But this was to change, due in part to the stores getting wise and devoting more shelf space to video software, and mail order consumers getting burned by cowboy outfits failing to deliver what they promised or, in some instances, cashing cheques and not delivering anything at all. The most significant turnaround, however, came when record wholesalers moved into video distribution and utilised their sophisticated supply networks for films from major studios.[22] (A move which would ultimately have a devastating effect on independent wholesalers, as will be seen later.) Department stores, record stores, newsagents, pharmaceutical chains and supermarkets all became stockists of video software.

The Bellford Service Station near Guildford was one of the first garages in the country to offer videos, a scheme so popular with motorists that the garage switched the operation from their forecourt accessory shop to new custom-built premises. Super 8 specialists, with an established customer base and often the support of a familiar stockist – such as Fletcher and Intervision, who had also moved on from Super 8 to video – were ideally equipped for the formative marketplace. Even some ice cream vans are known to have carried a small stock of videocassettes on their rounds.

Video was open to anybody. Companies established in other fields might diversify into video, or perhaps the redundancy money of those hit by recession might be pooled into a new video outlet. Market stalls trading in videos opened. Vacant high street properties on the outskirts of town were leased and turned into dedicated video stores. A more personal touch came from video dealers who operated out of a car boot, bringing a videocassette direct to a customer's door and exchanging it for another from their list of titles on a designated return trip. Expanding upon this concept were mobile video libraries, walk-through vans equipped with a selection of tapes, travelling from district to district on a weekly basis.

(The antithesis of this concept were the standalone automated rental booths for use on high streets announced in January 1987. Called Movie Machines, this American import was operated with the use of a credit card. Offered a choice of 374 videocassettes, the customer would rent a title and return the tape after use, whereupon the machine would issue a receipt and debit the customer's card accordingly. It isn't believed that Movie Machines ever saw commercial use on the streets of Britain, although, as noted, automated video dispensers did become a reality in cinema chains for a brief period.)

"Video was a growth market," recalls Christopher Glazebrook, a TV and Radio Section Supervisor selling televisions, video recorders and other electrical equipment in a department store in the late seventies. "Deciding to stock the software, as well as the hardware, was a natural progression to aid sales."

> It must have been about 1980 when I first became involved with videocassettes. Initially my job was to purchase the tapes and oversee the running of the library. As the business expanded, I was appointed the Video Libraries Manager responsible for seven outlets.
>
> At this early stage there was only one other retailer in the vicinity dealing in videocassettes. As the popularity of video grew, several more soon sprang up, but mainly on the outskirts of town, too far away to have any effect on our trade.
>
> Reps would call once a month. Demand was very high for anything available, both on VHS and Betamax, and we would order all the new feature films released.[23]

One of the independent retailers on the outskirts of town was Phoenix Home Leisure, whose operation soon expanded into wholesale distribution and the supply of videos to other retailers. Steve Ellison gives an insight into the unexpected quarters from which a video competitor was likely to originate:

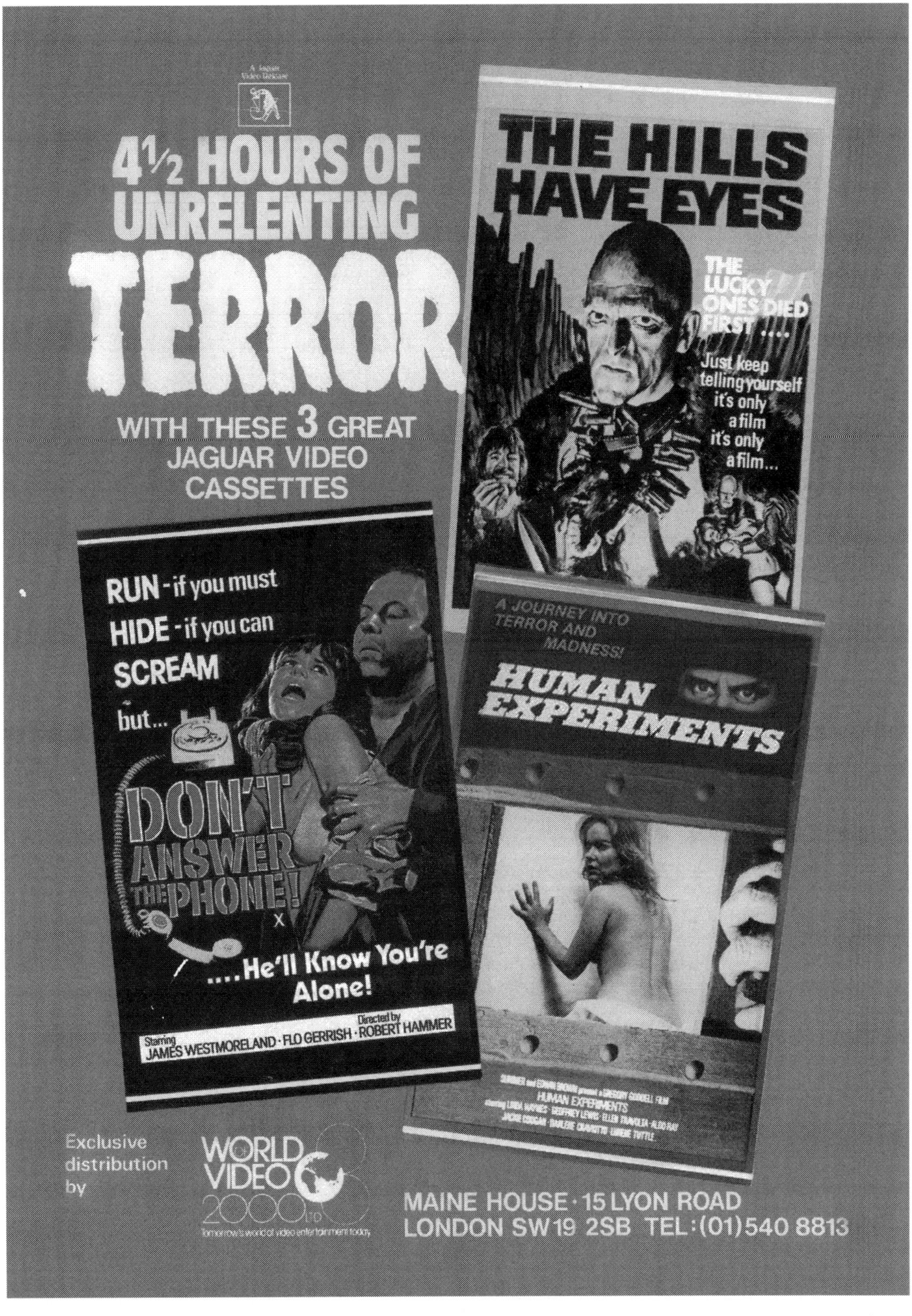

A Jaguar Video Release

4½ HOURS OF UNRELENTING TERROR

WITH THESE 3 GREAT JAGUAR VIDEO CASSETTES

THE HILLS HAVE EYES

THE LUCKY ONES DIED FIRST....

Just keep telling yourself it's only a film it's only a film...

RUN - if you must
HIDE - if you can
SCREAM
but...

DON'T ANSWER THE PHONE!

X

....He'll Know You're Alone!

Starring JAMES WESTMORELAND · FLO GERRISH · Directed by ROBERT HAMMER

A JOURNEY INTO TERROR AND MADNESS!

HUMAN EXPERIMENTS

Exclusive distribution by

MAINE HOUSE · 15 LYON ROAD
LONDON SW19 2SB TEL:(01)540 8813

I had a competition at the time with another wholesaler who, strangely enough, used to be my accountant. By virtue of being my accountant, of course, he got all the names and addresses of all the film distributors and suddenly announced he was leaving accountancy and becoming a video wholesaler. And he really got serious about it and supplied all his reps with the new Escort XR3, these fast cars so they would whiz down to London, pick up films, and guarantee to have them back in the shops the same day of release. There was always a bit of a bone of contention because London shops would get the films, and it would be a couple of days by the time the carrier got them up to the North. In actual fact, three reps — not his reps — were killed on the M6 and the M1 during this short period of time, because of all the dashing around with films.[24]

The various video clubs didn't adhere to a common customer protocol or membership scheme; this was down to whatever the individual dealer chose to implement, be it video rental, straight sale, exchange, or a combination thereof. However, there were certain conditions imposed on the dealers by distributors and film companies, which became increasingly convoluted as the market expanded and the impetus shifted from mail order to the high street.

Exchange schemes had been the preference for mail order companies, who required that a customer first become a member, then purchase one videocassette outright, which could be exchanged for another of the same price range – for a small fee and the price of postage.

For a membership fee of £40, Video Unlimited of Bournemouth ran a tape exchange scheme at a cost of £6 per tape (or, if payment was made in advance, £60 for twenty exchanges). Relocating to prestigious quayside premises in Dorset after eighteen months of trading, the company became something of a video superstore in 1981 with a stock of 3,000 different film titles; the largest of its kind in Britain, if not Europe.

Some dealers offered lifelong membership and free tape exchange for a one-off fee of £150 (Cathedral Films of Worcester), while others required no membership at all but the purchase of one tape and £2.95 per exchange thereafter (Caramel Video of Devon). The concept of the videocassette exchange scheme was intrinsically a straightforward one and considered a breach of copyright or suppliers' trading terms. The same cannot be said for the options that came to dominate as mail order and exchange schemes waned.[25]

Most source companies – whether videocassette distributors or major film studios – had their own idea of how best to bring their product into the hands of the consumer. Retailers were often faced with a boggling array of paperwork when they stocked films by different studios, each with different conditions and rates because of the royalty agreements that had anxiously been established with the various copyright holders. United Artists and Guild Home Video were among the companies operating a 'rental only' policy on their titles. Warner Home Video and IPC on the other hand, stipulated 'straight sale' only. In time the companies adhering to the latter system were forced to reconsider, as the choice of rental titles increased, and consumers were less willing to pay the high asking price for outright sales. Magnetic Video – holding out until 1982 – was the last company to switch to the rental idea.

However, rental wasn't a straightforward alternative. Rental included club membership fees, deposits, hire charges and forms to be filled by both dealer and customer for every rental transaction undertaken. In the case of Warner Home Video, the lease scheme that replaced their 'sales only' policy was off-

puting and many wholesalers refused to participate anyway. (The retailer was required to pay Warner £12 a month for their films and take a minimum of twenty titles.) Rank and Precision Video both stipulated that their rental tapes had to be rented for a three-day minimum period. Because many of the major video companies had negotiated special deals with the larger retail outlets, independent dealers wishing to stock their films had to do so via third party suppliers. In the case of Thorn EMI this was Intervision, one of the earliest independent suppliers of videocassettes. Intervision required more paperwork than anyone else – different forms for different titles – and also required the dealer to lodge a sizeable cash bond for Thorn EMI's tapes, which could take up to a year to recover should the deal be cancelled.

Steve Ellison recalls the tumultuous era of video retailing.

> Intervision had a whole rack of feature films and a rental system whereby you sign the contract with them, and were charged, I think, £5.95 for three days hire or £7.95 for a week — you kept the odd £1.95 or £2.95 and sent the rest to them. They invoiced you and you sent all the copies of the forms to them. It was very complicated and long-winded. Then very quickly a lot of people just started buying the videos and hiring them out even though they weren't supposed to. The first big controversy in video was tapes that were supposed to be for 'sale only' being hired out. Magnetic Video came on the scene with a whole string of Twentieth Century-Fox stuff that was supposed to be for sale only at £39.95. But what was happen-

> ing was people were buying piles of this stuff and renting it for £1.50 or £2.00 a night. The only stuff that should have been rented was the Intervision stuff. The rest of it was purely and simply for sale. It actually said on the video box 'For Sale'. That was the first thing in video that caused some bones of contention. But eventually, like most of these things, people just ignored the law anyway. And to get anywhere you had to start renting when everyone else was renting anyway. [26]

Dealers simply refused to adhere to the sales and lease guidelines stipulated by film companies and suppliers, which they saw as unnecessarily restrictive and convoluting. Intervision urged dealers to play ball with a motto that threatened "Reckless Exploitation of Copyright Programme Material Can Seriously Damage Your Business," and incorporated a spoken warning on their tapes – the remonstrative tones of actor Patrick Allen[27] – whose pre-feature announcement hammered home the importance of filling in the correct rental documentation. Viewers who experienced any irregularity in their rental agreement were urged to contact Intervision, receiving a free blank videocassette should their claim be justified.

But independent companies were finding it increasingly difficult to stay afloat as the major film companies got a grip on the market, no longer looking to the likes of Intervision to distribute their product. The sparse landscape they had once monopolised was by 1981 rapidly changed, and the independents were forced to invest large sums of money in exclusive distribution deals or go under. As a result VCL – who had a penchant for music videos – signed a deal with GTO Films for the likes of *Phantasm*, *Scum* and *Breaking Glass*. Intervision sought to raise $2.5

million for the rights to a number of films from United Artists, a company who wanted to break the British market without having to set up their own subsidiary.

Phoenix Home Leisure was one of the many independents forced into closure. "I was wholesaling mostly the second-rate stuff," says Steve Ellison, "because the 'big boys' wouldn't let us have wholesale terms."

He explains:

> I liquidated in 1982. By 1982, all the big companies like Warner Brothers, EMI, Fox, RCA, Columbia, had got their own national capability for distribution so they didn't need local wholesalers anymore. They just cut us up for price. They had their own reps on the road, and they just started going straight to the shops. The same kind of thing that had happened previously with the long-playing record business was happening with video. With records, Music For Pleasure had come along and put racks into newsagents and everywhere else, and it killed these local little wholesalers.
>
> When I liquidated, I owed EMI £18,000 for blank tape. And in those days, a blank three-hour tape retailed for round about £8. We were invoiced by EMI at a distributor price of £5 a tape, to sell to the shops at £6. I had something like 10,000 tapes at this price. I was walking round the wholesalers in Eccles [Greater Manchester] the next week and saw that they were selling tapes at the same price I was paying. I rang EMI and they told me, "Oh, the price has gone down." I asked them to send me a credit note for the difference. "We can't do that," they replied. "It's not our fault if the market fluctuates." So, we got left with a lot of blank tape which we ended up trading off to

> Surrey Video or something. A lot of local wholesalers did go under because national wholesalers took over. [28]

While leasing obligations were being ignored by some retailers, the 1959 Copyright Act – which had yet to catch up with video – allowed many other dealers to happily operate in a legal twilight. There was no High Court test case on which video suppliers and film companies could fall back and until there was, no dealer was technically breaking any copyright law. Nonetheless, it seems inconceivable today that legitimate companies – like Video Exchange in Bath – could ever have entertained such copyright-scamming notions as trading programmes taped off-air, actively encouraging customers to send in their unwanted 'time-shift' recordings. Even Palace Video, celebrated distributors of award-winning arthouse and cult movies, decided in their inaugural months to introduce a scheme that seems nothing short of a legal time bomb. As a means of reducing the cost of films, Palace provided its customers with the opportunity to buy selected titles at a discount price of £13.50 so long as a blank tape was provided on which to copy the films. *Pink Flamingos*, *Eraserhead* and *The Enigma of Kaspar Hauser* were among those films requiring a two-hour blank tape, while *Mephisto* and *Aguirre, Wrath of God* (a double bill of both German and English language versions) required the purchaser to provide a three-hour tape. The idea was enough of a success to warrant Palace repeating the scheme with a concert film of Gary Numan at Wembley Arena, called *Micromusic* (a title that probably derived from the fact the film was also available in Technicolor's innovative micro videocassette format).

Legal problems surrounding video software were the subject of a major conference in the UK in October 1980. The following month, the British Videogram Association (BVA) came into existence to create a "healthy environment for business" – as stipulated in their remit – tackling copyright issues such as unauthorised home copying and off-air taping.[29] A levy on blank videocassettes and possibly even hardware was seen as the best solution to the problem,[30] but this threat – a proposed ten per cent of the cost of a videocassette – was ultimately dropped, leaving the contentious issue of home-taping unresolved.[31]

As video wholesalers sought to protect themselves against the major studios, their movie catalogues expanded with product from a growing selection of sources. Material had as much chance of coming from a supplier who had sought out the required permissions, as it did someone offering, say, vaguely public domain films.

Unlike some of the smaller distribution companies, Guild Home Video acquired the correct licences for all its releases. Says Iain Muspratt:

> Mostly they were for five or seven years. The longest license we ever did was for the *Dallas* TV series, which was for twenty-one years. We also did a lot of cartoons and what people forget is that we helped finance them as well. We co-financed *Super Ted* with S4C, and we co-financed the first six episodes of *Thomas the Tank Engine*. We had all the Hanna-Barbera stuff, we had all the Filmation stuff. We were even in the discussions to make the first live action version of *Spider-Man*.[32]

Other suppliers simply transferred material to video tape with no licensing agreement whatsoever, hoping nobody would notice. Recalls Ellison:

> The very first year we were wholesaling we were offered a stand at a video trade exhibition organised by *Video Trade Weekly*, because someone had pulled out. I was this little wholesaler in Wigan. I said, "How much is it?" and they said, "Well what can you offer?" I actually offered them a crate of wine. We got use of this exhibition for a crate of wine! I was also tied in with Fletcher Video as their northern agent at the time, so I rang Fletchers and said, "You know this exhibition that starts next week? I've got a stand there but I've nothing to put on it." And they gave me a whole pile of cartoons that had just come in from Techno in Italy — plastic-cased cartoons, Bugs Bunny, Daffy Duck and all that. They were old, prewar and early fifties cartoons that Warner Brothers had originally hired down to a company called AAP — an American firm, I think, who were pretty big in 8mm. All this stuff had been on 8mm. In Italy Bugs Bunny is called just "Bunny". Well, our stand turned out to be right by the entrance opposite Twentieth Century-Fox with Magnetic Video, who had built a replica of the spaceship from *Alien* as their stand. And next to them was Warner Home Video and the guy from Warner Brothers was looking over at our stand, at all our cartoons, and he comes over saying "That's Bugs Bunny". I'm saying, "No, it's not, it's *Bunny*. If you look at it closely, the ears are shorter."[33]

And, in another case:

Hokushin put a few videos out. Basically Hokushin was a company that supplied 16mm projectors — there's a Hokushin 16mm projector that was made in the seventies — and they brought over some American tapes from Magnetic Video and transferred them to the PAL system. They got into trouble quite quickly with Twentieth Century-Fox and had to stop it, but by then they'd got hold of the rights for *The Playbirds* and *Come Play With Me*, the Mary Millington films, and were able to put those out.

Ellison remembers a "clearing house for video rights" based in Paris where some early distributors in Britain got their films, Intervision among them. Fletcher Video, however, was a company importing films ad hoc, boxed up and ready for sale. They had a container full of films flown in, with the briefest of advance notification from the Italian suppliers of what to expect. Once off the plane, the tapes were taken to Fletcher's Space Way warehouse near Heathrow airport, and from there distributed around Britain.

Things were a little different for everyone. Says Steve Webber, formerly the marketing director of VCL Video Services: "The thing was, we used to put stuff out without the rights and sort the rights out afterwards, that was the way you could do things then."[34]

There was little chance of beating the major studios in terms of big-name blockbusters. But with the influx of cheap, exploitative features and plenty of hard-nosed promotion, the territory formally dominated by the majors came under considerable pressure.

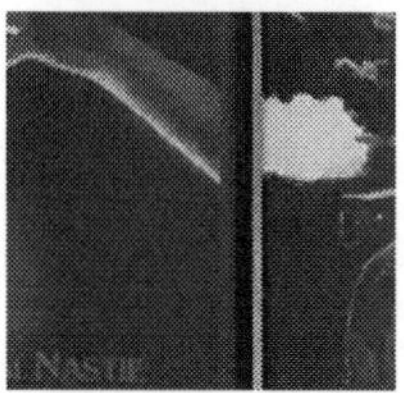
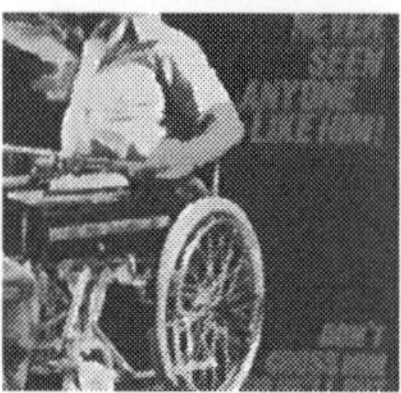

Unease

'AN ORGY OF COMMERCIALISM'

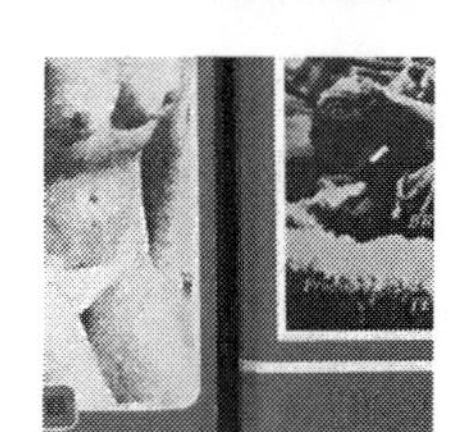

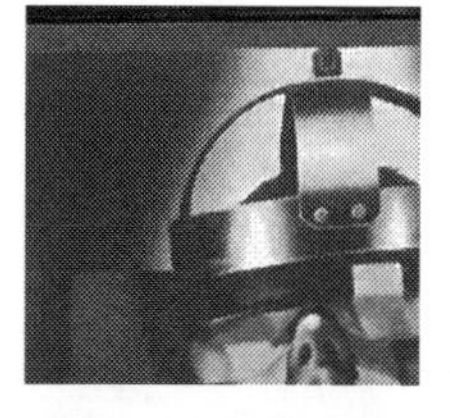

Unease

'AN ORGY OF COMMERCIALISM'

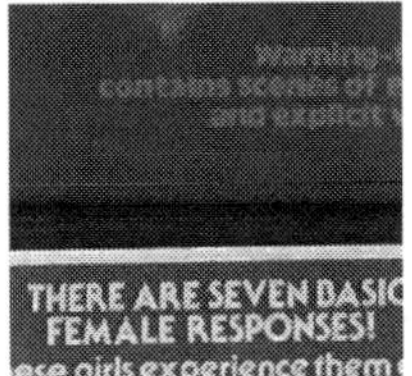

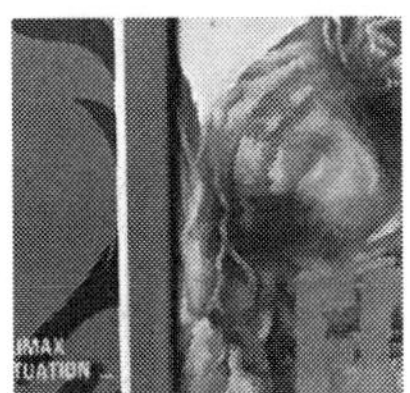

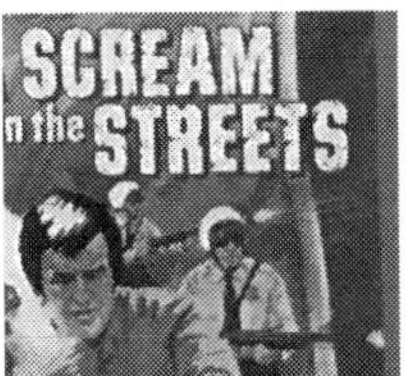

THERE WAS NO such thing as all-night television.

When video arrived, television networks in Britain were in the habit of ending broadcasts at around midnight. And, as was the tradition in cinemas, the BBC signed off with the National Anthem. Video helped eradicate such scheduling constraints and gave people the opportunity to watch what they wanted when they wanted. The growing likelihood that cable and satellite television would soon take off didn't seem to hinder sales of video recorders. Instead these technologies were seen to offer the video public an even greater choice for time-shift taping – which remained the most common use for video up until the middle of 1981 when the upsurge in pre-recorded titles began. A glut of faddish gadgetry and paraphernalia arrived on the market to assist the video owner in their hectic video recording schedule. These included the Videolog, Video Organiser, Videoplanner and write'n'wipe label kits. The hopeless enthusiast could even attire themselves in a "Video Freak" or "I Love Video" T-shirt (£5.99 each from BBS in North Humberside).

Video wasn't a substitute for TV viewing, but a reason to watch for longer. As noted by Laurie Taylor and Bob Mullan in their book *Uninvited Guests*, "Extra time has to be found to accommodate the extra viewing."

For many, playing tapes deep into the night provided the answer – a habit that often drew unwelcome attention from opportunist crooks, trawling darkened streets for the give-away flicker of an 'after hours' TV screen. A Ferguson Videostar, a popular model of VCR, cost one of your authors £379.99

to purchase from electrical retailer Rumbelows in December 1985, plus £37.50 extra for the cover plan, and £4 delivery. Theft was a worry. But protection from thieves – poised outside homes, waiting the cathode glow to terminate and make their move[1] – could be obtained in the guise of VCR alarm systems.

"In Coventry, about fifteen video recorders are stolen each week," the Midlands-based manufacturer of Videoalert told the *Sunday Times* in May 1983. With advance orders for 300, it was estimated that annual sales of Videoalert – a gadget that attached to the outside of the VCR, emitting a ninety-eight-decibel shriek should the unit be moved or lifted – would hit a rather optimistic 25,000 mark. A window sticker served to ward off the crooks.

Another concern came from a different quarter. It was feared that people were becoming *addicted* to watching videos, especially late at night. Without the discipline of television's midnight termination, it was believed that video would create a nation of insomniacs. At the height of the video boom, counselling was even established in some areas to help so-called "videoholics."

"There was certainly one lady who could be described as a videoholic," recalls Chris Glazebrook of his days as a video libraries manager. "She would work out how long the tapes lasted on a piece of paper and decide when the family could have dinner."

At a Methodist Conference held in Portsmouth, Reverend Pat Brown attacked the National Children's Home (NCH) for its association with what he perceived "a tainted industry."[2] The Video Charity Day, held in May 1987 and organised by the BVA with the support of the whole industry, raised £150,000 from donations, proceeds of videocassette rentals and a series of fundraising events across the country. The Reverend Brown accused the charity of accepting "blood money."

In 1987, turnover for the video industry was an estimated half-a-billion pounds. This swift ascendance was not without a price, and a backlash that started at the beginning of the eighties would have a lasting effect on the medium, irrevocably shaping its image in the public eye. Mounting pressure from lobby groups and the media led to the creation of the 1984 Video Recordings Act, which resulted in many films on videocassette being outlawed. Renewed concern came in 1987, when the press laid the cause of a massacre in the small English town of Hungerford almost exclusively on the influence of video. (See THE BIG INFLUENCE.)

The appearance of lurid advertisements in the early months of 1982 sparked criticism from members of the public and the BVA. In their monthly case report for May 1982, the Advertising Standards Authority (ASA) upheld complaints against

Left to right: A typically arresting advertisement from Go Video for the release of *The Demons*. But, following the complaints upheld against lurid advertisements for horror videos, Go Video returned with a full-page ad for the same release – arguably more lurid thanks to the impromptu penned warning.

three video film advertisements and condemned any publication prepared to print advertisements in which, increasingly, films of a violent or sexual character were described in terms calculated to appeal only to the most degraded tastes and cause unnecessary offence to readers.

The three ads in question pertained to *Cannibal Holocaust*, *The Driller Killer* and *SS Experiment Camp*. The latter film, with its depiction of a semi-naked woman tied upside down to a cross with a swastika hanging from her wrist, was singled out by the Authority as particularly vile. In response, a meeting took place in which magazine editors who shared the ASA's concern agreed to carry out "much more careful vetting in future." From now on, went the theory, there would be consultation between the publishers, and any advertisement deemed objectionable would be collectively rejected – although the contentious ad for *SS Experiment Camp* continued to appear through June 1982.[3]

The backlash against video started as these things often do: relatively innocuously. The general anxiety that comes with any innovative technology manifested in public fears of burglary and addiction, while the various pressure

groups – having doggedly rallied against 'permissiveness' per se – found in video a brand-new menace.

Most vociferous of these groups was the National Viewers and Listeners Association (NVLA[4]), founded in the early sixties by a sanctimonious schoolteacher from Shropshire called Mary Whitehouse and her friend, Norah Buckland. These two middle-aged Englishwomen became appalled at the shape of cultural change and the shift away from middle class Christian principles – a change personified in the BBC's growing penchant for gutsy 'kitchen sink' drama, scathing satire and current affairs programmes. In 1964, after rallying support in a highly publicised meeting at Birmingham's Town Hall, the Clean Up TV campaign was the first action proper of what was to become the NVLA.

Whitehouse was the single most influential figure in the NVLA. Following a hotly debated BBC panel show in October 1967, she also became its public face (through to her retirement in 1994; she died in 2001).[5] According to Whitehouse, television was in such a state that even BBC personnel, "so deeply troubled about the kind of material [they were] expected to transmit,"[6] were anonymously turning to the NVLA. Come the following year and the resignation of the BBC's Director General (Whitehouse's arch enemy Sir Hugh Greene), the NVLA moved its emphasis away from television and toward pornography in general. Indeed, the NVLA doesn't identify any distinct group to which it is opposed, but lumps them all together as one nebulous, ungodly whole.

"Radicalism is the keynote to the NVLA's work," state the authors of a study that appears in *Censorship and Obscenity*. "Theirs is a total disenchantment with, and critique of, the existing social world... the complex and disturbed world 'out there' which they see as more and more likely to engulf their own world of Christian truths."

Wrote one reporter for the *Observer*: "The real trouble is that she [Whitehouse] doesn't seem to be able to tell the difference between a sensitive documentary about being a homosexual... and someone saying 'git' in [the sitcom] *Till Death Us Do Part*."

Considered a crank and prudish busybody by many people, Whitehouse was nevertheless persistent enough to succeed in getting TV programmes dropped, and landing stage plays and periodicals in the dock with alarming regularity. *The Little Red Schoolbook* and 'School Kids' *Oz* were two publications brought to trial and successfully prosecuted because of her intervention (published in Britain in 1970, the former advocates that young people think for themselves; the latter is a special edition of the underground newspaper, *Oz*, edited by children). Whitehouse took these two items to show the Pope, whereupon they were deposited in the Vatican archives (supposedly comprising the finest collection of erotica in the world). Hers wasn't the voice of reason, but rarely did she face any opposition.

The NVLA claimed to gain strength by "providing timely information to the Prime Minister, the Secretary of State for National Heritage, the Home Secretary and other members of HM Government; also lobbying Members of Parliament". Yet, more than anything else, public apathy fuelled its campaign and brought a disproportionate impression of controversy to the things it deemed

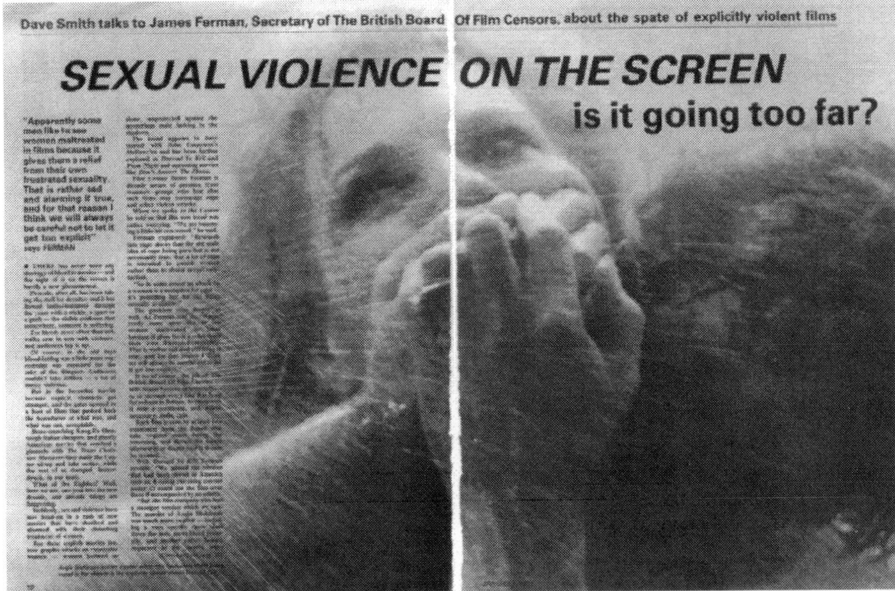

Dave Smith talks to James Ferman, Secretary of The British Board Of Film Censors, about the spate of explicitly violent films

SEXUAL VIOLENCE ON THE SCREEN
is it going too far?

"Apparently some men like to see women maltreated in films because it gives them a relief from their own frustrated sexuality. That is rather sad and alarming if true, and for that reason I think we will always be careful not to let it get too explicit" says FERMAN

objectionable.[7] With support from the Prince of Wales and political factions that saw an opportunity to win votes, Mary Whitehouse – later made a CBE by the Queen[8] – was able to posit herself as matriarch for the nation.

The moral standards dictated by the NVLA were decided upon by the Association's founders. Everyone else was expected to accept their definition of what was 'acceptable'. Although statistics indicate that NVLA activity was tremendously unpopular, the organisation insisted that it functioned for the majority. Few people who signed up for the NVLA's philosophy could be aware of how deep the protective knife cut into personal and public freedom of choice.[9] They claimed to be *opposed to* any form of government censorship, yet stressed that a tightening of the Obscene Publications Act was long overdue. (What is the Obscene Publications Act if not government censorship?) Instead of censorship they advocated self-restraint, but of course the NVLA wished to set the parameters of that restraint.[10] NVLA propaganda is riddled with references to criminal acts reported in the media. A report on, say, television violence will be interspersed with press snippets relating to rape, murder, robberies and other acts of violence, leading the reader to believe that all violent crime is the direct result of acts of violence portrayed on television. (See also THE BIG INFLUENCE.)

Whitehouse is considered a goodly person yet on more than one occasion

Top: Teaser advertisement for *The Devils*.
Above: With a sensationalistic cover like this, it was little wonder that Lord Longford's anti-porn tract could also be found in Soho sex shops.

implied that those who break the 'moral code' should be put to death. In *The Little Red Schoolbook* trial, she quoted from the scriptures and warned a defence witness that "it were better for him that a millstone were hanged about his neck, and he were cast into the sea."[11] Sociologist Howard Becker described such fervent campaigners as "moral entrepreneurs," and dissected them thusly:

> The existing rules do not satisfy him because there is some evil which profoundly disturbs him. He feels that nothing can be right in the world until rules are made to correct it. He operates with an absolute ethic; what he sees is truly and absolutely evil with no qualification. Any means is justified to do away with it. The crusader is fervent and righteous, often self-righteous.[12]

Becker concludes that if a crusade shows signs of success, it may encourage the entrepreneur to become a professional rule creator. Becker's theories were published in 1963. The following year the NVLA took its first steps, and after that came other groups for moral armament, notably the Nationwide Festival of Light (NFOL) and the Community Standards Association (CSA), both of which had a representative in Whitehouse.

The Nationwide Festival of Light was launched in September 1971 with a series of meetings and processions throughout the country. Sponsored by Christians, but open to anyone concerned about love, purity and family life, the gathering of some 30,000[13] people in Trafalgar Square on the twenty-fifth of that month was the hub of the festival. Here, the NFOL made their "Proclamation to the Government" regarding media representations of sex, drugs and violence:

> The present trafficking in sadistic and obscene material and the ridiculing of purity and family life are placing in peril the innocence of children, the dignity and equality of women, and the true fulfilment of human personality. The health of society is now endangered, and those in authority in national and local government must act at once.[14]

The group followed with Operation Newsagent, a scheme requesting the boycott of newsagents that sold pornographic magazines (years later, the CSA were to award a "Family Seal of Approval" to shops that forfeited said magazines). At the annual meeting of the Wales and Monmouth Advisory Committee of Llandrindod, the government was urged to promote moral values by every means possible. Mrs Madge Westmoreland spoke of the press pandering "to the baser instincts of the 'sick' minority" and added, "I don't want to see photographs of unmarried mothers with their babies or to read of the love life of a hippie, or how families started wife-swapping." Another spokesperson said that foreigners should be stopped from having abortions in Britain.

Films like *The Devils*, *Straw Dogs* and *A Clockwork Orange* played amidst cries of outrage, and, in the case of *Flesh*, earned a fine for its exhibitor the Open Space Theatre. The 'health of society' may have been at risk, but concern over the issue of pornography was becoming obsessive.[15] Into this flurry of protest and police raids came the Earl of Longford, teacher, politician, journalist, author, Labour convert, Roman Catholic peer and amateur missionary. On April 21, 1971, Longford initiated a debate in the House of Lords on pornography and proposed that the government might set up a far-reaching inquiry whilst volunteering an immediate unofficial inquiry of his own. Sixteen months of work resulted in *Pornography: The Longford Report*, a 500-page paperback book published by Coronet, a London-based firm in which Longford had an interest. The fanfare that surrounded the investigation led many to believe it was nothing more than an exercise in self-promotion. "Lord Porn" – as he came to be known in the pages of *Private Eye* – delighted the tabloid press with research that took him and his entourage to the seedy sex shops and clubs of Soho and Copenhagen (customs allowed him to keep the twelve sex mags in his possession on his return to Britain). In one establishment, having declined to flagellate a semi-naked girl whose whip had become tangled around his neck, he informed news hounds, "I have seen enough for science and more than enough for entertainment."

No surprise the book became a bestseller given the subject matter,[16] the publicity that surrounded its writing and the profile afforded by some of its celebrity committee members, such as Kingsley Amis, Jimmy Savile and "the pious pop star"[17] Cliff Richard. Mary Whitehouse attributed its success to the fact that many people in Britain – "four-fifths" of the population to be exact – objected to the rising tide of pornography. But remained blissfully ignorant to the conundrum this created or indeed why the book should be such a hit in the very porn shops it vilified.

Despite the report's "Christian approach," and the fact that its findings and recommendations were applauded by the NVLA and NFOL, Longford was at pains to distance himself professionally from Whitehouse et al should the association tarnish the credibility of his report. In the end it didn't seem to matter. Most critics dismissed the work as ineffectual, claiming it offered no basis for legal reform. The *Times* considered it a piece of "good campaigning," the *Spectator* regarded it as "funny," while Robert Robinson in a Radio 4 interview programme called it the "lost cause of the year" and even managed to extract an apology from Longford for being rude. Having no direct impact on parliament, the reactionary report did however exert an influence, not least on the police, who embarked on raids following its publication. The police netted 150 tons of Paul Raymond's *Club International* and *Men Only*, two magazines that Longford had paid particular attention to, commenting that a crude cartoon strip in the latter was "a clear attraction to young children." An unexpected twist came when journalists at the *Sunday People* and *News of the World* embarked on an exposé of the smut trade, and unearthed corrupt dealings between the porn barons of Soho and members of Scotland Yard's Obscene Publication Squad. Pornography – in Soho at least – was flourishing on account of deals made with bent coppers stretching back twenty years.[18]

Moral crusaders also found support within 'enemy' ranks when Women's Lib and Gay Lib – two groups that would do their utmost to disrupt the Nationwide Festival of Light in Trafalgar Square before the year was out – attacked the

KEEP NASTIES FROM OUR KIDS

A PARENTS revolt against sick video nasties has been sparked off in Cleveland.

I want to protect youngsters — MP Bright

Encouraged by parents' views — Mrs. Whitehouse

By ANDREW THOMPSON

underground press for having "a sexist viewpoint" and for carrying ads for "pornography and those which offer jobs posing in it." One leaflet protested that "Lately, porn has been mistakenly associated with sexual freedom."

Women in the north of England entered the 1980s with a series of protests, ranging from sloganeering and the defacement of posters through to city centre marches and attacks on men. Such acts were an angry response to the reign of terror created by the 'Yorkshire Ripper' – the killer of at least thirteen women – and the fact that he still eluded capture after five years. It was the murder of twenty-year-old Jacqueline Hill, a student at Leeds University, that galvanised women across the country into fresh action. Some of the principal objections included men being on the streets after dark,[19] and films considered pornographic or containing violence against women.

Video was an obvious target for the lobby groups who had doggedly rallied against permissiveness since the early seventies. Fuelled by the media, who perhaps saw video as a refreshing twist on a tired argument, moral crusaders reiterated their arguments about pornography and reservedly supported the women's groups that embraced a more direct form of protest. Into this equation came the notion of *sadistic* pornography and the insidious effect it might be having on children.

The cry was for censorship and the 'banning' of videos.

FEAR . . . for Colleen Dewhurst in When a Stranger Calls

FEAR : He Knows You're Alone

FEAR of a razor . . . in the controversial murder movie Dressed to Kill

FEAR of a maniac husband . . . in Jack Nicholson's film The Shining

SPECIAL REPORT By LIZ GILL

SCANDAL OF THE X-CERT RIPPERS

"The idea is to make women afraid and vulnerable"

CONSIDER these four horrific stories.

Real-life victims

SINISTER

TERROR

VIOLENCE

PUNISHED

By and large, theatrical film distributors have to obtain a certificate prior to releasing a film into cinemas. There was no such obligation when it came to video in the early days. Feature films that had been cut for cinemas – or, in some instances, rejected outright – often appeared on video intact. Consequently, the video market quickly expanded with movies of all types, as an increasing number of distributors trawled for fresh and exclusive product. Because there was no legal requirement to submit videos for classification, companies could put out a film relatively cheaply – a set-up that led to the influx of obscure exploitation movies on some equally obscure video labels. These might be films made in less censorial climes, say Italy, or films that played the drive-in circuit of North America – the sleazy crowd-pleasing content of which would undoubtedly have caused consternation with the British Board of Film Censors if presented for a theatrical release.

Before the advent of video, films like this were near impossible to see in Britain (unless they were considered a genre classic, in which case there was a slim possibility they might turn up at a film society screening someplace). But that isn't to say video created a market for them. The following letter, printed in the winter 1982 edition of US movie magazine *Midnight Marquee*,[20] identifies the mood of frustration felt by some fans of horror films living in Britain:

> I was particularly pleased to find that you have changed to 'capsule comment' style reviews: I do not mean that to sound as if I did not enjoy your full reviews, but this change does mean that you can now review low-budget minor films (*I Spit on Your Grave*, *Final Exam* and *Student Bodies*) which, since they are unlikely to be released theatrically in England, we do not hear about normally.

The moral panic that inspired the crusade against so-called 'video nasties' was a cyclic one, fitting a pattern that can be traced back to campaigns against comics books and cheap paperbacks in the 1950s, Hollywood gangster and horror films in the 1930s, and the penny dreadfuls and penny theatres of the Victorian era. Each of these inspired a clampdown of some form or a complete ban, the primary motivation invariably cited as the protection of juveniles. More recent concerns have included the 'freedom' press of the underground in the sixties and seventies, violence on TV, gangsta rap, computer games and the Internet.

"The technical and cultural competence young people gain as spin-offs of media use," states John Springhall in *Youth, Popular Culture and Moral Panics*, "pose a potential threat to existing power relations within society."

The panic that accompanies any burgeoning popular culture or new technology occurs when the parental generation, suddenly insecure, feels it wants to be back in charge. In contrast to threats in the Victorian era, video was not perceived as exclusively the domain of the working class.

"I think this is the trouble with video. It changes the times of everything." So said a parent in *Uninvited Guests* with regard to time-shift recordings she made of sit-com *The Young Ones*, only to be shocked by the programme's content when she finally sat down to watch an episode. The parent implies the problem lies not in the fact she allowed her children to watch material typically broadcast after their bedtime, but in the technology she utilised in order that they could do so. Elsewhere in the book, another parent expresses a similar fear:

> There was a time when I videoed various things and then I realised my six-year-old could work it himself. He'd take it out, put it in, and I'd find him watching *The A-Team*.

A couple of older moral panics...
Comic books: Jack Cole's strip 'Murder, Morphine and Me!' from *True Crime Comics* May 1947 was regarded as typically lurid and objectionable. Penny dreadfuls: Boy Savages from Percival Wolfe's *Red Ralph, or The Daughter of the Night*, 1860.

A report published in May 1983 by the National Association of Head Teachers outlined concerns over the amount of time children spent watching television, as well as the easy access many children had to video films of a violent and pornographic nature. At a conference in Harrogate the following month, head teachers spoke of the "orgy of commercialism" which allowed the availability of such videos to go unchecked. Peter Roberts, headmaster of a school in Suffolk, suggested that youngsters were pooling cash to hire films clearly not suited for them. He feared they would ape the behaviour they saw on the screen or become desensitised to it. (Aside from protecting children from films of sex and violence, the conference demanded greater protection for head teachers, who were said to risk suspension following "mischievous" allegations made by children.)

We can turn the clock back over a century for much the same rhetoric. Springhall in *Youth, Popular Culture and Moral Panics* reflects on newspaper reports pertaining to penny theatres in the mid to late 1800s, and the general belief that such popular, unlicensed entertainment was responsible for the apparent rise in juvenile crime. Featuring comedy acts, magic tricks, melodramas, farces and dancers, the penny theatre – or "gaff" – was staged primarily for working-class children and adolescents who could not afford entrance to 'legitimate' theatres and music halls. But the idea of an autonomous youth subculture didn't sit well with the establishment, and with the introduction of controls such as the 1843 Theatres Act, there followed a crackdown in which the gaffs were banned from showing performances of a theatrical or musical nature without a licence.

Springhall points out, in a statement as pertinent to the rising video culture as it was the penny theatres, 'Whenever the introduction of a new mass medium is defined as a threat to the young, we can expect a campaign by adults to follow.'

"It used to be drink, smoking and drugs," said Detective Superintendent Peter Kruger, head of Scotland Yard's Obscene Publications Squad. "Then there was a fourth thing, porn, and now there's a fifth, horror."

Kruger was reflecting on the changing face of the nation's leisure pursuits, specifically an increase in complaints received from people who had been shown videos at parties, or whose children had been shown videos. From 1979 through to March 1982, the police seized in excess of 22,300 videocassettes of a pornographic nature.[21] Although the interview with Kruger in the *Sunday Times* dated May 30, 1982, makes no mention of the fact, the confiscated material was comprised of hardcore pornography only available under-the-counter or from sex shops, as opposed to being openly available on the high street. (See chapter on BLACK MARKET & PIRATES.)

The arrival of video caught the legislative bodies off-guard, and its explosive growth created a whole new industry in which few of the existing rules and regulations applied. One apparent exception was the Obscene Publications Act (OPA), whose ethereal test for obscenity – defined by law as "having a tendency to deprave and corrupt" – could be brought against horror comics and

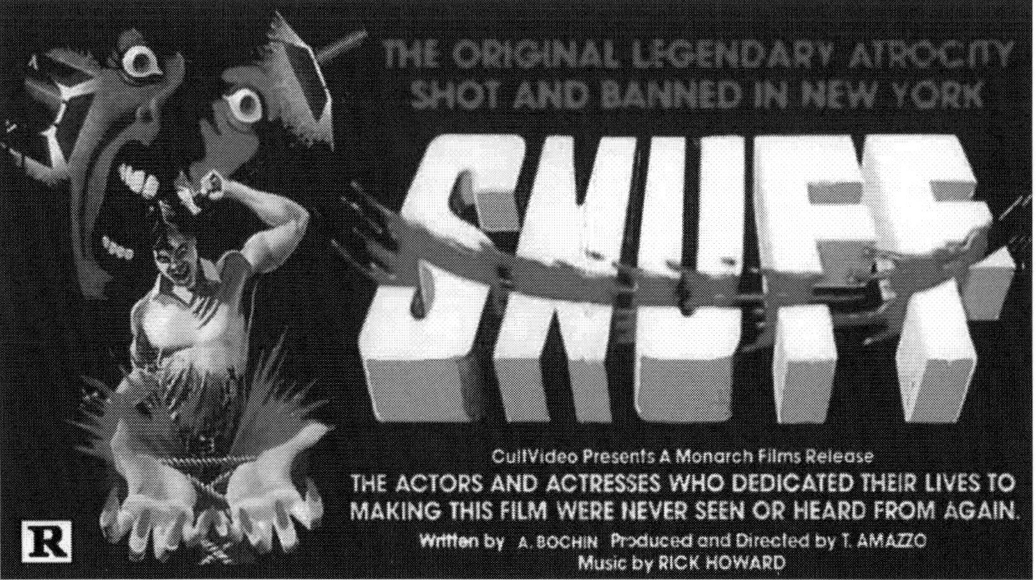

contemporary literature, as easily as it could images of a sexual nature. It was under this act that police seized the many thousands of pornographic videocassettes noted above and – with growing outrage directed at the high street – with which police sought to prosecute material of a different type: horror and terror videos.

"The horror videos are a new concept," Kruger told the *Sunday Times*, "and I think we are going to get involved with them more and more."

The video backlash had started in earnest and a new moral panic was created.

May of 1982 was the month the ASA announced it had upheld complaints against advertisements for *Cannibal Holocaust*, *The Driller Killer* and *SS Experiment Camp*, and the month a working party was mobilised to try to address the videos issue. It was also the month police seized copies of *SS Experiment Camp*, the first horror video taken with a view to prosecution.

"Some small companies seem to be cashing in on a minor boom in violence on video," reported the *Daily Mail* on May 20, 1982, "But sometimes what's on the packaging may not represent what's actually on the tape."

This adroit observation was in response to the ASA's ruling regarding offensive advertisements. A more emotive full-page article appeared a week earlier, on May 12, in the section of the newspaper devoted to mums. "Could these be your children... and this your home?" ran the header. The report centred on a survey by a careers teacher, which revealed that the top ten video films amongst youngsters comprised titles like *Scum*, *Zombie Flesh Eaters*, *The Exorcist*, *Flesh Gordon* and *The Texas Chain Saw Massacre* – "all films they were far too young to see in the local cinema." Parents not owning video players, the article determined, shouldn't necessarily feel their children were safe as there was every likelihood they would be watching videos at a friend's house.

Although the *Mail* would play a major part in forcing parliament to take a stand on video software, their campaign to "Ban the Video Nasties" was still a year away; it was a series of reports by Peter Chippindale in the *Sunday Times* that fanned the flames of dissent. Reproducing images that the ASA had condemned, the first of these reports, "How High Street Horror is Invading the Home," dated May 23, 1982, warned that

> Uncensored horror videocassettes, available to anybody of any age, have arrived in Britain's High Streets. The videos — called 'nasties' in the trade — are freely available for hire or sale off the shelves of hundreds of shops catering for the video boom. They cost as little as £2 to hire for up to four nights. They exploit extremes of violence, and are rapidly replacing sexual pornography as the video trade's biggest moneyspinner.

Whether the term 'nasties' was a colloquialism bandied around by those 'in the trade' isn't known, but its first appearance in print in connection to videocassettes dates to the *Sunday People* in December 1981, where it was used to describe a tape of pornographic content. Following Chippindale's report the term came to identify a strain of horror films supposedly removed from the traditional concept of horror, and which were a by-product of the inherently dangerous new medium of video.

> Video viewers use the freeze-frame, slow-motion and rewind buttons on their recorders to revel in the gory bits as often as they like.

Naturally, the people who peddled these 'nasties' were portrayed as an unscrupulous lot and also a little smug, as per the flippant remarks they made to Chippindale concerning films like *Snuff* and *The Driller Killer*. Said Mike Behr, managing director of Astra Video: "There's no censorship laws on video at all. What can they do about it?" A spokesperson for Vipco admitted:

High Street "nasties": three films that are helping the video boom in Britain

How High Street horror is invading the home

by Peter Chippindale

UNCENSORED horror video cassettes, available to anybody of any age, have arrived in Britain's High Streets. The videos—called "nasties" in the trade—are freely available for hire or sale off the shelves of hundreds of shops catering for the video boom. They cost as little as £2 to hire for up to four nights. They exploit extremes of violence, and are rapidly replacing sexual pornography as the video trade's biggest moneyspinner.

The "nasties" are far removed from the suspense of the traditional horror film. They dwell on murder, multiple rape, butchery, sado-masochism, mutilation of women, cannibalism and Nazi atrocities. The films have such titles as The Driller Killer—the cassette box of which carries a colour photograph of a man screaming while an electric drill is driven through his forehead. Then there is SS Experiment Camp, which features experiments on women in a Nazi concentration camp. Other titles are Cannibal Terror, Cannibal Holocaust, Blood Feast and I Spit on Your Grave.

Great adv[...] in special eff[...] have [...] that realism [...]

the reports were true or merely a sensational sales ploy, the product is horrifyingly convincing—and can now be viewed at home by anyone with a video recorder. The cassette's cover pushes the ambiguity. It reads: "Are the killings in the film for real? You are the judge."

Despite the US ban on Snuff, Mike Behr, the managing director of its British distributor, Astra Video of Croydon, says he is not worried about it being stopped here. "There's no censorship laws on video at all. What can they do about it?"

A Home Office official said last week that video cassettes

about £2 for the hire of one video cassette for between one and four nights.

A spokesman for VIPCO, the London company that distributes The Driller Killer, among other videos, said: "We are feeding a demand, not creating it. People want to see this sort of stuff, and we are giving them what they want.

"I agree that there's a lot of violence, and that is probably bad. But who are we to decide? Ideally there ought to be a line drawn somewhere — but there isn't."

This new phenomenon of video violence sparked off by technological change which has brought a huge boom in video recorders and cassettes in Britain, has left the law far behind. The Williams Committee on Obscenity and Film Censorship, which reported in 1979, did not even mention video.

Peter Lloyd, Conservative MP for Fareham, whose Cinematograph Bill is now before the House of Lords, said that his private member's bill did not even begin to touch the problem of video at home. "What worries me is not so much the pornography but [...] really harmful [...]

> We are feeding a demand, not creating it. People want to see this sort of stuff, and we are giving them what they want... I agree that there's a lot of violence, and that is probably bad. But who are we to decide?

A survey in 1983 put it into figures: two per cent of people who bought videocassettes and fifteen per cent of those who rented "chose 'horror' titles, a category that included 'nasties' but also covered the traditional horror film."[22] The ethereal 'other horror' that was the 'nasty' slowly manifested over the coming months into a quantifiable enemy – the unacceptable face of the phenomenon that was video. These 'video nasties' were the subject of much concern in the media over the next few years. This served to exaggerate the issue and prevented public interest in cheap horror movies from arguably running a natural course. (Indeed it increased it, as will be seen in the chapter to come.) "Many people, including many MPs, do not seem to appreciate how violent, brutal and sadistic these sort of films are," said Conservative MP Peter Lloyd.

> My girl raped! Two seventeen-year-olds. Said they thought girls enjoyed it after watching videos. Yes, I think that kids "grow up thinking this is the way it is" — how can they think any different when they've had no other experience?
>
> Who do I blame? I blame shit-holes like you who don't know the difference between sexual liberation and pornography. So you think that "nasties" don't affect people? "Nasties" affected two young lads, giving them a distorted view of reality.

Unease gives way to panic and a clampdown.
Previous: The *Sunday Times*, May 23, 1982. Below: *Daily Mail* headlines, June 28, 1983.

Daily Mail
TUESDAY, JUNE 28, 1983
18p
SUPER SNOOKER

Boy, 18, attacked women after seeing films

FURY OVER THE VIDEO RAPIST

By TIM MILES

DEMANDS for action on video 'nasties' mounted last night following the case of a teenage rapist who struck after watching pornographic films.

An Old Bailey judge was told that 18-year-old Martin Austin, emotionally

Virginia wins but it all goes wrong for Jimbo

Your chance to get in on the £1·7m game

> "Nasties" affected my girl, who's mentally dead for the rest of her life. "Nasties" affected me. Yes, me! And I've never even watched one. Yes, it's changed me because now I hate! I just hate! I fucking hate!
>
> —Letter from Anon, *NME*, March 31, 1985

'Video nasties' were used by some lawbreakers to try to vindicate themselves of their crimes via the negative publicity given to video. In April 1983, a sixteen-year-old boy admitted to the charge of burglary with intent to rape, claiming that *Confessions of a Window Cleaner* – a British sex comedy in the mould of the *Carry On* films – had made him do it. "I watched the film and then went out because I wanted to have sex with a girl," the boy said. The *Times* reported the incident as "Youth Tried Rape After Seeing Video." Soon to follow was the case of eighteen-year-old Martin Austin, found guilty on June 27, 1983 of two counts of rape and seven charges of burglary. The unemployed youth, emotionally immature with a low IQ, was described by the press as a habitual glue-sniffer

Below: The *Sun*, December 17, 1976. Inset: Sixteen-year-old Danny Logan is driven to kill because of the 'brutality and unending murders flashed across the screen' in *Telekiller* (NEL, 1978), a novel cashing in on the cause-and-effect argument raging in the media.

The Sun examines a new sickening glut in blood and guts films

By BRIAN WESLEY

FANCY a nice night out at the pictures? How about sitting comfortably while Gregory Peck stabs a woman in the face with a fork?

Or Laurence Olivier tortures Dustin Hoffman with a dentist's drill?

VIOLENCE

Will you ever dare go to the pictures?

It's too gory even for the censor

WHAT DOES IT DO TO US?

Blood

Hunters

Chase

Censor

Excited

Scenes of violence from The Texas Chain Saw Massacre and Marathon Man

who lived in a fantasy world ruled by a daily diet of films like *I Spit on Your Grave*. "I got the ideas for the rapes from a so-called video nasty," Austin told the police, before receiving six years in youth custody. Ignorant to the fact that her son was hiring such films and watching them at home, Mrs Joan Austin told the press, "These films have helped destroy my son's life. They must be banned before another boy's mind is infected by them."

The case acted as a catalyst. The *Daily Mail* responded with the front-page headline "Fury Over The Video Rapist," and reported how Austin – whose "moral values had been obliterated by the video films" – had intended only to burgle on the two nights he committed rape. Their editorial comment[23] queried "How many more women will be savaged and defiled by youths weaned on a diet of rape videos...?" Pulling out all the emotive stops, the *Mail* accused the government of dithering while

> our children can continue to buy sadism from the video-pusher as easily — and as cheaply — as they can buy fruit gums from the sweetie shop...

In reference to *SS Experiment Camp*, seized by police some months previously, the *Mail* lambasted depictions of Nazi atrocities that were "complete with the screams of the Jewish girl victims, played for kicks. And rape, rape, rape."

> Britain had fought the last World War against Hitler to defeat a creed so perverted that it spawned such horrors in awful truth. Now the nation allows our own children to be nurtured on these perverted horrors and on any permutation of them under the guise of entertainment.
>
> Are we insane? Are we bent on rotting our own society from within?

Two months later, the "soul-soilers that deaden decency and encourage depravity" struck again in the guise of Christopher Meah, aged thirty, who received two life sentences for separate counts of sexual assault and rape, and for using a knife with intent to cause grievous bodily harm. Having suffered brain damage in a car accident some years earlier, the defendant was said to have been driven completely out of his head by drugs, drink and video films "of the most vile kind." The court heard how Meah acted as if "he was looking at himself playing a video nasty film role." Mrs Christine Meah claimed that her husband "was loving, kind and considerate until he became addicted to watching an endless string of horrifying video films containing detailed scenes of the most depraved and vicious kind."

She added:

> When my husband first began watching these videos, we treated them as a bit of a sick joke. Now I am convinced that they changed his personality and that they should be banned... He began watching them day and night and they obviously turned him into a Jekyll and Hyde. Things got so bad that our daughters were waking up in the early hours and switching the video on.

The furore surrounding 'sadistic' videos in the early eighties had also surrounded 'sadistic' films in the seventies. In December 1976, the *Sun* had ruminated on recent cinema releases, including *Marathon Man*, *Rolling Thunder* and *The Texas Chain Saw Massacre*, and asked, "Will you ever dare go to the pictures?" It reported that Dr Malcolm Carruthers, a consultant clinical pathologist of the Maudsley Hospital in London, took a dozen volunteers to see

'The latest fashion... in murder.' Nancy Allen, Brian de Palma's *Dressed to Kill.*

A Clockwork Orange and *Soldier Blue*. Measuring heart rate and testing urine, he recorded that the volunteers[24] "got very, very excited at the violent scenes... They were also revolted. Their heart beats slowed down. In any person there are always these two divided reactions – excitement and revulsion." Despite the apparent normality of his findings, the doctor deduced that audiences are becoming "blasé about violence... And if youngsters in particular turn to violence how can we blame them?"

In the early eighties there was concern over a cycle of horror films whose plots revolved around a lone killer hunting and butchering the other characters. These films, known as 'stalk-and-slash,' created controversy on both sides of the Atlantic when accused of signifying a trend for misogynistic violence. In Britain, the likes of *He Knows You're Alone* and *When A Stranger Calls* were released amidst the anxiety of the Yorkshire Ripper murders.[25] "The idea," wrote Liz Gill in the *Daily Express*, "is to make women afraid and vulnerable." She asked the reader to "consider these four horrific stories":

> An attractive middle-aged woman is slashed to death by a maniac wielding a razor.
>
> A pretty teenager is sexually assaulted and so badly battered that her body is identifiable only by her jewellery.
>
> Another teenager soon to be a bridesmaid for her best friend is found brutally murdered, her head has been severed from her body.
>
> A young girl student is viciously killed as she walks home alone. Her body is grotesquely mutilated.

Stories two and four happened, stated Gill, while the first and third were episodes from films on release in Britain at the time. A caption beneath pictures showing two women who had been recently murdered (including Ripper victim Jacqueline Hill), reflects "Could their killers have been aroused by horror films?"

The film most often criticised for its portrayal of sex and graphic violence was Brian de Palma's *Dressed To Kill*, a stylish remodel of *Psycho* – a film which Gill applauded – starring Angie Dickinson and Michael Caine. Critics, care workers, former sex symbols and film directors were unanimous in their outrage. James Ferman, secretary of the British Board of Film Censors (BBFC), on the other hand offered that it was wrong to make any one film pay the price for a whole genre and claimed that films had become less violent over the years. "As far as violence is concerned," he told *Photoplay* in January 1981,

> I don't think we're getting the same kind. We had an awful lot of very, very violent Hong Kong and Italian movies in the mid-seventies; blood everywhere, loads of rape scenes... from America too, like *The Texas Chain Saw Massacre*, a film we've never given a certificate to.

Unfortunately for Ferman, both the violence of the mid seventies and the films to which he never gave a certificate were about to return on video. And, for women who had attacked cinemas and hurled red paint and eggs at screens showing *Dressed To Kill*, a new target arrived in the form of any video shop that carried X-rated material.[26]

Staging protests outside shops selling violent and X-rated videocassettes in December 1982, fifty women took part in a two-hour protest at the Video Centre on Tottenham Court Road in London, resulting in three arrests for obstruction. In Liverpool, seven women who sat down in the doorway of Cut Price Records were dragged on to the pavement by shop assistants. The following month, a group calling itself Angry Women launched attacks on video shops in West Yorkshire, breaking windows and lighting fires. Other shops were spray-painted with slogans.

The *Daily Mail*'s "Fury Over The Video Rapist" headline coincided with the announcement that a damning report on the police handling of the Yorkshire Ripper investigation was to be made public.

The video trade was preparing itself for a police purge on 'nasties' following the successful prosecution of *The Driller Killer* and *Death Trap* at Willesden

Magistrates Court at the end of August 1982, and *I Spit on Your Grave* in Croydon the following month. These were the first films found obscene for content of "ultra-sadistic horror and terror, rather than straightforward sexual pornography."[27] The DPP brought charges under Section Three of the Obscene Publications Act, which meant forfeiture and destruction of the videocassettes under a magistrate's warrant. (In the case of *I Spit on Your Grave*, this meant a total of 234 tapes that had been removed by police from the offices of Astra Video.)

A far more serious ruling would have been a Section Two prosecution, which requires the publisher of an obscene article to face a full criminal trial, and the prospect of a jail sentence of up to three years.[28] The leniency in this instance was based on the case having no precedent, and the fact the distributors willingly handed over the master tapes to police. Also to be considered was that under Section Two the case may have taken several months to hear, and the DPP were anxious to be seen to make a move. Mary Whitehouse, however, thought the leniency to be a public scandal, and accused the DPP of protecting the interests of the video nasty distributors.

But the illogical notion that 'nasties' were "a tangible concrete genre removed from other forms of video,"[29] did little to help traders determine what films to look out for and avoid in future. There existed no official set of guidelines. Following the ruling against *The Driller Killer* and *Death Trap*, the Video Trade

Association – who represented the owners of rental shops – informed its members and the press

> We now believe that a lot of police forces will be keen to take action, often spurred by complaints by members of the public. We have had a lot of calls from traders who are very worried. Half are concerned that they might be doing something illegal, and the others are worried about a substantial loss of profit if they withdraw the nasties.
>
> We are advising them to take the two titles which have already been through the courts off the shelves immediately, but we are also warning them that any film which exploits gratuitous violence may now be open to the same sort of prosecution as pornography. There are probably lots of other uncensored films around as bad as the ones which have been convicted and they may be liable under the act.[30]

Indeed there were, as witnessed in the many thousands of horror film videocassettes seized over the coming year and a rapidly expanding list of blacklisted titles. But what exactly constituted "unnecessary violence," one of the damning allegations levelled at the nasties? And by what comparative scale were such scenes and these films being measured? No one knew, least of all the police who were seizing them.

"The forthcoming election and the threat of video nasties has given a new impetus to our campaign." Speaking for the NVLA in the run up to the June 1983 General Election, Mary Whitehouse warned the political parties of the perils they faced should they ignore the issue of video legislation. Not one to take the ex-schoolteacher's views lightly, Margaret Thatcher, soon to win a second term as Prime Minister, pledged in her election manifesto to protect the young against video pornography and horror.

Video's golden age was fast becoming a twilight zone.

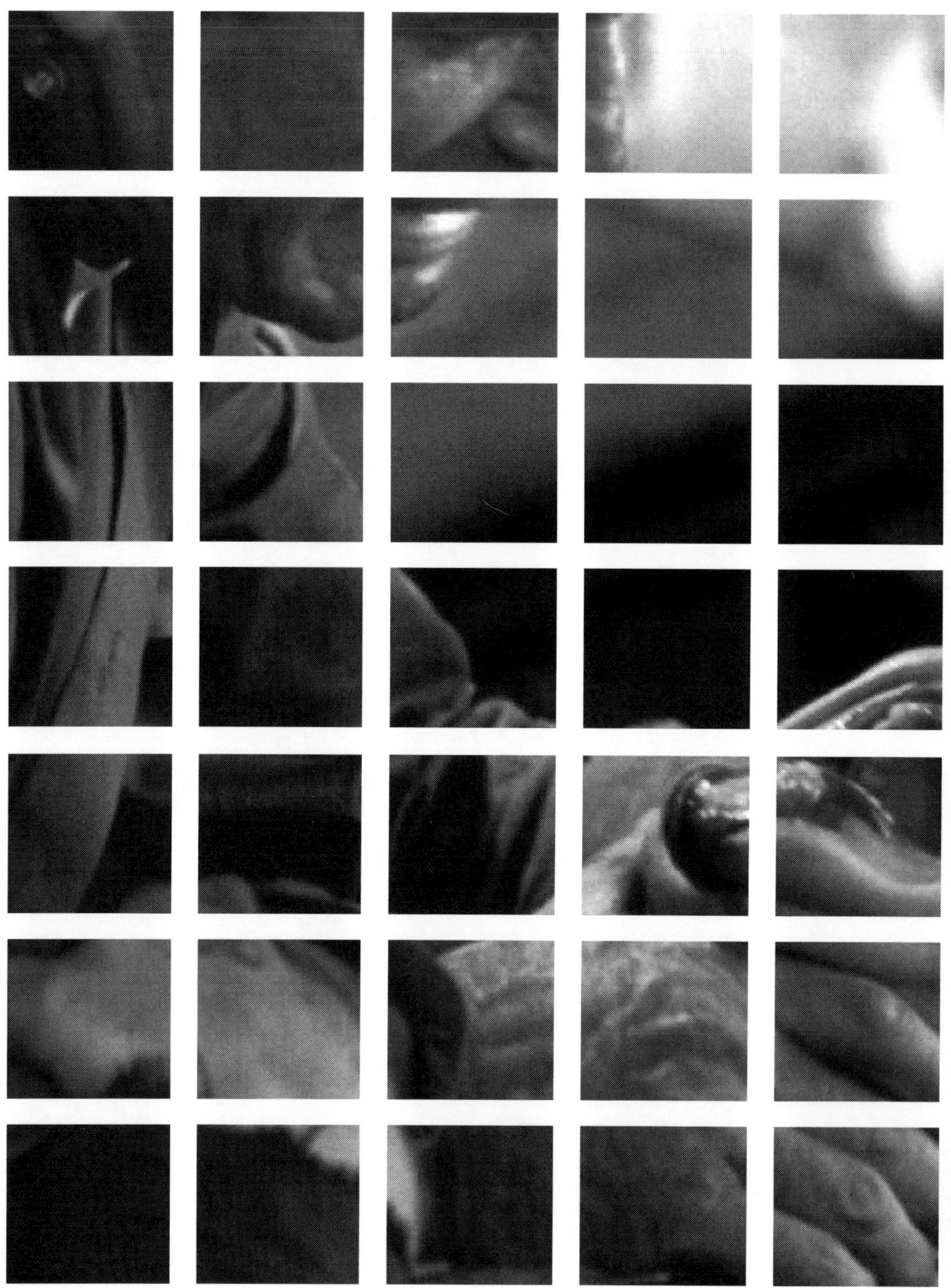

Clampdown

'PRIVATELY FUNDED BY INDIVIDUALS AND CHURCHES'

IT DOESN'T TAKE an awful lot to trigger the machinations of the Obscene Publications Act. A police constable may apply for a warrant to search any premises in which he has 'reasonable cause' to suspect obscene articles are being kept for gain. This reasonable cause may be an unverified complaint from a member of the public or observations the police themselves have made. Under the original 1857 Act, a magistrate would require some evidence of sale to issue a warrant, but with the reformed 1959 Act, the police could base their action on a mere suspicion.

Suspicion in the case of the 'video nasties' arose from an article published in a Sunday newspaper. In exposing the violent films that were supposedly "replacing sexual pornography as the video trade's biggest moneyspinner," the *Sunday Times* dated May 23, 1982,[1] provided the police with reasonable enough cause for action. More than that, it put them in a position whereby they couldn't be seen *not* to act. Playing devil's advocate, the article effectively put video distributors above the law, while its author pressed the Home Office for comment. Consequently, Scotland Yard's Obscene Publications Squad secured a warrant and raided the offices of Astra Video, removing copies of *SS Experiment Camp*, one of the films cited in the report. As Detective Superintendent Peter Kruger speculated in the *Sunday Times* the following week, this was undoubtedly just the first in a line of video horror films deserving of police attention.

It was. But little did the detective realise quite how far the line of videos stretched or the ramifications of trying to police it. Two years of police raids and questionable charges under the Obscene Publications Act would come to a head in 1984, with the formation of a highly controversial parliamentary bill known as the Video Recordings Act. This legislation marked the official end for many video titles, not all of them 'nasty'.

Charges of obscenity against the written word[2] were effectively abandoned in January 1976 following the acquittal of *Inside Linda Lovelace*, a book in which the star of *Deep Throat* revealed how to suck cock and perform anal sex. In his summing up, the judge lamented, "If this book is not obscene within the definition of the [Obscene Publications] Act it might well be difficult to imagine anything that would fall into that category." (Not unreasonably, given publicity of this calibre, the circulation of the book rose from 20,000 to 600,000 within the space of three weeks.) From here on, pictorial depiction of the labia and the erect penis were considered the main taboo subjects, so too any depiction of anal, oral, animal or group sex. (Child sex was covered by the Protection of Children Act 1978.) This became the 'rule of thumb' by which police gauged obscenity, and such matter invariably stood to be charged. But things were rarely clear-cut, particularly if the contentious material didn't originate from a sex shop.

British obscenity law is decidedly vague and elastic. What constitutes an obscene article in one part of the country may be freely available in another. This may have as much to do with, say, the religious beliefs of the area's Chief Constable of Police as it does the available manpower.[3]

A confidential memorandum issued by Scotland Yard's Assistant Commissioner (Crime) in March 1970 highlighted the difficulties in policing pornography and obscenity. Raids on "dirty bookshops" resulted in no real protest, and it was a relatively simple matter "to assert that the seized articles [were] 'filth for filth's sake'..." However, the report also posited there was a level of pornography designated "exceptionally delicate, where any police action will obviously attract much publicity, subsequent analysis and criticism." Pornography of this latter type was said to comprise

(a) Displays in recognised galleries and books expensively published.

(b) Works of alleged or real masters.

(c) Exhibitions of famous, infamous or notorious individuals.

(d) Films at private clubs and associations, etc.

The memorandum appears to have been influenced by *Flesh*, a film from the Andy Warhol stable, containing nudity, sex and swear words. Or rather,

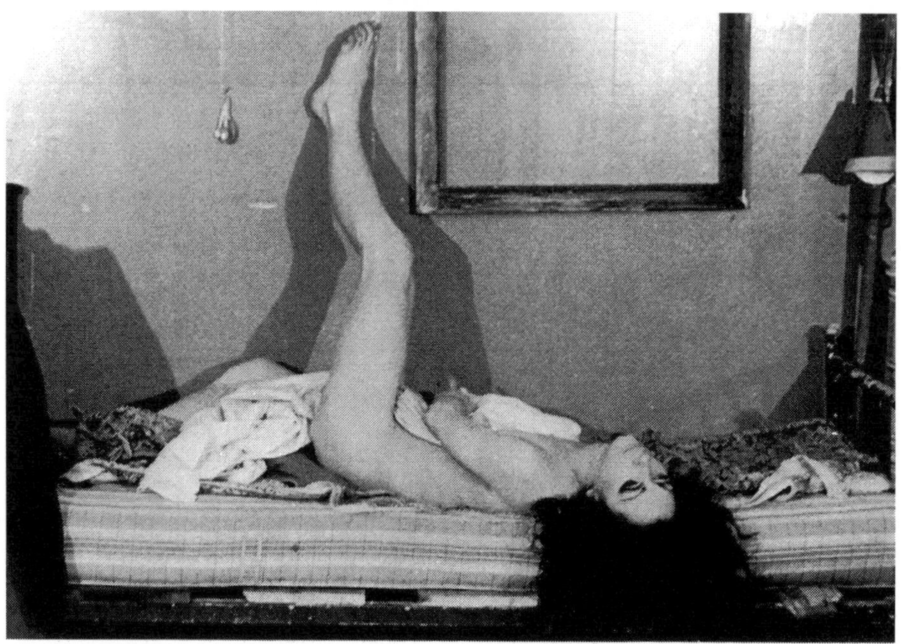

VAUGHAN FILMS LTD. present
ANDY WARHOL'S

influenced by media reactions following a screening[4] which was halted after no less than thirty-two policemen descended on the theatre. Not only did the invading officers take the print, but also the projector, screen, and the name and address of everybody in attendance. *Flesh* was a critically acclaimed film, and the Open Space Theatre where the screening took place was a "reputable theatre club, supported by the Arts Council, with a membership of intellectuals."[5] The incident made headline news, with most newspapers showing support for the theatre.[6] Questions were even raised in the House of Commons. Ultimately, the owners of the Open Space Theatre were not prosecuted for obscenity but did plead guilty to failing to uphold a members-only policy on the door. It may have been a conviction – albeit not the one envisaged – but the police weren't entirely off the hook. In a publicity masterstroke,[7] Andy Warhol flew in and paid the fines imposed on the theatre owners, telling reporters that it "was the least he could do to fight against censorship in Britain."

Despite the *Flesh* debacle, the police were to spend a good deal of the 1970s seizing material of an "exceptionally delicate" nature. The result being, as per the cautionary advice from the Assistant Commissioner, "much publicity, subsequent analysis and criticism." Throughout the decade, the underground press was a prime target because of their use of pornography for political ends. The trials of *International Times*, *The Little Red Schoolbook*, *Nasty Tales*, *Libertine* and *Oz*[8] all took place amidst a blaze of publicity and critical disdain. In the *Oz* case – at twenty-seven working days, the longest obscenity trial in British history – the resultant guilty verdicts brought riotous crowds outside the Old Bailey and saw the presiding judge burned in effigy. On appeal the charges of obscenity that had landed the publishers in jail were quashed, and at a cost of some £100,000, the press was unanimous in condemning the trial a disaster.

Previous and above: The films of Paul Morrissey and Andy Warhol were championed by the BBFC, disliked by police.

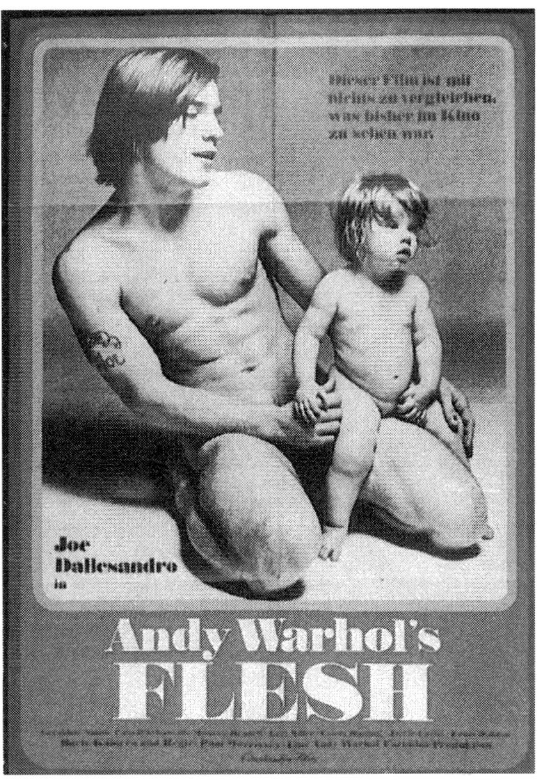

The Obscene Publications Act was capricious and unreliable. Unlike the material which fell within the ridiculous criterion of "filth for filth's sake" – constituting the sex shop smut seized by police with little ado or objection – almost everything else brought with it defence lawyers and expert witnesses willing to testify in its favour.

When material is seized by the police, it is examined by the Crown Prosecution Service (formerly police lawyers) and the DPP, whose office will then decide on what action to take. If the decision is made that the material is obscene and liable to have a corrupting influence, its publisher faces proceedings under one of two statutory alternatives. As noted in the previous chapter, these consist of either a prosecution for a criminal offence under Section Two of the 1959 Obscene Publications Act, or a civil forfeiture hearing under Section Three.[9]

Not all material has to go through police hands to reach the DPP. Outraged members of the public are entitled to submit work they consider to be obscene directly to the department themselves. "Custodian of public morals" – as Geoffrey Robertson labels the DPP in his book, *Obscenity* – is not a role that many directors would like to project however, particularly when in prosecuting they are forced to act as censor. Director Sir Theobald Matthew said of the Obscene Publications Bill in 1957, "I do not know, and I do not suppose anybody else knows, what corrupts." His successor, Sir Norman Skelhorn, stated in 1973:

> The DPP is not acting as a censor, he is not judging the moral standards of the day. All we try to do is predict what a jury is likely to do. We try to assess the prospects of conviction if we prosecute. Of course, it is not easy to predict what a jury is likely to do, but one is guided by the statutory definition of obscenity and one's experience of how the courts have reacted in previous cases.

But court cases are hardly consistent, and the statutory definition of obscenity offers little guidance. Indeed the Test of Obscenity – the tendency to deprave and corrupt – is ambiguous to the point of meaninglessness. (In the case of the *Oz* trial, the judge decided to broaden the scope of the Act by incorporating the literal meaning of the word 'obscene.'[10] It was this serious misdirection that helped to overturn the charges on appeal.) It comes as no surprise therefore that the law is unwilling to pre-empt what might constitute an obscene item prior to it being published. Indeed, when the firm of Calder & Boyars took the precaution of contacting the DPP for just such advice in the matter of *Last Exit to Brooklyn*, the response was apologetic:

> If you find — as I am afraid you will — that this is a most unhelpful letter, it is not because I wish to be unhelpful but because I get no help from the Acts.

Hubert Selby Jr's *Last Exit to Brooklyn* was published in the UK in January 1966. The following August a search warrant was issued for copies to be seized from bookshops, and in November, under Section Three of the Obscene Publications Act, the book was ordered to be destroyed. As one reporter put it, Britain once again had "made herself the laughing stock of the civilised world." These proceedings had been launched, not by the DPP, who hadn't considered the book obscene, but by a private individual who believed the book was.[11] The destruction order given in court obliged the DPP to change its mind.[12]

If the 1959 Obscene Publications Act was vague when it came to differentiating serious literature from pulp pornography (the purpose for which it was intended), its application to videocassettes in the 1980s proved even more problematic.

"Videos are difficult to deal with because you cannot flip through them like a publication," was one of the obvious drawbacks of policing video obscenity, as voiced by Peter Lloyd MP. A bigger pitfall, however, was that over the course of the next few years, more than ever the police would be working as arbiters of public taste. And in so doing they would chase a nationwide phenomenon with a law that was far from dependable.

'This much fun couldn't be legal.' *The Best Little Whorehouse in Texas* – a musical comedy seized by eager police as liable to prosecution.

Indeed, the first obscenity case concerning video resulted in the court deciding that the medium fell outside the scope of the Obscene Publications Act. Film club owner Tom Hays and two of his employees were charged with showing a sexually explicit videotape in a Soho basement cinema. Defending the case at Knightsbridge Crown Court was Geoffrey Robertson QC who argued that a videotape was not a film or "article" as defined by the Act,[13] but a "piece of plastic storing invisible electrical impulses capable of being converted into audio-visual signals."[14] This was a fact supported by a BBC TV engineer called as an expert witness. Hays was acquitted in July 1980 and the offending tape – comprising material copied from 8mm film – was returned to him. "As it stands," Hays optimistically told reporters, "I could, if I wanted to, show whatever I liked on video."

With some urgency the matter was redressed. In September 1980, the Court of Appeal ruled that obscene displays from videotape were "indistinguishable to the watcher from conventional film shows" and therefore would be covered by the Obscene Publications Act. Police wasted no time clearing shelves of anything they thought suitable for prosecution. When it came to 'video nasties' quite often titles were seized by mistake, while other titles would be acquitted but then seized again. As had happened with other media, the zeal with which the police undertook their purge on video varied from one force to the next.

Armed with search warrants, copies of Francis Ford Coppola's *Apocalypse Now* would be taken by police – for no reason other than it sounded like the cheap Italian horror movie *Cannibal Apocalypse*, which was already considered suitable for prosecution. In another incident, police took away a copy of Vernon Sewell's *The Blood Beast Terror*, a 1967 film starring Peter Cushing that regularly airs on television. The film was eventually returned to the shop and placed by the owner in the 'for sale' section so as to avoid it being seized again. Copies of *The Best Little Whorehouse in Texas* were also netted, an innocuous musical comedy starring Burt Reynolds and Dolly Parton, but with a tantalising box blurb: "This much fun couldn't be legal."

The Evil Dead, having already enjoyed a successful run in cinemas, was a horror film that seemed to galvanise forces across the country in a video raiding frenzy. When a Leeds-based video firm was finally acquitted of obscenity in June 1984 for having stocked the film, its distributors asked the DPP for no less than forty-seven other cases pending *The Evil Dead* to be dropped.

The truth of the matter was that the video nasty wasn't a quantifiable entity;

it wasn't a definable genre alongside, say, the western, thriller or sci-fi. The BVA, unable to get the DPP to disclose details of any guidelines, shrewdly noted that 'video nasty' was, simply,

> A phrase coined by the press that generally refers to material that can include disembowelling, castration, cannibalism, and humiliation.

Pressured by the industry and seeking to help police with some semblance of a directive for its many raids, a Parliamentary Question on July 23, 1984, led the DPP to draw up a set of guidelines. Maintaining that it was for the court to decide what was and wasn't obscene, the department recommended that a video work

> is likely to be regarded as obscene if it portrays violence to such a degree and so explicitly that its appeal can only be to those who are disposed to derive positive enjoyment from seeing such violence.
> Other factors may include:
> violence perpetrated by children;
> self-mutilation;
> violent abuse of women or children;
> cannibalism;
> use of vicious weapons (e.g. broken bottle);
> use of everyday implements (e.g. screwdriver, shears, electric drill);
> violence in a sexual context.

Style was also acknowledged as important. "The more convincing the depictions of violence," stated the DPP, "the more harmful it is likely to be."

> Who is the perpetrator of the violence, and what is his reaction to it?
> Who is the victim, and what is his reaction?
> How is the violence inflicted, and in what circumstances?
> How explicit is the description of the wounds, mutilation or death? How prolonged? How realistic?
> Is the violence justifiable in narrative terms?

These signposts didn't really benefit anyone much. They could be interpreted in a variety of ways, and just as easily absolve those films they sought to identify.

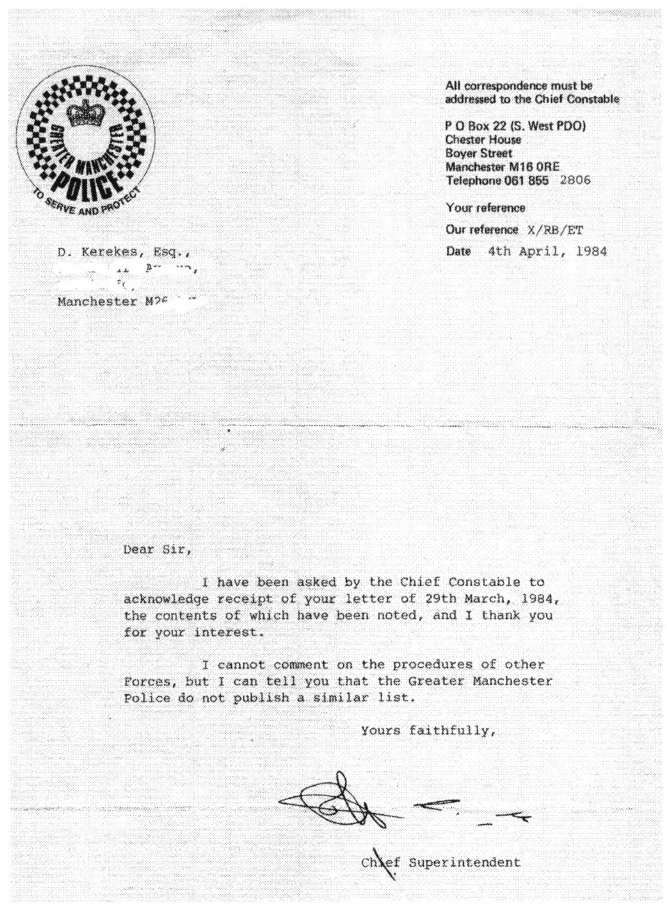

GREATER MANCHESTER POLICE
TO SERVE AND PROTECT

All correspondence must be addressed to the Chief Constable

P O Box 22 (S. West PDO)
Chester House
Boyer Street
Manchester M16 0RE
Telephone 061 855 2806

Your reference
Our reference X/RB/ET
Date 4th April, 1984

D. Kerekes, Esq.,

Manchester M2

Dear Sir,

I have been asked by the Chief Constable to acknowledge receipt of your letter of 29th March, 1984, the contents of which have been noted, and I thank you for your interest.

I cannot comment on the procedures of other Forces, but I can tell you that the Greater Manchester Police do not publish a similar list.

Yours faithfully,

Chief Superintendent

(The rape victim in *I Spit on Your Grave* avenges herself by gruesomely murdering her assailants in a series of violent acts that few viewers would deny was justifiable.) The guidelines didn't enable the police to narrow down their scale of operations and they continued to raid indiscriminately. An exasperated Alf Morton, president of the Greater Manchester Retail Video Association, couldn't understand it. "They are spending an awful lot of money on raids," said Morton of the police. "If they would just give us the information about films which are likely to bring prosecutions they could be taken out of the shops almost overnight."

This sentiment was shared by every retailer in the country who lobbied Sir Thomas Hetherington, then Director of Public Prosecutions, to do something about it.[15] As a result, Scotland Yard compiled a list of titles that had been prosecuted under the Obscene Publications Act, or were considered suitable for prosecution. This list came to be known as the 'DPP list', aka the 'video nasties' and 'banned' list, and initially comprised thirty-nine titles. With monthly updates the number of titles fluctuated, reaching more than sixty different titles before tailing off again. This rise was attributable to police finding fresh titles they considered obscene, while the drop came when films were acquitted in court or examined by the DPP who decided not to launch proceedings. There was much ambiguity. Early incarnations of the list didn't include *Death Trap*, prosecuted back in August 1982, but did include *Snuff*, a film pulled by its distributor and

Previous: Greater Manchester police reply to co-author David Kerekes' enquiry relating to the existence of a DPP list in April 1984. Below: Photocopy of perhaps the first list of videocassettes liable to prosecution as issued by the DPP – a total of thirty-nine titles.

HORROR VIDEO CASSETTES

Following the Attorney General's Statement in the House of Commons on 23 July 1984 a list of titles of video cassettes of the horror variety which have been the subject of prosecution under Section 2 of the Obscene Publications Act, 1959 or advised as suitable for such prosecution is as follows:-

HORROR

ABSURD (Uncut)
ANTHROPOPHAGEOUS BEAST
AXE
BEAST IN HEAT
BLOOD BATH
BLOOD FEAST
BLOOD RITES
BLOODY MOON
BURNING, THE (Uncut)
CANNIBAL APOCALYPSE
CANNIBAL FEROX (Uncut)
CANNIBAL HOLOCAUST
CANNIBAL MAN
DEVIL HUNTER
DON'T GO IN THE WOODS ALONE
DRILLER KILLER
EVIL SPEAK (Uncut)
EXPOSE
FACES OF DEATH
FIGHT FOR YOUR LIFE
FOREST OF FEAR
FRANKENSTIEN (BY ANDY WARHOL)
GESTAPO'S LAST ORGY
HOUSE BY THE CEMETARY
HOUSE ON THE EDGE OF THE PARK
I SPIT ON YOUR GRAVE
ISLAND OF DEATH (NICO MASTORAKIS VERSION)
LAST HOUSE ON THE LEFT
LOVE CAMP 7
MADHOUSE
MARDI GRAS MASSACRE
NIGHTMARES IN A DAMAGED BRAIN
NIGHT OF THE BLOODY APES
NIGHT OF THE DEMON
SNUFF
SS EXPERIMENT CAMP
TENEBRAE
WEREWOLF AND THE YETI
ZOMBIE FLESH EATERS (Uncut)

never officially released in Britain. Scotland Yard didn't agree with some of the verdicts returned on the more notorious videocassettes. *The Evil Dead* was begrudgingly dropped from the list several months after it was cleared of obscenity, while other titles never left the list at all. Among the latter were *I Spit on Your Grave*, *Cannibal Apocalypse*, *SS Experiment Camp* and *The Last House on the Left*, for which a London-based video shop owner was acquitted in April 1985.[16] (The full content of the list is discussed in THE DPP39.)

Knowledge of the list for most people came via the film magazines that reproduced it, specifically publications devoted to horror and fantasy. Very few people during the video clampdown of the eighties recall ever having seen an actual copy of the list, a fact that has led some traders and police to erroneously surmise that it never existed in the first place.

"There was never an official list," states Steve Ellison,

> There was a list that each Chief Superintendent of each constabulary probably had in his head and wrote down, but there was never an official list; nothing that the DPP put out to constabularies and said 'these are the films to seize.'[17]

The view is shared by Chris Glazebrook, buyer of video films for a chain of department stores. "I think the list is something of a myth. I never saw or heard of an official list."[18] However, the fact that a DPP list did exist is irrefutable: after much searching the authors of this book managed to secure a copy of it from a reliable source. But the confusion which surrounds it is understandable, deriving from the fact that to see it one had to seek it out, and to seek it out one had to know it existed. It was never officially made public, nor was it offered to those people one assumes needed it the most.

In theory, Scotland Yard's Vice Squad would distribute each new list to police authorities around the country. From here it would have been available to anyone who requested a copy. Many dealers had hoped that, if given a list, they could work with police in identifying the 'nasties,' remove them from shelves and thereby safeguard themselves against a raid. But plenty of local forces remained ignorant, denying knowledge of a blacklist,[19] as evidenced when one author of this book contacted Greater Manchester Police concerning police raids taking place around the country (see page 70). Or, perhaps police were unwilling to work with the retailers. The raids continued.

On February 3, 1984, three men were found guilty of possessing obscene articles for publication and gain. These comprised 212 videocassettes of *Nightmares in a Damaged Brain* which had been seized in October 1982 following police raids on premises in London and Leeds. The men were sentenced under Section Two of the Obscene Publications Act. Malcolm Fancey and Roger Morley both received suspended sentences and fines, while company secretary David Hamilton-Grant was jailed for six months.[20] This effectively marked the end of the grace period afforded the video industry; until now no one had

actually gone to prison for handling 'video nasties'. Defending the case was the distinguished Geoffrey Robertson, who several years earlier had rankled the courts in arguing that video was not covered by the Obscene Publications Act.[21] The expert witnesses included film critics Derek Malcolm and Marjorie Bilbow. It was while giving evidence on the film's competent camerawork that Malcolm was interrupted by Judge Christopher Beaumont, who unwittingly quantified the inanity of the whole 'nasties' debate in his remark:

> How is this relevant to the jury in deciding the case? You might say the German tank invasion of Poland was well executed. Does excellence and camerawork help the jury to come to a conclusion in the case?[22]

In what may have been a premeditated reversal on the corruption of minors argument, Malcolm defended *Nightmares in a Damaged Brain* as a work concerned with the likely perversion of children by the excesses of the adult world. A bloody decapitation scene at the end, he deduced, was the film's "least memorable part." Marjorie Bilbow agreed, believing that while the film showed promise and was on a par with "early Hitchcock", its bloodshed was over the top albeit "commercially important."

After watching the film, the jury of three women and nine men decided that it was likely to deprave and corrupt. "People who make money out of this sort of obscenity," concurred Judge Beaumont, "have got to be punished."

For April Electronics – distributing the film through their subsidiary label, World of Video 2000 – the verdict meant liquidation. Although the severity of the sentencing set a precedent, the trial of *Nightmares in a Damaged Brain* wasn't the first instance of a successful Section Two prosecution. That dubious honour fell to a video dealer in Leeds called Stephen Taylor, who in 1983 had received a fine of £600 for dealing in 'nasties'. Although he considered the sum to be excessive, Taylor was mindful that things could have been much worse had this not been the first prosecution. "If I had been the second, I might have got six months' imprisonment."

Taylor was interviewed for a Channel 4 documentary titled *A Gentleman's Agreement?*, which investigated the idea of a voluntary code of practice within the video industry. Driving around in his van and delivering videos to his clients – amongst them "the Speights and their five children", about to take receipt of *Nightmares in a Damaged Brain* – he told the film-makers that he often inquired as to what customers really thought about the 'video nasties'. "Not one of them objected," he said. This was the attitude of a good deal of the video viewing public. Chris Glazebrook, asked whether he had ever received complaints about a film during his years working in video software, told the authors:

> The only film we ever had any complaints about was *Monty Python's Life of Brian*, on the grounds that it was blasphemous. No one ever complained about violence or bad language.[23]

Of course, this runs contrary to the outrage expressed in the media and by lobby groups and MPs, intent on demonising video. So fired up were some that even a debate on the topic of horror films was out of the question, as per the aforementioned *A Gentleman's Agreement?*, which almost didn't air because of those who were hostile towards its subject matter. Its title derived from a statement made by Gareth Wardell MP. Withdrawing from Parliament a Private Member's Bill aimed at legislating against the nasties, Wardell made it clear that he thought it unlikely the industry would be able to control itself, as suggested by the BVA. The profits were just too large, he lamented; how could a gentleman's agreement be expected of "people who basically are not gentlemen"?

The documentary was scheduled for broadcast on June 8, 1983. The 8:30 PM time slot was moved back to 10:30 PM on account of the inclusion of scenes taken from video films containing "extreme violence,"[24] notably *I Spit on Your Grave* and *SS Experiment Camp* which had been found obscene the previous September. But the Independent Broadcasting Authority's decision to allow the documentary to be broadcast at all riled Mary Whitehouse, who requested that the DPP intervene and stop the screening. Mrs Whitehouse told the *Times* newspaper that she had not actually viewed the documentary, nor the scenes to which she objected. "It really would not have made the slightest difference," she asserted, "because I know very well what they are – we were responsible for bringing them before the courts." Police were also said to be alarmed that extracts from obscene material would be aired. The DPP pointed out that it wasn't an offence under the Obscene Publications Act to transmit the scenes, so the broadcast went ahead.

The following month, July 1983, it was reported that of the 5,000 accredited video shop owners in Britain,[25] almost half were in support of government legislation to control the 'video nasties'. Responding to the question "Would you prefer a clear law to govern what videocassettes you should stock rather than a voluntary certification system?", forty-five per cent said yes, fifty-three per cent said no, and two per cent of the dealers didn't know.

This shift of opinion away from the voluntary self-regulation volunteered by the BVA, reflected the concern dealers felt regarding the increasing negative press and prospect of a police raid. But the premature death knell for self-regulation was to come from outside the industry. Still smarting over the DPP's refusal to stop at her behest the screening of *A Gentleman's Agreement?*, Mary Whitehouse attacked the video medium with renewed vigour. In 1980 she had sent a letter to the Home Secretary citing video as being "the biggest threat to the quality of life in Britain." In 1983, along with the NVLA, she held special fringe meetings at the Conservative Party conference, showing excerpts from several 'video nasties' (outraged by the excerpts in Channel 4's documentary, this presentation however posed no dilemma to Whitehouse). These screenings led to a meeting at Conservative Party offices with Graham Bright, MP for Luton South, who was to take heed of Whitehouse's concerns over video.

The Prime Minister told the House of Commons that the Home Secretary was considering the introduction of a new law to curb 'video nasties'. Only a few weeks had passed since a Private Member's Bill from the opposition was

Fears grow at threat of increased cinema censorship

INDUSTRY OUTCRY OVER VIDEO BILL

THE GROWING outcry from the UK film and video industries over the implications of the Video Recordings Bill reached a peak this week as the Bill passed unopposed through the House of Lords on Monday (April 2).

By Alex Sutherland

The UK film industry fears that the Bill, designed to ban so-called "video nasties" and introduce a system of classification for all cassettes shown in the home, will result in increased censorship of films in cinemas.

The Directors Guild of Great Britain, representing over 500 film, television and theatre directors, described the Bill as "an infringement on the freedom of artistic expression", and believes the terms "go dangerously far beyond (the Bill's) declared purpose of controlling socially and morally unacceptable material".

"We now face a period of even stricter censorship in films from the British Board of Film Censors, who have already permitted films in Britain to be censored more heavily than in any other country in the free world," the Guild's chairman

● **Continued on page 2**

withdrawn to give the industry a chance to establish its own code of practice. Now came a sudden and complete reversal as the Commons prepared to debate a Private Member's Bill from Bright, which sought "to outlaw pornographic, obscene and horror video tapes." Come November 1983, the month in which it was given its second reading in the Commons, the MP had resigned from his minor position at the Home Office to dedicate more time to his 'Bright Bill.' Soon to become the Video Recordings Bill, this badly drafted piece of legislation would go beyond its intended remit, such as it was, and forever change the culture of video in Britain by unwittingly launching a black market industry whose revenue remains inestimable. (See BLACK MARKET & PIRATES.)

On November 1, 1983, a few days before his Bill was to get a second reading, Bright gave Members of Parliament "the experience of seeing a video nasty." In a Commons committee room a film of twenty-two minutes duration was screened comprising scenes from videotapes confiscated by Scotland Yard. With entrepreneurial aplomb, Bright warned his audience of rape, gang rape, sexual killings and a monkey having its head bashed in, and that none of the 100 or so MPs in attendence should feel ashamed if they were unable to sit through the horror and had to leave. MPs were suitably galvanised. After the screening, one told the *Times*:

> Some people think that the sight of two or three people making love is aesthetic, but there cannot be two conflicting views about seeing a girl chopped up and her entrails ripped out and eaten.

Another MP lamented:

> What we have just seen is bestial and horrific. To show this to youngsters would be deplorable.

Jeremy Hanley, Conservative MP for Richmond and Barnes, couldn't sit through the whole thing. He told the reporter:

> Many people did not want the showing to continue they were so horrified by what they saw. I am still shaken now by what I saw. I am not a believer in total censorship, but I am afraid I think I have just seen where the limit lies.

Screen International documents the Video Bill. Previous: April 7-14; This page, from top: January 28-February 4; July 14-21, 1984.

Bright Bill likely to restructure BBFC

MAJOR CHANGES to the structure of the British Board of Film Censors (BBFC) seem likely if Graham Bright's Video Recordings Bill becomes law, **writes Sue Newson-Smith.**

Home Secretary Leon Brittan has already made it clear that he favours the BBFC as the classifying authority for video cassettes.

However, this proposal has been questioned by several MPs, discussing the Bill at committee stage.

At the committee's last meeting (Jan 18), Home Office Under Secretary David Mellor announced four new proposals in an attempt to ward off s[illegible] criti[illegible]

Bill that the Home Secretary should himself name the four without anyone else having a say. The Government proposes to formalise the present informal arrangement by which the president and secretary are nominated by the cinematogaph industry with the tradition of their names being acceptable to the Home Secretary.

2) *Examiners*. At present there are 12 part-time examiners. This number will be greatly expanded and there will be a clear and definite need for their range of experience to be greater than at present.

3) *Accountability*: The G[illegible] see an [illegible]

Video Bill completed

THE Bill banning video nasties has finally completed its proceedings in Parliament and will soon become law.

By Sue Newson-Smith

It outlaws video recordings portraying explicit sex and excessive violence, and gives guidance to retailers, customers and parents on the suitability of other videos for particular age groups.

Welcoming the Video Recordings Bill's completion, Home Secretary Leon Brittan told MPs, "Parliament has acted speedily to deal with this new and evil trade. I am sure that it has done so with very widespread public support."

The Bill was sponsored by Conservative MP Graham [illegible]

Is that what Bright's bill entailed? Total censorship? On November 16, Bright took his film to Strasbourg to find European support. Euro MPs, parliament staff and journalists were amongst those who viewed the compilation tape. "Nasty is too weak a word for it," noted the reporter for the *Times*. "One girl had to rush from the viewing room to be sick and more than one journalist will be unable to give a full account of what happened."[26] Ironically, one of the arguments frequently used against video is that the technology allows violent or sadistic scenes to be played out of context. This is exactly what Bright was presenting in his showreel – violent and sadistic scenes out of context.[27]

The British Videogram Association commissioned a MORI poll. Two million questionnaires were sent to video dealers for distribution among their customers, the intention being to help "bring to the attention of both Government and Parliament the views of the video public." It was an obvious ploy to alert people to the ramifications of Government legislation, and avert the clampdown threatened by the Bright bill.

The confidential survey asked four questions of the public:

1. Do you believe that the video films which you watch at home should be more censored than the cinema, the same as the cinema or less censored than the cinema?
2. Do you believe that any film which is considered not to be obscene should be available to adults from their video library?
3. Do you believe that parents have the final responsibility as to what their children should or should not watch?
4. Do you believe there should be censorship on video films which are watched in the privacy of the home?

The result demonstrated that sixty-five per cent of the British public were against video censorship. And while in favour of a categorisation system, the general opinion was that government shouldn't determine what videos people watch in their own homes. However, another unrelated survey was already in progress, one which was to have far greater impact when its findings were presented. Published under the title *Video Violence and Children*, this survey was conducted among schoolchildren throughout the country, aged seven to sixteen years. Given the working party involved in the enquiry, it could come as no surprise that its findings fully supported Graham Bright. (In the words of someone associated with the party, the result was "exactly what we wanted.")

The topic was video and its effect on children, already the staple of news panics dating back to 1982 and the subject of an all-party Parliamentary committee led by anti-porn crusader Jill Knight MP earlier in the year. Having been postponed from its initial date in May, the Parliamentary Group Video Enquiry was formed following a meeting that took place in the House of Lords on June 27, 1983. Its chairman was Lord Nugent of Guildford, a supporter of moral legislation in the Lords. In attendance were representatives of the political parties and senior members of various churches.[28] Leading the enquiry was Dr Clifford Hill, who ran an evangelical mission in London.[29] Raymond Johnston, with whom Hill was to produce an outline of research proposals, was the director of CARE (Christian Action Research and Education), formerly the Nationwide Festival of Light. Johnston had told the assembly that children were "regularly hiring violent, pornographic and occult horror videos", and that he considered the Obscene Publications Act to be a "flawed instrument" that needed to be strengthened. The working party's directive, which concerned "the phenomenon of violence not pornography", was to provide Members of Parliament, the media and the public with (a) an overview of the current social, commercial and legal situation in Britain with regard to video films depicting scenes of explicit violence, (b) evidence of children's viewing patterns in relation to the suitability of the films seen, and (c) deal with the effects upon children of viewing scenes of violence in video films.

Data for the enquiry was amassed from 7,000 questionnaires given to children and parents. These were completed during school time, with children working independently from one another. Following this, they were encouraged to divulge their video viewing habits in a class discussion, and on occasion a member of the working party would attend to conduct taped interviews.

Director Clifford Hill stressed that "checks upon the honesty and reliability of the children's answers were carried out", but it became common knowledge that the report was rushed to completion in order to influence the later stages of the Video Recordings Bill. Indeed, the Commons had been influenced right from the beginning when, at the request of the sponsors, the working party produced an interim report to coincide with the early stages of the Bill. The interim report was published despite comprising, in Hill's own words, "incomplete figures which made it vulnerable to misinterpretation." That there were any figures at all – let alone assertions, conclusions and recommendations – was something of a mystery, as less than a fortnight earlier Hill was admitting that "the analysis of data had not yet begun."

Nevertheless, the inconclusive and misrepresentative statistics made good copy: Britain's schoolchildren, subsisting on a daily diet of violent and horrific films in excess of anything that cinema-going adults could legally see, was a topic lapped up by the media. Newspapers, TV and radio revelled in proclaiming that "nearly half" of the nation's youngsters had seen a 'video nasty' (a third by the time they were age eight).

Many people were supportive of a Bill that sought to protect kids from the supposed corruption that was the 'video nasty'. But others voiced concerns over the legal control of video films and the makeup of the enquiry's research. These included Brian Brown, whose name and research unit at Oxford Polytechnic were attached to the Report, but who repudiated its "framework, context and conclusions." Part of Brown's concern originated from the fact that Dr Hill was using material whose source was unknown to anybody else. This challenge resulted in Hill unexpectedly, in Brown's absence, raiding the unit at Oxford Polytechnic and removing all questionnaires, material and data pertaining to the report. Even computer tapes were wiped.[30] When *Video Violence and Children* was finally published on March 7, 1984, delegates for the Methodist and Roman Catholic Churches had already formally withdrawn from the enquiry, sceptical about its alarming findings. In response to its claim that forty-five per cent of British schoolchildren had seen at least one violent video film, Methodists told the press that more important social issues faced children, such as alcohol abuse and glue sniffing.[31] Brian Brown and his team suspected these figures were a gross exaggeration anyway, but of course were unable to follow up their suspicions on account of Hill having confiscated the research data.[32] Even Graham Bright himself appeared on TV and aired some doubts. "I do question the validity of the research," he told the BBC. "It points at the problem, but I don't think one can take that as concrete evidence."[33]

The validity of the evidence didn't deter the press from proclaiming that young people were addicted to violence like drugs. "The wave of video filth that has swept through Britain's homes," stated the educational correspondent for the *Daily Express*, was partly responsible for the increase in "child abuse, brutal sexual attacks, violent assaults and street rioting."

Palace Video prepared libel actions against the Hill Report for prejudicing legal hearings against their film *The Evil Dead* and "influencing the press into mistakenly categorising it as a video nasty."[34] Several other distributors complained that the Parliamentary Group was in contempt of court, given that the report detailed the synopses for several video films currently embroiled in legal proceedings. These allegations were rejected, and no action was taken. Neither were they made public. This was because the sponsors of the enquiry, according to Hill, "did not want any publicity that might have detracted from the main issues."

Contrary to what many believed, the Video Enquiry was not an official parliamentary investigation but a privately funded one ("funded by individuals and Churches" was Hill's vague declaration). Its political significance, however, was never in doubt, and the Prime Minister herself, Margaret Thatcher, took a personal interest in its development. Less than a week after *Video Violence and Children* was published, Graham Bright's Bill was well on its way through

Parliament. On July 12, with only two Tory MPs and one Labour peer dissenting, the Video Recordings Act 1984 reached the Statute Book.

Its official stamp was to "make provision for regulating the distribution of video recordings and for connected purposes", but in truth the Act was a major piece of legislation adopted at the height of a moral panic. Agitated by the press and the findings of the Video Enquiry, public concern over 'video nasties' was so great that the Bill met with only muted, belated protest. When it became clear that its implications went far beyond the censorship of mere 'video nasties', the rapidity with which the Bill had moved through Parliament meant that any opposition to it would invariably be too late. A handful of video titles had been exploited by the media as excessively violent and brutal, and yet, on the back of this, a wide-reaching law was hurriedly shaped and introduced. There arose an industry outcry. With the Act only weeks away from the Statute Book, the Directors Guild of Great Britain claimed it posed "an infringement on the freedom of artistic expression." This was a concern shared by the ASA, who had been instrumental in kick-starting the media interest in 'nasties' when they upheld complaints against advertisements back in May 1982 (see previous chapter). The ASA feared that the country was moving into a period of creeping censorship.

For the British Council of Churches, the law had to "strike [a] delicate balance between public good and the freedom of the individual." Protection of children, the Council insisted, lay foremost with parents and guardians.

Of the formative days of the Video Recordings Act, Steve Ellison recalls that

> As a member of the Video Trade Association I was invited down to London to Westminster Hall to a couple of the meetings with Graham Bright. Dear old Mary Whitehouse was there, and a few other people. I was there in a couple of the meetings when the actual terms of the Act were thrashed out. I remember saying at one of the meetings, "Why don't they make every film that was produced before 1940 exempt?" And Graham Bright said, "No. They were making pornographic movies in 1915." That was the problem. He was a bigger problem than Mary Whitehouse

BRITISH BOARD OF FILM CLASSIFICATION

VIDEO RECORDINGS ACT 1984

Tariff of Fees

July 1985

Type of work	Fee
Video works not previously examined in any form	
Works in which the spoken language is predominantly English (standard rate)	£4.60 per minute to 2 hours £3.45 per minute thereafter
Minimum charge	trailers/shorts up to 10 minutes: £46.00
Sub-titled works in a spoken language which is predominantly other than English	£3.45 per minute to 2 hours £2.30 per minute thereafter
Minimum charge	trailers/shorts up to 10 minutes: £34.50
Untranslated works in a spoken language predominantly other than English	£2.30 per minute to 2 hours £1.15 per minute thereafter
Minimum charge	trailers/shorts up to 10 minutes: £23.00
Charities and non-profit-making organisations are invited to apply for a reduced fee chargeable at the Board's discretion for works which are not to be distributed for private gain.	£1.15 per minute
Minimum charge	trailers/shorts up to 10 minutes: £11.50
Video works previously certificated as films or broadcast as British television programmes	£2.30 per minute to 4 hours £1.15 per minute thereafter
Minimum charge	trailers/shorts up to 10 minutes: £23.00

(For this purpose, television serials will be charged as one complete work, although episodes of a series which may be supplied and viewed independently will be charged as separate works.)

The above charges are subject to VAT at the prevailing rate.

ever was. Mary got the stick in the press because she was very outspoken. Really, what she wanted to do was to protect the kids. I remember standing on the steps at Whitehall and saying, "Come on, Mary. What would happen if I told you a dirty joke?" She looked around and said, "Well, there are no kids around — I'd probably laugh." She wasn't the matriarch that people make her out to be — she was actually quite a normal, warm human being. But Bright was difficult to deal with.[35]

Conan Le Cilaire's pseudo documentary, *Faces of Death*, had been available in Britain in the early days of video, but quickly found itself on the DPP's list of 'banned' films once the clampdown got under way. (One sequence, in which diners at a Turkish restaurant supposedly feed on fresh monkey brains, had been included in Graham Bright's inflammatory showreel shown in Parliament.[36]) During the brief period in which *Faces of Death* was legitimately available, access to this "particularly offensive and revolting" film[37] was hindered only by extraneous factors like limited distribution and the reluctance of some rental outlets to give shelf space to a supposed documentary feature. There was no regulation on the actual content or restrictions on who should and shouldn't be allowed to see the film. Indeed, as noted earlier, there was nothing to stop any enterprising businessperson from putting any old thing out on video. The result was that video shelves were crammed with all manner of diverse films from around the world. And whenever quality was lacking, the promise of sex and violence was always a workable substitute.

The sales pitch on the reverse of the *Faces of Death* box included the statement:

> Scenes in this video film are of explicit and shocking nature [*sic*]. They should not be viewed by young persons, or those of a nervous disposition. In the opinion of the distributors many of the scenes contained herein would not pass the British Board of Film Censors.

Previous: BBFC tariff of fees for video at the implementation of the VRA 1984. Below: A typical BBFC cuts sheet.

CUTS

THE THRILL KILLERS (Video Feature) Palace Video 14 10 88 '18'
The title is likely to prove unacceptable for this video even if it is successfully cut, as follows:

At 16½ mins Reduce sadistic killing in bedroom by removing entire humilation by threat and slapping to woman, cutting from killer advancing with scissors saying "I'm going to kill you" (TC 13:26:32:21) to shot of her trying to reach door for second time (TC 13:27:15:16).

At 32 mins Reduce sequence of maniacs taunting woman by removing suggestion of rape, cutting away after frightened woman says "Oh, no..." (TC 13:41:53:00) and resuming on group shot (TC 13:42:20:00) just before man runs across to grab her.

At 32½ mins Then reduce assault on woman and maniacal laughter by cutting from face of husband being held down on floor (TC 13:42:30:12) to shot of struggle in middle of room (TC 13:42:53:01) shortly before woman is rescued.

At 33½ mins After husband is punched at door, remove second assault on him by cutting from man crouching in corner before he says "hit him" (TC 13:43:23:18) to shot of man hitting floor with head at bottom of screen (TC 13:43:30:00).

At 33½ mins Immediately after close-up of worried wife, remove shot of man picking up axe (TC 13:43:33:13) resuming on man in corner after axe is pushed across room (TC 13:43:39:05).

At 36½ mins After woman escapes from house, reduce chase and taunting with axe and gun by removing whole sequence round van, cutting from end of tilted shot of man chasing her round house and past camera (TC 13:46:19:23) to shot of her entering room (TC 13:47:11:03).

At 37½ mins Reduce final chase and exhilaration of killers by cutting away after men chase woman up staircase past camera (TC 13:47:46:06), resuming on mid shot of man sitting against wall taking off glasses (TC 13:47:56:15), then cutting (TC 13:48:02:09) to long shot of axeman rushing forward for kill (TC 13:48:06:16).

At 47½ mins After blonde woman in close-up says, "You're awfully brave with a gun in your hand," remove threat to her with axe (TC 13:57:10:21), together with threat to others by hysterical axeman and sight of man taunted with gun in neck, face and eye, resuming on man with gun saying "OK, coffee..." (TC 13:57:34:01).

Resubmit.

Further cuts may be required.

A shrewd observation, but presumptuous. At the hands of the BBFC the film would undoubtedly have suffered cuts or perhaps been rejected outright. But *Faces of Death* was never submitted to the Board because, prior to the Video Recordings Act 1984, it didn't need to be. Material destined for theatrical release required examination by the BBFC and a certificate (although local councils could overrule any of the Board's decisions on appeal), whereas distributors of video material operated – initially – under no such obligation,[38] because the new medium fell outside the parameters of existing Home Office guidelines.[39]

By default the BBFC landed the job of videocassette classification. They were, in the words of Graham Bright, "the only classifying board in operation at the moment."

The BBFC is an independent, non-profit making body that derives almost all its income from the examination fees it charges. Apart from some works that qualify as exempt, this includes all feature films, short films, trailers and advertisements.

Formed in 1912 under the aegis of the Incorporated Association of Kinematograph Manufacturers – a trade collective representing manufacturers of cinema equipment and film processors – the BBFC provided a uniform, national alternative to the various local authorities who were imposing their own disparate forms of censorship on films.

The Cinematograph Act had been introduced in 1909 and required that all cinemas carry a license issued by the local council. Primarily concerned with safety of the public, the Act brought cinemas into line with similar regulations which were already applicable to music halls and pubs. But a wider ruling shortly after – which sought to restrict the showing of films on Sundays – was interpreted as giving local authorities the power to censor films.[40] Film companies were unhappy with this and approached Parliament with a view to establishing a recognised central censorial board. Initially viewed with some suspicion by the local authorities, the BBFC was eventually adopted as the unofficial body that would classify, cut or reject the films destined for the nation's cinema screens.[41]

However, not until the Cinematograph Act 1952 – which sought to prohibit children from gaining admittance to works designated as unsuitable – did Parliament formally acknowledge the BBFC.[42]

Two major pieces of legislation were to have a direct impact on the Board in the 1980s. These were the Cinematograph Act 1982[43] and the Video Recordings Act 1984. Both incorporated recommendations made some years earlier by the Committee on Obscenity and Film Censorship, which had been chaired by the philosopher Bernard Williams.[44] Appointed by the Labour government in July 1977 with the charge of reviewing the obscenity laws, Williams had been an expert witness in the defence of *Last Exit to Brooklyn* a decade earlier. His choice as head of the Committee angered the Festival of Light and many other moral crusaders, who regarded the appointment of a non-Christian as prejudicial. Indeed, the Committee favoured a rational approach as opposed to a moral one, deducing that pornography was an effect of the new permissiveness, not a cause, and posed no threat. "Terms such as 'obscene', 'indecent' and 'deprave and corrupt' should be abandoned as having outlived their usefulness," was one common-sense approach to the issue.

Upon its presentation in 1979, Mary Whitehouse demanded that the government reject the report, as did politicians and many newspapers.[45] But while its findings would have no immediate impact, certain recommendations were to be incorporated into fresh legislation over the coming years. In the case of the Cinematograph Act 1982, this meant tighter control over bogus cinema clubs and the introduction of a new film category, the troubled R18 rating (which the BBFC designated "for restricted distribution only, through specially licensed cinemas or sex shops to which no one under 18 is admitted"[46]). Regarding the Video Recordings Act 1984 – despite there being no provision for video in the report itself – an updated set of classification categories were among the proposals adopted, whose display in the form of a symbol would appear on all screenings and advertisements for a film.

The Williams Committee also suggested that a statutory body be introduced to take over the censorship powers of local authorities, and proposed the authority should be called the Film Examining Board. Under the Video Recordings Act, the BBFC found itself exercising a statutory function on behalf of central government. Although they didn't become the Film Examining Board as a result, they did undergo a change of name, from the British Board of Film Censors to the less draconian sounding British Board of Film *Classification*.[47]

The Video Recordings Act 1984 was a means to outlaw the 'video nasties' and classify all video material as to its suitability for viewing in the home. Pivotal was the fact that a film destined for video should be subject to greater scrutiny than one destined for a theatrical release (what might be a 15-certificate film in the cinema may carry a stricter 18 rating on video, or even require cuts). A film which was refused a certificate could still play in cinemas if the local authority authorised it, whereas on video – although there existed a Video Appeals Committee – such a refusal invariably represented a legal ban.

The Bill was devised to eliminate the element of chance that accompanied any prosecution under the Obscene Publications Act (which required proof that material seized, if taken as a whole, was liable to deprave and corrupt). Now, with a classification system supported by the state, video was a quantifiable commodity and the industry in turn was bound by clear-cut legislation: anyone supplying material for gain that hadn't been classified as suitable for viewing in the home, transgressed the law, as did anyone who supplied material to persons below the age stipulated in the packaging or supplied an R18 video on premises other than a licensed sex shop. The penalty stood as high as £20,000.[48]

The government was under pressure to implement the Act – *any* Act, it seemed, given those MPs sickened by Graham Bright's showreel, the media blitz, and lobby groups baying for an end to the 'video nasties'. "Why was the Act delayed for more than a year?" queried the *Daily Express* in October 1985. No better reason, determined the newspaper, than because "Whitehall civil servants were busy reworking such peripheral details as labelling regulations and details of consumer protection... meanwhile, children were without the protection of the new law."

Even as the Bill made its way through Parliament, the vocal Mary Whitehouse was picking holes in it. She spent an hour in discussion with the Home Secretary, Leon Brittan, whose later Parliamentary statement regarding "this new and evil trade" was uncannily attuned to the feeling and phraseology of the moral reformist. Whitehouse believed the BBFC were the wrong body for the job of classifying videocassettes and explained to the *New Video Viewer* in November 1983 that, "Inevitably, when a group is dealing with the kind of material which over the years [the BBFC] have seen, their judgement becomes de-sensitised." (Whitehouse doesn't volunteer who she considers better suited to the job, but one suspects she'd have been happiest doing it herself.)

However stringent the Video Recordings Act was likely to be, it wasn't stringent enough for Whitehouse. "Whatever goes on to videotape," was her portentous message, "children will inevitably see it. There's no way you can be sure of protecting them."

> The degree of corruption and fear and terror in those films wouldn't be allowed by any society in its right mind. It would ensure that the legislation was such that the children were protected. If that meant that adults who have a weakness for corrupting and violent material of that kind couldn't see it, so be it.

The Act took effect on September 1, 1985, after which date all new video releases required a BBFC certificate and appropriate labelling prior to release. Of the video titles already in circulation, the Board was given until September 1988 – an additional three years – to clear the backlog. (This it was required to do incrementally: an English language title theatrically distributed in 1980 would need to be certified by March 1987; an English language title theatrically distributed between 1975 and 1979 would need to be certified by September 1987; all foreign-language material would be due for classification by September

1988, and so on.) Three years to examine, impose cuts, classify or reject some 10,000 videocassettes already on the market. As we shall see later, many films were never submitted – for economic reasons, companies going bust, and so forth – so the actual number of videocassettes examined by the BBFC would have been considerably lower. Nevertheless, the added responsibility saw the BBFC grow from "a small, family-sized operation with a staff of twelve" in 1982, to an organisation comprising fifty in 1985.[49] As is the case now, every video passing through their doors at Soho Square in London would have been seen by a minimum of two examiners. Most classifications were straightforward and could have been based on this initial observation, in which case the Board aimed to release their decision seventy-two hours after viewing. However, if a film proved problematic, classification would have been delayed indefinitely, with the original examiners referring the work to a second team or even to senior staff. Should the Board feel the need for changes or cuts, these requirements were put to the film company in writing.

The credo of the Board is that the integrity of a work should be preserved whenever possible, whilst balancing the requirements of the law and the public interest. Imagery – and in some instances 'taste'[50] – can often throw this balance. One area singled out as unacceptable by the BBFC in their *Annual Report 1985*, was that of genuine, unsimulated cruelty to animals, said to be "a particular problem in foreign-language works which have been produced in countries where animal welfare is not generally accorded the same importance as in the English-speaking world." But the major concern remained rape and sexual violence, regarded in the report as a worrying trend in cinema since the seventies.[51] "The Board is even stricter with such depictions on video than on film, since the fact that a scene might be searched out and repeated endlessly out of context in the privacy of one's own home could condition some viewers to find the behaviour sexually exciting, not just on film, but in real life."

By way of example:

> For the cinema, the sight of a man scarring the breasts of a prostitute with electric curling tongs had been excised; on video the whole idea was cut. Threats and injury to breasts with knives, razors and lighted cigarettes were cut from video works classified '18', as was the sexual taunting of a woman bound and gagged.

Graham Bright had assured the press that the objective of his Bill was to stamp out the 'video nasties' "straight away." But to determine what would be suitable for viewing in the home and by whom, all material would need to be evaluated. This meant that not only 'sadistic' and 'violent' films, but everything else, from children's cartoons to sitcoms, would require examination by the BBFC. In the case of feature films already passed by the Board for viewing in a cinema, further examination was necessary. This factor Bright and his stalwarts hadn't anticipated (and which, according to the BVA, Bright reputedly thought absurd). The MP had optimistically told the *Guardian* that on top of the "thirty nasties that will not get a classification", there were only some 200 to 300 films which needed to be looked at.

With the introduction of the Video Recordings Act, a register of films released theatrically in Britain[52] – some 58,000 titles – was made available by the Home Office. What benefits were to be had in owning such a list isn't clear (though at a cost of £20, the list was obviously beneficial to someone): many titles on video had never seen a theatrical release and so wouldn't be featured, while those titles that did feature wouldn't necessarily receive on video the certificate they had carried theatrically. Far more relevant was *A Trade Guide to the Video Recordings Act*, a booklet compiled by the BVA to assist the industry in carrying out the requirements of the Act. Providing explanatory notes and using plainer language than that of the Act itself, the booklet nevertheless struggled to offer much relief in the face of such a sudden and serious legislative slab. Fundamental aspects of the Act, even in translation, must have seemed unfathomable.[53]

As the BBFC undertook the task of examining and classifying thousands of videocassettes, film distributors would supply retailers with an update on those films granted a certificate. It was then the duty of the retailer to check their stock and keep it in line with the classification process, either by attaching the appropriate BBFC certificate label to videotapes or removing material from the shelves altogether. "Each day we would receive lists from various companies indicating the certification category granted and would have to put the correct label on the tape and display box," recalls Chris Glazebrook. "Where a cut had been requested, the original tape had to be withdrawn and replaced with the new certified version."

One film that was denied a certificate after years of availability was Sam Peckinpah's acclaimed *Straw Dogs,* released by Guild Home Video. Says Iain Muspratt, "It was one of the best films we ever distributed. We released it years

'Talking about bits of the female anatomy.' Del Henney and Susan George in *Straw Dogs*.

before the VRA. The BBFC's James Ferman was a strange chap; he'd done the job for too long, he was obsessed by sex, in my opinion. And he would analyse it in a very clinical way. You'd sit there [in a meeting] and he would be talking about bits of the female anatomy as if he was a gynaecologist. He said there was an anal rape in *Straw Dogs*. But I asked Susan George, some years later, if that was the case, and she said no, it wasn't. But by the time the VRA banned it it had made its money anyway."[54]

Not all videos required a certificate from the BBFC. Exempt works included those which, if taken as a whole, were designated to inform, educate or instruct, or were concerned with sport, religion or music.[55] However, in a sub-clause which seemed primarily directed at *Faces of Death* – a documentary that was arguably informative, educational and instructive, and fit the above criteria – a work could not be deemed exempt if, to any significant extent, it depicted: (a) human sexual activity or acts of force or restraint associated with such activity; (b) mutilation or torture of, or other acts of gross violence towards, humans or animals; (c) human genital organs or human urinary or excretory functions.[56]

Everything else did require a BBFC certificate.

In 1985 it cost £4.60 a minute to have the BBFC view previously uncertified material, putting the examination of, say, a video of 1hr 30min duration at £414 (excluding VAT) – payable in advance. If the Board demanded cuts, the film would need to be resubmitted at further cost. Lower rates were applicable to films examined previously for a cinema release.[57]

Left to right: BVA newspaper announcement, and the BVA guidebook for retailers.

A TRADE GUIDE
TO THE VIDEO
RECORDINGS ACT

BVA

British Videogram Association
21/22 Poland Street
London
W1V 3DD

Few small companies could afford the cost of submitting their entire back catalogue for classification, much less when there was some uncertainty as to whether the films would come out unscathed – or indeed, come out at all. Many distributors opted for liquidation, and consequently retailers were left with a surfeit of stock that wasn't going to see certification. Once the examination schedule was met, any unclassified videocassette on display in a store or rental library would result in prosecution. These tapes, recalls Chris Glazebrook, were supposed to have been destroyed by retailers, "breaking the case and pulling the tape from the spool." But with some dealers fearing they might end up losing eighty per cent of their stock this way, an alternative was eagerly sought. The guidebook issued by the BVA stated that prosecutions couldn't be brought under the Video Recordings Act for material currently pending classification. This was an invitation for dealers to try and recoup some cash while they still had the chance. Rather than destroying tapes, they chose instead to sell them off to the public.

The Video Recordings Act effectively cleaned contentious video titles from the high street, and a lot more besides. The transitional period granted by central government didn't stop some local authorities from continuing to carry out raids. One person still seizing videocassettes yet to be awarded a certificate was Chief Constable James Anderton, whose campaign in Greater Manchester is described by Steve Ellison as "a witch hunt."[58]

> He would raid all the shops and take out all videos that he felt were obscene. This was after the Video Recordings Act had been put into place and there was a changeover period. Anderton and his men just went all over Manchester looking through video stores, and seize everything that didn't have a certificate. They were seizing children's cartoons, they were seizing everything. And they were making a lot of money for whoever gets the money from the fines that people pay — the courts were full of people having to plead guilty to carrying obscene material.
>
> The way the whole thing was handled was very unfair and it really caused a lot of heartache and caused a lot of people to go out of business. You had a situation where a shop in Walkden, or someplace, would be raided and virtually everything taken — yet a shop fifteen yards down the road, carrying the same stuff, wouldn't be touched because it happened to be outside the Manchester jurisdiction. This was happening all over the place in Greater Manchester. It was alright if you were in Wigan; it was alright if you were somewhere else. But anywhere that Anderton had control... He took issue with films that you might consider to be bad taste.[59]

The major film distributors came through the Video Recordings Act with minimal damage. If anything, they were better off. The way was clear to monopolise the industry, as envisaged a couple of years earlier when the majors created their own distribution networks and cut out the independent wholesalers. (See BEGINNINGS.) For a government in favour of an open market, the Video Recordings Act proved cataclysmic for small business.

The fall-out continued. One development in the immediate wake of the new Bill was a period of excessive self-censorship conducted by the film companies; another was the emergence of a video black market. The underground trade created in the wake of any censorial policy was conveniently overlooked in the eagerness to establish the Video Recordings Act.[60] Once uncertified videos were outlawed, they quickly became sought-after items by an increasing number of collectors. Video had brought an exciting new entertainment medium to Britain, and access to a wide range of films hitherto denied. In creating a ban, a subculture soon developed for whom the DPP 'video nasties' blacklist became a checklist of sorts.

Video controversy was far from over. Titles like *Faces of Death*, *I Spit on Your Grave* and *SS Experiment Camp* may have been removed from the visible landscape, but the mark they left was indelible.

Seige

'DRAINING THE BLOOD OF THE INNOCENT!'

Seige

'DRAINING THE BLOOD OF THE INNOCENT!'

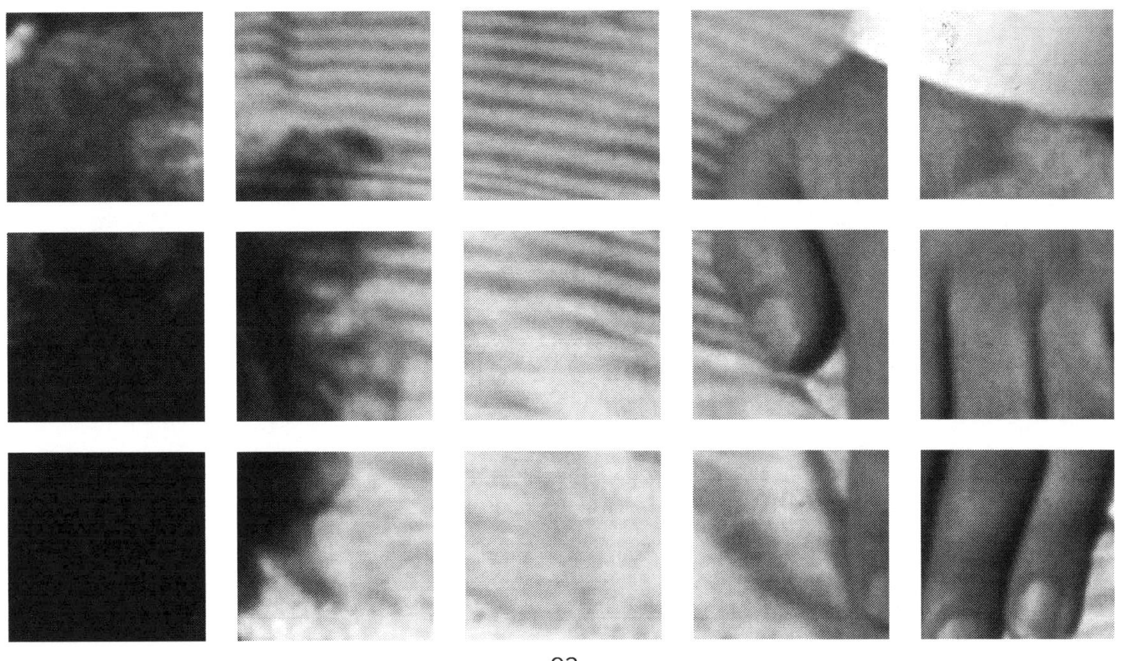

THE INTRODUCTION OF video into the domestic market was a blessing to the film aficionado. For the first time a huge variety of full-length feature films could be watched in the home. The dawn of the video age in Britain saw films that were not normally accessible become suddenly available. The nannying system of censorship and the selection criteria of cinema chains were temporarily breached and avid film viewers had a short-lived freedom. Horror movie fans were the best served, as titles never seen in the UK became available for rent from a seemingly endless and unlikely range of outlets – from corner shops through to laundromats, all cashing in on the video phenomena. Prior to the Video Recordings Act, the distribution system benefitted the smaller scale films and distributors, putting them on a par with major studios – literally, on the shelves next to Hollywood blockbusters. Indeed, low-budget films and obscurities outnumbered the big studio efforts. William A Levey's *Blackenstein*, Ed Adlum's *Invasion of the Blood Farmers*, Eddie Romero's *Beast of Blood*, Inoshiro Honda's *Matango: Fungus of Terror*; Don Dohler's *Night Beast*, Larry Buchanan's *Mistress of the Apes*, and Michael Findlay's *Shriek of the Mutilated*, films like this began to spring up like uncontrollable weeds. To some people they were an ugly, misunderstood irritant, but to many others they were a much-appreciated delight. Says Steve Ellison:

> Video was a godsend to the producer of crap films that were never likely to get anywhere near the cinema.[1]

The packaging for such videos became increasingly lurid as independent companies struggled to get their product noticed. Blood-dripping monsters, flesh-chewing cannibals, Nazi torturers, knife-wielding maniacs and gore-choked power tools were common sights. "The covers of the nasties were terribly important to their image," James Ferman would

Two examples of child-like, 'coloured-in' video sleeve art: *Scared To Death* (1947) and *Don't Open the Window* aka *The Living Dead* (1974).

later deliberate.[2] The covers for Ruggero Deodato's *Cannibal Holocaust*, Abel Ferrara's *The Driller Killer*, and Pete Walker's *Frightmare*, for instance, didn't leave much to the imagination. Yet others would lose the plot entirely and try to sell a genuinely superior horror film in utterly asinine packaging. A fine example of terribly conceived artwork was LVC Video's[3] release of *Don't Open the Window*. This, the American R-rated version of Jorge Grau's excellent *Living Dead at the Manchester Morgue*, had a sleeve with no discernible connection to the film contained within. The illustration of a woman closing a window appears to have been painted by a child. Similarly, Christy Cabanne's creaky 1947 shocker *Scared To Death*, starring Bela Lugosi, featured hurried 'coloured-in' artwork that was unlikely to draw the interest of any would-be video viewer.[4] Medusa's release of Umberto Lenzi's *The Iron Master*, on the other hand, had spectacular Frank Frazetta-like artwork, but this merely disguised a cheap *Quest for Fire* rip-off starring the redoubtable George Eastman.

Many of the earliest videos were packaged in simple boxes made from thin card.[5] Some companies used a standard slipcase for their genre releases, the art being the same but with a small label stuck to the box and cassette to identify the film. Several titles from Intervision came in this format, including *Onibaba*,

Satan's Slave, and *Dead of Night*.

Companies were quickly established to take advantage of the new medium of video, and they capitalised on its lack of restrictions. Vipco released on tape Lucio Fulci's *Zombie Flesh Eaters* in both an X certified version, which had played theatrically, and a specially labelled "strong, uncut version", giving potential consumers a choice between the hard or soft. For most people this was the first time a strong horror film had been seen in all its uncensored glory, and the difference in the two versions was startling. Throats are torn out and the blood flows in torrents, eyeballs are punctured on wooden splinters and intestines are pulled out to be devoured.

It wasn't just horror that was available in a new light. TCX was a label specialising in edited hardcore sex movies. Practically everything but penetration and erections were shown in films such as Alex de Renzy's *Baby Face*, Jim and Artie Mitchell's *Behind the Green Door*, and FX Pope's bizarre *Nightdreams*.

Palace Video could be relied upon for obscure gems. Not only did they release Sam Raimi's *The Evil Dead*, one of the most notorious and popular horrors on video, but they also brought out John Waters' early cult atrocity *Pink Flamingos*. This bad taste shocker showed larger-than-life transvestite Divine consuming dog excrement *for real*, a brief glimpse of fellatio *for real*, and a man showing off his dilating anus – *for real!*[6] The sleeve advised "parental guidance."

Intervision supplied David Cronenberg movies, *Rabid*, *Shivers* and *The Brood*, in addition to rare curiosities like Norman Foster's *The Deathhead Virgin*,[7] Jerry Jameson's *The Bat People*, Sean MacGregor's *Devil Times Five*, Ray Danton's *Crypt of the Living Dead*, Al Adamson's *Death Dimension*, and Ray Austin's *House of the Living Dead*. Packaged in flimsy card slipcases, these may not have been the connoisseur's first choice, but the fact they were available at all mattered more.

Seige

'DRAINING THE BLOOD OF THE INNOCENT!'

Once the campaign against the 'video nasties' got underway, this matter of choice was greatly diminished. As noted earlier (see UNEASE), scare stories were generated that claimed videos were a threat to the moral stature of the country and a particular menace to children. The Video Recordings Act 1984 was ushered in – a law to control and censor video, preventing any film from being released on video without a certificate. The cost of certification was prohibitively expensive and caused many independent distribution companies to collapse. In addition, few of the companies that remained solvent were prepared to sink money into the low-budget end of the film market. It was risky to spend close on £1,000 to release, say, a complete obscurity like *Death Bed: The Bed That Eats* – regardless of whether it would pass without cuts.[8] Would the film break even?

Some films would certainly have required cuts, and this raised another problem. The marketability of Herschell Gordon Lewis' cult classic *Blood Feast*, for example, was dependent entirely on its excessive bloodletting. Gore was its *raison d'être*. To obtain a certificate, *Blood Feast* would most certainly need to be censored, effectively robbing the film of its purpose as well as audience.

During the height of the 'video nasties' scare and the phasing in of the certification process, some companies, concerned with the possibility of prosecution, cut scenes from their own releases in a bid to play safe. (In effect, showing a complete disregard towards customers and supplying damaged goods.) The original release of Cronenberg's *Videodrome* on the CIC label provides one example of this over-cautiousness. To determine whether their films could be

Below: *Death Bed: The Bed That Eats* – the kind of cinematic oddity that became commercially redundant once distributors had classification fees to consider.

Bottom: The generic slipcase of early Intervision horror releases – only the labels differed. In this instance, Norman J Warren, director of *Satan's Slave*, told the authors he had no idea that the Intervision print contained "revolting" gore footage that he himself had removed prior to the film's release.

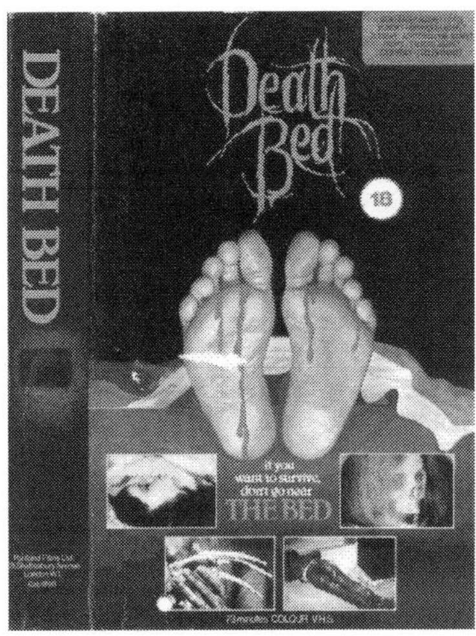

construed as obscene by law, larger distribution companies would employ the services of Geoffrey Robertson, a QC well versed in Media Law who has appeared as counsel in many landmark court cases (see CLAMPDOWN). It was on his advice that CIC removed scenes from *Videodrome*. The film was submitted to the BBFC for video classification in 1987, pre-cut by several minutes with a running time of 80m 41s. In 1990, when the 'video nasty' hullabaloo had died down, the film was resubmitted with a running time of 83m 41s and passed without cuts.[9]

When Polygram Video removed scenes from *Christiane F.*, which Robertson had advised could be problematic, James Ferman encouraged the film company to put them back again. Robertson also advised Electric Video in regards to the all-star adult historical drama, *Caligula*. Scenes removed by the film company included those displaying phallic – or "indecent" – bottles, a particularly asinine decision and often erroneously attributed to the BBFC; Ferman would lament years later, the Board has "been blamed for that cut ever since!"[10]

Robertson was trying to serve his employers' interests during a highly volatile and unusual period. He may have over-reacted in some instances, but the fact remained that film companies and distributors *were* being prosecuted and their offices raided on account of the content of their films.

Apex Video took self-censorship to an extreme. Their release of Andrea Bianchi's eerie zombie opus, *Nights of Terror*, was cut by one-third of its running time – reducing it from ninety-two minutes to an astonishingly limp and violence-free fifty-nine minutes *before* submitting it for classification. The film had evidently been selected for distribution before the Video Recordings Act became law. Having no desire to submit it more than once to the BBFC, who would undoubtedly have requested cuts, Apex removed all the vaguely contentious scenes themselves, ensuring no further cuts would be required and a certificate guaranteed on first submission. It is also possible that Apex thought submitting a full version of *Nights of Terror* might result in outright rejection, giving them no opportunity to make any cuts. Whatever the reason, it seems that the video sleeve had already been printed because it displayed images Apex cut from the film – much to the chagrin of those who rented the thing.

Another confusing consequence of the VRA panic was the availability of alternate versions of the same film with identical packaging, circulating at the same time. Paul Donovan and Maura O'Connell's *Siege*, featuring urban warfare and home-made weapons, was one example. An opening sequence where rednecks execute the patrons of a gay bar was intact on some tapes in circulation, while on others it was truncated. Fate decreed which version ended up in the hands of the consumer. It isn't known who made the decision to cut *Siege*, or whether the release of an unabridged version was an oversight. Likewise VTC's release of *Zombie Holocaust* and Interlight's *City of the Living Dead* were available in minutely different versions. Copies of the former sometimes showed a hand being severed in the pre-credit sequence, while copies of the latter sometimes showed a split-second head-drilling sequence unavailable in other identically packaged prints. Other films on the market were also available in alternate versions, sometimes for no discernible reason (*Madhouse*) and sometimes the result of a mistake (*The Burning*). More on this later.

In the formative days of the 'video nasties' campaign, attention was focused on the more extreme examples of uncertified films. *Snuff*, *The Last House on the Left*, *The Driller Killer*, *SS Experiment Camp*, and *I Spit on Your Grave* were among the first casualties. Their explicit viciousness ensured them little chance of support or room for appeal. Cinematic mutilation, multiple rape, and dismemberment were considered indefensible, even if the films themselves contained an anti-violence sentiment, or moral message, and were in turn condemned by the media and summarily executed without trial. As discussed in the previous chapter, the DPP was forced to compile a list of video titles put to them – mainly by pressure groups – as possibly being in contravention of the Obscene Publications Act 1959. The list was astonishingly inconsistent, containing BBFC certified and censored films on the one hand (Tobe Hooper's *The Funhouse* and Lucio Fulci's *The Beyond*), while on the other it omitted titles that positively revelled in contentious imagery (such as Ferdinando Baldi's *Terror Express!*, effectively a remake of *Late Night Trains*, a film that *did* feature on the DPP list).

The titles said to have been included on the DPP list peaked at seventy-five, but gradually the number dwindled to thirty-nine. As films were vilified in the media and removed from the shelves of video retailers, they became instant collector items, the outcome of which we shall see next.

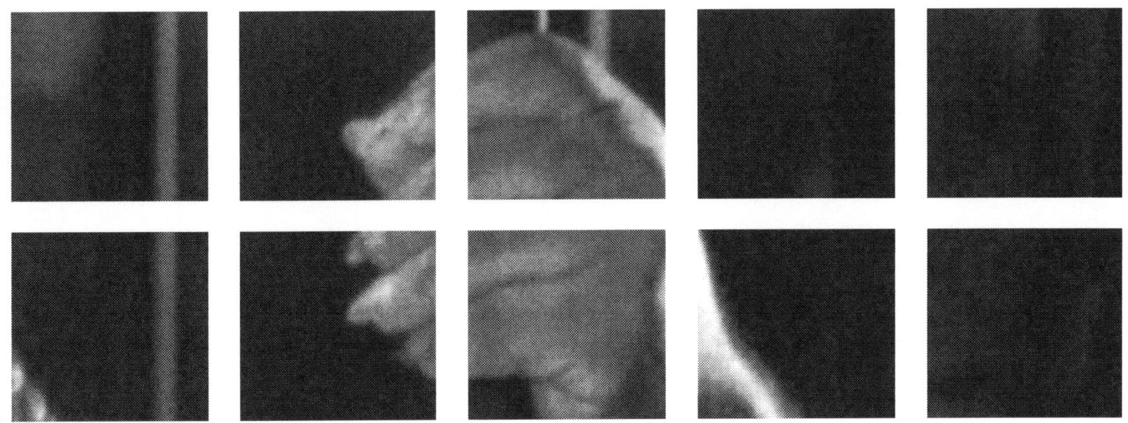

Black Market & Pirates

'HARD TO FIND RARITIES'

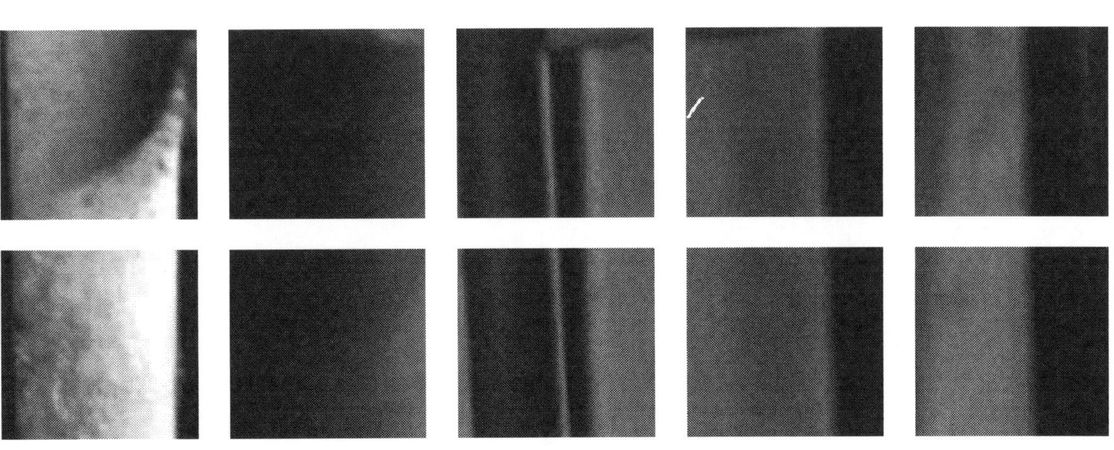

CANNIBAL ERROR

I REMEMBER SEEING displays for *I Spit on Your Grave*, *Cannibal Holocaust* and *SS Experiment Camp* in the video rental shop and thinking that films like that were somehow devaluing horror. I was always interested in horror films but I felt no urgency to see those. There were plenty of other films I wanted to see first. Then one day I walked into the shop and asked for *Tenebrae*, only to be told it was "banned." I couldn't believe it. I got a burning urgency to see all the "banned" stuff. Part of me wanted to know what all the fuss was about, and part of me was desperately missing what I had never been too concerned about in the first place.

—Adam *(this and following anecdotes circa 1997–1999)*

It's great fun being a horror fan in the UK. It's exciting trying to track down uncut horror films. —Andrew Allard[1]

I came across an antiques shop in a country village which doubled as the local video store. A sign in the window said "Video Nasties for Sale." I went in and entered a veritable Aladdin's Cave. Standing in neat rows on a polished wood writing bureau were numerous videos. The first to catch my attention was *Cannibal Ferox* — both versions: the 18 rated and the XX uncut print. Immediately behind it was *Snuff*, the first time I'd seen it since its nationwide disappearance many months ago — a pristine copy, too, by the look of it. Beyond that, *I Spit on Your Grave*, *Cannibal Holocaust*, *Gestapo's Last Orgy*, *Last House on the Left*. The antiques dealer said they were £8 each and I cursed my lack of ready cash. I picked up *Ferox* and *Snuff*, never having seen the former. However, *Ferox* was out on loan, so I opted for *I Spit on Your Grave* instead. I asked the chap if he would be interested in trading. I'd give him films he could safely rent out and take the banned titles off his hands. He agreed and over the next few days I picked up a selection of dirt-cheap ex-rental tapes (sold as 'watch 'n' wipes' at my local video store). I took the lot to the antique shop and traded them tape for tape. *Ferox* was back in the shop. I exchanged [1986 comedy] *The Money Pit* for that particular title. I got the best part of my collection from this one shop. Pretty much all the tapes were in excellent condition. The cases were a bit grubby — the shop owner was a heavy smoker, and a yellow film coated the protective plastic sleeve. There was a musty smell to the videos, too. Not an unpleasant odour — just what became an associative 'video nasty aroma.' I still have the films after almost fifteen years. The smell lingers vaguely and a quick sniff transports me back to the halcyon days of seeking out banned movies.

—Kevin

Black Market & Pirates

'HARD TO FIND RARITIES'

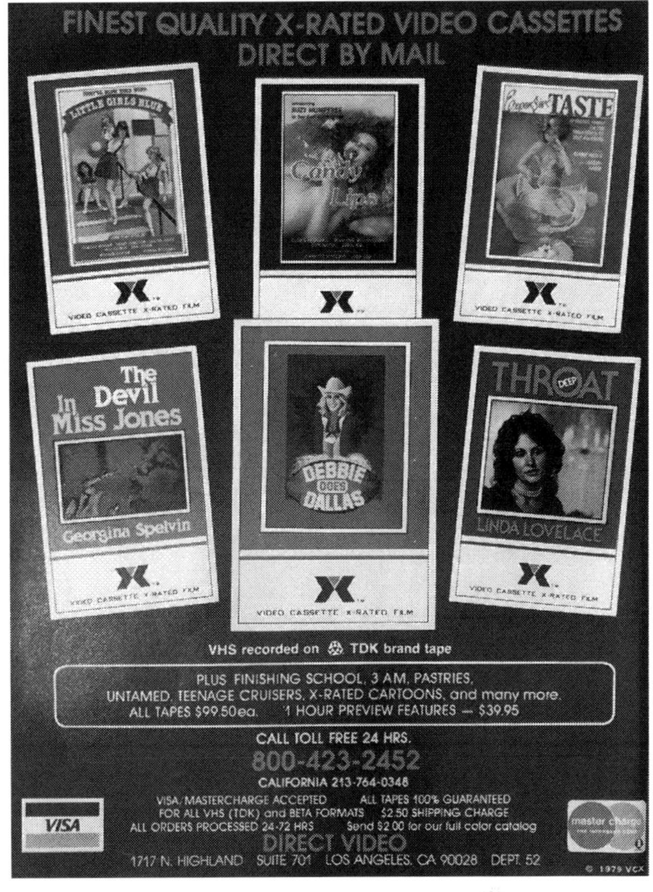

I started dealing in 'video nasties' when I was fourteen-or-so. You'd buy them from video shops — to the shop owners they were crappy old gore films no one rented anymore — and sell them through ads in the likes of [magazines] *Fear* and *Samhain*. One time I bought *Anthropophagous*, *Deep Red* and *Bloody Moon* for £5 each and sold them for £40, £60 and £40, respectively. I made a lot of fucking money, most of which I squandered on McDonald's and Space Invaders. You made a copy before selling the tape and sold copies of that, usually for £10-or-so a go. Likewise imported titles: *Nekromantik*, *Ilsa*, *Texas Chainsaw 2*… all very popular.

When I was seventeen, rumours started of police raids. One of my best contacts, A——, rang to tell me to stash my stuff. K—— in Birmingham had had a row with a neighbour, who told police he was a dealer. They raided him and found, amongst videos and so on, a package to be posted to A—— in Hull. On the outside was written "I know someone who's after porn." (A—— dealt in a lot of porn. Most people, me included, had *Deep Throat* and *The Devil In Miss Jones*, but little else.) So they raided him as well. They found 1,250 tapes, six VCRs, and his letter files, including all correspondence I'd sent him, which was a lot! So he rang me to warn me the Old Bill would be round — pretty good of him as he'd been warned not to, with the threat of a harsher sentence if he did.

Suddenly, the seventeen-year-old who had hitherto felt pretty cool about having his own video business turned into a rather scared little boy. My dad was

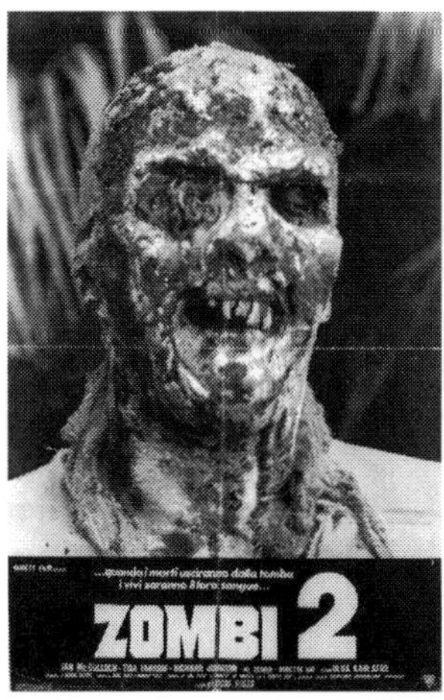

very helpful and cool-headed. He was well aware of the situation and had helped me run the business, seeing it as a display of initiative. My mum wasn't – she cried and threatened divorce and various other things unless we burnt all the films. She'd never been any good at handling a crisis. We hid the 250-plus tapes in a suitcase at my grandmother's flat around the corner, telling her it was stuff we'd confiscated from my younger brother. She suspected nothing, even when I kept coming round to retrieve films every few days – I was still dealing, albeit on a low-key, much reduced level. I always went to a phone box to call people, though, fearing I'd had my phone tapped!

Shortly after, I came home from school one day to find my bedroom disturbed. The Old Bill had called. They'd taken a few films I'd left lying around to give the impression I hadn't known what was coming – harmless stuff like *Suspiria*, *The Brood*, and so on – plus they got a load of unrelated stuff, like old diaries, one of which had some gibberish poems that I'd done with a friend way back, containing rhyming couplets about our school teachers. Maybe they thought it was a code, who knows? I could have hidden the videos in the garage, kitchen, living room, anywhere – the police only searched my bedroom. At one point my dad excused himself to go to toilet and nipped into his own room to stash his Swedish Erotica films under his bed.

A week later, I went with my dad to the local cop shop for an 'interview.' To say I was shitting myself would be something of an understatement. However, the first thing I was told was, "Don't worry, you're in no trouble. We just want to know who you know." Turns out they were basically interested in kiddie porn and 'snuff.' At no point had I ever been offered either – the network selling uncut copies of *Zombie Flesh Eaters* and *Cannibal Ferox* is entirely separate and distant to that of paedophile porn and so-called snuff films. The interview was all nice and chummy. I made up some bullshit about giving it all up six months earlier and burning all my stuff. They seemed to swallow it, despite there being one inconsistency: "If you did, how come we have a Xerox of a letter to A— asking for animal porn dated two months ago?" I said whilst I'd stopped dealing, I was still curious to see this stuff, but always burnt it once I had. The WPC didn't seem entirely convinced I'd buy a tape for £10, watch it once then destroy it, but she let it ride. They asked me for addresses, so I gave those of people I knew had already been busted. Tell a lie – I also gave them the address of a fucker in Essex who'd ripped me off to the tune of £500... I could hardly complain to Trading Standards, could I? The police gave me back everything they'd taken, and I left the station a happy boy.

I got the search warrant framed, and it still hangs proudly on my wall. Poor old A— had to give up his Teacher Training course, as his high-profile case was perfect for the scumbag local papers to scapegoat him. *"Is this the sort of man you want teaching your children?"* Doubtless they claimed he was a child-pornographer and personal friend of the Horned Beast. He faced a maximum £10,000 fine and six months inside, I think, but ended up with just a £50 fine. I haven't heard from him in years but wish him well wherever he may be.

I made a *lot* of money from dealing and had a gas. Built up a great video collection, too. Still got them – 400 films and not one of them legal in the UK! I was recently tempted to start dealing again, but I don't think the market's there as it once was. Also, I don't think the police would be as lenient on a twenty-two-year-old as they were a spotty faced adolescent. I'll just have to find a new way to make over £1,000 a month, tax free.

—Eddie

AS THE VIDEO RECORDINGS ACT was making its way through Parliament, interest in the films the law was destined to prohibit began to increase. A good indication of the titles that were unlikely to see their way through the clampdown came courtesy of the DPP index, which remains something of a "shopping list" for collectors. As noted in the previous chapter, rental shops took advantage of the changeover period allotted by Parliament and sold off stock to the public which invariably would need to be destroyed once the legislation came into effect. This became the prime source for the first 'nasty' collectors, who would spend their weekends frequenting out-of-the-way places for possible video goldmines. When the changeover period ended and the law came into effect, many shops risked a heavy penalty

Top: *Samhain*, a magazine whose classified ads section resulted in a smear campaign against its publisher. Bottom: The halcyon days of the long-running horror film magazine, *Fangoria*, the first issue of which appeared in 1979 (on the cover of No 8 is an image from *The Funhouse*, soon to be a 'video nasty' in the UK). Following the Hungerford massacre, a copy of *Fangoria* (No 68 or 69) was brought to the attention of Prime Minister Margaret Thatcher by an MP "disgusted" with its content. At least one shopkeeper removed their stock when he heard investigations were afoot to see whether *Fangoria* fell foul of the Obscene Publications Act 1959.

for continuing to sell what remained of their now illegal videocassettes.

Market stalls were another source for collectors. Even into the early part of the nineties, outlawed videocassettes could still be found on market days in some towns. Although many traders unwittingly displayed these tapes together with legitimate releases, others understood their black market value and the potential risks involved, offering them only to select clients (and often running parallel with a brisk under-the-counter trade in porn).

The third, perhaps most accessible and important source for banned videos was the classified ad pages in key magazines. (Indeed, this is how the authors of the book you are reading became acquainted.) Several publications devoted to video and fantasy films offered readers a classified ads service, among them *Video—The Magazine*, whose monthly free ads give us a clear indication of how collector interest was influenced by the Video Recordings Act: introduced in the latter part of 1984, the service was limited to commercially released tapes. It becomes apparent over the months that more readers are searching for contentious videocassettes, specifically targeting the films on the DPP list. By 1986, a substantial number of the tapes offered or wanted for exchange were those no longer available on the high street.

Ironically, another source for black market videocassettes seemed to be the police themselves. The fact that officers were taking videocassettes away didn't necessarily mean they were being removed from circulation. Illegal items such as hardcore pornography and pirate movies sometimes found their way back into public hands after they had been seized. In one instance, a school teacher was told by a pupil that their policeman father had brought home a seized pirate copy of Steven Spielberg's *ET*, many months before its official video release. The video was subsequently passed around for others to view. In March 2000 there was a case highlighted by the *News of the World*.[2] Following a serious domestic accident, a young couple called for an ambulance. The police also showed up but, rather than assisting, spent their time "snooping around the house," particularly the bedroom where they found two VCRs and a collection of video tapes. The police decided to confiscate the tapes on the suspicion they might have uncovered some video piracy.[3] The couple denied the tapes were pirates. On examination, officers found the couple were telling the truth. What the tapes did contain were home movies of the couple having sex – not illegal as the material was made for private viewing only. When they asked for their property back, police informed them that a number of the tapes had gone missing and they were about to launch an internal investigation.

Trading tapes and swapping them by mail drew collectors together and provided the

Top: *Roaaaaagh!*, a one-off 'video nasty' supplement given away with *Video World* magazine in 1985. Above: *Video Horror*, part one of a two-part zine primarily reviewing films that featured on the DPP list. Circa 1984.

beginnings of a network. Not everyone who had a videocassette to trade was interested in becoming part of a fan community, but the classifieds provided a gateway for those who did. Once initial contact was made, the network acquired another link and another source for the acquisition of videocassettes.

"I think most collectors would like to own a full set of nasties," one individual told the authors of this book. "What self-respecting collector wouldn't?"

As the number of collectors increased, the stockpile of pre-certified videocassettes in circulation was depleted. Many titles on the DPP list had never been widely available in the first place, and distribution of several key films – notably *Faces of Death*, *Anthropophagous the Beast* and *Beast in Heat* – had been particularly poor. Once films like this became the target of adverse media attention and police scrutiny in the run up to the Video Recordings Act, they became even more scarce, with stockists diligently removing them from shelves fearing a raid. In the case of at least one 'nasty,' *I Spit on Your Grave*, the distributor gave retailers a full refund and took away any copies they had in stock.

Although many people had originally been happy to acquire an original tape simply to view it before trading it on again for another, this type of friendly dealing was soon inhibited by dwindling supplies. Fewer collectors were willing to let videocassettes go that were clearly becoming scarce. Another factor that curbed any amicability was the increasing likelihood that some unscrupulous trader would try and pass a cheap duplicate off as an original.

'Video nasties' that were comparatively harder to find naturally fetched higher prices on the black market. According to one dealer,[4] up until several years ago the ten most sought-after nasties were:

Anthropophagous the Beast
Beast in Heat
Cannibal Ferox (uncut)
Death Trap
Devil Hunter
Flesh for Frankenstein
Island of Death (Nico Mastorakis)
The Last House on the Left
Night of the Demon
Zombie Flesh Eaters (uncut)

Depending on the quality of the tape and packaging, prices would range from £15 to £70. Some tapes fetched more, the most notorious example being *Beast in Heat* which is known to command up to £350 on the black market. In 1994, the prestigious *Lyle Price Guide for Film & Rock'n'Roll Collectables* valued *I Spit on Your Grave* on the Wizard label at £250, while the same film on the Astra label was said to be worth only £80.[5]

Says 'Adam', a disgruntled collector:

> I did actually own an original *Beast in Heat*. I'd bought it for something like £2 off a market stall run by this enterprising young lad – a nice guy, but a little clueless. A couple of times a week he would offload several cratefuls of videos from his van and set up his stall near to the fish market. I tried to get over there at least once a week. This was around about the late eighties. I remember picking *Beast in Heat* up from his table and thinking it was no big deal, because I never seemed to have much difficulty in finding stuff that had been on the DPP list. I think the tapes he was carrying came from out-of-business video shops, as all the cassettes had labels like 'Please Rewind' or 'Regent Video Centre, Salford'! On one occasion he asked me if I'd like to earn a little cash looking after his stall on Friday as he wouldn't be able to make it. I agreed and he told me that the guy who collects the rent for the stalls would come around, but that I wasn't to give him any money as it would be settled the following morning. Anyway, throughout the day this guy kept coming over for the rent and I kept telling him in good faith it'd be settled the following morning. It never was, of course, as the lad picked up his stock that evening, shared the takings with me and was never seen again! Anyway, getting back to *Beast in Heat*...
>
> To be honest, at that time I didn't have much idea of quite how scarce that particular title was becoming. Like most of the originals I got, I traded it on after I'd made a duplicate for myself. That was the last time I ever traded any tapes because what

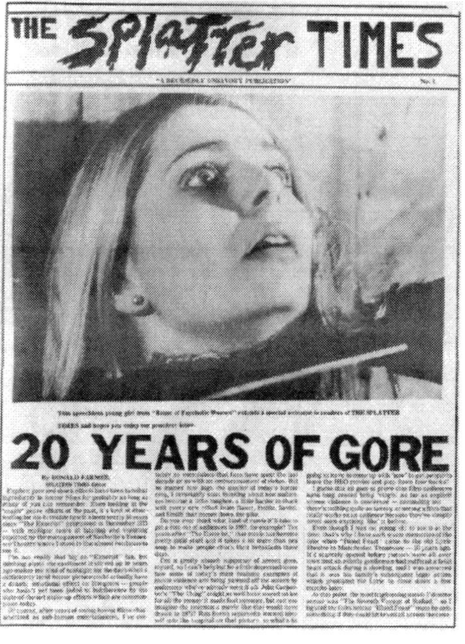

Horror fandom on both sides of the Atlantic owed a debt to the 'video nasties' – and, tellingly, punk rock. Top: *DOA*, Vol 2 No 0. Jul–Aug 1986; Bottom: *The Splatter Times* No 1, circa 1983. Four of the twelve films reviewed in this American tabloid zine would later be 'banned' in Britain.

I got back in return for *Beast in Heat* was a bootleg copy of (the uncut) *Absurd*. [See THE DPP39.] It breaks my heart now whenever I think that I had an original *Beast in Heat* and let it go!

Interestingly, the copy of [*Beast in Heat*] that I made for myself suffered a defect that I couldn't sort out. Although the original played fine, I couldn't make a decent copy. No matter how I tracked the original, the duplicate kept on breaking up at the precise same moment in the film. Having long since got rid of the duplicate, I was surprised many years later to watch a bootleg that a friend had picked up which had exactly the same fault in exactly the same places! Perhaps my original *Beast in Heat* has been used as the master for countless boots!

Before long more people were in search of 'nasties' than there were 'nasties' to go around.[6] Of course some ardent collectors were prepared to pay the sometimes exorbitant prices for original pre-certificated films, but most people were resigned to seeing banned titles via bootleg cassettes. This became the preferred method of trading and distribution. Anybody who was able to get their hands on a second VCR could, for a nominal cost, pick up a set of suitable co-axial cables from any electrical store, connect their machines together and run off duplicate tapes to their heart's content. Says one collector:

Black Market & Pirates

'HARD TO FIND RARITIES'

> I bought a double bill of *Zombie Flesh Eaters* and *I Spit on Your Grave* from this one guy who assured me that his copies were better than most because he was using specialist equipment. His prices were £10 for one film or £15 for two films on a single three-hour tape. When the tape arrived the films looked like any other second or third generation copy might. In fact, the tracking was out on *I Spit on Your Grave* and the picture kept rolling.

Originally, classified ads were the means by which collectors could contact one another and trade tapes, but the ads eventually became a front for a growing cottage industry. People who had initially traded for nothing got greedy and began selling their bootleg videocassettes. Numerous lists were in circulation, with dealers offering films at a price of anywhere up to £10 a copy. Straight trades would be accepted should the dealer be offered a film he[7] didn't already have, or an original pre-record he could sell on. As the network extended and trading intensified, no film on the DPP list, and many others besides, were out of the reach of dealers.

Quite often it wasn't enough to trade by mail. The underground network attracted its fair share of curious characters, many of whom desired to make impromptu social calls on fellow traders. Says 'Kevin':

> After responding to an advert in a video magazine an exchange of tapes was agreed. I had a spare copy of *Absurd,* the uncut version, and this guy was shifting *Cannibal Man*, a title I was having difficulty in finding. After speaking on the phone, B—said he would be passing by my place and could drop the tape off, even though he lived many miles away. I didn't want callers coming round to my house, so I asked him to mail the video. He would only do a hand-to-hand swap he insisted, and a few hours after the call arrived on my doorstep and handed me a scrappy-looking *Cannibal Man*. I said I'd like to check it out first and slotted it into the video player. He seemed itchy as I perused the quality of the cassette. "I can't hang around too long, my dad's waiting in the car outside," he remarked. "He's just had a heart attack," he added after a pause. I wondered whether he meant his dad had suffered a coronary on the trip over or had had an attack in recent months. But my proper attention was on the film, and I wasn't too happy. "I'm not sure about this," I said. The copy of *Absurd* was good quality and at the time I considered it a rarer film, so I was a bit dubious about letting it go. "I do a lot of body building, I'm fit and strong," responded my visitor and he flexed his muscles to further push the point. He went on to tell me how

> he had a collection of mounted animal heads and other objects of taxidermy. Not sure what his taxidermy hobby had to do with anything, I told him I'd keep *Absurd* and offered him a lesser title instead – I think it was *Forest of Fear*. B—countered with an additional offer of a copy of *Night of the Bloody Apes* as well as *Cannibal Man* for *Absurd*. I agreed and handed him my tape. "I'll put the film in the post," he promised and disappeared. Weeks passed and no tape arrived. I phoned B— to ask about the video and he told me that a friend had borrowed it and taken it to America, but he'd send it to me on his return. B—was never to be seen or heard from again. The copy of *Night of the Bloody Apes* was also never seen.

It was enough to put some fans off altogether. "The phone calls started to drive me mad," recalls Adam.

> Many people didn't seem to have a life outside of trading and watching videos. I got lists off a couple of contacts, contacted a couple more and before I knew it I was getting phone calls virtually every night – such-a-body had such-a-film and would I be interested in trading it for this or that? One particular guy, who I remember quite vividly because he always sounded as if he had sinus trouble, would often phone several times in the same evening. Very little small talk or familiarities, just him reeling off fresh titles he had to offer and me doing likewise. It got to be not much fun anymore. He phoned me back twice just to remind me how to pack the cassettes so they didn't get damaged in the mail!
>
> I always considered myself a film fan and only ever swapped videos – a copy-of-yours-gets-a-copy-of-mine sort of thing. I was well aware that a heavier penalty faced anyone who got caught doing this stuff for profit, but at the end of the day I wasn't in it to get rich. The only time I took money off anyone for a bootleg tape was when this guy desperately wanted a film I had but had no film to offer in return. He was quite insistent and in the end I told him to send me the cost of a blank tape and I'd run him a copy off. That was the only money I made, the price of a blank videocassette.

The sense of community that came with collecting was aided by a growing number of film-based publications. On the heels of *Fangoria*, a US-based glossy news-stand horror movie magazine launched in 1979, the video boom of the mid eighties had seen something of a revolution in cheaply produced fanzines devoted to obscure and exploitational movies. Interestingly, zines on both sides of the Atlantic started to spring up around the same time and brought to film the

Black Market & Pirates

'HARD TO FIND RARITIES'

Trading via classified ads, post Video Recordings Act 1984. This is a sample of ads that appeared in *Video–The Magazine*.

SWAPS SWAPS SWAPS SWAPS

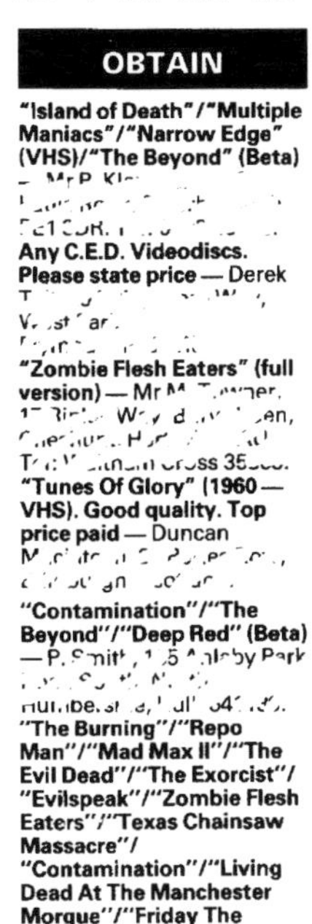

OBTAIN

"Island of Death"/"Multiple Maniacs"/"Narrow Edge" (VHS)/"The Beyond" (Beta) — Mr P. Kl[illegible]

Any C.E.D. Videodiscs. Please state price — Derek [illegible]

"Zombie Flesh Eaters" (full version) — Mr M[illegible]

"Tunes Of Glory" (1960 — VHS). Good quality. Top price paid — Duncan [illegible]

"Contamination"/"The Beyond"/"Deep Red" (Beta) — P. Smith, 15 Ashby Park [illegible]

"The Burning"/"Repo Man"/"Mad Max II"/"The Evil Dead"/"The Exorcist"/"Evilspeak"/"Zombie Flesh Eaters"/"Texas Chainsaw Massacre"/"Contamination"/"Living Dead At The Manchester Morgue"/"Friday The 13th"/"The Beyond"/"House By The Cemetery" (VHS) — David Wright [illegible]

"Caged Heat" by Jonathan Demme/"The Story of 'O'" by Just Jaeckin (VHS) — J. [illegible]

"Neil Diamond — Love At The Greek" — Mr H. Johnst[illegible]

EXCHANGE

"The Warning"/"The Changeling"/"Samurai Reincarnation"/"Private Eyes" (Beta) for "Cataclysm"/"Mad Max 2" any other good films (Beta) — Stev[illegible]

"Videodrome"/"1984"/"Incubus"/"Spaceship"/"Nightcomers"/"Looking For Mr Goodbar"/"Satan's Slave"/"The Awakening" — J. [illegible]

"Zombie Flesh Eaters"/"Zombie — City Of the Dead" for "The Deer Hunter"/"Daredevil Drivers" — S. [illegible]

"She-Freak"/"Blood Devils"/"The Devil's Men"/"Mausoleum". Offers — [illegible]

"Give My Regards To Broad Street" (Beta) for "Romancing The Stone"/"War Games"/"Risky Business" (Beta) — Steven [illegible]

"Tenebrae"/"Zombie Flesh Eaters"/"Hills Have Eyes Part 2"/"Dawn Of The Dead"/"Halloween III" for other good horror films (VHS) — G. Jackson [illegible]

"Gremlins"/"Romancing The Stone"/"Trading Places"/"Police Academy" for "Porky's"/"Young Warriors"/"The Key"/"Grizzly"/"Black Sunday" (Barbara Steel) — Marc [illegible]

"Alien Terror" (Beta) for any Elvis Presley film (Beta) — [illegible]

"The Link"/"Screamtime"/"Cujo"/"Blow Out"/"Cat People"/"Schizo"/"Christine"/"The Octagon"/"An Eye For An Eye"/"Forced Vengeance" — [illegible]

"Eating Raoul"/any good comedy (VHS) — C. B. [illegible]

"Straw Dogs" for "The Evil Dead" (VHS) — Scott [illegible]

"S.O.B."/"Jaws III" for "Attack Force Z"/"The Evil Dead" (VHS) — A. M[illegible]

"Don't Go In The Woods Alone" (VHS) for "Absurd"/"Suspiria"/"The Beyond"/"Nightmare Maker"/"Madhouse" and others (VHS) — Mr R. Allen, [illegible]

same anarchic attitude of the punk rock zine explosion a few years earlier. Indeed, the irreverent attitude that the small press had towards *Fangoria*, considered mainstream, was identical to the music zines before them, scornful of the likes of the *NME* and *Rolling Stone* which were perceived as staid and out-of-touch. ("Fuck the Critics," was the philosophy of Jeff Queen's *D.O.A.*, a US film/punk crossover zine that regarded exploitation as an art form.) Utilising cut-and-paste layouts and photocopy reproduction, British zines like *Cold Sweat*, *Video Horror* (by the erstwhile 'Horror Consultant'), *Yeeeuuch!*, *Samhain* and *Whiplash Smile* had a natural inclination towards the films that featured on the DPP list, and were predominantly concerned with issues of censorship, often comparing cut prints of domestic video releases with their European and American counterparts. Not suffering the same censorial background, American zine publishers were less inhibitive in their range of subject matter. Nonetheless, the likes of *Sub Human*, *Hi-Tech Terror*, *Video Drive-In!*, *Gore Gazette* and *Slimetime* piqued the interest of British videophiles, reviewing material that, if not already banned in Britain, was unlikely to see a release given the dragnet of the Video Recordings Act.

Fanzines were networked in a similar way to videos, inasmuch as they could be found via the classified ads of news-stand magazines. From here the reader would be patched into other, like-minded small press publications courtesy of the review roundups which zines invariably carried. Interest in British pre-VRA videocassettes even extended to overseas collectors, eager to seek out the films causing so much fuss in the United Kingdom. The Dementia Horror Shop in Sweden was one outlet operating in 1987, which advertised British videos for sale and trade, as well as uncut imports, underground oddities, experimental music, books and zines.

With fanzines, the communal identity of video fandom was established and with it a channel of communication that generated social activities, such as late-night video parties and film fairs. These events offered fans the opportunity to meet and make further contacts, as well as buy or trade videocassettes, fanzines and assorted memorabilia. In August 1987, the British exploitation film journal *Shock Xpress* launched Shock Around The Clock, a marathon eighteen-hour horror film festival held at the Scala cinema in London.[8] Featuring ten movies and a celebrity panel discussion, the Shock festival was an instant sell-out, repeated with equal success on an annual basis over the next few years. It also provided the blueprint for numerous unrelated marathon screenings, such as the northern equivalent Black Sunday.

'Geoff' recalls the camaraderie among collectors:

> The film fairs were good fun when they first started on a regular basis. We'd arrive before the doors opened and meet up with some friends in the queue. Swap tapes and stuff. After about an hour-or-so looking around the fair we'd go to a nearby pub, have a couple of drinks and then go back again and maybe pick up some more crap in our semi-inebriated state! I got to know quite a few of the traders, and it was still relatively easy to pick up bargains like, say, originals of *The Toolbox Murders* and *The Witch Who Came From the Sea*, which I got for £15 the pair. Stalls selling pre-certified material and bootlegs weren't that common initially, but they did seem to be a couple more traders dealing in that stuff with each fair. I remember there was a guy who regularly drove over from France just to sell Dutch videos of stuff that was cut or banned over here. And these fairs weren't big events back then, either! It was obviously worth his while bringing a suitcase full of videos all that way, through Customs, for half a day's work. *Crazy Breetish!* His videos were £20 apiece, in the original Dutch sleeves. He had stuff from the banned list, like *House on the Edge of the Park*. I got that off him and that other *Last House* rip-off, *The House by the*

> *Lake*... Ultimately, these fairs became bigger, and a lot more business oriented. It seemed that some of the people getting into videos were doing so purely for gain, picking up films simply so that they could generate a catalogue and sell boots.

Forerunner to Frightfest, the UK's biggest fantasy festival, was Shock Around the Clock. Pictured is the programme for its fourth and final year (August 1990).

The 'nasties' trade wasn't going unnoticed. Film fairs took place in major cities around the country, some for years prior to the arrival of video, but it's accurate to say that video collectors were a new breed galvanised by such spaces. While the fairs may have offered anonymity to collectors in search of elusive, pre-certificated films, not so dealers – they were taking a chance and faced prosecution for selling such material. As the video subculture grew, so it drew the attention of moneymakers and the authorities alike. Says 'Geoff':

> There were two guys who started to attend the fairs for a while, who walked around with a list of bootlegs they kept in the boot of their car. They would flash this list in front of anyone they thought might be interested. It didn't take a brain surgeon to figure these guys weren't collectors as such, nor really concerned with films apart from the fact they could make a bit of money from 'banned' tapes. At one fair they clocked me offering someone an original *Blood Rites*, and that's how I got to know what they were up to. They saw me with this tape and came dashing over, offering to trade it for a couple of boots on this list of theirs. When I said I wasn't interested, they offered me a bit of cash and I let them have it. They gave me the impression they were trying to get 'heavy.' Some months later I ran into these two jokers again at the next fair, where they told me that the tape I'd sold them was faulty. I knew it wasn't. When I offered to take the film back, they told me they'd already sold it for double what they had given me, plus had made a boot of it and were selling that on their list. They disappeared shortly after that, and I heard they'd been nicked.

Chris Glazebrook recalls that once the Video Recordings Act came into force, unscrupulous video shops would rent out the likes of *SS Experiment Camp* under-the-counter at £5 or £10 a night, a higher price than usual rentals. These were the people authorities were most concerned with – dealers operating for profit. Although the VRA brought legitimacy to the industry, outlawing the worst excesses of sex and sadism, piracy and bootlegging had become more of a problem as a consequence. Raids continued through the latter part of the eighties and into the nineties, except the onus was not now on the police but on Trading Standards officers and the Federation Against Copyright Theft (FACT). The intensity of the raids was only marginally less than it had been pre-VRA, now so commonplace that prosecutions rarely extended beyond the local press. "Two jailed over sick videos," was a headline in an October 1995 edition of the *Manchester Evening News*. The story was a fairly typical one, concerning market traders "selling obscene and unclassified movies like *Erotic Clips*, *Cannibal Holocaust* and uncut versions of *The Exorcist* and *Straw Dogs*."

> [W]atchdogs began their investigation after a tip-off. One trading standards officer went undercover and bought illegal tapes on sale with mainstream movies. [One of the stall holders] then showed him boxes marked 'horror' and 'adult' which were stored under the counter and the officer bought some of these.
>
> When officials identified themselves they seized dozens of pornographic and horror films.

More tapes were said to have been recovered from the pair's car and homes. Admitting to a total of forty offences under the Obscene Publications and Video Recordings Acts, each man received three months imprisonment. The Video Recordings Act made it an offence for anyone to supply a videocassette without a classification certificate; however it led to few prosecutions. The custodial sentence in this case was influenced by the fact the "videos were being sold on a public, open market where they could have been purchased by children."

A series of raids that did make the pages of the national press occurred in May 1992. Video collectors across the country feared the worst when their underground network was infiltrated by Trading Standards officers. Reported as the largest operation of its kind, officers in Liverpool were alerted to the operation ("racket") following a raid on a suspected computer software pirate. Other local authorities became involved as officers spent six months undercover and entered correspondence with dealers. The raids on homes across Britain netted some 3,000 videocassettes and recording equipment and saw ten

MR NASTY SELLS DEATH VIDEOS TO OUR KIDS

NEWS OF THE WORLD INVESTIGATES

EVIL Tom Halloran is the Pied Piper of Horror.

He plays the fool to attract a crowd of impressionable children ...then sells them stomach-churning videos of **REAL-LIFE** death, gore and mutilation.

The kids, sucked into believing that anything Halloran does is fun, part with their pocket-money and rush home with films that could warp them forever.

His biggest seller is a video called Faces Of Death. It despicts sequences from real tragedies including a parachutist landing in an alligator park and being eaten alive by the reptiles.

In another scene, a live monkey's head is smashed open with a hammer.

Asian diners are then seen eating the whimpering creature's brains.

There are also close-ups of the mangled victims of fatal car crashes and surgeons carrying out autopsies.

Sinister

Yet another clip shows a woman falling to her death under a lorry.

"Kids are the best customers," said ex squaddie Halloran with a sinister chuckle. "Adults don't want them.

"A customer is a customer. The kids may be robbing their mums so they can pay them, but that's not my problem.

"As far as I'm concerned, if kids are old enough to be walking around with a tenner, they're old enough to be buying a video off me."

The 35-year-old monster, who touts his grisly wares around the East London borough of Newham, also has a video called Being Different. It shows sad, seriously disfigured people with growths on their heads and stunted limbs.

Wounded

Not content with even that, he hopes to get Army perverts to smuggle him copies of a medical training film, featuring operations on soldiers seriously wounded in the Falklands and Gulf wars.

"A couple of blokes in Germany I'm speaking to soon may bring some back," he jeered. "They nick them, you know."

Halloran, who served with the Royal Engineers, boasts that business has doubled since Home Secretary Michael Howard announced tough laws to protect children from video nasties ...and drove his wares underground.

"I'm storing up lots of the Faces Of Death videos," he said.

"They're really popular because it's all blood and guts.

"I'm waiting to see what happens about this new legislation thing, because the price will go up."

The Home Secretary's crackdown on violent videos came after teachers protested at their effect on children.

The British Board of Film Classification will be given powers to ban the worst examples. Jail sentences will also be included in measures to curb under-the-counter supplies of unsuitable videos to children.

The Professional Association of Teachers found in a specially-commissioned study that children secretly deal in horror videos in about 1,000 primary and 800 secondary schools.

Billions

Lavinia Carey, director of the British Video Association, said that the illegal trade in video nasties—worth billions of pounds a year—"needs to be stamped out."

Hopefully Halloran's filthy tricks can be stamped out too.

We have sent our dossier on the Pied Piper straight to the police.

HALLORAN: 'Kids are the best customers'

By GARY JONES

Video nasties seized as ring is smashed

Ian Katz

TRADING standards officers yesterday claimed to have smashed a nationwide underground "horror" video ring after a series of raids across the country.

In the largest operation of its kind, the council investigators, supported by police, seized almost 3,000 videos depicting scenes including torture, mutilation and cannabalism.

Duplicating equipment was also discovered and 10 people were yesterday helping police inquiries after the raids at eight addresses in the North-west, the Midlands, South Wales, Kent and Cornwall. The seizures followed a six-month undercover operation in which Liverpool trading standards officers posed as dealers. Peter Mawdsley, Liverpool's Chief Trading Standards Officer, said children as young as 12 were involved in trading the videos. Titles included Faces of Death, Cannibal Holocaust, and Blood Sucking Freaks.

It is cl[illegible]med th[illegible] some[illegible]os [illegible] movies, in which the victims are killed during filming: "Some are billed as snuff videos but I believe it is more a matter of marketing because most of the people in them are easily identifiable."

His officers were alerted to the racket after a raid on a suspected computer software counterfeiter. Four Liverpool officers spent months infiltrating the ring and 10 other local authorities became involved.

Mr Mawdsley said the network was made up of "enthusiasts" who corresponded. The videos, which sold for between £12 and £90, reportedly include the removal of eyes, tongues, limbs and scalps and people eating human excrement.

The Liverpool investigators have alerted Interpol to the network's connections in Finland, Germany and Ireland. Next week officers start viewing the haul to establish what charges can be brought. They are likely to be charged under the Video Recordings Bill and the Obscene Publications Act. They face fines of up to £20,000 per tape and up to three months' im[illegible]isonment.

Main: *News of the World*, May 8, 1994.
Inset: The *Guardian*, May 8, 1982.

people brought in for questioning. "Some of the films are so sickening," said the chairman of Consumer Protection in Liverpool, "they would be unwatchable for most people." Journalists noted how many of the films confiscated were 'video nasties' that had appeared on the DPP blacklist, while other reporters keyed into more sensational aspects. The *Daily Star*, for instance, managed to associate the raids with supposed 'snuff' films and the murder of schoolboy Jason Swift two years earlier – the sole connection being that the sting had uncovered a boy of twelve trading horror videos with his friends. Even the so-called quality press was not immune to such exploitative tactics, and scenes from films that were evidently works of fiction were presented ambiguously, as possibly genuine instances of torture, mutilation and murder.

Following the haul, a scene from *Anthropophagous the Beast* (see THE DPP39) was used by the press and excerpted on television as something of a 'video nasty' nadir, contextless and indefensible: The cannibal in the movie devours a foetus.

"MR NASTY SELLS DEATH VIDEOS TO OUR KIDS" was the supercharged headline of a report in the *News of the World* on May 8, 1994. It told of a thirty-five-year-old ex-squaddie by the name of Tom Halloran, who

> plays the fool to attract a crowd of impressionable children... then sells them stomach-churning videos of REAL-LIFE death, gore and mutilation.
>
> The kids, sucked into believing that anything Halloran does is fun, part with their pocket-money and rush home with films that could warp them forever.

Halloran, operating in East London and described in the report as "evil," a "monster," and "the Pied Piper of Horror," admitted that *Faces of Death* was his biggest selling video. Several graphic scenes from the film were described by the newspaper, following which Halloran is quoted as saying "Kids are the best customers... kids may be robbing their mums so they can pay them [*sic*], but that's not my problem."

The report stated that stringent laws governing video violence had driven Halloran's "wares underground" – a curious point to make, as Halloran's illegal operation could never exist anywhere but underground in the first place. Wherever it resided, the trade seemed nothing short of endemic amongst the young and impressionable, as per the admonition that "children secretly deal in horror videos in about 1,000 primary and 600 secondary schools."

Children and *Faces of Death* were the subject of another news report when, on April 8, 1995, the *Manchester Evening News* declared, "'SNUFF' VIDEO IS FOUND IN SCHOOL." The sensational front-page story brought the video into the apocryphal realm of the 'snuff' film, circulating in a school playground no less!

> The sick 'snuff' movie called *The Face of Death* [*sic*] ended up in the hands of 15-year-old girl. [*sic*] She was so horrified that she handed it over to her parents.

Facts pertaining to this particular case did not come from police or the government, but an "inter-denominational Christian group called Marantha."[9] Said to "feature more than twenty deaths," the descriptions of several sequences actually fit those of *Faces of Death IV* and not Conan Le Cilaire's original film. This mistake was repeated in a piece that featured in the Irish paper *Sunday World*, dated September 27, 1998, offering some indication of time scale regarding pirate videocassettes and their circulation, given that three years had lapsed since the report in the *Manchester Evening News*. It also shows that widespread concern is primarily focused on the same old films. Beneath a reproduction of the original *Faces of Death* video sleeve, the *Sunday World* caption read:

> SICK COVER. The vile video that contains bloody scenes.

The report went on to describe several "slaughterhouse-like scenes" taken from *Faces of Death IV*, concentrating particularly on a sequence depicting Michael Stone. At an IRA funeral in Belfast's Milltown cemetery in 1988, loyalist terrorist Stone had launched a gun-and-grenade attack which killed three people and wounded sixty others. The footage shows mourners scattering and falling under Stone's hail of bullets, and Stone himself being pursued and attacked by a mob before police were able to pull him to safety. Stone received three life sentences. Under the Good Friday peace agreement between the British and Irish governments, however, he was amongst those eligible for an early release (in July 2000). There can be no doubting the political intent in associating Stone with the film. A picture of him with his hands up victorious is printed alongside an image of a man 'tied between two horses and ripped asunder on camera' – both may feature in the same film, but beyond that have no connection. Once free, the article proposed that Stone's intention was to live in Ballynahinch and open a business. His evil past however, "will still haunt him – through the pirate video."

The outlawed film is not the outrage in this instance, but a propaganda tool.

> To some in the loyalist community the video will be a vindication of a man they consider a hero. To others, the video will be the vilest footage they have had to relive and a reminder of how low the human soul can go.

Suspicion of video piracy could be based on nothing more damning than owning two VCRs, as in the case involving a couple's home-made sex films, noted earlier. It was the mere suspicion of piracy, together with the stigma attached to horror videos, that lost 'Jimmie', the author of the next tale, his job.

Last year, shortly after being made redundant, I started an office position through an employment agency on a temp-to-perm basis, with an initial four-week trial period. Although a large company, the office consisted of only the department head and three other employees, one being a temp who had been there for some time. After a while it became obvious I had been brought in to replace this person on a permanent full-time basis.

During the trial period I was determined to make a good impression, so I kept my head down and got stuck into my work, spending as many hours as possible learning the job. While my training period progressed, I tried to get along with everyone (as you do), and we occasionally talked socially about our pastimes and hobbies, my primary one being collecting horror movies.

Now, let's bear in mind I *did not* gibber fanatically about Giannetto de Rossi's goriest effects, nor did I babble on about the various versions of *Cannibal Holocaust*.

By the fourth week I was able to do the job without any supervision with all deadlines and quotas met. I was sure I had secured the position I had worked so very hard for – until came 'the final Friday.'

I returned back from lunch early (yes, I was that conscientious!) when the department secretary came over to the three of us with a dilemma: she said she was taping a film on Channel 4 that night which she wanted to keep, but that she was going out so it would be full of adverts. What could she do?

Someone suggested she get someone else to tape it for her, leaving out the adverts... but alas she knew no one. I suggested that if she brought the cassette in on Monday, I could re-tape it and edit out all the adverts. Everyone looked at me in astonishment and the secretary said to me with a gasp, "What? You mean you've got more than one video recorder?!"

I really did not know what to make of her reaction! I just shrugged it off and returned to work.

Later on in the afternoon my telephone extension rang. It was the woman from my employment agency.

"How's it coming?" she asked. "Any problems?"

I told her that I was sure I had got the job as I had progressed very well during my four-week trial. There was this short uncomfortable silence at the other end of the line, then she replied, "That's not what I heard. I've been told that you're involved in video piracy. You're finishing at five o'clock and I'm taking you off our records. We can't have someone like you working for us because you'll give us a bad name."

And she promptly put the phone down on me, leaving me shocked... What the fuck was going on?!

Five o'clock came and I still hadn't heard a word from the department head. (In fact, no one had said anything to me at all!) So I grabbed my jacket and went in to see her. She completely ignored me as I entered her office, so I asked whether I had got the job or not. After a short pause she said, "I'm not employing anyone in this department who deals in video piracy and enjoys watching 'snuff films.'"

I was shocked and told her I didn't know what she was talking about. I demanded to know how she came to these conclusions. She said it had been brought to her attention that I watch horror films and had offered to pirate a film for a member of staff. This was something the company took a very dim view of indeed. She further informed me that I was lucky the police hadn't been alerted to my criminal activities, and then called for me to be removed from the premises. Within moments I was being manhandled from the office by two large security guards. I couldn't believe this was happening, or that such a scenario could be so overblown...

It has been nearly a year now and I am still out of work. The local employment agencies won't touch me, as these things have a habit of getting around.[10]

Having infiltrated the underground 'video nasties' network, Trading Standards diligently kept up the subterfuge long after their high-profile sting of May 1992. Officers continued to bait unsuspecting video dealers with the pretence they were collectors in search of 'banned' movies. One fresh strategy was the perusal of classified ads in British horror publications like *The Dark Side* and *Samhain*.[11] Although the magazines themselves never advocated that readers should deal in 'video nasties', it was patently obvious what lay at the heart of some of the carefully worded ads. Phraseology used to mask the black market trade typically comprised of "Uncut films for sale," "Copies of rare films available," "VHS and Beta originals," "Good prices/swaps wanted" and "Hard to find rarities." Invitations to make your collection look authentic with colour photocopied video covers were also a bit of a give-away. Often it wasn't even as complex as that. The May 1993 edition of *The Dark Side* carried an ad from one K Howell which read:

UNCUT FILMS. *Beyond*, *Zombie Flesh Eaters*, *Cannibal*, *Cannibal Ferox*, *Faces of Death*, *Anthropophagous*, *Xtro*, *Exorcist*. Any two films on one tape £16.

In February 1994, Trading Standards officers undertook a second major series of raids. These covered twenty towns nationwide, resulting in a haul of 5,000 videocassettes and twenty people brought in for police questioning.[12] Meeting with markedly less media fanfare than the first raids, it was noted that Trading Standards had used the classified ads of the horror press to construct their latest campaign. Jim Potts, chief standards officer in Preston where the operation was coordinated, called for tough action against magazines that allowed dealers to advertise. (Some people suspected that bogus ads had been placed by officials in order to lure dealers into the open.[13])

On February 12, two days after the raids had taken place, Exeter's evening newspaper the *Express and Echo* launched a series of leading and defamatory articles against local man John Gullidge, whose magazine *Samhain* was said to specialise "in films and books with titles such as *Zombie Holocaust*, *Driller Killer*, *The Virgin Witch* and *I Spit on Your Grave*." Printing a picture of Gullidge beneath a headline that read "Cult horror mag probe," the article implied via a series of contradictory statements that the publisher himself was under investigation and had a pivotal role in the distribution of illegal videos. Furthermore, Gullidge was made to look as if he had declined to comment when contacted by the journalist writing the story. On the contrary. The reporter had chosen to omit the fact that Gullidge had spoken with Trading Standards officers the previous month about printing classified ads, whereupon the publisher was informed he was within his rights to run such a section so long as he had a "no video nasties" disclaimer.

The Trading Standards link was ignored in subsequent articles on Gullidge, with the *Express and Echo* concentrating instead on the ruckus they had created with their original report. "Resign call to mag boss" was the headline for one story some months later. Gullidge was well liked by staff and children at the playgroup, but several parents expressed concern that a "cult publisher" – as Gullidge was described by the newspaper – should be employed as a helper with young children. A claim made by the reporter that the Reverend Richard Jeffrey had called for Gullidge to resign, was refuted on publication of the story; the vicar denied having said it and apologised to Gullidge for what had appeared in print.

Someone whose mail was placed under surveillance and who consequently fell victim to a raid was William Black. A freelance journalist by profession, Black was a collector of horror films amongst other esoterica, but the circumstance surrounding his case was unique amongst those we heard about while researching this book. In this instance it was police and not Trading Standards who cast the net.

Black explained that it began with a different variety of classified ad:

> After answering a personal ad placed by a woman in a national newspaper, we began exchanging letters (I used a nom de plume). The letters, on both sides, were erotic, openly sexual and, over time, S&M based.
>
> When photos of the woman began arriving, she looked as good as her writing, a young-looking forties. In later photos, leather gear, ropes and a riding crop were in evidence. Other photos showed her in restraint and tied to chairs, sofas, bedheads, a stable door and spread-eagled in an X-position in an open doorway. She made a neat package in an elegant living room, a bathroom, a stairwell and in what appeared to be a basement or cellar. Not all the pictures were taken in the same house. One could have been described as a manor house, another a step above a council dwelling.
>
> That she had access to money was obvious in one picture where she posed in a full kit of riding gear alongside a handsome black mare. The woman was married. Her husband agreed to all she was involved in. Occasionally they swapped partners. Sometimes they accepted visitors who stayed at their house. I was obliquely invited. She wrote to a number of other people, men and women. Much later she sent me photos of a number of her correspondents. The women, like herself in her own pictures, were half-naked or sometimes nude or often involved in sex acts. One shot had a girl with the neck of a wine bottle inserted into her vagina, while she herself used a vibrator between her legs.
>
> Her letters were those of an intelligent, even sophisticated woman, feminine and not at all threatening, even when in one photo she posed like a skimpily dressed Nazi guard wielding a whip.
>
> Though she was the submissive in the photos (there were rarely men in the house) I could tell she was no unthinking sex ragdoll, to be ordered around haphazardly. She appeared fully aware of the reaction she was creating in the dominant one, and the resulting erotic charge she too was experiencing in fulfilling his – and sometimes her – desire. Her husband never wrote but she said he read all the letters. He was a mysterious figure who was sometimes in the outer regions of my mind when I wrote to her. Someone approving of my sexual ramblings. Someone who would take her to bed to read the sex-charged missives and turn the fantasy writings into heightened sexual reality.

Once she sent me a picture of a semi-nude and slightly buxom girl, who resembled something out of a Russ Meyer movie and resided close to where I lived. I drove past her house, with the knowledge that inside was a young woman with her boyfriend who were into the 'swapping' scene. Though a little too well-fed for my tastes, I wrote but received no reply. Not in your own back garden, perhaps?

Partway through our correspondences, the woman began to reply with letters written on a word processor. The letters were always signed but gone was the intimacy of hand-written material. I also felt the contents had changed slightly. There appeared to be a new interest in me as a person, a little more probing. Not something I could put my finger on. My letters were answered more quickly but were shorter in length. Questions I would ask about particular subjects were left unanswered. I began to doubt it was even her writing. That may have been the reason I ended the correspondence – or it could have been that I simply became bored.

Some months later I happened to glance from my bedroom window to see a police van in the street. I assumed they had been to a neighbour's house, though it's not that kind of neighbourhood. After showering and dressing, the phone rang. It was a wrong number, the caller explained. In fact it wasn't. It was the police's way of discovering if I was actually in the house. A few minutes later they arrived at the door... five uniformed policemen and two detectives. Some of them carried hammers, screwdrivers and crowbars and a search warrant was waved before my unbelieving eyes...

I asked three times of nobody in particular what they were looking for. By then I was backed-up into the living room. It was then that the alarm I felt changed to fear. I tried to remain calm. I felt cold. I couldn't swallow. My mind began to distance itself from what was happening.

The police asked me whether I had any pornographic material in the house. I led them to a box containing videos. I also showed them my collection of mondos and 'banned' tapes.

When I was informed the warrant had been issued on behalf of the police station's Child Care unit, I sat down and attempted to hide my shaking hands. I watched the events happening as though I wasn't there. It was a medium shot from a scene in a movie. A climatic act in a stageplay. It was a Roger Cook door-storming incident. But it wasn't. It was my house, and me, surrounded by police searching for something I knew not what...

The police were searching the house room by room... They expressed no hostility toward me and went about their business quickly and quietly. No hammers or crowbars were needed. My study – like a set for the film *Twister* – caused a groan or two, but otherwise it was under the bed, over the wardrobe, into the attic, and through every drawer in the house.

My mondo and 'banned' collection caused the older of the detectives to mutter soberly about the "wild titles." Then the police began to gather all the tapes; those with photocopied covers, tapes in boxes without covers, tapes in dust jackets with details of their contents written on them by myself all piled together.

Originals such as *The Texas Chain Saw Massacre* I to III, *Martin*, *Nightmares in a Damaged Brain*, *Blood Sucking Freaks*, *The Driller Killer*, and many of their ilk were added to the pile.

"I see you have a copy of *Snuff*," said the younger detective with a wry smile. He stared at me when I said it was a badly made old thriller.

The tape was added to the growing heap assembled on the living room carpet.

From my mondo collection, the police took *Signal 30*, *Uncensored News*, *Mondo Cane* I and II, *Of The Dead*, *Ecco*, *The Killing of America*, *This Violent World*, *Faces of Death* 1 to 5, *Death Scenes*, and others.

I sat rock still. My body had become part of the chair. If they dragged me away, the furniture would come with me. I felt I was gasping for breath, yet I was calm and barely breathing. I felt almost drunk. The fishbowl I was looking out from appeared to expand, taking me even further away from the events around me.

A constable lifted my copy of *Guinea Pig 2* from a shelf. And *Guinea Pig 3*. And *Guinea Pig 4*. They made a neat stack all on their own.

I love the cinema. I have attended a number of film festivals and I have a large collection of movie documentaries on video, mostly taken from television. They cover the cinema in general, with features on directors, actors, special effects experts, script writers, and interviews with the likes of David Lynch, Clive Barker, David Cronenberg, and others. A few are copies I obtained from advertisers in various cinema and horror magazines, as recommended by Jonathan Ross in the back of his *Incredibly Strange Film Book*.

Other documentaries – again all taken from TV or purchased across the counter at the likes of Virgin – cover true crime. Some are rare: Ted Bundy's last interview, *Charles Manson Superstar*, *Manson: Live from Death Row*, and many more.

All these were also taken in the search.

My book library was left untouched. No interest was shown in *Porn Gold*, *Araki*, *Memories of an Erotic Bookseller*, *Dada and Surrealism*, or *The Erotic Arts*. Nor even in the book of the film *Death Scenes*. (Why should the representation of an image differ in one medium from that of another?) *Final Truth*, *Hunting Humans*, *Alone with the*

Left: Police officers viewed William Black's confiscated video collection and made notes. This is a typical comment sheet. Right: A minute-by-minute description of one examined video tape.

CURRENT EXH. NO: G.C1

NEW EXHIBIT NO:

DATE VIEWED: 15.11.95

FILE NO / /

NECROPHILIA
PAEDOPHILIA
SCATOPHAGY
ENEMAS
DEFAECATION
BESTIALITY
VAGINAL FISTING
ANAL FISTING
SADO-MASOCHISM
URINATION
ANILINGUS
BONDAGE
BUGGERY
MASTURBATION
EJACULATION
CUNNILINGUS
FELLATIO
INTERCOURSE
TITLE
OTHER COMMENTS
QUANTITY

19

\- 3 -

Male No 2 rubs his hand between female No 2's legs.

2943 Male No 2 pulls out his penis from female No 2's vagina and ejaculates.

2954 Female No 1 receiving a vaginal fisting from female No 3.

3022 Male No 3 ejaculates into female No 2's mouth while Male No 2 penetrates her.

31.01 Female No 3 continues to give Female No 1 a vaginal

31.23 Male sticks needles into Female No 1's vagina.

31.30 Male No 3 masturbating himself over Female No 2.

32.22 Female No 2 sucking Male No 3's penis.

33.32 Male No 1 placing needle into the area of Female No 1's vagina.

34.30 Female No 2, on all fours, sucking Male No 3's penis.

3614 Weigh placed and attach to needles in the area of Female No 1's vagina.

3632 Female made to stand up with weigh hanging between her legs.

3639 Sex Aid pushed inside Female No 2's vagina.

37.56 Female No 2 and No 3 sucking and fondling at Male No 2's penis, while No 3 pushs sex aid into Female No 2.

38.54 Female No 2 having Oral Sex with Male No 2.

39.04 Male No 3 licking between female No 3's legs.

39.08 Quality of Video poor becoming fuzzy.

39.10 Close up of Female No 2 having Oral Sex with Male No 2.

39.15 Female No 3 licking between Female No 2's legs while Female No 2 sucks Male No 2's penis and Male No 3 licks between Female No 3's legs.

39.18 Quality of Video poor becoming fuzzy and intermittent.

39.20 Male No 3 pushs Sex Aid into Female No 3's vagina.

39.34 Male No 3 pushing Sex Aid in and out of Female No 3's vagina

40.17 Male No 3 continues to push Sex Aid in and out of Female No 3's vagina while Male No 2 has his penis sucked by female No 3.

41.15 Male No 2 ejaculates into female No 3's mouth.

Devil, works by [Brian] Masters and [Colin] Wilson, and none of the other titles among my true crime books got a look in. And my photographic art books didn't appeal to the police either, books by the likes of Thornton, Knoll, Valleso, Bailey and Klimt.

But the police did find a number of notebooks that I had listed my videos in, and address books going back something like twenty years. A number of ex-girlfriends and mates of old were, I presumed, in for a surprise. Also discovered was a small packet of photos I received from my correspondent. All those involving bondage and any sort of sex act (vibrator use, basically) were taken. Other pictures I had of women who had posed for my camera (I fancy myself as a photographer of pretty girls) were given back to me – and some of the poses were explicit.

The search lasted in total two hours. The detectives questioned me briefly (or in my dazed mind it appeared so) and showed me copies they had of some of the letters I sent to the woman. I noted a number of paragraphs on various pages had been marked in red or green ink. I was asked for the letters I had received from her. But months before I had ended the correspondence, and discarded them.

I had not, however, disposed of a number of video tapes she had sent me. They were among those in the box I had handed over earlier. All her tapes had an S&M theme. She had no interest in 'video nasties' or mainstream cinema.

The police informed me that all the tapes would be viewed and assessed, and that it would take some time. I was not arrested or charged with any offence at this stage. As the officers left the house carrying a number of black bags, a solitary neighbour saw them go. He and a policeman he knew exchanged what seemed like knowing looks. Later they must have got together for a chat because my neighbour began ignoring me after that for a time.

Five months later I was summoned to a police station for an interview. I arrived with a solicitor. I was questioned about my letters and those of my correspondent – they had all of mine, but none of those she had sent to me. I was also asked about the contents of a small number of the videos taken from my house.

In the cold light of a police cell interview room, inhabited by two determined detectives and an elderly solicitor, where your every whispered reply is taped (twice; once for the police and once for my solicitor), talking about sex seemed suddenly akin to being caught naked with a hard-on by your mother.

I was offered a TV and video to review the tapes as their content was read out for the tape recorder. I declined. I wanted, at this stage, to keep my solicitor on my side. The interview lasted two hours.

The police told me my correspondent had received a video tape containing child porn, allegedly sent by me. And that she had sent it back to me. The police search was an attempt to find the tape and anything along similar lines. Nothing relating to child porn was found in my house.

I was shown a photocopy of pages put together by the woman, with the titles of videos on one side and on the other side some comments on their content and their 'hardness' or otherwise, all hand-written: hardcore, softcore, extreme, etc. Each entry was numbered, with the highest number I saw being 150, but there could have been more listings beyond the page I saw. The name of the person she had sent each tape to was also recorded.

There was no record of any of the few tapes I had sent to the woman. The disputed child porn tape was listed on her record sheet as having been sent to me. And then the entry had been scratched through, as though the sender had changed their mind about sending it.

Needless to say, I did not possess, send or receive the tape in question. The tape I was supposed to have sent to her – and she allegedly back to me – was, in fact, found at her house, I was informed during questioning...

I was told boldly: "You were not writing to a woman, you were writing to a man." Yet, no matter what I was told, I knew the early letters were written by a woman genuinely in search of sexual excitement. Later perhaps they were from a woman (or a man) wearing a uniform sitting behind a desk in an office in a police station.

I am not suggesting I was set up. I think I just happened to be caught up in the ripples emanating out from some 'stone in the water' – the further the ripples spread, the weaker the waves, the less important the lone surfer caught up in them.

But I was still in the water and I had to keep my head above it. And I don't think I had helped myself during the long wait by having my solicitor contact the officers a number of times to try and reclaim my videos. At that stage I had been unaware of the kiddie porn angle of the investigation. I just assumed that porn and 'video nasties' were the items they were looking to take action on.

A year later I was charged, and summons were issued. My solicitor, and by now a barrister in tow, had the original date of the hearing delayed by four months. The charges related to a small number of video tapes I was accused of publishing contrary to common law. In other words, I had copied an obscene article, or articles. I was also charged with sending a postal package containing indecent or obscene written communications.

I would plead not guilty with the backing of my solicitor and barrister, the charges being trivial and technical they said. However, after an arranged viewing session of the named tapes at the police station, my barrister's attitude changed completely. (Not so with my solicitor.) Viewing the tapes in court, as the police intended, I was told, would influence the magistrate enough to come down heavily on me. Yes, I suppose a little oral, anal, and heavy bondage at a 10 AM sitting would be too much even for the most liberal of magistrates.

I pleaded guilty.

A few of the written communications – the letters – were on the charge sheet along with a small number of the videos. But a large number of the tapes were left off. The child porn angle was not raised in court. The case was presented by the police prosecutor without aggression or revealed distaste. It could have been worse, I was told.

The magistrate commented on the "perverts" who get "some form of perverted pleasure from these things" and that the transactions – the tape swapping – was not commercial, but a private affair between two people. The fine was nominal.

There was a feeling that, with all the work undertaken in the investigations, someone would have to carry the can at the end of the day. Almost certainly the authorities knew that I, and people like me in the same position, would plead guilty to lesser charges to save time, expense and embarrassment.

If the charges against me had not been tainted by the child porn angle (though, as mentioned, they were not part of the case), I may have pleaded not guilty. After all, we are part of the EC where, across the channel, pornography is legal.

In Europe, my case would not have gone to court. But sadly it will take a stronger man than me to take the fight against an injustice levelled on us all by our government, the British media, and – the biggest enemy of all – our own hypocrisy.

After the hearing I was approached by the case detective and told I could arrange to pick up those video tapes that did not constitute part of the charges. In due course I collected a huge box containing the tapes. *Guinea Pig*, *Faces of Death*, *Snuff*, *Blood Sucking Freaks*, *Death Scenes*, *SS Experiment Camp* were all there, as were my movie documentaries and true crime tapes. However, one part of the *Faces of Death* series was missing. Another cassette that had on it the title *Faces of Death IV* was, I later discovered, actually a John Wayne western. I couldn't figure that one out...

The address books and notebook listing the videos had all been returned to me much earlier.

I never learned what happened to my penpal, nor her husband, nor her other correspondences.

In a case that generated much publicity and the cause of some irritation and embarrassment for the police, porn historian David Flint was raided by officers from Manchester's Obscene Publications Unit in March 1998. Having amassed material over a twelve-year period, and working on *Babylon Blue*, a book about the history of sex cinema, Flint was in possession of several hundred videocassettes. These were removed from his home in the raid, along with VCRs, computer equipment and paperwork. He later described the operation – conducted at 7:30 in the morning and lasting three hours – like being burgled, but "having the burglars wake you up to watch, and constantly tell you that there's worse to come."[14] The police suspected Flint of possessing obscene material for gain. As noted previously, suspicion is all that is required to obtain a search warrant.

Flint was informed that his formal arrest would take place two weeks hence, allowing police time to examine the seized items. Said the author, "They doubtless thought that I would follow the usual pattern of behaviour: keep my head down, try to get off lightly, avoid publicity, and hire a local solicitor who had no special knowledge of the obscenity laws. That's what most people do."

A half-page report in the following morning's *Guardian* was critical of the police raid. The negative sentiment continued over the coming weeks, with factions of the media angry that police would focus time and energy on a historian involved in credible research.[15] When the time arrived for Flint to go to the police for an interview and a formal charge, he had the leverage of the press coverage as well as the services of a "heavyweight London barrister." More importantly, the police had no evidence that the accused had sold any tapes to anybody, and he was bailed until July. Meanwhile, Flint was re-arrested on another charge: conspiracy to produce obscene material for gain, on account of police having found a mock-up video sleeve on his computer and correspondence in which he discussed the idea of shooting a porn film.

Flint was bailed until September, but at the end of August received a call from the Crown Prosecution Service telling him that there was no case to answer and all charges were dropped. What material hadn't already been handed back some weeks earlier was now returned.

"To be fair to the police," states Flint in hindsight, "they were as honest as they could be with me. Never once did they try threatening behaviour or lie to me. They were, in the end, just doing their job. I just wish that their job had something to do with the real threats to the people of Manchester..."

Flint is adamant that it was a mean-spirited neighbour who made the initial complaint to the police, leading to a series of mysterious phone calls prior to the raid, which he now believes were made by police. The caller said he got Flint's number from a mutual acquaintance – a name not in fact familiar to Flint – and that he was in the market to buy some porn videos. Flint smelled a rat. But foolishly in hindsight, he decided to string the police along and perhaps get a "witty article" out of it (by way of some vague promises, return calls and cancelled meetings). The plan backfired and resulted in months of stress for Flint, as well as other people who were raided because of material seized from his home.

Flint had been raided once before in 1994. In this instance he was detained by HM Customs on returning from a trip to Amsterdam when he was found carrying some twenty VHS tapes. The tapes included vintage porn as well as horror and mondo films. Flint was charged, arrested and detained in a Manchester airport cell. It was while being detained that a raid was carried out on his home. ("I had to hand over my keys," he says.) With the help of a lawyer, most of the videocassettes seized from his home would be returned. However, legal aid fees dissuaded him from pursuing an appeal and Flint settled for a reduced fine of £200. (See also the interview with David Flint in the APPENDIX.)

Raids conducted by HM Customs & Excise[16] on the homes of film collectors are not unheard of. Flint had attempted to bring videocassettes into Britain in his personal luggage, but a raid could be instigated by items intercepted in the mail on entering the country, should they be considered obscene. Alas the guidelines governing this practice are arbitrary to say the least, and in most instances the addressee would simply receive a written "Notice of Seizure." Left uncontested the goods would be destroyed without any criminal consequence. Should the addressee contest the forfeiture, they have one month to do so in writing, upon which HM Customs "are then required to institute proceedings for a court to decide the matter." The prospect of a civil action is enough to put most people off and so claims are rarely made by individuals importing videocassettes and other material for their own use. (Less common is that HM Customs will lose a case that has gone before a court.) Anyone receving a Notice of Seizure who then bothered to call the provided number to check with HM Customs what might happen next, as did the authors of this book, would be informed by a member of staff that there was "nothing to worry about."

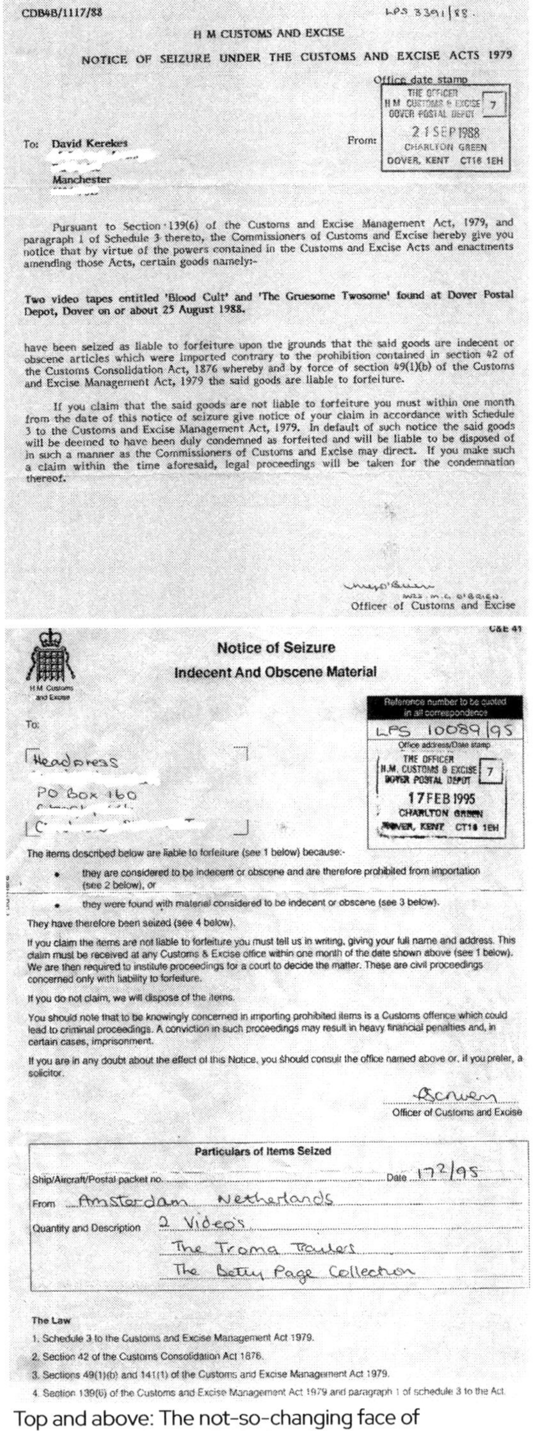

CDB4B/1117/88 LPS 3391/88.

H M CUSTOMS AND EXCISE

NOTICE OF SEIZURE UNDER THE CUSTOMS AND EXCISE ACTS 1979

To: David Kerekes

Manchester

From: Office date stamp
THE OFFICER
H M CUSTOMS & EXCISE 7
DOVER POSTAL DEPOT
21 SEP 1988
CHARLTON GREEN
DOVER, KENT CT16 1EH

Pursuant to Section 139(6) of the Customs and Excise Management Act, 1979, and paragraph 1 of Schedule 3 thereto, the Commissioners of Customs and Excise hereby give you notice that by virtue of the powers contained in the Customs and Excise Acts and enactments amending those Acts, certain goods namely:-

Two video tapes entitled 'Blood Cult' and 'The Gruesome Twosome' found at Dover Postal Depot, Dover on or about 25 August 1988.

have been seized as liable to forfeiture upon the grounds that the said goods are indecent or obscene articles which were imported contrary to the prohibition contained in section 42 of the Customs Consolidation Act, 1876 whereby and by force of section 49(1)(b) of the Customs and Excise Management Act, 1979 the said goods are liable to forfeiture.

If you claim that the said goods are not liable to forfeiture you must within one month from the date of this notice of seizure give notice of your claim in accordance with Schedule 3 to the Customs and Excise Management Act, 1979. In default of such notice the said goods will be deemed to have been duly condemned as forfeited and will be liable to be disposed of in such a manner as the Commissioners of Customs and Excise may direct. If you make such a claim within the time aforesaid, legal proceedings will be taken for the condemnation thereof.

MRS. M.C. O'BRIEN.
Officer of Customs and Excise

C&E 41

H.M. Customs and Excise

Notice of Seizure

Indecent And Obscene Material

To:
Headpress
PO Box 160

Reference number to be quoted in all correspondence: LPS 10089/95

Office address/Date stamp
THE OFFICER
H.M. CUSTOMS & EXCISE 7
DOVER POSTAL DEPOT
17 FEB 1995
CHARLTON GREEN
DOVER, KENT CT16 1EH

The items described below are liable to forfeiture (see 1 below) because:-

- they are considered to be indecent or obscene and are therefore prohibited from importation (see 2 below), or
- they were found with material considered to be indecent or obscene (see 3 below).

They have therefore been seized (see 4 below).

If you claim the items are not liable to forfeiture you must tell us in writing, giving your full name and address. This claim must be received at any Customs & Excise office within one month of the date shown above (see 1 below). We are then required to institute proceedings for a court to decide the matter. These are civil proceedings concerned only with liability to forfeiture.

If you do not claim, we will dispose of the items.

You should note that to be knowingly concerned in importing prohibited items is a Customs offence which could lead to criminal proceedings. A conviction in such proceedings may result in heavy financial penalties and, in certain cases, imprisonment.

If you are in any doubt about the effect of this Notice, you should consult the office named above or, if you prefer, a solicitor.

Officer of Customs and Excise

Particulars of Items Seized

Ship/Aircraft/Postal packet no. .... Date 17/2/95

From Amsterdam Netherlands

Quantity and Description 2 Video's
The Troma Trailers
The Betty Page Collection

The Law

1. Schedule 3 to the Customs and Excise Management Act 1979.
2. Section 42 of the Customs Consolidation Act 1876.
3. Sections 49(1)(b) and 141(1) of the Customs and Excise Management Act 1979.
4. Section 139(6) of the Customs and Excise Management Act 1979 and paragraph 1 of schedule 3 to the Act.

Top and above: The not-so-changing face of HM Customs & Excise's Notice of Seizure.

HM Customs don't take any notice of trial acquittals.[17] They draw their interpretation of obscenity from Section 42 of the 1876 Customs Consolidation Act, which is no less ambiguous than that of the Obscene Publications Act. For instance, Customs Officers have on occasion intercepted and seized the film *I Spit on Your Grave*, and at other times examined it and let it go. A perfectly innocuous film will be impounded if packaged with an item that Customs believe is indecent, though sometimes the reverse may also happen. Customs will exercise discretion and will not detain small quantities of obscene material if intended for personal or professional use, yet guidelines to travellers entering the UK ranks pornography amongst those prohibited goods "which are banned completely."[18]

The transit of horror films is supervised in a similarly indiscriminate and contrary manner. Apparently, Customs will call the BBFC to see whether an intercepted title already carries a certificate in Britain, although this doesn't explain why some unclassified material is examined and subsequently allowed to pass through. Customs have on occasion seized and destroyed films which an importer intends to submit to the BBFC for classification (as in the case of Screen Edge and *Shatter Dead*; see APPENDIX). Contrarily, a thirty-five-minute preview copy of Olaf Ittenbach's *The Burning Moon* was seized, determined to contain obscene imagery, but reprieved once the importer (Headpress) explained to Customs officials that it intended to review the film and, if suitable, submit it to the BBFC with a view to a release.[19]

'Kevin' relates his own dealings with Customs & Excise:

> I received a Notice of Seizure in lieu of an expected package of three videos – *Cannibal*, *Primitifs*, and *Night of the Devils* – which I'd ordered from a source in Holland.[20] Confident that not all of these titles could be considered obscene, I phoned the seizing officer at Mount Pleasant [sorting office] for some kind of explanation. I was put through to the person dealing with the case, who clarified that all the films had been watched; two of the titles were to be sent on to me, while the third was to be destroyed as it was considered obscene. I was told that the one marked for incineration was actually *Night of the Devils*, an atmospheric and stylish vampire movie made in 1972. Indeed, the woman I spoke to (she sounded middle-aged and was very pleasant, friendly, and sympathetic) said that the "jungle films" were actually quite good – in spite of the fact that one of them was the uncut version of Ruggero Deodato's notorous *Cannibal*, complete with animal killings, mutilations and eviscerations! If any of the three films were destined for seizure, I thought

> that particular title would have been it. Somewhat naïvely thinking it would make a difference, I explained that the films were for my personal viewing alone and I didn't find such material offensive. How then, I asked, could Customs justify preventing me from receiving my own private matter? The response I got was astonishing: "There is always the possibility that you may be burgled and the video will fall into the wrong hands." As far as I was concerned my private mail was already in the wrong hands, but I concluded from that response there was no point in continuing arguing. I didn't push the issue any further, not wanting to jeopardise the fact that I was to get at least two of the films. A few days later *Cannibal* and *Primitifs* arrived with a note saying that *Night of the Devils* would be destroyed. A few weeks after that I obtained the film from a different source.

"Such cases are often not examples of people deliberately breaking the law," one Customs officer told *Sight & Sound* in May 1998. "They attempt to import the material either in good faith or in ignorance and we prevent them from doing so."

There are exceptions. Sometimes items intercepted by Customs officials intended for personal use will not result in a forfeiture notice but a raid. This doesn't necessarily have to be material that poses a threat to national security or of a sexual nature involving minors, as outlined by law,[21] but can include 'objectionable' or 'questionable' material as per cases involving the importation of 'squish' videos.[22] Unlike a raid carried out by police, Customs & Excise are only entitled to seize "material of foreign origin which cannot be traded lawfully in this country." This fact was pointed out to 'E.W.', raided by Customs in December 1992 following the interception of five videocassettes of an adult nature. The tapes in question – *The Story of K*, *Caught*, *You'll Love the Feeling*, *Top Secret* and *Bittersweet Revenge* – were sent by a fellow collector in Ireland. All the tapes had been lawfully available and obtained by mail order in London, prior to the introduction of the Video Recordings Act.

Although cleared of conspiring to import two further videos from France – a fact that officers would have been blissfully unaware of were it not for the honesty of the accused – 'E.W.' was found guilty of the obscenity charge pertaining to the five videocassettes above. In summing up, the stipendiary magistrate made it clear that he believed both charges to be fairly trivial and gave 'E.W.' a two-year conditional discharge. 'E.W.' maintained that the officers who dealt with the case were in abuse of their powers, i.e. seizing material indiscrimately. Complaining to HM Customs & Excise in July 1993, he writes:

> During the search of my house Customs & Excise removed items "loosely described as 199 video tapes, twelve boxes of various documentation, magazines and books, and two computer discs." They are now claiming that most of these items are forfeit and will not be returned to me. They are in fact prepared to return sixty of the 199 tapes, and most of the magazines, but this in itself is an empty gesture. Their seizure of material during the course of the search was virtually indiscriminate. For example, amongst the seized tapes were titles like *Crystal Gale in Concert*, *Everyday Yoga* and a number of others, equally innocuous. These of course make up a large part of the tapes to be returned. Similarly they are prepared to return copies of such things as *Men Only* amongst the magazines, but precious little else.
>
> I find it difficult to understand how they can seize tapes that I have made direct from films shown on public television, e.g. excerpts from films shown on the Adult Channel on cable TV. In the enclosed press cutting the statement is made that "mildly erotic scenes that have long been shown on national television and other satellite services, such as BSkyB, (which) all conform to ITC regulations." If this is true, by what right do Customs & Excise confiscate such material?
>
> They are also seizing copies of videos that are manufactured and sold quite openly and legally in the UK [as well as] admittedly more contentious material such as videos in the *Slave Sex* series, which show scenes of whipping etc...
>
> I have of course protested to my solicitor about this high-handed action by Customs & Excise, but he tells me that I have no recourse to the law to recover my property. We are in the process of preparing a detailed list of those items for which there seems to be absolutely no justification for their being confiscated, but my solicitor tells me that, in his opinion, there is very little chance of them giving way on so much as a single item and I have absolutely no chance whatsoever of recovering any of the more contentious material. It is his view that under the terms of the Customs & Excise Management Act they are quite at liberty to confiscate anything they might find during their search of my home if in their opinion it is obscene, and I have no right of appeal. Their opinion is not subject to the law.

Nonetheless, prepared to take the case to the High Court, 'E.W.' was notified by Customs in February 1994 that all material would be returned to him (apart from the five tapes for which he had been prosecuted, subsequently destroyed). It was still their belief that the material seized was liable to forfeiture but having weighed this "against the potential costs to the taxpayers", Customs declined to take the matter further.

Following discussions with Customs, author and academic Dr Mikita Brottman also had success in convincing Customs to forward material they had intercepted and initially found to be obscene. Mikita isn't sure if there is any lesson to be learned here, other than you can get your videos back so long as you've got the right kind of headed notepaper, and promise both to burn them and write a book about them afterwards... "During the whole of 1995," she says,

> I'd been ordering "outlawed" videos on a regular basis from the US, all of which came through HM Customs on a regular basis, without any difficulties at all. In December, whilst working on my book *Meat is Murder*, I needed two films that the company I'd been using in the US couldn't provide – Deodato's *Cannibal Holocaust* and Conan Le Cilaire's *Faces of Death*, and so – foolishly, in retrospect – I ordered them from a European company instead (I think it was Cult Video in Amsterdam). I also ordered a copy of Kubrick's *A Clockwork Orange* in the same shipment. Sometime in the middle of January 1996, I received my copy of *Clockwork Orange*, accompanied by the familiar "Notice of Seizure" from HM Customs informing me that *Cannibal Holocaust* and *Faces of Death* had been "seized."
>
> I thought I might have a chance of getting these videos back, since my purpose in ordering them was a "legitimate" one – they were to be used in "academic research" rather than to satisfy a voyeuristic curiosity (remember, I was trying to put myself in the mindset of a senior officer at HM Customs & Excise). So, on the headed notepaper of my university department, I sent them a long, detailed description of my proposed research project, detailing its (admittedly somewhat minor) emphasis on censorship, accompanied by a copy of an article I wrote on Nick Bougas' *Death Scenes* for an academic film journal, *Cineaction*. I stressed that these videos had been ordered for use in a "legitimate, academic" project (rather than to be... what? enjoyed?) and would be watched by myself alone, "in the privacy of my own home."
>
> On February 23, I received another letter from HM Customs requesting further information. They wanted "written confirmation from the head of your department... that this is a specified research project for which the videos are an integral part, that the work is conducted under the supervision of the head of department, and that the end product is endorsed by him/her", and "a written understanding from yourself that the videos in question will be viewed only by you, in connection with the research project, and that when your work is finished you will return them as seized material in due course."
>
> So I sent them back the further "confirmations" they needed, and they sent

'Soon they will be banned...' As well as enabling a black market in pirate hardcore pornography to flourish, the Video Recordings Act 1984 helped pornographers to pressure-sell legitimate softcore.

me my videos. They haven't been "disposed" of yet, but should I ever come to the conclusion that I've got nothing else to learn from them, they can easily be replaced. Here in the US, where I'm currently living, both *Cannibal Holocaust* and *Faces of Death* are prominently displayed on the shelves of my local video shop. The US Midwest is supposed to be a very conservative place – and in some respects, it really is. But unlike England, they don't require you to have a Ph.D. from Oxford to watch a low-budget horror film.

In an unrelated case that occurred in April 1998, Customs officials stopped a horror video entering Britain and called on the home to which it was addressed. They took numerous videocassettes in the raid, but later returned them all. The importer had already lost seven other packages to Customs, receiving the usual Notice of Seizure. This was his eighth offence, and the resultant raid seemed to comply with the general suspicion that Customs keep a record of individuals who repeatedly have items seized. This cannot be verified. Although interception of mail is supposedly random, Customs do admit to being familiar with the packaging that accompanies contentious material, whilst trying "to isolate the likely routes through which it would travel."[23] Any contentious material which is stopped and found to be dishonestly labelled or in some way disguised, will be viewed as smuggling and elicit more serious attention, possibly resulting in a raid.

The idea of a Customs blacklist doesn't explain why some people should be raided following their first unsuccessful attempt at importing contentious material. As in the case of 'Paulo' from East London, whose tale further highlights the irregular – and some might say dubious – way in which Customs sometimes conducts itself. 'Paulo' ordered two magazines from a company called Nu-West in the USA, specialising in spanking and corporal punishment (CP)...

> Instead of receiving the magazines, I got a knock at my door on a Sunday afternoon by three men who introduced themselves as HM Customs. They asked me my name and whether I'd bought any magazines from Nu-West. When I let them in the events went like this: I was asked whether I'd brought into the country any other similar material to which I said 'no.' They then asked how I got hold of the address of Nu-West. I said through a UK magazine – which they then asked to see (my heart dropped!). One of the men came up to my bedroom and I showed him my collection. He looked at each magazine. If it wasn't clearly of UK origin he flicked through the contents. As all of my CP mags were from the UK he didn't bother about them. However, there were a couple of hardcore adult mags which I'd brought back from a trip to Holland. I was questioned as to where I'd got these and I said I'd bought them in London. I'm not sure he believed me, but as he decided to seize these mags as well it made no real difference.
>
> At this time I was still living at home with my mum. I made this point to the three men, and that she was likely to be back home soon. The officer who checked my magazines went and discussed something with the other two men and they decided to continue my interrogation in their car.
>
> I was told that if they had found any other imported material, or I was discovered trying to import any adult material in the future, then I would be prosecuted. They then left with my magazines.
>
> I have to say that the whole incident was a great shock, but also left me seething with rage. The material I imported was not offensive by any means – you can buy similar stuff in the UK – so what right did they have?

In this chapter we have dealt primarily with the black market that grew out of the formation of the Video Recordings Act. We have concentrated on the

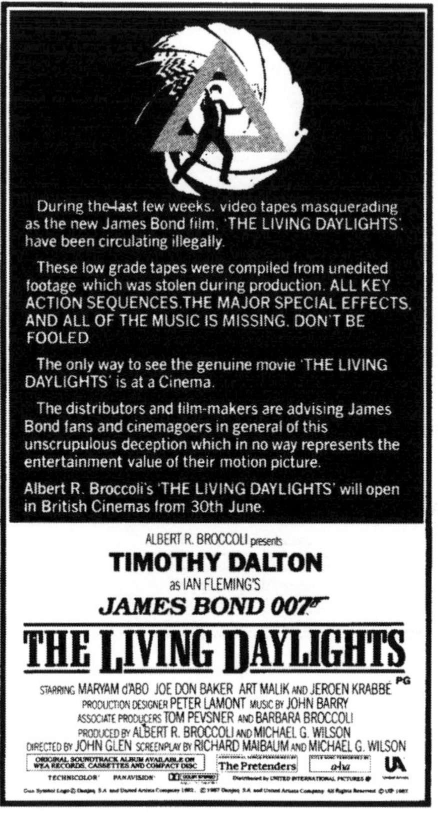

dealers of unclassified films for whom the VRA made collecting not simply "fun" and "exciting" – to quote one of the dealers at the opening of this chapter – but also profitable and risky.[24] However, this is just one side of the black market, and to the video business probably not the most contentious side either, dealing as it does with low-budget or independent films from companies that have no commercial clout and cannot afford to pursue pirates.

Whenever networks of video horror fans are infiltrated by Trading Standards and handfuls of collectors are busted, it's a "terror" or "sick film racket" said to have been smashed, and rarely an issue of piracy or copyright. Compare this to any new blockbuster release from Hollywood, which will invariably be preceded by a campaign in the media warning of the perils of pirates and copyright theft. One of the first and most intensive of these campaigns accompanied CIC Video's release of *ET–The Extraterrestrial*.[25] (Pirates still managed to get their copies on the market first.)

Video piracy is the copying and subsequent sale of feature films or any other programme without the consent of the copyright holder. A pirate might deal in material already on the market, offering cheap duplicates of desirable movies, or he may offer copies of films that haven't yet officially been released on video. Either way, the money the pirate generates is considerable and almost pure profit, his only outlay being the price of blank cassettes on which to duplicate his master tape and perhaps the packaging.

Piracy was rife in the early days of video. The lack of quality product and high prices helped to see to that. By early 1982, it was estimated that sixty-five per cent of all videos sold in Britain were pirated copies, with the film industry claiming it was losing international revenue of around £100 million a year. London was regarded as the pirate capital of the world.[26] The high concentration of film facilities "gives the pirates very easy access to the films themselves", said Peter Browne, head of the anti-piracy unit of the Motion Picture Export Association of America (MPEAA). In 1981, the MPEAA claimed there were 5,000 pirates operating in London, with virtually every film finding its way onto pirate videocassette within two or three weeks of its West End theatrical release. Unscrupulous projectionists, laboratory workers and even cinema managers were said to be responsible for helping to put films on the black market, taking the print away from the cinema overnight and allowing pirates to run a copy off using professional tele-cine converters. Unless hardcore pornography was involved – in which case the police could be brought in – it was the responsibility of the MPEAA and the Society of Film Distributors to investigate such crime in Britain.

The power and resources wielded by these organisations was less formidable than the FBI, who handled piracy across the Atlantic. A report published by the Economist Intelligence Unit[27] in May 1983 stated that British video laws were "weak and toothless", resulting in the climate of piracy.

Asked about the kind of material being pirated in these early years, an anonymous source told the authors:

> The first pirate tapes that I heard of were basically all the Disney cartoons, which of course weren't officially made available on video until years later. I remember a colleague ringing me one day and saying, "There's a guy in Bolton who's got all the Disneys. Nip over and get some!" I had this old transit van at the time, and I remember going over to this house and putting a hundred of these tapes in the back. *Snow White* and all that stuff. Very, very poor pirated copies of Disney films.[28]

In an attempt to address the situation, the MPEAA and the Society of Film Distributors joined forces with the British Videogram Association to form the Federation Against Copyright Theft (FACT). The Federation comprised a large team of investigators and administrative staff, whose dedicated role was to combat piracy and illegal public performances. By the end of 1983, FACT had seized some 30,000 illegal tapes, and supposedly reduced the pirates' share of the market to under thirty-five per cent.

At a press conference, Peter Duffy of FACT revealed that most pirated films in circulation were not now mastered in Britain but had originated overseas. Evidence of US origin was demonstrated in the way some pirate tapes had flaws systematic with duplication between the nominally incompatible American

NTSC format and the British PAL format. One primitive way around the problem was to sit a PAL video camera on a tripod and aim it at a TV screen on which an NTSC film was playing and record it that way. The end product was understandably terrible, with washed out colours, a constantly flickering image and an unshakeable, ghostly after-image that clung to every movement and action that happened onscreen. However, this eye-straining method of piracy did offer moments of unintentional amusement, as in one instance recounted by 'Kevin':

> This copy of Buddy Giovanni's *Combat Shock* I got from abroad – the US – whenever the screen darkened it revealed the reflection of the person making the copy, who was sitting naked in an armchair!

London lost the stigma of the piracy capital of the world.[29] But the Federation's claim that no new films had been pirated since its formation were proven inaccurate when copies of *Educating Rita* and *Scarface* turned up in the hands of dealers prior to their official video release. Also erroneous was the assertion that FACT had stamped out the counterfeiting of tapes, in which videos were made and packaged to look identical to genuine releases, even down to incorporating copyright warnings. Special reflective security labels and even the introduction of Macrovision to pre-recorded videocassettes – a process that ostensibly caused picture deterioration in an illegal duplicate – didn't curb the pirates.[30]

"Bootleg videos are pouring into Britain," was a report in the *Daily Express* dated December 18, 1995. Illegal copies of new movies such as Disney's *Pocahontas* and the James Bond blockbuster *GoldenEye* had been discovered at car boot sales and market stalls. Reg Dixon, director of FACT, said, "People think they are simply getting a video on the cheap but they are helping finance crime at its worse."

FACT had a detrimental effect on the illicit video trade, but they couldn't seriously hope to bring it to an end. Indeed, in years to come, they would be forced to change tactics and increasingly target the consumer as opposed to the pirates directly, trying to halt the trade with campaigns that pricked the public conscience. One shocking FACT advertisement posited that children were put at risk by blasé parents who purchased pirated tapes.[31] Another common attempt to deter consumers was the suggestion that profits accrued from illegally duplicated films, Disney films in particular, funded the IRA,[32] the drug trade,[33] and the manufacturers of child pornography.[34] As no evidence was forthcoming to support such claims, they can only be construed as a type of aversion propaganda.

But it wasn't only the film industry that alleged a link between movies and criminal activity – albeit, in this instance, pirated movie revenue funding crime. The news media and politicians are the worst offenders when it comes to making these allegations. But, as we shall see in the next chapter, these supposed links are self-serving propaganda.

The Big Influence

'WHO SUPPORTS VIOLENT FILMS NOW?'

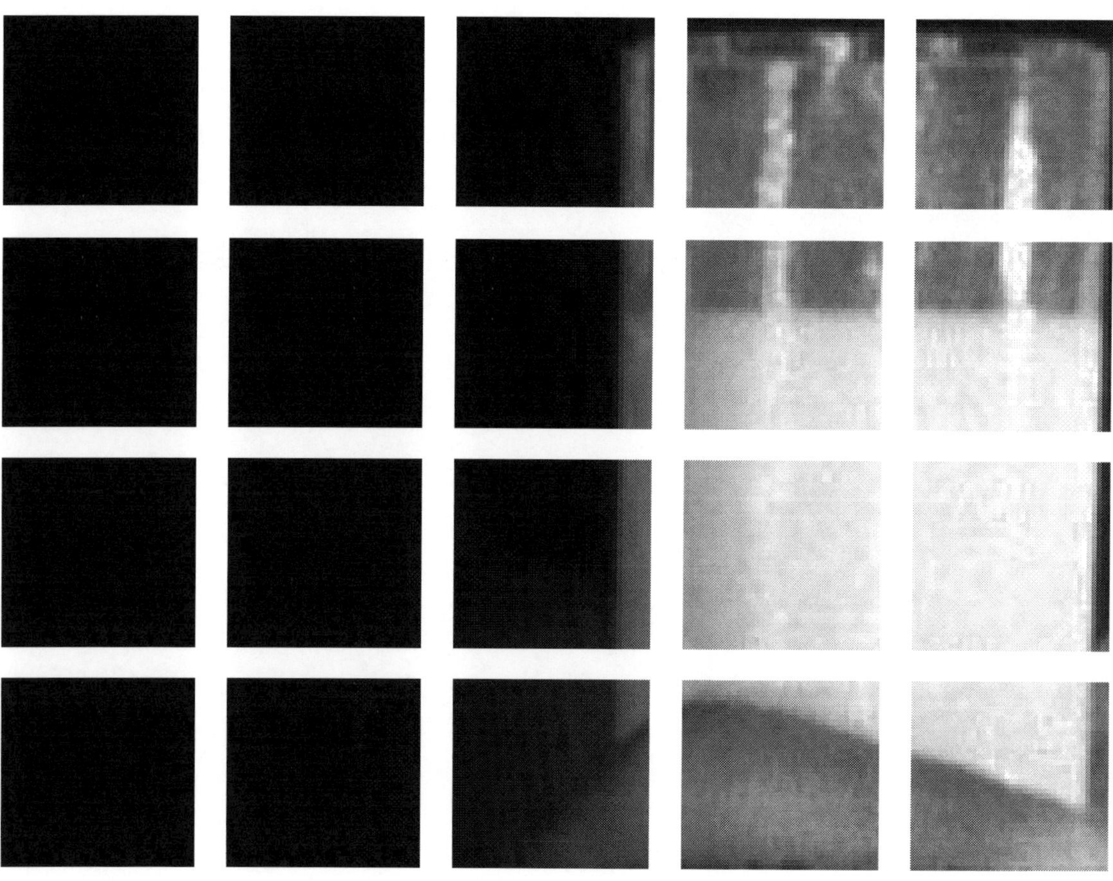

The Big Influence

'WHO SUPPORTS VIOLENT FILMS NOW?'

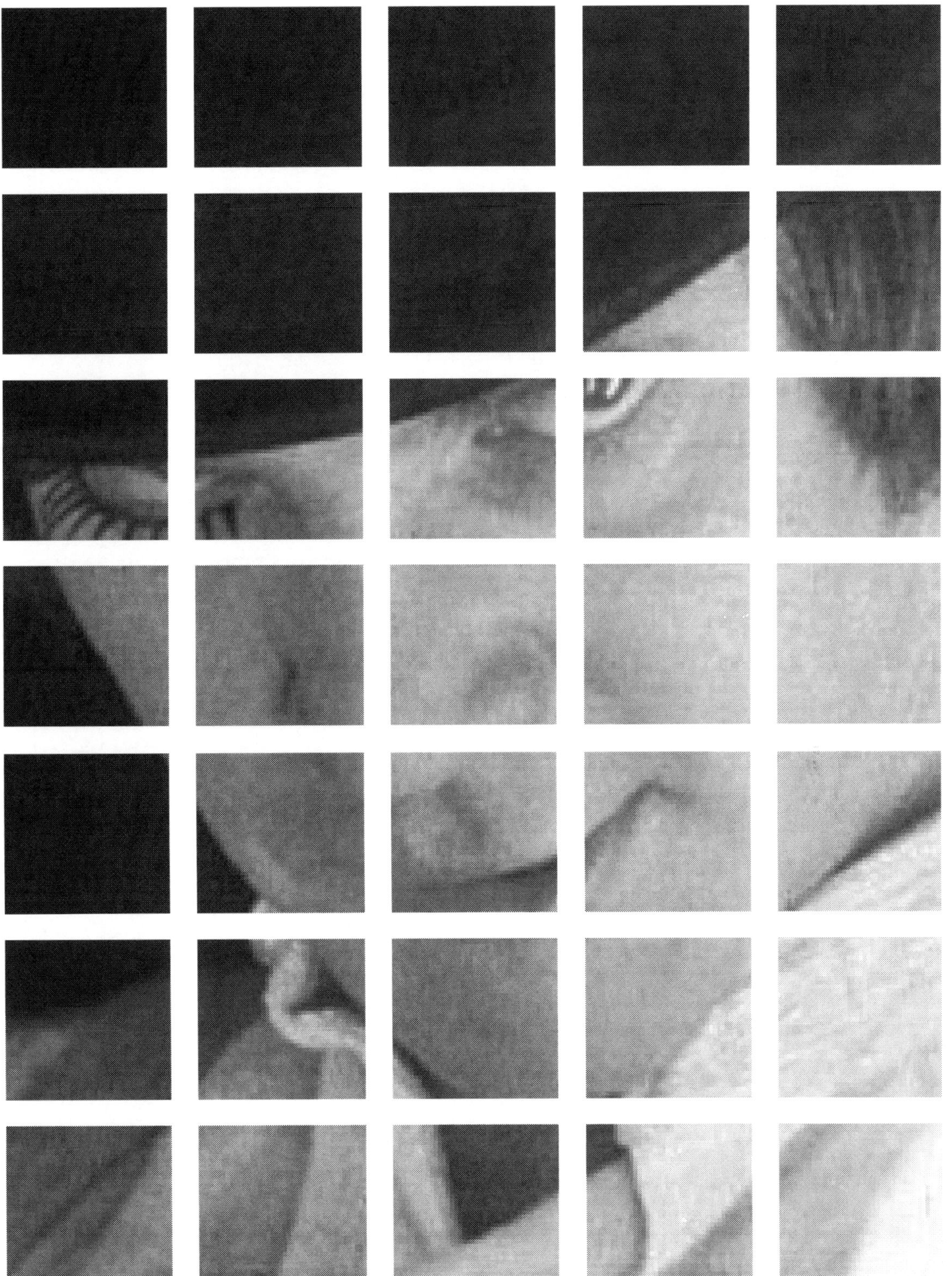

CANNIBAL ERROR

SOME CRITICS SAY the coercive influence of motion pictures – its ability to make people do what they wouldn't ordinarily do – is corroborated by the fact that companies spend vast sums of money advertising products on television: if viewers are not influenced by commercials, the argument goes, then manufacturers wouldn't waste money producing them. Such critics fail to understand that advertisers can only make potential customers *aware* of a product – there is no influential effect because a viewer isn't going to purchase something they wouldn't ordinarily buy. If critics were right in their argument, that advertising is influential, we would all be purchasing goods we had no use for, while not being able to understand why we were doing so. If you haven't got a cat you won't buy a tin of cat food simply because you see it advertised on television. Every toy advertised isn't the latest craze. Similarly, if you are not a violent person and have no intention of committing a violent act you do not do so simply because you have seen a violent scene in a film.

The cause-and-effect argument was used during the debate for amendments to the Criminal Justice and Public Order Bill in the House of Commons on April 12, 1994. (See SEX & WRECKS.) The discussion was focused on videos, primarily David Alton MP's attempts to add a clause to the Video Recordings Act which would deny adults the right to purchase or hire any video work not suitable for children. Frank Cook MP stated,

> I am anxious to nail the argument of those who say that such material is innocuous and does not cause harm. If that were so, what is the justification for the amount that we spend on video material to train our military, our tank and air crews, and those in industry and education? Why do we waste so much money on that if it does not have an impact on the recipients?

Alton added, "why does the advertising industry spend £1.6 billion trying to sell us its wares if such material does not have an effect on anybody? [...] The honourable gentleman is right, which is why we must take such issues very seriously."

Both men were so focused on their goals they became blind to commonsense. Cook's claim that movies have the same effect as educational videos is utterly preposterous. An educational video is instructive, and the viewer aware of its nature and purpose and therefore receptive to its content (the effect being erudition). A movie is emotive, and the viewer likewise perceptive of its content (the effect being entertainment).

The Big Influence

'WHO SUPPORTS VIOLENT FILMS NOW?'

Since the earliest days of cinema, films have been the scapegoat for many of society's ills. Commonsense eventually prevails but whenever a new format is released to the public, say video, the moral crusade peaks again. (See UNEASE.) Indeed, the press has censured films and videos so openly and for so long that lawbreakers will try to mitigate their criminal acts by blaming a movie. Usually this occurs with the full cooperation, even initial prompting, of a defending lawyer or progressive psychologist (per *Natural Born Killers*, below). Parents, too, will often attribute their children's offensive behaviour to television, videos, computer games, and now the Internet. Indeed, they will blame anything other than themselves, seemingly ignorant to the fact they have provided their children with the very things they censure.[1]

Some aspects of media can influence behaviour. Not advertising or films, but news media. In a social climate where it is viewed as healthy to have a positive "role model" – in other words, to deny your own distinctive attributes and replace them with those of, say, a successful celebrity – imitating those people in the media is a current trend. Role models do not take the form of movie characters but movie stars, sports personalities, successful businesspeople, pop stars, and so on.[2] Certain people's publicised achievements tend to emphasise other people's lack of attainment and the "underachiever" may react accordingly, by trying to emulate the achiever. This is often recognised as a positive response, and actively encouraged. However, it only diminishes individuality and offers unattainable goals for the imitators (plus ego boosts for the imitated). But, as we shall see, people do not always choose "positive" role models.

The media tends to outline real-life events as being 'film-like.'[3] A shooting incident or police pursuit will be described as 'like something out of a film'; an arsenal of illegal weapons seized by police will be outlined in the press as resembling something out of *The Terminator* movie. Hazel Savage, the detective who launched proceedings against serial killer Fred and Rosemary West, was likened in a *Daily Express* article about the case to "TV's *Prime Suspect* Detective Jane Tennison, played by Helen Mirren." When Paul Britton's book *The Jigsaw Man*, a biographical account of his work as a criminal psychologist, was published, a press critic called it a "real-life *Cracker*" after the popular television crime/psychology drama. Even in analysing the Budget report for 2000, the *Express* newspaper used pictures of soap opera characters to illustrate the types of people who would be affected by the new taxes.

It would seem that the general public is unable to appreciate the realities of society without cinematic reference. This may be because most people have only 'experienced' shooting incidents and criminal psychology in movies or on TV, but the immediate, off-the-cuff link paves the way for accusations of undue movie influence. So when an incident is described as being like something out of a film, the conclusion is that a film inspired the event. A typical example is a report in a local newspaper, the *Stockport Express,* on Wednesday, September 8, 1999, which described a sword attack. Ian Morrison used an ornamental sword to break through a door of his ex-wife's house. The police were called, and Morrison attacked them in the street with the sword before he was run down by the police van, overpowered and arrested. Though films had nothing to do with the incident, the headline for the page-one report was "*The Shining*" and illustrated with the famous image of actor Jack Nicholson grinning though a smashed bathroom door. The link was contrived simply to generate an eye-catching, though utterly irrelevant, headline.

On Saturday, March 16, 1996, in relation to Thomas Hamilton's horrifying Dunblane school massacre, a piece appeared in the *Times* headlined, "Who Supports Violent Films Now?" The question in most people's minds was likely "who supports legalised guns now?" as Hamilton was a legitimate gun club member and gun owner. But somehow films had been brought into the equation despite there being absolutely no link between movies and Hamilton's moment of insanity. The reporter, speaking for the population, regardless of any contrary opinion, said, "This week... we would willingly burn every violent book, film and magazine that we could lay our hands on if we felt that we might be stopping another madman from tipping over the edge." Burn books, films, and magazines? Why not also newspapers? Or is the writer only prepared to destroy things that don't impact his life adversely? It is ironic that the press reports that garlanded Hamilton's action would themselves be the key source of inspiration for future acts of violence, as we shall see.

One of the first high-profile and effective media attacks on a contemporary movie was against Stanley Kubrick's 1971 film, *A Clockwork Orange*. Because Kubrick's film was original, daring, and controversial, it inevitably drew condemnation. Although it did also receive critical acclaim, moral crusaders vilified the movie and proceeded to ascribe virtually every criminal act that occurred during its first cinema release as a spontaneous reaction to the film.[4] The British press, with the support and encouragement of MPs, claimed that juveniles were imitating scenes from the film, dressing in a manner similar to the

A clockwork scapegoat?

main characters and behaving violently. Indeed, Jill Knight MP (see also 'The Fox,' below) claimed there existed a link between the film and a murder committed by a juvenile, despite there being no evidence to support the allegation. In another case, sixteen-year-old Richard Palmer assaulted a tramp; a psychiatrist said that viewing *A Clockwork Orange* was "the only possible explanation for what this boy did." Palmer's defence lawyer also asked, "what explanation can there be for this savagery other than the film?" Such conclusions suggest that no vagrant had ever been beaten up before *A Clockwork Orange* was made.

In fact, Anthony Burgess' novel on which the film was based was modelled after vicious street gangs operating in the north of England in the late 1800s. Amongst other nefarious preoccupations, these gangs – 'scuttlers' – were not averse to knifing innocent people for kicks. Sometimes blame was attributed to penny dreadfuls (see UNEASE); moving pictures had yet to become a form of popular entertainment. General William Booth, founder of the Salvation Army, lamented in 1890:

> The lawlessness of our lads, the increased license of our girls, the general shiftlessness from the home-making point of view of the product of our factories and schools are far from reassuring. Our young people have never learned to obey. The fighting gangs

Taxi Driver – art imitating life?

of half-grown lads in Lisson Grove, and the scuttlers of Manchester are ugly symptoms of a social condition that will not grow better by being left alone.[5]

Kubrick withdrew his film from circulation in the UK, not because of its alleged corrupting influence (as was believed for many years) but because of anonymous death threats made against him and his family by groups and individuals opposed to movie violence – the self-proclaimed moral crusaders. It is bizarre that those condemning fictional violence seem so willing to administer violence themselves.[6]

Incriminating *A Clockwork Orange* for unlawful behaviour was so well publicised that it became a mitigating defence argument. On May 15, 1972, in the USA Arthur Bremer attempted to shoot dead Alabama Governor George C Wallace. Wallace survived the public attack but was permanently paralysed. During the trial it was claimed that Bremer's diaries revealed he had decided to kill Wallace while watching *A Clockwork Orange*. But Bremer's original plan was to assassinate President Nixon. Realising it would be impossible to get close enough to the President because of security, he opted for Wallace instead. It was while biding his time waiting for an opportunity to get near Wallace that he went to see *A Clockwork Orange*. In his diary Bremer writes, "I had to get away from my thoughts for a while. I went to the zoo, the lake front, saw 'Clockwork Orange' & thought about getting Wallace all through the picture – fantasing [*sic*] myself as the Alek on the screen come to real life..." Clearly, he had already settled on killing Wallace before seeing the film. Contrary to the allegations that the film influenced his actions, Bremer admitted that he had committed the crime with the desire for media attention distinctly in mind.[7] By the time of the trial, indicting Kubrick's film had become a common defence tactic. Over twenty years later Oliver Stone's *Natural Born Killers* would find itself in an identical situation.

But the story has a further twist. Screenwriter Paul Schrader used Bremer's diaries as inspiration for the 1976 movie, *Taxi Driver*. Director Martin Scorsese used television footage of Bremer's attack as a blueprint for the scene where the armed and dangerous protagonist, Travis Bickle (Robert De Niro), gets close to a presidential candidate. In the news footage, the casually dressed Bremer is caught on camera moments before he opens fire. He has an unusual hairstyle, dark glasses and a beaming smile, just as Bickle modelled. Even more ironic, five years after the release of *Taxi Driver*, John Hinckley became infatuated with Jodie Foster who played the role of an underage prostitute in the film. Hinckley began stalking Foster and sending obsessive letters, telling her that on occasion he had been close enough to kill her. When she failed to respond to his letters, Hinckley tried to assassinate President Ronald Reagan, on March 31, 1981, as a means of impressing her. *Taxi Driver* was instantly indicted as the cause of the attack when Hinckley's letters revealed he had seen the film on several occasions. Indeed, his behaviour certainly seemed modelled on that of the Bickle character, at least according to his parents who wrote a book about their son, *Breaking Points*.[8] The book, of course, may have been a cathartic reaction or a prerequisite 'we're not to blame – Hollywood is' declaration. But Hinckley's obsession was with Foster, a real person, not the film or the character of Iris who Foster portrayed. Hinckley was nothing more than a deranged stalker, a dangerous schizophrenic who became fixated on an actress. The only way he was able to relate to Foster was in reference to *Taxi Driver* – he had seen it; she was in it. To play devil's advocate: if he *was* influenced

More like Bambi than Rambo. *Daily Mirror*, August 21, 1987.

DAILY Mirror

Trigger happy Ryan aged 11

FORWARD WITH BRITAIN

20p

MANIAC IN THE MAKING

Mother who adored him

'He was a mummy's boy . . much more like Bambi than Rambo'

FULL REPORT—Pages 2, 3, 4, 5, 6 and 7

by Bickle, Hinckley would surely have sported a Mohican haircut and shot pimps, not the President. Moreover, in the film, Bickle doesn't open fire, so Hinckley's attack is therefore in imitation of Arthur Bremer's attempted assassination of a political figure – i.e. Hinckley mimics a news media event. Bremer shot Wallace to get media attention; Hinckley shot Reagan to get Foster's attention.

In 1987, Michael Ryan carried out what would become known as the Hungerford Massacre. The press called it the "Rambo Killings", implying the trigger source derived from *First Blood*, a fifteen-year-old novel and five-year-old film adaptation. Efforts were made to homogenise the fictitious John Rambo (played by Sylvester Stallone) with the real-life Michael Ryan. Was this correlation by the media justified, or nothing more than deliberate misinformation?

On the morning of Wednesday, August 19, Michael Ryan drove from his home at 4 South View in Hungerford to the Savernake Forest, a Wiltshire beauty spot some miles from his house. There he came across Sue Godfrey and her two children who were packing their car following a picnic. Ryan parked next to Godfrey's car and approached her carrying a Beretta 9mm automatic pistol. He picked up the groundsheet the family had used and put the children back in their car, then forced Godfrey into the woods for about 75 yards where, it is speculated, he intended to rape her (the groundsheet was discovered laid out on the grass). Instead, Ryan shot Godfrey ten times in the back. As she collapsed into a wire fence, he fired three more bullets into her. The back wounds indicate Godfrey tried to escape.

Up to this point, Ryan had fired his pistol only at paper targets, albeit human-shaped ones. With a dead woman at his feet Michael Ryan had crossed the Rubicon. He left the scene without harming the children and drove to a petrol station, filled the car tank and a canister with petrol, and approached the cashier Kakoub Dean, with every intention of shooting her dead. The first shot, now from an automatic rifle he had stored in the boot of his car, missed its target. As he moved closer and re-aimed, the rifle misfired, and Ryan's intended second victim survived. As Dean telephoned the police, Ryan returned to the car and drove to his home where he collected his survival kit and bullet-proof vest and loaded the boot with his remaining weapons. He doused his house with petrol and set it alight. The car, however, failed to restart, so he strafed it with gunfire and set off on foot. At the back of the burning house he shot dead his neighbours Ronald and Sheila Mason. Moments later, seventy-seven-year-old Dorothy Smith confronted Ryan about making so much noise. He didn't open fire on her, but shot and wounded

Margery Jackson instead. Ryan followed a route that eventually led him to his old school, opening fire on everyone he encountered along the way. Those to die after the Masons were Ken Clements, PC Roger Brereton, Abdul Khan, George White, Dorothy Ryan, Francis Butler, Marcus Barnard, Douglas Wainwright, Eric Vardy, Sandra Hill, Jack and Myrtle Gibbs, and Ian Playle.

There was no apparent purpose to Ryan's actions other than the destruction of his only known world. He killed his mother and his pet dog, ruined his car and destroyed his home before casually walking around the town, shooting at everyone. Sixteen people lay dead with as many injured before Ryan finally sought refuge from the pursuing army of police, which he did in his old school. After futile negotiations, he decided the only way out was to kill himself. He placed the Beretta to his head and pulled the trigger. Then it was over, and the truth about what really pushed Ryan so far over the edge was blasted from his head with that single pistol round. The cause of Ryan's rampage was open to speculation, and yet, within hours, the news media had unanimously agreed on a designated patsy: Rambo. In the 1982 movie, *First Blood*, itinerant war veteran John Rambo (Stallone) is forced to retaliate when the sadistic sheriff of a small town tries to hunt him down.

Whatever Michael Ryan was, he most certainly wasn't a film buff. A military fanatic, definitely; a gun obsessive, yes; a friendless loner still living with his mother, positively – all idiosyncrasies that may be indicative of some psychological instability. No available information on Ryan suggests he had any interest in either films or film characters. To purport that he had allowed reason to be overwhelmed by a movie character, without evidence to suggest so, is an extravagant speculation. But something did push Ryan over the edge, and there are subtle pieces of evidence that help pinpoint the catalyst that transformed Ryan into a cold-blooded killer. The most telling is when Ryan made his final purchase of stockpile ammunition. The date was August 12, seven days before he summoned the courage to put the ammunition to its intended use. He went to the Wiltshire Shooting Centre shop and bought a reconditioned M-1 Carbine rifle and fifty rounds of ammunition. Had *First Blood* aired on television on August 11, then the press would have had credible, if circumstantial, evidence to aggrandise their claims of movie influence. However, the BBC had shown the film only once – almost a year prior to the shootings – in September 1986.[9] If we are to believe that Ryan had watched and was influenced by the film, surely the Hungerford massacre would have occurred closer to its air date? There was a theory that Ryan owned

a video recorder and a VHS copy of *First Blood*, which he repeatedly watched, although this was supposition to support the argument. If Ryan had seen *First Blood* – and he may well have, when it played cinemas or was aired on television – there is absolutely nothing to suggest he was influenced by its content.

One of the staunchest partisans of the Rambo connection is journalist, author, and self-proclaimed born-again Christian, Tom Davies. Davies' book, *The Man of Lawlessness*, attempts to establish a link between films and real-life incidents of violence, although it fails to offer any credible evidence. One person credited in the acknowledgements is Dennis Coggan, who was behind the seriously flawed study, *Children and Video Violence*, from which Davies draws much of his data. Davies states early in *The Man of Lawlessness* that "I must always try to honour the fire that God has built in me," which gives some indication of the book's true aims. This pious rhetoric continues throughout: "We glory in the greatness of God's creation...," "God spoke directly to me...," "I knew then that God was at work in my life again...," "God has finally raised the curtains for the Son of Man to make his reappearance on the world's stage." Disturbing stuff. Indeed, we are to believe it was a "vision", which Davies claims took place while in Malaya working on a novel of violence and homosexuality, that inspired him to write *The Man of Lawlessness*.[10]

The Big Influence

'WHO SUPPORTS VIOLENT FILMS NOW?'

Davies clearly has decided on the book's conclusion before embarking on his investigation, and manipulates evidence to fit his theory. He relates an incident in Walsall, September 11, 1988, when Anthony Haskett (named by the press "Rambo Boy") shot three youths with a shotgun before turning the gun on himself. Davies claims that Haskett was influenced by the Rambo films. He makes an issue of the fact that camouflage paste was found in Haskett's bedroom and that similar paste "crops up a lot in the Rambo stories." However, as Davies himself points out, Haskett was in the Territorial Army, where cadets are supplied with, and trained in, the use of weapons and camouflage materials. According to Davies, Haskett wasn't the only one corrupted by the Rambo films, so were James Huberty, James Purdy, Julian Knight (see below), Michael Ryan, and Darren Fowler (see below).

John Rambo isn't Davies' only cinematic target. "*Taxi Driver* is still widely available in most video shops," he states, "but after Hinckley's widely publicised trial, the British Video Association should have known of the vital role that it played in the attack on President Reagan. Why is it still available?" In a bizarre contradiction, he also says, "Nowhere in this book – or in my mind – is there an argument – either covert or overt – for banning a film."

Davies notes an incident in which a man rammed a police roadblock following a chase. The court was told the defendant was re-enacting a scene from *Vanishing Point*, a 1971 road movie starring Barry Newman. But if he were re-enacting a sequence from a film then the police must also have been re-enacting the same scene. It was either a remarkable coincidence that both parties were acting out the same scene on the same stretch of road at the same time, or perhaps they colluded beforehand. Such an explanation is, of course, preposterous. The driver wasn't re-enacting any film scene – he was being pursued by police and tried to evade arrest by smashing his way through a roadblock. After the event it may have reminded some people of a scene from a film. Davies unreservedly accepts the claim the incident occurred because of *Vanishing Point* simply for the reason it amplifies his argument. Elsewhere he blames the film industry for football violence and drunken brawling.

What is the evidence that Michael Ryan was imitating *First Blood*? Davies asserts that, together with journalist Robert Peart, he found the remains of a video recorder in Michael Ryan's burned-out home. "Just standing there and looking at that charred recorder, all God's grief came flooding back to me. Just look at what they're doing to all my babies," he writes. He offers the following as proof that Ryan was influenced by *First Blood*:

- ▷ Ryan liked to wear military-style clothing
- ▷ He owned a video recorder
- ▷ He had a Second World War helmet
- ▷ He had a thin beard
- ▷ Ryan wore a black bandana[11]
- ▷ Ryan attacked a petrol station just as Rambo had[12]
- ▷ Both were surrounded by police
- ▷ Both were shadowed by helicopters

He points out that Rambo had spared children, implying this was the reason Ryan failed to shoot Sue Godfrey's children in Savernake Forest. If Ryan was imitating Rambo to such a degree, why shoot and seriously wound fourteen-year-old Lisa Mildenhall, and why kill several women? To suggest that the police surrounded Ryan, and that a helicopter shadowed him because it does Rambo in *First Blood*, implies police, too, were mimicking the film. Davies is desperate to prove the movie is to blame. He continues: "It is true that no one ever actually saw Michael Ryan watch *First Blood*, but the overwhelming body of evidence [the bulleted points above] suggests that he watched it again and again." He offers nothing to suggest Ryan saw the film even once.

DAILY Mirror

FORWARD WITH BRITAIN 20p

14 DEAD

Then gunman kills himself

DAY OF THE MANIAC

SEE PAGES 2, 3, 4, 5, 6 and 7

Daily Mirror, August 20, 1987.

It's reasonable to say Michael Ryan may have had Rambo on his mind the day he stockpiled his ammunition in preparation for the massacre – and equally that he may have been inspired by a true life case. It was around this time the press reported the killing spree of a young Australian failed soldier and gun fanatic named Julian Knight, who was predictably likened to John Rambo.

Melbourne, Australia. On the evening of August 9, 1987, Julian Knight, after drinking in the Royal Hotel, decided to go home "and get my guns and start shooting." Armed with two rifles, a Mossberg repeating shotgun and ten-inch sheath knife, Knight embarked on a killing spree. He found a vantage point overlooking a busy road then randomly fired at passing motorists. By the time of his arrest that night, following a brief shootout with police, six people were dead and forty-six injured. Knight claimed he intended to commit suicide rather than be arrested or shot by police but had not done so because he ran out of ammunition and lost the single bullet he had placed in his pocket for that purpose. In custody, the day after the incident, Knight was observed in his cell searching the newspapers for reports about himself.

Most important here is that British newspapers reported the event on Monday, August 10, and Tuesday, August 11. The first report in the *Daily Mail* ran the following, under the headline "Rambo Sniper on the Loose Kills 6":

> 6 people were shot and at least 16 others injured after a sniper went berserk last night. The gunman dressed in Rambo-style clothing shot at police and motorists from bushes in a busy street. One woman was gunned down as she sat in her car at a service station... Other victims were picked off at random as the gunman walked down a suburban street in Clifford Hill, Melbourne Australia.

The next day, the *Mail* followed up the story with "The Misfit who Killed 'For Love'" suggesting that "a broken romance may have triggered the rampage..." Further details about Knight's character came from neighbours who described him as "a weird type of boy who stalked around wearing military fatigues... He kept a library of military books and magazines." The report offered details of the shootings, the weapons and pictures of the killer and Knight's dead victims.

Knight's description fitted Michael Ryan's persona perfectly, and his behaviour suggests an affinity with Knight. On August 12, Ryan attempted to purchase a rifle like Knight's M-14 semi-automatic, as described in the newspaper report (but settled for an M-1), and stockpiled ammunition as Knight was reported as having done. Eight days after the *Daily Mail* glorified Knight's rampage, Ryan duplicated the events almost exactly, pointing to a clear and direct influence by the press coverage.

Following the Hungerford massacre, the *Daily Mail* tried to concoct an unequivocal link between Ryan's actions and the plot of *First Blood*. The report pointed out that Rambo started killing deputies in a forest, ignited petrol pumps in a service station, and set a building on fire. These incidents were analogised to the killing of Sue Godfrey in Savernake Forest, the attempted murder of Kakoub Dean at the petrol station, and the igniting of Ryan's own home. Police believe Ryan intended to rape Godfrey and that her attempt to escape led to her murder, a scenario brutally echoing the *Mail*'s "Misfit who Killed 'For Love'" reference to Knight. Similarly, Ryan's attempt to shoot the female service station attendant doesn't correlate with anything in *First Blood* (Rambo shot the petrol pumps) but closely mimics the *Mail*'s claim that Knight shot a woman in a service station. Ryan walking through the streets of Hungerford shooting innocent people at random doesn't conform to any scene in the film but reproduces identically the *Mail*'s report. It is also worth noting that on the morning Ryan embarked on his killing spree, the *Mail* had a front-page report on the suicide of Rudolph Hess, an original member of Hitler's inner circle. It stated that by killing himself Hess was "outwitting and humiliating his allied captors." Within hours Ryan would do likewise.

Hungerford is undoubtedly a copycat of the Melbourne incident. It is extremely unlikely that journalists at the *Mail* didn't tie the two together, although clear why they would fail to acknowledge and publicise the fact: they chose to divert evidential blame from themselves by indicting *First Blood* as the likely cause.

It wasn't only the *Mail* that promoted a connection between Ryan and *First Blood*; other popular tabloids were equally parochial. The *Sun* called the event the "Rambo Shootings", the *Daily Mirror* the "Rambo Killings", while the *Daily Star* stated simply, "Rambo" – all perhaps indicative of Fleet Street collusion. One year after the event, *Rambo III* was released, with Sylvester Stallone reprising the role of war veteran John Rambo. The film gave the press the opportunity to resurrect old headlines and reopen wounds. "Fury as Sly's new movie revives the horror of Hungerford" shouted the *Mirror*, although the 'fury' was only provoked by the author of the piece. Hungerford's Reverend David Salt requested that "the townsfolk just want the anniversary to pass by quietly." Another resident, former Mayor Ron Tarry, said, "A lot of people identify Ryan with Rambo. We don't need this film as a reminder." Public perception had been influenced by the press-invented link between Ryan and Rambo. Any incident involving a firearm was attributed to the Rambo films and this happened not only when the films were popular, but inflamed on a whim. When fifteen-year-old Oliver Bennett received an eye injury from a paintball pellet, one report likened the innocent adventure to "a Rambo-style wargame," illustrated with a picture of actor Stallone. Such a trivial accident would never have made the national press without the contrived link. As late as March 26, 1998, the *Mirror* ran the headline "MY RAMBO GRANDSON" in reference to the Jonesboro school massacre in which five people (four pupils, one teacher) were shot dead. The killers were eleven-year-old Andrew Golden and thirteen-year-old Mitchell Johnson, referred to in the report as the "Rambo Boys," along with the claim that Golden "thought he was Rambo." In the multiple-page article there is no direct reference to the Rambo films to suggest any causative link; indeed, the name is only used twice in the body text yet used three times as headers.

Just as the press reports on Julian Knight had potentially stimulated Ryan to kill sixteen innocent people, the subsequent reports on Ryan would influence others. On Wednesday, January 6, 1988, sixteen-year-old Darren Fowler, using a shotgun, fired at and wounded people at his school in Northamptonshire. Deputy headmaster Michael Cousins and two pupils were hit in the face, neck and chest. Fowler was eventually overcome by a PE teacher and disarmed. Following his arrest, police discovered he had a great interest in Michael Ryan. This obsessive fascination was generated by intensive press coverage of the Hungerford massacre. An even stronger link between press enthusiasm for Ryan and copycat murders was made appararent when Robert Sartin took up arms.

"The Satan Boy" was the ostentatious headline the *Daily Mirror* used on May 1, 1990, to describe Robert Sartin, on trial for murder and attempted murder. One year earlier, on Sunday, April 30, 1989, twenty-three-year-old Sartin had wandered around the streets of his hometown, Monkseaton, carrying his father's shotgun and shooting people at random. Confronted by an elderly resident, Vera Burrows, he was asked, "What the hell is going on?" Sartin replied that he was killing people and was going to kill her, too, but suddenly changed his mind saying, "Oh, you're old, I'm not going to kill you." Of the seventeen people he fired upon, one died – Kenneth Mackintosh, shot in the chest at point blank range. Others received injuries that varied in severity, due to the nature of Sartin's weapon as opposed to any intention to inflict less-serious damage. Had Sartin carried an automatic rifle then he would have achieved a death toll like that of his role model, Michael Ryan. Indeed, the Monkseaton shootings virtually duplicated the Hungerford massacre, and Sartin himself admitted visiting Hungerford to tour the route of Ryan's kill-spree eight months before he decided to re-enact it. The actions of Sartin were incredibly similar to Ryan's: he commenced his attack after a car journey, his first victim was a female motorist and he even refrained from shooting an elderly lady who verbally confronted him, exactly as Ryan had done.

The *Sun*, May 1, 1990.

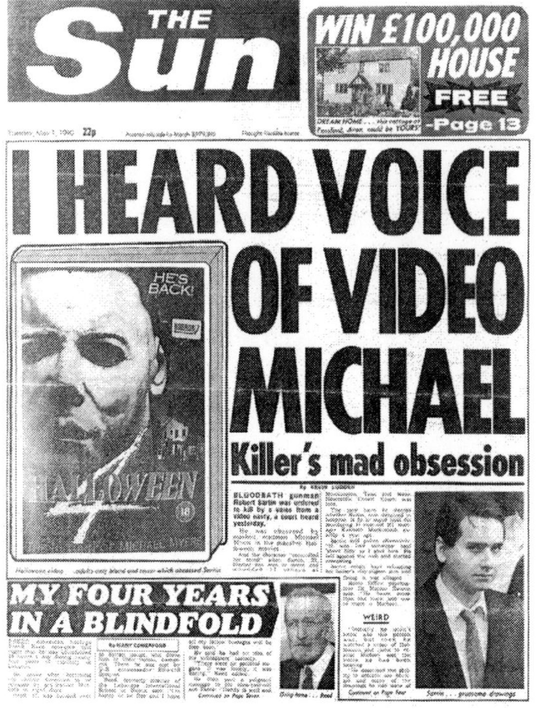

THE Sun

WIN £100,000 HOUSE FREE -Page 13

I HEARD VOICE OF VIDEO MICHAEL

Killer's mad obsession

BLOODBATH gunman Robert Sartin was ordered to kill by a voice from a video nasty, a court heard yesterday.

WEIRD

Continued on Page Four

Sartin . . . gruesome drawings

MY FOUR YEARS IN A BLINDFOLD

Continued on Page Seven

Sartin was finally diverted from his rampage by a police officer. Unlike Ryan he didn't have the courage to take his own life.

Despite the evidence identifying the source of Sartin's influence (the news media), consultant psychiatrist Marion Swan posited in his trial that the "Michael" that had impelled Sartin was not Michael *Ryan*, but Michael *Myers*, a fictitious character from the popular *Halloween* series of horror films. Remarkably, it came to light that a psychiatrist had been treating Sartin for three years before he took the gun to the streets. Sartin had even told his psychiatrist that voices in his head were instructing him to kill. Evidently, the therapy failed catastrophically. Considering the outcome it seems that little effective treatment was given to deter him from carrying out his threat.

Sartin, the *Mirror* reported, was so obsessed with everything evil – satanism, cannibalism, murder – that he acquired the nickname "Satan." Such a claim makes good sensational copy, although the similarity between "Sartin" and "Satan" is more likely the origin of the sobriquet. Moreover, school peers had given him the nickname, which perhaps may have formulated his interest in the occult in the first place.

The *Sun* covered the story under the front page banner, "I Heard Voice Of Video Michael." The report stated that "Bloodbath gunman Robert Sartin was ordered to kill by a voice from a video nasty..." A photograph of the killer was dwarfed by a picture of the video sleeve for *Halloween 4*, a film described in the report as having "gallons of blood flying about" and the Michael Myers character as a "teenage psychopath who hacks his family to pieces one by one." (The newspaper does not reveal that the fictional Myers is a mute who never speaks, much less gives orders.)

Had the accusation of influence been directed at its proper source, the real-life Michael Ryan, then the question should be asked: how was Sartin influenced by a dead killer? At that time, the only readily available source of information on Ryan's methods of killing was the press. It is from here that Sartin undoubtedly drew his inspiration.

On Friday, February 12, 1993, six years after Michael Ryan's massacre, James Bulger was tortured and murdered. In this instance there was one fatality on a railway track. Yet this case was more disturbing and its repercussions more extensive than Hungerford. The victim was an infant. He had been snatched in full view of the public (the event being caught on security cameras), and most astonishingly, the killers were children themselves.

Every new detail of the crime compounded the tragedy. Several members of the public admitted to seeing James Bulger in tears while he was being dragged, kicked and punched through the streets by his abductors. Needless to say, no one intervened, everyone minded their own business, aware (in the burgeoning climate of 'political correctness') of the criminal liabilities involved in accosting a juvenile – delinquent or otherwise.

Before it was discovered the infant had been tortured, mutilated and killed, every household in Britain had watched him being led away by his killers-to-be on television: blurry security video was aired in the hope of leading to the safe retrieval of James. Everyone reasoned that the child must have been okay because his abductors were only kids. Once news broke that Bulger's body had been found, the video footage took on a more disturbing, 'snuff' movie-like quality. In some ways the case could be seen to equate to that of the Moors Murders some thirty years previously. Ian Brady and Myra Hindley were deviants who fed off each other's depravity, anomalous sex being the prime motivation for their crimes. The children they assaulted and murdered were discreetly snatched off the streets, bundled into a car and driven away. Bulger was lured from his mother and dragged in full view of the public to be battered to death simply to alleviate boredom. It wasn't long before two ten-year-old boys, Jon Venables and Robert Thompson, were arrested. They were tried and found guilty of the crime.[13] The general public was in a state of shock, and as any newspaper editor and politician knows, people in such a state are easy to deceive and manipulate. The deception and manipulation of emotions began the day after the trial.

During Judge Morland's summing up of the perplexing case, he made the speculative comment: "It is not for me to pass judgement on their [Venables

Daily Mirror, 1994.

Soul-searching needed after James Bulger trial

WHY SICK VIDEOS MUST BE BANNED

and Thompson's] upbringing, but I suspect that exposure to violent video films may in part be an explanation." This was a very indeterminate statement that would subsequently be swallowed and modified by the sensation-hungry press.[14] Following Morland's comments, a campaign was launched against the video industry by the tabloids, spearheaded by David Alton MP, a self-appointed moral crusader. The purpose of the campaign, it was claimed, was to protect the nation's children. Such an emotive aspiration is guaranteed success, no matter how unreliable or ludicrous its foundation. At the time, Alton (compared by some to Goebbels, the propaganda expert of the Third Reich[15]) was a Liberal Democrat MP from Liverpool, but as of writing he is Professor of Citizenship at Liverpool John Moores University and a cross-bencher in the House of Lords. Like Tom Davies, Alton is unreservedly pious. He is parliamentary advisor for the Movement of Christian Democracy. Speaking in 1997 to a Christian group, referring to film director Oliver Stone and his like, Alton stated, "Their abolition of God – and the man made in His image – has left us poor beyond belief."

The film that was unanimously held up as causative in James Bulger's murder was *Child's Play 3*, probably because the title fitted well with the fact that the killers and victim were three children. It was suggested that a copy of the film had been in Jon Venables' home three weeks before he and Thompson murdered Bulger, though there was no evidence of this. As with *First Blood* and Hungerford, similarities were made between scenes in the film and the incident itself: Bulger had been splashed with paint and the doll in the film is struck with a paintball; Bulger died on a railway line and a set-piece in the movie takes place on a ghost train ride; the killers admitted that Bulger constantly got back on his feet no matter how hard they hit him and the doll in the film shows a similar indestructibility. (The suggestion that Bulger repeatedly rose to his feet after being struck down because of a scene in the film, poses the ridiculous and outrageous notion that Bulger must have seen the film and was mimicking it himself.) So ambiguous are the supposed links that if we were to transpose *Child's Play 3* with *Home Alone 2* the results would be just the same – indeed, the latter film would be more fitting as it features a child being separated from his parents and terrorised by two older males.

One newspaper printed stills from the film (including shots of the Chucky doll with half its face hacked away) next to a reconstructed photo of two young boys dragging a toddler along a railway line. They were attempting to illustrate Bulger's facial wounds with pictures from the film,[16] a tactic that surely would have caused great distress to the dead boy's parents. Because of the speculative nonsense published in the press, many tabloid readers became convinced that the movie really was to blame for the boy's murder. The *Daily Star* claimed to have asked a "cross-section" of people to view the film and report their responses to it. "Outraged father-of-two Les Clayden," said, "The message children could draw is that murder, blood, mutilation... well, that's entertainment. It should be withdrawn from video shops immediately." Natalie Miller said, "Having seen this I am sure this is where the two boys who murdered James got their evil ideas from." Neil Carroll said, "This should really be banned. We can't risk other children copying what these boys did." Anne Naughton said, "I can imagine that certain children watching this couldn't wait to experiment afterwards." We can't know whether the above are genuine vox pop reactions or ones influenced or embellished by the *Daily Star*, but if anyone did hold a contrary opinion the paper chose not to print it. The adjective "evil" was frequently used to describe the film, no less than five times in one report. Anyone wanting to check out the claims of the newspapers and hire the film were branded "ghouls" by tabloid journalists ignorant of the true definition of a ghoul, a legendary creature that disinters graves to feed off the dead). Feeding off the death of James Bulger is exactly what the tabloids were doing, and Alton was, metaphorically, using the boy's tiny coffin as a soapbox.

Proper investigation revealed nothing to indicate any of the children had seen *Child's Play 3*. Venables parents claimed their son had not seen the film. Those closely involved with the case – police, the parents of the killers and Mark Thomas, author of the detailed account, *Every Mother's Nightmare: The Killing of James Bulger* – insisted videos played no part in the events. Detective Superintendent Albert Kirby, who led the murder case from beginning to end, concluded that no evidence had been found to indicate that either Venables or Thompson had access to videos any worse than those found in many homes. Inspector Ray Simpson said, "We looked at all the videos in their houses and checked their lists of rentals from the shop. We did not find *Child's Play 3*, nor did we find anything in the list that could have encouraged them to do what they did. If you are going to link this murder to a film, you might as well link it to *The Railway Children*."

After questioning, Venables and Thompson revealed they at first tried to get Bulger to fall in the canal so he would drown, but only managed to drop him headfirst on the towpath as he struggled to avoid the water. Then they considered leaving him by the roadside in the hope that he would step in front of a moving vehicle – something they confessed to having planned to do to a child in the past.[17] The fact that they failed to get the boy drowned or run over helps to explain why they took him to a railway line: these are the three main dangers impressed on children at school – bodies of water, roads, and railway lines. Venables and Thompson were probably hoping to see the toddler get hit by a train, but no trains passed because the line they chose only carried freight and was infrequently used. They made Bulger lie on the track but as he kept getting up, they beat him with bricks and a discarded metal fishplate[18] until he stayed down. It was the severity of the beating, resulting in multiple fractures of the skull, that ultimately killed him. Even so, the boys laid Bulger's body across the line in the naïve hope his death would appear an accident, as it would have had he drowned or been hit by a car.

Psychiatric study of Venables in detention showed he was not just uninterested in scenes of violence but repulsed by them. Of course, it seems peculiar that he should be disturbed by make-believe violence, considering what he had done to Bulger. It may have been that such scenes reminded him of what happened on the railway. Perhaps Venables really was offended by violence: the nature of the crime is such that neither boy would have committed it alone. A sadistic area of the brain was tapped into, and each boy spurred the other to greater atrocities. They knew exactly what they were doing and probably thoroughly enjoyed the experience, likely regretting what they had done once it was over and went their separate ways. Both children were misfits. Robert Thompson – who eventually admitted murdering Bulger seven years after the event – was an urban recidivist brought up in a family led by a violent, indifferent father, also named Robert. Venables by all accounts was a simple-minded tag-along. The fact that there were signs of sexual interference with Bulger – his trousers and underpants had been removed, his foreskin had been retracted and batteries may have been inserted into his anus[19] – points to a possibility that either one or both killers are victims of sexual abuse themselves. It would seem they are the product of defective upbringing, rather than innocent children corrupted by a ninety-minute fantasy film. Even Susan Venables, Jon's mother, called the link to the film "rubbish", stating that her son was never allowed to watch adult films. A school friend of the killers told how they often tortured animals and had a long-standing plan to push a child under a bus at Bootle Strand shopping centre.

David Alton was generally unknown outside of Liverpool, but following Bulger's death he became a nationally recognised figure. Rational thinkers would conclude that he was manipulating the tragedy to enhance his political career, hoping that the attention generated for himself would guarantee he retained his seat in Parliament, which, indeed, it did. To corroborate his claim that video violence did influence the action of children, Alton commissioned an investigative report. The report was supposed to be an independent inquiry into whether children were adversely affected by video imagery, but proved to be a politically motivated piece designed to "confirm" Alton's claims. The resultant work is worth looking at in some detail as it proved widely influential and helped lead to a strengthening of the law concerning videos (see SEX & WRECKS).

The rushed paper, titled *Video Violence and the Protection of Young Children*, was written by Professor Elizabeth Newson of Nottingham University. It runs for eight pages and opens by directly referring to the Bulger case: "Two-year old James Bulger was brutally murdered on February 12, 1993, by two ten-year-old children. This stark fact has prompted a long overdue focus upon what conditions in our society could precipitate such an unthinkable act." In the very first sentence, Newson unequivocally sustains the myth that a video film was connected with Bulger's death. In the third paragraph she shrewdly

The Newson report as received by the *Daily Mail*, April 1, 1994.

Video nasties do cause violence

By JENNY HOPE

Professor admits the danger to children

EXPERTS have admitted they seriously underestimated the effects of screen violence on children.

In an amazing U-turn, 26 top specialists conceded they had been 'naive'.

Computer

refers to the two killers as "the two children who survive" and "victims themselves", as though they were not somehow responsible for their actions, further implying that an outside force was to blame for the murder. Newson goes on to detail the attack and describe the wounds suffered by Bulger. Leaving the infant draped across the railway line, she points out that the killers "wander down to the video-shop where they were known," again drawing an irrelevant link with video. To illustrate how such a terrible crime is a new and contemporary phenomenon, an idea that is the foundation of the theory, she writes:

> Shortly after this trial, children of a similar age in Paris were reported to have set upon a tramp, encouraged by another tramp, kicked him and thrown him down a well. In England an adolescent girl was tortured by her 'friends' over days, using direct quotations from a horror video (*Child's Play 3*) as part of her torment, and eventually set on fire and thus killed; while the following note appeared in a local newspaper on December 7, 1993:
>
> Two schoolboys were today expected to appear in court accused of torturing a six-year-old on a railway line. The youngsters, aged ten and eleven, allegedly tried to force the boy to electrocute himself on a track in Newcastle upon Tyne last week. They are also accused of stabbing him in the arm with a knife.
>
> We do not have the information to be able to comment on the full background of any of these crimes at present...

Newson admits to not having proper details of the crimes, yet selectively uses what scant tabloid information is available to promote her/Alton's theory. The adolescent girl to whom she refers is Suzanne Capper (see below), tortured and murdered by a gang of drug-addled adults – something Newson fails to mention, along with the fact that no videotape of the film was discovered. The case of the two schoolboys assaulting a child on a railway line was accepted as mimicry due to the excessive media coverage of the Bulger case. It had nothing to do with any movie.

Other possible causative factors mentioned in the report as driving Thompson and Venables to kill Bulger include emotional neglect, physical/sexual abuse, disturbed family relationships, poverty, and more. These are swept aside because they "have been part of many children's experience over the years." Newson declares that none of the above factors are relevant but ponders instead what different factor "has entered the lives of countless children in recent years." This, she claims, must be "the easy availability to children of gross images of violence on video." Are these her own theories or is she merely writing to Alton's requirements? Alton was quoted in a newspaper, many months before publication of Newson's paper, saying, "I strongly believe the easy availability of videos, often containing highly explicit scenes of violence, helps to explain the level of violence today compared with fifteen years ago."[20] One point neither Alton or Newson seem to realise is that over a decade before the Bulger murder, videos were uncensored and unrated, and many contained far more violent scenes than those available at the time of the killing. Uncertified videos had been withdrawn from circulation under the Video Recordings Act 1984 (see CLAMPDOWN). If there was any truth in their theory that videos were to blame for serious juvenile crimes, incidents would have surely peaked in the early eighties.

Contrary to Newson's claims, the Bulger killing is not so special or unique, nor a sudden insidious development in the nineties. Unfortunately, children murdering children is not a new phenomenon. Cases are rare, but hardly a sign of the times. The case of Mary Bell is a remarkably similar example. Mary Bell was eleven when she murdered four-year-old Martin Brown and three-year-old Brian Howe in 1968. The killings occurred on separate occasions and Howe's body was mutilated with a pair of scissors and a razor. When questioned, Mary tried to blame her friend Norma Bell (no relation), but the ploy failed. Although Norma admitted to being at the scene and witness to the murder of Howe, it was determined she was under the complete control of Mary and was acquitted. The parallels between the two cases are plain and significant. Newson's failure to acknowledge the Bell case suggests she was striving to offer the Bulger killing as something unique rather than attempt to discover the true cause of child brutality, and therefore

The *Sun*, November 28, 1993.

THE Sun

FREE MINCE PIE FOR YOU TODAY

20p

Brave Roy's cancer is back

FRENCH REVOLUTION

For the sake of ALL our kids...

BURN YOUR VIDEO NASTY

PLAY £26,000 SUN BINGO AND £48,000 NOUGHTS AND CROSSES – PAGE 40

the apparent validation of Alton's claims. Appalling as it was, Bulger's murder was incorrectly evaluated by those wishing to gain reputation or reward from it.[21]

Newson adds to the report that "industry finds it worthwhile to spend millions of pounds on advertising," as though this statement – another one of Alton's favourites – serves to prove her case. Following publication of the report, Newson was quoted in one newspaper, saying, "Violence may continue. The government has not addressed the question of video games, or the effect of violent videos on adults." The clear implication is that videos and video games are responsible for violence in society. Does she believe that if all films were erased overnight violence would not continue? Newson aired doubt about another, genuinely independent report,[22] one which indicated there was no discernible link between films and behaviour, and thoroughly contradicted her own dubious findings.

The false allegation that *Child's Play 3* was embroiled in the death of James Bulger has been repeated so often that it is accepted as an established fact by the ill-informed, becoming an urban myth. On Wednesday, April 13, 1994, the *Daily Mirror* (whose erroneous masthead claims, "Honesty, Quality, Excellence") reproduced the *Child's Play 3* videosleeve beneath the headline "Banned–Thanks To Your Daily Mirror." The headline was dishonest – another tabloid fabrication to justify their campaign to ban the film "after the *Child's Play* video was linked to the murder of Merseyside toddler James Bulger." The film wasn't banned at all. The first *Child's Play* was given a BBFC 15 certificate on December 8, 1989, *Child's Play 2* received the same certificate on March 21, 1991, and *Child's Play 3* was given an 18 certificate on November 18, 1992. No video certificates were revoked. It would seem the newspaper was tiring of sustaining a bogus story and so invented a conclusion to appease their beguiled readers. Indeed, if the *Daily Mirror* truly believe, as they claim, that the film was powerful enough to cause the death of a child, their campaign should never have ended and should still be demanding the banning of the video. Evidently they have become wearied with the subject, and it is no longer a lucrative theme. Instead of achieving their goal they simply lied to their readers by claiming their goal was met.

On Monday, March 30, 1998, during a BBC current affairs programme concerning violence among children, the narrator stated, "The judge in the Bulger case said, 'video nasties played a part in the role.'" This is evidence of a hypothesis being transposed into fact by the simple omission of the words "may have." The campaign against *Child's Play 3* is another powerful example of how news media influences public behaviour. The film was regularly rented and remained unremarked upon for months before the campaign. Following it, people were calling it "sick" and "obscene" and literally burning copies in the street at the behest of the press. In one of the most sinister and hypocritical moves by the tabloids, the *Sun*, on November 26, 1993, ran the front-page headline "For the sake of ALL our kids... BURN YOUR VIDEO NASTY." Their copy ran:

> A video chain boss yesterday torched his entire £10,000 stock of tapes linked to the James Bulger murder. And last night the *Sun* launched a nation-wide campaign to get all other copies of *Child's Play 3* burned. If you own one yourself, burn it safely. If you have rented one, take it back to the shop and ask the dealer to destroy it. Last night Liverpool MP David Alton praised the *Sun*'s campaign. He said burning was the answer...

Though very few members of the public followed the newspaper's instructions to the letter, many readers were influenced by its fascistic principles. Trading Standards Officer Peter Mawdsley stated, "The Bulger case brings into focus the problems of children getting hold of films." Perhaps most ironic, Judge Morland himself later spoke of the film and incident as though inseparable – he, too, being influenced by the press. (See also multiple murderer and *Sun* reader Colin Ireland, below.)

In an introduction to an in-house article, 'Television Violence', the NVLA president Revd Graham Stevens makes the following statement:

> The shocking murder of Merseyside toddler James Bulger in 1993 by two older

> children was seen by many observers — expert commentators and ordinary people alike — as one more piece of evidence of the link between real life violence and the violence that we see every day in TV dramas, movies and videos.
>
> But even after such an horrific event there are, of course, many others — academics and film directors, as well as broadcasters and even a number of leading politicians — who still refuse to recognise any connection between violence on our screens and violence in our society. No wonder. For them to admit a clear cause and effect would mean they would have to admit that they have been wrong about a major cause of social ill, and wrong not to take corrective action. Thankfully, there are some people in high places who have the right idea.

Following Bulger's murder, the Strand shopping centre, where Bulger was abducted, provided a crèche where mothers could safely leave their children when shopping. It was reported recently that the crèche was to be closed due to lack of funding. Consider for a moment the amount of public attention and financial gain the likes of David Alton and the tabloid press generated from Jamie Bulger's death – all claiming concern for the safety of children. None of them, it seems, were concerned enough to be benefactors of a tiny safe haven once the Bulger case was no longer valid as a means of self-promotion.

On Tuesday, December 15, 1992, sixteen-year-old Suzanne Capper was found wandering naked and terribly burned near Stockport, Greater Manchester. In intensive care she lived for three days and was able to tell police of the circumstances that led to her condition. Capper had been abducted by known associates. Investigations soon uncovered the people responsible, and details of her ordeal began to filter out. Her torment had included being chained to an inverted bed, shaved of body hair, scrubbed with a yard broom and raw bleach, injected with drugs and having teeth removed with pliers. The press was more interested in the audio tape that Capper was subjected to, playing at full volume on headphones taped to her head. It was techno music, but one track, often heard on a local radio station, comprised samples of dialogue from *Child's Play 2*. For some factions of the press, this was 'proof' that the movie series was indeed evil and caused viewers to commit murder. The *Daily Mirror*, on December 18, 1993, ran the front-page headline "Murdered by Chucky's Children" and showed a photograph of the murder victim dressed as a bridesmaid, doctored to appear that the Chucky doll was looming over her shoulder. The report claimed that her attackers "were fascinated by the occult, practised with Tarot cards and rune stones and kept a 'black library.' Behind their sick obsessions lurked the demonic figure of Chucky, also mentioned in the Bulger murder trial." The report not only took the opportunity to reiterate the erroneous Bulger connection, claiming the film title was referred to in the trial, but offered what it considered links in Capper's ordeal:

> In *Child's Play*, Chucky breaks a man's arm and leg – Suzanne's arm was battered. The doll is burned in the face with a cigarette lighter – Suzanne was burned with cigarettes. The doll kills a psychiatrist by electrocuting him with a headset – a headset was forced over Suzanne's head. Finally, the doll is apparently destroyed by fire – just like Suzanne.

Nothing is said of the shaving of body hair, the scrubbing with bleach, or injecting with drugs, real-life atrocities committed on Capper that do not occur in the film. But then, contrary to the report, none of the cinematic attacks on Chucky were played out on Capper: she didn't have her arm and leg broken, she wasn't burned with a cigarette lighter, and she wasn't electrocuted. The only similarity is that Capper was burned. Her torture was conjured from the minds of her sadistic captors. Despite its attempt to take some blame away from Capper's tormentors, the *Mirror* admitted that police found "no video in the torture house." Alas, as there was no film, how could it be classed as an "obsession" by the newspaper? Capper's parents appeared on a television chat show and aired their disgust with the press for attempting to associate their daughter's death with a horror movie, attaching her terrible ordeal to a movie character rather than her real-life killers.

Les Reed was kicked to death by a gang of thugs on a Cardiff estate. During the trial, the attack was attributed to the film, *Juice*, because it was alleged that one of Reed's attackers had said, "I've got the juice." The only "juice" in evidence, noted the court, was the lager and cider the thugs had consumed prior to the attack. Nonetheless, the press concluded that here was "irrefutable evidence of the link between violent videos and crime on our streets," and pointed to a scene in *Juice* where a man is kicked to death by four youths for remonstrating about their destructive behaviour. According to James Ferman, there is no such scene in the film – "no one is kicked to death in *Juice*, which is a serious anti-violence film." The Ely estate, where the assault took place, is a notoriously troubled area, rife with crime and violence – one part of it had been declared a no-go area by police well before the film *Juice* had even been made.

In his opening statement regarding proposed amendments to the Criminal Justice and Public Order Bill (see SEX & WRECKS), David Alton said:

> ... a number of cases have come before the courts which have involved the use of videos and videos have been cited in the course of those court cases. I think particularly of the Suzanne Capper case in Manchester, where a young woman was tortured and brutally murdered while the sound tape of the movie *Child's Play 3* was transmitted to her. Quite recently, in a case in Cardiff the video *Juice* was cited as an influence on the young people who were involved in a terrible murder.[23]

On June 29, 1994, the House of Commons published *Video Violence and Young Offenders*. Paragraph nine illuminates Alton's remarks:

> ... the present debate about violent videos was sparked by the grotesque murders of Jamie Bulger, Suzanne Capper, and Les Read [*sic*], and the allegation made, following the trials of those three cases, by some parts of the media that the videos *Child's Play 3* and *Juice* had played some part in motivating the murders. Closer analysis of these three cases has indicated that these allegations were in fact unfounded.

Memorandum 16 of the report was submitted by James Ferman, Director of the BBFC. Members of the Video Consultative Council, an advisory body appointed by the Home Office, were, said Ferman, invited to view *Child's Play 3* and *Juice* following the allegations made against the films:

> Their unanimous view was that *Child's Play 3* was 'irrelevant' to the Bulger case and that it was properly classified 18. *Juice* elicited an even stronger reaction: they considered it an excellent film, exploring moral issues in a constructive fashion.
>
> It is a pity that the issue of research should have been muddied by assumptions about the supposed link between *Child's Play 3* and the killing of James Bulger, a factor which weakened the paper circulated by Professor Elizabeth Newson and a number of distinguished academics and child carers.

The press persisted in ignoring the truth. As late as February 7, 1999, six years after Bulger's murder, the *Sunday Telegraph* reported that

> A NEW horror film featuring "Chucky", the psychopathic doll blamed for inspiring the murderers of James Bulger, has been passed for release in Britain by the British Board of Film Classification.
>
> Three previous films in the same series were removed from shops after the court case which convicted James's two killers. *The Bride of Chucky* is already a box office hit in America but Universal Pictures, distributors of the previous films *Child's Play* I, II, and III, have refused to be associated with the new movie.
>
> Denise Bulger, James's mother, refused to comment on the new film last night. But Mary Whitehouse, the anti-sex and violence campaigner, said: "It's utterly irresponsible. The Director for Public Prosecutions should have a look at it. But it is really up to the public to react. They should write to their MPs."

The fact that the reporter contacted Denise Bulger to provoke a reaction is quite appalling and identifies what little sympathy is felt by the press towards the loss of her son.

The Chucky doll would be mentioned again after a twenty-year hiatus. When Nathan Maynard-Ellis and his boyfriend David Leesley were convicted of the 2019 murder of Julia Rawson in Tipton, West Midlands, police photos released to the press showed the contents of the Maynard-Ellis flat. Standing prominently on a shelf of horror movie memorabilia was the Chucky doll. The shelf also contained books about serial killers and crime. It was also reported that he collected newspaper clippings of murder cases and had DVDs of horror movies, *Nekromantik* and *Nekromantik II*. Evidently the fervour by this point had passed and attempts to project the doll as an influential aspect of the brutal crime were not taken up.

On March 10, 1993, forty-five-year-old Peter Walker was found dead in his flat in Battersea. He was a frequenter of gay bars and diagnosed HIV-positive. Walker was discovered lying on his bed naked and bound with nylon cord. He had a condom in his mouth and another on his nose. Cigarette burns and small puncture wounds were visible on his body. His penis was blemished with what appeared to be a "love bite." Two small teddy bears had been placed against his body in a curious pose. Death was a result of suffocation. After the discovery of the body, a man telephoned the *Sun* newspaper and took anonymous credit for the murder, promising there would be further killings.

On May 30, thirty-seven-year-old Christopher Dunn was discovered murdered in his Northwest London home. He was wearing a bondage-style harness and studded belt. Like Walker, Dunn was a homosexual and had been strangled with some kind of ligature. A "love bite" was evident on his back. Five days later the body of Perry Bradley III was found in his West London flat. He too had been strangled in his bed, but it wasn't commonly known that Bradley was a homosexual. A doll had been placed on his body. Five days after the discovery of Bradley's body, thirty-three-year-old Andrew Collier was found murdered in his flat. A dead cat with a condom on its tail had been laid across his body. Collier was HIV-positive.

It became known that all the victims had frequented the Coleherne pub in West London, a place frequented by sadomasochistic homosexuals. It was at this location that Dennis Nilsen and Michael "The Wolf" Lupo had selected victims many years earlier. Following the discovery of Collier, the police received a call from a man claiming to be the killer, who threatened to kill one person every week. Later he phoned again, telling the police he had killed another man and asked if they had found the body. The fifth victim was Emanuel Spiteri – a regular of the Coleherne. The police theorised that Spiteri had likely used the Underground to travel from the pub to his flat. Examining CCTV footage from Charing Cross station, they identified Spiteri, who was with another man. The second man's image was made public and, shortly after its broadcast, Colin Ireland notified police that it was him on the videotape, although he claimed to know nothing of Spiteri's murder. The police took Ireland's fingerprints and checked them against a single unidentified print lifted from Andrew Collier's apartment. They matched. When confronted with this evidence, Ireland confessed to all five murders.

In December 1993, Colin Ireland – an ex-soldier and 'survival fanatic' – was convicted of the murder of the five men and sentenced to life imprisonment. Even though the victims were all homosexuals, and the killings of a sexual nature, Ireland claimed to be heterosexual, a detail corroborated by Ireland's girlfriend: she resolutely put the blame for his conversion from a decent man into vicious killer on "video nasties," although no films were identified by title. Ireland would have other scapegoats in mind, one being the television police drama series, *The Bill*. "They should ban *The Bill*," he declared, "it gives people ideas." It was also implied that he'd been inspired to kill by true crime books, in particular Brian Masters' *Killing for Company* and Robert K Ressler's *Whoever Fights Monsters* and *Sexual Homicide: Patterns and Motives*. Ireland later claimed that the "FBI manual" he owned stated a murderer was classified as a serial killer if they killed at least four people. Recognition by the *Sun* as a serial killer of homosexuals was likely to be Ireland's goal; "I've got the book. I know how many you have to do," he told police during one of his phone calls. He apparently wanted to achieve the same kind of media fame as had Dennis Nilsen. A neighbour confirmed Ireland's obsession with true crime literature and claimed to have been loaned a copy of the Nilsen book, and that Ireland later wanted it back to re-read. Author Brian Masters was taken aback by the suggestion his work may have inspired a murder. He wrote in a *Mail on Sunday* supplement: '...it cannot be stated too often that there is no evidence whatever to support the notion of a pure "copycat" crime undertaken in emulation of a visual or literary experience.'

It is no great surprise that Colin Ireland chose the *Sun* with which to collude[24] – it is officially the most popular newspaper among Britain's criminal population.[25] Geraldine Bedell, writing in the *Independent on Sunday*, describes it as "a newspaper read widely by persistent young offenders," while Anne Nagell showed it to be the favourite amongst the juvenile delinquents she interviewed. During the House of Commons debate on the Criminal Justice and Public Order Bill, Angela Eagle MP posited that "offenders are in large numbers readers of the *Sun*." David Alton, in league with the tabloids, countered, "I will resist the temptation to be drawn into a wider debate about the quality of our newspapers..."

Peter Moore was a movie aficionado who started his own small cinema chain in Wales. He was an only child and archetypal mother's boy. He was also a violent homosexual and had been carrying out random attacks on people for over twenty years. In May 1994, his mother died, and Moore progressed from assault to murder. In September 1995, he murdered fifty-six-year-old Henry Roberts, a Nazi enthusiast living on the island of Anglesey. Roberts was found with his trousers around his ankles and almost thirty stab wounds to the body. In November, Moore attacked forty-nine-year-old Keith Randles in his caravan and stabbed him to death. The following month, thirty-five-year-old Anthony Davies was discovered stabbed to death in an area known as a homosexual meeting place. Traces of blood that did not belong to the victim were found at the scene. The police opened a telephone hotline and encouraged local gay men to report any violence they may have encountered. The name Peter Moore was reported on several occasions. When police went to question Moore and search his house, they discovered items stolen from his victims. A blood test matched the sample taken from the Davies murder scene.

Moore confessed openly to the killings but would later claim he had an accomplice and that this second man had committed the murders. He said the name of this other man was Alan, then changed it to Jason. It was suggested that the Jason he spoke of was not a real person, but the homicidal character in the *Friday the 13th* series of films. Another film implicated in the crimes was the 1971 action thriller, *Dirty Harry*: referring to his assault on a lorry driver, Moore said, "I think I got the idea out of the Clint Eastwood film..." Another film link was Alfred Hitchcock's *Psycho*, likened to the case by the press because Moore was a 'mummy's boy.'

Thomas Hamilton spent eight months as a Scout Master with the 4th/6th Stirling Scout Group when, in 1974, he was forced to resign from the association after two children in his charge had suffered from hypothermia on an outing. Still wanting to work with young boys he formed a youth group called the Stirling Rovers but in 1983 became entangled in a dispute with the Central Regional Council on how he ran the club. He complained about his treatment to a local Government Ombudsman which ruled in Hamilton's favour. However, the council then refused him access to a hall in the town's high school that hitherto he had been using for the weekly group meetings. The parents of seventy of the boys who attended the meetings were puzzled by the decision and wrote letters praising the way in which Hamilton ran the group. But because of the council's action, and rumours now circulating, his kitchen fitting business lost custom and collapsed. Hamilton was increasingly concerned about unsubstantiated claims that he was a child molester. He requested permission to defend himself against the allegations, but the authorities refused to listen. In 1993, he was investigated by police; nothing was found to substantiate the rumours. On March 24 of that year, he wrote to Michael Forsyth, the Scottish Secretary, outlining his concerns. Extracts from that letter follow:

> With the horrific murder of little James Bulger, possibly by two ten-year-old boys, the whole question of juvenile crime is in greater debate across the country. The work of my group in providing sporting and leisure time activities for young boys has the effect of channelling young energies into creative and worthwhile pursuits. Sadly, having run for eight years, our two Dunfermline Boys' Sports Clubs closed last year. It is ironic the decline of these clubs was caused by the irresponsible actions of over-zealous police officers from Central Scotland police, obsessed with child abuse, in carrying out their failed pervert hunt using unfair tactics. Mr Forsyth, in twenty years

> of operation of our lawful activity, there has never been any lawbreaking or any suggestion of sexual child abuse from any boys against either myself or any of my leaders. I know that sexual child abuse must be identified and the abusers rooted out as a matter of national priority and this, in concept, is wholeheartedly supported by the general public. Nevertheless, such a complaint against myself, claiming that I was taking photographs of the children and the purely malicious innuendos [*sic*] associated with this claim, should not have resulted in a full-scale pervert hunt. The officers themselves confirmed that there was no suggestion of improper or indecent photographs having been taken but that the taking of photographs of children in itself is a cause for concern. The proper and legitimate purpose of the need to take such photographs had been fully explained previously to their superiors. When senior officers had been shown these photographs in earlier years, their only comments had been that "the colours were nice." Serious and lasting damage has been caused to our work and ability by these modern day witch-hunts where ordinary everyday events are given sinister slants by police officers. In my work with children, any suggestion of child abuse, however vague, will do great damage to public and parental support. However, to have police officers suggesting to parents in Dunfermline that I am a pervert, even on a nod and a wink basis, in the hope that they will be forthcoming with information of a sinister nature, is gross injustice. There can be reams of letters of communication with Central Scotland police over a twenty-year period and still young officers appeal in a panic stating that they do not know me from Adam and have never heard of my group; hence the gross over-reaction. Such action seems to be condoned by senior police officers, the Scottish Office, etc. The officers involved are protected in an elaborate cover-up and whitewash and the officer in charge is promoted. Any legal action is ruled out, as legal aid is not available to me under Government rules and the Citizen's Charter seems ineffective. If the government is going to effectively condone the police undermining, smashing and destroying voluntary youth groups in modern day witch-hunts, it is perhaps hardly surprising that bored children with little or nothing to do turn their energies to crime from a young age.

The letter and its sentiment appear out of sorts with someone trying to hide their guilt, only serving to draw further attention to Hamilton and the allegations made against him. Acting on hearsay and rumour, Doreen Hagger boasted that she and a friend confronted Hamilton outside a youth club in Linlithgow and showered him with eggs, oil, shampoo and flour. Such actions succeeded in isolating Hamilton further and no doubt contributed to his mental degeneration.

Already a member of the Stirling Rifle and Pistol Club, Hamiliton applied to join the Callander Rifle and Pistol Club in 1996, but was refused membership. He wrote directly to the Queen claiming that the Scout organisation had ruined his reputation and, as a result, he was branded a pervert. Shortly after this he made a decision to commit suicide, but not before taking revenge on the community he felt had persecuted him. On March 13, 1996, at 9.30 in the morning, forty-three-year-old Hamilton strode into Dunblane Primary School carrying his handguns and shot dead sixteen children and one teacher before placing a pistol in his mouth and taking his own life.

Little was known about Hamilton. The press sought to attribute superficial details to the killer, as if the crime was not enough in itself to report.[26] Some papers made clumsy attempts to link Hamilton's actions to movies. *Scotland on Sunday* reported that he chatted to young club members about the 1984 film *The Terminator*, described as "the movie which features Arnold Schwarzenegger as a crazed killing machine pursuing a young boy." The reporter has changed the character pursued by a time-travelling robot from that of a woman, played by Linda Hamilton, to a "young boy," fabricating a hypothesis that links the film to Hamilton's mindset. The *Times*, as we have seen, followed the massacre with an article titled, "Who Supports Violent Films Now?" Unable to think of any specific movie to fortify their argument, the newspaper accused violent films in general.[27]

On April 29, 1996, shortly after the international publicity given to Thomas Hamilton, a similar shooting spree occurred in Port Arthur, Tasmania. Twenty-eight-year-old Martin Bryant, dining in the Broad Arrow Café, lifted two semi-automatic rifles from his sports bag, shot dead twenty customers and wounded eighteen. He then casually strolled around the streets and shot dead a further twelve people before coming close to losing his own life in a house fire where three other bodies were discovered. The short amount of time that elapsed between Hamilton and Bryant suggests an imitative act, and that Bryant was seeking similar notoriety afforded to his ephemeral role model. The press, however, had other ideas and in typical simplistic fashion blamed Chucky, the doll and by now familiar scapegoat from the *Child's Play* films. On Friday, May 3, 1996, the *Daily Mirror* ran the facetious headline, "Psycho surf boy mad on Chucky." The piece continued: "Monster Martin Bryant was obsessed with Chucky, the evil video doll who figured in the murder of toddler James Bulger..." The story, written by Mark Dowdney and derived from foreign news sources, was composed from details supposedly given by Bryant's onetime girlfriend, Janette Hoani. How much Hoani was paid for the information is not disclosed but it is unlikely she gave it for free. The luridly sensational story concluded with suggestions that Bryant slept with a pig, had sex with animals, and wanted sex with other men. The suggestion that he may have had homosexual tendencies, like his counterpart Hamilton, would figure strongly in the mind of one particular reader. See Horrett Campbell, below.

It wasn't only the tabloids that promoted a film link. The *Times* on May 5, 1996, undoubtedly using the same source as the *Mirror*, reported that, "Renewed fears about video nasties were raised last night after it was revealed the Tasmanian mass murderer Martin Bryant was obsessed with a film that has already been linked to killings in Britain." On May 7, the *Daily Mail* ran the headline, "...Chucky Doll was Killer's Inspiration" but were unable to follow the claim with anything to suggest that had been the case. Quoted in the report was David Alton. Reaffirming his role as an original rumour-monger in the James Bulger case, Alton asked: "How many more tragedies must occur before the world takes notice?"

More reports attempted to implicate films as the main cause of Bryant's deranged state of mind, asserting that he had a collection of videos depicting violence and hardcore pornography, including bestiality. "Massacre suspect's violent video hoard," headlined the *Daily Telegraph,* claiming that, "more than 2000 violent and pornographic videos have been found at the home of Martin Bryant." Understandably concerned, Australia's chief censor John Dickie tried to determine exactly what the contents of the films were and contacted Tasmania's Department of Justice and Perpetual Trustees, which was holding the assets of Martin Bryant. Far from the violence and pornography touted by the media, the collection consisted of early romance films and musicals, starring the likes of Clark Gable and Bette Davis. These had belonged to the previous owner of the house, Helen Harvey, Bryant's benefactor. Out of the entire collection only four videos did not fit the romance/musical category: two episodes of the sitcom *Blackadder*, and the movies *A Nightmare on Elm Street* and *Taxi Driver*. The gulf between the truth and the report is staggering – the press declared there were 2,000 violent videos in Bryant's possession when in fact there were only two. Following disclosure of the true nature of the films, Dickie stated, "I have no doubt that misreporting such as this has contributed substantially to the perception that some violent incident on the television or on some video has led to this tragedy."

As a result of false press, sixty-five per cent of the community in the Bryant case believed a connection existed between violence in films and violence in real-life. Outrageous fabrication of this sort is not new, as can be evidenced in the case of Alan Derek Poole in June 1951. Anti-comics sentiment was on the rise in Britain, with horror and crime comics in particular seen by some factions as harmful for the nation's youth. Twenty-year-old Poole, from Chatham, Kent, shot and killed a policeman after he was disturbed breaking into a farm building. Poole himself was later killed in a shootout with police. The press claimed that hundreds of crime and horror comics had been discovered at Poole's home, implying this was the cause of his criminal behaviour. In truth, only one comic was found and it wasn't crime or horror related, but a western.

Dr Park Dietz, the FBI's leading forensic psychiatrist, claimed the likely catalyst that triggered Martin Bryant's assault was television coverage of the Dunblane massacre. He stated, "Were it not for the experience of someone else's actions, such people would more likely just kill themselves." And added, "[Bryant] probably thought to himself, 'I am as powerful as [Hamilton] is. The world needs to know my suffering and feel my rage.'" Speculative, for sure, but Dietz has far greater insight, experience and understanding of psychotic behaviour than any journalist writing for a mass-market tabloid. Defence psychiatrist Paul Mullen would also state that media coverage of the Dunblane massacre triggered Bryant: "He followed Dunblane. His planning started with Dunblane. Before that he was thinking about suicide, but Dunblane and the early portrayal of the killer, Thomas Hamilton, changed everything."[28]

If media coverage of Dunblane did indeed trigger Bryant, then the press wouldn't want to implicate itself. Direct evidence of the news media's influence is currently lacking in this case, although future psychiatric examination of Bryant may well confirm it. However, other incidents can be exclusively associated with excessive and lurid press coverage of crimes.

Horrett Campbell fell under the influence of the tabloids and, on Monday, July 8, 1996, attempted to re-enact what he had read in the newspapers about the Dunblane and Port Arthur massacres. Thirty-three-year-old Campbell didn't have access to a firearm, so used a machete instead. He entered the grounds of St Luke's nursery school in Blakenham, Wolverhampton, and attacked children and staff with the heavy blade, on which was written "you filthy devil" and "666 marks the devil."[29] Despite some severe head wounds, none of his seven victims died. When Campbell was arrested, police discovered newspaper cuttings in his flat relating to Thomas Hamilton and Martin Bryant. He had drawn a heart-shape pierced with a Cupid's arrow around the photograph of Bryant. Campbell was possibly "turned-on" by the newspaper allegation that Bryant wanted sex with other men and perhaps imagined himself as one of those men. He was also said to regard Thomas Hamilton as a "kindred spirit."

After serving a thirty-month jail sentence for assault, fifty-year-old David Jenning told a prison chaplain that he planned to "do a Dunblane" once he was released from prison. He claimed he wanted to protest the treatment of his children who were in council care. Because of the threat, Jenning is now banned from approaching schoolchildren, teachers, and from going near the local school. He has previous convictions for assaulting a council officer and carrying a firearm in public. Like Campbell, he had been made aware of Hamilton's attack by the media, and had been inspired to contemplate an attack of his own.

The *Daily Express*, on Wednesday, June 14, 1995, reported the case of two juveniles who committed robbery at gunpoint with an unambiguous byline, "Crime Spree Caused By *Reservoir Dogs*." The father of one of the juveniles suggested that the film drove his drug-induced, gun-toting son to commit the crime. Using a blank-firing pistol to threaten staff, the two youths robbed local shops. Earlier, fourteen-year-old Scott Richards had held the gun to his mother's head and threatened to kill her. Such behaviour suggests the Richards were a dysfunctional family. "It's outrageous that someone as young as Scott can get hold of a film like *Reservoir Dogs*," said Scott's father, Chris, a former soldier. And yet his statement says more about his own failure to take responsibility for his son. The fact that the two youths watched *Reservoir Dogs*, if indeed they did, was used to divert attention from the shortcomings of the parents in the matter.

On March 7, 1995, in Hernando, Mississippi, Bill Savage was shot twice in the head at point blank range and robbed of $200. The following day, some 300 miles away in Ponchatoula, Louisiana, a female robber shot shop assistant Patsy Byers in the throat. The event was recorded on the shop's security camera and images of the attacker were made public. Following a tip-off from an informant, nineteen-year-old Sarah Edmondson was arrested on June 2. Her apprehension led to the arrest of her boyfriend, eighteen-year-old Ben Darras. The couple were charged with the murder of Bill Savage and the attempted murder of Patsy Byers. It transpired that the couple were regular drug abusers. Edmondson had serious psychiatric problems from the age of thirteen and

Darras' father had been an alcoholic and committed suicide. Despite such dysfunctional backgrounds, claims would be made that they were driven to commit their crimes because of Oliver Stone's 1994 movie, *Natural Born Killers,* starring Woody Harrelson and Juliette Lewis. Chief promoter of this notion was best-selling novelist and onetime-lawyer John Grisham, who would declare that "The artist should be required to share the responsibility along with the nut who pulled the trigger." He said there was overwhelming evidence to link the film to the crime, and that the perpetrators had no history of violence. (But that applies to everyone – no one has a history of violence until they have committed their first violent act.) Edmondson's father claimed that the two teenagers watched *Natural Born Killers* more than twenty times and, in an interview with *Vanity Fair*, said that "on one occasion they watched it six times in one night." As the movie has a running time of 118 minutes, this seems unlikely, however drug-addled the viewer may be. Some parents seek to criticise any influence but their own, perhaps more when the prospect of a multi-million-dollar lawsuit is at hand. Grisham hoped to employ the product-liability laws against Oliver Stone and Warner Bros, whereby manufacturers are responsible for any injury or death caused by their product. He argues that *Natural Born Killers* is an artistic product that caused the death of Bill Savage. However, if his lawsuit were successful, he would leave himself in an extremely vulnerable position and open to similar claims against his own arguably violent novels and film spin-offs (which include *The Firm*, *A Time to Kill* and *The Chamber*). If Grisham wanted to utilise the product-liability law it would make more sense to target the manufacturers of the guns that were used in the killing, for there is no grey area in this argument. The fact that he doesn't may suggest he has a personal vendetta against Oliver Stone.[30]

One tabloid tried to link murderers Eric Elliot and Lewis Gilbert to the same movie. "Sick Killers Copy Woody's New Film" screamed the headline in relation to multiple murders committed by the two Ohio men. The report stated the crimes were "a real-life imitation of a brutal, new Hollywood blockbuster. The actions of the sick pair, arrested in America last week, were a copy-cat of killings featured in *Natural Born Killers*..." Robert Hawk, an FBI agent, said in earnest, "There are a lot of movies that imitate life. Whether these two picked up on that, we don't know." His inconclusive statement provided sufficient grist for the press: Elliot and Gilbert were two killers operating as a team, as actors Woody Harrelson and Juliette Lewis are a team in the film.

Next in the firing line - *Natural Born Killers*.

France, too, got in on the act when Audry Maupin and Florence Rey shot dead three policemen and a taxi driver in Paris on October 4, 1994. They were christened by the press as "France's natural born killers." Maupin and Rey had raided a police pound armed with sawn-off shotguns and pistols stolen from the policemen. They hijacked a taxi as an escape vehicle, but the driver rammed a police car. Maupin shot the driver in the back of the head and a shootout ensued, resulting in the deaths of two policemen. The couple hijacked another vehicle and were pursued by a police motorcyclist, also killed in the gunfire. They were eventually forced to a standstill at a police roadblock and in the subsequent shootout Maupin was fatally wounded. Rey – who the *Sunday Times* described as a "Natural born killer [who] was a fool for love" – was arrested at the scene. It was later reported that a poster for the film *Natural Born Killers* was found in the room the couple shared.

Still in France: The *Daily Express* reported a "Video murder hunt" on March 6, 1996. Police were searching for seventeen-year-old Sebastien Dubois and his eighteen-year-old girlfriend, Veronique Malarme, after the body of a sixteen-year-old boy was found buried at Dubois' home in Gournay near Paris. A video copy of *Natural Born Killers* was found in the home, prompting investigator Jean Michot to remark, "This horrific video could well have inspired the boy's lust to kill." There was no mention of any other items found in the home, which indicates that attention was only drawn to the video because of questionable claims of causative effects, publicised in the United States. Indeed, here we have a case of police officers being influenced by press reports of what other police officers have theorised. It was fashionable to blame Stone's movie for any dyadic criminal act.

An eleven-year-old hooligan and his gang attacked a brother and sister on waste ground in Ipswich, Suffolk, beating them with a stick. He also forced the two children to suck on the stick and told them he was going to kill them. When the case came to court, child psychologist David Morgan claimed the child may have been imitating a scene in the film *The Krays*. "The film shows a gun being put into someone's mouth to humiliate and degrade. It could be this is a case of him learning behaviour from the film," he said. Despite the psychologist merely making a wild guess, the *Daily Express* accepted the comment as fact and ran the story under the headline "Bully 'copied Kray gun scene in film.'"

Sixty-four-year-old Bryn Price, a gun enthusiast from Mid Glamorgan, was accidentally shot and killed by his six-year-old granddaughter. Price had handed the girl his Magnum revolver, unaware it was loaded, and she had fired a round into his throat. He died later in hospital. Newspaper coverage ran under the headline "Girl, 6, Shot Man Dead In Imitation Of Video Comedy." The film she supposedly imitated was the Sylvester Stallone slapstick, *Stop! Or My Mom Will Shoot*.

In November 1984, forty-one-year-old Vanessa Ballantyne went to a night-club and picked up John Parr. Unknown to Parr, Ballantyne was carrying a five-inch kitchen knife. Later in the evening, she lured Parr into a dark alley. "I've got something for you," she said, and drove the knife into his stomach. Parr survived the attack, removed the blade and sought assistance. Ballantyne was arrested and told police that the film, *Basic Instinct*, had made her attack the man. "*Basic Instinct* made mother stab stranger" and "Mrs Average turned into stab maniac after watching *Basic Instinct*" were two headlines in the *Daily Express* following Ballantyne's trial. Ballantyne was described in a sympathetic manner in the reports, a "respectable housewife", and Sharon Stone, star of *Basic Instinct*, a "sex siren" and "knife-wielding temptress."[31] The fact that Ballantyne chose to deliberately stab an innocent man shows she certainly wasn't "Mrs Average." The film was no guiltier of the crime than the knife.

Sandy Charles was fourteen-year-old when he lured seven-year-old Jonathan Thimpsen into the woods near his home in La Ronge, Canada, and murdered him. Charles stabbed the youngster several times then crushed his skull with a rock. He mutilated the body by cutting away portions of flesh. After his arrest Charles told police, "There's a strong spirit in my room that gave me these thoughts... I was going to commit suicide until this thing popped into my head. I started thinking about killing someone else." However Charles' defence lawyer Barry Singer claimed it was the film *Warlock* that drove the defendant to murder. His evidence for such an assertion was that the film showed that "if you cut the fat off a virgin or an unbaptised child, then boiled it down and drank it, it would give you the power to fly."

An incident related in the *Sunday Post*, October 18, 1987, under the headline "Terror of Man in Silver Mask," described how a twelve-year-old girl had been pursued by a strangely dressed man wielding a machete. His mask was silver, he also wore a black cloak and spurs, and had been seen by many other children in the area. The report went on: "He's nicknamed Freddy because he dresses the same way as the murderer in the horror film Freddy's Revenge." The children who described the attacker were said to be of similar age, i.e. twelve, a fact which disputes their knowing how Freddy in *Freddy's Revenge* dressed – the film was on general cinema release with an 18 certificate. The description of the attacker is far removed from Freddy's trademark fedora and striped pullover, and instead sounds remarkably like the costume worn by the Phantom in Andrew Lloyd Webber's stage musical, *Phantom of the Opera*. This isn't mentioned in the report – it would be unseemly to attribute a "copycat" crime to such an esteemed and popular production. The press is discriminating when it comes to condemning a movie – first taking account of its popularity or its "class" distinctiveness. Fourteen-year-old Imtiaz Ahmed hanged himself, leaving behind a note that referenced Walt Disney's *The Lion King:* "I want to die, Allah. Please make me the Lion King." The press reported on the incident, but despite its links with the death of a child, there were no calls for the film to be banned.

When a ten-year-old schoolboy fought with classmates and scratched their faces, his teacher, Carol Shields, stated, "He has been exposed to violent videos and is exhibiting violent behaviour." The report in *Today* on April 20, 1994, claimed the youngster was copying Freddy Krueger in *A Nightmare on Elm Street*.

When two robbers poured petrol into a ticket clerk's office on a New York subway and set the clerk alight, the crime was attributed to *Money Train*, in which a similar incident occurs.

Thirty-six-year-old Stuart Hulse was jailed for life in 1998 after being convicted of the rape and murder of Shirley Brown in Lowton, Greater Manchester. Because

The Fox is video nasty fan

By PETER HOOLEY

THE VICIOUS rapist dubbed The Fox is a video nasty freak, police believe.

Detectives have made urgent checks on video libraries, clubs and postal outlets in their hunt for the perverted beast who has struck five times in the triangle of terror at Leighton Buzzard, Beds.

The man leading the hunt Detective Chief Superintendent Brian Prickett, said yesterday: "We think there is a link.

Identical

"There are many video nasties which depict scenes identical to some of his actions."

Meanwhile the Mayor of Leighton Buzzard, Councillor Robert Cook, hit out at police failure to catch the Fox. He said: "People's confidence is low. It's bordering on complete panic."

Yesterday police ruled out any link between the Fox and a burglary at a house in Great Gaddesden on Sunday night.

Hulse had been to a party where a pornographic video was played, his action was attributed to the viewing of the film: defending the killer-rapist, Roderick Carus QC said he had become "inflamed" by the video. Ann Winterton MP stated, "This case gives the lie to those who claim, with supposed authority, that violence in the media does not affect the behaviour of people who watch it." But it was also reported that everyone at the party paired off, leaving Hulse alone. Hulse, a married man, had gone to the party hoping for sex but found himself isolated while everyone else was "at it". Because his victim lived only 300 yards from his home, he murdered her to prevent being identified.

Thirty-two-year-old Malcolm Fairley was a multiple rapist who was known as The Fox prior to his identification and arrest. Fairley showed no sexual preference during his attacks, raping both male and female victims – even a family's pet dog, it was reported. Prior to his arrest, the press made speculative connections to films, running headlines like, "The Fox is a video nasty fan." Two videotapes had been stolen from one home he invaded: a copy of John Carpenter's cult sci-fi horror film, *The Thing*, and John Landis' *National Lampoon's Animal House*, a comedy starring John Belushi. Neither film has ever been classed as a "video nasty" by the DPP or any other organisation. However, the fact that Fairley chose to steal *The Thing* may be linked to press reports concerning one Christopher Meah, who was sentenced to two life terms in 1983. Meah was a violent rapist who desperately tried to apportion blame on the John Carpenter film as an influencing factor. Months after the report, Fairley would focus on the same film and behave in a similar manner to Meah. When he was finally caught, Fairley tried to blame his sex attacks on pornographic videos. Joan Fairley, his first wife, described him as "a compulsive liar." Curiously, the *Daily Mail* said that Fairley was just a burglar[32] who turned into a rapist after watching "pornographic video nasties." A similar standpoint was taken by the *Daily Star*, sympathetically describing Fairley as "A quiet, non-smoking teetotaller with a wife and three children," but "turned into a monster by the most disgusting hard-core pornography imaginable."

Pre-empting the Bulger case by a decade, the police said that too much significance had been put on the video connection. Fairley had been watching pornographic films for years before any sex attack took place. The first time he assaulted a person was on April 11, 1984, when he entered the home of a seventy-four-year-old woman. Finding her in bed, he had the urge to touch her, but ran from the house when she started screaming. From that point, most of his home invasions had a sexual motive. During one burglary he stole a shotgun, sawed off the barrel and removed the butt to make it easy to conceal. The weapon was used threateningly on subsequent attacks. With this new element, the press tried to link his crimes directly to a film called *Sex Wish*,[33] which included scenes of a rapist wearing a Balaclava and carrying a shotgun (Fairley wore a hood made from a trouser leg).[34] The police didn't find a copy of *Sex Wish* in Fairley's collection and he denied ever having seen it, even though admission to viewing it could have aided his defence. He told police that he wore the mask when he committed burglaries, and no sex attack was planned. Most of the porn videos he amassed had been stolen from the houses he had burgled.

Previous: *Daily Star*, July 24, 1984. Below: *The Mail on Sunday*, March 3, 1985; *Daily Mail*, February 27, 1985.

Fox's rape video is still on sale

A PORNOGRAPHIC video which a judge blamed for influencing the rapist called The Fox in his depraved sex crimes was still available in Britain last night.

The 45-minute film Sex Wish, condemned by Mr Justice Caulfield last week when he sentenced Malcolm Fairley to six life sentences, was to be found on the shelves of some lending libraries and corner shops.

Sex Wish, made in America, portrays violent rape by a man carrying a shotgun and wearing a Balaclava helmet — the way The Fox operated.

Legislation could soon lead to such videos being banned, with a £20,000 fine for anyone dealing in them.

The British Board of Film Censors will begin classifying all videos after Easter, when Parliament has given formal approval to regulations piloted into law by Tory MP Mr Graham Bright.

Mr Bright, MP for Luton South, said: 'The chance of The Fox, or anyone like him, getting hold of such material if this legislation had been in force at the time would have been reduced significantly.'

Like so much on the British porn market, the cheap budget movie began in Los Angeles, at the studios of Cal Vista Inc.

They shared profits with their British distributors, David Gold and Tommy Harris — but both were said last night to have withdrawn the film.

Daily Mail 20p

He started as a petty burglar—then Malcolm Fairley discovered porn videos

THE FOX —EVIL BEYOND WORDS

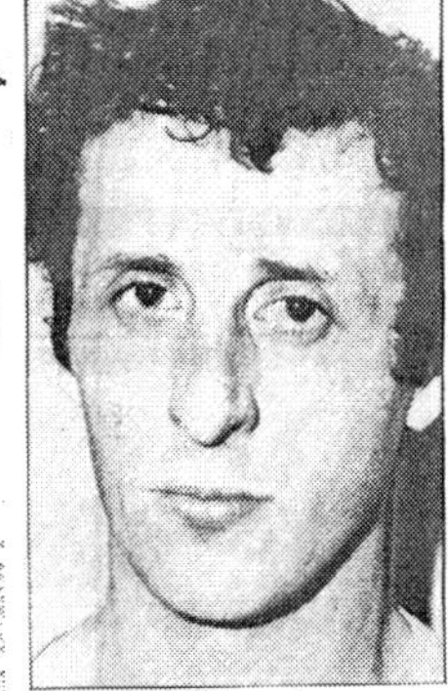

THE man they called The Fox was behind bars for life last night for his horrific sex crimes.

Accent

Turn to Page 2, Col. 3

The face his victims never saw

Jill Knight MBE MP wrote an article for the *Sunday Express* (it was never printed). In it she states,

EVENING MAIL, THURSDAY, JANUARY 22, 1998

PORN FILM KILLER JAILED FOR LIFE

Falklands vet raped and strangled mum after watching movie

Headlines following the arrest of Stuart Hulse.

> Malcolm (the Fox) Fairlie [*sic*] had been an avid watcher of porno-videos and his particular favourite was a charming American-made seventy-minute movie called *Sex Wish*... What Fairlie saw over and over again on the screen he finally went out and re-created for himself in real life. He openly admitted to the police that watching pornographic films had turned him into a rapist. *Sex Wish*, astonishingly, does not come under Section 2 of [the Obscene Publications Act] because the sex act in the film was simulated and not real. However, it was real enough for Malcolm Fairlie and his victims.

She concludes with a nonsensical cliché: "Is the freedom to see porno movies more important than the freedom from rape, murder and terror?"

The *Daily Mail* reported a case on July 7, 1983, as part of its campaign to "Ban the Sadist Videos." It related to Kevin Cooper, who murdered four people in Chino, north of Los Angeles. Under the headline, "Cruel movies fan hacks four to death", the report stated that Cooper, after escaping from the California Institution for Men, "hacked to death a married couple and their two children after regularly watching violent video films." The film link was an illogical non sequitur, established because "two days after the killings inmates at the Chino Institution watched a video of the film *The Texas Chain Saw Massacre*." It failed to explain how people watching a film after a murder committed by another person could somehow be linked. As is seen so often, the *Mail* was twisting facts and proffering misinformation to bolster its misguided crusade against its own definition of "evil."

On May 12, 1996, the *Mail on Sunday* was congratulating Dustin Hoffman for speaking out about movie violence. Hoffman, star of the film, *Straw Dogs*, unable to gain a certificate in the UK at the time because of its violent content, suggested the Dunblane and Port Arthur massacres may have been sparked by violence in movies. He failed to elaborate or give credence to his theory, but it was noted that he also failed to take any responsibility for crimes of violence that occurred in the early seventies, which, by his argument, may have been sparked by *Straw Dogs*.

James Ferman said of the film,

> *Straw Dogs* has been cited by men in prison as having turned them on to rape because of the way that the woman responded to the rape at first and therefore appears to welcome the advances of men. Now we passed that uncut on film in the early 1970s before I came to the Board. We have never passed it on video because if you cut the scene you destroy the motivation of the film and it is rather a good one. We just think it does not belong on video because certain men with certain proclivities could watch that scene selectively out of context over and over again obsessionally and turn it into masturbatory fantasy and we are not very happy with that.[35]

Ferman may have been getting a bit carried away, but Hoffman is simply speaking out against an industry in which he is no longer a major player. The report sanctimoniously stated that "if anyone is triggered into murder by a film, then the film-makers have a lot on their conscience." It was a tell-tale statement following the newspaper-inspired Hungerford massacre and St Luke's attack.

On May 14, 1998, Graham Wallis and Neil Sayers were drinking alcohol around a campfire in woods with their friend Russell Crookes. All three had an interest in the Special Air Service (SAS). Students at Hadlow agricultural college, near Tonbridge in Kent, their friendship was bonded by the formation of a clique called

Below: The *Sun* reports the Wallis and Sayers case. May 8, 1999. Next page, from top: *Time* ponders the Columbine High School shootings; *Daily Express*, April 21, 1999.

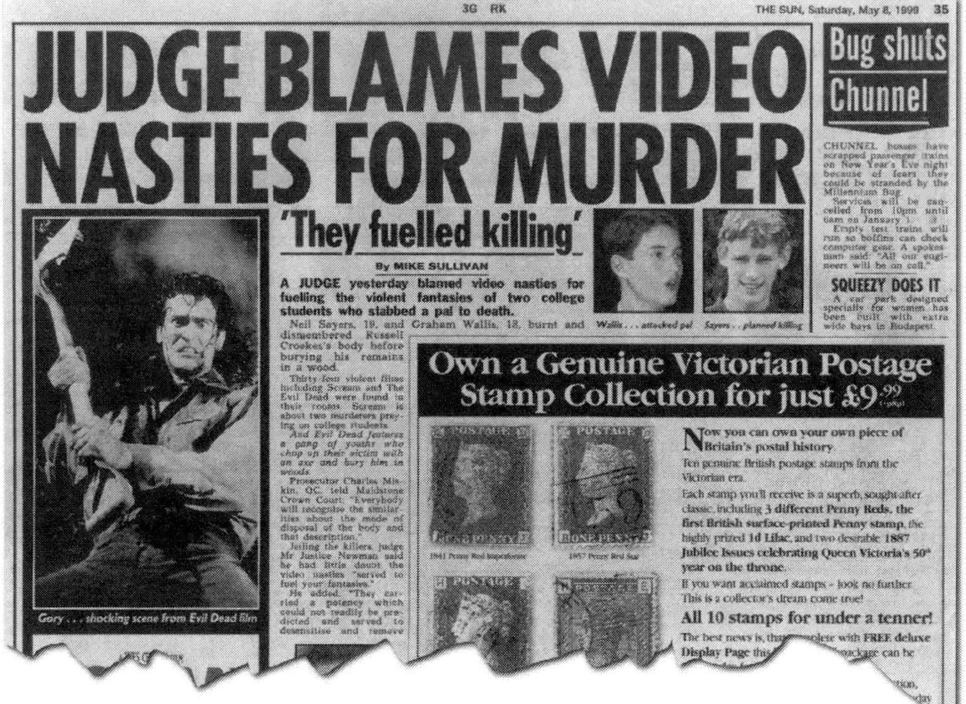

3G RK THE SUN, Saturday, May 8, 1999 35

JUDGE BLAMES VIDEO NASTIES FOR MURDER

'They fuelled killing'

By MIKE SULLIVAN

A JUDGE yesterday blamed video nasties for fuelling the violent fantasies of two college students who stabbed a pal to death.

Neil Sayers, 19, and Graham Wallis, 18, burnt and dismembered Russell Crookes's body before burying his remains in a wood.

Thirty-four violent films including Scream and The Evil Dead were found in their rooms. Scream is about two murderers preying on college students.

And Evil Dead features a gang of youths who chop up their victim with an axe and bury him in woods.

Prosecutor Charles Miskin, QC, told Maidstone Crown Court: "Everybody will recognise the similarities about the mode of disposal of the body and that description."

Jailing the killers, judge Mr Justice Newman said he had little doubt the video nasties "served to fuel your fantasies."

He added: "They carried a potency which could not readily be predicted and served to desensitise and remove

Gory . . . shocking scene from Evil Dead film

Wallis . . . attacked pal

Sayers . . . planned killing

Bug shuts Chunnel

CHUNNEL bosses have scrapped passenger trains on New Year's Eve night because of fears they could be stranded by the Millennium Bug.

Services will be cancelled from 10pm until 6am on January 1.

Empty test trains will run so boffins can check computer gear. A spokesman said: "All our engineers will be on call."

SQUEEZY DOES IT

A car park designed specially for women has been built with extra wide bays in Budapest.

the Brotherhood, based on military-like survivalism. Sayers – whose father was a former army officer – was the self-styled leader of the group and called himself the Emperor. Crookes had been vying for leadership of the Brotherhood and constantly tormented and humiliated Wallis and Sayers. For this reason, Sayers and Wallis made plans to kill him. Crookes was stabbed repeatedly in his body, neck, and head, then carried onto a pre-prepared woodpile, doused in lighter fuel and set alight. The following day, Wallis and Sayers returned to the scene to dismember and bury the remains of their victim. When the body was discovered some weeks later, the two students were arrested. A simple and straightforward case with a trivial motive, it would seem.

During the trial, the police, prosecution and judge focused much attention on the thirty-five video films owned by Wallis and Sayers, among them Sam Raimi's *The Evil Dead*. Prosecuting, Charles Miskin QC pointed out that in the film a zombie is chopped up with an axe, carried in a sheet into woods and buried. Miskin implies parallels between the killers' actions and the film, stating,

"Everyone who has heard the evidence in this case would recognise the similarities between the mode of disposal of the body here and in that description." In a sense, Miskin is partially right, as he only mentions disposal of the body and that it was buried in the woods. But there the similarity ends. Crookes wasn't killed indoors, he wasn't killed with an axe, he wasn't carried into the woods in a sheet. Sober judgement dictates that Crookes was buried in the woods because he was murdered in the woods, not because such a scene happened in a zombie film. Also among the films owned by the defendants and named in court were Wes Craven's *Scream* and Fritz Kiersch's *Children of the Corn*, both horror. As these were the only movies mentioned by title, we might surmise that the rest of the collection was non-violent in nature. *Scream* was said to be influential in the crime because it depicted college students killing and being killed. *Children of the Corn* was linked to the case because it contains stabbings and corn is an agricultural product and the three students were studying agriculture.

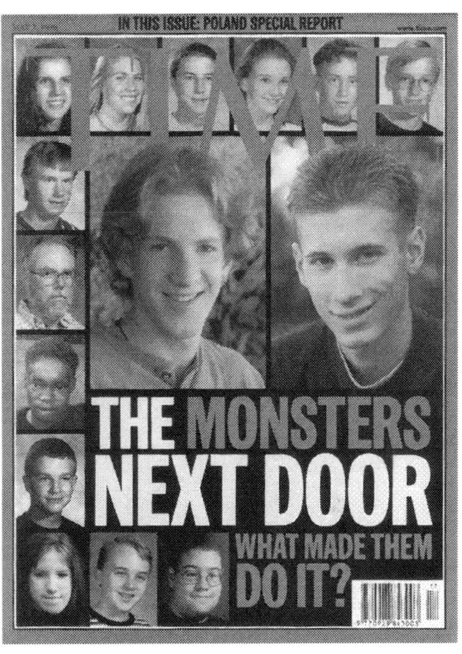

IN THIS ISSUE: POLAND SPECIAL REPORT

TIME

THE MONSTERS NEXT DOOR

WHAT MADE THEM DO IT?

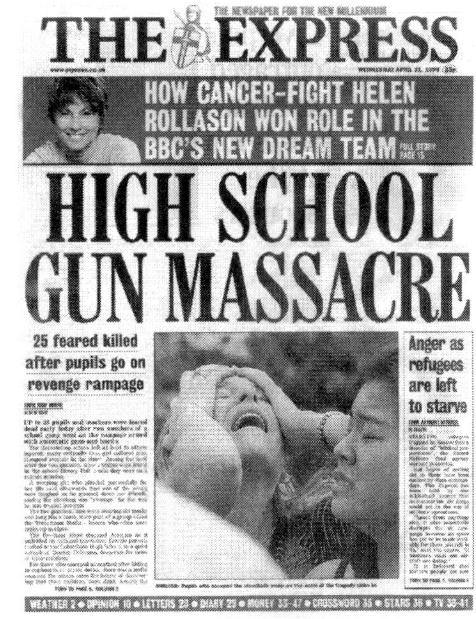

THE NEWSPAPER FOR THE NEW MILLENNIUM

THE EXPRESS

HOW CANCER-FIGHT HELEN ROLLASON WON ROLE IN THE BBC'S NEW DREAM TEAM

HIGH SCHOOL GUN MASSACRE

25 feared killed after pupils go on revenge rampage

Anger as refugees are left to starve

Chief Inspector Dave Stevens said "The videos were pretty innocuous in one sense. They were not banned, they could be purchased in the shops. But I suppose it was the context in which they were watched, what they did to the minds of the defendants."

Stevens seems in no doubt that the films affected the minds of the killers. But in what context does he believe the films were watched? Though his statement is confusing, it seems to imply the defendants watched them with murder in mind, which invalidates the view that the films had made them kill.

Summing up the case, Mr Justice Newman stated, "Videos – not recognisably extreme and designed to be seen for entertainment – have, I have very little doubt from the synopses, served to fuel your fantasies and isolated you from conventional counterbalancing. They carried a potency that could not be readily predicted and served to desensitise you and remove you from the enormity of killing another person by stabbing them."

It's a remarkably similar statement to one made by Judge Morland in summing up the Bulger case, and which undoubtedly influenced Newman. The statement also shows that Newman based his conclusion on synopses of the films. Furthermore, these synopses had been presented to the judge out of context, with every intention of demonstrating their causality.

The story made front page news in the tabloids because of the insignificant film link. "Murder By Video" was the ridiculous front-page headline in the *Express*. "Judge Blames Video Nasties For Murder," stated the *Sun*. "Life For Horror Video Copycats," said the *Daily Star*. The *Daily Star* did a follow-up piece some days later, reporting that, "After being mutilated, [Crookes] was burnt then buried. It was *identical* to scenes in *The Evil Dead*, which was watched by the killers." [Our emphasis.] What was initially described as 'similar' has become 'identical.' The only readers who would know it wasn't true were those who had seen the film. No newspaper attempted to challenge or oppose the Judge's conclusion, and even the comparatively level-headed *Guardian* ran the headline, "Horror videos inspired student killers." The *Daily Mail* didn't use the story as one might expect, relegating it to page forty-one, likely because it was busy on another crusade at the time: generating hatred towards the impending influx of Kosovan refugees who were escaping the Balkan crisis.

Ever on the tailcoats of tragedy, MPs were quick to take advantage of the judge's comments. Alan Beih, Liberal Democrat, said, "This is a very distressing case and should be looked at carefully by the Home Secretary and British Board of Film Classification." Julian Brazier MP, president of the Conservative Family Campaign, demanded stricter control of violent videos. He said, "This case is further proof that innocent people can become victims of crime because of the widespread culture of violent videos and films. There has to be a mechanism whereby films which have passed the classification in the past can be reviewed in the light of new evidence." Dr Adrian Rogers, director of Family Focus, espoused opinions cognate to John Grisham's, stating, "The makers of these films should be held responsible for the dreadful consequences of their work." Jonathan Bartley of the Movement for Christian Democracy said, "We recognise the link between what we see on the screen and how we act are complex, but this is another piece in the jigsaw of cause and effect. There is little doubt now there is a relationship." Roger Gale MP said, "I believe there is a direct relationship between violence on the screen and violent behaviour." Asinine observations like these are self-serving propaganda. They are not made in order to discover the actual truth of the matter, only to serve an agenda.

April 20, 1999. News of the Columbine High School massacre in Littleton, Denver, was broadcast around the world. It was only a matter of time before it would be imitated. Two students, Eric Harris and Dylan Klebold, were members of a small gang known as the Trenchcoat Mafia. Subjugated over the years by the school élite – or 'jocks' as those who excel in sport are known – Harris and Klebold became increasingly segregated and viewed the glorified jocks as enemies. One pupil at the school said, "The ones who are the worst at spreading rumours and lies are the jocks and the cheerleaders." Carrying home-made bombs and guns, Harris and Klebold invaded the school premises and shot dead thirteen people before killing themselves. Some media factions chose to ignore eyewitness accounts – explaining that the killers were specifically targeting the jocks and saying it was their way of getting revenge for the torment and humiliation administered over the years – and invented their own theories as to what inspired the attack. Blaming the school massacre on films was the obvious and most simplistic route. The 1995 crime drama, *The Baseball Diaries*, starring Leonardo DiCaprio, has a dream sequence in which a character wears a long coat and shoots teachers and classmates in school. Other films postulated by the press as potential triggers were *The Faculty*, in which students rebel against alien teachers; *Heathers* – a pupil plots to eliminate despised classmates; *The Craft* – schoolgirls adopt the powers of black magic; and *The Matrix,* because a character wears a long coat and carries guns. The governor of Colorado suggested TV violence may be to blame. Actor Charlton Heston, president of the National Rifle Association, and vehemently opposed to gun control, chose to blame trenchcoats and suggested such items of clothing should be banned.[36] Also targeted as a possible influence was rock star Marilyn Manson. Attempts were made to suggest that Manson's lyrics contained subliminal messages and that his philosophy may have inspired these and other killings. The *Express*, under the header "Shock rocker who filled pair with a thrill to kill", quoted Manson as saying, "if someone hurts me, I'll hurt them back," an ideology plucked from the Old Testament. The quote was immediately followed by, "one of Tuesday's gunmen had apparently spoken of his schoolmates having made his life hell," implying a link between the Columbine revenge shootings and Manson's words.[37]

Computer games were also cited as causative. Shoot-em-ups were said to be regularly played by the two killers. The *Express* picked up on this loose connection and, under the title "Video nasty you can't buy because it's for free," stated, "games such as *Quake* and *Doom* were alleged to have influenced US teenagers Eric Harris and Dylan Klebold who massacred thirteen of their Colorado classmates." The report then referenced a cover disc supplied with *PC Zone* magazine that contained a free demo of a new game called *Kingpin*, rallying that "If the game escapes a UK ban it would give manufacturers a green light to make their products as cinematic and gruesome as possible." The killers had referred to *Doom* in a videotaped statement recorded in the build-up to the massacre. "It's going to be like fucking *Doom*," Klebold said, with Harris adding, "That fucking shotgun is straight out of *Doom*." Klebold spoke of his family: "You made me what I am. You added to the rage."

But, like Dunblane and Hungerford, the foremost problem was gun accessibility. Even the motive reflected that of Thomas Hamilton, who had felt persecuted by the community before taking revenge. A public Internet poll as to where the blame for Columbine lay brought the following results:[38]

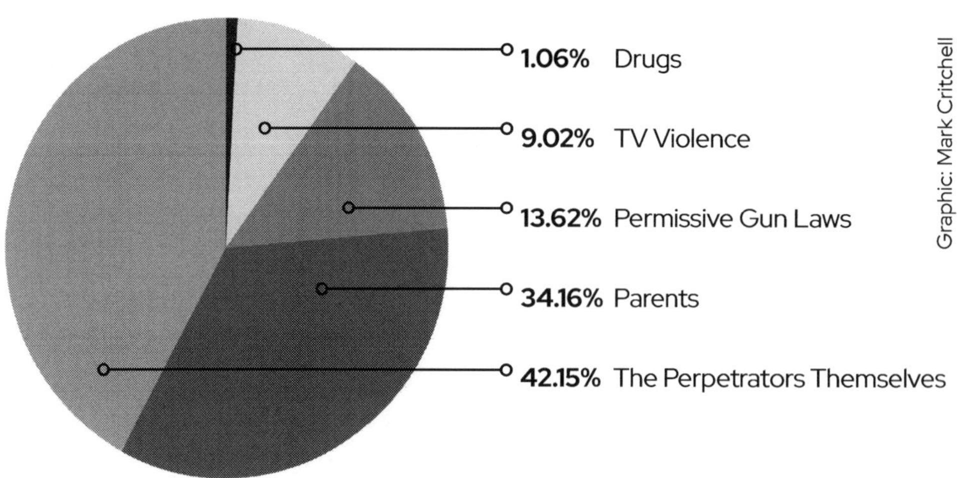

It is remarkable how low TV violence scores, despite the attempts to influence public feeling. Interesting also is the high rating of parents. Klebold's father was a military man, and a military connection is a statistic that appears in many cases – see also Michael Ryan, Julian Knight, Anthony Haskett, Scott Richards, Neil Sayers, and Colin Ireland.

Time magazine ran an oddly slanted article on the school shootings. There is no doubting the appalling nature of the crime, but the article went out of its way to demonise the killers and beatify the victims. One victim "dabbled in witchcraft before she was born again", another was "an avid soccer fan", others were "into wrestling, golfing and fishing"; "writing poetry, composing songs..."; "planned to become a missionary..."; "earned a spot on the football team"; "travelled with his dad to Mexico to build a house for the poor." Survivors are quoted as saying, "God made us invisible," "God put an invisible shield around us," "God gave me an inner peace," "God told me to get out of there," and so on. The killers are simply quoted as saying, "Oh, you fucking nerd. Tonight's a good time to die." The purpose is to present the perpetrators as abnormal and unpleasant. But the truth is, prior to committing their crime, they appeared no different to anyone else, which is why people who knew them were totally taken aback by their actions.[39]

On Wednesday, April 28, 1999, in Taber, a small farming town in Canada, a fourteen-year-old schoolboy mimicked the media reports of the Columbine school shootings. He entered his local school and shot two pupils with a sawn-off automatic rifle. It was reported that he wore a trenchcoat similar to those the media said were worn by Harris and Klebold. One of the pupils died, the other was seriously injured. The time lapse between the Columbine news flash and the Taber event is remarkably similar to that of Michael Ryan mimicking Julian Knight. On the same day, a gun attack occurred at Gloucestershire College of Art and Technology. A sixteen-year-old fired three shots through an open window. However, no injuries occurred, and the firearm proved to be an air pistol.

On July 22, 1999, the *Express* ran the headline, "Horror film boys left stab friend for dead." The report began, "Two teenage boys stabbed a friend after watching a horror film..." and mentioned four paragraphs later that the attackers were using cocaine. The accused film was Wes Craven's *Scream*. To persuade readers that the movie was indeed responsible, a brief and selective synopsis concurred that "some American teenagers are stabbed to death by two of their friends." Drug-fuelled delinquents had carried out a violent attack. Because they had watched a movie doesn't suggest implication.

The *Express*, November 14, 1999, reported that the David Fincher film, *Fight Club*, starring Brad Pitt, Edward Norton, and Helena Bonham Carter, had inspired violent scenes in North America and Brazil:

> The victim of the Seattle fight, 16-year-old Jonathan Wills, suffered convulsions and bleeding from nose, mouth and right ear. Local Sheriff John Urquhart said the teenager and his friends had been re-enacting *Fight Club* after going to see the film. The fighters wore gloves but no head gear... In another outburst linked to the film, a 24-year-old Brazilian medical student at a screening of *Fight Club* in Rio de Janeiro earlier this month opened fire in the cinema, killing three people and wounding five.

When neo-Nazi David Copeland was tried and convicted for a series of nail bombings in London in 1999, the media made baffling attempts to draw movies into the final analysis. Copeland admitted that he had wanted to spread fear and start a race war, targeting ethnic minorities, and was later diagnosed as having paranoid schizophrenia. But Copeland's warped political views were often sidestepped or embellished: Channel 4 made a casual reference to Copeland having repeatedly watched the 1986 psychological horror film, *Henry: Portrait of a Serial Killer*. The *News of the World* took another leap when it alleged that he had watched all three *Hellraiser* movies, not omitting the fact that the films had been "turned into videos" – as though the transfer process from film to video tinctured them with some kind of influential evil. One of Copeland's bomb attacks left a victim with a six-inch nail in his skull, later extracted in hospital. The *News of the World* tastelessly posted a mug shot of Copeland next to Pinhead, the most prominent character in the *Hellraiser* films, whose entire head is embedded with nails. The picture was the same size as that of the mad bomber, as though both characters were equally responsible for the atrocities. The tenuous film association appeared to be, once again, a covert attempt to deflect blame from deeper rooted issues, in this instance extreme right-wing factions.

Scapegoating movies is part of society, a vicious circle in which an accusation is made, picked up by the press, embellished, and disseminated into the public domain. The original accuser will then adopt the press reports as independent corroboration. The charge snowballs out of all proportion, yet, if the clutter and nonsense is cut away, the original catalyst is revealed to be the pea of an idea. It may only be fabricated accusation, but it makes for sensational headlines and

Several press reports concerning nailbomber David Copeland concentrated more on the fact that he watched horror videos than his actions or far-right associations. *News of the World*, July 2, 2000.

HELL RAISER

Horror movie drove Nazi bomber to kill

HORROR: Burned drinkers stagger from Soho pub blasted by Copeland

FACE OF EVIL: Nailbomber Copeland blew victims apart

FACE OF EVIL: The nailed head of film villain Pinhead

EXCLUSIVE

BY NADIA COHEN

WARPED Nazi maniac David Copeland hatched his nailbomb plans for mass murder after watching the infamous Hellraiser horror films. His favourite was Hellraiser III: Hell On Earth.

The blood-curdling hit was one of the series of graphic movies-turned into videos–about a serial killer called Pinhead whose head and face is embedded with nails.

The monster–played by Doug Bradley–rips his victims apart with hooks. And the film's chilling slogan is: "What began in Hell will end on Earth."

Last night Copeland's brother Jonathan, 28, told the News of the World: "David would always repeat that line. There were three Hellraiser videos available then and he owned all of them." Copeland, 24, would wallow in his bedroom, festering with hatred for gays and the black, Asian and Jewish communities–then rewind the videos and watch them again, formulating his plan.

Jonathan recalled: "I once watched one of them ... and that was ...

the grim theme of the Hellraiser videos, he boasted ... intention was to cause murder ... damage ...

... round snarling all the time looking at the floor, so he always bumped into people. I think he liked the nickname, but nothing made him laugh. In all our family photos he never smiled. He lived up to his nickname and just looks angry."

Sexually David was a late developer. He ... reach puberty until he ...

... immediately race out to meet her in a playground near our house. He told me that they used to have sex on a toy train in the playground.

"It sounded really funny to me but David said he loved doing it on that toy train."

In 199? David left home to travel ... Thailand for six months but ... weeks ...

... fore and Jonathan talked him out of it. David never managed to forge any lasting friendships with other lads either.

But he adored the pet rat he named Heinrich Himmler after Hitler's right-hand man in the Nazi party.

When he was arrested David–who slept under two Nazi flags ...

newspaper sales, and provides much needed attention for ideas-redundant politicians and self-proclaimed moral crusaders. It also offers potential lenient treatment for criminals who don't wish to take proper responsibility for crimes they have committed.

Many media reports are founded on prevarications, as we have seen, but they still have an influential impact on public perception and, ironically, the workings of the BBFC – as we shall see in the next chapter.

Sex & Wrecks

'AT THE LEAST PROVOCATION'

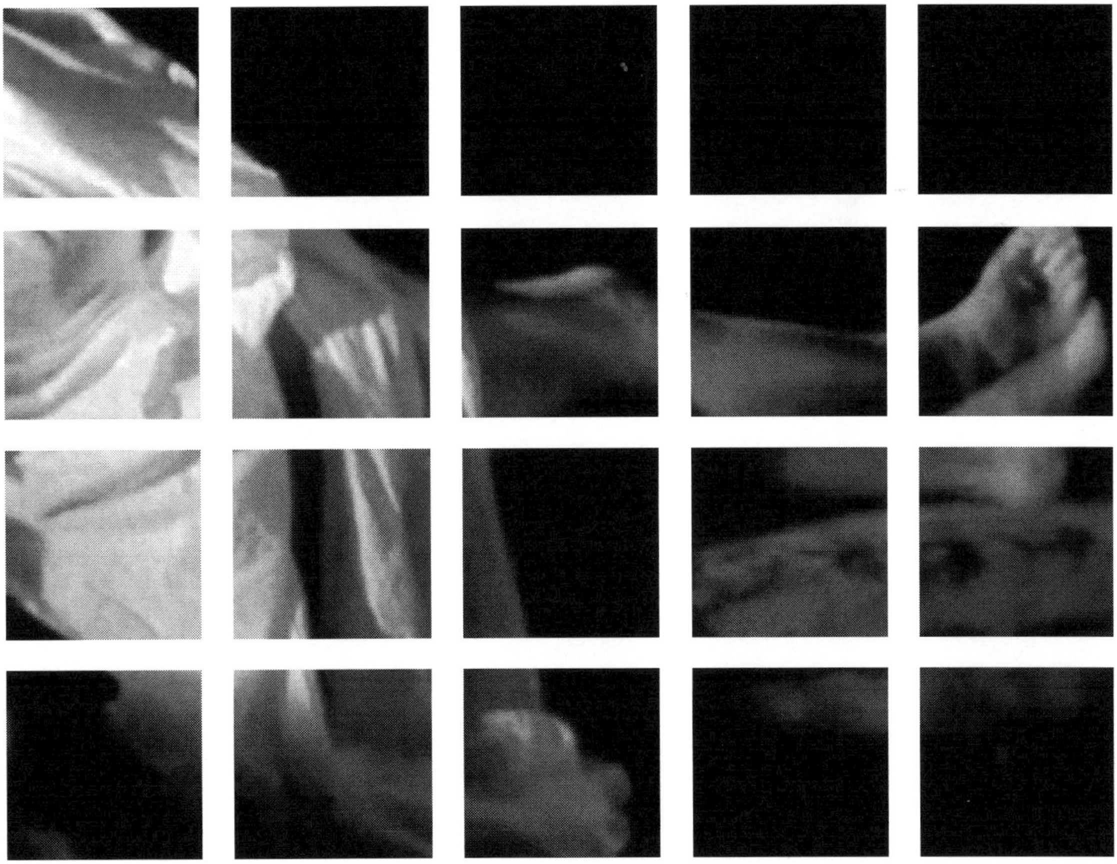

WITH THE MEDIA furore that followed the murder of the infant James Bulger, and the publication of Professor Newson's *Video Violence and the Protection of Young Children*, Parliament bowed to pressure and supported a strengthening of the Video Recordings Act. This came in the form of amendments contained within the Criminal Justice and Public Order Act 1994.

As outlined in a press release issued in July 1994, the BBFC originally regarded these amendments as pertaining exclusively to works exempt from classification, such as music videos and videos "designed to inform, educate or instruct." Under the new law, the depiction of drug use (added to the criteria already outlined in CLAMPDOWN) would now also forfeit exemption. In fact, the amendments as they finally appeared were wider ranging and not restricted to exempt works. Instead – as the following excerpt indicates – they required the BBFC to consider whether a video was likely to cause harm to its potential audience, or to society through the behaviour of its audience.

> 4A. (1) The designated authority [the BBFC] shall, in making any determination as to the suitability of a video work, have special regard (among the other relevant factors) to any harm that may be caused to potential viewers or, through their behaviour, to society by the manner in which the work deals with—
>
> (a) criminal behaviour;
>
> (b) illegal drugs;
>
> (c) violent behaviour or incidents;
>
> (d) horrific behaviour or incidents; or
>
> (e) human sexual activity.
>
> 'potential viewer' means any person (including a child or young person) who is likely to view the video work in question if a classification certificate or a classification certificate of a particular description were issued;
>
> 'suitability' means suitability for the issue of a classification certificate or suitability for the issue of a certificate of a particular description;
>
> 'violent behaviour' includes any act inflicting or likely to result in the infliction of injury; and any behaviour or activity referred to in subsection (1)(a) to (e) above shall be taken to include behaviour or activity likely to stimulate or encourage it.[1]

As with the Video Recordings Act, this new legislation was passed quickly, rashly and was only deemed necessary because of the influence of a moral panic.

Few films are rejected outright by the BBFC. From September 1985 to April 1989, a period when film companies were still coming to terms with the Video Recordings Act, the Board refused a certificate to twenty-six videos. The titles included the 1967 psychedelic opus, *The Trip*, through to the DPP branded 'nasty', *Island of Death*, submitted to the Board under the title of *Psychic Killer II* – presumably in an attempt to hoodwink the BBFC into thinking the film was a follow-up to the unrelated *Psychic Killer*, which had been passed for theatrical release in 1979.[2]

1967's *The Trip* also falls foul of the new Video Recordings Act.

Why so few rejections? Film distributors were less willing to submit possibly contentious titles – the whole classification process being too expensive to take unnecessary risks – hence the BBFC can truthfully say they reject very few films. In 1998, five films were rejected on video, three between 1995-96, one in 1993, three in 1992, and none in 1991. Rape as titillation, sexual subjugation and scenes of sexual violence feature in many rejected works; persistent spanking between clearly consenting adults, which results in the "reddening of the buttocks",[3] will also lead to rejection. Law Lords state that the consent of a victim in masochistic practice is no defence to a charge of actual bodily harm. Films have been banned on other grounds, notably criminal libel (*International Guerillas*), excessive violence and dangerous combat techniques (*Kickboxer 4: The Aggressor*), schoolgirl uniforms (*Sixteen Special*), blasphemy (*Visions of Ecstasy*), and a focus on the details of torture (*Boy Meets Girl*). Manga animation has always proven problematic with the Board, and two such films were refused a certificate in 1996 (*Urotsukidoji IV Part One: The Secret Garden* and *La*

Rejected by the BBFC. Below: *Visions of Ecstasy* – 'contemptuous of the divinity of Christ.'
Bottom: *Boy Meets Girl* – a film about 'torture and captivity'.

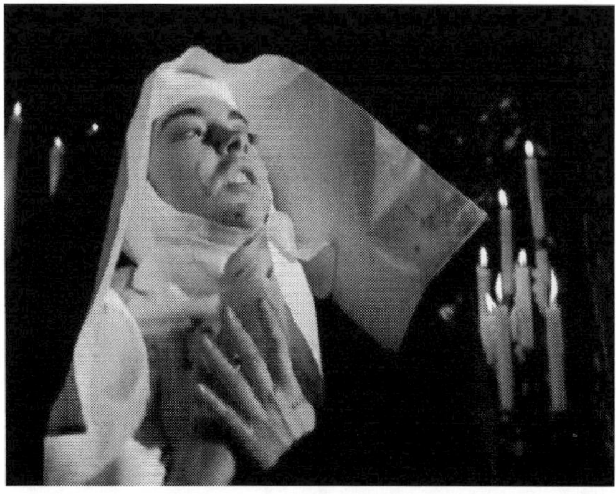

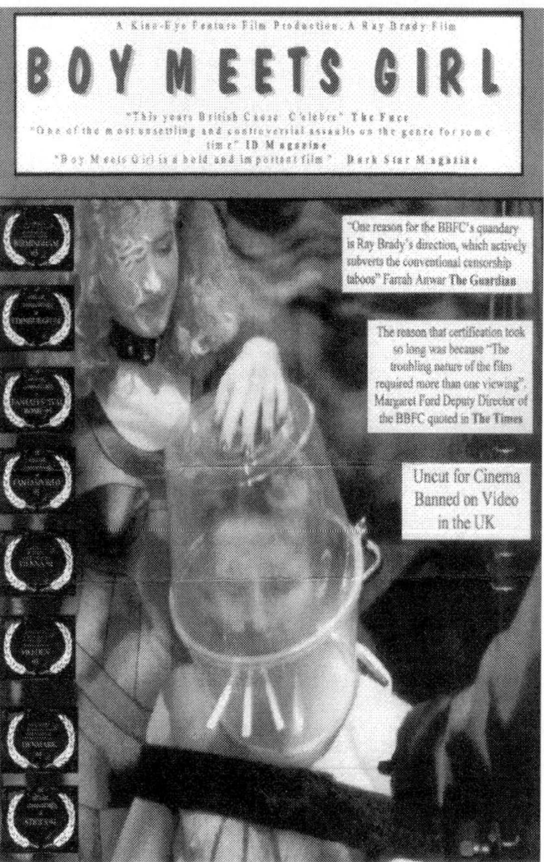

Blue Girl). Several documentaries have been banned for including imitable weapons (*SAS Weapons & Training*) and for "promoting gross violence and selling its pleasures" (*Bare Fist: The Sport That Wouldn't Die*). In the case of at least one film (*Banned from Television*), the BBFC appears unable to provide a quantifiable reason for rejection.[4] (See APPENDIX for more.)

Films are rejected when the Board decides that cuts will "not make sufficient difference to the nature of the work to prevent its being found depraving and corrupting under British obscenity law." In some cases, a film has been rejected because the distributor declines to make the cuts required by the Board. But then, the fact that the Board examines a film and requests cuts is no guarantee the work will be granted a certificate anyway – as was proven with Jim VanBebber's *Deadbeat at Dawn*, a low-budget action thriller concerning urban warfare. After examination, the BBFC informed the distributors (Exploited) that *Deadbeat at Dawn* would need to be resubmitted with a total of fifteen cuts (2m 12s) before the proposed 18 certificate could be given. However, several weeks after its decision, the Board informed the distributors that even in this trimmed form the work would not now be suitable for classification. A letter from James Ferman, the Board's director, outlined some reasons for the change in stance:

> By requesting the cutting of all shots glamorising the use of imitable weaponry, we hoped to reduce the violence sufficiently to make the video acceptable as an '18', but this cutting merely revealed that the frequency and intensity of violent behaviour and incidents was an insuperable problem in itself. All the male gang members resort to violence at the least provocation, and the violence they inflict results in maiming, mutilation and death. Violent problems provoke violent solutions, and the acting out of violent impulses provides the only pleasure on offer. Given the problem of violence by youth gangs in Britain, the Board is concerned that this video could attract viewing by young offenders whose own behaviour might be validated and confirmed by the behaviour of the characters, resulting in harm to society and members of society.

Along with Screen Edge, Exploited were one of the few video companies dedicated to releasing obscure, low-budget cult films in Britain. (See APPENDIX.) This sort of material doesn't sit well with the BBFC, who are more comfortable and lenient with what it perceives to be 'art' as opposed to 'commerce.'[5] Take, for instance, the Board's defence of Lars von Trier's controversial *The Idiots* following their decision to classify it as 18 without cuts:

> This challenging art film, in Danish, concerns a group of young people who have formed a commune founded on 'anti-middle class ideology.' As part of that philosophy, they pretend to be 'idiots' (i.e. people with learning difficulties) and behave accordingly in public places.
>
> The BBFC considered the possible offensiveness of this behaviour to members of the public who are disabled, and to those who are concerned with them. The view of the film, taken as a whole, is however a positive and sensitive one – particularly when real disabled characters are involved.

The Board can be even more patronising when it comes to ventures that fall short of its artistic yardstick. In these instances, the Board might request cuts or suggest some post-production tampering. This happened with *Henry: Portrait*

Henry and Otis watch their exploits on tape in *Henry: Portrait of a Serial Killer.*

of a Serial Killer. A sequence in which two killers murder a family had originally pulled back to reveal that the event was a video recording, watched now by the killers. To secure a video release, not only did distributors Electric Video have to appease the BBFC with cuts to *Henry*, but they also had to juxtapose this sequence to make it clear much earlier that the killers were in fact watching a tape recording of their actions. As a result, the potency and whole point of the sequence is lost.

If this 'hands-on' approach failed to turn *Henry* into a better film (just a classifiable one), there are plenty of other instances in which the Board claim a film has benefited from their intervention.

The character played by Arnold Schwarzenegger in the theatrical release of *Eraser*, for instance, is not the same as the character in the video version. To attain a 15 rating on video, thirty-eight cuts were made to the film (on top of the five already required to secure a theatrical 18). This change in category was at the behest of the distributor after the film flopped at the box office. The result was a less sadistic hero and, according to the Board, a film "which proved to have far greater appeal to the British audience".[6]

For *Lethal Weapon 2*, scenes were removed that showed Mel Gibson slamming a car door into the head of a bad guy following his girlfriend's murder.

Replacing these scenes, Gibson now carries his girlfriend's body along a beach, vowing revenge. According to James Ferman, this change didn't simply remove excessively violent footage, but allowed the Gibson character to grieve – and the film was the better for it.

Not only is the Board "prepared to read scripts for British film-makers"[7] advising how best to make films that accord to BBFC standards, they also take receipt of major international films in 'rough cut' form so that film companies can tailor the end product to the widest possible audience. This was the case with three films during the period 1995-96 – amongst them James Bond's *GoldenEye*, which was "carefully crafted to achieve a 12".[8]

The messed-up *Batman Forever* was re-edited by distributors on both sides of the Atlantic, with the BBFC requesting even more cuts to achieve a rating suitable for British children. This was heralded as another success for the Board when the advisory Parental Guidance (PG) enabled *Batman Forever* to top the box office charts for 1995.

"He likes the idea of being in Hollywood," one ex-examiner said of James Ferman in a TV documentary.[9] When Steven Spielberg was working on *Indiana Jones and the Temple of Doom*, Ferman flew out to the US to "help" the director with cutting the film for British audiences. Spielberg's films have met with remarkably little resistance with the BBFC. At a time when the Board was exercising a stricter policy in order to – amongst other things – "protect children from excessive fear",[10] *Jurassic Park* was only classified PG but had children cowering in fear wherever it played.[11] *Saving Private Ryan* was another Spielberg film that was given a seemingly lenient (15) certificate and, as a result, met with public outcry. The film comprises some of the most brutal and realistic depictions of mutilation and carnage committed to celluloid – not to mention one of the most protracted stabbing scenes.

When the Board rejected Exploited's intended debut release, the stalk-and-slash movie, William Lustig's *Maniac*, they did so on the grounds that it was "unhealthy and dangerous because of the way that the killing of women is linked with the sexual arousal of men." The Board's decision to reject *Maniac* came back-to-back with their decision to pass Adrian Lyne's *Lolita* uncut for the cinema. The latter was afforded more analysis, with the BBFC explaining that Lyne's film of Nabokov's novel – concerning a middle-aged man's infatuation with a "precocious under-age girl" – was viewed by the police and distinguished experts in the fields of child psychiatry and sex abuse before a decision was reached. Ironically, given the decision to ban *Maniac*, the BBFC determined that the confrontational *Lolita* should be passed on the pretext that "adult cinemagoers have a right to judge for themselves."[12]

Exploited had acquired the rights to *Maniac* and submitted it to the BBFC in November 1997. An initial search by the Board revealed the film hadn't previously been classified and Exploited were quoted a classification fee of £941+VAT. This figure was dropped to £535+VAT when the Board subsequently discovered that *Maniac* had indeed been submitted previously, for theatrical release in 1981, but rejected.[13]

The BBFC normally expect to reach a decision on a film within seventy-two hours of viewing. They are, however, under no obligation to stick to this timeframe and the processing period can take considerably longer.

"I was obviously curious to know how long the classification process would take so I could plan my release schedule around it," Exploited's David Gregory wrote in *Samhain*.[14] "The BBFC themselves were unwilling to commit to any length of time, not even a ballpark figure. In any other business paying anything like that for a service would get you all kinds of feedback, certainly including a delivery date. But what I was starting to realise was that the BBFC do not consider their work a service, it is a privilege."

Exploited finally received word on *Maniac* in a letter dated January 12, 1998. The film had been examined but was being referred for further consideration, and it was unlikely a decision would be reached within the next five working days. Time rolled by and Exploited were once again forced to chase up the matter. When Gregory finally got through to James Ferman, he was told that *Maniac* had been rejected, and that he really should do his homework before submitting material in the future – a reference to the fact that *Maniac* had already been submitted and rejected by the Board some sixteen years earlier (notwithstanding that the BBFC itself had originally overlooked this fact). Exploited received written confirmation of the film's status on March 20, 1998, eight months after submitted it.

Low-budget films that had proliferated prior to the Video Recordings Act were all but gone. But suddenly, hitherto problematic films *The Exorcist*, *The Texas Chain Saw Massacre* and *A Clockwork Orange* were granted a certificate (for cinema and video release).[15] The decision was profound; the ban imposed on these three particular films had been so long and often debated that their unavailability was absorbed as part of British culture, the status quo. Even *The*

MANIAC
JOE SPINELL · CAROLINE MUNRO
WILLIAM LUSTING
JAY CHATTAWAY
JOHN PACKARD
ANDREW GARRONI e WILLIAM LUSTIG
C.A. ROSENBERG e JOE SPINELL
UNA MAGNUM MOTION PICTURE
colore
distribuzione
eurocopfilms

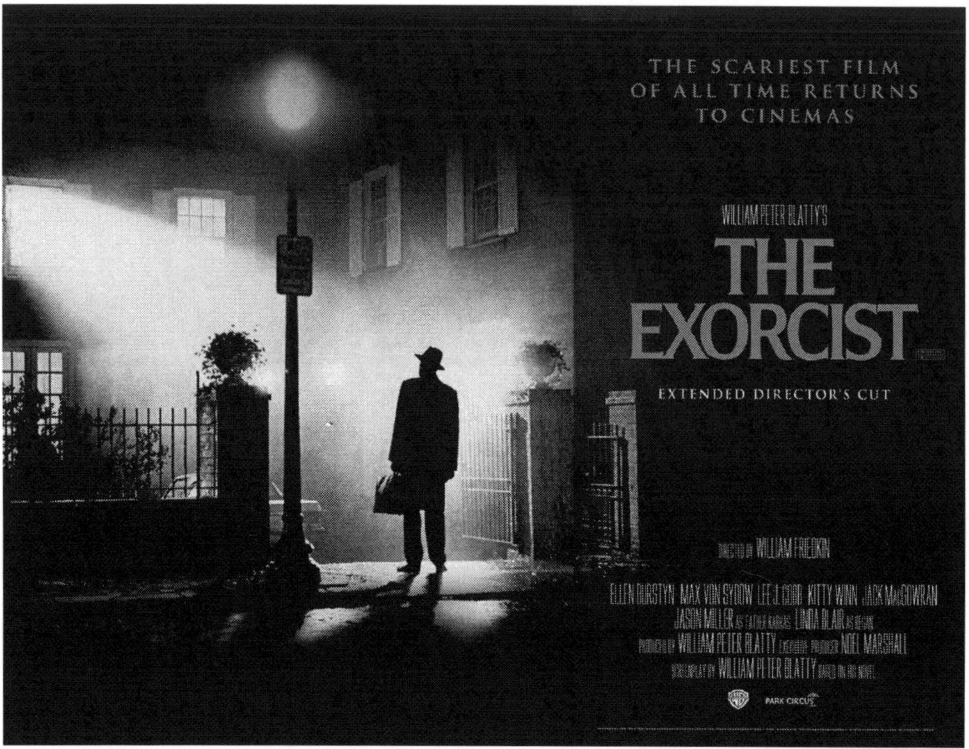

Driller Killer, one of the most vilified of the 'video nasties' and one of the first to be prosecuted under the Obscene Publications Act, found itself with a certificate in 1999, and a terrestrial television airing, after a fifteen-year ban. No doubt this decision was primarily due to director Abel Ferrara's subsequent credibility as a 'serious' film-maker, with his more recent films, *King of New York* and *The Addiction*.

Following in the footsteps of *The Driller Killer* were other films that had once languished on the DPP list, including *Shogun Assassin*, *Tenebrae*, *The Toolbox Murders*, and *Axe*. But the BBFC wasn't about to call an amnesty on all the former 'nasties' – they rejected *The Last House on the Left* for its "explicit and sadistic sexual violence" – but evidently some were seen to have merit, and perhaps nothing too offensive that couldn't be remedied with a few snips.

The newly classified former 'nasties' didn't appear in the same versions that were available pre-VRA. Tainted by their inclusion on the DPP list, they were now released in different form to that which had been considered obscene and liable to prosecution in the eighties. In the case of *Tenebrae*, this difference is courtesy of a few seconds of excised gore;[16] for *Axe*, nineteen seconds of cuts

Censorship extends to promotional artwork. Original poster art for *Tenebrae* included a neck wound and trickle of blood (see page 410), replaced by a bowtie for the 1990s re-release.

were made, replaced in part by scenes lifted from elsewhere in the movie, played in slow motion; in *The Driller Killer*, the difference was one slight cut and the addition of material of nearly six-and-a-half minutes by distributor Visual Film.

The apparent relaxation of BBFC attitudes and the emergence of formerly 'banned' material came after James Ferman's retirement in December 1998. Director of the BBFC for twenty-three years, Ferman regarded himself as the last of the 'traditional' censors; his successor, Robin Duval, would not simply have to contend with film and video as he had done, but also digital technology and the Internet. Ferman announced his retirement on the cusp of some particularly hostile press, and the Board's decision to pass several highly contentious films.

Ferman ran the BBFC with a draconian hand, contractually binding those who worked there to secrecy. When one employee transgressed this rule, she received a solicitor's letter informing her of her duty and obligation to the Board. Maggie Mills, another examiner, called Ferman "a control freak" and described how he:

would sit in his office alone, late into the night, obsessively watching videos. His lack of contact with the normal human world showed; he ran the BBFC as his personal fiefdom, overriding those who disagreed with him.[17]

Another disgruntled employee told the *Guardian* in February 1994 that "censorship here is not a democratic process… in reality, James Ferman calls the shots." That same month Ferman proposed to sack thirteen part-time examiners who had passed a vote of no confidence in the director. It was primarily Ferman's decision that kept *The Exorcist* from seeing a video release for so long. He flatly refused to review his position on the matter until December 1991, when examiners forced a vote. But even with a majority vote to grant the film a video certificate (fifteen voted yes, one wanted to maintain the ban and three abstained), the video remained shelved.

Ferman defended his stance on *The Exorcist* many times, offering a whole gamut of reasons why the film shouldn't be made available for video. These ranged from the predictable (the harm the film might inflict on impressionable young girls viewing it in their bedroom) through to the downright peculiar (the problem it raises with regards to the power of the supernatural). In 1992, principal examiner Guy Phelps offered another explanation: the Board feared "the potential use of the film in terrifying children as a part of 'satanic' abuse. We know that videos are used in this way..."

(Although it didn't result in a video certificate for *The Exorcist*, satanic ritual abuse was exposed as a myth in 1994, following a three-year investigation.)

Another film that suffered a long and meaningless ban under Ferman was *The Texas Chain Saw Massacre*, despite most of the violence being implied, while Ferman himself considered the film "a very good piece of craft".[18] Paradoxically, the power tool of the film's title became an issue in itself: *Hollywood Chainsaw Hookers* – an otherwise unrelated low-budget horror-comedy – had to have the word "chainsaw" removed from its title and replaced instead with an image of a chainsaw. The Board conceded, when it passed *The Texas Chain Saw Massacre* in March 1999, that "The notoriety of the film may owe a lot to its original rejection by the BBFC in 1975."

The threat that video was said to have posed in the early days of the Video Recordings Act was to return anew a decade later. Throughout the nineties the pressure was on again to curb video sex and violence – or, as some argued, any video that wasn't suitable for children. Following the massacres in Dunblane and Tasmania (see THE BIG INFLUENCE), Warner Home Video considered the scheduled video release of *Natural Born Killers* "inappropriate" and pulled the plug on it indefinitely (despite already having obtained a video certificate). The theatrical release of the film had met with substantial fuss in the media, with calls for it to be banned on account of supposed copycat crimes.[19] Addressing these concerns, the BBFC issued a press statement outlining their reason for passing *Natural Born Killers* 18 without cuts.

When Ros Hodgkiss resigned from her job as an examiner at the BBFC, she told the *Guardian* that whenever stories condemning violent culture broke in the tabloids,

Like the VRA never happened...
Below: The Home Secretary is forced to tighten video legislation. *Daily Mail*, April 2, 1994.
Next page: Lost innocence. *Daily Express*, November 26, 1993; Michael Medved's influential book.

Daily Mail, Saturday, April 2, 1994

AFTER EXPERTS FINALLY ACCEPT THE CONNECTION BETWEEN SCREEN VIOLENCE AND YOUNGSTERS' BEHAVIOUR

Howard on fast-forward

Home Secretary will act to keep video nasties out of the home

By JOHN DEANS, Political Correspondent

HOME SECRETARY Michael Howard is ready to put pressure on film censors to stop more video nasties from being viewed in the home.

He plans to meet members of the independent British Board of Film Classification to stress the need for tougher action to prevent so many violence and sex films corrupting the nation's children.

Mr Howard: 'Deep concern'

Clare Short: 'Time to act'

THE HORRORS ON SALE IN ANY HIGH STREET

COMMENTARY

by ROY HATTERSLEY

Phoney freedom that damages us all

whatever the facts, there was a reigning in [at the Board]. Decisions undoubtedly became more conservative. In such a climate it is difficult to keep your cool and remain objective.[20]

The press reported on March 4, 1993, that American TV networks were turning down BBC dramas – like *The Men's Room* and Melvyn Bragg's *A Time to Dance* – on account of their sex and violence. Home Secretary Kenneth Clarke urged programme makers to show common sense in the battle against crime. (When in July 1994 the BBC's licence fee was confirmed for another five years, it was on the understanding that the corporation publish a statement of promises to cut back sex and violence and deliver the promise to everyone with a TV licence.)

Following a remark made by actor Sir Anthony Hopkins, that he may pull out of a sequel to *Silence of the Lambs* because he didn't want to contribute to a climate of violence, the onus shifted from television to the BBFC. Hopkins may have been smarting from remarks made about *Silence of the Lambs* in *Hollywood vs. America*, a highly publicised and inflammatory book by US film critic Michael Medved. The book accused the entertainment industry – in particular, Hollywood – of following "its own dark obsessions, rather than giving the people what it wants." Hollywood was said to ignore and assault the values of ordinary, God-fearing American families.[21]

VISIONS OF VIOLENCE

Children have grown used to scenes of simulated slaughter

SICK SCRIPT: Was James Bulger's killing a video-inspired act of brutality?

Corruption of the video generation

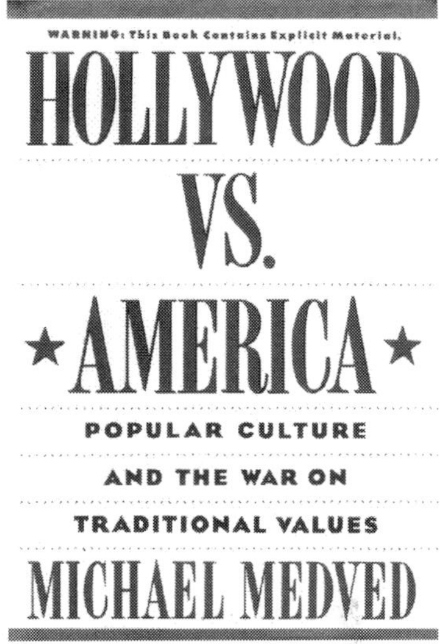

As noted, towards the end of 1993, the media was awash with speculation concerning the death of James Bulger, with many reports linking the murder to the video *Child's Play 3*. The *Daily Express*[22] claimed to have a list of the videos the young killers had watched in the weeks leading up to the fateful day, but weren't going to divulge it because doing so "might persuade youngsters to go out and rent copies." If they had divulged it, readers would have seen that *Child's Play 3* wasn't listed.

Home Secretary Michael Howard was set to put pressure on the BBFC and introduce tougher measures for video shops that rented films to the wrong age groups. Liberal Democrat MP David Alton wanted to go further and ban the home rental of any video containing "inappropriate models." He intended this restriction to take the form of a new classification: "Unsuitable for Children." Even though Alton's madcap proposal would effectively ban anything that wasn't made specifically for kids, the panic generated by the media brought him much support, and the backing of 300 MPs from all parties. In light of this, Howard was pressured to concede to some of Alton's demands or run the risk of almost certain Commons defeat. The result was a new clause added to the Criminal Justice Bill (which can be found at the beginning of this chapter).

Having faced the daunting prospect of Alton's original proposal, James Ferman told the *Times*, "From now on, we are going to have to cut more and classify higher." The victory that was the "toughest-ever crackdown on violent videos"[23] put the BBFC into a panic and placed a halt on classifying any film it believed

might be affected by the legislation. Under the new ruling, the Board had a statutory obligation and a responsibility to protect viewers from harmful video material. One film on hold was the British horror thriller *Beyond Bedlam*, despite initially having been given an interim 18 certificate for video only a week earlier.[24] *Heavenly Creatures*, the true story of two girls who murdered a parent in 1950s New Zealand, was given an 18 certificate rather than the proposed 15 for no reason other than that the killers were adolescent.

Any film that associated killing and juveniles became problematic in light of the Bulger murder. "Terror is as close as the boy next door" was the tagline for Douglas Jackson's *The Paperboy*, one such film that idled away for several months, until November 1994 when it was passed 18. Shedding his *Home Alone* persona, Macaulay Culkin was an 'evil' child in *The Good Son*, which was granted an 18 with cuts in September 1995. *Mikey*, on the other hand, was rejected outright in December 1996. The furore over *Child's Play 3* resulted in CIC withdrawing its forthcoming release, *Dollman vs. Demonic Toys*.

Newspaper headlines at the end of April 1994 focused on 'lost innocence'. In a world dominated by television, computers, drugs, crime and career worries, only three per cent of children considered themselves to be living the carefree lives depicted by Enid Blyton – so claimed psychologist Dr David Lewis.[25] More curbs on video were suggested by MPs. One idea was to hand a notice to any adult buying or renting an 18 certificated film, reminding them not to let children view the film. Another idea was a compulsory identity card for all schoolchildren visiting a video shop.

Before its release in Britain, British transport police requested a viewing of the comedy crime drama, *Money Train*, starring Wesley Snipes, Woody Harrelson and

Jennifer Lopez. It had scenes that concerned them, and which had supposedly encouraged the murder of a subway toll booth operator in New York. Columbia Tristar released a press statement condemning an "isolated act of senseless violence."

The screen violence debate raged on. The world and its filmmakers were divided. Some considered the idea of a movie inciting real-life violence to be absurd (including directors John Landis, Paul Verhoeven, Michael Winner, and Quentin Tarantino), some believed that film-makers had a responsibility to society to refrain from violence (David Puttnam), while others blamed everyone but themselves (Jon Amiel).[26]

Experimental psychologist Michael Yardley counted, frame by frame, the number of guns and killings in the most popular videos of 1995 and deduced from the high volume that viewers were being given an unspoken justification for real violence. "It is time to challenge film-makers who routinely peddle this pornography of violence," he determined. In August 1996, the National Viewers' and Listeners Association released figures from their own poll concerning the movies of the previous year. Not surprisingly, they called for more control in dealing with Hollywood action and thriller movies.

"Time to sack this feeble censor" opined the film critic for the *Daily Mail* on December 13, 1996. The remark was in reference to a statement made by James Ferman earlier in the week, where the BBFC director put the culture of violence permeating mainstream filmmaking "beyond the reach of British law." There was, said Ferman, no scope to make further cuts because the BBFC were already rigorous in their approach. Ferman may have been "fighting a losing battle," concurred the *Mail*, "but he is losing it partly because of his own half-heartedness."[27]

The tabloids whipped themselves into a lather over Ferman's proclamation. The government tried to impress upon the public that it shared their concerns over video violence, and the danger it presented to the nation, its youth and, seemingly, its thugs: "Young offenders are set to be barred from watching violent videos in institutions," reported the *Express*, August 18, 1997.

The relationship between the BBFC and the new Labour government was never a particularly good one. Labour, promoting moral values in their party conferences, as did all politicians, came to office in 1997 amidst the furore surrounding several particularly controversial films. No sooner had the brouhaha on one film died down (invariably after it had been passed, released and people got a chance to see it), another film jumped up to take its place. First it was violence, with the likes of *Reservoir Dogs*, *Pulp Fiction* and *Natural Born Killers*, then followed sex, or rather 'unnatural' ideas about sex, which colluded in *Kids*,[28] *Crash*,[29] *Kissed*,[30] *Lolita* and *The Idiots*, to further embarrass the authorities. The fad that was the 'educational video' also brought its share of problems, notably in the form of *Executions*,[31] *Hookers: Sex for Sale* and *Everyday...Operations*.[32]

In December 1997, the newly elected "people's government" intervened to block the automatic appointment of Lord Birkett as successor to Lord Harewood, the retiring president of the BBFC. This unprecedented step was taken in "a bid to make the board more accountable to Parliament and public taste"[33] and resulted in the appointment of Andreas Whittam Smith, founding editor of the *Independent* newspaper, whose knowledge of film was meagre to say the least. Whittam Smith felt that public accountability could best be achieved through these stated objectives:

> (1) to promote consistency in the classification process, (2) to encourage the Board to be as open as possible, and (3) to make sure that the Board is well informed about the public's attitude to its work.[34]

Labour Home Secretary, Jack Straw, also considered it necessary to halt measures the Board were taking to liberalise the R18 category, material only available in licensed sex shops and specially licensed cinemas. Discussions between Tory Home Office Minister Tom Sackville and the Board back in 1996 concluded that the R18 guidelines, as they stood, did not permit enough sex to lure purchasers away from black market hardcore. Straw, having once described porn as "nasty, degenerate and worthless",[35] didn't agree. When news reached him that BBFC-approved sex films (in the form of *The Pyramid* and *BatBabe*) now contained erections and glimpses of penetrative and oral sex, Straw ensured that the porn breakthrough went no further.[36]

James Ferman steadfastly denied that it was the media and government backlash that had influenced – or forced – his decision to retire. Nevertheless, as soon as he made the decision, he let his views be known on matters that would undoubtedly have had to remain private had he stayed at the BBFC. His farewell message was a call to make hardcore pornography legal. In what appeared a provocative rebuttal of Jack Straw's intervention on the matter of R18 videos, Ferman told the press that "The more you try to ban it the more it grows".

The ban on 'conventional' pornography had encouraged a black market ready to deal in far more obscene material, Ferman claimed. In his twenty-three years of office, it was the influx of (under the counter) violent sex videos that he considered his biggest failure. As to cutting sex videos in 1996, he felt this to be "the most soul-destroying use of professional expertise yet invented."

The BBFC Annual Report for 1997-98 said this:

> In response to a steady increase in the public's tolerance of screen sex, confirmed by a wide range of research, the Board relaxed its stringent standards to allow marginally more explicitness in sex videos sold through licensed sex shops. This move was promptly curtailed when it became apparent that these standards were out of line with those of enforcement agencies such as Customs & Excise and the police and Magistrates' Courts. In October 1998, the Board reverted to its previous standards, but it is concerned that the failure to distinguish between harmful forms of pornography and those which are merely offensive will fuel the already flourishing black market which mixes pornography with obscenity. Mr Ferman says that this is one of the biggest problems he leaves for his successors and calls for a solution to be found.

After his retirement, the BBFC undertook to remove the stigma brought about by Ferman's directorship and craving for secrecy. For the first time, the Board published Draft Guidelines for Classifying Films and Videos, detailing "the criteria used to arrive at the decisions it makes on behalf of the public." Then there was the Public Consultation Programme, a nationwide roadshow to which members of the public were invited. Problem scenes from recent films were screened, alongside insight into the process that led the Board to pass or cut them. Afterwards, the audience put its questions to members of the examination team. "Maybe it's a subjective opinion but it's mine," responded one examiner to a question in the roadshow attended by the authors.

As film producer Stephen Woolley points out in the documentary *The Last Days of the Board*, these are "the censors who want to be loved."

The first contentious film for Robin Duval, Ferman's successor, came in the form of Gaspar Noé's *Seul Contre Tous*. French and subtitled, it contained scenes showing a pregnant woman being beaten, hardcore footage being played in a porn cinema, and a protagonist who dreams that he rapes and murders his daughter. Given its arthouse aspirations, Ferman was of the unofficial opinion that *Seul Contre Tous* should be passed uncut. Duval however, wanted the porn

Two films and BBFC decisions unpopular with the tabloid press. Below, from left: *Daily Mail*, November 9, 1996; *Daily Express*, March 24, 1998. Next page: Chucky is dangerous.

Daily Mail

SUPPORT POPPY APPEAL 1996

Britain's very best TV guide

WEEKEND

7 FREE INSTANT SCRATCH CARDS PLUS WIN UP TO £50,000

Campaign to stop depraved movie being shown in Britain

BAN THIS CAR CRASH SEX FILM

THE Heritage Secretary called last night for a depraved new film to be banned.

Premier concedes free vote on caning

THE EXPRESS

Whatever happened to the Tiller Girls?

FURY AS CENSOR PASSES LOLITA

Concern over film's paedophile risk

JENNIFER FLIES IN WITH SOME CLOSE FRIENDS

in the cinema scene removed before granting it an 18, leaving intact the two violent and arguably more objectionable sequences.[37] It was a telling decision for the new director, and an almost complete turnabout for the Board in light of Ferman's twenty-three-year legacy.

"People are all excited that they're relaxing standards," commented one video distributor of the new BBFC,[38] "and that's completely not true."

There is something inherently ridiculous in opening a newspaper and seeing the face of Chucky, the doll from *Child's Play 3*, and the warning "DANGEROUS" beneath it. As noted in the previous chapter, quite often the news media is the catalyst for serious criminal incidents. The reporting of Julian Knight's massacre induced the Hungerford massacre, reporting of which in turn induced the shootings in Monkseaton and Northamptonshire. Reports on the Dunblane massacre were followed by the killings in Tasmania and indubitably linked to the attempted murders by Horrett Campbell at St Luke's nursery school. These are facts the newspapers fear and that is why they generate public distaste for films and other entertainment mediums – diverting responsibility for the crimes they themselves provoke.

DAILY EXPRESS Saturday April 2 1994 5

over video nasties

'eme'

lger had both
Play 3.
ndment to the
Justice Bill to
orror videos.
classificiation,
and make it an
youngsters.
alled that the
ct the amend-
e Bill. He said:

S: Page 9

"We are tightening the law to enable prosecutions to be brought more easily.

"But to ban a video which may be inappropriate for children when most households do not contain children would be an extreme step."

Mr Alton hit back: "The Police Bill and the Criminal Justice Bill have been PR disasters for the Government. Here is a chance to do something in line with public and Parliamentary opinion.

"To fight efforts to curb grotesque violence in videos is ridiculous. Most people would applaud him."

CHILDS PLAY 3

DANGEROUS: Chuckie

Of course, not all criminal acts inspired by the press are as serious as the above. 'Ram-raiding' – driving a vehicle into a shop front or commercial property to commit theft – was an isolated incident, demonstrated to the nation by the news media, after which it became a national problem overnight. The value of computer RAM chips and the ease with which they might be stolen was highlighted on one television news report, and the crime suddenly escalated. When Ayatollah Khomeni placed a fatwa on *The Satanic Verses* author Salman Rushdie, and a $2 million purse on his head, it was the news media that informed all potential assassins of the prize, thus compounding Rushdie's dilemma. Los Angeles burned following media coverage of the Rodney King beating and subsequent trial. Terrorist attacks are generally carried out for media attention.

We understand this is a simplistic view of some rather complex issues. Do we advocate media censorship? News blackouts? No, but those opposing films often take such a reactionary stance. Let's paraphrase words spoken by Jill Knight MBE MP (now Dame Knight) and direct them, not at "porno movies" as her original intent, but at news media instead: Is the freedom to report news items more important than the freedom from rape, murder and terror?

News media incites imitative crime, whereas films don't. Politicians and journalists use emotive language to further their campaigns and secure public attention. They may claim to be protecting children but in truth are protecting their own interests and promoting themselves.[39] The tabloid press is constantly seeking to invent a new menace, not unlike a parent warning a child of a monster in the closet so they can then comfort and protect them. Politicians and the tabloid press enthuse about the child-eating monster that awaits around every corner, say, horror comics in the fifties, and later satanic abuse, "devil dogs", horror videos, and the Internet. These are perils that exist on the pages of newspapers and to remain vigilant and 'safe', one must buy the next edition and await the all-clear... by which time the next threat is upon us.

Going in a blaze of glory... James Ferman makes a controversial announcement on his retirement. The *Express*, August 12, 1998

THE EXPRESS

WEDNESDAY AUGUST 12, 1998 35p

I can't forget my little dead daughter, by Cilla Black

• PAGES 28 & 29

MAKE HARD PORN LEGAL

Censor calls

Battle to ban porn is lost says censor

FROM PAGE ONE

into the country as the biggest failure of his 23-year term of office.

He argues that the ban on "conventional" pornography has encouraged the growth of a black market ready to deal in far more obscene videos involving children, animals and violence.

He also suggested a former Conservative Home Office Minister had favoured the policy of legalising hard-core pornography.

Mr Ferman admitted the report could be seen as a provocative parting shot.

"Yes, I feel strongly about it because the black market will just grow and grow," he said.

"A little of what people want is OK as long as it's on the harmless end of the spectrum. The more you try to ban it the more it grows." However Mr Ferman, who said he was aware that there were bestiality tapes circulating in Britain, stressed that anything involving violence should not be legalised.

John Beyer, director of the National Viewers' and Listeners' Association, said: "We agree entirely with Mr Ferman that violent pornography undermines a healthy society and that this problem must be tackled urgently."

But he called for harsher penalties for those trafficking in obscene videos.

"A new restrictive definition of 'obscene' is absolutely vital with more severe penalties for those found guilty," said Mr Beyer.

FERMAN: Warning over growing black market

Statistics can be used and manipulated to mislead the public and advance a political career or moral crusade. The community will be temporarily deluded into believing that the reformist is campaigning for an improvement in their rights. It will be argued that failure to follow and offer support will result in an unprecedented danger to the children. Cuckolded public opinion will then carry the acclaimed reformer into a higher-ranking or higher-salaried position. Once this step-up in status is achieved, from MP to Lord for instance, the campaign will suddenly cease. One dubious statistic thrown around during the early days of the video controversy indicated that half the nation's children had seen a 'video nasty'. Had this and the theorised effects of viewing such material been true, then half the country's present adults would be depraved and corrupt.

When an incident as inexplicable as the Bulger murder grips the nation the simplest form of action is to blame a movie. This way the film can be made a pariah, with the instigator of the mitigation claiming credit for a great public service when in fact nothing has been accomplished at all. In the wake of the

Bulger case, after the government announced its crackdown on violent videos, *Today* (April 13, 1994) printed an assortment of horror video sleeves and the word "BRANDED" stamped over them. That same day, the *Daily Mirror,* not a newspaper to let facts get in the way of a good campaign, went a step further and reproduced the sleeve to *Child's Play 3* beneath the fatuous claim the film was "BANNED – Thanks to your *Daily Mirror*." The film wasn't banned and never has been, thanks but no thanks.[40]

Blame for such incidents as the Bulger murder cannot be laid unequivocally on films – the causes of crime are far more deeply rooted than that. To find the source would take time and much effort, something politicians refuse to give. For every study that determines a causative link exists between film and crime, another one appears whose findings are quite the opposite. Television violence is good for you, researchers in Germany concluded in 1994. It makes people less likely to act aggressively and more likely to identify with victims. However, this is not an opinion that fires the editorial imagination, and research like this is rarely afforded the space or sobriety that the counterargument tends to receive.

In November 1990, a psychologist named Jeffrey Goldstein determined that youngsters aged six were able to spot when they were being brainwashed by commercials. By the age of ten, most had become sceptical of claims made by advertisers, the research revealed. A decade later, in August 1999, the American Academy of Paediatrics suggested that television at too early an age could lead to irreversible brain damage or psychological impairment.

Research into juvenile crime, conducted by the BBFC no less, found that

> young offenders were watching very much the same films as non-offenders of the same age, with neither group showing undue interest in horror films or films about violent criminal lifestyles.[41]

If it is true to say that crime has increased since video came into homes, it is equally true to say that violent crime has increased since the formation of the NVLA, or since the introduction of the Video Recordings Act, or since the spread of fast-food burger chains. Evidence can be used to mislead. It was noted that serial killer Jeffrey Dahmer had a copy of *Exorcist II: The Heretic* in his flat – but what does this actually mean and why was it thought so important? Right-wing Christian groups used it as proof that malevolent films engendered malevolent people, yet the same groups chose to ignore the fact that a copy of the Bible was

Banned, or maybe branded. Thanks to the *Daily Mirror* or *Today*? April 13, 1994.

DAILY Mirror

Woman GET SLIM FAST 4 PAGE EXTRA INSIDE

HONESTY QUALITY EXCELLENCE

Jane on a Princess in torment

BANNED

Thanks to your DAILY Mirror

CHILD'S PLAY 3

Nude Fergie photos fury

SEE PAGE 5

ONLY 25p

TODAY

Anne Robinson INSIDE TODAY ANOTHER POINT OF VIEW Page 5

PLAY TODAY GET Rich £10,000 TO BE WON EVERY DAY Full details on Page 15

Maniac hacks couple to death and attacks girls

BRAINDEAD

CHILD'S PLAY

BRANDED

BODY

well in Toyland

Now Chucky can't come out to play

also found in Dahmer's flat. Dahmer openly admitted that throughout his killing spree he was "living on nothing but McDonald's." The killers of James Bulger were also fast-food consumers and burger bars are the supposedly favourite haunts of America's gun maniacs – does such evidence identify a link? Does it imply a potential peril of food additives? Should fast-food products be banned for the sake of children? The increased use of aspartame, the artificial sweetener in soft drinks, also correlates to the increase in juvenile violence.[42]

This does not mean of course that children should be allowed to watch any type of film, because the argument isn't about children – despite attempts by groups and individuals to put them in the line of fire. BBFC consumer guidelines, the regulation of video outlets and parental control should suffice to keep children from unsuitable material. Of course, there are parents who care little about what their children watch; should the entire adult population be subjected to prohibition because some children are unrestrained or left unsupervised?

If there was any truth to the notion that screen violence influences actions, then the most dangerous people in the country would not be the inmates of Broadmoor's maximum-security wing but the BBFC staff and members of the

NVLA,[43] people who watch more scenes of violence than any average member of the public. Following the Russell Crookes murder case, the NVLA was quick to use the tragedy as propaganda. John Beyer, the NVLA director, said that broadcasters should stop showing violent films, and asked, "How many more murders will there be before someone does something about the violence?" During a TV debate on screen violence, Beyer mentioned that Channel 5 had aired Oliver Stone's *Natural Born Killers*. When asked whether it should have been shown, he responded in the absolute negative. Because he is so blinded by his organisation's crusade, he failed to comprehend that the film had been shown and nothing untoward had happened as a consequence. There was no increase in crime, no mass murders, no collapse into anarchy. The film was aired again on Channel 5 with similar non-events.

Members of organisations such as the NVLA, Customs & Excise, and the BBFC believe themselves to be immune to the effects of viewing violence – that is to say, the effects these groups insist exist in the first place. They do not perceive that viewing such material inspires no imitative reaction, but that it identifies their own intellectual superiority and mental stability. It is everyone else who is susceptible to an adverse effect. When it comes to viewing violent imagery, BBFC examiners are said to have "ways of defending themselves."[44] While they may become, at worst, "desensitised" to certain scenes, we, the public, will become "depraved and corrupt." This distinction in the classes was highlighted when the controversial faux documentary, *Man Bites Dog*, was certified for video without cuts. The BBFC argued that the film ("a savage lampoon of media complicity") would not appeal to certain social classes because it was b&w and subtitled. As a result, its excessive violence – far stronger than anything in the banned *Straw Dogs* (colour/English language) – was left intact. Conversely, the violent scenes in James Cameron's *True Lies* underwent cuts, as the movie had more of an appeal to the 'lower' social classes (the easily influenced feeble-minded) and little attraction to art-intellectuals (the resistant secure-minded). This theory of the susceptible and easily influenced residing on the deficient side of the intellectual divide is merely self-aggrandising speculation by those believing they occupy the opposite side. The adversely affected can never be identified by example, only alluded to hypothetically – or the accuser would stand to lose support and favour from the stated group.[45]

What was really gained by the Video Recordings Act and the banning of, for the most part, a bunch of rather cheap, ineffective horror movies? Everything, one suspects, that the authorities wanted to avoid. Some of these same movies have returned with an official BBFC stamp of approval and been heralded in some quarters as renaissance pieces. Understandably, distributors have promoted re-released films like *Axe*, *Zombie Flesh Eaters*, *Shogun Assassin*, *The Slayer* and *The Driller Killer* on the back of their association with that most tumultuous of times.[46] If the 'nasties' weren't a "term of art" to begin with, that's what banning them has turned them into. Critics now extrapolate and analyse ideas and meanings from these films. Academic presses publish books devoted to them. A new generation of collectors – some too young to remember the controversy that sparked the VRA in the first place – are tuning into the subject. Where once trade was conducted via the pages of fanzines and magazines, now, of course, it's the Internet, as per this early seller's website, circa 1999:

> WE HAVE A WIDE RANGE OF FULLY UNCUT HORROR MOVIES WHAT HAVE TAKEN US AGES TO COLLECT ALL FILMS ARE 10+++ QUALITY AND ONLY PROFESIONAL EQUIPMENT IS USED TO TRANSFER THE FILMS FROM NTSC-PAL MENNING NO QUALITY LOSS FOR FULL LIST E-MAIL ME AT ––– ALL FILMS ARE £13 INCLUDING P & P. FOR A QUICK EXAMPLE WE HAVE CANNIBAL MOVIES, ZOMBIE MOVIES, AND LOADS MORE AND ALL FILMS ARE THE TRUE UNCUT VERSIONS SO YOU WON'T BE DISSAPOINTED.

Arguably, there would be no underground niche and much less interest in cannibal and zombie movies if the video 'fad' of the early eighties had been left to run its natural course. The VRA succeeded only in creating a locked groove; cinema has moved on, 'video nasties' haven't. It is almost inconceivable that – let's admit –terrible feature films like *Werewolf and the Yeti*, *Contamination* and *Evilspeak* could ever be perceived as a danger, much less a national threat. But they were, and to a large degree still are – thanks to a news media that continues to label every questionable celluloid matter a 'video nasty'.[47] These are exploitation films, whose only mind-altering threat comes via an abundance of stilted acting, poorly-dubbed dialogue, cheesy plots, cornball special effects and occasional lapses into poor taste.

Responding to questions raised by the Home Secretary concerning its responsibilities under the Video Recordings Act, a brooding BBFC stated in a report dated December 6, 1996, that "the 'video nasties' are still the most violent videos ever submitted to the Board, but they were never a part of mainstream cinema." Not only had the Board decided in 1985 to avoid media generalisations like 'video nasties,' but very few of the films on the DPP list had been submitted for classification in the first place, hence their 'banned' status. This blatant self-justification tactic is followed by scare-mongering:

> Fringe industries were created in South America, Asia, and Europe, with Italy specialising in scenes of rape, torture and mutilation, many of them played by a small American group of porn performers allegedly funded by the Mafia. In Britain such films were banned or heavily cut...

Whether or not one considers the public accountability of the new BBFC to be something of a façade, or the apparent leniency to be an empty gesture, things undoubtedly are changing. Access to the Internet and the evolution of DVD and Blu-ray (and now streaming) formats have globalised the film market to a greater extent than videotape – much to the chagrin of those who wish to control not only their own viewing habits but those of everyone else. Virtually any film can be imported from any country (or downloaded) at the click of a button. When *Tenebrae* was re-released on video and DVD, the several seconds of footage excised at the behest of the BBFC was made available on the Internet. Consumers could watch the cut print of the film on their TV sets, and then, on their computer monitor, the bloody sight of actress Veronica Lavia getting her arm severed with an axe (but out of any context and streaming in an endless loop). It is this kind of accessibility that brings the censorial capacity of the BBFC one step closer to redundancy and quantifies reformists like the NVLA as an even more pointless governance.

Shortly before his retirement, James Ferman conceded that with advancements in technology the future of the BBFC lay as an advisory body, not as governors of what should and shouldn't be seen. As to whether this was a prospect that bothered him much, he replied, "No, I think history moves on and standards change."[48]

Which is where we came in...

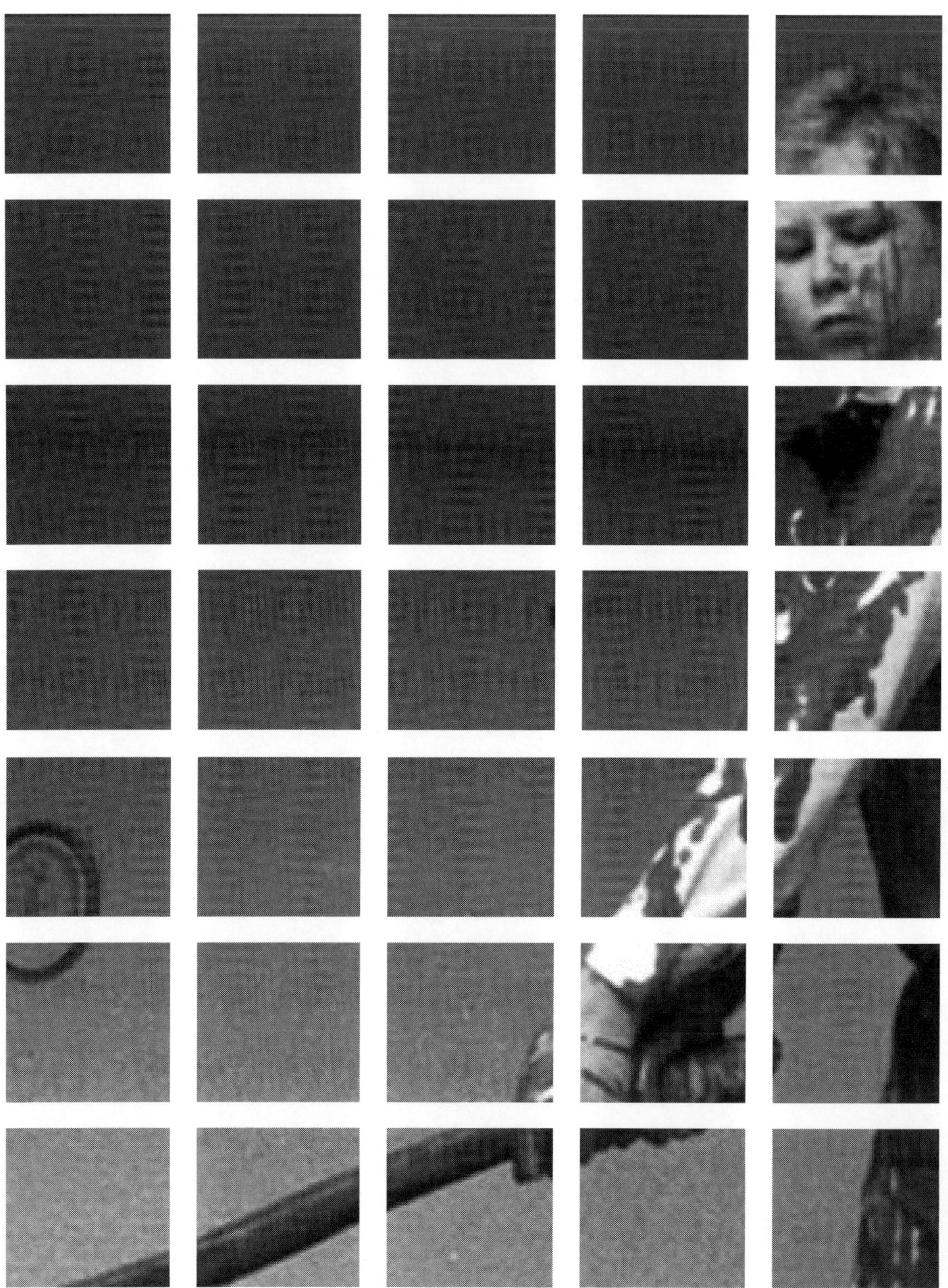

The DPP39

'SCENES OF EXTREME AND EXPLICIT VIOLENCE'

The DPP39

'SCENES OF EXTREME AND EXPLICIT VIOLENCE'

THE FILMS THAT follow were cited at various points as comprising the Director of Public Prosecution's 'video nasties' list, an inconsistent and ever-changing list that ostensibly revolved around a core thirty-nine titles (see page 71), and appeared occasionally in its various forms in newspapers and film magazines from the mid 1980s onward. These were films said to be of the 'horror variety,' openly available on videocassette prior to the Video Recordings Act 1984, but either prosecuted under Section 2 of the Obscene Publications Act 1959, or considered suitable for prosecution. Some titles became mainstay 'video nasties' (*The Driller Killer*, *Snuff*, *I Spit on Your Grave*...), while others disappeared from the list relatively quickly (*The Evil Dead*, *Cain's Cutthroats*...). Samuel Fuller's critically acclaimed war movie, *The Big Red One*, appeared on some lists but was never truly considered a 'nasty' nor was it collectable, and isn't included here. This chapter looks at what we shall call the expanded DPP39, seventy-five films that inspired a collector's market.

Film synopses have been truncated for this edition of the book – the original long-form storylines have been removed,[1] given that the majority of these films are now commercially available in the UK. However, we have retained the commentary much as it originally appeared, being an important document on the so-called 'nasties', as well as contemporaneous attitudes towards them – from the media, film fans, the British Board of Film Classification and ourselves as authors. A newer perspective can be found in the APPENDIX.

ABSURD

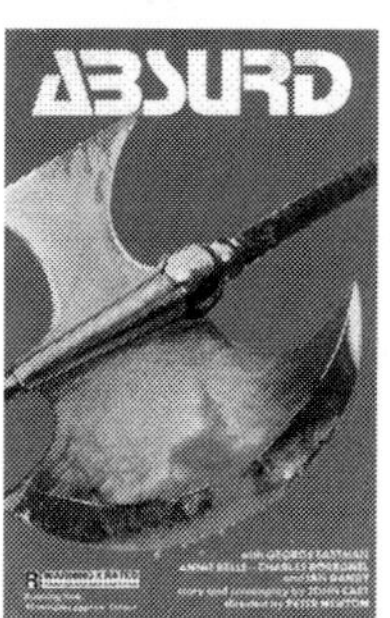

aka: Rosso sangue (original title); Horrible; The Monster Hunter

Italy 1981

cast: George Eastman, Annie Belle, Charles Borromel, Katya Berger, Kasimir Berger

story: John Cart [Aristide Massaccesi]

producer: [not credited]

director: PETER NEWTON [Aristide Massaccesi]

A homicidal maniac with superhuman regenerative powers is on the loose. A priest, who claims to serve God with biochemistry, tries to stop the slaughter.

The DPP39

'SCENES OF EXTREME AND EXPLICIT VIOLENCE'

PETER NEWTON IS another pseudonym for Italian director Aristide Massaccesi, better known as Joe D'Amato.1 Not only is this one of his more entertaining films, in many ways it epitomises the romance of the 'nasties' with its excessive bloodletting, dodgy prosthetics, arcane dialogue, clumsy dubbing, competent direction, and simplistic, free-rolling plot.

George Eastman (real name: Luigi Montefiore) plays Nikos, the homicidal monster whose origins are vague but include Greece and the pseudo-scientific babble of a Roman Catholic priest. Eastman together with Massaccesi conceived *Absurd* as a sequel to their own successful *Anthropophagous the Beast*. However, all that links the two films is that Eastman stars in each as a homicidal brute who loses his intestines at the end of one film and then again at the start of the other.[2]

Absurd stands as a 'non-sequel.' In the book *Spaghetti Nightmares*, Eastman relates how he got a part in *Absurd* because of certain scripting problems. Unable to offer a completed script due to other work, Eastman originally gave Massaccesi an outline for the film. He later returned to the project and was presented with a poor script completed in his absence. "Since I needed the money," claims Eastman, "I offered to revise the script in return for a part in the film."

Original press announcements for the film state that it was to have starred Black Emanuelle actress Laura Gemser. This fact, coupled with Eastman 'buying his way into the title role,' suggest that *Absurd* may have been planned as an altogether different film – possibly one in keeping with a straight thematic follow-up to *Anthropophagous*. One thing's for sure however – there was never any doubt that the film should be completely outrageous and over the top.

"We really wanted people to be shocked," Eastman said of both *Absurd* and *Anthropophagous* in an interview with *The Dark Side*.[3] "When we wrote them, we kept making them more and more shocking."

There is little point trying to rationalise the story. Tim Ferrante, in a review for *Filmfax*,[4] calls *Absurd* "HALLOWEEN ALL'ITALIANA!" and accuses it of ripping off John Carpenter's *Halloween*. One curious aspect of *Absurd* is that a priest (played by Edmund Purdom, the narrator of many Mondo films) should be unwittingly responsible for the maniac that is Nikos. Why make him a priest? With Massaccesi's track record, and Eastman's insinuation that they were only out to shock with the film, there is probably no intended agenda behind it. But nevertheless it does throw an interesting slant on the picture, one that is critical of the Church. Despite the scientific anomaly which he himself has created, the priest still regards Nikos as "evil" and claims he is possessed by the devil. It's an oxymoron, just like the

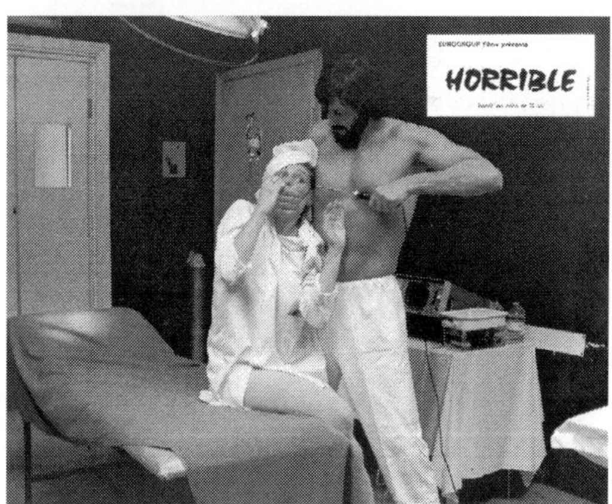

Scenes from *Absurd*, under the title *Horrible*.

insistence of the gutter press that so-called 'video nasties' – feature films; spools of magnetic tape encased in plastic – are "evil."

Absurd does occasionally touch on the brilliant, notably in the sequence where Nikos gets his eyes gouged out. (An equally memorable inversion of this scene occurs earlier when Nikos' eyes pop open whilst he is undergoing major surgery.) Here the film loses its humble exploitation trappings and seems more like a twisted homage to Polanski by way of Pasolini – specifically, Polanski's *Repulsion* and the doomed hero of Pasolini's Sophoclean drama, *Oedipus Rex*. It also owes a tip of the hat to Walter Grauman's *Lady in a Cage*, a film which, in its closing moments, features a homicidal James Caan searching blindly for crippled Olivia de Havilland after she has stuck metal strips into his eyes.

In the latter stages of *Absurd*, Nikos breaks into the home of the Bennett family and terrorises bedridden daughter Katya and her carer, Emily. Having escaped the clutches of the sightless monster in her bedroom, Katya hobbles as best she can down the darkened corridors of the house, supporting herself on its walls. At one point she falls to her knees as the monster suddenly appears in the brightly lit background, silhouetted in the centre of the frame. He too supports himself on the walls of the corridor, searching blindly for the girl. It's a tense, magnificently crafted scene that compromises the director's reputation for being "one of the topmost boring Italian directors,"[5] deflating somewhat his own assertion that "I'm a businessman and not an artist."[6]

Although it could never top the abortion and auto-cannibalism scenes of *Anthropophagous* for sheer tastelessness, *Absurd* is eminently better paced, with one horrific set-piece following another. None of the prosthetic effects are particularly convincing (flesh and bone offer no resistance to the assortment of objects that sink into them), but they're all executed with bloodthirsty relish and a liberal spattering of gore. Given these factors, it's unlikely the film would ever be submitted to the BBFC for classification in an uncut state. Indeed, the murder of Emily the babysitter would be justification enough for the Board to reject this film outright. Even though Nikos kills whoever he can lay his hands on, whatever sex they might be, there is misogynistic relish to his cooking of Emily's head in the oven. Filmed from within the oven itself, Emily cooking in agonising close-up lasts for over a minute[7] but doesn't even end there – she gets stabbed in the neck with a pair of scissors when she pulls herself from death's door to try and stop Nikos capturing Willie.

(Talking of death's door: A lot of emphasis is placed on the door of the Bennett house. It seems that whenever it opens, something horrible is revealed behind it. First it opens to show Nikos spilling his guts, then Peggy being murdered, and finally Katya displaying a severed head.)

There is a concerted effort to displace the setting of *Absurd* from Italy to the USA, presumably because the film would be met with greater favour in its home territory if it looked like an American product. As a result, every street shot has a fake fire hydrant in view, with characters watching lots of American football on television. But they snack on pasta, which is a bit of a give-away.

Medusa released two versions of *Absurd*: one cut, the other uncut, both in identical sleeves. The only way to tell the two apart was via the spine of the video itself. If it had a sticker with the film's title, it was uncut; if it had a holographic Medusa seal, then it was the cut version. Some unscrupulous dealers are known to have duplicated uncut copies of the film over cut versions to tout them as more desirable full-uncut originals. Second or even third generation quality playback ought to have alerted dubious viewers to these pirated tapes – by which time, of course, it was invariably too late to do much about it.

Massaccesi freely admits that he will turn his hand to any kind of movie, and his filmography is testament to this fact, touching on all genres, from thrillers through action adventure to hardcore pornography. With hardcore, there is no risk of *not* making money. Profit is guaranteed, claims the director. But softcore is Massaccesi's forte (he directed the dire *Ladies' Doctor* in 1977, a sex comedy about a gynaecologist). *Absurd* marked the end of his brief foray into horror cinema, and Massaccesi joined the post-apocalypse sci-fi bandwagon before returning to porn and his most successful movie to date, *11 Days, 11 Nights* (1989). He took pride in the fact that some of his films are banned in Britain. "Somebody saw my movies and it had this effect," he told *Flesh & Blood*.[8]

ANTHROPOPHAGOUS THE BEAST

aka: Anthropophagous; Antropofago; The Grim Reaper; Gomia, Terror en el Mar Egeo; Man Beast; Man-Eater; The Savage Island
Italy 1980
cast: Tisa Farrow, Saverio Vallone, George Eastman, Margaret Donnelly, Vanessa Steiger, Mark Bodin, Bob Larsen, Simone Baker, Serena Grandi, Rubina Rey
story: Luigi Montefiori & Aristide Massaccesi
producer: Oscar Santaniello
director: JOE D'AMATO [Aristide Massaccesi]

On a seemingly deserted Greek island a group of tourists must avoid a lumpen homicidal maniac.

ALTHOUGH HE HAD ventured into the realms of horror with previous films – the sexually motivated though visceral *Emanuelle in America*, *Emanuelle and the Last Cannibals* and *Erotic Nights of the Living Dead* – *Anthropophagous the Beast*[1] was D'Amato's first specific horror movie and one he was quite rightly proud of.[2] Without resorting to any sexual content D'Amato needed to generate unease as opposed to titillation, something he had failed to achieve in his earlier genre composites. He had provided scenes of abject violence in the two *Emanuelle* instalments but never induced any sense of atmospheric horror or dread. However, with *Anthropophagous*, he succeeded in producing a viable tale of terror in the EC horror comics tradition. The deserted island location and washed-out film stock create a unique atmosphere – even the soundtrack is unnerving at times. The fact that George Eastman doesn't have a speaking role helps and he is rigorously disturbing as the lumbering, skin-diseased cannibal.

Un Chien Andalou? No, *Absurd*.

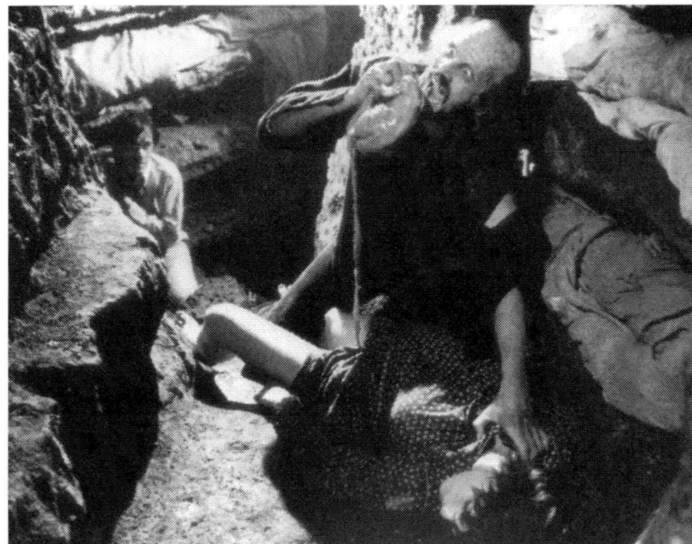

Another major bonus point is the absence of children and wise-cracking teenagers, commonplace in today's formulaic horror movies.

A backstory reveals that the Eastman character was shipwrecked on the island and developed a taste for human flesh when forced to eat his dead son. This, we are to believe, has made him insane. The film contains several grisly moments, but it is the realistic scene depicting the aborting and devouring of a near full-term foetus that causes much anxiety. It is a moment of genuinely shocking screen horror. Indeed, the build-up to the scene, with one of the visitors to the island walking amongst the subterranean shelves of skeletons, followed by the ponderous, heavy-breathing killer, is the most atmospheric moment in the film – pure gothic horror punctuated with an extreme grand guignol finale. In a way it is comparable to the eye-slitting scene in Buñuel's *Un Chien Andalou*. In each instance, the viewer is made fully aware of what is about to happen but so appalling is the anticipated climax, he or she doesn't really expect it to be followed through on screen. In *Un Chien Andalou* we see the razor being stropped and the eye being forced open. For a moment we feel 'let off' with a symbolic image of a sliver of cloud cutting across the moon but then the camera abruptly cuts back to the fullscreen view of the eye being sliced open. In *Anthropophagous* we see the man throttling the pregnant woman, as his other hand goes beneath her dress and forces its way between her legs. The shot cuts back to the woman's face as she dies from strangulation. For a second the sequence seems over, but then it cuts back to the killer pulling the foetus from between her spread legs and raising it to his mouth.[3]

Another tremendously effective scene is when one character is suspended above the well and the scabrous Eastman rises from the murky water.

Unfortunately, the final climax where the cannibal devours his own intestines, in spite of its poetic symmetry, is a bit too hokey and doesn't have the impact of the foetus-eating scene – possibly because the guts are too thin and stringy to pass off as a human digestive tract. Effective atmosphere is something D'Amato rarely achieves in any of his films yet in this one he succeeds admirably. He is better known for generating tedious longueurs of which, admittedly, there are several here, including an endless walk to the store to collect antibiotics. But these are only minor quibbles and take little away from the film.

Contrary to popular belief, D'Amato knows exactly what he's doing (even if he can't always afford the time to do it). Courtesy of an article by Thomas M Sipos that appeared in *Midnight Marquee* (No 60), here's how he achieved some of the cost-cutting atmosphere on *Anthropophagous*:

> *Anthropophagous*... cleverly uses day for night photography to simulate lightning: Tisa Farrow (Mia's sister) is chasing Zora Kerova through a forest during a storm. As Farrow's costume and the trees are nearly white, the film stock records an image even though underexposed. We see only the bright trees and Farrow, the

> underexposed surroundings appearing lost in nighttime darkness. But every so often director [Joe D'Amato] opens the lens aperture – briefly! – to admit more light. When such instances are cued with thunder on the soundtrack, the impression is of lighting illuminating the landscape. But freeze the frame on your VCR and you'll see the 'lightning' is daylight, the entire landscape evenly lit.

Anthropophagous the Beast was released uncut by Videofilm Promotions, and in a truncated, hard-to-find R-rated form on the Radio Shack video label. At one period it achieved notoriety as a 'snuff' film, identified as such by the ill-informed press, and even excerpted on national television news programmes. A sequel of sorts was *Absurd*, again directed by D'Amato and featuring George Eastman in another mute role.

AXE

aka: Lisa, Lisa; California Axe Massacre; The Axe Murders
USA 1974
cast: Jack Canon, Ray Green, Frederick R Friedel, and introducing Leslie Lee
story: Frederick R Friedel
producer: J G Petterson Jr
director: FREDERICK R FRIEDEL

Three gangsters lay low in an isolated farmhouse inhabited by a sick man attended to by his granddaughter, Lisa. One by one Lisa kills the men.

ONE OF THE most striking things about *Axe* is its use of sound. The main theme – which also serves to accentuate Lisa's psychosis – is perhaps the singularly most annoying pieces of music set to film,[1] consisting of a toy keyboard making a shrill noise that starts high and gets higher. The dubbing is strange, too, no less during the opening sequence where the three protagonists – Steele, Lomax and Billy – break into the apartment of an associate, Aubrey, and torture and murder him. A succession of punches produces the same lifeless thud; Aubrey gives a strange non-human gurgling sound when the cigar is extinguished in his

Lisa – hiding something in *Axe*.

mouth; and a fey looped "Ooh" emits from the corner of the room, where a friend of Aubrey cowers. *"Ooh... Ooh... Ooh... Ooh..."*

Things are deliberately ambiguous. There is no clue as to what Aubrey has done wrong that merits being taught a lesson. He has squealed on something, that much is clear. But not once does the gang discuss events prior to his murder, and no mention is made of loot, or a heist, for which the gang appear appropriately dressed. (One might assume that the intended crime never took place, seeing how the only reason they decide to head off and lie low for a while is because they killed Aubrey.)

Lisa on the other hand is hiding something. We first see her pottering around a farmyard, doing chores, during which she drops an egg. It smashes and she rubs it into the dirt with her bare foot. Later, she opens the refrigerator, and we see only broken eggs on a shelf. There is something dark and troubling weighing down on the girl.

The video box states that Lisa is thirteen-years-old – which would make Lomax and Steele's assault on her even more despicable – but as there is no mention of the girl's age in the film, it's a fact presumably lifted from a pressbook or distribution notes.[2] However, it is evident that Lisa is supposed to be much younger than the actress playing her, given her demeanour and the fact that the outlaws don't suspect she is capable of anything untoward.

Where are Lisa's parents? (She tells the outlaws she has none.)

Why isn't she afraid?

Why is she alone in running the farm and caring for her grandfather?

What is causing her mind to collapse like the eggshells in her fridge?

Bill Landis, in *Sleazoid Express*,[3] describes Lisa as "one of the most haunting female characters ever in an exploitation film." While Lisa is a cinematic mystery, not much is known about the film's real-life director Frederick R Friedel. Besides *Axe*, Friedel is known to have directed at least one other movie, *Date with a Kidnapper*,[4] which also starred Jack Canon (in the same business suit no less) and shared some of the same production credits. *Date with a Kidnapper* even takes several of the ideas from *Axe* and uses them to a much more confident – if no more logical – end. It's about a guy who kidnaps the daughter of a millionaire and holds her to ransom. Both films have teenage girls at their centres, suited gangsters whose past crimes are never elaborated on, psychotic rural folk, lonely farmhouses, and rapists who are murdered whilst on top of their victims.

The comparatively more polished and satisfying *Date with a Kidnapper* makes *Axe* look like a dry run, and leads one to believe that Friedel kept himself busy in other film work between the two productions. Interesting to note is that *Date with a Kidnapper* failed to make the nasties list, despite several scenes that are no less harrowing or confrontational than some of those found in *Axe* – an example of how poor distribution[5] and an innocuous title could sometimes save a film from the clutches of the DPP.

Everything in *Axe* is protracted to the point that otherwise mundane actions take on a Zen-like quality. The aforementioned beating up of Aubrey and the succession of punches, or Billy taking the trunk containing Lomax's body into the attic – it isn't enough to establish the act, we have to watch it every step of the way. There seems to have been a reluctance to edit and tighten the movie, perhaps because it is already barely feature-length at less than seventy minutes.

But then it goes overboard with 'interesting' camera angles, and Friedel lets slip from the menagerie his aspiration to create 'art'. (The minimalist cast and one-house setting bely a certain Bergman influence.[6]) In one sequence, a noise heard by Steele and Lomax alerts them to a prowler outside the farmhouse, who then runs off. We haven't seen enough of the man to establish just what it is he is supposed to be doing or who he is, and nobody makes any further reference to the incident – not even the two outlaws after they return from their pursuit of him. In another sequence, Lisa ponders her reflection in the bathroom mirror. The reflection is suddenly bloody. She spots a small black snake curled up in the bottom of the bath. Later, when disposing of Lomax's body – hacking him to pieces and putting what's left in the trunk – at the bottom of the bath, curled up like a snake, is his black necktie.

Axe is relatively gore free. The bloodiest moments come from a headless chicken, while Lomax's dismemberment is implied rather than shown – cutting from Lisa's raised axe to shots of her grandfather's blank face, or courtesy of a silhouette of the scene through the window blind. Even when Billy opens the trunk, we are treated only to his reaction and a momentary replay of Lomax's death throes.

One possible point of contention comes with an early sequence in a store, given that it serves only to humiliate and terrorise an innocent victim without furtherance to the plot.[7] Indeed, it was here that the film lost three minutes when released theatrically as *California Axe Massacre* in 1982. (This footage was replaced when the film was passed for video release in 1999, see APPENDIX.)

Elements that might have helped make *Axe* an 'undesirable' film include the video box claim that Lisa is only thirteen (Lomax calls her a "Nice lookin' woman"), the insinuation of cannibalism, the headless chicken (not in itself, but the tone it conveys through the rest of the film), Aubrey's murder, a child as killer, and the rape sequences (particularly the one accompanied by the sporting commentary on the TV, the dialogue of which was toned down in the recent re-release)...

Executive producer J G 'Pat' Patterson, prior to *Axe*, directed and starred in the terrible *Dr Gore*, which got more attention than it deserved when re-released in the eighties with a tagged-on introduction by Herschell Gordon Lewis. It is Patterson's involvement with *Axe* that makes it unlikely the production is as late as 1977, as some sources suggest. Patterson died in 1974.

Prelude to a horrifing [*sic*] experiment. *The Beast in Heat*.

THE BEAST IN HEAT

title on print: Horrifing [*sic*] Experiments Of S.S.Last Days
aka: La Bestia en Calor; SS Hell Camp; SS Experiment Part 2; Holocauste Nazi–Armes Secrets III Reich
Italy 1977
cast: Macha Magall, John Braun, Kim Gatti, Sal Boris
producer: Eterna Film
director: IVAN KATANSKY [Luigi Batzella]

Dr Ellen Kratsch, a lieutenant of Hitler's Third Reich, is responsible for inhuman experiments. The Italian Resistance press ever closer.

BEAST IN HEAT opens with a swastika coming into focus, accompanied by a woman's piercing scream and an odd electronic score.[1] The swastika remains centre-screen for the duration of the credits – which comprise the production company and all of five names. Following the credit for 'Sal Boris', the actor who plays the 'Beast' of the title, a sex-crazed throwback created by the Third Reich, there is an uncomfortable wait of almost a minute-and-a-half before the next name appears, during which time nothing is on screen but that swastika![2]

One reason why parts of *Beast in Heat* seem detached lies in the fact that the director has constructed much of it out of *When the Bell Rings*, an earlier war film of his (described as "tedious" by the *Delirium* guide to Italian exploitation). This material is easily identifiable due to the ill-matching stock and scenes of heavy artillery, aircraft and impressive explosions. In contrast, the rest of the film is noticeably down-market and consists of interior shots, lame 'action' and footage of people arguing. This would explain why an exodus of local villagers serves no purpose but simply concludes when an infant is thrown in the air and shot. Several minutes later the villagers are back in their homes as if nothing has happened. We also see Dr Kratsch discussing the whereabouts of the Italian Resistance with a superior but doesn't seem to be in the same shot or even the same room or village as him. (Alas, it's unclear whether this fusing of different films is responsible for the curious sequence where Irene, the village whore, is chased by angry locals for fraternising with the enemy. The chase comes to a dead halt with a Mack Sennett-like gag – a bucket of water is thrown at her but misses and hits someone else.)

The grisly excesses of *Beast in Heat* are unevenly paced, and director Katansky appears torn between making a straight war film and a clone of the *Ilsa* series, which had starred Dyanne Thorne as a busty, sadistic, sex-crazed Nazi officer.[3] Indeed, the previous year Katansky had covered similar ground with *Desert Tigers*,[4] a film featuring a Nazi camp with a sadomasochistic lesbian doctor called Erika.[5]

Dull action and unnecessary dialogue marks time between each ridiculous appearance of the Beast – played not very seriously by Sal Boris (real name: Salvatore Baccaro), a comedy actor called on more than once to appear in exploitation movies.[6] He gurns at great length into the camera (which gets so close that at one point the lens steams up), mugging wildly while furiously pummelling his flabby buttocks. This surreal performance reaches its nadir when he munches pubic hair. Why does this happen?! What train of thought must have been running through the screenwriter's mind to arrive at a point where a rape victim has her pubes ripped out and eaten?! This absurdity, coupled with the general ineptitude of the film, makes it difficult to qualify *Beast in Heat* as the most revolting entry in the Italian Nazi cycle, which some critics have suggested. It's simply too dumb, and more competent exercises – like *Gestapo's Last Orgy* – are far more alarming and unpleasant. But it's not difficult to see why *Beast in Heat* should have ended up on the 'banned' list: Nazis, rape and titillation are not an acceptable combination.

Other than the video sleeve, the title *"Beast in Heat"* is nowhere to be found. A Spanish language certificate pops up before the film starts, carrying the original title *La Bestia en Calor*, but it is the rather ham-fisted *Horrifing* [*sic*] *Experiments of S.S. Last Days* that appears on the print itself. *Monthly Film Bulletin* (November 1984) suspected the film was Walerian Borowczyk's female masturbation fantasy *The Beast* under a different title – an error that has been compounded elsewhere many times since.

Katansky – who also uses the pseudonyms Ivan Kathansy (with an 'h') and Luigi Batzella – directed many giallos and horror films under his real name Paolo Solvay, including *The Devil's Wedding Night*. *Beast in Heat* remains the most sought-after tape on the DPP list (see BLACK MARKET & PIRATES).

THE BEYOND

aka: L'aldilà (original title); Seven Doors of Death
Italy 1981
cast: David Warbeck, Catriona MacColl, Sarah Keller, Antoine St John, Veronica Lazar, Giovanni de Nava, Al Cliver, Anthony Flees, Michele Mirabella, Gianpaolo Saccarola, Laura de Marchi, Maria Pia Marsala
story: Lucio Fulci
producer: Fabrizio de Angelis
director: LUCIO FULCI

Liza Merril inherits a rundown hotel in Louisiana, location of a public execution years earlier. The discovery of a mysterious book and painting leads to many strange events, zombies and death.

THE BEYOND IS one of three films directed by Lucio Fulci to have been included on the DPP list. Judging by the selection criteria, however, there could well have been more – notably *City of the Living Dead* and *The Naples Connection*, the latter an extremely violent *French Connection* imitation whose different genre class probably helped it to escape the clutches of the DPP.

The Beyond is a horror story involving a warlock called Shvyke, a mysterious painting, and the resurrected dead plaguing mankind. Cobbled together with

All the Fulci hallmarks... *The Beyond*.

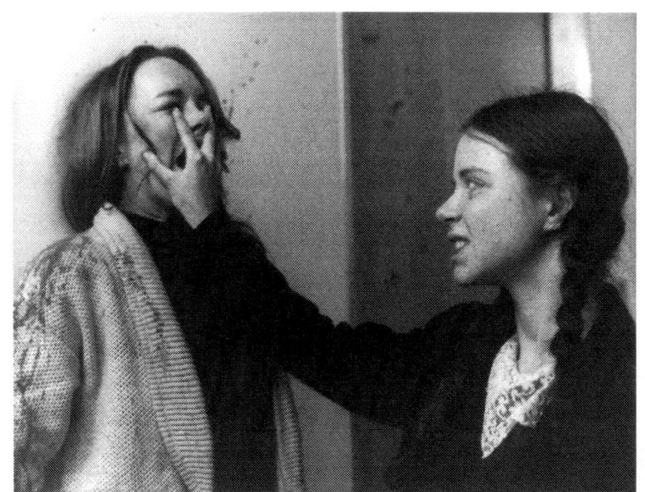

ideas from other sources – such as *The Sentinel*, *Suspiria*, and *Inferno*[1] – it carries all the Fulci hallmarks: sudden lingering close-ups of eyes; exaggerated sound effects; punctuating moments of graphic horror; and a seriously bleak – though confusing – ending. Some scenes fail and the film would have been better without them. The spider attack sequence, for instance, is unrealistic, the arachnids looking every bit like the mechanical puppets they obviously are. Intercutting the sequence with real tarantulas only emphasises the clumsiness of the automatons and consequently the scene is more amusing than horrifying. Having inherited a rundown hotel, Liza (Catriona MacColl) sees the image of the crucified warlock in one of the upper rooms, yet the prologue shows him being dragged from his room and nailed to a wall in the cellar. Although the film is effectively composed, there remains a lack of continuity and scenes don't make much sense. The latter parts take place in a hospital, with Liza meeting Dr McCabe (David Warbeck). Here a hospital technician places an EEG-type device on the head of an obviously long-dead corpse, and everyone must destroy zombies to survive.

Unlike Fulci's earlier *Zombie Flesh Eaters*, which has a straightforward, even simplistic, narrative and startling set-pieces, *The Beyond* trips over its own confusion. It almost tries to be too clever with its esoteric mystery and unexplained characters and as a result the film's pace is adversely affected. Moreover, the film lacks any genuinely memorable sequences – unlike the superbly rendered underwater fight in *Zombie Flesh Eaters* or Christopher George's desperate attempt to save Catriona MacColl from a partially buried coffin with a pickaxe in *City of the Living Dead*. The only noteworthy and genuinely creepy image in *The Beyond* comes in its closing moments, when Liza and McCabe find themselves locked in the nightmare landscape of Shvyke's painting. But Fulci is unable to muster the enthusiasm to do anything with it and the film simply ends here. The director, it seems, had run out of verve and daring ideas, content instead to play around with the obvious horror a paralysed man being overrun with (toy) spiders would invoke. Indeed, Fulci's career went into the gutter after *The Beyond* and, with the possible exceptions of *The House by the Cemetery* and *The New York Ripper*, he failed to make another film of worth. He even resorted to self-parody in the truly dreadful *A Cat in the Brain*, in which he played the lead role: a demented film director.

The Beyond was released on video with an official BBFC X-certificate – the same version that had been released theatrically in Britain in 1981. Several cuts totalling two minutes were made to the original film to achieve this classification, including the removal of the gorier aspects of the spider attack. With the original violence toned down, the only scenes which may have brought the Vampix release to the attention of the DPP are those depicting the torture and crucifixion of the warlock in the sepia-toned prologue. But even these scenes had been trimmed to remove some of the impact-blows while the victim was being chain-whipped.

The film was later re-released on the Elephant Video label in an utterly worthless version with all the scenes of violence removed.

Blood Bath

aka: A Bay of Blood (original title); Antefatto (working title); Carnage; The Ecology of a Crime; Twitch of the Death Nerve; New House on the Left; The Last House on the Left Part II

Italy 1971

cast: Luigi Pistilli, Claudine Auger, Claudio Volonté, Chris Avram, Anna Maria Rosati, Leopold Trieste, Laura Betti, Brigitte Skay, Isa Miranda, Paulo Rubens, Guido Boccaccini, Roberto Bonanni, Giovanni Nuvoletti

story: Mario Bava, Joseph McLee, Filippo Ottoni, Dardano Sacchetti, Franco Barberi

producer: Giuseppe Zaccariello

director: MARIO BAVA

Mario Bava – hardly any story. *Blood Bath*.

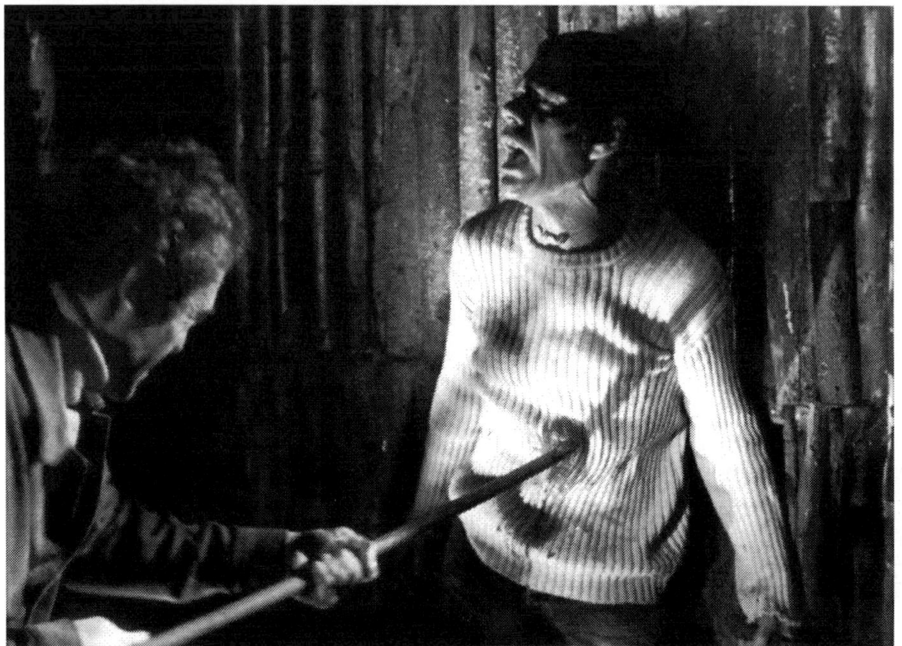

Puzzling murders take place in and around a house on the edge of a bay. Everyone has motive but two children are responsible. They consider murder a game.

THERE WEREN'T MANY classy films in the DPP listings but Mario Bava's *Blood Bath* was certainly one of them. This is a stylish, plot-twisting whodunnit marred only by the severely frivolous finale. The element of mystery is sustained throughout and even though the violent incidents are graphic they aren't its *raison d'être*. The same can't be said of most of the plot-redundant gore films that were spawned in its wake.

Mario Bava has made many influential films, or to be more precise, influential *sequences*. For example, his 1960 *Black Sunday* contains a startling eye-piercing scene that was honoured in Fulci's *Zombie Flesh Eaters*; his *Blood and Black Lace* features a drowned girl's face peering lifelessly from the bottom of a bathtub filled with water, a scene recreated in Roger Corman's *Bloody Mama*; while *Planet of the Vampires* has a sequence depicting the discovery of a fossilised alien life-form, mimicked almost fifteen years later in Ridley Scott's *Alien*. *Blood Bath* is often cited as being the inspiration for the abundant stalk-and-slash movies of the eighties. However, films like *Friday the 13th* and its many sequels (most notably part 2), copied only the grisly murders and abandoned – or simply lacked the skills to realise – the style and panache of Bava's original.

The first graphic murder in *Blood Bath* shows a half-naked girl having her throat chopped deeply with a machete. In another particularly brutal scene a man is struck full in the face with a machete. Although the impact isn't shown in detail the blade is seen buried deep in the face, then being prised from the massive wound. Effective editing makes the scene horribly realistic. A couple having sex are speared through and pinned to the bed, the spearhead seen penetrating naked flesh. There are other scenes of violence, such as stabbing through clothing.

Blood Bath was released on the Hokushin label with an unofficial 18 certificate. Later it was re-released by Redemption Films with a proper 18 certificate. Forty-three seconds of cuts were required to achieve this rating.

Martin Scorsese has a great fondness for Bava, calling his films "a kind of Italian gothic." There's "hardly any story," he says in *Scorsese on Scorsese*,

> just atmosphere, with all that fog and ladies walking down corridors... I could just put them on loops and have one going in one room in my house, one going on in another, as I have many televisions around. I do that sometimes, put different tapes on and just walk around creating a whole mood...

BLOOD FEAST

USA 1963

cast: Connie Mason, Mal Arnold, Thomas Wood, Lyn Bolton, Scott H Hall, Toni Calvert

story: A Louise Downe

producer: David F Friedman

director: HERSCHELL GORDON LEWIS

Fuad Ramses is a caterer who specialises in rare and exotic dishes. He is also responsible for brutal killings in the city, using human body parts in a ritual he believes will bring the goddess Ishtar to life.

"I'VE OFTEN COMPARED it with a Walt Whitman poem," H G Lewis once said of *Blood Feast*, "it's no good but it's the first."[1]

Made in 1963, *Blood Feast* is the oldest film to appear on the DPP list.[2] It seems strange that a clumsy, semi-professional film from the early sixties should be caught up in the controversy surrounding an altogether new era of ultraviolent movies on video. The entire film took about a week to make – though some sources claim production ran to a full nine days on account of rain – and is populated with a cast of unknown actors. The only person whose name may have been familiar at the time of its release is Connie Mason – not an actress per se, but a *Playboy* model. Even director Lewis himself was under no illusions and in 1981 claimed that the film's producer, David Friedman, had "found her under a rock... Connie Mason was not known for her thespian talent. She had talents but they didn't lie in that direction."

No attempt is made to disguise the film's cheapness or the ineptitude of its actors. Mal Arnold, who plays Fuad Ramses, can at times be seen reading his lines – his eyes scanning an off-screen prompt-board. In one flashback sequence he portrays an Egyptian pharaoh carrying out a sacrifice. A woman lies on an altar constructed from concrete blocks as Arnold approaches with a snake. As he backs away, he obviously catches his heel on something out of shot – an electric cable perhaps? – and stumbles. The filmmakers had no time or inclination to do a re-take. But then, the skill of the actors, the quality of the plot, and the abilities of the production crew were irrelevant to the fundamental purpose of *Blood Feast*. The film was made as a vehicle to test a new concept on a movie-going audience: excessively graphic violence.

Within its first minute, *Blood Feast* has given the audience its first violent incident. A woman is stabbed in the eye. The attack may happen offscreen, but the resultant carnage is there for all to see, as the killer gloats over a knife smeared with blood and from which hangs loose slivers of flesh. When the woman loses her leg, the process of amputation is obscured by the killer's head and shoulders, but again there is some revelry in the aftermath – a grisly stump of flesh and bone protruding from the soap suds. Later in the film, a victim has her head split open. Again, budgetary restrictions prevent our witnessing the infliction of the injury. But this is amply compensated for by the lingering aftermath, which provides a close-up shot of loose brain matter being fondled by the killer. The final excessive gore effect is an offscreen tongue removal, followed by the ghastly sight of the killer holding a dripping (sheep) tongue, roots and all, above the cranberry sauce-filled mouth of his victim.

In 1973, the *Monster Times*[3] classed *Blood Feast* as a negative groundbreaking film and a cinematic-miracle-in-reverse. In other words, one of several films "that have succeeded in establishing totally unprecedented standards of atrocious acting, technical ineptitude and execrable [*sic*] bad taste." Said magazine editor Joe Kane, "We're sorry to report that *Blood Feast* director Herschell G Lewis did not at once fade into the oblivion he so richly deserved."

Indeed he didn't. Sights as gruesome as these in *Blood Feast* had never been seen in cinemas, and the film launched a very profitable film career for Lewis – as well as cementing cult status for him in years to come. *Blood Feast* was to horror cinema what the Sex Pistols were to rock'n'roll. Lewis and his cohorts had a hit on their hands which was to have an impact on a generation of equally influential filmmakers like Tobe Hooper, and wannabes like J G 'Pat' Patterson. They fully intended to exploit their veritable gold mine. The novelty of gore meant that prints of the film would often come back from theatres with key scenes excised by souvenir hunters. At the first anniversary bash of Rick Sullivan's fanzine *Gore Gazette* in November 1981, guest of honour H G Lewis told those in attendance:

> ...one of the problems we always had was getting prints back mangled. Projectionists would cut ten feet out of it, it was a terrible problem because 35mm colour prints were not cheap... some of the prints circulating were cut to shreds

> and the best effects were gone. What somebody could do with a ten foot 35mm motion picture is beyond me.[4]

(As if this in itself wasn't enough, the film for a time fell into the control of a producer called Stan Kohlberg, who was to cut the front titles off many of the prints and replace them with a card that read "*Blood Feast* made by Stanford Kohlberg.")

Not only did the new popularity and portability of video enable *Blood Feast* to be seen by a completely fresh audience in Britain (thanks to distributors Astra), but it also brought the film renewed interest in its native America. In the seventies *Blood Feast* was regarded by many promoters as kitsch and played as a midnight attraction for a time, billed as the "worst film ever made." It took the more discerning video distributors of the eighties to find the right audience for the gore film that started it all.

Lewis followed *Blood Feast* with other gore-oriented works, notably *Two Thousand Maniacs!* and *Color Me Blood Red* (which, along with *Blood Feast*, constituted Lewis' 'gore trilogy'). Although he made films in other genres, most of Lewis' output was horror and he would later direct *Monster a Go-Go*, *A Taste of Blood*, *The Gruesome Twosome*, *The Wizard of Gore* and *The Gore Gore Girls*. Although this latter picture extended the atrocities Lewis had begun with *Blood Feast*, offering even more redoubtable carnage (onscreen as well as off), it also showed that after all this time the director had no intention of betraying his cost-cutting acumen:[5] when the finished picture came up short, he didn't bother getting any actors back to shoot additional scenes, but instead stuck two mannequin heads on a table and dubbed dialogue over the top! Many viewers found *The Gore Gore Girls* particularly offensive and misogynistic (one scene shows a woman's nipples being snipped off, with milk pouring from one mutilated teat and chocolate from the other). Lewis determined there was nothing else left for him to show, and with *The Gore Gore Girls* ended his career as a director to concentrate instead on other lines of work, which included writing books on mass communications.

Renewed interest in *Blood Feast* in the eighties led producer Johnny Legend to contact H G Lewis with a view to directing *Blood Feast II* – or *Gore Feast* as it was also announced. Although he had little intention of leaving the "good life" as a writer, word got around that *Blood Feast II* was a viable direct-to-video project in which Lewis had shown serious interest. The film was officially said to be "on ice" in the Winter 1983/84 edition of the *Splatter Times*, no less because

Legend had lost the potentially lucrative British market thanks to the 'video nasties' campaign. However, in 2002, after a 30-year break from filmmaking, Lewis himself would direct the sequel *Blood Feast II: All U Can Eat*.

Blood Feast was made in the same year as *Carry On Cabby*.

Blood Rites

aka: The Ghastly Ones (original title)
USA 1967
cast: Veronica Radburn, Anne Linden, Maggie Rogers, Richards Romanos, Fib La Blaque, Hal Borske, Hal Sherwood, Eileen Haves, Don Williams
story: Andy Milligan & Hal Sherwood
producer: Jerome Fredric
director: ANDY MILLIGAN

The turn of the last century. Three sisters and their husbands convene at the isolated family estate for the reading of a will. The staff is strange. Death follows.

BLOOD RITES IS so amateur a film there are times when the director's agitated instructions to the actors are audible. The colour is washed out and grainy, the film having been shot originally in 16mm on a $700 Auricon camera. But, like the period piece setting, these are characteristic anomalies of an Andy Milligan production and it is Milligan's obvious enthusiasm that makes his films watchable and oddly enjoyable, despite their prevailing inanity.

The soundtrack alternates between static, muffled lines of dialogue and portentous library music. In the pre-credit sequence, set on the grounds of the family estate, one character looks around (staring into bushes and up at trees as he wanders along). The sound of the foliage thumping the microphone is clearly discernible. To pad out the running time, characters ruminate at great length over the most basic details – such as lawyer H H Dobbs' name, and the fact that he's still alive after all these years. Richard:

> H H Dobbs? *The* H H Dobbs? Hubert Humphrey Dobbs? ... I can't believe it! I thought he'd be dead by now! The first books I read in law school were by H H Dobbs!

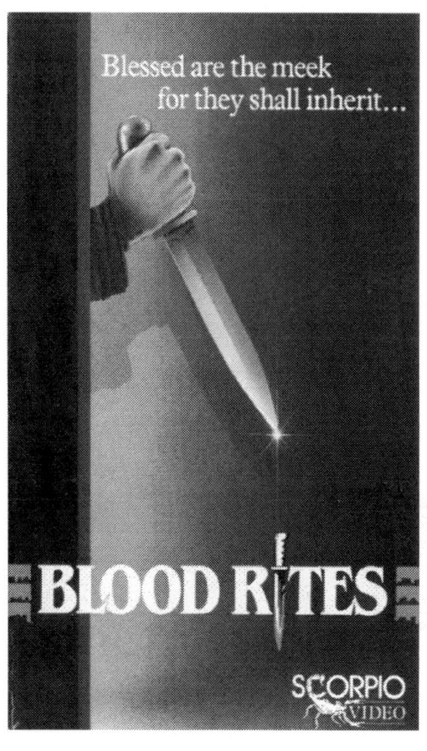

The plot of *Blood Rites* has been used countless times over the years; Paul Leni first employed it in his 1927 film *The Cat and the Canary*. Heirs to a will are called to a lonely mansion and systematically killed off. Milligan receives no awards for his own red herring ploy, and indeed seems to have completely missed the concept of the diversionary tactic altogether: There is no doubting that Colin the hunchback is the prime suspect, because we see him murdering two people in the opening shot! So, it's baffling to be told that someone other than him is behind the mystery murders.

However, what Milligan lacks in storyline he amply makes up for with his bouts of full-frontal gore. The violent moments are few and far between, but they stand as particularly gross, a fact aided immeasurably by the obvious shortcomings of the budget – their shoddy execution makes them seem somehow all the more horrible. (The effects were created by Milligan himself, who also made the costumes for the cast, drawing on the skills he learned as a dressmaker.[1]) When Colin attacks the lovers in the pre-title sequence, he yanks out the man's eye, only to hold aloft an object that appears to be the size of an apple! His attack on the girl is equally violent and equally unrealistic – he chops off her hand, then lifts her skirt to repeatedly hack at what is clearly a mannequin. The murder of Donald (Richard Romanus, who would secure a central role in Martin Scorsese's *Mean Streets*) is the other main scene of controversy, said by Walter L Gay in *The Sleaze Merchants* to be "realistic enough" to have offended Stephen King. He is secured to a bench and his shirt is lifted to reveal his bare stomach. The killer then plunges a knife into the abdomen, twisting it, turning it, and pulling out handfuls of bloody matter. Finally a wood saw is used to cut the torso in two. Such scenes are Milligan trademarks. "The apparent recklessness of the camerawork," noted Tim Lucas in *Video Watchdog*, "lends a tone of accidental, snuff movie authenticity to the slayings."[2]

Another trademark was Milligan's penchant for flailing with the camera in scenes

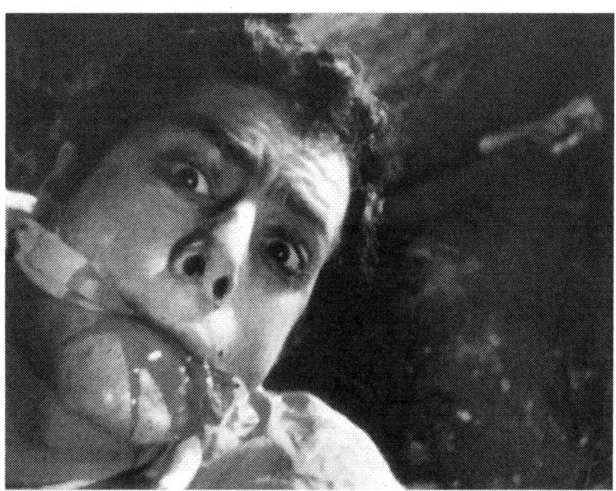
Richards Romanos, later to star in Martin Scorsese's *Mean Streets*. *Blood Rites*.

of carnage, a corner-cutting effort to heighten the horror or chaos. During the scene in which a character is impaled with a pitchfork, the swirling camera inadvertently reveals a crew member. Other shots are framed peculiarly and are often underlit. Everything is tight and in close-up – indeed there doesn't appear to be a long-shot in the whole movie.

To *Castle of Frankenstein* magazine, Milligan's camera provided some of the "most bleary, indistinct photography ever yet seen."[3] *Demonique* said it was sure to induce eye-straining headaches.[4]

Milligan made films with titles bigger and wilder than their content. *Torture Dungeon*, *Bloodthirsty Butchers*, *Guru the Mad Monk*, *The Rats are Coming! The Werewolves are Here!*, *The Man with Two Heads*, *Blood*,[5] and *Carnage* were his most audacious efforts. He tended to include an effeminate male character at the centre of his films. In *Blood Rites* it is Robert's brother (an incestuous relationship is also heavily implied between the brothers). In *Torture Dungeon* the Duke of Norfolk describes himself not as bisexual but as "tri-sexual" because he'll "try to have sex with anyone." These characters might be considered an expression of Milligan's own homosexuality, though in real-life few people knew he was gay, a fact that only became public with his death from AIDS in June 1991.

Blood Rites was released on Scorpio Video without cuts, with a video sleeve that was reversible: one side contained bloody stills from the film, while the other compromised with an inoffensive blood-free artistic representation of a knife.

In 1972, Milligan remade *Blood Rites* as *Legacy of Blood*. Also released on video in the UK this goreless adaptation brought nothing new or different to the story but served to recoup for Milligan some of the cash he lost on *Blood Rites*. Although *Blood Rites* had turned a tidy profit for its backers J.E.R. Pictures, with whom the director was bound in a three-picture deal,[6] Milligan had received only $1,000.

Bloody Moon

aka: Die Säge des Todes (original title); Colegialas Violadas; Profonde tenebre

Spain/West Germany 1981

cast: Olivia Pascal, Christopher Moosbrugger, Nadja Gerganoff, Alexander Waechter, Jasmin Losensky, Corinna Gillwald

story: Rayo Casablance

producer: Wolf C Hartwig

director: JESÚS FRANCO

A language school situated on a holiday resort in Spain is beset with problems, not least incest and murder.

MORE OF A 'proper' movie (in that it has a plot) than Jesús Franco's usual efforts, *Bloody Moon* remains an ordeal to sit through. "You hope the camera remains focused," was the best one critic could wish for of a Franco movie.[1] Using a tired murder-to-gain-a-family-inheritance plot, like *Blood Rites* it opens with a scene identifying a murderous character – in this case Miguel – who happens to be in the vicinity of each subsequent murder but ultimately turns out to be a red herring.

A certain porno quality pervades the film, thanks to the fact that every female character looks like a glamour model for whom the boarding school setting is nothing more than an opportunity to lounge around the pool and hold dance-mad disco parties. (They dance to a weird hybrid of Europop and rock'n'roll, jiving to one particularly asinine record whose lyric comprises only this: "Shake your baby / Rock your baby.")

The implied incestuous relationship between Manuela and Miguel, which is afforded plenty of angst-ridden screen time, is, unsurprisingly, just another red herring. "If we could just get rid of everyone around us," a frustrated Manuela says at one point, "then things could be as they were." Miguel stares into the distance with menacing intent.

There is one sequence in *Bloody Moon* that does threaten to conjure genuine atmosphere, when Angela hears the killer's voice on her tuition tape. But Franco is more content to take easier routes, and bestow the story with half-hearted, curiously inappropriate diversions in a bid to build and sustain suspense. Anytime a student at the language school is alone in a darkened room and we believe the killer is about to strike, Franco interjects an unlikely alternative to the perceived threat – such as a cat or mannequin throwing a shadow on the wall. In one especially hapless ploy, a little boy is outside the house selling "souvenirs" in the middle of the night.

All the murders take place at night under a full moon. Why this should be the case isn't clear, although it does provide the film with plenty of foreboding full-moon cutaways. Without doubt, the most convincing and engaging aspects of *Bloody Moon* are the gruesome special effects (although this doesn't extend to Miguel's disfigured face makeup, which looks like pancake mix gone wrong). The prologue depicting the murder of a girl by Miguel shows him stabbing his victim in the abdomen. The scissors are seen repeatedly penetrating the girl's bare midriff in close-up. When Eva is murdered, the knife is shown entering her back and exiting in similarly fine detail through her right breast. Blood on breasts and knives in contact with breasts have always been a sticking point with the BBFC, and it is no surprise that this scene was removed from the certified version of the film released some years later.

A decapitation on a stone-saw is the most gruelling sequence. Not simply because it is depicted in graphic detail, but because the whole process is so slow and protracted – thanks to Franco's unwillingness to waste a single frame – as the heavyweight machine encroaches on its victim in real time. (The actress is secured to real cutting equipment and the machinery propels her alarmingly close to the spinning blade.) To lend credibility to the unlikely scenario, the victim is under the misconception that being tied up by a masked stranger is a prelude to kinky sex. Her unintentionally ridiculous dialogue comprises lines like, "I said I was game for anything!"

The sequence is a parody of the cliché from early westerns, where the female lead is captured by a masked villain and tied to a railway line. Like the train being stopped at the last moment by the hero, in this instance the blade is stopped inches from the victim's neck by an intervening child who happens to be playing nearby. However, the girl is not rescued from her fate and the man in black restarts the equipment. This time there is a decapitation from which the camera doesn't flinch. The blood that spurts from the resultant stump could be construed as a cheap porn-gore pop shot, if one suspected the wayfaring Franco to be so inclined...

Bloody Moon was released by Interlight Video in both cut and uncut versions. Following its ban it was later re-released heavily cut with an 18 certificate on the resurrected Vipco label.

The Bogey Man

title on print: The Boogey Man
USA 1980
cast: Suzanna Love, Ron James, John Carradine, Introducing Nicholas Love, Llewelyn Thomas
story: Ulli Lommel
producer: Ulli Lommel
director: ULLI LOMMEL

Lacey and Willy are haunted by the image of a murdered man. He appears in a mirror and is 'freed' when Lacey smashes it, embarking on supernatural mayhem.

THE BOGEY MAN is a modestly effective horror movie that invigorates the teens-in-peril sub-genre with a supernatural twist and some extraordinary deaths. It accomplishes what it sets out to do without the chest-beating of its follow-up, *Revenge of the Bogeyman* (also on the DPP list), and is masterly by comparison.

Belying its *Halloween* influence: *The Bogey Man*.

With a protagonist whose face remains obscured and who doesn't say a word it's safe to assume that director Lommel was inspired by John Carpenter's *Halloween* – a film that would be lambasted as being "old hat" in Lommel's follow-up – even down to his use of a main theme that is reminiscent of Carpenter's synthesiser score.

There's a lot of wandering around in almost complete darkness (table lamps provide no discernible illumination), some lame shock tactics (hands reach out menacingly but belong to friends and family not monsters), and one protracted sequence which fails to go anywhere (the overwrought carving of a chicken at a dinner table). Lommel, however, does come up with a few solidly paced scares, notably when Lacey, one of the protagonists, is menaced by a reflection in a mirror that doesn't correlate with the room behind her.

The emphasis placed on mirrors gives *The Bogey Man* not only an unusual twist, but also strains of folklore and superstition. For instance, the aforementioned sequence has origins in the belief that peering into a mirror in a death-chamber will reflect a corpse looking over your shoulder. It's a sequence that works well in itself, but the reluctance of the filmmakers to exploit the lore to which they're subscribing leaves other scenes quirky and abstract. On the surface there is no rhyme or reason why Willy should get spooked by his own reflection in the barn, or why he should paint all the mirrors in the house black. But looking deeper, these actions carry a mythical significance that the film is reluctant to divulge.[1] Similarly the mysterious appearance of a paper bag containing mirror shards may seem weird on the surface, but it represents an undisclosed symbolic link: i.e. placing the pieces of a broken mirror into a bag and burying it was thought to counteract any bad luck generated by breaking it in the first place. Apart from a few oblique references – a smashed mirror that frees everything it's seen – the filmmakers don't share the mythology drawn upon in their story, which is a shame as given this context one feels *The Bogey Man* would be a much stronger work.

Some German critics read the film as less a horror film and more a social commentary on American teenagers.[2] A curious stance, no doubt influenced by Lommel having had tutelage under Rainer Werner Fassbinder, the leading voice in Germany's "new cinema."[3] After *Bogey Man*, Lommel's work remained steadfastly in an American vein but with some idiosyncratic ideas and occasional arthouse diversions.[4] This, his American debut, has a peculiar fluidity to the way murder scenes are orchestrated. The deaths of two sisters and their annoying younger brother, for instance, are a case in point. These killings happen in close succession, but the 'hierarchy' of the attacks seems wrong. Furthermore, a scene in which a young man gets a knife through his neck whilst seated in his car is laughably contrived, but at least it has a satisfyingly bloody, genuinely eerie climax.

The above death scenes feature close-ups of sharp objects penetrating flesh and rank high in reasons why *The Bogey Man* should have ended up on the DPP list. Other contributing factors may have included early scenes of the infants Lacey and Willy, gagged and threatened with knives, and the general proximity of sex and violence when their drunken mother entertains a masked male friend.

Rumour has it that *The Bogey Man* encountered several production problems, notably the disappearance of the soundtrack and a freak snowstorm. These may or may not have contributed to the boom microphone straying into shot and staying there for the duration of one lengthy dialogue scene. (The 'arty' composition of this sequence – via a mirror no less – ensures that the rogue microphone takes prime position.)

THE BURNING

USA 1980
cast: Brian Matthews, Leah Ayres, Brian Backer, Larry Joshua, Jason Alexander, Ned Eisenberg, Carrick Glenn
story: Peter Lawrence, Brad Grey, Bob Weinstein, Harvey Weinstein, Tony Maylam
producer: Harvey Weinstein
director: TONY MAYLAM

At Camp Blackfoot a group of campers play a prank on caretaker Cropsy, which backfires and leaves him horribly disfigured. He seeks revenge.

THE BURNING IS an uninspired retread of *Friday the 13th* even down to the similar summer camp setting in which a group of teenagers are selectively murdered in grisly fashion. Cropsy (Lou David) is this movie's Jason Voorhees. Such a basic idea when attached to a simplistic plot yields very little in the way of absorbing entertainment. Indeed, for things to happen and the story to 'progress,' people behave in a stupid and irrational manner: having sex in unlikely places, for instance, or wandering alone in dark woods.

There is an attempt to inject some *Porky's*-style slapstick humour (a film made the same year and aimed at a predominantly teen audience). At times it succeeds, notably in the scene where the obnoxious Glazer (Larry Joshua) is shot in the pants with an air pistol. When *The Burning* endeavours to shock however, it fails miserably, simply because it declines to stray from over-familiar clichés. A bird suddenly flying out from behind an opened door accompanied by a jolt on the soundtrack, for example, irritates rather than startles. The teen sex sequences, and imperilled shower scene, are simply *de rigueur* – as is the sudden lunging into shot of the apparently dead killer at the end.

Matters aren't helped by a soundtrack by former Yes keyboardist Rick Wakeman, comprising "electronic janglings"[1] wherever the vengeful Cropsy goes, or the apathetic performances of the cast. However, two young actors who marked their debut in *The Burning* did go on to greater things – Jason Alexander and Holly Hunter.[2]

Unremarkable but for the gore effects. *The Burning*.

The clever special effects were created by Tom Savini, considered something of a maestro in horror prosthetics at the time, having worked on *Friday the 13th* and many subsequent successful genre productions. (Savini turned down *Friday the 13th Part 2* to work on *The Burning*.) As tended to be the case on many of the films in which he was involved, Savini's gruesome decapitations and imaginatively staged mayhem provide the focus. It's fair to say that the American stalk-and-slash genre owes as much to Savini's ingenious prosthetic skills as it does the influence of Mario Bava's *Blood Bath*.

Thanks to Savini, for a time during the eighties special effects people were held in as high regard as the director. Many fans flocked to see horror films because they featured the talents of Rob Bottin (*The Thing*), Rick Baker (*Videodrome*) and other rising stars creating unique, mind-blowing fantasies on the screen. The popularity of these artists meant that their name attached to a film was interpreted as an endorsement, and would often draw audiences into an otherwise unremarkable picture – as was the case with Savini and the likes of *Rosemary's Killer*, *Nightmares in a Damaged Brain* and *The Burning*.

When Thorn EMI submitted *The Burning* to the BBFC, fifteen seconds of cuts were requested for a pre-VRA X-certificate. These cuts were agreed upon, but the company inadvertently mass-produced and released duplicates of the uncut master. The result was that in September 1983, police raided Thorn EMI offices and seized the master tape and videocassette copies of the film. On June 21, 1984, Uxbridge Magistrates Court cleared the company of obscenity charges. (Defending, Richard Du Cann said that *The Burning* was "simply a bogeyman story... The horrific scenes take up only a minuscule amount of a film predominantly made up of some of the most boring teenage dialogue you are ever likely to witness.")

Although Thorn EMI recalled the uncut tape and offered to replace it free of charge with the slightly shorter certified version, not everyone returned the offending video. The company repeated its offer when the film was cleared of obscenity and warned dealers that continued distribution of the uncensored print would be liable to prosecution. The cut version was identifiable by a date stamp on a two-colour label, as opposed to the uncut version which was date-free with a single-colour label. Another give-away was that the two versions could also be identified by the thickness of the video box lid: the cut version was released in a standard video case, while the uncut film was enclosed in a more substantial heavy-duty box.

The censored film was re-released by Vipco.

CAIN'S CUTTHROATS

aka: Cain's Way; Caine's Way; The Blood Seekers; Justice Cain
USA 1969
cast: John Carradine, Scott Brady, Bruce Kimball, Russ McCubbin, Tereza Thaw, Valda Hansen
story: Will Denmark
producer: Kent Osborne & Budd Dell
director: KENT OSBORNE

1870. Captain Justice Cain is visited by members of his former regiment, now outlaws, who want him to lead an army in a new war against the Yankees. Cain refuses and violence ensues.

CAIN'S CUTTHROATS IS an obscure western using a regularly utilised plot in which a decent man, Justice Cain (Scott Brady), seeks revenge on those who murdered his kinfolk. (The film was virtually remade as *The Deadly Trackers* starring Richard Harris in 1973.) Although the film slows down considerably after the first twenty minutes it is unusually brutal for its time – the racially-motivated gang rape of a mother in front of her young son being particularly truculent. The cast are typical B-movie types and the ubiquitous John Carradine obviously revels in his role of Simms, an ambiguous preacher-cum-bounty hunter, delivering Biblical platitudes one moment and hacking the head from a corpse the next. He also delivers some of the best lines, saying of one outlaw who is killed whilst having sex: "He wenteth before he cameth." At times, the camaraderie between Simms and Cain is reminiscent of the light-hearted episodes that would off-set the violence in westerns from Clint Eastwood's Malpaso film company (such as *The Outlaw Josey Wales*, which also bears a thematic resemblance to *Cain's Cutthroats*).

Cain's Cutthroats appeared briefly on a list of banned and 'suspect' titles that appeared in the video trade press, a fact that has largely been forgotten by collectors and genre historians, due to it being a western as opposed to a horror picture. The violence consists of brief though fairly bloody shootouts in the style of *The Wild Bunch* – made the same year – with outlaws revelling in their brutality. The gang, led by the one-eyed Amison (Robert Dix), bicker like schoolchildren when not committing acts of violence; murder and rape cause them to laugh uncontrollably. One of the first victims to fall to the gang, a Yankee soldier on a payroll wagon, is shot in the belly, leading to a fleeting glimpse of a gaping, offal-wound. (Notably, *Soldier Blue* was made the following year.) But it is the rape sequence that caused most concern, even if it isn't unduly explicit. The continuous racial insults and the fact that a minor is forced to watch certainly intensifies the unpleasant event.

The film was released uncertified on the VTC label under the category of "violent western." Prior to this, in 1978, it had a theatrical run as *Cain's Way*, shorn of four minutes. Nevertheless, under this title, the film appears to have run on slightly longer, making more of the futility of Cain's plight. (Cain is abandoned because, as the preacher Simms puts it, he is no longer motivated by revenge but by "a lust for killing.") According to the *Monthly Film Bulletin* (*MFB*), the execution of Amison at the film's end inspires Cain, cheated of his prey, to fall to his knees in front of the body. The VTC print, on the other, hand ends suddenly with a freeze-frame of Amison's slumped body, over which the credits play.[1]

As an actor, Kent Osborne appeared in a number of movies by low-budget film-maker Al Adamson, one of which was a western entitled *Five Bloody Graves* made in 1969 (featuring a narrator in the form of Death!). The two productions share several of the same cast members, no less Scott Brady and John Carradine – who plays a preacher in both. There is every likelihood that the films were made back-to-back, and the respective film-makers certainly appear to have spurred one another on with a desire to make a raw and gritty western, far removed from the other westerns of this era: Walter L Gay in *The Sleaze Merchants* describes Adamson's *Five Bloody Graves* as a "savage storm of ferocious Indian assaults, shooting, rape, torture, and assorted other mayhem."

Before the rot sets in: John Morghen in *Cannibal Apocalypse*.

CANNIBAL APOCALYPSE

aka: Apocalypse Domani (original title); Cannibals in the Streets; Invasion of the Flesh Hunters; Savage Apocalypse
Italy/Spain 1980
cast: John Saxon, John Morghen, Elizabeth Turner, Tony King, Cindy Hamilton, Ray Williams
story: Anthony M Dawson, José Luis Martinez Molla, Dardano Sacchetti, Maurizio & Sandro Amati
producer: Maurizio & Sandro Amati
director: ANTHONY M DAWSON [Antonio Margheriti]

An American extraction team in Vietnam is attacked by the prisoners of war they are trying to help. The team return to the US as flesh-hungry cannibals.

CANNIBAL APOCALYPSE WAS a spin-off from the fading Italian cannibal genre and the Vietnam resurgence initiated by Francis Ford Coppola's *Apocalypse Now*.[1] The Vietnam sequence is over almost before the opening credits have finished, however, and the film comes across as a confused hybrid of both genres. John Saxon plays Norman Hopper, a deteriorating war veteran, and is the only character that holds any interest as he fails to align himself back in society. But it is a mystery virus that ails him, not psychological trauma as one might expect. In this respect director Antonio Margheriti (using the name Anthony M Dawson) tries to break from tradition, though in reality he has only produced a contemporary modification of the Dracula and vampire myth: Saxon travels to a distant and uncivilised country (Vietnam substituting Transylvania) where he is bitten and contaminated with a behaviour-modifying virus. Though he tries to fight off his desire for human blood he eventually succumbs and sides with the contaminated soldiers who infected him. Those people who survive attacks by the pack also become flesh-eating psychotics. Viewed today, scenes where the precocious Mary makes a pass at Saxon are far more alarming than any of the film's flesh-rending. She seems hardly older than twelve, but at one point Saxon lifts her dress to reveal a tiny G-string and barely visible fringe of immature pubic hair.[2]

Saxon told *Is it...Uncut?*[3] that he found the English version of the *Cannibal Apocalypse* script interesting,[4] but that it gave no clue as to the filmmakers' real intent: to cash-in on Japan's and Germany's penchant for "bloody cannibalism at its most vulgar." Saxon claims to have only discovered this

> later when we were ready to do a scene, and I asked "Where did this meat we are all supposed to be devouring like this come from?" ... did I find out this was supposed to be human flesh. And more specifically when I came to understand (not clear in the English translation to me) that this meat included the testicles of one of our brother soldiers, I asked Margheriti to exclude me from the scene which he did. However, I was now in almost suicidal despair...

The film was a big hit in Korea. Margheriti denies it was his intention to include so much gore, and puts this fact down to the producers, who he says wanted to cash-in on the trend launched by George Romero's *Dawn of the Dead*. "I've always tried to capture an effect of gracefulness and gentleness," the director said in *Spaghetti Nightmares*.

The British video release of *Cannibal Apocalypse* was an unexpurgated version. Although the gore effects are extreme, they are not particularly well done. The penchant for splatter results in some strangely protracted scenes. A shot of a garage mechanic having his leg severed with a grinding disc, for instance, with arteries and bone visible in the wound, seems to go on forever. Other mutilations include eyeballs enucleated with fingers, chunks of flesh being bitten and torn, and John Morghen (playing Bukowski) having his entire body contents blasted out of his abdomen in the final sewer scenes. (The resultant gaping hole which is used as a framing device for the background action is an idea lifted wholesale from John Huston's *The Life and Times of Judge Roy Bean*.)[5] Replay's video sleeve displayed a self-imposed, though unofficial, XX-certificate.

CANNIBAL FEROX

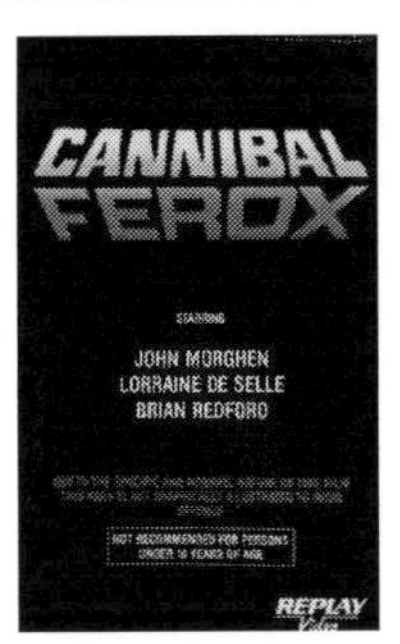

aka: Make Them Die Slowly; Let Them Die Slowly; Die Rache der Kannibalen; Woman from Deep River
Italy 1981
cast: John Morghen, Lorraine de Selle, Brian Redford, Zora Kerowa, Walter Lloyd, Meg Fleming
story: Umberto Lenzi
producer: Antonio Crescenzi
director: UMBERTO LENZI

A group ventures deep into the jungles of South America where they encounter primitive cannibals and violent, drug-addled emerald hunters.

CONSIDERING THAT DIRECTOR Umberto Lenzi went to the Amazon to film *Cannibal Ferox*,[1] he doesn't make an awful lot out of the fact and the locations could be pretty much anywhere. Even the opening shots – looking down on the jungle from a plane with the superimposed legend "RIO DELLE AMAZZONI" – are ill-matched and appear to be taken from some other source. More exasperating is the New York sub-plot that serves only to provide this Italian movie with its quota of American cutaways (each accompanied by a brash 'Big Apple' score): Mike Logan (Giovanni Lombardo Radice) rips off a drug gang to the tune of $100,000 and goes on the run, ending up in the Amazon, which happens to be where anthropology student Gloria (Lorraine De Selle) is headed. Although he had made *Deep River Savages* back in 1972, it was only the success of Ruggero Deodato's *Cannibal Holocaust* almost a decade later that prompted Lenzi to return to the genre, a purely financial decision the director claims.[2]

Indeed *Cannibal Ferox* is essentially a rehash of Deodato's yarn but without the technical embroidery that makes Deodato's movie so special. It even incorporates similar sounding musical passages for its similarly composed shots. Most blatant of these is Rudy (Danilo Mattei) photographing the mutilated body he finds tied to a stake on first entering the village, a direct lift of the scene in *Cannibal Holocaust* where the filmmakers happen upon a native woman impaled on a stake. But it is not enough to merely mimic scenes; Lenzi must be seen to go one up. His *coup de grâce*: a live and screaming female victim, impaled through each breast.

Lenzi also employs the inverted racism of Deodato's film by teaming primitive flesh-eating savages with belligerent white protagonists, who are amoral and completely unsympathetic, but whose presence serves only to demean the primitive peoples yet further. In the end, Gloria's anthropological bent serves to point out the obvious (in a dialogue that virtually paraphrases the closing line in *Cannibal Holocaust*):

> What a fool I was, thinking I had to leave New York to find the reasons behind cannibalism... It's us and our superior society!

Elsewhere in the movie, the cannibals play with twentieth-century artefacts such as a credit card,[3] a wristwatch and a camera. But the out-of-place objects have no significance in this film – they are just images that Lenzi has borrowed from Deodato.

Lenzi jettisons the film-within-a-film framework of Deodato's movie and cranks up the viciousness. Not content with the usual consortium of real animal mutilation[4] and prosthetic limb hacking, we are treated to graphic depictions of eye gouging, genitals being hacked off and breasts being punctured with meat hooks (for a tribe still reliant on stone cutting tools, where these iron hooks might have come from is a mystery).[5] *Fangoria* described the result as "a stupefyingly vicious piece of garbage with absolutely no redeeming values whatsoever."[6] The film was evidently too much for horror hostess Elvira as well: its release on the US Thrillervideo label came without the traditional endorsement she bestowed on other movies from the same company.

In Britain, Replay Video released two versions of the film: the first was complete and carried a self-imposed "XX"-certificate, in a package that carried nothing but the title on the cover, some cast credits, and the warning:

> Due to the specific and horrific nature of this film this area is not graphically illustrated to avoid offence.

Inverted racism. *Cannibal Ferox.*

The re-release carried a BBFC 18 certificate and was cut. The sleeve featured the same warning as above, but also a drawing of bones and a nonsensical axiom:

WOULD YOU BELIEVE IRON-AGE MAN STILL LIVES
THEY FOUND OUT!

The video sleeve for the latter was without two strong scenes that had featured on the reverse of the sleeve before it. Both sleeves however, carried the same running time and reference number. The DPP list makes no differentiation between the two versions, and both are effectively banned. However, it's impossible to verify whether *Cannibal Ferox* is "Banned in 31 Countries," as several of its American distributors have claimed. (It's not an unreasonable figure, but who would collate such information?) For *Eaten Alive*, Lenzi's next digression into cannibal territory (his third and final entry in the sub-genre), opposition seems to have increased proportionally and the distributors boasted of a ban in not thirty-one but thirty-eight countries.[7]

Cannibal Holocaust director Ruggero Deodato was mortified by the censorship of nipples in this Spanish film still, prior to signing it at the Festival of Fantastic Films 2005, Manchester.

CANNIBAL HOLOCAUST

Italy 1979
cast: Robert Kerman, Francesca Ciardi, Perry Pirkanen, Luca Giorgio Barbareschi, Salvatore Basile
story: Gianfranco Clerici
producer: Giovani Masini
director: RUGGERO DEODATO

A team of documentary filmmakers is missing in the jungles of South America. A search party is mobilised, who discover the missing party via rolls of found film.

DESPITE ITS CLICHÉS and portentous dialogue, *Cannibal Holocaust* is a very clever and powerful film. What is a threadbare adventure yarn – and a return to the themes of Deodato's earlier *Cannibal* – has been given a complete refurbishment thanks to shaky handheld camerawork! Together with gratuitous animal slaughter and indigenous actors who aren't afraid to munch on ugly looking food, the handheld camera infuses the film with a newsreel veneer – one that has succeeded in fooling people for decades into believing what is shown on screen is real, including the murders.[1] (Many of those who aren't fooled tend to read the film as a piece of social commentary but then denigrate it because it's only exploitation.)[2]

Controversy has hounded the film from the start. Shortly after opening in Italy, it was confiscated and declared obscene by the High Court, while an old law pertaining to cruelty against guinea pigs, no less, helped to get the film banned outright.[3] The ruling was overturned in 1983. In France, following an article in the magazine *Photo*,[4] news began to spread that *Cannibal Holocaust* "was the [film] in which men were really dismembered, beheaded, castrated and *mangiati vivi*!"[5] This completely erroneous fact continues to be trotted out by the ill-informed and lazy journalists. In Britain in April 1993, a raid on a comic mart in Birmingham (emotively referred to as a 'children's fair' by the press) was reported as having resulted in "the first known seizure in the city of a snuff video"[6] – in reality, a copy of *Cannibal Holocaust*.

Far from being a snuff film, *Cannibal Holocaust* does however contain scenes in which people are shot dead for real. This footage comprises 'The Last Road to Hell' segment, a film the documentary crew are said to have made prior to their ill-fated trip into the jungle. In fact, this footage shows what appear to be black civilians executed under a dictatorship, footage that director Deodato "bought from an English company."[7] (The same material is utilised in several Mondo documentaries.) The undeniable authenticity of this segment, despite it looking nothing like the rest of the movie, helps to re-enforce the misconception that *everything* about *Cannibal Holocaust* is real. Writes Mikita Brottman in *Offensive Films*: "The 'Last Road to Hell' is a fleeting and crucial glimpse of the unimaginable reality that *Cannibal Holocaust* (falsely) disguises itself as."

Cannibal Holocaust exists in a multitude of slightly differing prints of various running times. (Although the fabled 'piranha baiting' sequence – a still for which has appeared in several fan publications over the years – has yet to materialise in any of them.) The British video print of *Cannibal Holocaust* is one example of the film's many different forms: not content with censoring whole passages, someone down the line has taken to removing bits of other scenes. These part-expurgated sections include a sequence in which Professor Monroe

(Robert Kerman) and his search party observe a heavily pregnant native being clubbed about the belly, an act described by the professor as "social surgery." The clubbing part is still in the British version but, outside of a single long shot, all other shots that show the woman is pregnant have been cut. The reason for Monroe's diagnosis will be lost on all but the most eagle-eyed viewers. (The complete sequence, which can be found in European prints of the film, not only shows the woman's bloated belly being clubbed, but also the foetus which is induced by the primitive abortionists.) Another trimmed sequence concerns the native found impaled on a stake by the documentary film crew. Here, all shots below the woman's waist have been removed, revealing the stake exiting the woman's mouth, but not the part entering between her legs.

It is difficult to ascertain why one scene should be cut and another left intact. In another sequence, Monroe's team encounter another woman who is violated with a grotesque makeshift dildo for being an adulteress. Unlike the abortion meted out earlier, this sequence remains intact in the British print. (Curiously, the British print repeats – back-to-back – a sequence in which men from the documentary team chase a girl prior to raping her.)

Unlike some directors who have worked in the exploitation field, Deodato isn't embarrassed about the excesses of his film past. Indeed, he stands by *Cannibal Holocaust* and to this day claims it to be his best film. "*Cannibal Holocaust* is a splendid film," he says in *Spaghetti Nightmares*. "Even when I see it today, I can't understand how I managed to direct it with such finesse and expertise! It certainly couldn't have been done any better."[8] As to his own handheld camerawork, Deodato has claimed the result to be "realistic beyond belief."

> To be a good director you have to be at least fifty years old, before that age you are really nothing. When you are young you shoot movies from your heart like I did with *Cannibal Holocaust*, not really from your head. At the time I directed that film I was very depressed due to [a] terrorist group called Brigado Rosso (Red Brigade). I saw all that violence in the newspapers and many journalists exploited that violence in a very bad way I think.
>
> —Ruggero Deodato[9]

Deodato's film seems to have been the prime inspiration for *The Blair Witch Project*, which can fairly be described as *Cannibal Holocaust*-Lite. Here a team of young filmmakers set out to document the legends surrounding a wood (in which a group of teenagers have already supposedly gone missing) and come up against much more than they bargained for. The consequence is that they are neither seen nor heard from again. But, thanks to the cameras they so resolutely refused to switch off, their story lives on in the form of found footage.

THE CANNIBAL MAN

aka: The Apartment on the 13th Floor; La semana del asesino (original title)
Spain 1972
cast: Vincent Parra, Emma Cohen, Eusebio Poncela, Vicky Lagos, Lola Herrera
story: Eloy de la Iglesia & Anthony Fos (dialogues by Robert H Oliver)
producer: Joe Truchado
director: ELOY DE LA IGLESIA

A lowly food factory worker falls into a spiral of murder. His victims end up in the food chain and an admiring neighbour secretly observes his crimes.

IT IS UNFORTUNATE that Eloy de la Iglesia's *La semana del asesino*[1] was titled *The Cannibal Man* for British distribution. Not only is it a misnomer, with the lead character never devouring human flesh (nor do we see anyone else doing so), but without such an inflammatory title there is the possibility that this obscure movie would have been overlooked in the trawl for 'video nasties'.

Made in Spain while the country was still under the rule of General Franco, *The Cannibal Man* is one of several horror films that emerged in the slightly liberalised years prior to the dictator's death in 1975.[2] There is a theme of observing and being observed running through the movie, beginning and ending with scenes of the labourer Marcos (Vicente Parra) being spied on by the well-to-do Nestor (Eusebio Poncela) while passers-by give wayward glances. Along the same lines there is the desire among characters to see what lies behind closed doors, close-ups of eyes, mirrors, and Marcos positioning the bodies of his victims face-down (prompting a father to accuse his dead daughter of being unable to look him in the face, before he himself gets a meat cleaver between the eyes), and so on.

Running concurrent to this theme is repressed sexuality. Marcos doesn't consider himself to be homosexual, despite the fact that his only happiness in the movie arises from the short time he spends relaxing with Nestor.[3] His sexual relations with women all end in murder ('little death,' indeed!),[4] and even masturbating to the tacky bikini-clad beauties on his wall at the beginning of the film proves an arduous, uncomfortable task.

There can be no transgression for the working class, and homosexuality for Marcos is as far removed as the expensive apartments that he faces daily. When he and his fiancée are thrown out of a taxi for petting on the backseat, Marcos accuses the cab driver of being "Some kind of homosexual". The comment is absurd as well as derogatory, because, for Marcos, the concept of homosexuality is completely alien. This is the first and only time the word "homosexual" is used outright in the film, and it can be perceived as a veiled reference to Marcos' own self-doubt.[5]

In his native Spain de la Iglesia made something of a name for himself for provocative subject matter, usually with a homoerotic element. His first film was *Fantasía... 3* (1966), a trilogy based on the fairy tales of Hans Christian Andersen. By 1987, de la Iglesia had directed something like twenty-one films (including an adaptation of Henry James' ghost story *The Turn of the Screw*), after which drugs got the better of him and he was more or less living on the streets as a heroin addict – as one source claims. He appears to have overcome this problem and returned to film-making in recent years. Given the dictatorial climate in which it was made and de la Iglesia's track record, it's inevitable that we should find political and sexual subtexts in *The Cannibal Man*. However, some ideas are so subjugated they are open to almost any kind of interpretation, not least the emphasis placed on dogs: Nestor is always out walking his dog; packs of wild dogs constantly roam the area; dogs sniff at doors and are locked into other rooms. Most pointed of all, a sick dog draws a crowd of onlookers. This scene is symbolic overload: having just killed a playful waitress, his final victim, a deathly pale Marcos happens upon a sick dog surrounded by onlookers. Someone in the crowd suggests they call a veterinarian for the sick animal. After what seems an eternity, someone replies, "Is there one nearby?" Raising half a smile Marcos continues on his way.

The cheap dubbing sits uneasily with the film's arthouse aspirations, while the gratuitous shots of Marcos in the abattoir environment of his factory seem to have been inserted only to draw a parallel with *Blood of the Beasts*, George

Social comment in *The Cannibal Man*.

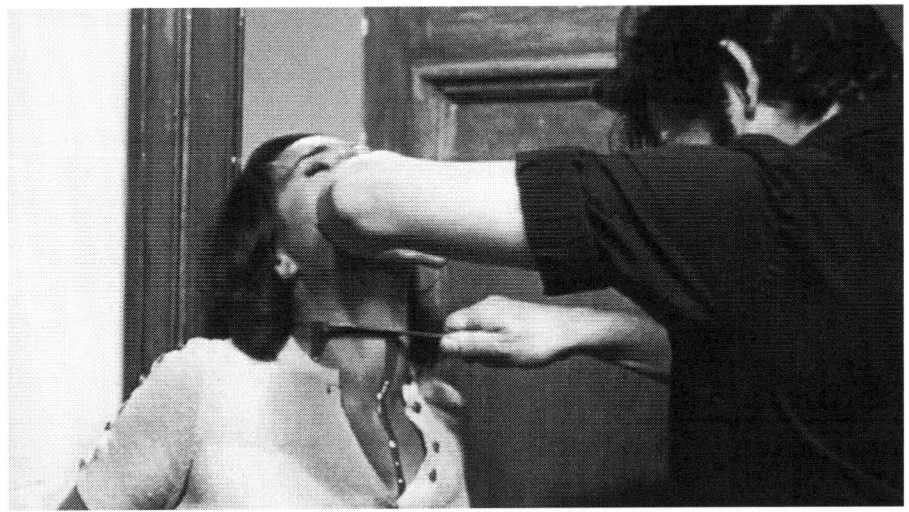

Franju's arthouse documentary on the slaughterhouses of Paris. The first of these sequences plays before the opening credits roll and show Marcos nonchalantly munching on a sandwich, while around him workers hack at cows suspended on hooks. The beasts have their throats cut and the torrents of blood are caught in buckets or mopped into rivers along the tiled floor. Returning to this environment later in the film, a sequence in which Marcos wheels meat parts from one end of the building to the other cleverly segues the (real) carnage of the slaughterhouse with the fictional tale unfolding.

It's not clear whether the director intended these scenes to be indicative of Marcos' unbalanced state of mind. Given the ghastly ads that play on TV, which promote Flory soups as being like "mama used to make", the slaughterhouse seems more a wry social comment on consumerism and commercialism.[6] ('Wry' like the pinball game called 'Top Secret' that Marcos plays in Rose's café.)

The gore in *The Cannibal Man* is fleeting but effective. A head struck with a wrench creates a plume of blood, while the meat cleaver in the face is an image that recurs in *Friday the 13th Part 2*. The dismemberment of the bodies is represented by shadows on a wall or carried out behind the closed door of Marcos' bedroom (onto which a crash zoom accompanies each sound made by the striking meat cleaver).

The Cannibal Man was certificated and released by Redemption in the nineties, with one second cut.

The fabulous 'savages' – *Cannibal Terror*.

CANNIBAL TERROR

Spain 1981
cast: Tony Fontaine, Sylvia Solar, Burt Altman, Pamela Stanford, Gerard LeMaine, Michael Lavry
story: H L Rostaine & Ilona Kunesova
producer: Marius Lasoeur
director: ALLAN W STEEVE [Julio Perez Tabernero]

Petty crooks concoct a kidnap plot and hide in the jungle with their child victim. To their dismay, the location is the habitat of cannibals.

MANY PEOPLE ORIGINALLY suspected that Allan W Steeve, director of *Cannibal Terror*, was actually Jesús Franco under another one of his pseudonyms. However, the film is now widely regarded to be the work of Julio Perez Tabernero, a former actor who took up directing in the early seventies with *Sexy Cat*, a horror movie centred around the mysterious murders that befall a film crew.

Nevertheless, there is the unmistakable imprint of Jesús Franco about *Cannibal Terror*. While it is difficult to believe that anyone could or should want to mimic Franco's torpid directing style, there is the strongest likelihood that Franco did have considerable input into the project. For a start, the film was made at the same time as Franco's two ultra-cheap cannibal movies, *The Devil Hunter* and *Cannibals*, both of which shared stock footage and many of the same actors. Some of the same footage, actors and locations also appear in *Cannibal Terror* (the start of which could "easily be mistaken for a holiday ad," according to a review in *Hi-Tech Terror*).[1] The plots for *Cannibal Terror* and *Cannibals* are virtually interchangeable, with each story revolving around parents in search of their jungle-captive offspring. John Boorman would utilise this basic idea several years later for his considerably more upmarket *The Emerald Forest*.

Other Franco characteristics in *Cannibal Terror* include a lack of filmmaking tolerance and scant regard to matters of detail and realism, disjointed musical accompaniment,[2] actors statically pondering non-events (usually behind a bush) and flesh-munching in extreme close-up.

Cannibal Terror is a chore. It is cheap and inept, with a fatuous story that is at once stupefyingly simple and yet convoluting to the point of distraction. Dialogue is dubbed, seemingly without the benefit of a script.[3] The party at the hideout is a cacophony of arrhythmic musical sounds with someone's voice "la la la"-ing tunelessly over the top. The jungle soundtrack comprises an unending loop of a single birdcall. The heart of the jungle is a cluster of palm trees some 100 yards from a busy road with vehicles visible in the distance. Most of the jungle natives are white, wearing body paint and carrying sticks mounted with cheap plastic skulls. Some tribesmen sport Elvis Presley sideburns, or moustaches, and several look every inch like out-of-condition businessmen, without their clothes on. Few of them can barely refrain from laughing when they are supposed to be engaged in a tribal dance (of which there are many) or cannibalising their victims and tugging on raw offal.

One inexplicable scene that is bestowed some importance (it's shown more than once) features a native crawling into shot and trying to snatch a bone from the big chief's bone collection. He is turned away in the manner of a bad comedy sketch, only to return later whereupon the routine is played out again.

Much of the film's running time is devoted to characters wandering from one location to another, simply looking at the surrounding flora. But then, no matter how many miles they travel, that same bird is still audible in the background! The blurb on the video box calls *Cannibal Terror* "fast-paced," but it takes a dialogue-free half-hour for the cast to wade across a shallow stream.

Cannibal Terror was marketed on the strength of its gore content ("Don't view on a full stomach!" warned the posters). The video sleeve depicted a group of cannibals gorging on raw flesh – an effect comprised of genuine offal and coloured foodstuffs. Some of the scenes of carnage were achieved by concealing a slaughtered pig carcass in an actor's clothing and hacking it open. The 'natives' then drag out the entrails. "Nyam, nyam, nyam," go the actors as they chow down on the meat. The depiction of anthropophagy wasn't tolerated by the DPP. As with almost any film with 'cannibal' in its title, *Cannibal Terror* quickly found itself on the 'video nasties' list. Curiously, *Cannibals*, the film that was almost identical, escaped the DPP unnoticed.

Originally released on Modern Films Video, uncertified and uncut.

CONTAMINATION

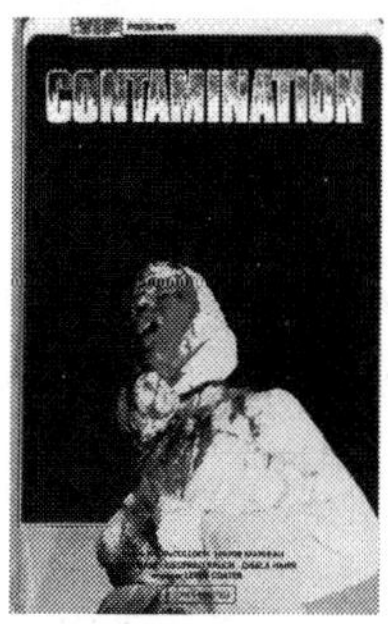

aka: Alien Contamination; Toxic Spawn
Italy/Germany 1980
cast: Ian McCulloch, Louise Marleay, Marino Masé, Siegfried Rauch, Gisela Hahn, Carlo de Mejo
story: Lewis Coates & Erich Tomek
producer: Claudio Mancini
director: LEWIS COATES [Luigi Cozzi]

A crewless ship enters port carrying a mysterious and deadly cargo. Investigators trace the source to a coffee plantation hiding a link to lifeforms from Mars.

LUIGI COZZI HAD a modest hit in 1978 with *Starcrash*, a film the director describes as "science fiction for kids." He intended to follow this surreal *Star Wars* cash-in with two sequels, but problems with potential investors and producers ensured that neither got off the ground.[1] Fortuitously, another box office smash arrived and Cozzi was able to stay with sci-fi for his next film, albeit less for kids. The major talking point of Ridley Scott's *Alien* was the chest-burster scene, and for Italian scriptwriters and financiers intent on jumping on the next money-spinning trend, chest-bursting found a place in Cozzi's new adult-oriented sci-fi movie. (Its intended title, *Alien 2*, was dropped for fear of legal repercussions from Twentieth Century-Fox.[2]) But why stop there? *Alien* was a success with one chest-burster scene, why not a movie with lots of chest-bursting scenes?

Contamination is content to play the same special effect over and over. Nothing distinguishes one chest-burst from the next, as most victims are attired in identical protective white overalls and face masks. But the bloody entrails are consistently spectacular[3] and – together with Goblin's musical soundtrack – provide some remuneration for the sorry dialogue and storyline.

Because of its scenes of erupting viscera, *Contamination* was quarantined on the DPP list. Following their removal, European Creative Films were able to secure an 18 certificate and release the film with an advertising campaign that boasted "At last it's legal – BBFC Certificated." The promotion also promised that *Contamination* "reaches beyond *Alien* to new extremes of terror," whilst cheekily incorporating the same gory image that VIP had used for their original (uncut) video packaging.

'At last it's legal.' Ad for the BBFC certified, cut, re-released *Contamination*.

With a love for science fiction, particularly "trash movies from the fifties,"[4] Cozzi considers *Contamination* to be his most effective film. When pressed on the similarity between his opening sequence and that of Lucio Fulci's earlier *Zombie Flesh Eaters* – both having a deserted ship sailing into New York – Cozzi claims not to have seen it because "I don't like that style of movie."[5] This is difficult to accept because Cozzi even borrows the leading man from *Zombie Flesh Eaters*, the classically trained British actor, Ian McCulloch. *Contamination* was the last of three horror pictures McCulloch made in Italy and effectively marked the end of his career, with the actor not having had an interview for a film since. "I thought I was absolutely terrible in *Contamination*," McCulloch told *The Dark Side*.[6] Nevertheless, it's his solid performance that holds the movie together. While not hostile toward his Italian film work[7] – indeed he embraces these films as "the best working vacations an actor could have... and they made money"[8] – McCulloch doesn't pretend *Zombie Flesh Eaters*, *Zombie Holocaust*[9] and *Contamination* are anything other than "silly." He recalls in his *Dark Side* interview the reservations he had while working on *Contamination*:

> I went out one night with the actress Louise Marleau [who plays Colonel Holmes in the movie] and I mentioned to her that it was a pretty bad script. The next night we met Cozzi, and I was aghast when she said "Ian thinks this is crap!" I may have thought it, but I would never have had the bad manners to say that to someone who was employing me.

The original theatrical trailer for *Contamination* can be found on VIP's video, *The Living Dead*. Between teasers for the gore explosions on offer, the trailer repeatedly flashes up the title, *Contamination*. It pounds dramatically closer and closer with each appearance. Alas, no concession has been made for the transfer to the small screen, leaving the final appearance of the title truncated and the viewer left watching a trailer for a movie that appears to be called *TAMINAT*.

DEAD & BURIED

USA 1981
cast: James Farentino, Melody Anderson, Dennis Redfield, Jack Albertson, Robert Englund, Lisa Blount, Nancy Locke Hauser
story: Ronald Shusset, Dan O'Bannon, Jeff Millar, Alex Stern
producers: Ronald Shussett & Robert Fentress
director: GARY A SHERMAN

The small town of Potter's Bluff is plagued by a series of murders. Deceased victims reappear and go about their daily business. Sheriff Gillis investigates.

Too much on contrivance. Dead & Buried was eventually dropped from the DPP list.

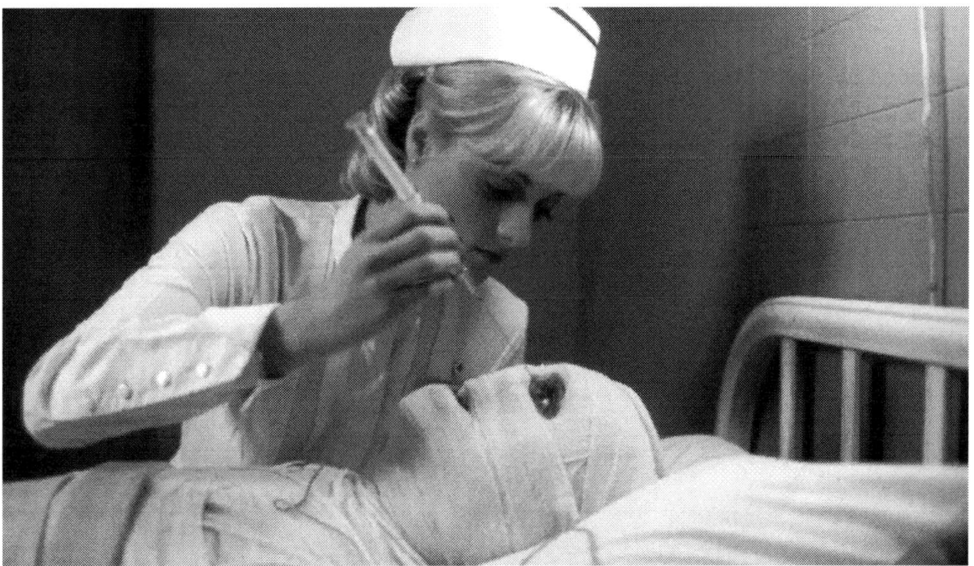

AT A PRODUCTION cost of $6 million, *Dead & Buried* is one of the unusual high-budget – therefore 'respectable' – movies that offended the DPP, even though the violence content is nothing remarkable. The film comes across as a modified version of *Invasion of the Body Snatchers* but falls far short of attaining the quality or calibre of that film. Indeed, *Dead & Buried* at times resembles an amalgam of classic horror movie moments. When Sheriff Dan Gillis (James Farentino) finds a book on demonology and has suspicions about his wife, it is a situation we recognise, having been done before, but better, in *Night of the Eagle*.

Another film that appears to have proven a big influence on the *Dead & Buried* scriptwriters is *Scream and Scream Again*. This too has a plot that involves a mad doctor creating superhuman zombies. In that movie, Michael Gothard is apprehended and handcuffed to the bumper of a police car. To the surprise of the police however, he escapes, and his torn-off arm is discovered hanging from the front of the vehicle. In *Dead & Buried*, the scene is recreated when Gillis finds a detached arm on his car radiator, the mutilated owner getting up and running away. Both films have other noteworthy similarities: a zombified murderous nurse, a scene in which a killer and victim meet for the first time and try to guess each other's names, and a climax where an apparently normal person is revealed to be a 'zombie.'

The overwhelming impression is that *Dead & Buried* is bereft of any real weight.

The film struggles to make a feature-length production out of a basic, one-note plot that would perhaps be better suited to a half-hour episode of *The Twilight Zone* or five pages of an EC comic. It takes an awfully long time to arrive at its thin denouement – one that is patently evident from an early stage. The film relies too much on contrivance to generate any kind of tension. One of the few ominous moments comes when Gillis exhumes the body of a freelance photographer but finds only a bundle of clothing in a coffin containing the man's heart.

Dead & Buried was released by Thorn EMI. The scenes that probably caused offence are the ones depicting the hypodermic needle in the eye and acid to the face of a lab assistant. It was eventually dropped from the list and re-released. *Dead & Buried* derived more publicity than it deserved because of its association with the box office smash *Alien*. Dan O'Bannon worked on the screenplays for both films, a fact prominently displayed on the unimaginative *Dead & Buried* poster and video sleeve.

The most memorable aspect of seeing *Dead & Buried* on its original theatrical run – for one author of this book at least – was the fact it was supported by a short British obscurity, *The Orchard End Murder*; its atmosphere and imagery had a far more lasting impact than *Dead & Buried*.[1]

One correspondent told the authors that, in the early eighties, "the first video shop in Burnley town centre informed its customers that *Dead & Buried* was a genuine snuff film."

DEATH TRAP

aka: Horror Hotel; Eaten Alive; Starlight Slaughter; Legend of the Bayou; Swamp Beast (working title)
USA 1976
cast: Neville Brand, Robert Englund, Mel Ferrer, Carolyn Jones, Marilyn Burns, Stuart Whitman, William Finley, Kyle Richards, Roberta Collins
story: Tobe Hooper, Mardi Rustam, Alvin L. Fast, Kim Henkel
*producers***:** Mardi Rustam, Mohammed Rustam, Samir Rustam, Larry Huly, Robert Kantor, Alvin L Fast
director: TOBE HOOPER

Neville Brand is Judd. *Death Trap*.

A deranged hotel owner has a hungry pet crocodile to feed. His guests ensure a lasting supply of food.

DEATH TRAP IS Tobe Hooper's flawed follow-up to *The Texas Chain Saw Massacre* and comparisons between the two films are unavoidable. Hooper tries in vain to recreate the atmosphere of his vastly superior debut, even down to a thrifty reprise of *Texas Chain Saw*'s 'final girl' sequence. Originally it was Marilyn Burns narrowly escaping a weapon-wielding psychopath in the guise of the pig-squealing Leatherface, here it is Janus Blyth (as Lynette) chased by a babbling Neville Brand (as Judd). "Where? Where? *Whe-e-e-e-re*?" Judd bewails when his intended victim is whisked away by an anonymous passer-by (just like in *Texas Chain Saw*), falling to his knees and hacking at nothing with his scythe. It's a poor substitute for chainsaw-reeling dementia. Hooper also tries to recreate the 'prolonged climax' that defined *Texas Chain Saw*, wherein the whole film was one long adrenaline rush. In *Death Trap*, however, the result is more a caustic irritant, with the incessant screaming of the victims – sometimes several at once – blurring into Judd's inane mutterings, and a musical soundtrack that comprises country and western songs with industrial-strength electronic blips and bleeps.

The psychotic Judd has a bugbear about 'loose' women, but all visitors to his hotel are potential targets and end up as food for his crocodile – even Judd is eaten in the end. Although the assembled performers attack their roles with gusto, the fact that *Death Trap* utilises 'name' actors robs it of the power and verisimilitude that the cast of unknowns lent to *Texas Chain Saw*. The all-too-obvious studio sets illuminated with primary coloured lighting also give the suggestion of a theatrical play ("menacingly unreal," said a delighted reviewer in the *Splatter Times*).[1] Whereas *Texas Chain Saw* was shot for the most part in blazing sunlight, *Death Trap* is dark and shadowy to the point of total screen blackout. This achieves nothing other than eyestrain and apathy. The earlier film seemed all too credible – as the poster campaign posited, audiences really did agonise over "Who will survive and what will be left of them?" But it is difficult to take anything in *Death Trap* seriously at all. Why do all these people want to stay in such a decrepit hotel as the Starlight, "an hour from town" no less? More to the point, what are they all doing in the middle of nowhere to even find the place?

What *Death Trap* lacks in atmosphere, it tries to make up for with bloody deaths. Not overtly gory, there is still a good deal more blood spilled than in *Texas Chain Saw*. The opening murder by rake is particularly brutal – even though the weapon blows occur offscreen – and Mel Ferrer's demise with the scythe through his neck is explicit enough to have landed the film on the DPP list.

Commentators have noted that *Death Trap* bears a resemblance to comic stories published by EC in the fifties, such as 'Horror We? How's Bayou?' and in particular 'Country Clubbing!' (*The Haunt of Fear* Feb 1954). With their swamp settings, crumbling isolated shacks, mad men and crocodiles, similarities between these strips and Hooper's film are easy to draw. However, it's only fair to note that EC themselves weren't averse to lifting ideas. Like *The Texas Chain Saw Massacre* (and no doubt some of the EC stories), *Death Trap* was based loosely on a true crime incident. Judd of the Starlight is a rendition of Joseph Ball who, in the late 1920s, owned The Sociable Inn, a gin mill that had a concrete-lined pool containing five alligators. To entertain his buddies he would throw stray cats and dogs to the reptiles. Ball also murdered around twenty-five women and fed their chopped-up remains to the alligators. After police started to make inquiries about a missing person, Ball shot himself on September 24, 1938.

Hooper claimed that studio interference together with a disagreement with the producer resulted in a film that he wasn't entirely happy with. Similar circumstances were said to have plagued and spoiled his later productions.

Death Trap was released uncertified by Vipco in video cases that sometimes carried the same "strong uncut version" sticker that appeared on the uncensored version of *Zombie Flesh Eaters*. This may have been a packaging error, because, unlike that other film, there was no discernible difference between either the *Death Trap* that carried the warning and copies that didn't. Vipco re-released the film in a cut and certified version a decade after it was banned.

Hooper would direct a made-for-TV adaptation of Stephen King's *Salem's Lot* next, before returning to the big screen with *The Funhouse*. This too found itself on the DPP list.

DEEP RIVER SAVAGES

aka: Il paese del sesso selvaggio (original title); The Man from Deep River; Sacrifice
Italy 1972
cast: Ivan Rassimov, Me Me Lay, Pratitsak Singhara, Sulallewan Suwantat, Ong Ard, Prapas Chindang, Tuan Tevan
story: Francesco Barilli & Massimo d'Avack
producer: M G Rossi
director: UMBERTO LENZI

Bradley, an English photographer in Thailand, becomes embroiled in the customs and rites of a native tribe. First, he is a prisoner. Later he embraces the life.

THIS WAS THE first in a long line of popular Italian cannibal movies. *Deep River Savages* uses a plot and several scenes characteristic of the 1970 western, *A Man Called Horse*: a civilised Englishman encounters a primitive culture, undergoes intolerable initiation, accepts the antediluvian ways as an improvement on his own 'advanced' culture and finally attains a high-ranking status in the adoptive society. Ivan Rassimov in the role of Bradley at times looks like the young Richard Harris, who starred in that earlier film, and some effort is made to have him sound like him too. ("I can't take any more, do you understand? You bloody savages!")

Like most cannibal films there seems to exist an evolutionary timeline within the jungle. The further along this line one progresses the more feral the

Deep River Savages

inhabitants become. As such it is the unclean, ugly men from deeper in the forest who are the cannibals, not the tribe by the river into which Bradley is assimilated. The more distant from civilisation they are, the more brutally they behave.

Although anthropophagy plays only a small role,[1] throughout are scenes of genuine, thoroughly unpleasant, animal slaughter and mutilation. An alligator has a knife pushed through the base of its head, whereupon blood foams from the wound and the creature is skinned alive. A mongoose and cobra are forced to fight to the death. A live monkey has the top of its skull cut off to reveal its brains. When tribeswoman Mariya (Me Me Lay) marries Bradley and gives birth, a sacrificial goat has its throat sliced clean open.

Often the case in Italian cannibal movies, a disclaimer appears after the opening credits, which in this instance posits:

> even though some of the rites and ceremonies shown are perhaps gruesome and repugnant they are portrayed as they are actually carried out. Only the story is imaginary.

Director Umberto Lenzi would go on to make two further 'Third World' cannibal films after this one, *Eaten Alive* (1980) and *Cannibal Ferox* (1981), each sleazier and more violent than its predecessor. Lenzi claims not to be proud of these forays into the cannibal sub-genre and considers himself primarily a director of action and horror pictures. His expansive filmography incorporates historical melodrama, spy adventure, war, westerns, comedy, and crime, and Lenzi is recognised as a director who can readily adapt to whatever genre is in vogue (albeit not always with satisfying results). Unfortunately for Lenzi, it is the cannibal genre for which he is best known. "I really hate those movies!" he said in one interview.[2] "It is very sad that I am always mentioned because of those cannibal movies."

For all his protestations however, Lenzi wasn't about to let someone else steal his thunder. When fellow Italian, Ruggero Deodato, received the accolade of having invented cannibal movies, Lenzi waded in. "I'd like to make something clear," he said of the genre he so despised:

> Deodato said in an interview that he invented this type of film, that Umberto Lenzi copied his ideas and his successful films. This is not true! The first cannibal film was mine, *Deep River Savages*; it went very well so the producers wanted to make a second part. I was already busy with other projects and so I refused. The film was given to Deodato and called [*Cannibal*]. If you check the actors, you'll find Me Me Lay and Ivan Rassimov in both films.[3]

Deep River Savages looks every bit the forebear of a genre that would, in a few short years, transmute into a riot of animal mutilation and innards-chomping. Also of note is the fact that much of the dialogue is presented in the natives' original tongue, without the benefit of subtitles, and whenever Me Me Lay gets her smiling flowery face into shot the soundtrack goes all gushy.

DELIRIUM

aka: Psycho Puppet
USA 1979 [?]
cast: Turk Cekovsky, Debi Chaney, Terry Ten Broek, Barron Winchester, Bob Winters, Garrett Bergfeld, Nick Panouzis
story: James Lowe, Eddie Krell & Richard Yalem
producers: Sunny Vest & Peter Maris
director: PETER MARIS

VTC issued *Delirium* in two different video sleeves. See also previous page.

A psychotic Vietnam war veteran is the puppet of a secret vigilante organisation.

IT COMES AS a shock when *Delirium* loses its central character forty minutes into the film; the drive and focus that the psychotic Charlie (Nick Panouzis) brings is lost, and with him the few 'objectionable' scenes of bloodletting: a spear bursting messily out of a chest (replete with a squirt of blood); a pitchfork penetrating a neck; repeated blows from a meat cleaver (including a close-up impact wound); and Charlie's manhandling and murder of a hitchhiker, after she berates him for not being able to "get it up". As if to compensate for the dry spell following Charlie's exit, the climactic shootout features squibs in close-up.

Without Charlie, the emphasis shifts to a love interest and some dull, tail-chasing detectives. These two clowns, Dollinger (Turk Cekovsky) and Mead (Terry TenBroek), do little more than collate lots of information that is redundant to the viewer, already privy to it. When a sheriff informs the detectives that prime suspect Charlie is dead, we have already witnessed the murder with a shotgun.

Delirium overstretches its limited budget and scenes that ought to be tense or horrific come over as plain silly. The 'Nam flashbacks are a case in point: a building site doubles as a cut-rate jungle and a dilapidated prefab represents a Vietnamese village. Gunfights between a handful of motley US troops and an unseen enemy comes courtesy of 'The World War II Re-enactment Society', which receives special credit at the end of the film. An abundance of library music doesn't help matters.[1] Nor do the incidental characters who look to have been written into the script in exchange for a small non-refundable cash payment. These include an elderly police chief, constantly poised on the steps of the Police Department, asking how the case is going, and a motorist who knocks someone over by mistake.

Some dumb scenes are not without charm: An outwardly respectable businessman with sinister connections suspects his secretary is listening in on his calls, and thereafter uses a public phone to hold his irate conversations. Elsewhere, a bald man in sunglasses, the pint-sized Stern (Barron Winchester), 'drags' a considerably taller person through an abandoned warehouse (a funny image accompanied by bizarre exclamatory noises: "Ow... Yow... Oh!"). In a scene where Charlie advances on his next victim, a woman having a bath, he makes plenty of noise banging into things, but the intended victim remains painfully oblivious, shrugging off each new noise as being nothing untoward. One scene even has a certain (unintentional) arthouse quality: A group of children playing on a beach spot the corpse of the naked hitchhiker floating past. Calling their parents, they then run out of the frame one by one.

At the heart of this illogical movie is an interesting conspiratorial-vigilante idea, in which a secret committee, believing the law is too lenient, take matters into their own hands. The idea was borrowed by Peter Hyams for his 1983 film, *The Star Chamber* – with equally disappointing results.

With sixteen seconds of cuts, *Delirium* was given a certificate and released by Viz Movies and Vidage as *Psycho Puppet*. The producer is a man called Sunny Vest.

THE DEVIL HUNTER

title on print: Devil Hunter
aka: The Man Hunter; Mandingo Manhunter; Il Cacciatore di Uomini
Spain/France/Germany 1980
cast: Ursula Fellner, Robert Foster, Antonio de Cabo, Gisella Hahn
story: Julius Valery
producer: JE Films
director: CLIFFORD BROWN [Jesús Franco]

Film star Laura Crawford, working on location, is kidnapped and held for ransom in the jungle. She is abducted again by tribespeople who want to sacrifice her to a cannibalistic man-monster.

Too much Laura Crawford and not enough monster in *The Devil Hunter*.

DEVIL HUNTER STARTED out under the directorship of Amando de Ossorio – responsible for the *Blind Dead* series of films[1] – but Jesús Franco stepped in and completed it under the pseudonym Clifford Brown.[2] It doesn't look like de Ossorio made much headway as *Devil Hunter* looks every inch a Franco film, utilising some of the same actors as his jungle adventure of the previous year, *Cannibals*. It's also laced with such familiar Franco traits as crash zooms to nowhere, dreamy music, and the general impression that he wants to get the whole damn thing out of the way as quickly and painlessly as possible. The result is an even more alienating Franco movie than most, with no concession whatsoever towards the viewer: the film supinely unfolds, failing to generate tension, suspense, or emotion. This may explain why the few reviews contain glaring plot inaccuracies. *Aurum Film Encyclopedia* states erroneously that a "priestess tears out young mens' hearts and eats them," while *The Psychotronic Video Guide* suggests that the film contains "Nam-vet cannibals". It doesn't.

There are two plot strands at work, which never satisfactorily gel. The kidnap of the actress Laura Crawford (Ursula Buchfellner) becomes enmeshed with a local horror story involving a cannibalistic killer. Part of the film's ethereal quality is due to many characters speaking with their backs to the camera, or hiding their face behind an object, such as a hat – or talking nonsense, which happens a lot.[3] These things help with lip syncing and post-production embroidery.[4] But things become quite surreal when a whole conversation takes place with no direct evidence who is having it. The dubbing is some of the worst committed to celluloid, with completely lacklustre deliveries from everyone concerned. The dialogue is in the tradition of a porno loop, and bad enough to suggest that it's being made up on the spot. ("Back in my country, we have these flowers and we used to offer them to the virgins." "Flowers – Shit! Damn it! Damn it! Damn it! Damn it!") Characters blabber inanely and often contradict themselves. Many of the male voices are dubbed by the same person, who adopts as many diverse accents as he can muster. Pretty terrible to begin with, the accents come and go on a whim. A pilot called Jack has what could loosely be termed a Texan twang, while stiff upper lip Thomas talks as though he has marbles in his mouth.

Audio effects are no better. Characters walking through the jungle sound as if they are treading a gravel path. Punches thrown in fight scenes land with a sound reminiscent of a hand slapping water. Everything has a horrible resonance to it, as though events have been dubbed within a small cardboard box. The musical soundtrack – composed by Franco himself – comprises two main themes. The first is a strange, alluring lounge-type number, replete with haunting vocals. The second is a wild, percussive piece, pounding out a tribal rhythm. Both are competent in themselves, but the manner of their use is jarring. As the film cuts between the beautiful actress Laura Crawford, touring the city at the beginning of the film, and a native girl running through the jungle, the music jumps abruptly between the two. Back and forth, back and forth.

The jungle tribe fears a cannibalistic monster. The monster is played by a tall, athletic black man in a loin cloth – according to Franco, a six-foot Polish basketball player. As if to compensate for the lacklustre makeup, which constitutes large stuck-on white eyes, each appearance of the creature is accompanied by a cacophonous roar on the soundtrack.

Several of the tribespeople in the one-hut village are undoubtedly crew members. As was the case in Allan W Steeve's *Cannibal Terror*, no attempt has been made to hide the fact they're white (and dance apprehensively to a white guy playing bongos). Other unintentionally humorous shortcomings include a scene where the monster bludgeons one of the kidnappers with a rock, resulting in a spray of blood. The actor makes no attempt to hide his amusement when the spray of blood strikes him in the face. Later, when the monster is killed, the tribespeople are quick to destroy the totem pole effigy that stands in their village. Insecure and lightweight, the first touch topples it. Under a barrage of gunfire, Weston, the man sent to rescue Laura Crawford, is in plain view but manages to dodge bullets by rolling up and down, flipping this way and that. And while it can be nighttime on one side of the island, it is sunny on the other – as per a scene where Weston speaks on a walkie-talkie with Thomas, head of the kidnap gang.

Devil Hunter has little gore. Apart from one victim of the monster, whose intestines are exposed following an attack, gore is implied or off screen. Franco appears not to have the time or patience to offer much in the way of special makeup effects. When the monster rips open the stomach of a sacrificial victim early in the film, it's courtesy of sleight of hand, except that a poor camera angle and late cutaway destroy the illusion. As for why the film has not been submitted for certification following the Video Recordings Act 1984, scenes such as Weston beating a kidnapper's head repeatedly against a rock wouldn't win it any favours. There's also a little too much emphasis on women being held captive, molested and raped – we see more of Laura terrorised in chains than we do of the monster, or anything else for that matter. The camera lingers a long time on the pubis of the captive Laura as she is transported through the jungle, and also on the backside of a village girl who does a frenetic dance. (US distributor Trans World Entertainment labelled the film "Adult" as opposed to "Horror".) Cannibalism is a clear point of contention, outlined by the DPP as one factor that may render a film obscene, even if, as with *Devil Hunter*, it is far from convincing.

Franco has claimed that *Devil Hunter* was the unaccredited inspiration for the Arnold Schwarzenegger blockbuster *Predator*. "It's exactly the same," the director said in an interview,[5] "except instead of a creature from another planet we had a sort of Yeti."[6] That said, Weston's battle with the monster on the clifftops at the film's end might be construed as a kind of Franco re-enactment of the Empire State sequence in *King Kong*.

DON'T GO IN THE HOUSE

aka: The Burning (working title)
USA 1979
cast: Dan Grimaldi, Robert Osth, Ruth Dardick
story: Joseph Ellison, Ellen Hammill, Joseph R Masefield
producer: Ellen Hammill
director: JOSEPH ELLISON

Donny Kohler's mother burned his arms on the gas stove when he misbehaved. Now an adult, guided by the voice of his late mother, he kills women in his private incinerator.

Don't Go in the House – morally formidable.

DON'T GO IN the House is the progeny of Tobe Hooper's *Texas Chain Saw Massacre* (with a flamethrower substituting for the chainsaw), Alan Ormsby's *Deranged* and Alfred Hitchcock's *Psycho* – all of which were rudimentarily based on the real-life crimes of Edward Gein. It lacks the impact and panache of these other films but does provide some incisive and genuinely creepy moments of its own.

Stephen Thrower, in his review for *Eyeball*,[1] rightly claimed the first fiery murder to be "one of the most outrageous scenes ever to feature in a 'video nasty.'" *Don't Go in the House* was shocking on its release back in the eighties, and more so now. Today it is so wide of social perceptions of acceptability it looks like it comes from a different planet entirely. It is impossible to imagine any contemporary theatrical production subjecting an audience to such morally formidable imagery.

Donny (Dan Grimaldi) skips work to create a crematorium in his house, lining the walls of one room with steel sheeting and buying an asbestos fire-proof suit. A kindly florist called Kathy is the first victim. Having been knocked unconscious, she finds herself naked and suspended in Donny's home-made crematorium. Clinical panelled walls offer no clue as to what fate awaits her. Dressed in his asbestos suit, Donny enters and without uttering a word pours gasoline over her. While the helpless Kathy screams, he ignites her with a flamethrower and watches her burn. She continues to scream as the flames engulf her.

This is the only murder that is played out in any detail, but it sets the tone for the entire picture. Other excesses found on the DPP list of movies pale next to this: no amount of dodgy cannibal gut-munching or eye-gorging zombie effects work comes close to this sight of a woman being incinerated. It seems to epitomise – forgive us a moment – the 'nasty' in video nasty. Those who label it a misogynistic film may want to note that the producer/co-writer is a woman. What may also have been intended as a serious comment on child abuse –identifying with the popular theory that Donny, abused in childhood, himself becomes an abuser in later life – is lost in the first kill scene.

The film was shot without sound for European distribution only (which might explain the full frontal nudity, uncommon for an American R-rated production). Film Ventures, a small independent studio, saw potential for a wider market and paid for it to be dubbed into English. Special makeup expert Tom Brumberger told *Fangoria* how he achieved such convincing burn effects on the slim budget afforded *Don't Go in the House*:

> I suggested to [Film Ventures] that we try not to attach prosthetics to the actresses, because the prosthetics could only make them look larger – and when you're burned, you *shrink*, as you lose fluid. The director wanted the victims absolutely charred black, and skeletal, so I suggested that he use dancers who would be much slimmer than the actresses, but the same height. So that's what we did...[2]

Outside of his burn-chamber, Donny is just a simple-minded boyish misfit suffering oedipal withdrawal. In one scene, we see a pal of his prominently reading a copy of *Mad* magazine, as if that detail somehow paints a picture we don't already know. In anticipation of a date, Donny shops for a "dynamite outfit". It appears for a moment that an effeminate salesman will undermine the dense atmosphere with cheap laughs, but it doesn't happen. Director Joseph Ellison wants nothing to undermine the tone established in the opening murder scene.

In a recent interview, Alan Ormsby claimed that he interjected his similarly themed film *Deranged* with black humour because he felt he couldn't make it any other way; the story was simply too gruesome – and in a sense, ridiculous – to translate in a po-faced fashion. We have the opposite situation in *Don't Go in the House*. Void of humour – and a markedly less rounded film than *Deranged* – it's difficult to imagine any attempt at levity after the first murder scene.

When the film was released theatrically in Britain in January 1982, the reviewer for *Screen International* gave credit to director Joseph Ellison for "stressing the gothic horror elements instead of exploiting the gruesome potential of the murders." The two minutes of cuts excised by the BBFC might well have made it seem that way. There was no such concession when *Don't Go in the House* appeared on video courtesy of distributors Arcade, who released the film uncut. As noted, it is clear where the contention lies. The video sleeve alone would likely have been enough to land *Don't Go in the House* on the nasties list. Over a blackened corpse, suspended by its hands, the blurb on the video box reads: "In a steel room built for revenge they die burning... in chains."

The film was later reprieved from the prosecution list and re-released with over three minutes of cuts on the Apex label.

Don't Go in the House was filmed under the title *The Burning* – not to be confused with Tony Maylam's film of the same name, which also featured on the list.

DON'T GO IN THE WOODS... ALONE!

title on print: Don't go in the Woods
USA 1980
cast: Jack McClelland, Mary Gail Artz, James P Hayden, Ken Carter, Larry Roupe, Angie Brown
story: Garth Eliassen
producers: Roberto & Suzette Gomez
director: JAMES BRYAN

A disparate collection of people explore a wild terrain unaware that a primitive throwback lives in the forest. He kills the intruders invading his territory.

IN TERMS OF budget[1] and technical competence, this film sits at the bottom of the nasties list. Director James Bryan appears not to have grasped even the rudimentary aspects of film-making, and *Don't Go in the Woods* (surely his one and only feature)[2] suffers every cinematic pitfall imaginable – from being underlit through to utilising characters who look, dress, talk and behave exactly the same as each other (in the same woodland setting no less). It also has the most ham-fisted editing ever to grace a theatrically released production (it had a cinema release in the US, but not Britain).[3] Indeed, frayed to begin with, continuity comes to a complete standstill in the 'action' sequences, courtesy of editing that doesn't adhere to any rational sense of rhythm or timing.

Nothing about this film draws the viewer in (other than the fact that it has been 'banned'). The musical soundtrack consists of synthesised 'themes' played back-to-back without a break, underpinned by a succession of digital beeps and squeaks. This drone starts with the opening titles and doesn't stop until the final credits, where a terrible song based upon 'The Teddy Bears Picnic' takes over. A series of electronic 'wows' is offered in lieu of any actual tension. One of the hikers is a man alone in his wheelchair, attempting to navigate the rugged terrain, which is a tasteless stab at humour, given that each appearance has a 'comedy' musical accompaniment.

Like the music, the film plays without any sense of depth or dynamic. Although events take place over a period of only a day or two, the timeframe could easily be spanning weeks, months or even years. Everything is unclear and confusing.

Donald Farmer, in the *Splatter Times*,[4] determined, "Another reason to stay away is the constantly shaky camerawork – anyone sitting too close to the screen could probably get motion sickness."

Most bloodletting is lost to the overall ineptitude of the film. Several of the early attacks in the woods[5] – when the identity of the attacker is still being guarded – are so spectacularly incompetent and surreal that they could effectively be depicting anything. (And detractors read more into these scenes than is taking place.) The only gore sequences clear enough to make out feature an attack on a backpacker in the wildman's lair (the wild man slashes her repeatedly with a knife as she clambers through a skylight) and the death of the wild man himself, a frenzied stabbing by two of the backpackers. The special effects don't extend to anything more gratuitous than close-ups of slashed and bloodied clothing, but both the above sequences are needlessly protracted, with the death of Joanne (Angie Brown) – caught in the skylight[6] – being particularly unpleasant.

The non-actors don't bring enough unintentional humour to the proceedings, although the sequence with eager lovers in a camper van will likely raise a smile. "Dick... Dick..." the woman hollers in a completely dispassionate manner while her man takes an inordinately long time investigating a noise outside. When the camper van is subsequently sent tumbling down the mountainside – undoubtedly the single greatest expense in the movie – the viewer gets a sense of relative extravagance. But it's wasted as the incident is filmed in almost complete darkness.

One of the earliest entries in the generic stalk-and-slash cycle, *Don't Go in the Woods* is a shining example of how inclusion on the DPP list has bestowed a piece of complete crap with notoriety and near-legendary status. Why else are we still discussing James Bryan?

For reasons unknown, US distributors Manson International, extended the original title for their poster artwork to reflect the advice of one of the characters in the film: *'Don't Go in the Woods... Alone!'*[7] It is this artwork that adorns the British video box.

Though the sub-genre that comprises yeti and Bigfoot cinema is minuscule, several films on the DPP list are part of it: *Night of the Demon*, *The Werewolf and the Yeti*, and *Don't Go in the Woods*. Arguably we might include *Anthropophagous the Beast* and *The Devil Hunter* as a sub-subgenre of stalking-hairy-man-thing type movies.

DON'T GO NEAR THE PARK

aka: Night Stalker
USA 1979
cast: Aldo Ray, Meeno Peluce, Tamara Taylor, Barbara Monker, Linnea Quigley, Crackers Phinn
story: Linwood Chase & Lawrence D Foldes
producer: Lawrence D Foldes
director: LAWRENCE D FOLDES

Gar and Tra are cursed to grow old but cannot die. To lift the curse a human sacrifice is required when the planets are aligned a certain way, an opportunity that arises only once every 12,000 years.

DON'T GO NEAR the Park would undoubtedly have faded into oblivion, unnoticed and unmissed, had the DPP not immortalised it with 'nasty' status. At times it has the air of a made-for-TV film, but then suddenly swings into graphic mutilation and cannibalism. In these occasional and very short gore scenes, abdomens are torn open, their contents scooped out and devoured. No review of the film prior to or during the media backlash had a good word for it (ditto after the 'nasties' furore, but this is now a moot point because it's highly desired by collectors). Reviewing the latest horror releases, Liam T Sanford in the July 1983 edition of *Video Viewer* called *Don't Go Near the Park* "brainless junk." So

brainless in fact, he felt compelled to advise readers that

> Many moronic movies now being made available on videotape were originally perpetrated by used-car salesmen, opticians, lawyers, dentists and greengrocers. Whether intended as a tax fiddle or a money-spinner, they don't give a gnat's earlobe about quality.
>
> Enlisting the dubious aid of family friends, in-laws, outlaws and casual acquaintances to fill in on both sides of the camera, they then proceed to toss together the sort of trash that gives 'splatter' a bad name...

Having established the quality of the few gore scenes, let us peruse the sleazy underbelly that seems to have passed most commentators by. *Don't Go Near the Park* has an odd mix of dubious themes: cannibalism, incest, and subliminal paedophilia. First, the use of the barely-of-age Linnea Quigley in an adult role (complete with shower scene). Although she would go on to become a B-movie queen featuring in the likes of *Return of the Living Dead* and *Graduation Day* (hired to replace an actress who refused to remove her top), this was one of the first parts for Quigley. The film may have had nudity, she later confided, but it "also gave me a few lines."[1] Pretending to be a 'normal' family, the undying Gar and Tra have a daughter called Bondi (Tamara Taylor). At one point an eight-year-old runaway tries to grope her breasts, but she wakes and tells him that he'll have to wait until he's at least twelve before he does anything like that. In another scene, Bondi remarks that she is sick of being molested. The molester who rips open her blouse, bares her immature breasts and gropes her is played by director Lawrence D Foldes. In many scenes the camera is positioned to get an unobstructed view up Bondi's skirt, nowhere is this more evident than a scene in which she climbs out of a window and down a tree.

Not even the once respected Aldo Ray[2] gets away untarnished. He plays Taft, an old man, who picks up Nick from the street. He takes the boy home and invites him to stay as his special friend. Towards the end of the film, Nick is among the three children sleeping half-naked in Taft's apartment, while he looks on with a smile.

Sleazy moments such as these throw a different slant on the ridiculous onscreen proclamation that *Don't Go Near the Park* "is based on actual occurrences which happened over the centuries"!

Foldes went on to direct the altogether more competent *Young Warriors* and *Nightforce*, the latter starring Linda Blair.

DON'T LOOK IN THE BASEMENT

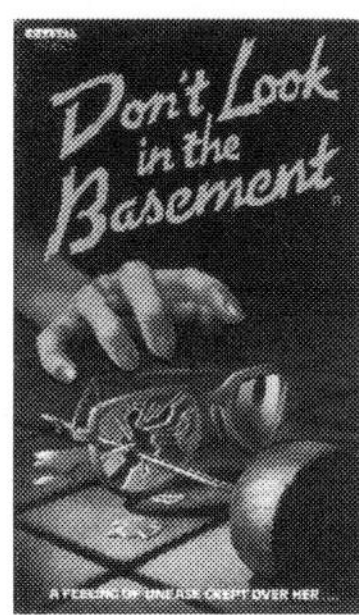

title on print: "Don't Look In The Basement"
aka: The Forgotten (original title); Death Ward #13
USA 1973
cast: William Bill McGhee, Jessie Lee Fulton, Robert Dracup, Harryette Warren, Michael Harvey, Jessie Kirby
story: Tim Pope
producer: S F Brownrigg
director: S F BROWNRIGG

Dr Stephens runs a sanatorium and has radical ideas about psychiatry. But when he is murdered, the unstable Dr Masters takes his place and soon the patients are out of control.

IT'S NOT MUCH of a surprise to learn that Dr Masters (Annabelle Weenick) is insane, having established at the beginning of the movie that the patients are her "family." She is responsible for the murders of the patients in her charge and put on trial and found guilty by the other patients, a case of the lunatics having taken over the asylum. What is a surprise is the fact that a new staff member, Nurse Charlotte (Rosie Holotik), might also be delusional.[1] From the moment she arrives, Charlotte is viewed as an outsider and never is there a suggestion she might be anything other than a nurse.[2] In the film's climax, when

Masters' real place in the sanatorium is revealed – madder than everyone else – Charlotte confronts the other patients for confirmation and is informed by 'the Judge', "You too are a patient my dear." When she arrives at the sanatorium to take up her new post, through to the end when she leaves, we don't see Charlotte go anywhere but the grounds. From the onset, she is a part of the insular world of *Don't Look in the Basement*.

"Yet another slice of raw garbage," David Bartholomew wrote of the film in *The Monster Times*. But out of his budgetary shortcomings, director S F Brownrigg successfully creates an oppressive atmosphere and several supremely weird moments. The curiously framed low angle shots, for instance, reach a subjective nadir in one conversation in the grounds: half the frame is focused on grass blowing in the wind, despite the human activity in the top half. Most noteworthy is a sequence near the end, where Charlotte decides she must escape the place but... but... cannot find the door! "I can't find a way out!" Charlotte cries in desperation, ending up in the basement. There is also the unnecessary twist that Dr Stephens, having been axed in the opening of the film and presumed dead, is still alive. (Now's the time to mention the limp promotional blurb from the video box: "A feeling of unease crept over her...")

We never get a clear glimpse of the exit, not once throughout the entire film. Like some psychological black star, the little world of *Don't Look in the Basement* is in a state of collapse, drawing its residents inexorably towards its bloody cataclysmic breakdown and taking all means of escape with it. Charlotte lost in the tiny building in which she lives is a masterstroke of paranoiac cinema, but one arising as much out of low-budget necessity as it is design. In what might be the director's only published interview, Brownrigg explained in *Draculina*[3] that *Don't Look in the Basement*

> was put together rather hurriedly... and we did put it together along the lines that I try to do the low-budget pictures, and that is we try to keep the script, until after

we get the thing financed, kind of loose so that we can go to the actual location and write the script around the location where we're going to shoot.

Sherold F Brownrigg worked in commercial and industrial films for a company in Dallas, Texas, before turning his hand to feature films. His first stint was as a soundman on several of Larry Buchanan's early movies. As a director, he made just five movies, the first of which was *Don't Look in the Basement*.[4] Shot in just twelve days, it introduced the actors that would become repertory players in Brownrigg's other movies[5] and enjoyed a brief theatrical run in the South under its original title *The Forgotten*. When Hallmark picked it up, the title was changed to *Don't Look in the Basement* and distributed in a succession of horror double-bills and triple-bills across America.[6]

In its unexpurgated form, the film has a reputation of being something of a gore opus. The version released in Britain is cut, however, with almost every gore scene showing evidence of tampering. It seems that this truncated version is the responsibility of an American video company, who, according to *Demonique*, excised twelve minutes from the film to create "what seems their own nearly-PG-rated version."[7] Even the final axe massacre is a reserved affair, constituting for the most part 'reaction shots' and blood being spattered on walls.[8]

"We were trying to outdo everybody in blood and everything," Brownrigg told *Draculina*. Not a big horror film fan, Brownrigg's ambition was first to create a suspense movie in the manner of Hitchcock but, lacking any commercial clout, he went the route that offered "less chance for an investor to lose their money." Sure enough, *Don't Look in the Basement* was a success. Brownrigg stuck with horror through the seventies, directing *Poor White Trash Part 2*,[9] *Don't Open the Door* and *Keep My Grave Open*.[10]

Despite turning a tidy profit for his distributors, Brownrigg claims not to have made the type of money he should and got disillusioned to the point that, after this quartet of horror, he made only one more movie – a teen sex comedy called *Thinkin' Big*, which he subsequently disowned. After this he returned full-time to commercials, sales films, and "producing an outdoor hunting and fishing show for Star Sportsmen."

In John McCarty's book *The Sleaze Merchants*, exploitation director Bret McCormick[11] says that he and Brownrigg – "a close pal" – had penned a sequel to *Don't Look in the Basement* which they hoped to get onto the video shelves someday. Alas, Brownrigg died in 1997 at the age of fifty-nine.

THE DRILLER KILLER

USA 1979

cast: Jimmy Laine, Carol Marz, Baybi Day, Harry Schultz, Alan Wynroth

story: N G St John

producer: Rochelle Weisberg

director: ABEL FERRARA

Reno is a struggling artist, unable to pay his rent, and disgusted by vagrants. When a punk band moves into the apartment beneath his, he takes to the streets with a portable hand drill.

THE DRILLER KILLER is more an arthouse film than a horror film, yet too much of a horror film to sit comfortably with the former's convention and as a result tends to alienate both audiences.[1] Had Reno gone out and murdered in a more conventional manner, say with a gun, things would have been much simpler. The focus would have been taken away from the means of murder. But, as the title of the film corroborates, the emphasis is on how he kills rather than why.

What confounds matters further is the fact that director Abel Ferrara doesn't suggest there is anything deeply significant in Reno's modus operandi. "To me it's a comedy," he said in an interview for *Shock Xpress*.

> Like drilling people, that's a joke, that was our sense of fun! The idea is a documentary about a dear friend of mine. I played the role of my friend. He lived in that attic with those two girls, they were his real girlfriends. I played the role because it was shot over a long period of time, and we couldn't interest an actor in staying with a film shot in bits and pieces.[2]

When we see Reno go on his kill-spree, running unnoticed around the streets and brandishing his power drill like a revolver, we can well believe that the film is a comedy at heart. Reno sees his world collapsing and his greatest fear is that he will soon be joining the 'degenerate bums' he so despises. Killing them, wiping them out, will forestall the inevitable – so he believes. He can't pay the rent, or his bills, and his partner Carol leaves him. When the Roosters, an awful punk band that move into his apartment building, secure a lucrative contract he can't comprehend the injustice and feels he's on a road to nowhere. Losing a painting deal, Reno ceases to focus his anger on vagrants and instead begins to destroy his peers.

When James Ferman reflected on gory video sleeves in the early eighties and their part in the 'nasties' backlash, he singled out as a particularly pertinent example the artwork for *The Driller Killer*. Given the film's arthouse aspirations, however, the director of the BBFC had no qualms that *The Driller Killer* could be passed with only a few cuts. Ironic then that the killings and their lingering grisliness should detract from the film. When Reno murders his first victim, barely has the drill bit touched the clothing of the vagrant than a fountain of blood is gushing in the air. Though the effects themselves are cleverly realised –particularly the drilling of the head as shown on the garish sleeve – they seem almost superfluous.

The Driller Killer was released on the Vipco label uncertified and with the few gore scenes intact. After fifteen years in uncertified limbo, the film was finally submitted to the BBFC in 1999 by Visual Films and passed 18 with cuts. This version also reinstated some non-violent scenes that had been missing from Vipco's original print and utilised considerably tamer video sleeve artwork.

Part of *The Driller Killer*'s regeneration as something of an 'acceptable' nasty is

EVIL
DEAD
Can they be stopped?
STARRING
Bruce Campbell • Sarah York • Betsy Baker • Hal Delrich • Ellen Sandweiss
Special Make-up Effects by Tom Sullivan • Produced by Robert G. Tapert • Written and Directed by Sam Raimi
SCREENINGS
THE FINAL SCREENING TONGHT STAR III, May 22, MIDNIGHT
Tickets Required First Show Only - Available At Films Around The World Office
Worldwide Representation
Irvin Shapiro
Films Around The World
In Cannes:
Carlton Hotel
Room #501
Films Around The World
745 Fifth Avenue, New York, New York 10151
Telephone: (212) 752-5050 Telex 420572 Film UI

down to Ferrara's partial assimilation into the mainstream, with a remake of Don Siegel's *Invasion of the Body Snatchers* and episodes of *Miami Vice* under his belt (we say 'partial assimilation' because other features, like *Dangerous Game* and *The Funeral*, are far from mainstream). On top of this is the recognition that *The Driller Killer*, Ferrara's first major feature, offers social comment. Ferrara said of its New York City setting:

> That's where I live, the awfulness is there... A lot of the film is real, but if we staged something, we were sure there was something twice as bad going on two blocks away![3]

Alongside the importance and reverence attributed to the punk rock era, where once *The Driller Killer* was perceived as a horrible scruffy lout, now it's seen as 'art' (as if the two couldn't co-exist before historians got a handle on them). Punk credibility is provided in an early intertitle advising the viewer to play the film loud. There is a rumour that Ferrara tried to get David Johansen of the New York Dolls to play the role of Reno.

THE EVIL DEAD

aka: Book of the Dead (original title)
USA 1982
cast: Bruce Campbell, Ellen Sandweiss, Betsy Baker, Hal Delrich, Sarah York
story: Sam Raimi
producer: Robert G Tapert
director: SAM RAIMI

Young people on vacation in a secluded cabin discover a tape recording and mysterious book and inadvertently invoke evil spirits that want only to kill them.

THE EVIL DEAD was Sam Raimi's debut feature and, as often is the case, remains his best and most striking work. It was Raimi's maverick style as much as the outlandish special effects and camera work that propelled the movie into instant cult classic status. From the opening moments when the camera glides over a sinister-looking pond the film rarely lets up. Whether rushing through the woods knocking down trees in its path, or providing forced perspective shots of characters, the camera technique generates an excitement of its own.

Raimi – an ardent horror movie and Three Stooges fan – borrows ideas from many sources yet manages to convert them into something wholly unique. Scenes in the forest evoke the chilling woodland chase sequence in Jacques Tourneur's *Night of the Demon*. The 'above the rafters' point-of-view shot in *The Evil Dead*'s latter half appear remarkably similar to the Steadicam shots in Kubrick's *The Shining*, in which Danny rides his pedal car through hotel corridors (even replicating the strange on-off sound effect of that film as the car crosses rugs and wooden floor surfaces).[1] There are also some cryptic references in the film, such as a poster for Wes Craven's *The Hills Have Eyes*, torn in half on a cellar wall. This isn't so much a homage to Craven as an amicable dig at a movie that frightened Raimi. In *The Hills Have Eyes* a torn poster for *Jaws* can be seen on a wall, as if to signify that, however scary that film was, things here are scarier... Raimi considered his own film to be even scarier.[2]

There are times when the pace slips and its amateurish origins are revealed. While this serves to enhance the charm,[3] there are moments when it can be merely exasperating, such as scenes in which Ashley (Bruce Campbell) is entangled in collapsed bookshelves. There is no discernible reason why he can't get back on his feet, yet he struggles under the flimsy woodwork as though he were trapped beneath a truck. Minor complaints aside, *The Evil Dead* achieves exactly what it set out to accomplish and provides a relentless assault on the senses. Even the limited acting capabilities do nothing to diminish the impact of the film. If anything, the sight of Bruce Campbell desperately trying to express fear and panic serve to amplify the madness. He shakes and babbles in a hyper-nervous state as objects around him take on hallucinatory qualities. Blood starts to pour from the walls, a mirror loses its natural solid state and – most inspired of all, when Ashley finds he needs only to stave off the demons a little longer before dawn breaks – time itself reverses! If Raimi never picked up a camera again, this scene alone ought to secure for him auteur status.

Having made Super-8 shorts together, Sam Raimi, Bruce Campbell and Robert Tapert raised money for *The Evil Dead* by showing potential backers *Within the Woods* – a half-hour condensed treatment of their *Evil Dead* screenplay. With a budget ranging between $90,000 to $420,000, depending on the source, *The*

Evil Dead took three years to make. Raimi claims not to have had high hopes but was happy to simply see the film play the drive-in circuit. "We wanted a film that would stop people kissing in their cars and turn their attention to the screen," he told *Starburst*.[4] The picture soon became an international success, with an endorsement from Stephen King, who considered it a work of genius and "the most ferociously original" horror movie of the year.[5]

A possible influential source for the story can be found in a horror comic. Issue No 4 of *Eerie*, published by Warren in 1966, features a Joe Orlando and Archie Goodwin strip titled 'House of Evil'. A man goes to an isolated house in search of his brother. The house seems deserted, and he finds a tape recorder. He plays a tape and hears the voice of his brother, claiming the original owners of the house had summoned demons. The tape lures a hideous zombie-like creature into the room, which he attacks with a chair and witnesses the thing decompose into a slimy mess. It turns out to be his brother, infected by the house's evil. Now he himself is infected and transforming. As if 'House of Evil' wasn't enough to draw a comparison, in the same issue of *Eerie* is a strip where a man decapitates his lover, who then returns from the dead, her severed head talking to him while the headless body wanders around – a striking parallel to the killing and resurrection of Ashley's girlfriend in *The Evil Dead*.

The Evil Dead was released on the Palace Video label in the same slightly censored state it was released theatrically in the UK. The film is gory but in such a cartoonish, over the top manner that it would seem impossible to be offended by it... although evidently it did offend some people. For no other reason than it had 'evil' in the title, *The Evil Dead* was singled out by anti-'nasties' protestors led by Mary Whitehouse as particularly objectionable – this in spite of it being a good old fashioned scare story, a criterion many campaigners claimed differentiated 'video nasties' from traditional, more acceptable horror. The film was the subject of many courtroom battles around the country (film director David Puttnam was among the defence witnesses ready to give evidence). After it, and Palace, were cleared of obscenity at Snaresbrook Crown Court, in what was regarded as something of a test case, Judge Owen Stable QC criticised the DPP. In summing up, he said:

> I regard it as quite lamentable that in relation to a single film that there should have been over forty separate pieces of litigation up and down the country. I am concerned with what this chaotic state of affairs does to the reputation of the administration of justice.

The Evil Dead was re-released with a few additional cuts, though again the reasoning behind some of these decisions – i.e. trimming a shot where a pencil is twisted into an ankle – was baffling. In an interview with *Killing Moon*, principal examiner Guy Phelps was asked why *The Evil Dead* should be cut while other over the top films, such as *Society* and *Bad Taste*, were passed intact. He replied:

> *Society* and *Bad Taste* didn't seem to have any handle on reality; they were clearly placed in the completely fantasy world. You can obviously say the same about *The Evil Dead*, but within that there were moments where the violence to the people took you into a much more realistic handling of violence. The wriggling of a pencil deep into someone's ankle gives you a very real jolt of pain in a way the taking of the top of the man's head off in *Bad Taste* clearly didn't – it was obviously ludicrous and fairly painless as well!
>
> I think the particular problem with horror is that there are two ways of looking at these things. The public at large see them as quite real, whereas the horror buff sees them as totally unreal. So for them the horror film is not at all dangerous; for the public at large, as we all saw in 1982–3, it clearly is. [6]

The film was followed by two sequels which, despite higher production values, played more for laughs and were inferior to the original.[7] The best thing to be said about the third instalment, *Army of Darkness*, is that it had a great tentative title in 'The Medieval Dead'.

EVILSPEAK

USA 1981
cast: Clint Howard, R G Armstrong, Joseph Cortes, Claude Earl Jones, Hatywood Nelson, Don Stark, Charles Tyner, Hamilton Camp, Louie Gravance, Jim Greenleaf, Lynn Hancock, Loren Lester, Kathy McCullen, Lenny Montana
story: Joseph Garofalo
producers: Sylvio Tabet & Eric Weston
director: ERIC WESTON

The DPP39

'SCENES OF EXTREME AND EXPLICIT VIOLENCE'

West Andover Military Academy. Bullied student, Coopersmith, discovers occult paraphernalia. With this, and a computer, he avenges himself.

CHILD STAR OF the sixties TV show *Gentle Ben*, with some ninety film appearances in thirty years, *Evilspeak* marked the first star part for the young adult Clint Howard. He attacks his role with gusto, perfectly attuned to the downtrodden, ham-fisted student, Coopersmith. Indeed, because of *Evilspeak*, the diminutive pudgy-faced actor would appear in more and more films in the horror genre (though it would be over a decade before his next leading role, a homicidal mental patient in *Ice Cream Man*). Thanks to his brother Ron Howard, director of hits like *EdTV*, *Splash* and *Backdraft*, Clint's career is not relegated to low-budget dreck but occasionally crosses over to big-budget Hollywood productions. For his role in *Apollo 13* – Ron's most successful movie to date in which Clint played a mission control technician – he received a shared cast award.

Howard doesn't denigrate the more modest productions he's called to work in, and rarely turns any part down. The fact that, in his own words, he's "a funny looking guy," hasn't hindered his career in the least. "God has seen fit that I'm a character actor," he told *Psychotronic*.[1] "In my own head, I'm not a leading man. I'm not a hero in my own head."

Of all the movies he's appeared in, it is *Evilspeak* that Howard has a fondness for. Because the story incorporated a computer, the actor considers it ahead of its time. The computer isn't called to do much beyond flash digital text on the screen and project swirling pentangles. At one point it looks like the sixteenth-century devil worshipper that possesses the computer has his own logo.

Eric Weston never managed to break through with *Evilspeak*, despite the relative competence he showed as a director. Howard has suggested that the movie was the first in a prospective trilogy, hence the tagged-on digital message warning that the wrath of Coopersmith can be invoked in a ritual. For all of Weston's directorial promise and Howard's capacity as an actor, the premise of *Evilspeak* is not so good you'd want to see it pan into a second or third instalment. Indeed the story is formulaic to the point of tedium. With everything stacked so unfavourably against Coopersmith it ought to be a pleasure to see him avenge himself. (He doesn't belong. He's overweight. Everybody hates and deceives him, even the Reverend. He's hopeless at sports. He's an orphan. Sarge wants to sodomise him. He is called names. His cute puppy is killed, and so on.) But Coopersmith's revenge is an inevitability – a particularly lame one at that – about which the only good thing is the fact that it draws the film closer to an end.

The gore effects are few, but visceral. They include the decapitation of a topless woman, a brief shot of a pig drawing innards from a naked secretary, and a hand sinking into a chest and removing a heart. With a few cuts, the Board had no problem passing *Evilspeak* as 18 some years after it featured on the DPP list.

EXPOSÉ

title on print: The House on Straw Hill
aka: Trauma
Great Britain 1975
cast: Linda Hayden, Fiona Richmond, Patsy Smart, Karl Howman, Vic Armstrong, Udo Kier
story: James Kenelm Clarke
producer: Brian Smedley-Aston
director: JAMES KENELM CLARKE

Boorish novelist Paul Martin employs a secretary, the promiscuous Linda, to help meet the looming deadline for his next book. But Linda has murder on her mind.

JAMES KENELM CLARKE'S sex and horror hybrid was released theatrically in Britain in 1976 as *Exposé*. Under this title it was packaged for video release by Intervision, despite the title on the video print itself being *The House on Straw Hill.*[1] These differing titles give some clue to the problem that faced Clarke's film. Although Udo Kier (who plays novelist Paul Martin) and Linda Hayden (his new secretary, Linda) were both familiar names in exploitation cinema,[2] the big selling point was Fiona Richmond (Suzanne) – "Britain's Number One Sex Symbol." A celebrity in most part due to the monthly column she wrote for Paul Raymond's *Men Only* magazine, much of the film's promotion was geared around Richmond and the fact that *Exposé* marked her feature-length movie debut. Fiona's piece in the January 1976 edition of *Men Only* was a set-report for the soon-to-be released movie. It might not have offered much insight – the guys in the crew are said to be "dishy" and Fiona "could cheerfully have given them all one" – but suggests the title change was a last-minute decision. Fiona refers throughout her article to *The House on Straw Hill*, and that its release is "very soon." Not two months later, *MFB* had reviewed the film as *Exposé*. British distributors Target International were responsible for the title change,[3] an obvious attempt to make the whole thing appear more 'naughty' than it was – as evidenced in the advertising blurb that promised of Fiona, "Nothing is left to the imagination."

Soft-porn lovemaking in the sex-horror *Exposé*.

The initial, better-suited title is derivative of Sam Peckinpah's *Straw Dogs*, a film from which Kenelm Clarke draws some inspiration.[4] But the new title and marketing, as *Exposé*, was directed elsewhere.

> Proves that if adult-filmmakers would add explicit sex to a good story they might produce more interesting films. This one has the story, but implied sex, including rape, is not detailed.
>
> –*The X-Rated Videotape Guide I*

> Slow, pointless softcore porn number... horror fans should fast forward their VCRs to the last twenty minutes.
>
> –*Hi-Tech Terror* No 20

Paul, under pressure to finish his new novel, isolates himself in a country cottage. But there is a procession of interruptions, some of them real: bloody nightmares or flashbacks, lesbian sex, sex toys, unpleasant locals, rape, and murder.[5] The film's uneasy combination of eroticism and horror could have won little favour with the powers that be. Scenes of soft-porn lovemaking are either interrupted by Paul's violent hallucinations, or, in the case of the lesbian romp between Linda and Suzanne, followed by vicious, sadistic murder. Linda's bout of masturbation and subsequent rape in the field makes for a particularly uneasy alliance, given that she shows no signs of fear or emotion throughout the ordeal. The

Udo Kier is nervous in the elusive *Exposé*.

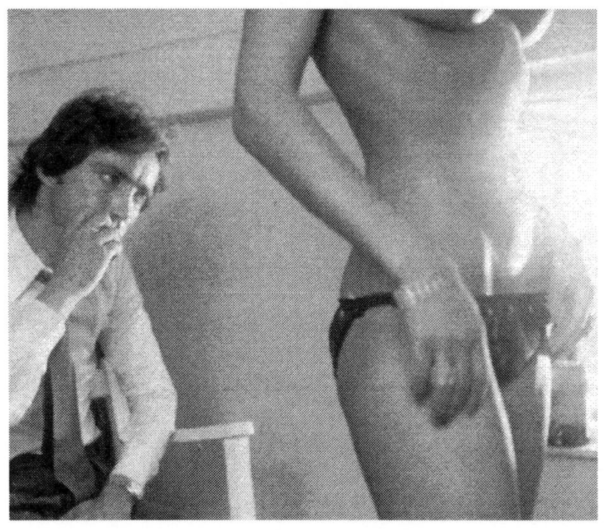

BBFC would undoubtedly construe the victim's failure to respond to the sex attack in the same negative way as they would the sight of a victim who suddenly enjoys her ordeal – as evidenced in their cuts for *Exposé*'s re-release in 1997.

Director Clarke worked on the BBC2 documentary series *Man Alive*, and it was a report on the British sexploitation business that prompted him to take up film-making. No sooner had the report aired in 1975 than Clarke acquired funding from Paul Raymond[6] and was directing Fiona Richmond in a trio of films: *Exposé*, *Let's Get Laid!* and *Hardcore*. Clarke resorted to sex comedy for the latter two films.

Exposé was one of the more elusive films to make the DPP list. While it suffered from poor distribution, one suspects it also fell foul of its own marketing, in that the drawing power of Fiona Richmond had diminished by the time it made it to video. She may well have been "Britain's Number One Sex Symbol" in 1975, when the film was made, but by the eighties her crown had been relinquished. Porn's hierarchy shifted in favour of a more explicit stable of models, courtesy of Mary Millington, and the publishing empire of Raymond's rival, David Sullivan. People who wanted pornographic videos could relatively easily get hold of cut-down versions of notorious American titles (like *Deep Throat* and *Debbie Does Dallas*), and fully uncut hardcore courtesy of mail order companies like Videx and Taboo,[7] who advertised regularly in film and video magazines.

Fiona Richmond once again came to the fore as "Britain's Biggest Sex Star of the Seventies," thanks to retro chic and modest success of the Saucy Seventies series of movies re-released by Medusa.[8] Siren Video remastered and reissued *Exposé* – together with *Let's Get Laid!* and *Hardcore* – with Fiona as the key selling point. Passed with fifty-one seconds of cuts, Siren's video is missing much of Suzanne's murder as well as the rape of Linda.

The *Aurum Film Encyclopedia* noted that on its original theatrical release the censor cut thirty minutes – a fact repeated by *Psychotronic*[9] in their review some years later. However, this is unlikely. Producer Smedley-Aston recalls that only a little self-imposed cutting was ever made, specifically a shot of blood running down Suzanne's legs following her murder.[10]

Clarke is reported as saying he intends to remake *Exposé*.

Faces of Death

aka: Junk

USA/Japan 1979

consultant narrator: Dr Frances B Gröss [Michael Carr]

producer: Rosilyn T Scott

writer: Alan Black

director: CONAN LE CILAIRE

In this pseudo-documentary, a forensic examiner by the name of Frances B Gröss offers film clips for a better understanding of man's greatest fear: death.

GIVEN THE 'SHOCKING' nature of some of the footage left intact, it is puzzling why Atlantis Video Productions chose to remove a whole chunk of *Faces of Death* for the British market. The excised footage – which can still be found in the American print of the film – comprises all the material that originally fell between sequences showing a Los Angeles autopsy room and stock footage of WWII.[1] It is probable that the reason for this wholesale removal lies in the video company wanting to save cash on magnetic tape, a fate which befell at least one other film on the nasties list (*The Driller Killer*).

According to the press book for the film's US theatrical release, *Faces of Death* took three years to make, comprised a team that "could have been hired by the United Nations," and answers "the unasked questions we've always had about death." But the production is shrouded in mystery, and all the credits are obviously pseudonyms.[2] The film's host, Frances B Gröss,[3] self-proclaimed "doctor of the pathological sciences," works as a county coroner we are informed in a US press booklet, while director Conan Le Cilaire:

has directed adventure stories from diving to scalling [*sic*] mountains. He is a man with a great love of celluloid. The intensity of *Faces of Death* will no doubt place him in a league all his own amongst his associates in the film world.

'FACES OF DEATH' DUE AT CANNES 'MARKET'

Tokyo.

Having recently had its preem in Los Angeles, "Faces of Death" by Rosilyn T. Scott and directed by Conan Le Cilaire, will be given its international launch in the market of the Cannes Festival. World-wide distribution rights have been picked up by Telecas of Japan, whose president Kenzo Kuroda will be on the Riviera, supported by two principal aides.

Among the "Faces of Death" described in the film are sequences dealing with a flesh-eating cult in San Francisco; self-immolation by a Buddhist monk; a game warden in Florida being mutilated and devoured by an alligator; and an execution by decapitation in the Middle East.

In other sequences two pit bull terriers fight to the death, while in a restaurant in India a waiter serves a live monkey with its head secured in the middle of a table. The diners are then presented with mallets and bang the monkey's head until it dies. The waiter then serves the brains.

Announcement in *Variety*, May 7, 1980.

In a league of his own unquestionably, but no hint at what these other works might be. Ambiguity also surrounds producer Rosilyn T Scott (said to have "worked on several documentaries and docu-dramas"), writer Alan Black ("a 'film doctor' for numerous movies throughout the world"), composer Gene Kauer (responsible for composing and conducting "the music for many major pictures out of Hollywood"), and director of photography Michael Golden ("a leading cinematographer in the United States").

The inspiration for *Faces of Death* undoubtedly lies in an earlier film: Robert Emenegger and Allan Sandler's 1975 *Death: The Ultimate Mystery*. More reserved in its use of grisly imagery, it looks like a dry run for *Faces of Death* and the two films share many striking similarities. Most obvious is the use of a lone figure on a journey of self-discovery, each starting their trip with a visit to the mummies of Guanajuato, Mexico.

Faces of Death is part of a cycle known as Mondo films – or 'shockumentaries' – feature-length documentaries that seek more to entertain and shock than inform. The Mondo film had its golden age in the sixties and seventies, exciting audiences with exotic and ghoulish images from around the globe. Thanks to recent camcorder technology and the home video market, the Mondo film has seen a recent rejuvenation in the form of cheaply produced, direct-to-video compilations, consisting of true gore footage captured by newshounds or culled from police files and the like. It was Gualtiero

Jacopetti who created the blueprint for the genre in 1962, with his film *Mondo Cane*. Subsequent productions adhered closely to Jacopetti's successful formula – a haughty narrator guiding the viewer through a succession of perilously linked film clips, accompanied by an overblown musical score and a sappy closing song (in *Faces of Death* the closing song is 'Life'). Some films devoted themselves to a specific topic, such as witchcraft, the mysterious continent of Asia, or sex. As decades wore on, the world these films helped to span was getting smaller, and material that had once appeared exotic and alluring now seemed dated and quaint. *Faces of Death* changed that, stripping all extraneous matter away to leave the only subject still regarded as taboo. After hardcore pornography had crossed into the mainstream with movies like *Deep Throat* and *The Devil in Miss Jones* in the early seventies, sex as a draw for Mondo audiences was effectively redundant. Conan Le Cilaire helped to reshape Mondo, shifting into a territory that brought to the viewer a barrage of gruesome deaths and disasters.

Made in 1979 by an American team for the Japanese market, *Faces of Death* proved enormously popular in Asia and even secured a place in Hong Kong's All-time Top Twenty Grossers list for 1980. It fared less well when released theatrically in the US in 1981. Later, on video, it was a surprising success and established itself as one of the top rental hits in the country. Several sequels were spawned, with *Faces of Death* parts 2, 3 and 4 directed again by the "man with a great love for celluloid," Le Cilaire. All followed the same pattern, with Dr Gröss[4] – substituted by a Dr Louis Flellis in part 4[5] – guiding viewers, via footage, on his thoughts and theories relating to death. The series appears to have come to its true end with the fourth instalment, but the title continued for a spell thanks to a German entrepreneur by the name of Uwe Schier who bought the rights to the title at the beginning of 1990. His instalments in the series – aimed solely at the German market – bear little relation to the earlier films and consist of footage culled from already available sources and set to classical music.[6]

Not all the footage collected in this franchise was authentic. As with most Mondo films, fabricated scenes are included with authentic scenes. No attempt is made to differentiate one from the other – everything is presented as cold fact. While it is hard to imagine that audiences could be fooled by some of the fabricated sequences,[7] they were and continue to be. The camera most certainly can lie and a deceptive narrative can often go unquestioned. Back in the eighties, *Faces of Death* dazed an audience yet to experience a daily influx of Reality TV shows and true crime reconstructions. In the nineties and beyond, the fact that the film is unobtainable in Britain and attitudes governed by hearsay and jaundiced news reports, it is little wonder that *Faces of Death* has acquired legendary status and figured prominently in the government spearhead to outlaw the 'nasties'.

In 1998, some of the mystery surrounding *Faces of Death* appeared to have been solved. Gorgon Video, then US video distributor, made *Faces of Death: Fact or Fiction?* a short feature that featured as a DVD extra.[8] It purports to offer background information addresses the contentious issue of passing fabricated material off as genuine. A man hidden in shadow with a voice distortion box is introduced as director Conan Le Cilaire, described as a "dark genius… born in the slums of Marseille." Le Cilaire admits that many scenes in the films are simulated, the reason being that last-minute legal responsibilities prevented him from using the source material. Other insights have more of a ring of truth. One notorious yet fake scene shows a restaurant that serves live monkey brains as a delicacy[8] (which begins with a monkey being clubbed unconscious by hesitant diners). Japanese clients for the film, Le Cilaire explains, didn't want to show Asians in a bad light and demanded that the original setting of a Southeast Asia restaurant be changed to one in the Middle East. With regard to another notorious sequence, a commercial airline incident over San Diego and its bloody aftermath, the director claims the footage was in a can marked "Body Parts" and cost him $50 from a news agency.

FIGHT FOR YOUR LIFE

aka: I Hate Your Guts; Blood Bath at 1313 Fury Road; Getting Even; Stayin' Alive; The Hostage's Bloody Revenge; The Killing Machine; Held Hostage

USA 1977

cast: William J Sanderson, Robert Judd, Reginald Blythewood, Lela Small, Daniel Faraldo, Catherine Peppers, Yvonne Ross, Peter Yoshida

story: Straw Weisman

producers: William Mishkin & Robert A Endelson

director: ROBERT A ENDELSON

Three violent felons take refuge in the home of the Turners, a God-fearing black family, and subject them to intimidation and abuse.

FIGHT FOR YOUR Life is an extremely uncomfortable piece of cinema and one of the most powerful films on the DPP list. The theme of intruders breaking into a secluded house and degrading the inhabitants is not uncommon in exploitation cinema – several other titles on the 'nasties' list share it, as does William Fruet's *Death Weekend*, released the same year as Endelson's film, and *Hostage Girls*,[1] a hardcore porn variant. It's a cinematic tradition that appears to have its genus in William Wyler's *The Desperate Hours* (1955).[2] However, *Fight for Your Life* substitutes the class divide usually evidenced in this type of film with race[3] – a turnabout owing much to the success of blaxploitation movies, which hit their stride in the mid seventies with the *Shaft* series and the likes of *The Candy Tangerine Man*, *Welcome Home Brother Charles*, *Dolemite*, *et al*.

Jesse Lee Kane (William Sanderson)[4] is leader of a violent gang that escapes from a police truck and makes a getaway in a pimp's Mercedes, eventually arriving at the home of the Turners on Thanksgiving. A news bulletin warns that all three are extremely dangerous, "especially Kane." After much squirm-inducing racist dialogue, the tables are turned, and the Turners get the upper hand. The promotional campaign for *Fight for Your Life* sometimes used this fact as its selling point. "Stand up and cheer the Brother who taught America the meaning of the word 'courage'... and experience the joy of total revenge," ran one tagline, making the film look even more like a blaxploitation movie.[5] In reality, it's a cleverly ambiguous blast of high-octane exploitation.

Although the film appears to side with the Turner family, it doesn't do them any favours. For the entire time on screen, the Turners are subjected to ridicule and abuse. Beyond that, the first racial slur in the film comes not from the convicts but from Mrs Turner herself, and her opinions regarding a local white girl.[6] Certainly, Turner 'wins' out in the end and kills Kane, but his 'joy of total revenge' as an act seems anticlamactic, taking all of two minutes. Not exactly the most satisfying denouement, given the humiliation he's had to endure to get to it. So swift is Turner's retribution, the filmmakers try to give it extra clout by running Kane's demise in slow motion. However, these couple of minutes of retribution are a commercial necessity. Without them, Kane's racism would remain unchecked, and the film possibly unmarketable as a result. With this ending, the film opens itself to part of the audience it has so completely alienated for most of its running time. As Steve Puchalski notes in his review for *Shock Cinema*:[7]

> You couldn't have paid me to be the only white face in a Harlem theatre when [*Fight for Your Life*] was first shown! But the most frightening aspect of the flick is the fact it was probably enjoyed on both sides of the Mason-Dixie, for totally different reasons.

On the one hand it was marketed as a piece of black power propaganda, while for white liberal audiences it was promoted as an action film with no hint of racial intolerance – as per the blurb on the British video box, which simply states that *Fight for Your Life* is "eighty-nine minutes of sheer terror."

The racial slurs are relentless and inflammatory but not likely the primary reason for the film's ban in Britain. Only a few years prior to *Fight for Your Life*, the BBFC had deliberated over another film which they feared might stir up racial feelings. This was *Uncle Tom*, a pseudo-historical reconstruction filmed in a documentary-like manner. Made by the Italian team of Gualtiero Jacopetti and Franco Prosperi – co-directors on *Mondo Cane*, and the 'fathers' of Mondo cinema – it was supposedly an inquiry into conditions of slavery in the Deep South during the early nineteenth century. But, as Guy Phelps notes in his book *Film Censorship*, the film was "in fact totally voyeuristic and exploitative. The blacks are shown to be little more than animals and the camera gloats at the treatment they receive from whites."

Uncle Tom received a theatrical release in Britain in 1973, after cuts of forty minutes,[8] which included the removal of the last reel in its entirety. According to Phelps, the BBFC in general would have liked to have banned the film outright. Director Stephen Murphy, however, "was not eager to expand the issues upon which 'social undesirability' becomes cause enough for rejection." As a result, *Uncle Tom* was screened for the Race Relations Board, who agreed with Murphy and felt it shouldn't be banned because the social issue was not entirely relevant

– the film degraded both blacks and whites. The Board then consulted the Race Relations Act which stipulated that to secure a conviction, it had to be proven that the handlers[9] of a work fully intended to stir up racial hatred. This was unlikely as *Uncle Tom* was dealing with a real, albeit emotive, era in history, and that the despicable treatment of black slaves served to degrade the white characters.[10]

The Board didn't suffer the same consternation over *Fight for Your Life*, rejecting it without hesitation when submitted in 1981 with a view to a theatrical release.[11] It was never submitted for video classification following the introduction of the Video Recordings Act.

Something else draws the two films together: The Ted Turner character in *Fight for Your Life* is obviously a 'nod' to Nat Turner, the slave leader and religious fanatic who, in 1831, mounted the only sustained slave revolt. The final reel in *Uncle Tom* – the one the BBFC excised completely – focused on the writings of Nat Turner and brought them 'up-to-date' in a hypothetical scenario that shows white families being slaughtered by blacks.[12] Given these parallels it's highly likely that *Uncle Tom* was the inspiration for Endelson's film.

Everyone is tarred with the same brush, with ethnic slurs directed at other members of Kane's own gang, Chino Rodriguez and Chow Ling.[13] *Fight for Your Life* is part of a very isolated tradition of commercial cinema, whereby filmmakers present racial stereotypes and slurs in an almost amoral fashion with seemingly no underlying racist agenda of their own. It doesn't fit in with the blaxploitation films of the seventies, nor more recent anti-KKK message films, like *Mississippi Burning* and *A Time to Kill*.

This raises another issue. While cuts may be made to, say, *Cliffhanger* on the basis that some audiences in East End cinemas supposedly cheered the racist remarks made by a cockney villain about his black accomplice,[14] what cuts can be made when the central character in, say, *Dawn of the Dead* gets jeered by audience members for being black, as witnessed by one author of this book?[15] Neither the DPP with regard to horror videos nor the Video Recordings Act 1984 (and its numerous amendments) make any reference to racism.[16] Speaking at the ICA[17] James Ferman voiced his concerns that the heroin use in Tarantino's *Pulp Fiction* was a potentially harmful influence. Responding to a question from the audience on the abundance of the word "nigger" in that same film, he said, "At 18, we don't ban language."

So would *Fight for Your Life* be granted a video certificate if submitted to the BBFC? Not likely, with or without cuts.

FOREST OF FEAR

aka: Bloodeaters
USA 1979
cast: Charles Austin, Beverly Shapiro, Dennis Helfend, Kevin Hanlon, Judy Brown, Pat Kellis, Roger Miles, Philip Garfinkel, Bob Larson, Hariet Miller, Paul Haskin, John Amplas
story: Charles McCrann
producer: Charles McCrann
director: CHARLES MCCRANN

The government drops Dromax, a powerful new herbicide, on a marijuana farm, intending to destroy it. A side effect is that the hippie farmers become rabid killers.

SAD IT MAY be, but the most exciting thing about *Forest of Fear* is spotting a baby-faced John Amplas – an actor who had previously played the lead in George Romero's *Martin* – in the role of Agent Henry Phillips. Acquiring Amplas was presumably something of a coup for the *Forest of Fear* film-makers: not only is he the only 'name' actor in their movie, but his presence accentuates a connection – albeit tenuous – between their work and that of Romero's (whose *Night of the Living Dead* and *The Crazies* obviously influenced *Forest of Fear*).[1]

McCrann doesn't appear to have made any other film besides this 16mm effort, and nothing outside of *Forest of Fear* is known about him. He is one of the great unknowns of low-budget cinema, obscure to the point that even the most persevering of film zines has yet to come up with a feature or factoid on him.

McCrann's characters completely lack colour and depth. Everyone is a cipher, operating under ambiguous epithets like "agent" out of tiny offices in "Washington," or – as in the case of Jimmy – have a mental disability. (Jimmy is one of two children played here by young adults, who appear to be in their mid twenties.) Jimmy really doesn't have much to do. He rubs a curiously phallic teddy bear and delivers a half-dozen mumbled words which have no bearing on anyone or anything.

McCrann takes a couple of stabs at generating tension, but these instances fall flat or come across as just plain weird. None weirder though than the mother who momentarily escapes death by driving a knife into a hippie's eye and finds herself on a dirt track. Crawling along, hysterical with fear, she spots a pickup truck in the mid-distance. (Considering the film is set in a remote area of forest, an awful lot of people are converging on this spot.) The truck driver, who has been fiddling under the hood, drives away blissfully unaware of the woman who desperately tries to attract his attention. Not far down the road the truck pulls over again and the guy checks under the hood a second time. About to drive off he spots the woman in his rear-view mirror... This all constitutes a laborious set-piece, the whole attitude skew-whiff thanks to the radio upon which everything hangs: the guy can't hear the woman because he has the radio in his pickup switched on – but it's not enough that the radio should be on, it is on very loud because it's not playing music but conversation. But it's not even real conversation; it's playing what sounds like a made-up language. The driver of the pickup is driving around listening to a very loud made-up language on his radio.

Below: Trade ad. Bottom: Otherwise unrelated, this 1957 Corgi paperback appears to have lent its title and poster art to Charles McCrann's film, *Forest of Fear*.

For no logical reason, the British release of *Forest of Fear* is missing a chunk of footage. This missing sequence adds little to the film but does highlight another miserable misfire on McCrann's part to incorporate elements of tension, suspense and shock.

Where the British print concludes with Tom and the children gathering around the body of Polly – a scene that jumps abruptly to the end credits – the original version continues to run for several more minutes, showing Tom clearing his desk, having quit his job and heading off to see how the children, Jimmy and Amy, are coping. He pulls in for gas and – snapped out of a daydream by the pump attendant – continues his journey until the end credits roll. Presumably, this coda is meant to impart a feeling of the horror being far from over, that the hulking pump attendant – who pops out of nowhere with a sneeze into the camera – is yet another Dromax-infected crazy. But nothing about the sequence works and the jolt simply comes over as absurd.

The gore effects in *Forest of Fear* fare marginally better and mercifully aren't locked on screen too long (a major failing with low-budget film work is a reluctance to cut away). There is a passable hand-being-lopped-off scene and a couple of instances of spilled offal, but an aversion to depicting the actual killings, which tend to take place out of shot.[2]

There is little reason why *Forest of Fear* shouldn't be granted a certificate if submitted to the BBFC. Perhaps the opening scene with the federal agents being garrotted and stabbed repeatedly would be truncated (it follows lengthy shots of a hippie girl soaping her breasts), but nothing beyond this ought to hinder the film in getting a release.

Two things to note: The title of the movie likely derives from a book, *The Forest of Fear*, recollections of an Amazonian adventure by Ernst Löhndorff; the cover of the Corgi 1957 edition also seems to have inspired McCrann's poster artwork. *Forest of Fear* has the most succinct opening credits of any film on the DPP list. They read, in their entirety, "CM Productions presents *Forest of Fear*."

FRANKENSTEIN (ANDY WARHOL'S)

title on print: Flesh For Frankenstein
aka: Il mostro e in tavola... barone Frankenstein! (trans: The Monster is on the table... Baron Frankenstein!); Andy Warhol's Frankenstein
Italy/France 1973
cast: Joe Dallesandro, Monique van Vooren, Udo Kier, Arno Juerging, Dalila Lazzaro, Srojan Zelenovic
story: Paul Morrissey
producer: Andrew Braunsberg
director: PAUL MORRISSEY

Baron Frankenstein is determined to create the most beautiful man and woman. Together they shall produce perfect children. Things don't go to plan.

The DPP39

'SCENES OF EXTREME AND EXPLICIT VIOLENCE'

Waiting for a script? *Flesh for Frankenstein*.

FLESH FOR FRANKENSTEIN[1] is inexorably linked with *Blood for Dracula*. Shot back-to-back in Italy over a two-month period, both films star Udo Kier in the title role and utilise virtually the same cast and crew.

Despite lending his name to the posters and credits, Andy Warhol didn't contribute anything to either movie.[2] However, this association with Warhol and actor Joe Dallesandro was necessary in securing the deal with the Italian backers. Paul Morrissey joined Andy Warhol's Factory in the sixties where he worked as a production assistant and cameraman. He gradually moved to directing and brought to the Factory's rash cinematic work a formality and accessibility lacking in its earlier output. Indeed his trilogy of *Flesh*,[3] *Trash* and *Heat* – each starred Dallesandro – are perhaps the most popular films the Factory ever produced.

Having no interest in the horror genre as such, the idea that he could make a film in 3-D and in Europe with European actors appealed to Morrissey, leading him to accept the offer to make a Frankenstein picture. Estimating he could bring the film in for $350,000 within three weeks, the response from the backers was one of surprise and Morrissey was offered a budget of almost a million dollars if he would make not one but two films. The backers wanted Dallesandro and understood the kudos Warhol's name would have, but were concerned that the result would somehow be systematic of the Factory and therefore not commercial enough – at least, this is the reason Antonio Margheriti gives for having been asked to "supervise" *Flesh for Frankenstein* and direct some sequences himself. In an interview with *The Dark Side*,[4] Margheriti claims that Morrissey had no script,

> just fourteen pages of what is to happen, and they made decisions with the actors about what the dialogue would be, writing the script all night for the next day. Because Carlo [Ponti, executive producer] was worried about all of this, he worked a kind of blackmail on me, he said: "Tony, you want to make that picture in Australia we talked about? If so, you have to be with the Morrissey shoot first."

Margheriti unquestionably did film parts of *Flesh for Frankenstein*, although what parts and how much is open to question. The general consensus is that he filmed only pickup shots that feature the Baron's two children wandering around the lab and castle, although Margheriti claims also to have shot some of the gore effects.[5] Margheriti's name doesn't appear on prints of the film outside of Italy (because the American distributors believed it would detract from Warhol and the film's arthouse alliance); in Italy, under the pseudonym 'Anthony Dawson', Margheriti is credited as director. This curious turnaround owes itself to the fact that, in Italy, a film with an Italian director became eligible for a state subsidy.

Initially, Warhol's name on both *Flesh for Frankenstein* and *Blood for Dracula* took precedence over that of Morrissey's directorship.[6] (Morrissey has said that "Andy's idea of making a movie is going to the premiere.") Of late, Morrissey is usurped once again as some sourcebooks and critics erroneously credit his work to Antonio Margheriti. Both films have an attitude that is completely removed from Italian horror. For instance, they have humour and irony, attributes alien to Italian genre pictures (certainly they're absent from the films of Margheriti). And it's debatable whether Udo Kier would have landed the title roles in the two films without a chance meeting with Morrissey on a plane. Morrissey, always keen to cast players who sound right as well as look right, made the perfect choice with Kier, and it's impossible to perceive these films being anywhere near as entertaining without the presence of the German actor. Although he had already appeared in the highly controversial and altogether more sombre *Mark of the Devil* (also as a baron), it was his role in Morrissey's films and the association with Warhol that established Kier as a cult figure. Suddenly he was in *Vogue* magazine.

Wild abandon. Udo Kier in *Flesh for Frankenstein*.

As the bombastic Baron in *Flesh for Frankenstein*,[7] Kier espouses demented ideas about sex, death and power, and admonishes his assistant Otto for being "filthy," in an accent and manner at once hilarious and a little sad. In one of the most notorious sequences, the Baron fist-fucks his female zombie's stomach cavity and cries, "To know death, Otto, you have to fuck life in the gall bladder!" This oft quoted dialogue,[8] states Michael Ferguson in his book *Little Joe Superstar*, was inspired by the director's disdain at the critical idolatry heaped upon Bertolucci's *Last Tango in Paris* the previous year. In Bertolucci's film, having sodomised Maria Schneider and prior to a request to stick her fingers in his rectum, Marlon Brando explains that the man she is looking for will remain elusive until she goes "right up into the ass of death; right up in his ass until you find a womb of fear, and then maybe, maybe then you'll be able to find him." Morrissey thought this to be a ridiculous line of dialogue.

Ferguson also makes the valid observation that Kier may have mixed up "life" and "death" in his delivery, which is understandable given that the actors only saw what passed as a script hours before shooting commenced. (One particularly lengthy diatribe is clearly being read by Kier from pages placed on the workbench before him.) The most priceless moment comes at the end of the film, when the male zombie revolts and the Baron loses a hand trying to flee it. With blood gushing from the stump, the Baron staggers around the lab, trying hopelessly to join his hand back to his wrist before throwing it at Nicholas, a shepherd boy, in frustration. "It's all your fault!" he yells.

Flesh for Frankenstein was heavily cut when released theatrically in Britain in 1975, losing about seven minutes. The critic in *World of Horror* deduced that the film's 3-D process – so proudly boasted in the advertising – had only really been successful in one scene of the film. In truth, almost all the scenes that did exploit the gimmick had been removed – ironic given that a supporting feature on this first run was *Violence in the Cinema Part 1*,[9] a "convincing and grisly" short which included an eye gouging and a woman having a breast hacked off.[10]

Flesh for Frankenstein was later re-released 'flat' on a double bill with *Blood for Dracula* – a film that reverses the political accent of the former from fascism to socialism. Enjoyable it is, but *Blood for Dracula* stands as a sanitised and unevenly paced work by comparison. Despite initial arrangements that it too would be made in 3-D, the idea was scrapped when the confines of the location in which much of *Dracula* takes place proved impractical for the Space-Vision camera.

Vipco's video release of *Flesh for Frankenstein* – residing on the DPP list – is uncut. Viewed today, the wild abandon with which real sheep guts are brandished remains a little shocking, particularly given the sexualised context in which the Baron conducts his business, holding the raw (spoiled and stinking) offal to his cheek and plucking oversized seminal vesicles from containers. Guts are gleefully thrust into the camera, or tumble towards it, as in the scenes where a maid is killed by Otto and the male zombie tears open his own sutures. When the Baron decapitates Nicholas' buddy with a pair of shears in an ambush, Otto clubs the headless torso as it stands bolt upright spraying blood into the air. One of the last shots of the film features the Baron delivering a soliloquy with half his stomach swaying from the point of a lance, several feet in front of his face. It's an arresting image that seems several light years removed from any other horror film made before or since.

It should be noted that *Flesh for Frankenstein* was made the same year as Hammer's *Frankenstein and the Monster from Hell*, the last of the British studio's lengthy run with Mary Shelley's monster. The two films are as removed as Hammer's original Monster was from the Universal *Frankenstein* of the 1930s. Except for one convoluting link... Following their work together on *Four Flies on Grey Velvet*, Dario Argento and Luigi Cozzi began looking to their next venture, intended to be a new interpretation of the Frankenstein legend. They planned to transpose the original story to 1920s pre-Nazi Germany, with the Monster allegorising the birth of Nazism. According to Cozzi, interviewed in *Psychotronic Video*,[11] no backers were interested. "They said Frankenstein was dead, and anyway, no one who wanted to see a horror movie cared about politics."

It's odd that Argento and Cozzi should be given the thumbs down only to have Morrissey's Italian-backed Frankenstein project appear shortly thereafter, even more so given the political, fascistic charge of Morrissey's film. And the convoluting link? Hammer was one of the potential investors approached by Argento and Cozzi to fund their *Frankenstein*.

FROZEN SCREAM

USA 1981
cast: Lynne Kocol, Renee Harmon, Thomas Gowen, Wolf Muser, Bob Rochelle, Lee James
story: Renee Harmon, Doug Ferrin, Michael Soney, Celeste Hammond
producer: Renee Harmon
director: FRANK ROACH

Experiments into immortality are taking place and people are being murdered to keep the research a secret.

WHEN IT FIRST gets underway this film looks like it might turn out to be an obscure, hitherto unknown gem. Unfortunately, it quickly becomes evident this isn't going to be the case. *Frozen Scream* is strange and dream-like, but it's not the result of a talented auteur. On the contrary, the film is a mess. Everyone appears to be in a somnambulistic state, regardless of whether they are the resurrected dead, courtesy of the experiments conducted by Dr Lil Stanhope and her colleague-lover, Dr Sven Johnson.[1] Characters talk to one another as if nailed to the spot, not moving in case they slip out of focus. None of the cast appears to have grasped the basic principles of acting, and emotions are conveyed through a succession of stares. Ann Gerhard (Lynne Yeaman) is the locus of the film. When confronted by hooded intruders[2] with crazed, excitable expressions, she simply stares back, only harder, as if unable to muster up feelings of fear or confusion. So, too, Lil, who just stares for no reason at all, often in tight close-ups. Only once in the whole movie do the filmmakers attempt a panning shot. (Panning onto a character who stares past a telephone.)

The plot is confusing and made more arduous by the curious accent Renee Harmon (as Lil) adopts at times, uttering lines like, "I could stay vivver avile."

Some of the confusion can be attributed to the fact that four writers are credited with scripting the story, which they may well have done without collaboration between themselves. Clumsy editing, in which characters suddenly appear out of context, adds to the chaos, as do the dream sequences and flashbacks that occur with startling regularity in the film's first half and then cease altogether. The continuity is also flawed. When a hooded killer is seen carrying a female victim to the lab in the opening reel, her face appears horribly mutilated, yet once inside the lab she is completely unblemished. The music, an irritating synthesised score of a type unduly popular amongst the nasties, is the same as that used in *Don't Go in the Woods* and credited to H Kingsley Thurber III (the two movies also share a similar transcendental quality).

There are many unintentionally humorous incidents, notably the footsteps that are wildly out of sync when Ann is being chased at the film's end (she stops running and they carry on going) and the big hand that slips into the confessional to strangle a priest (he doesn't notice it's there, despite it lingering in front of his face). Lil reprimands a reanimated killer with the line: "Feel your forehead, Kirk... It's hot in here."

Frozen Scream is another example of a film that was unnecessarily targeted by the DPP. Maybe its junior-grade appearance and the lowly video sleeve – images seemingly lifted straight off a TV screen – were enough to land it on the list? The only scenes that may have designated *Frozen Scream* a nasty are those depicting the aftermath of an axe attack, with the tool implanted in a woman's head, and the attack on a night watchman that results in a sliver of glass protruding from his eye. There is also a trauma-to-the-eye scene implied at the film's end, with a hypodermic needle approaching a screaming face before the screen turns blood-red and the credits roll.

Frozen Scream is tame enough for late-night television.

THE FUNHOUSE

USA 1981

cast: Elizabeth Berridge, Shawn Carson, Jeanne Austin, Jack McDermott, Cooper Huckabee, Largo Woodruff, Miles Chapin, David Carson, Sonia Zomina, Kevin Conway

story: Larry Block

producers: Derek Power & Steven Bernhardt

director: TOBE HOOPER

The DPP39

'SCENES OF EXTREME AND EXPLICIT VIOLENCE'

Teens witness a murder at a travelling carnival. They take refuge in the funhouse and are slowly picked off by one of the attractions. Only the virginal Amy survives.

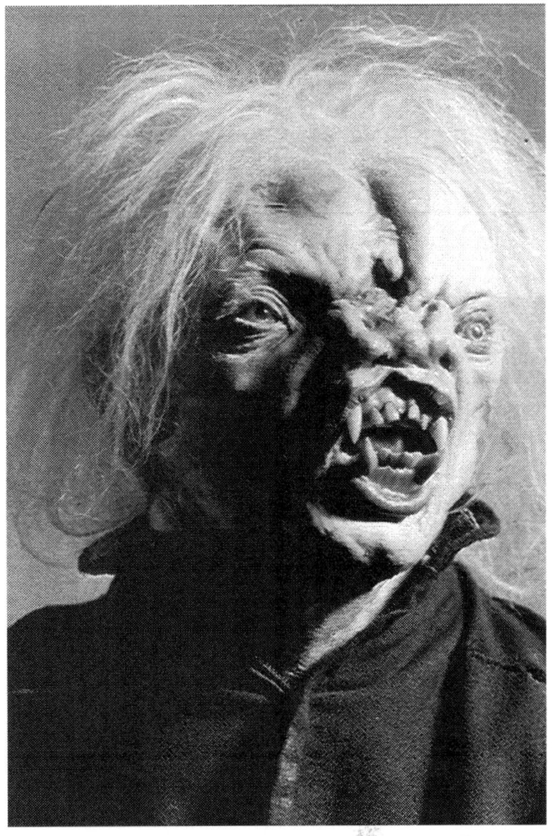

"Alive! Alive! Alive!" *The Funhouse*.

THE FUNHOUSE MET with disappointment among fans expecting another *Texas Chain Saw Massacre* from director Tobe Hooper, and it confirmed the slide into mediocrity evident in *Death Trap*, his second feature.

The Funhouse is Hooper's first movie with major studio backing and it completely lacks the gritty, claustrophobic edge of either *Texas Chain Saw* or *Death Trap* – which, unfortunately, is an argument that can also be levelled at every subsequent Hooper production. Hooper clearly intends *The Funhouse* to be a homage – or a return – to the traditional scares of early horror films.[1] Not content with the trite *Psycho*-inspired shower scene that opens the movie, he feels compelled to signpost his intention through the entire first half. There are posters featuring classic Universal monsters adorning bedroom walls; the killer wears a Boris Karloff Frankenstein's Monster mask; and should any viewer still be missing the point, a clip from *Bride of Frankenstein* plays on TV as Amy (Elizabeth Berridge), the final girl, leaves the house on a date.[2]

Even the violence and bloodshed are always just out of frame.

But Hooper fails to add any depth to his characters (the two protagonists, the carnival barker and the monster, don't even have names).[3] Amy is a virgin,[4] and is content to display the fact in a little-girl outfit that belongs to a completely different era. Her friend Liz – big-girl outfit – chides her for "saving it," but her own promiscuity proves her downfall. These are attributes drawn without aforethought from other movies in an attempt to lend a contemporaneous air to proceedings – which, it has to be said, is infinitely more preferable to the film's own trite efforts, courtesy of such embarrassingly 'hip' dialogue as "When you're stoned, Charles Manson is a terrific guy."

Distancing oneself from Hooper's earlier, better pictures, *The Funhouse* might provide the less-discerning viewer with some pleasing moments. Most notable are the garish carnival attractions with their bright neon lights and art brut murals; the barkers – all played by a suitably weary, and excellent, Kevin Conway – draw crowds with cries of "Alive! Alive! Alive!" and "Terrifying! Terrifying! Terrifying!" The inside of a freakshow tent, a guaranteed attention-grabber, is unfortunately only afforded a fleeting glimpse here. There is a burlesque attraction in which a motley bunch of women flash their leather hides to an eager male audience. While this curiously displaced segment doesn't serve to develop the plot, it does add to the atmosphere – a facet attributable to Hooper's insistence on using an actual working carnival for the film. But it's a double-edged sword: relocated to the Ivan Tors studio in Florida from Akron, Ohio, the carnival came with a price and soon production was beset with problems.

The limited shooting schedule was a major handicap, particularly given union rules with regard to shooting at night.[5] Ultimately many sequences had to be compromised in order to try and bring the film in on time – pressure that weighed on the film-makers in the guise of a completion guarantor who wandered around the set, looking to protect the investors' money.

Some scripted shots were left out entirely, which may or may not explain why *The Funhouse* has a particularly unsatisfying ending (Amy simply wanders into the distance) and nagging subtexts that go unexplored. For instance, the supernatural flourishes, Amy being drawn to the barkers and they to her, and two different adult males coming on to Amy's little brother, Joe, over the course of the movie. All of these unrealised aspects suggest a better movie.

Hooper was only able to deliver one rough cut before leaving the film for another commitment (an aborted involvement in *Venom*, shot in England).[6] He returned to *The Funhouse* for the final stages of post-production.[7] There is no logical reason why this innocuous little film found itself for a brief spell on the DPP list. The bloodletting is very discriminate, and there is no twisted sexual activity. Perhaps the reference to Hooper having directed *The Texas Chain Saw Massacre* on the video box was reason enough?[8]

GESTAPO'S LAST ORGY

title on print: The Gestapo's Last Orgy
aka: L'ultima orgia del III Reich (original title); Caligula Reincarnated as Hitler; Orgies du III Reich; Des Filles Pour Le Bourreau; Bourreaux SS
Italy 1977
cast: Daniela Levy, Marc Loud, Maristella Greco, Fulvio Riccardi, Atineska Nemour, Caterina Barbero
story: Antonio Lucarella
producer: Ruggero Gorgoglione
director: CESARE CANEVARI

Visiting the ruins of a Nazi death camp, a former camp commandant and a surviving prisoner meet. Flashbacks to their former lives are intercut with the Nuremberg trials.

LIKE THEIR SHORT-LIVED series of cannibal movies, the Italian-lensed Nazi camp genre was more intent on depicting brutality and sadism than it was a means of making any moral statement. Derived in part from Liliana Cavani's *The Night Porter* and in whole from the works of de Sade, *Gestapo's Last Orgy* depicts a lot of extreme cruelty yet has very little to say. Other entries in this unpleasant cycle also found their way onto the DPP list (see *Beast in Heat* and *SS Experiment Camp*), while some managed to slip by seemingly unnoticed (*SS Girls* and *The Red Nights of the Gestapo*, albeit cut). However, compared to the greasy sexual and sadistic excesses of *Gestapo's Last Orgy* they all seem positively slight and frivolous.

The use of a familiar quotation from Nietzsche[1] which follows the opening credits in no way raises the film from the level of the toilet pan. Everything about it stretches credibility. Former commandant Conrad von Schtarke (Adriano Micantoni) is said to have received a lenient prison sentence for overseeing a camp that tortured, raped and murdered nearly 4,000 prisoners. When the story flashes back from the present day to WWII, von Schtarke and the prisoner with whom he is besotted, Lise (Daniela Poggi), don't look a day younger. Lise's moment of passion with the Nazi doctor, where they roll back and forth across a bed, goes on for so long it becomes a laughing matter. The sequence is made even more humorous by the song, Lise, in tandem with their naked frolicking.

There are moments of cinematographic clumsiness. When Alma, the female commandant, first comes to the camp she is seen arriving on an open boat. As the camera circles the craft a man can be seen hiding in the bottom of the vessel crouched on his knees with his backside thrust up in the air. He is not a character in the film, but perhaps the real-life boat owner keeping an eye on his craft. Supposedly some months later, when Lise herself is using the boat, the man is seen again in the same position. At one point he even peeps over the side and looks directly at the camera before quickly ducking back down 'out of sight.'

When von Schtarke threatens Lise with rats, he demonstrates their voracity by placing his hand into the tank containing them. The creatures are clearly not rats at all but gerbils that sniff curiously at his hand. "They're voracious little beasts, aren't they?" intones von Schtarke. "My blood excites them." The gerbils don't look threatening whatsoever and are hardly bigger than von Schtarke's thumb.[2]

Lise's character is incomprehensible. Her desire to die stems from the mistaken belief that she betrayed her family to the Nazis. Once this error has been rectified and Lise learns she wasn't to blame, she is ecstatic with an absolute desire to live. Yet, she becomes thoroughly unpleasant and begins to betray her friends and conform to Nazi ideals. At one point she willingly wears a human hair girdle made from the scalps of her onetime companions to please von Schtarke.

Of course, it isn't technical ineptitude and an asinine screenplay that landed *Gestapo's Last Orgy* on the banned list. Yet these characteristics serve somehow to make an unpleasant film even sleazier. The content of the lecture and slideshow (should that be sideshow?) that von Schtarke presents to his troops are straight out of Krafft-Ebing's *Psychopathia Sexualis*. Forcible incest and half-starved women required to eat from dog bowls are regarded as "the object of a certain sexual stimulation." The whole thing comes over like loose-leaf case studies lifted from the good doctor's book. In one of the film's typically objectionable diatribes, von Schtarke advises his troops that

> a soldier of the Third Reich never makes love to a girl of the Hebrew race. He limits himself to taking pleasure, dominating her, demonstrating to her that she is nothing but filth and he is perfection. He should cause her great suffering. Pain of body and of mind. Never must a Jew be allowed the honour of orgasm with an Aryan.

Gestapo's Last Orgy. The reverse of the videosleeve originally contained a warning notice, while some covered this with a sticker highlighting the film's content – 'full of intrigue sex and violence'.

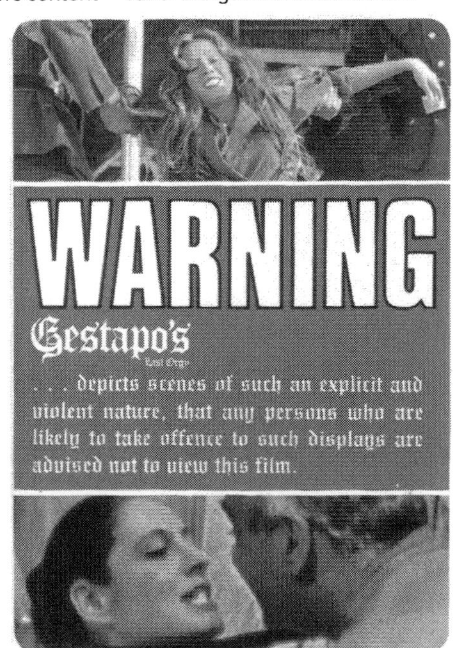

The only time the film rises above cheap sexploitation and manage to instil a sense of real drama is when elderly and infirm women are sent to the cremation oven. As they walk through a brick tunnel, the film loses its colour temporarily. It may be a technical fault rather than deliberate, but it does afford the sequence a truly sinister and disturbing significance – perhaps because the momentary colour loss transforms the movie into what looks like newsreel footage and gives the feeling that suddenly it's 'all too real.'[3] There is also something uniquely disagreeable in seeing a heavily pregnant naked woman running back and forth between huge plumes of burning gas – which is as much a medical concern as an ethical one.

There are no singular scenes in *Gestapo's Last Orgy* that could be attributed to its ban, and there is less actual bloodletting than in, say, *Schindler's List*. Like the other films of its ilk, it is the entire context that lies at the root of the problem; the subject matter and the way the filmmakers have handled it. But as reprehensible as these films are, racism is not the intention. The sexual tortures and horrors are not here to remind the audience of a historic atrocity, but to titillate and excite. Nowhere is this so blatant as in the scene where soldiers begin to masturbate while viewing von Schtarke's slides (despite the commandant's insistence that masturbation is non-Aryan animal-like behaviour). Nevertheless a film such as this doesn't need to be banned. It is so unappealing, uninteresting and unexciting that it fails as a piece of film entertainment on every level. Had it not been drawn to the public's attention by the process of classifying it as a nasty, like the Nazi camp genre it would have long since died a natural and unmourned death.

THE HOUSE BY THE CEMETERY

aka: Freudstein (announced under this title); Quella villa accanto al cimitero (original title)
Italy 1981
cast: Katherine MacColl, Paolo Malco, Ania Pieroni, Giovanni Frezza, Silvia Collatine, Dagmar Lassander
story: Elisa Livia Briganti
producer: Fabrizio de Angelis
director: LUCIO FULCI

Dr Boyle moves his family into a sinister house to continue the work of a deceased colleague. It is haunted by a deranged anatomist from a previous century.

THE FOURTH AND final instalment in Fulci's 'living dead' series, *The House by the Cemetery* doesn't adhere to the narrative trajectory of *Zombie Flesh Eaters*, *The Beyond*, or *City of the Living Dead*, but there is continuity in common motifs, familiar actors and gory pay-offs. It's more insular, focusing story and action on an autumnal New England house, next to a cemetery.[1] Here, Dr Norman Boyle (Paolo Malco), his wife, Lucy (Catriona MacColl), and son, Bobby (Giovanni Frezza), stay while on a business trip. Facets of the story seem to exist only to disorientate the audience. Various townspeople are adamant they remember Norman from a previous visit, although he denies ever being to the town before. Norman is unfazed at the discovery of a tombstone beneath a rug in the hall, but destroys audio recordings made by his deceased predecessor, Peterson, who also stayed at the house. Peterson had become obsessed with Dr Freudstein, another previous owner, a surgeon banned for his bizarre experiments. Also of note is the sinister way the babysitter, Ann, goes about her business.[2] Whatever secrets she and Norman may have, in the end they both die trying to save Bobby – who suffers from particularly appalling *adult pretending to be a child* dubbing. The obtrusive dubbing extends to footfalls through the house: everyone clomps about as if they're wearing hobnailed boots.

Dynamic – *The House by the Cemetery*.

The most tantalising element of the story – enforced in the early stages but allowed to peter away – is that Lucy is taking prescription pills said to induce hallucinations. How might the final nightmare, featuring a rotting Dr Freudstein, have played had the 'acid' idea been carried through? The imposing Freudstein looks great, so too his cellar domain filled with bodies. There are many well-crafted scenes in *Cemetery*, but if we have to single out one it would be Bob's discovery of Ann's decapitated head: entering the cellar alone, the boy arrives at the foot of the steps when he hears the pounding of something bouncing behind him – it may be one of his toys, but somehow he knows it won't be – and out of the shadows the babysitter's head rolls into view.

After the dynamic head-stabbing in the opening minutes, *The House by the Cemetery* settles down to some restrained mood-building and a blood-free sobriety not often seen in Italian exploitation of this era. It isn't until the halfway mark that the film embarks on its series of remarkably gory set-pieces. The first of these is a corny bat attack that breathlessly intensifies until a mini-bloodbath ensues and the creature succumbs to multiple stab wounds. Subsequent killings are of the human kind but are conducted with the same unnerving intensity.

There aren't many tell-tale signs that the Vampix release is victim to cuts; indeed the only real evidence of censorial tampering comes with the death of an estate agent (which has an 'irregular' feel about it). But while everything else might appear intact – i.e. without discernible jumps in sound or picture – this impression is conveyed by the sheer length of the gore scenes, as opposed to, say, the dexterity of a film censor's hand. The gore is interminable and horribly brutal – so, what could be missing? A lot.

Trapped beneath the tombstone in the hallway. Wonderful imagery in *The House by the Cemetery*.

The estate agent in the Vampix release gets a poker rammed into her chest. After some twisting and turning and pooling of blood, the tool is removed and sunk through the victim's blouse into her left breast. In its original uncut form, these shots are complemented with plenty of bloody close-ups and the penetration of the left breast is considerably more protracted. But it doesn't end there: in a sequence excised in its entirety from the Vampix release, the killer then drives the poker into the victim's neck. Its withdrawal results in a spectacular explosion of blood from the perfectly formed wound, shot from several camera angles and played in both real time and slow motion.[3]

Other excised scenes include *cinéma-vérité* camerawork in the Freudstein cellar (over which Peterson's tape recording is played), revealing a close-up of a mutilated, innards-on-display torso. When Ann is decapitated, the Vampix print shows a single neck slash before cutting away. In its entirety, the sequence continues with the knife being brought down a second time, creating two horrendous wounds. When Bob's head is pressed by Freudstein against the cellar door that Norman tries to break down with an axe, Vampix omit one final blow where the axe strikes the boy's head and draws blood. Both Freudstein and the boy reel from the impact, the preposterous consequence of which is that Bob is merely grazed and Freudstein loses a hand. Apart from the truncation of more gory debris in Freudstein's subterranean laboratory, Norman's throat ripping is the last scene to suffer cuts.

Vampix's *House by the Cemetery* is the same print released theatrically in Britain (even opening with the original X-certificate). Despite the cuts, and the fact the print is discernibly much darker than it ought to be, the film positively shines when compared to its subsequent British releases on the Elephant and Vipco video labels

– where less discerning, more brutal censorship, serves to completely eradicate the 'point' of the film (the latter print missing seven-and-a-half minutes).

Fulci's next film would be *The New York Ripper*, a psychotic and misogynistic visual blowout that was rejected outright by the BBFC. Stories of the print receiving a police escort out of the country are true.[4]

HOUSE ON THE EDGE OF THE PARK

aka: La casa sperduta nel parco (original title); Der Schlitzer; Trampa para un violador; The House at the Edge of the Park
Italy 1980
cast: David A Hess, Annie Belle, Cristian Borromeo, Giovanni Lombardo Radice, Marie Claude Joseph, Gabrielle di Giulio, and with a special appearance by Lorraine de Selle
story: Gianfranco Clerici & Vincenzo Mannino
producer: Giovanni Masini
director: RUGGERO DEODATO

In return for a good deed, Alex and Ricky are invited to a private party. They object to the rich lifestyle of the other guests and become increasingly violent.

DIRECTOR RUGGERO DEODATO attempts to elevate this odious film with some rather ineffectual stabs at issues of class and society and seems to imply that, compared to the world of 'toffs', a reprobate like Alex (David Hess) isn't so bad. The film suggests that for all his shortcomings, if misguided and insane, at least Alex is honest and loyal. Even his devotion to the dim-witted Ricky (Giovanni Lombardo Radice), his best buddy, is tainted by association. When it all goes pear-shaped and Alex stabs Ricky in the belly, Alex crumbles with a heartfelt plea:

> They did this to you! ... They're all fuckin' bastards – all of them! They did this to you! They're trying to turn us against each other! Just look at them – what do they know about friendship anyway!

The main theme is a lullaby.[1] Sophisticates are painted as a type bored with their lives. Money has brought them plenty but robbed them of even more. Into

Alex and Ricky take over the rich people party.
House on the Edge of the Park.

this flam of finery and etiquette come our two protagonists, who are the brunt of some humiliation but at the same time hold a rugged appeal for the other guests – particularly Alex, who the women regard as a "stud." Alex and Ricky are first portrayed as a couple of 'regular' guys simply out of their depth, and their hosts a scheming lot who not only make fun of the mentally challenged Ricky but are prepared to take advantage of him also. Alex quickly gets wise. He isn't fooled by the charade and in his own callous way manages to make a valid observation or two, inadvertently recognising Glenda – a black girl with a bald head – as not so much a guest but a symbol of 'polite society' decadence like himself. They tell him he should be in a cage; he calls Glenda "Roots."

House on the Edge of the Park is a virtual reprise of Wes Craven's *The Last House on the Left*, lifting David Hess from that movie and typecasting him forever as one of cinema's most degenerate villains. Like that earlier production, here a family avenge the rape and murder of a loved one, albeit in a more cold and calculated way. By the end of *House on the Edge of the Park*, revenge has become something else entirely – a turn-on for some of the guests, another twisted kick for those who can afford it.

House on the Edge of the Park has lost none of its shock value. If anything, it's more shocking viewed in these politically correct times than when it first appeared in the early eighties. It traverses an uncomfortable line, using rape for titillation and victims who get turned on by their ordeal – a major point of contention for the BBFC. But Deodato goes further than that. With the arrival of Cindy (Brigitte Petronio), a teenager who flirts with Alex before realising what is going on, the film charts a territory out of place even in a film as morally disjointed as this. The girl is displayed for the audience (she faces the camera in the centre of the shot) and humiliated; she is a virgin, for which she is humiliated even further. When finally Alex uses his cut-throat razor on her, the evident sexual satisfaction he derives in slicing her flesh is intercut with the orgasmic thrusts of Ricky and one of the other guests elsewhere. (After which the guest in question wishes to break up with her partner, the implication being that rich people aren't committed to relationships the way that Alex and Ricky are.) There aren't many ways this lengthy passage of sexual sadism can be interpreted. At the time *House on the Edge of the Park* was made, even hardcore pornographic features had given up trying to tackle this kind of fantasy extreme, not that many had ever bothered to do so with such conviction, anyway.[2]

It is around this sequence that a myth has evolved. Numerous people claim to have seen a questionable scene in *House* that certainly doesn't exist in the British print (which was released uncut) and has yet to appear in any video version elsewhere. These rumours appear to have originated in the US, where more than one viewer has stated they remember the scene from a theatrical screening around the mid eighties. Rick Sullivan wrote in *Gore Gazette*[3] around this time:

> *House* offers what has to be one of the sickest scenes ever committed to celluloid: [David] Hess rips the panties off one of the party guests and is about to rape her when he notices that a white string is dangling from between her legs. He crudely shouts "Hey, look what I found" and pulls out a bloody tampon for all to see while the humiliated girl sobs with embarrassment.

It's almost inconceivable that a bloody tampon would be dangled in front of cinema audiences, even those savouring the rare exploitational pedigree of a movie such as this one. On top of that, it's hard to imagine how such a scene would fit in what, when all is said, is a tightly edited sequence – in a close-up shot, the film has already shown Alex feeling through the girl's panties and declaring her to be a virgin. Hess himself in an interview has denied that such a scene was ever filmed.

So how has the idea of such a scene come about? It could simply be the ramblings of an overworked Rick Sullivan,[4] whose critique has since passed into legend (people who have never seen the film frequently speak of the 'tampon scene'), or it may be that the print playing theatrically back in 1985 was doctored. Such a thing happened with *I Spit on Your Grave*. In this instance the tampon scene mystery may simply be a confabulation of the episode in which Ricky sets about raping Gloria after the card game. He pushes her onto the sofa and after some groping reaches under her dress and rips away her panties. He holds up the small loose flap of bright red material saying, "Hey, see what I got," before tossing it away.

HUMAN EXPERIMENTS

USA 1979

cast: Linda Haynes, Geoffrey Lewis, Ellen Travolta, Aldo Ray, Jackie Coogan, Darlene Craviotti, Lurene Tuttle
story: Richard Rothstein
producers: Gregory Goodell & Summer Brown
director: GREGORY GOODELL

Incarcerated for a crime she did not commit, Rachel discovers that the resident psychiatrist of the Gates Correctional Facility is conducting radical experiments on the prisoners.

DESPITE ITS PROMISING opening, *Human Experiments* soon slips into a tiresome women-in-prison saga featuring the prerequisite hard-boiled guard and big butch prison dyke. The few male characters are redneck misogynists who come straight from the gene pool of *Macon County Line* and *Jackson County Jail*, films that had similar plots concerning outsiders wrongly accused of a serious crime. However, *Human Experiments* dwells more on the psychological torment of the heroine rather than the physical abuse administered to the female characters of those two earlier films.

The concept of Dr Kline's (Geoffrey Lewis) bizarre experiments at the Gates Correctional Facility is interesting but not explored in any depth. He has developed a method of rehabilitation in which the patient is regressed to childhood and brought back to adulthood as a different, 'much-improved' person. We only witness the outcome of the experiments, even when Rachel (Linda Haynes) – the central character – is the subject.

We are never too sure about what exactly is going on in the prison and who amongst the other prisoners are wise to the experiments, if indeed any of them. Following Rachel's 'rebirth' as Sarah, none of the other inmates remark on the transformation. It is also unclear whether Rachel is at times hallucinating – the noises she hears at night, the bodies she discovers, the masses of insects – or embroiled in some hideous reality. Such a lack of clarity is detrimental to the film.

There is no one scene that could warrant *Human Experiments*' status as a video nasty (though when it played theatrically in 1980, *MFB* recorded cuts that totalled a mind-boggling eight minutes). It can only be concluded that it was placed on the DPP list because of its title alone – in that the word 'experiment' may have somehow erratically linked the film to *SS Experiment Camp*. Indeed, *Human Experiments* would not be out of place on television – though perhaps with a single expletive dubbed out (Aldo Ray's utterance of the word "cunt").

Human Experiments was released on World of Video 2000. Vipco re-released Michael Laughlin's unrelated *Dead Kids* under the title of *Human Experiments* in the nineties, no doubt in an attempt to fool people into believing that – along with truncated versions of *The Slayer*, *Shogun Assassin* and *Zombie Flesh Eaters* – it was another entry in their own line of BBFC-certified video nasty re-issues.

Husband and wife team executive producer Edwin Brown and co-producer Summer Brown were, prior to *Human Experiments*, better known for sex films. Under the name Sandra Winters, Summer co-produced the 1974 *China Girl* (a film apparently made before its star, Annette Haven, had her teeth capped) which also dealt with memory and featured a doctor experimenting on the human brain.

I Miss You Hugs & Kisses

title on print: I Miss You, Hugs and Kisses
aka: Left for Dead
Canada 1978
cast: Elke Sommer, Donald Pilon, Chuck Shamata, Cindy Girling, George Touliatos, Cec Linder, and introducing George Chuvalo
story: Murray Markowitz
producers: Charles Zakery Markowitz & Murray Markowitz
director: MURRAY MARKOWITZ

Entrepreneur Charles Kruschen is charged with the bloody murder of his wife. At the trial he reminisces about his past, beginning with the 1956 Hungarian uprising.

CANNIBAL ERROR

SEVERAL MINUTES INTO *I Miss You, Hugs and Kisses*, a notice rolls by:

> The film you are about to see is fiction although the basic idea for the film was inspired by an actual event, the circumstances and characters have been deliberately and extensively altered so that any resemblance to the actual events or actual persons living or dead is purely coincidental.

The same ambiguous disclaimer appears again during the end credits (on the tail of a notice that proclaims "This film is dedicated to Ms. Elaine Green on the occasion of her marriage").

Charles Kruschen (Donald Pilon) stands accused of the murder of his wife, Magdalene (Elke Sommer). Despite the sentence passed on him by the court, the filmmakers evidently don't believe he committed the murder – although they include his lurid daydreams and negotiation on how best to kill his wife. Instead, they suggest that any one of a number of people could have committed the crime, the emphasis being on a boxing coach by the name of Tibor Zanopek (George Touliatos) and madman John MacGregor (Miguel Fernandes) as the most likely perpetrators. Zanopek is said to have gone round to collect another "advance payment" from Magdalene on the night of her murder and was himself later killed in a high-speed police chase (but how this links to the murder is never explained); MacGregor, on the other hand, already having killed several strangers, was simply in the area at the time. Such unresolved hypothesising would have been better suited to a more widely known criminal case, but the 'actual events' on which this film is supposedly based are long forgotten.[1] Its open-endedness therefore comes over simply as sloppy, confusing and ultimately frustrating.

Not that the film is helped in having a structure that would give Peter Greenaway a headache. There are flashbacks within flashbacks, slotted together seemingly at random, and 'major' characters who don't get so much as an introduction but are dropped cold into the story (except for MacGregor, who literally drives down a road and into shot).

There are several contentious scenes in *I Miss You, Hugs and Kisses*. One of them is the sex-murder perpetrated by MacGregor, who drags his victim to the ground, stabs her and proceeds to rape her while the knife is jutting from her belly.[2] A flashback to the incident shows the girl being stabbed twice again in close-up, blood slowly pooling around the blade as MacGregor indulges in post-mortem sex. The other notable contentious scene features the brutal bludgeoning of Magdalene Kruschen, which is the hinge pin on which everything in the film hangs. Should there be any doubt about the importance of this event, the filmmakers trot it out with shocking regularity, first playing it during the opening credits and several times again in close succession. Here, as George Kruschen contemplates the guilty verdict just handed to him by the courts, the film attempts to undermine the sentence by placing each of the other suspects at the crime scene, weapon in hand, delivering the fatal blow. Gershen – Charles's buddy – jumps out of the shadows and strikes Magdalene across the head, as does Zanopek in a mirror scene, then MacGregor, and finally the boxing champ who had refused the $10,000 offer to kill Kruschen. Although clumsily executed from a technical viewpoint, the reign of slow motion blows and bright syrupy blood gushing through platinum blonde hair makes for an unsettling visceral onslaught.

Other scenes that might have raised a few eyebrows include the chicken slaughterhouse footage that serves to illustrate Kruschen's first job, and the police removal of clothes from Magdalene's bloodied corpse, which lingers unhealthily on scissors cutting through underwear.

Director Murray Markowitz made at least one other film, *Recommendation for Mercy*. Howard Shore, who composed the music for *I Miss You, Hugs and Kisses* went on to score David Cronenberg's *Videodrome*. The picture of Elke Sommer that adorns the sleeve for Intercity Video's pre-certificated video release is not a still taken from Markowitz's film. With 1m 6s of cuts, *I Miss You, Hugs and Kisses* was granted an 18 certificate when re-released by Heron Home Entertainment in 1986 under the title of *Drop Dead Dearest*.

Although it seems clear why *I Miss You, Hugs and Kisses* should be deemed a 'nasty', it belongs to no specific genre: it isn't a murder-mystery, a thriller, or a horror film. The DPP managed to give it an identity – not to mention a collector's price.

I SPIT ON YOUR GRAVE

aka: The Rape and Revenge of Jennifer Hill (original title); Day of the Woman
USA 1978
cast: Camille Keaton, Eron Tabor, Richard Pace, Anthony Nichols, Gunter Kleeman
story: Meir Zarchi
producers: Joseph Zbeda & Leir Zarchi
director: MEIR ZARCHI

Jennifer Hill leaves New York City for a summerhouse retreat. Here she draws unwanted attention from several local men. She is raped and later kills the men.

I SPIT ON Your Grave is the most notorious of all the titles on the DPP list, and its title was prominently featured whenever the media undertook their condemnation of the 'video nasties'. As a result, gang rape became another despicable factor of what the nasties were all about.

> *I Spit on Your Grave* has the distinction of being among the most loathsome films of all-time.
>
> –Kim Newman, *Nightmare Movies*

> Unpleasant as this film is, it at least shows a woman fighting back.
>
> –David J Hogan, *Dark Romance*

The controversy that surrounded the film in Britain was preceded by a storm of protest on the other side of the Atlantic, when film critics Roger Ebert[1] and Gene Siskel, on their PBS TV show *Sneak Previews*, urged people to boycott the theatres that screened it. Not everyone people heeded the advice. Nevertheless, the film fared badly in New York with only a handful of dates at 42nd Street's Anco Theatre and other decrepit joints. On video, however, sales went ballistic, and *I Spit on Your Grave* out-sold recent Academy Award winner *Ordinary People* by about twenty-to-one in some places, getting as high as number twenty-four in *Billboard*'s best-sellers list for 1981.

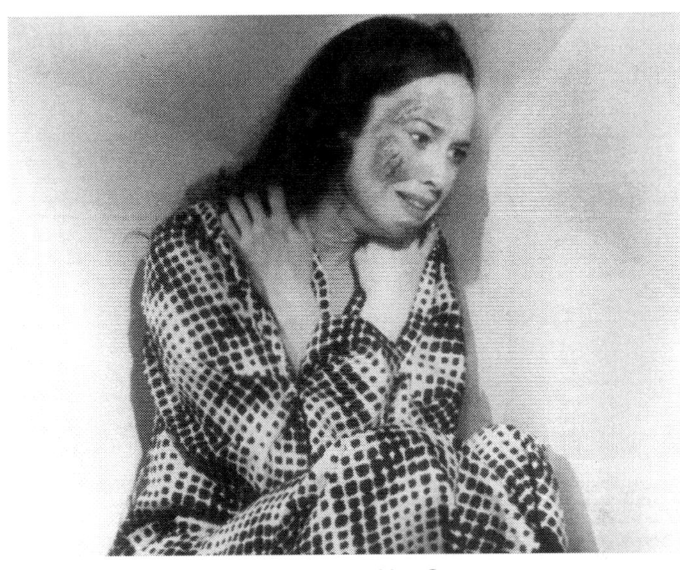
Camille Keaton in the notorious *I Spit on Your Grave*.

The star of the film, Camille Keaton (who plays Jennifer Hills), was moved to pen a reply to the critic for the *Los Angeles Times* who described *I Spit on Your Grave* as "a sleazy film about interracial sex."

> There is no interracial sex... Further, I personally resent the implication of [critic Lewis] Beale's sweeping generalisation... "films noted for their hilariously inept actors." Having made more than a half-dozen films in Europe and having won the Best Actress Award at the Sitges Film Festival for *I Spit on Your Grave*, my professional credentials are well-established.[2]

There was controversy of a different kind when it was discovered that theatrical and video prints displaying an R-rating – supposedly trimmed by seventeen minutes[3] – were in fact full uncut X-rated versions of the film. Bill Landis was one critic who figured something was amiss. "I agree with Ebert on this being the most extreme R-rated film," Landis wrote in *Sleazoid Express*.[4] The Motion Picture Association of America (MPAA) filed a federal lawsuit against Wizard Video and the Jerry Gross Organization – video and theatrical distributors – for misuse of their trademarked R symbol in advertising the film. But it took a year to catch onto the ratings masquerade, according to Keaton.[5] "You know the scene where I'm raped on the rock?" she told *Draculina*.[6] "If that's in the film, you know it's the [uncut] version."

I Spit on Your Grave has only ever had a video release in Britain, distributed under the Astra Video and Wizard Video labels. The latter was always much more difficult to obtain, but – outside of having a smaller label stuck on the cassette itself – is believed to have been identical to the Astra release in every way.[7] The British prints also carried the misappropriated US R-rating, which pops up at the end of the film, cutting the closing credits short.

According to director Meir Zarchi, the film has its genesis in a true-life incident that occurred one Sunday afternoon in October 1974. Driving to a park with his eight-year-old daughter and a friend, Zarchi spotted a girl wandering naked in a state of shock.[8] She had been raped. After dropping his daughter off at home, Zarchi and his companion took the girl to the police.

"Now of course I realise we should've taken her to a hospital," Zarchi reflected in *Fangoria*.[9] "We found out when we took her to the police just what the word bureaucracy means – How old are you? What's your name? Why were you in the park? What time was it? Should we notify your mother?"

The police insisted on filling out papers, despite the fact the girl was hysterical. Two men had raped, sodomised and beaten the girl, breaking her jaw. They were about to kill her, but she convinced them that she couldn't see anything on account of them having taken her glasses.

Zarchi was later to visit a friend in Kent, Connecticut, and saw the riverside house and petrol station that became the key locales in *I Spit on Your Grave*. They were his springboard for the rape-revenge story, which drew on his experience with the girl in the park and the further indignity suffered when taken to the police. "So Jennifer Hills did not report it," Zarchi said of his fictional rape victim, "and took the law into her own hands."

Further inspiration, which Zarchi fails to mention in his interview with *Fangoria*, undoubtedly comes from *Straw Dogs* and *Deliverance*, two hit movies dealing with themes of displaced city folk, rape and revenge. (Indeed, one early poster for Zarchi's film – under the title *The Rape and Revenge of Jennifer Hill*[10] – carried on it the blurb "More Devastating than *Deliverance*!") Other films to which *I Spit on Your Grave* bears a thematic relation include Michael Winner's *Death Wish*, Timothy Gulfas' *Revenge for a Rape*, a TV movie in which a pregnant woman on a deer-hunting trip is raped by three local rednecks, and Lamont Johnson's *Lipstick*, about a beautiful model who kills the man who rapes her and her daughter. Particularly worthy of note is *They Call Her One Eye*, a 1972 Swedish movie. As well as utilising a rape-revenge scenario it has a leading lady (Christina Lindberg) who bears more than a passing resemblance to Camille Keaton. Zarchi's own recollection of true-life events in 1974 bear a similarity to a TV movie of that same year called *A Case of Rape*. Directed by Boris Sagal and starring Elizabeth Montgomery, this told the story of a young woman who goes to the police after being raped, which only leads to red tape, further humiliation, scepticism, and the ordeal of a court case.

According to the BBFC, no topic is taboo if dealt with in the right way. Zarchi's film would seem to fall outside that criterion because it doesn't rise to the question of what is right or what is wrong. The film simply presents events without imposing on them any kind of morality – morality is left to the viewer. *I Spit on Your Grave* doesn't condemn rape, ergo it must be condoning it.

It doesn't criticise Jennifer's subsequent murder of the four men either, but that is never an issue with the film's detractors;[11] while the men pay for their crime, Jennifer rides off unchallenged following hers. No one who sees *I Spit on Your Grave* can be left in any doubt that the men deserve their fate. Jennifer's ordeal is perceived as inherently more terrible than the murder of her rapists, due to the way the film is structured. "How can you say anything bad about the way Jennifer Hills takes revenge?" queried Zarchi in his *Fangoria* interview. He offers the rapists no excuse for their crime, no shield to hide behind, no dysfunctional background... in fact, no background at all. The only instance in which any of the three men is presented as three-dimensional – a brief scene where one is shown to be a family man (tellingly only via long-shot) – serves only to provide Zarchi with the opportunity of dropping him from an even greater height, i.e. not only is he a rapist, but a cheat and a liar, too.

Sympathy throughout lies with Jennifer. She is the only 'real' person here.

We start the film with Jennifer and journey with her to the summerhouse; she is writing a book and we are privy to the work she does on her manuscript, eavesdropping as she mentally recites part of it; we share in the solitude and beauty of her riverside retreat, and also in her anger when the men arrive and disrupt the peace in their motorboat. When Jennifer changes out of her swimming costume, the camera modestly pulls back to the far bank of the river. Even the rape scenes when they come are largely played from her point of view – so that the viewer is also forced to endure the ugly, distorted, grunting faces of the men pressing down.

I Spit on Your Grave is in a way anti-cinema. The camera often comes to a complete standstill, locking onto shots for an uncomfortably long time without cutaways. The acts of rape appear to be played out in real time. In other words, the film utilises the convention of pornographic loops to further alienate its audience. ("The scope of the screenplay would've fit nicely into a twenty-minute Mitchell Bros peep-show reel," proffered Ralph Darren in his review for *Demonique*.)[12] The absence of music also imbues the film with a cold, callous edge. Not only does the film reject a main title theme, but it also refuses to diffuse the shocking nature of the story with incidental music.

The common notion that the film has no music at all, or that a harmonica played by one of the men is the only music in the film is, however, wrong. Music is playing in the church where Jennifer goes to ask forgiveness. She later plays a classical record[13] after taking revenge on one of her attackers, who lies bleeding to death in her bathroom. Of the three short musical pieces, it is only the harmonica that is used in a traditional filmic sense – changing tempo, heightening tension and working as a prelude to events on screen.[14] But it comes about in such a subtle, clever way, that it alone could testify to the skill at work behind the camera. Further examples of strikingly poignant and lyrical moments come with the scenes where Jennifer's swimsuit is casually tossed aside by the rapists as they leave the second rape scene, and with the terrible, haunting post-trauma shots of Jennifer sitting silently, unmoving on the staircase of the summerhouse. Without a doubt, the primitive, distancing quality of the film is a premeditated effort on the part of the film-maker (Zarchi wrote, directed, edited and cast the film[15] – his only other known directorial effort[16] is *Don't Mess With My Sister!*, a comedy that the *Psychotronic Video Guide* likens to Scorsese's *After Hours*).

After *I Spit* was remastered for a laserdisc release by Elite Entertainment, Michael Gingold in *Fangoria*[17] remarked that Zarchi's "simplistic approach comes to look less like low-budget craftlessness and more intentionally disaffected."

The men are dead and Jennifer Hill rides out of the picture. *I Spit on Your Grave*.

Following Zarchi's success, some films tried to tackle the rape-revenge story in a decidedly more mainstream manner. Most notable – or rather most similar – of these were Abel Ferrara's *Angel of Vengeance*, Tony Garnett's *Handgun* and Richard Gardener's *Deadly Daphne's Revenge*. Al Adamson's *Girls For Rent*, a film made before *I Spit on Your Grave*, found itself acquiring the title *I Spit on Your Corpse* when released onto videotape in the eighties. More recently there has been Todd Morris's *A Gun for Jennifer*, whose by-line is "Dead men don't rape."

I Spit on Your Grave is believed to have initially been released on the drive-in circuit in the late seventies as *Day of the Woman*.[18] According to some sources, under this title the film ran a few minutes longer. When Jerry Gross acquired it for distribution in the eighties, the title was changed to *I Spit on Your Grave* and some dialogue and several linking shots were excised.[19] The film has a history of being chopped up for no good reason. On a double bill with Lucio Fulci's *City of the Living Dead*, a rare early screening of *I Spit on Your Grave* was thwarted when the projectionist at the Fabian Theatre in Paterson discovered someone had stolen the print – not only had they stolen it, but they had gone to the trouble of splicing its title and opening credits onto another film in its place, in the hope that no one in the audience would notice! (The other film turned out to be John Newland's *The Legend of Hillbilly John*, about a man with a silver-string guitar who fights evil.)

An unofficial sequel, tentatively titled *Return to the Grave*, went into production but was never completed. Shot on video by Donald Farmer, former editor of the *Splatter Times*, the *raison d'être* for the sequel was Camille Keaton's willingness to reprise her most famous role.[20]

INFERNO

Italy 1980
cast: Irene Miracle, Leigh McCloskey, Daria Nicolodi, Eleonora Giorgi, Alida Valli, Sacha Pitoeff, Veronica Lazar
story: Dario Argento
producer: Claudio Argento
director: DARIO ARGENTO

According to an ancient book, a New York hotel is one of the buildings designed to house each of the evil Three Mothers. The inhabitants of the hotel are strange and strange things happen.

BEING A CONTINUATION of the 'Three Mothers' story that began with *Suspiria*, Dario Argento's *Inferno* comes across as much a remake as a sequel. Like

Suspiria the plot revolves around a protagonist being trapped within a stylised house of evil, culminating in a climactic confrontation and the fiery destruction of the house. Although it has its moments, *Inferno* lacks the terror invoked by its predecessor. Indeed, the film is more a series of glamorous, cleverly shot incidents than it is a coherent narrative. (Lucio Fulci was impressed enough to adopt a similarly free approach for his own *The Beyond* and *The House by the Cemetery* the following year, the latter even borrowing Argento's 'house of evil' environment.) The opening sequence, in which Rose (Irene Miracle), a central character, finds herself in a room submerged in water, looks good but it doesn't make much sense. How is the room lit, for instance? What is its purpose? Why does the floating corpse gravitate towards Rose?[1] Later, what is the relevance of the mystery girl in Mark's music class? She is credited as 'music student' but appears more a phantasm, whose unintelligible words could either be a warning or a curse. It seems all these elements are included for no reason other than visual appeal.

"This is an alchemist's picture," was Argento's justification, "if you don't understand it, well, me too, I don't understand! This is what the story is. Alchemy is a mystery, you know."[2]

Nevertheless, this disparate quality is a little too confusing and contrived in *Inferno*, detracting from the picture. It doesn't help that the visual composite is accompanied by a powerful (i.e. overbearing) and disjointed soundtrack by Keith Emerson – which tries to emulate the grandeur of Goblin's *Suspiria* soundtrack, but only once comes anywhere close. Thrown into this potpourri are some tantalising minutiae which serve no purpose. For instance, a title card informs viewers at one point that the setting is "New York – The Same Night in April," but the information is of no relevance. Similarly confusing are some of the characters, such as the able-bodied librarian in Rome who later appears in a wheelchair, unable to speak. Might they be one and the same character? Who knows? Doors in one chase scene are represented by fantastic close-ups of lock mechanisms being systematically engaged, the implication being that a revelatory significance is about to be divulged (or 'unlocked'). There isn't one.

However, the concept of infectious evil emanating into the area around the house is cleverly and subtly achieved. When Sarah, a character who locates a copy of the *Three Mothers*, alights from a taxi, a tiny needle extends from the door handle to puncture her thumb; Kazanian, the crippled owner of an antiques shop, cries for help but his apparent helper unexpectedly hacks him to death (one of the best sequences in the film). Anyone, it seems could be part of the conspiracy and such a prospect makes for good psychological horror.

The violence is tame compared to *Suspiria*, which, incidentally, wasn't banned.

Argento would use ideas from *Inferno* as a springboard for his next feature, *Tenebrae*, where a book would prove to be the key to an altogether more down-to-earth thriller.[3] The highly anticipated and long-awaited final part of the Three Mothers trilogy would be made in 2007 under the title *Mother of Tears*. It briefly stars Udo Kier and contains explicit violence, but Argento has lost his flair and innovation and it remains the shunned runt of the litter.

ISLAND OF DEATH

aka: A Craving for Lust; Island of Perversion; Psychic Killer II; Devils in Mykonos

UK/Greece 1976

cast: Bob Belling, Jane Ryall, Jessica Dublin, Gerarlo Gonalons, Janice McConnel, Clay Huff

story: Nico Mastorakis

producer: Nico Mastorakis

director: NICO MASTORAKIS

Christopher and Celia arrive on the Greek island of Mykonos, where they pursue a savage path of righteous debauchery and destruction.

REGARDED AS SOMETHING of a Jack-of-all-trades in his native Greece, Nico Mastorakis is not only a filmmaker but in his early days also applied himself to songwriting, radio production and quiz show hosting. His first directing work was in documentaries and a TV sci-fi series by the name of *Conspiracy of Silence*. His first full-length feature film was a slipshod ill-received erotic thriller with fantasy elements (inexplicably cut from the British theatrical print, reducing the running time by some thirty minutes) entitled *Death Has Blue Eyes*. His second picture was *Island of Death*, a film to which Mastorakis brings to bear much of his multi-faceted experience, not only directing, writing and producing it, but also penning the oddly inappropriate closing theme song ("Mother, I see the wonders of the day...").

Interviewed for *Video—The Magazine*, Mastorakis was surprised to hear that *Island of Death* featured on the DPP's nasties list because, he claimed, it had already been distributed theatrically in Britain by GTO, "a reputable company." In fact, it was distributed theatrically in 1978 by Winstone Films (under the title *A Craving for Lust*) and suffered some eighteen minutes of cuts. On video it had no cuts.

Said Mastorakis of the production:

> I had no money. All the people in it were amateurs. We were going up to people who looked American in the street and asking them if they could act! We shot it quickly and I did everything on it, wrote, produced, directed, photographed and edited.

Mastorakis, in the interview, reflected that the "movie was ahead of its time," and claimed he deliberately intended the violence "to be very realistic" to show "how horrible it was."

Let's quickly run through some of the film's 'realistic horror'. Christopher and Celia (Robert Behling, Jane Lyle) enjoy making love together in public spaces. The film's twist reveals they are brother and sister. As well as their incestuous relationship, and being exhibitionists, they are also voyeurs, and engage in any kink that comes their way. They murder a homosexual couple, as if on a righteous crusade, and later masturbate over photographs of the bodies. Later they murder a detective and anyone else who crosses their path, using a variety of methods, including a noose tied to a private airplane and a makeshift flamethrower. All in all it's debatable whether the violence in the film is realistic. However, there can be no doubting that *Island of Death* is horrible.

Whether it's intentional or not, the film would seem to be for Mastorakis a comment on his homeland Greece, where ninety-seven per cent of the population is Greek Orthodox. That Christopher attempts to clean up the streets

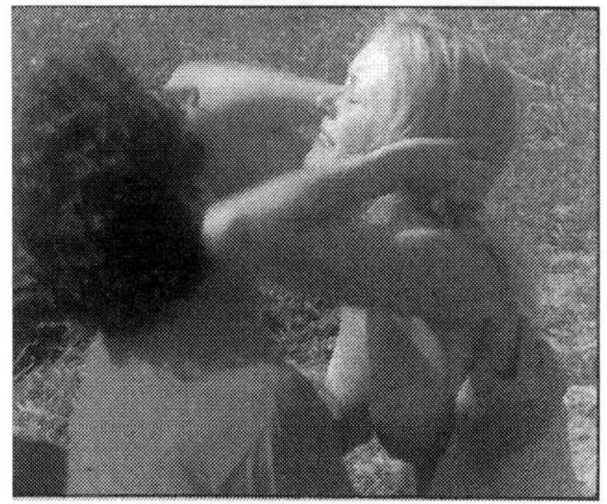

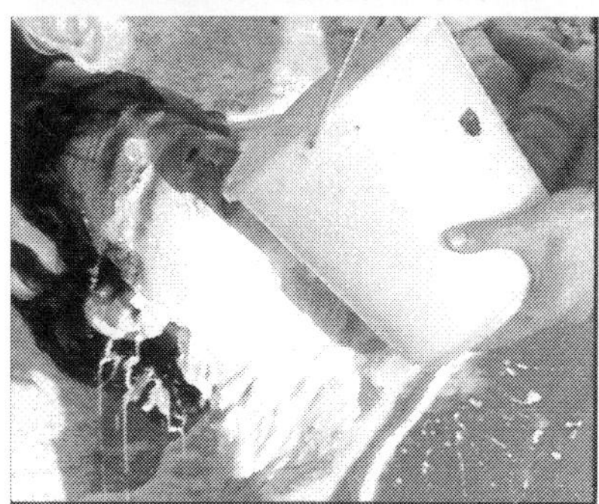

Island of Death is horrible and unusual.

of Mykonos seems to parallel the country's intolerance of anything that transgresses Christian values. Indeed, *Island of Death* can be read as a metaphor of the Crusades, with the aptly named Christopher remarking to Celia at one point that he is on a "crusade against perversion."

Yet Christopher is repulsed by the perversions of other people and blind to his own absolute wickedness. He is far more corrupt than any of the characters he castigates. The one person he believes is pure – a shepherd he encounters at the end of the film – is the one person as twisted as himself. Christopher is finally destroyed in a manner apt for the Middle Ages, in a lime pit, with rain and lime reacting to generate intense heat, burning him alive.

As part of all of this, Detective Foster (Gerard Gonalons) is an unnecessary addition. He is on Christopher's trail. No sooner does the detective arrive on the island than he is dispatched in one of the most implausible ways imaginable. To get into the position where Christopher can hang Foster from his own plane requires the utmost suspension of disbelief and would be arduous even in a teen stalk-and-slash picture.

It becomes clear soon enough that Christopher and Celia are not the ordinary vacationing couple they at first appear. (Mastorakis shot the film at out-of-season Mykonos locations, which gives the air of things being askew right from the outset.) When the couple jump into a phonebooth for sex, during which Christopher calls his mother to antagonise her, any initial feeling that *Island of Death* might be embarking on a familiar trajectory is quickly and irrevocably dashed.

The film is jaw-droppingly unusual, and its

excesses are completely absent from the director's later films (though *Zero Boys*, like *Island of Death*, also contains a scene in which a man is forced to suck on the barrel of a revolver). After its catalogue of sexual horrors, Mastorakis plays his final card, revealing that Christopher and Celia are in fact brother and sister.

"You've got to help me," cries Christopher from the lime pit. "I'm your brother!"

"Sh! You promised not to tell anyone," responds Celia.

By this point however, nothing can heighten the sleaziness and after all that has gone before, this revelation seems somehow inevitable.

For a film to include such a diversity of sexual kinks is unusual: homosexuality, incest, sodomy, bestiality and urolagnia. On top of this there is drug-taking, rape, mutilation and murder. But such spectacle does not make the film interesting or outrageous in the same way as, say, Tinto Brass' *Caligula*. Indeed, the film is dreary – the viewer endures a lot for the simple and obvious denouement: that perversion is a narrow thread made taut by those who seek to define it. It is this assortment of depraved themes rather than any particular scene that secured *Island of Death*'s banned status. (See also SEX & WRECKS.)

KILLER NUN

title on print: The Killer Nun
aka: Suor Omicidi (original title); Deadly Habit; La Petite Soeur du Diable; La Nonne Qui Tue
Italy 1978
cast: Anita Ekberg, Alida Valli, Massimo Serato, Daniele Dublino, Lou Castel, Joe Dallesandro, Laura Nucci, Paola Morra
story: Giulio Berruti & Albert Tarallo
producer: Enzo Gallo
director: GIULIO BERRUTI

The vindictive Sister Gertrude oversees the elderly and infirm residents of a hospice. She is addicted to morphine, believes she is dying and wallows in disturbing stories of martyrdom.

ACCORDING TO THE opening credits *Killer Nun* is based on a true incident (occurring recently in Belgium, states the video box). This may well be the case, as history is rife with accounts of sadistic sisters, lesbian sisters, and sisters who threaten to be an embarrassment to the Church. It would be nice to think there existed documentation of a sister smashing dentures underfoot while screaming "Disgusting! Disgusting! Disgusting!" as happens in this film.

Like Nazis and cannibals, nuns have provided inexhaustible potential for exploitation filmmakers, and their cloistered life was the focus of many productions through the seventies and eighties. Sometimes it didn't even have to stretch to a cloistered life. As with Hammer's *To the Devil–A Daughter*, a pretty face in a habit would often suffice.

The nun as an exploitable commodity stretches back beyond the aforementioned subgenres, and indeed beyond cinema itself. It enabled authors like Matthew Lewis to scandalise eighteenth-century English folk with *The Monk*, and Denis Diderot the French philosopher with his novel, *The Nun*, where the idea of chaste women living apart from men wasn't only titillating but also ammunition against the Church.

Killer Nun isn't typical of its oeuvre, introducing drug addiction, infirmity, and murder into the usual stocking-top sexploitative fare. The script is witty, too, another anomaly. Anita Ekberg is perfectly cast as Sister Gertrude, and it's refreshing that a central role in a film such as this has gone to someone who doesn't look like a glamour model and is over the age of twenty-five. (There are some concessions, however, like blue eyeshadow – not normally a requisite of nun life.) There is credibility to Gertrude's plea of "I need m-morphine!" And when she surreptitiously takes a ride into the city, there is a sense of genuine desperation in the old girl's attempts to entice a stranger with a flash of her stocking tops. Only a flash, mind you – lest he notices the bruises.

There isn't an awful lot of bloodletting or perversion, although the torture of an old woman near the end of the film – pins forced into her face and eyes – meant several seconds of cuts when *Killer Nun* was re-released through Redemption in the nineties. It is the sequence leading up to a bludgeoning with a lampshade that proves the film's standout piece. Indeed, with its pounding score and rapid editing of multifarious scenarios, it offers a frustrating glimpse at what director Giulio Berruti could really have achieved with *Killer Nun*.

After injecting herself with morphine and asking God for absolution, Sister Gertrude collapses on the floor. Discovered by one of the patients, she starts to suffer flashbacks and at the same time begins to hallucinate. She sees herself on the operating table, her cancerous tumour exposed ready for removal. This is intercut with shots of the sister about to interfere with the unidentified corpse of a naked young man in a morgue, as well as shots of her own eye in extreme close-up, her own drugged-up self being dragged to her bed by the old man, and a veiled woman dressed in black who – we assume – is the Angel of Death. On top of this is a pounding score by Alessandro Alessandroni that sounds like Morricone crossed with Goblin.

Nothing else in the film quite matches the flair and energy of this sequence, although some viewers will get a rise out of Gertrude tormenting an infatuated novice, demanding that she dons silk stockings or suffer a beating. "I'm the worst kind of prostitute," the novice is made to say – a sentiment that is evidently true, because later we see her lapping at the flies of a young doctor, promising him "anything" so long as she isn't reported for having supplied Gertrude with morphine.

The young sister obviously has got a lot more than this to hide, but the film is content to beat a hasty retreat once the church administers its "special treatment" to Sister Gertrude.

THE LAST HOUSE ON THE LEFT

aka: Sex Crime of the Century; Krug and Company; The Men's Room; Night of Vengeance (shooting title)
USA 1972
cast: David Hess, Lucy Grantheim, Sandra Cassel, Marc Scheffier, Jeraime Rain, Fred Lincoln
story: Wes Craven
producer: Sean S Cunningham
director: WES CRAVEN

Mari Collingwood and her friend Phyllis are abducted and murdered. The killers unwittingly end up at Mari's house, where they meet a similar fate.

A REMAKE OF Ingmar Bergman's *The Virgin Spring*, Wes Craven's *The Last House on the Left* contains a murder sequence that, for sheer brutal intensity, has never been surpassed in any film since. Even a quarter of a century after it was made.

On their way to a rock concert, Mari and Phyllis have the misfortune to encounter a criminal gang headed by Krug Stillo and Fred 'Weasel' Pudowski. They are travelling with Krug's heroin-addicted son Junior, and a female called Sadie. The gang torture the two girls and eventually murder them in a wood, close to Mari's home it turns out.

It was Craven's intention to portray what a real murder – as opposed to a cinematic murder – would be like, and he succeeded unequivocally. The uncompromising portrayal of the killers, their subjugation, torture and murder of the two young girls, and the *cinéma-vérité* style combine to bring a stamp of authenticity to proceedings.[1] The viewer is left with the impression that, by watching, they themselves are partaking in something truly dreadful.

Prior to *The Last House on the Left*, the director-producer team of Wes Craven and Sean Cunningham had only previously worked on a pseudo-documentary by the name of *Together* (and, it is rumoured, some porn). With little idea of film-making techniques, and no idea that it would ever be shown outside of Boston, they set out to make *Last House*. "Nobody was ever going to see it," reasoned Craven, "and nobody was ever going to know that we did it."[2]

With that proviso the team determined they could go all the way and make something that more reputable and proficient filmmakers would not dare to do.[3] Amazingly, given these sense-pummelling criteria and the film-makers' inexperience, there are many lyrical moments in the film – simple, almost overlooked aspects of comparative tranquillity that serve to heighten the horror.

Krug leaves his name in Mari's chest. *The Last House on the Left*.

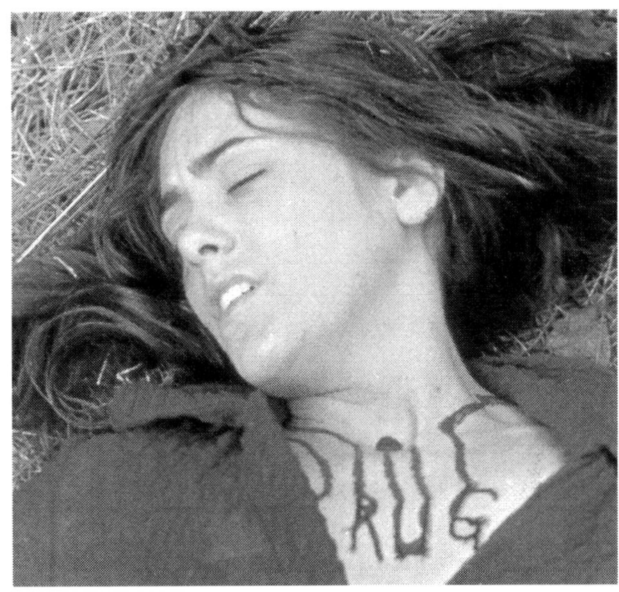

For instance, a scene where the killers idly clean their blood-covered hands (contrary to most movie gore, the blood looks real); or Weasel being momentarily sympathetic towards Phyllis and allowing her to dress before killing her; or the two petrified girls clutching one another naked, their sobs obscured by a sympathetic music score. The gang does nothing to prevent Phyllis crawling away into the woods, stabbed and dying. (We get tight close-ups of faces and then a low-angle shot, a familiar pattern during this whole torture and murder sequence.) If concern, guilt or sympathy is keeping the gang at bay, this dissipates and there follows the horrifying attack in which Sadie 'loses it' and disembowels the girl.

Having gone on to make many subsequent successful horror films, such as *A Nightmare on Elm Street* and *Scream*, Craven told *Shock Xpress*[4] he could never return to the intensity of *Last House* because now

> people can find out where I live. Back then, nobody knew where I was. I wasn't in nice hotels like this, I was sleeping on the producer's floor and shooting in people's backyards. As a matter of fact, we lost the first day's shooting because the people whose house we were using came back unexpectedly.

One of Craven's failings in *Last House* is the overstated nastiness of the outlaws. He introduces them by way of a radio news report which is so wildly descriptive – and so obviously the absolute antithesis of the neat and tidy Collingwoods – that it becomes Python-esque. We learn that Krug (who is seen popping a kid's balloon in the street) was convicted of killing a priest and two nuns, Fred was a child molester, Junior a heroin addict and Sadie an "animal-like woman" who kicked a police dog to death. So nasty are Fred 'Weasel' Pudowski and Krug Stillo that Craven saw fit to resurrect and remodel them as a composite monster called Freddy Krueger several years later in *A Nightmare on Elm Street*.

The latter half of the film is where Craven drifts from his goal of realism and returns to a more traditional cinematic model, a downslide which begins when the killers arrive at the Collingwood house. As if it isn't already enough of a coincidence they happen to turn to the family of their last victim for assistance when their car breaks down, the Collingwoods then invite the motley crew to spend the night as their guests – despite concerns about their missing daughter. Another stretch comes with the way Mari's mother chooses to kill the loathsome Weasel. Once she has the man's hands tied behind his back it is ludicrous to think she would fellate him to orgasm and bite off his penis.[5]

The bumbling sheriff and his dim-witted deputy, who arrive to take details of the Collingwoods' missing daughter, are an inexplicable appendage to the film. They are supposed to break the tension by offering light comic relief – coming across like Abbott and Costello or something out of *Cannonball Run* – but there is no need, nor any room, for their broadside buffoonery.

It would be comforting (and easy) to derive parallels between *Last House*, social unrest, and the Vietnam war, and indeed to an extent this is possible. But there is something telling in the fact that, as Phyllis and Mari drive to the city and the rock concert, the refrain of a horrible song promises that "The road leads to nowhere..."[6] This puts us in mind of Monte Hellman's *Two-Lane Blacktop*. The two girls are an inversion of the Driver and Mechanic in Hellman's film. Whereas, throughout that film there is disillusionment and, at the end, burn-out, the girls in *Last House* embark on a journey in which their joy for life only serves to make them look naïve and stupid. Two-Lane *Blacktop* finishes with the celluloid itself setting on fire, analogous of the end of the sixties, the era in which the film was made. *Last House*, which appeared only a few years later, has no patience for flower power or ennui. The sixties are burnt, and it'll take something more than love and peace to elicit change, or even motivate the world now.

"Few images," writes David A Szulkin in his book *Wes Craven's Last House on the Left*, "capture the burnt-out desperation of the early seventies as well as the shot of Junior Stillo sliding down a wall with his brains blown out and a peace-symbol ornament dangling around his neck."

The Collingwood home isn't last or on the left, and indeed Wes Craven regards the title of the film as a "nothing title" dreamed up by someone in advertising and liked by the producer.

The formidable David Hess went on to virtually reprise the role of Krug in Ruggero Deodato's *House on the Edge of the Park* and Pasquale Festa Campanile's *Hitch Hike*. Other filmmakers and distributors attempted to cash-in on the success of *Last House on the Left*, and a plethora of similar-sounding, similar-themed movies followed in its wake, amongst them *Late Night Trains*.

Craven himself did pen a script for an official sequel, but Krug and Weasel coming back from Hell, as Craven would have had it, wasn't a concept that particularly thrilled anyone. Thankfully the producer's own idea for a sequel didn't come to fruition, either: teens on a rafting trip who end up on Krug's island.

Last House on the Left was released uncertified in the UK on Replay video, missing incidental scenes of the two comedy cops having to hitch a ride on the roof of a truck when their squad car runs out of gas.[7] But in terms of gore it was essentially an uncut print. It should be noted however, that *Last House* is one of those movies that exists in a multitude of slightly different forms around the world. Outtake footage of Phyllis being disembowelled appeared in the pseudo-documentary *Confessions of a Blue Movie Star*, where it was presented as a genuine snuff film clip.[8]

LATE NIGHT TRAINS

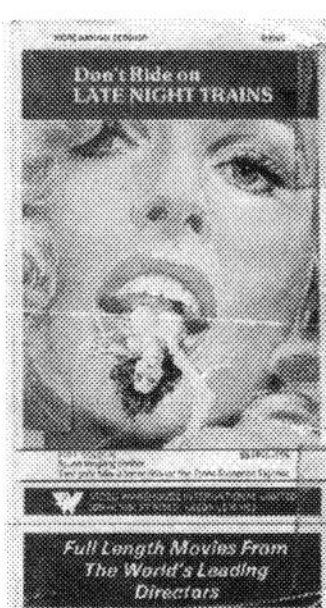

title on print: Night Train Murders
aka: L'ultimo treno della notte (original title); Don't Ride on Late Night Trains; Torture Train; Second House from the Left; Last House on the Left II; The New House on the Left
Italy 1974
cast: Flavio Bucci, Macha Meril, Irene Miracle, Gianfranco de Grassi, Enrico Maria Salerno, Marino Berti, Franco Fabrizi, Laura d'Angelo
story: [not credited]
producers: Pino Bucci & Paolo Infascelli
director: ALDO LADO

Two teenage girls, Margaret and Lisa, are travelling on overnight trains when they encounter a group of thugs. They do not make it home and the waiting parents inadvertently befriend the killers.

The end of a yob with no name. *Late Night Trains*.

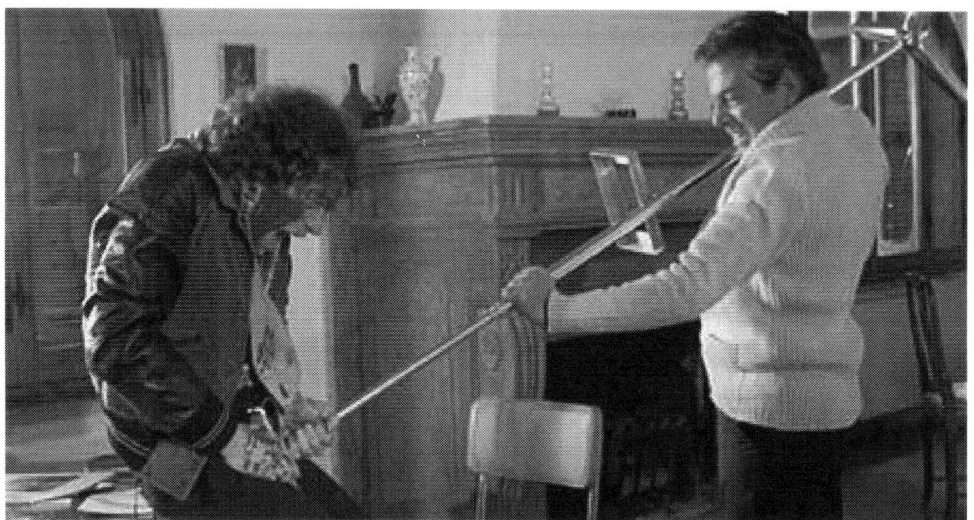

LATE NIGHT TRAINS is a direct imitation of Wes Craven's *Last House on the Left* but falls far short of the power and verisimilitude of that film. The similarities to *Last House* are intrusively prominent and include: (i) two upper-middle class teenage girls being held against their will, raped and murdered by deranged drug-infused yobs; (ii) parents who await the arrival of their daughter and prepare a celebratory party (in this instance for Christmas as opposed to a birthday as in *Last House*); (iii) a father who is a doctor; (iv) killers who end up as guests of the victim's parents; (v) a mother who becomes suspicious on seeing an item that belongs to her daughter, worn around the neck of a killer; (vi) a female gang member who is in many ways more ruthless than her male associates; (vii) one gang member who really doesn't want the girls to come to any harm, and so on.

One of the thugs (Flavio Bucci) even resembles David Hess, and it was probably for this reason he was cast for the part. The intensity of his performance, however – along with everyone else in the film – is prosaic and comes nowhere close to Hess' frightening portrayal of spiritual desolation. So derivative are the thugs in *Late Night Trains* that they don't even have names of their own. The credits do identify Bucci as 'Blackie' and Gianfranco de Gassi as 'Curly,' but nowhere in the film are these (ridiculous) names actually utilised. Macha Meril is credited simply as 'The Lady on the Train'. The villains are too unconvincing and stereotyped to generate any real antipathy (Blackie and Curly even mug a man dressed as Santa Claus in the opening reel). We are to believe that the woman who boards the train smartly dressed, well-spoken and knowledgeable (she strikes up a conversation on philosophy with a fellow passenger) requires just a good fuck with a stranger in the toilets to revert to her uninhibited, conscience-free, primordial 'other'. Should the audience misinterpret all the wriggling and commotion going on in the toilet as something other than sex, director Lado throws in a train-going-into-tunnel shot.

"We just want to have fun, nothing more," she tells the girls prior to their humiliation, torture and rape. She shows no remorse, even after forcing a knife into Lisa's groin, which brings about the girl's death.

"You're a mad woman, lady!" Blackie subsequently accuses the woman, to which she replies, "What did I do wrong? It was just one of those things."

The victims, too, are unrealistic and simply objects on which the villains can play out their misdeeds. Margaret and Lisa are said to be cousins. At the start of the film they are portrayed as naïve and silly, taking naughty pleasure in smoking a cigarette and rubbing themselves up against the vibrating walls of the train. It isn't much by way of characterisation, but after they switch trains, they do little more than simper and await their fate.

The confines of a train provide an ideal situation in which to create a claustrophobic atmosphere, but Lado spoils all efforts to capitalise on the opportunity. The means by which the carriage is suddenly isolated from the rest of the train – the connecting door handle coming away in a passenger's hand – is a bit too convenient and unintentionally comical. The same passenger then watches the girls being abused, remaining unnoticed at the compartment door for several minutes, despite being in plain view and constantly moving around to find a better vantage point. The lights are out for much of the ordeal.

A musical score by Ennio Morricone offers little help, although there is a nod in the direction of Sergio Leone's *Once Upon a Time in America* – also scored by Morricone. In Leone's movie Charles Bronson is always heard before he is seen, playing a sinister dirge on his harmonica. Likewise, similar downbeat phrases on the mouth organ introduce the junkie's appearance in Lado's film. A song by Demis Roussos, 'A Flower's All You Need,' provides the opening and closing song.

Although the film is a catalogue of unpleasantness, it implies more than it shows. The only gore is a brief stock footage scene at the film's beginning of a scalpel cutting flesh – part of a surgical procedure carried out by Lisa's father. The only nudity comes via brief scenes of the half-naked Margaret running from the gang down the corridor of the train, prior to hurling herself out of the window to her death.[1]

These factors aside, it is unlikely that the BBFC would grant the film a certificate if ever submitted – isolated incidents of sexual violence are often justification enough to warrant cuts or a rejection, let alone a film based entirely around such acts. However, *Late Night Trains* also contains that most reviled of concepts, 'porno-rape,' the rape victim who begins to enjoy her ordeal.

Released on the Video Warehouse International label, the sleeve for *Late Night Trains* claimed it had been voted "Best Late Night Horror Film" in 1978, although by whom and for what is not divulged. (The video box for *Nightmares in a Damaged Brain* carried a similarly obtuse accolade, in this instance hailing it "the American Cult Terror film of 1982.") *Late Night Trains* carried a self-imposed but unexplained certificate – "AX" – and a warning that its content "may contain scenes liable to cause distress to viewers with a nervous disposition."

In its favour, the circumstances that lead the killers to the family home of one of their victims – courtesy of stolen train tickets – is marginally more credible than that which led Krug and his gang to the Collingwood residence in *Last House on the Left*.

THE LIVING DEAD

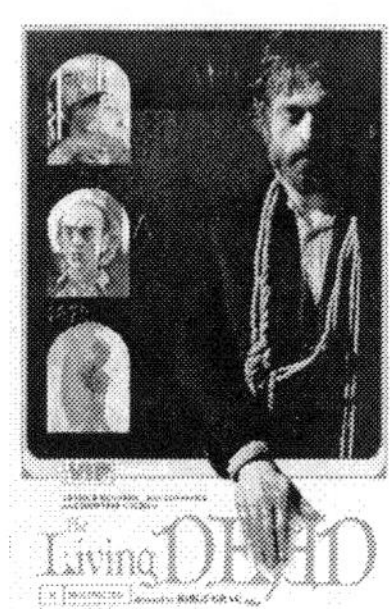

title on print: The Living Dead at Manchester Morgue
aka: The Living Dead at the Manchester Morgue; No Profanar el Sueño de los Muertos (original title); Don't Open the Window; Let Sleeping Corpses Lie; Breakfast at Manchester Morgue; Invasion der Zombies; Les Massacre des Morts-Vivants
Spain/Italy 1974
cast: Ray Lovelock, Christine Galbo, Arthur Kennedy
story: Sandro Continenza & Marcello Coscia
producer: Edmondo Amati
director: JORGE GRAU

A bigoted police chief believes that George, a "hippy", is responsible for a spate of grisly murders. In fact the attacks are perpetrated by reanimated corpses.

The DPP39

'SCENES OF EXTREME AND EXPLICIT VIOLENCE'

Shenanigans at the Old Olw [*sic*] Hotel. *The Living Dead*.

LET'S GET THE title of this film out of the way. The original theatrical print from the seventies carried the title *The Living Dead at the Manchester Morgue*. The subsequent video print carried a truncated variant of this, *The Living Dead at Manchester Morgue*,[1] and the video box simply called it *The Living Dead*.

> This is probably the most depressing film we've seen since *The Mutations*...
>
> —Lee Kennedy, *World of Horror*

> A step beyond in gore?
>
> —John Fleming, *The House of Hammer*

The early part of the 1970s were a time when cinematic horror shifted into a higher, more viscerally demanding gear – directly proportional to the nudity flooding British arthouse cinemas courtesy of continental soft-porn.[2] Warhol had put his name to Frankenstein and Dracula; a multitude of Italian *Exorcist* clones were intent on 'out-possessing' Friedkin's blockbusting original;[3] English-speaking audiences also managed to catch up on some of the burgeoning bloody obsessions of Hispanic horror (given a general release courtesy of small but enterprising distributors like Variety, Miracle and Grand National); and with

Frankenstein and the Monster from Hell, the institutionalised Hammer Films went into gore-frenzy, breathing life into its hideous creation one last time before tearing it apart again, literally. Exciting new glossy publications like *Kung Fu Monthly* made pin-ups of Bruce Lee, while *Monster Mag* did the same for such unlikely stars as vampires, skeletons and assorted grisly film moments – blowing them up to gory wall-dwarfing detail.[4]

The changing tide of horror cinema polarised in 1974 with the release of *The Texas Chain Saw Massacre*. Strains of the realism and unrelenting, almost ethereal, excess of this film could be found in other horror pictures of the same year, such as *Deranged*, *Vampyres*, and *The Living Dead at the Manchester Morgue*.

Common to all is the palpable, underlying threat of explicit horror that refuses to be swept politely out of shot come the pay-off. These films have a grittiness, a frisson absent from the even gorier heights scaled by the stalk-and-slash movies that proliferated in the decade to follow.

The Living Dead at the Manchester Morgue has often been described as a rehash of George Romero's *Night of the Living Dead*. (Alan Frank, writing in *Horror Films*, claims Jorge Grau's film to be superior to Romero's "in almost every way," but Frank is most certainly in the minority.) Seeing as Romero pretty much defined the lore of the zombie, parallels with *Night of the Living Dead* can be drawn from most every zombie film to have emerged since.[5] Like *Night of the Living Dead*, Grau introduces a lone zombie in the shadow of a cemetery at the film's beginning. And, like Romero, he has his anti-hero, an antiques dealer called George (Ray Lovelock), needlessly killed at the film's close. Contrary to Romero's unchallenged method of killing the living dead, bullets to the head fail to stop Grau's zombies (only fire can do that). But then, Grau seems uncertain of his own criteria – or at least his four screenwriters do – and his zombies at times appear to possess supernatural traits. It's an eco-horror film on one hand and something else on the other: George believes that a technology driven pesticide is reanimating the dead.[6] There's also the inference that it could be a type of "plague", as per a wonderful scene in a crypt where one reanimated corpse raises others by placing blood on their eyelids. But this itself smacks more of ritualism than contamination. Other curious disclosures about Guthrie, the first zombie we witness in the film, include his image failing to appear on photographs and his habit of appearing out of nowhere prior to each attack.[7]

The Living Dead came to be on the DPP list because of four key scenes depicting lingering, unflinching shots of cannibalism and flesh-rending. These comprise of George's attack on the undead in the crypt with a spike (which features a close-up impalement of a neck); the cannibalism of a policeman in a cemetery (which shows ghouls removing innards and feeding on them); an attack on a telephone receptionist at a hospital (ghouls tear one of her breasts off and feed on it);[8] and a zombie sinking an axe into the face of a doctor.

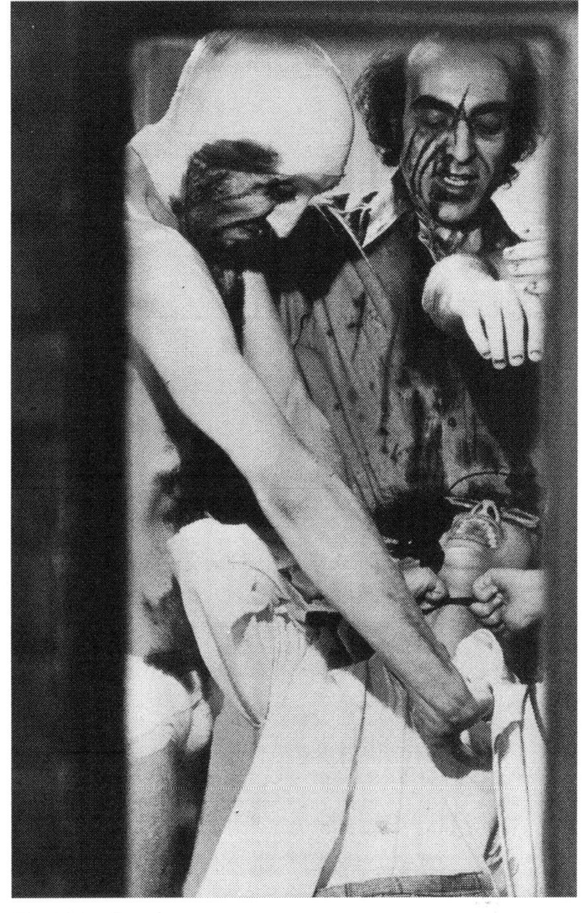
The Living Dead

In this respect, *The Living Dead* is a relatively 'easy' film for the BBFC – remove these scenes and the contention is gone (as proved the case with the re-release noted below).[9] Unlike, say, *I Spit on Your Grave*, where the problem is tone, i.e. the nature of the film itself, the potency of *The Living Dead* can be diffused with a few cuts of the censor's scissors, without having to disassemble the whole thing.

It would do the film a disservice to analyse it exclusively in terms of Giannetto de Rossi's gore effects. These are more than competent, coming from one who would later lend his skills to *Contamination* and *Zombie Flesh Eaters* amongst others,[10] but there is something else to the film that sets it apart. Several small details – such as the corpse in the crypt having nose plugs and the serenity of the zombies when feeding – help to make an unnerving whole. But it is Grau, a director working on foreign soil, seeing the English countryside as an outsider, who really sets the whole thing on edge. Grau engages the beauty of this blessèd plot, Windermere[11] – the bleakness, the isolation, the greens of the rolling hills – to haunting effect. So infatuated is he with preserving this vista, Grau goes to the trouble of removing all extraneous players from it.[12] With the exception of the opening shots in city centre Manchester[13] and the end 'crowd scene' outside the hospital, there is not a single person in *The Living Dead* who shouldn't be there. That is to say that everyone in the film has a design, a part to play; there are no 'extras.' As George heads for the hills at the film's beginning, the city and everyone in it is seen to methodically peel away. George is leaving a landscape that has emasculated its inhabitants only to enter one that looks to have devoured its inhabitants. By the time George reaches a garage for refuelling, there is no turning back: no one is left who doesn't belong; no one is left who George doesn't have to meet. Here, on the garage forecourt, Edna, in her Mini, knocks over and damages his motorbike. She gives him a lift and begrudgingly becomes his travelling companion. Later, in the hills, it is the farmer and the two men from the Department of Environment – no farmhands, no wife or family, no one out taking a stroll, no other travellers on the roads.

The landscape in *The Living Dead* comes alive, and an oblique reference to "ecological problems", announced on the radio, takes on a deeper meaning. The living landscape has dead things to do its bidding. The same sense of isolation is found in the village of Southgate, where the central characters, George, Edna (Christine Galbo) and Sgt McCormick (Arthur Kennedy) can wander streets but bump only into one another. There are no other guests in the Old Owl Hotel[14]... there is no one in the chemist shop but the man who develops the roll of photographs for George and Edna... George's friends in Windermere are faceless and voiceless entities on the other end of a phone line. The only people who inhabit *The Living Dead* are those with whom the principal characters – or the film/landscape – must have some direct interaction. Take for instance the hospital, whose corridors are always empty, and where three shadowy figures in beds – seen only once in medium-shot – represent the entire sick population of Southgate. When one of the babies attacks a nurse, there is nobody the doctor can call for assistance but George, who happens to be passing.

The film's soundtrack – boasting several variations on the excellent main theme, including the catchily-titled 'Manchester M2 6LD'[15] – incorporates strange guttural noises, which Grau himself describes as being the "voice of the dead." In an article that appeared in the Belgian magazine *Fandom's Film Gallery*, Grau relates how he was inspired by and sought to recreate sounds "that are sometimes uttered by corpses when they are moved and caused by exhaling the air from their dead lungs."[16] The effect is a chilling one. Interestingly, despite the sound accompanying each appearance of the zombies in the film, it never appears that the zombies are making the noise (returning us to the theory of the carnivorous landscape). *The Living Dead* is often regarded as being the first horror film to utilise a stereophonic soundtrack. However, André de Toth's 1953 *House of Wax* – as well as being presented with the attraction of 3-D – was originally screened with a stereo soundtrack.

The Living Dead was granted an 18 certificate when submitted to the BBFC by European Creative Films (ECF) at the end of 1985. Ron Gale, chief executive for ECF, told the press that he was "very pleased" and added, "I know there are a lot of people out there who want horror." Two minutes shorter than Grau had intended, the ECF print of the film the authors of this book viewed also suffered from an execrable soundtrack, obliterating much of the film's mood.

Grau has numerous film credits to his name, but his only other genre entry is *The Legend of Blood Castle*. As to why specifically a morgue in Manchester, the idea belonged to producer Edmondo Amati, who was obsessed with both Manchester and *Night of the Living Dead*. Speaking on Channel 4's *Eurotika!*, Grau said, "For [Amati] the magic word was Manchester. For him, a horror movie had to be set in Manchester."

LOVE CAMP 7

USA 1968

cast: R W Cresse, Maria Lease; Kathy Williams; Bruce Kemp; John Aiderman; Rodger Steel; Rod Willmouth; Dave Friedman
story: R W Cresse
producer: R W Cresse
director: R L FROST

WWII. Two officers of the Women's Army Corps are dropped behind enemy lines to infiltrate Love Camp 7, thus helping to win the war for the Allies.

LOVE CAMP 7 falls into a category of film known colloquially as 'kinkies' which, along with 'roughies' and 'ghoulies,' emerged in the politically volatile era of late sixties America and constituted a harder-edged form of sexploitation cinema. Key features in these films tended to be acts of sadism, rape, drugs and murder, peppered liberally with plenty of female flesh. Hardcore was still several years

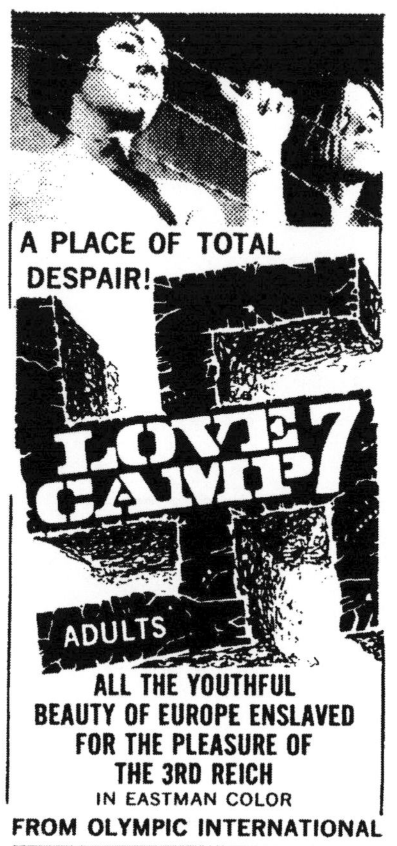

away but Kinkies et al went as far as possible with their sexual content within the law. Many scenes in *Love Camp 7* are awash with writhing naked bodies engaged in sex but are orchestrated to avoid depicting actual pubic hair.[1] Somehow this tends only to heighten the inherent nastiness of the film. The sex acts constitute naked women being pawed and mauled by overweight men who keep their trousers on. The camera wobbles and twists with each gasp and grunt.[2]

The story is told in flashback and purports to be true.[3] Ostensibly inspired by a prototype jet aircraft the Nazis are working on, the story is only really an excuse for gratuitous sadomasochism. With few exceptions the men in the film are horrid. Even the Italian Allied commander (who looks like a young Ron Jeremy and claims in a funny accent to be aged "forty sevron") has a leer on his face when he meets two female officers who must become "less than whores" to save the free world. One suspects that the dignified actor who plays Major Latham, a military bigwig at the start of the film, had little idea just what sort of film he would end up in. Worst of all is the camp commandant, a sadist with a yellow streak who thinks nothing of flogging the women for the slightest transgression, but turns into a snivelling wretch at the prospect of having to give up the luxury of his post for actual frontline combat. Indeed, the power-crazed way he lords over the camp, making unreasonable, effete demands from behind his desk, has more than a passing suggestion of Peter Ustinov's Emperor Nero in *Quo Vadis?*

Bob Cresse, the film's producer, cast himself in the role of commandment and throws himself heart and soul into the part. Having built a career in the transient world of exploitation filmmaking and distribution, Cresse made it clear he wasn't someone to be messed around with. He had in his employment two full-time bodyguards, and wasn't averse to flashing the revolver he carried, even sticking the barrel into the mouth of one reneging exhibitor and threatening to blow his head off unless he paid his fees.[4] Cresse also had a liking for Nazi regalia, so much so that it spurred him to come up with the idea of *Love Camp 7*. Distributor and film-maker Dave Friedman had a walk-on part in the film. In an interview for *RE/Search: Incredibly Strange Films*, Friedman said that

> Cresse was a weird kid... very domineering... Cresse really wants to be a Nazi more than anything else in the world, that's his whole thing. He *really* believed he was a Nazi.

But *Love Camp 7* gave Cresse more than just the opportunity to don a uniform and strut about with a swastika armband. It allowed him to engage in another predilection: flagellation – of which there is a lot in *Love Camp 7*. Cresse, "who apparently never cast an actress he didn't want to whip,"[5] flogs a woman with his crop in an early scene. For a film whose sets and special effects are sparse and unconvincing (the entire Love Camp consists of a single wall in a courtyard, painted blue), the resultant welts on the woman's chest and back are remarkably realistic. However there is no debating the authenticity of a thrashing Cresse administers later in the film. Naked and trussed with her hands behind her back, in a way that forces her to bend double in evident discomfort, one spy is flogged by Cresse without the sanctity of a cutaway as leather strikes flesh. As with all the scenes of debasement in the film, the flagellation lasts for some time, red welts materialising before the viewer's eyes.

Love Camp 7 – released by both Leeds based Abbey Video and (below) London based Mountain Video.

Contrasting this are the very funny scenes in which Cresse throws a fit of rage and starts to bark the only word in German he appears to know: "Schnell!" As if to compensate, he adds several impassioned pleas for help from a soldier with the name, Klaus Müller.[6]

The director of *Love Camp 7* is the prolific R L Frost, who had a long-running association with Cresse, working on a spate of Mondo documentaries[7] – their *Mondo Bizarro* featured Nazi-garbed actors in what is supposed to be a clandestine theatre performance filmed in Germany – and before that the nudie-monster crossover, *The House on Bare Mountain*.

As well as Frost's ability to make good, tight exploitation movies on next to no budget, his skill as a cameraman was called for in providing imported pictures with special sex inserts for the US market. Frost was hired by Twentieth Century-Fox to direct *Race with the Devil*, an action-horror film which Frost had co-written and whose name cast included Peter Fonda and Warren Oates. However, years spent working with meagre budgets betrayed Frost and he was swiftly fired[8] for unnerving "producers by not shooting an excessive amount of film, only what he needed."[9]

Love Camp 7 was a big success on the grindhouse circuit. But because of a growing rivalry, neither Frost not Cresse followed it up and it was left to the enterprising Dave Friedman[10] to make a deal with Canadian investors and produce a Nazi camp cash-in. However, so ineffectual was the result, *Ilsa, She-Wolf of the SS*, it wasn't released until 1974 (the same year as Liliana Cavani's controversial *The Night Porter*) and even then Friedman had his name removed from the credits.[11] The Italians, quick to tap a commercial vein, embarked on a cycle of sleazy Nazi-themed movies of their own, that ran in fits and starts through the latter part of the seventies. The cycle burned itself out before the decade was over.

Love Camp 7 was released in Britain by Market Video and Abbey Video. Although the respective artwork was different, both sleeves carried the same synopsis and the warning, "This is the film that goes beyond X. ADULTS ONLY."

MADHOUSE

aka: There was a Little Girl (original title; this title also appears on the British video, but is preceded by a tacked on card reading: Madhouse)

USA/Italy 1981

cast: Trish Everly, Michael Maere, Morgan Hart, Jerry Fujikara

story: Ovidio G Assonitis, Stephen Blakely, Peter Sheperd, Robert Gandus

producer: Ovidio G Assonitis

director: OVIDIO G ASSONITIS

Julia has concerns about the sanity of her twin sister. However, it is her preachy uncle, Father James, she should be worried about.

THERE'S NO SCIENTIFIC explanation, we are informed, for the virus that disfigures Julia Sullivan's hospitalised sister, Mary. We might argue, there's no reason why any of these murders should be taking place. Julia is a teacher at a school for deaf children. When she takes one of her pupils to church, Father James gives a sermon that attacks sisters who are selfish and deny kinfolk love and comfort, while great is the reward that awaits "those who honour familial love." There are lots of clues that Julia's clergyman uncle might be a homicidal psychopath, but his sermon is the nearest we get to an explanation for the big reveal, which is that he is an accomplice to murder alongside Mary.

Madhouse is a predictable and clichéd whodunnit that offers nothing original or particularly surprising. But if his sermon isn't enough indication that Father James is somehow complicit, he features on the video box holding a knife with a mad look on his face. *Madhouse* comes across like a bland TV movie save for the odd moment of violence. Trish Everly (as Julia) looks like she might have stepped straight out of *Dallas* or any one of a number of glamorous soaps, breathlessly emoting whole chunks of expositional dialogue. On the other hand, Dennis Robertson (as Father James) is a positive cauldron of seething, barely contained malevolence, happily singing nursery rhymes one minute and sinking a knife into a back the next.

In Britain, the film was available in two versions, one showing a dog being killed with a drill and the other missing this scene (there was no way to differentiate from the packaging which print of the film was which). In its uncut form, the sequence is particularly unpleasant; an over-the-top bit of nastiness in an otherwise compromising movie. (The dog, it should be noted, is substituted with a tacky fake for the scene in question.) It's unlikely that *Madhouse* would pose much of a problem with the BBFC if submitted with this one sequence excised.

The only other graphic scenes of violence occur in the opening and closing credits; a dummy having its face smashed repeatedly with a rock, and the axing to death of Father James, replete with streaks of flesh dangling from the wound.

The juxtaposition of maddening nursery rhymes and menacing strings in Riz Ortolani's score conjures up the composer's earlier work on Mondo films (such as *Brutes and Savages*) and on other banned titles, *Cannibal Holocaust* and *House on the Edge of the Park*. These soundtracks were similarly overbearing and cheery at times, counterpoint to the havoc onscreen.

The polished look and traditional scares of *Madhouse* are a million miles from the DPP films of some of director Assonitis' countrymen, notably such Italian films as *Absurd*, *Late Night Trains* and *Gestapo's Last Orgy*. Indeed, it seems a million miles from some of Assonitis' other work, which includes the more raw-edged and visceral *Beyond the Door* and *The Curse*.

Madhouse, with its dead bodies as party guests, was made the same year as the similar celebratory-motivated slasher *Happy Birthday to Me*.

MARDI GRAS MASSACRE

USA 1978

cast: Curt Dawson, Gwen Arment, Laura Misch, Cathryn Lacey, Nancy Dancer, Butch Benit, William Metzo, Ronald Tanet, Wayne Mack

story: Jack Weis

producer: Jack Weis

director: JACK WEIS

A killer on the prowl during Mardi Gras is sacrificing prostitutes to Evil.

ONE WONDERS HOW on earth the killer in *Mardi Gras Massacre* transports the enormous stone idol from town to town, present whenever he makes a human sacrifice – or, if we consider information supplied by Interpol, from country to country. His basic apartment doesn't look big enough to have an all-purpose sacrificial chamber, a sound-proof one at that.

Mardi Gras Massacre mixes film genres in the hope of hitting at least one target, combining elements of *Jaws* (town officials refuse to halt festivities and risk losing business!) and the disco craze sparked by *Saturday Night Fever*, yet fails to achieve anything of significance as a whole. The plot closely resembles that of *Blood Feast*, with the sacrifice of women to an ancient deity culminating in the ultimate sacrifice being thwarted at the last moment. Two cops on the trail fumble around doing very little other than appearing confused, although this does serve to generate unintentional laughter. For instance, they scour the night streets looking for clues, coming down heavy on a bum they beat up in a doorway and a crazed tap dancer they question in the middle of a crowd of people. All this is depicted in medium shot, which brings a greater sense of the absurd to an already absurd situation. The actors who play the cops behave as though they are Starsky and Hutch.

Mardi Gras Massacre – released by both Market Video and (below) Gold Star.

Given the incompetence of the cops and the weird surplus of individuals that inhabit the film, it seems almost plausible that the blatantly unstable killer should move from bar to club without attracting the slightest bit of attention. He asks for "evil" women with a Boris Karloff demeanour, as in the opening scenes when he approaches a hooker by the name of Shirley. "Hello," he says. "I understand you are the most evil woman here."

Catfish, the scat-singing rhyme-talking pimp is as big a nut as he is: "I may not be honest, but you've got my promise," Catfish tells the killer with completely nonexistent street credibility.

Dr Lewis,[1] the expert on ancient sacrificial rites whom the two detectives visit, blurts out with utmost conviction "Human sacrifice – not uncommon today," and then wrongly credits the Manson family with being devil worshippers.

The uneventful storyline is punctuated with infrequent acts of sacrifice, which are graphic but ridiculous. The scenes that resulted in the film being placed on the DPP list are easy to isolate, comprising shots of victims having their torsos cut open and their hearts extracted. This occurs on three occasions, but as each is filmed in the same way and at the same static angle viewers may be excused for thinking the same scene is being repeated over again. It is not clear why the filmmakers should go to the trouble and expense of creating several life-like torso models – it's safe to assume these are the single most expensive items in the entire production – only to film their destruction in a manner that renders them interchangeable. Astute viewers will notice differences in the way the sacrificial dagger slices through the (accommodatingly pliable) flesh, the way in which

"Hello. I understand you are the most evil woman here." *Mardi Gras Massacre*.

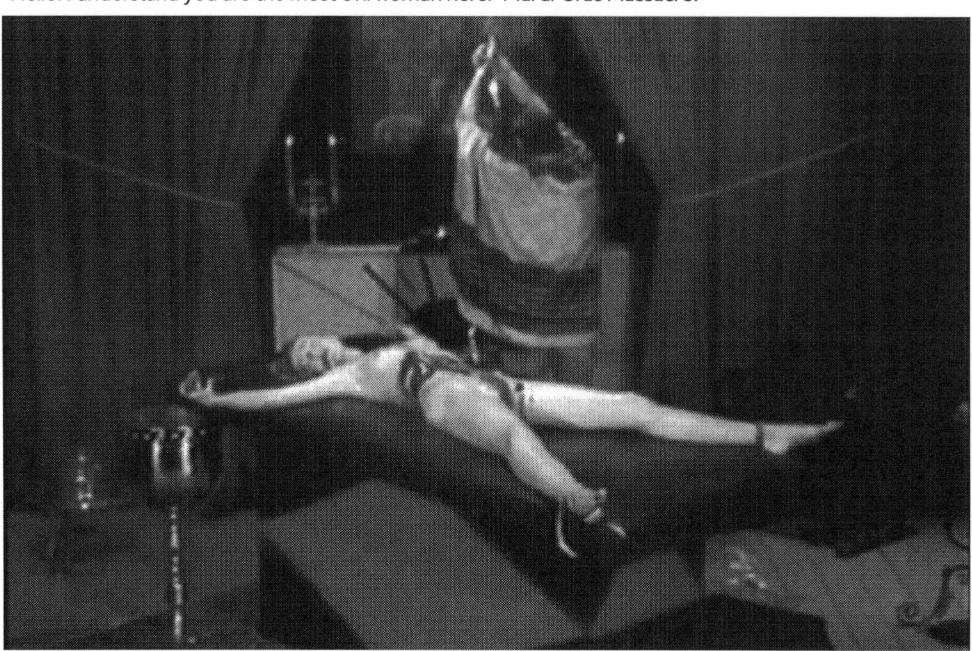

the killer places his hand so not to reveal too much of the emptiness that lies beneath the growing wound, and the way that each torso has differently shaped breasts and nipples to correspond with the live actress. These are prosthetics worthy of any major movie production.

Contrary to the title, all the killings occur before Mardi Gras, and none on the day of the festival. *Mardi Gras Massacre* tries to generate tension with a weird howling synthesised wind sound. Used indiscriminately, this will switch – usually mid-sacrifice – back to the pounding disco-funk score that otherwise dominates the soundtrack. Indeed, the film has a lengthy sequence set in a discotheque for no discernible reason other than to feature some gratuitous sign-of-the-times dancing (*Don't Go in the House* has a similar sequence). The soundtrack is at times reminiscent of the feel-good movie sounds of *Car Wash*, *Saturday Night Fever* and the like.

In February 1998, a professor at Lafayette University included clips from *Mardi Gras Massacre* in a lecture exploring stereotypes and inaccuracies in films that portray the Pre-Columbian people of Latin America – notably Hollywood's penchant for crazy, bloodthirsty Aztec priests.[2]

Crypt of Dark Secrets is often cited as being an alternative title for *Mardi Gras Massacre*, but it's actually an earlier – even more obscure – 1976 movie made by director Weis, which has found a recent video release in America under the title of *Dark Secrets*. It concerns a Vietnam veteran who is brought back to life in a voodoo ceremony, sharing the Louisiana setting and some of the same cast members as *Mardi Gras Massacre*. According to *Psychotronic Video*,[3] its "FX are surprisingly excellent". Not so *Video Watchdog*,[4] who claimed it to be "a truly excruciating sixty-nine minutes that will tax the patience of even the most devoted horror completist."

NIGHT OF THE BLOODY APES

aka: La Horriplante bestia humana (original title); Feast of Flesh; Horror y Sexo; Gomar, The Human Gorilla; Korang, La Terrificante Bestia Umana [?]
Mexico 1968
cast: Armando Silvestre, Norma Lazareno, José Elias Moreno, Carlo Lopez Moctezuma, Juan Fava
story: René Cardona & René Cardona Jr
producer: Alfredo Salazar
director: RENÉ CARDONA

Dr Krauman is a leading surgeon. His son, Julio, is dying from leukaemia, and so Krauman steals a gorilla from a zoo and transplants its heart into Julio, inadvertently creating a murderous man-ape.

RENÉ CARDONA SPENT five decades in the Mexican film business, as an actor, writer and producer, as well as a director of exploitation films, ranging from westerns to wrestling superheroes. He co-wrote *Night of the Bloody Apes* with his son, who was also to enjoy a film-making career. In many ways *Bloody Apes* comes over as a homage to the classic movie monsters, with its strain of mad scientist, Frankenstein-like monster and lycanthrope. The film opens with 'blood' pouring behind the credits and closes with a chase across the rooftops with frightened townspeople gathered below. Even the dramatic score echoes the Universal monsters era. The film bears a particular resemblance to William Beaudine's 1943 *The Ape Man*, wherein Bela Lugosi injects himself with ape serum and takes on ape-like attributes, resorting to killing others for

There is only one bloody ape in *Night of the Bloody Apes.*

the spinal fluid he needs to regain his human features. (Cardona appears to have been impressed enough by Beaudine's film to explore its ideas on at least one other occasion outside of *Bloody Apes* – his 1962 film *Wrestling Women Vs. the Aztec Ape* also features mad scientists and gorillas.) Cardona tries to modernise the archaic B-movie plot by throwing in scenes of wrestling, partial nudity and graphic gore, which raises laughs. The wrestling sequences (three in the first half-hour) are overlong and irrelevant, thrown in to appease fans of Mexican wrestling, around which an entire film genre had grown. Scenes that incorporated nudity were filmed in a cautious manner – not unlike early naturist documentaries – with conveniently placed objects obscuring certain areas of the body. A woman who is attacked in the shower by the monster manages to turn her leg discreetly while 'unconscious', thus obscuring any wisp of pubis.

The gore is plentiful, but remarkably cheesy and their rubber origins evident. When a victim has his scalp torn off, a plastic tube taped to the top of his head is clearly visible, supplying blood to the wound. An eye gouging seems to have been achieved with a rubber mask having mashed potato squeezed from the eyehole. The lengthy scenes depicting Julio's operations comprise stock footage inserts of transplantation surgery and a beating heart being cut from its donor (with plenty of cutaways to Dr Krauman[1] mopping his sweating brow). The fact that the footage doesn't correspond with the actors, their actions or the colour of the stock it is sandwiched between seems of no importance; there are more hands around the operating table than there are people in Krauman's lab.

The transformation of Julio into the ape is achieved with effects that are similar – but technically inferior – to those used on Lon Chaney Jr in 1941's *The Wolf Man*. However, as tends to be the case, the cheap makeup job somehow renders the sight of the creature more disgusting and horrific. On top of the gloriously wild and cut-price bloodletting, there are plenty of other factors that make *Night of the Bloody Apes* such an enjoyable experience. These include the Hispanic beat cop who speaks in a strange Irish accent; the police lieutenant's diminutive girlfriend, Lucy, a professional wrestler, who miraculously gains extra pounds once she has donned her mask and got into the ring; the small studio set that passes as an area of the park to which all the characters seem drawn (and in which a struggling victim inadvertently kicks up the artificial grass to reveal a concrete floor); the flimsy wooden boards that are nailed haphazardly across the lab window following Krauman's concern that no precaution can be great enough; the elderly woman who discovers a dead body in the street and screams "Oh! A dead man! A dead man! A dead man!" (pre-dating Edith Massey's Egg Lady in *Pink Flamingos* by several years).[2]

We almost hope that the phone never rings in the Krauman household because invariably, Goyo, the crippled assistant, will traipse through several rooms and up a staircase (in real time) to tell the doctor he has a call waiting.

As to why his son turns into a bloody ape, Krauman explains to his assistant:

> KRAUMAN: I was prepared for a case of refusal, for autoimmunisation which might affect the normal tissues – such as the pleura and the red blood cells – but I never thought it would affect the cerebrum.
> GOYO: The cerebrum?
> KRAUMAN: Yes. And what is more probable is that the heart of a gorilla is much too potent for any human, and the volume of blood to the cerebrum – which couldn't control this great pressure – damaged the superior parts. And when this happens man becomes... an animal completely without control, giving origin to the transmutation. The malignancy of the case is that the process might occur

each forty-five seconds, the time it takes for the blood to circulate through the normal body.

The film was described by *Monster Mag*[3] as one "based on an absolutely true and plausible occurrence". The unaccredited reviewer was aghast at the incredible advancements in medical science that made *Night of the Bloody Apes* so credible. "What horror can an eminent physician create in a state of terrible mental stress?" he wrote. Released theatrically in Britain in 1974 with one minute of cuts, *Night of the Bloody Apes* was made available on video by Iver Film Services (IFS) with a warning that "this film contains scenes of extreme violence."[4] The distinctive IFS packaging for its horror line tended to feature specially commissioned photographic work (the cover for *Bloody Apes* has a surgeon's bloodied hands; *Night of the Demon* was a darkened moonlight sky; *Pigs* was a pig's head with a bloody mouth) and often carried the film's American rating.

After the murder and mayhem is finally over, Lucy closes the film with the deadpan understatement: "It's unfortunate – really sad."

NIGHT OF THE DEMON

USA 1980

cast: Michael J Cutt, Joy Allen, Bob Collins, Jodi Lazarus, Richard Fields, Michael Lang, Melaine Graham
story: Jim L Ball, Mike Williams
producer: Jim L Ball
director: JAMES C WASSON

The heavily bandaged Professor Nugent explains from his hospital bed how he and his students were attacked by a Sasquatch – "a demon" – in the forest.

JAMES WASSON'S *NIGHT of the Demon* is an oddly engaging film. Despite its cheapness, lousy acting and trite script the film is immensely watchable, with a dynamism that kicks off right from the opening pre-title killing: a man preparing to go fishing is attacked and has his arm ripped off. Although this is only shown in

'Crazy Wanda' – *Night of the Demon*.

shadow, the victim manages to stagger into shot displaying his ragged wounds before falling to the ground and bleeding into the outsize footprint left by the thing that attacked him. Shoddily done, but nevertheless an attention-grabbing opening scene that hints at the mayhem ahead. Barely have the titles finished when we witness another Bigfoot attack. In what may be a tip of the hat to the famous Roger Patterson footage – scenes of a supposedly genuine Sasquatch taken in 1967[1] – this sequence is related to the anthropology students via footage accidentally caught on a home movie camera. Again the sequence is ludicrously awkward, but somehow transcends the humble budget to become greater than the sum of its parts.

Another attack features a couple making out in the back of a van in the woods (the lovemaking seems to go on for an eternity – not helped by the particularly unattractive couple doing the loving). Something outside the window catches the woman's eye. She suspects at first that it's a peeping tom and continues with a wry smile on her face. It turns out to be the creature. Having stared through the back window of the van and got a clear view of the man's naked pummelling backside, the creature pulls open the door and yanks him outside. Frozen to the spot, the woman listens to the creature pass across the top of the vehicle with her lover screaming in agony. With a handprint on the windscreen he finally comes into view again. For an awfully long time his bloodied face is perfectly still, emitting a strange guttural death rattle. The camera eventually focuses on the woman and stays with her as she slowly succumbs to shock and dies.

And, fundamentally, that is all the film is: a succession of events, generally in flashback – or flashbacks-within-flashbacks if one considers that the whole tale is being related by the convalescing Prof Nugent, who led his students into "Bigfoot territory" and paid the price. The flashbacks occur every ten minutes or so. It seems that wherever the team decamps in the woods, Nugent has a new story concerning people being "horribly mutilated". His team is comprised of the most disagreeable and incompetent students imaginable. A lack of rudimentary knowledge is highlighted when, in all seriousness, one of the team deduces that their boat has been pulled from its mooring by something "like an elephant."

The story takes an interesting turn when it establishes that Bigfoot is worshipped by the locals. Nugent's team is drawn to strange sounds in the woods. They observe a ceremony in which townsfolk are worshipping an anthropoid effigy and a woman is about to be ritually raped. The team eventually locate "Crazy Wanda", the woman in question, who, under hypnosis, relates that long ago she was raped by Bigfoot and gave birth to a monstrous child.

The flashback depicting Wanda's bestial impregnation and the conflict with her pious father are the most adept parts of the film. His attempts to induce a miscarriage in his daughter fail. When finally she gives birth to a malformed thing that screams like a chimpanzee, complemented by an expression on her father's face that is at once joy and terror, the result is quite chilling. Like *Cannibal Holocaust*, *Night of the Demon* appears to have been another inspiration for the makers of *The Blair Witch Project*. The sequence in which the team wanders around the small township asking people their opinion of the mysterious "Crazy Wanda" is similar to passages in that later film.

Segments that depict the Bigfoot attacks, narrated by Nugent, are the film's purpose (there is only one tight close-up shot in the whole movie that doesn't feature a grisly gore effect). Each is progressively more violent, culminating in the all-out assault on the anthropologists themselves – a sequence that is credited on the video sleeve as "the most gruesome blood bath ever filmed" (but is essentially another retread of Romero's *Night of the Living Dead*, in which those holed up in a barricaded shack are forced to fight off the ultimately overwhelming force of the aggressor).

The team constantly stray too close to the windows of the shack, despite the imminent danger should anyone come within reach of the creature's powerful claws. The dream-like state this sequence invokes is compounded once the creature breaks through the window-bars and gets into the building. As the Bigfoot contemplates its new environment, the team slowly manoeuvre their way around the room. Unable to get out through the front door, they make a run for a back room. The film switches to slow motion, and the creature embarks on an orgy of mutilation. One student is shaken to death; another is throttled; one student is forced onto a saw blade and from the resultant wound the creature rips intestines which it then uses to flail the boy's colleagues (the most memorable and silliest sequence); another student is impaled on a pitchfork, and another has his throat cut open on broken glass. Nugent has his face pushed onto burning coals – hence his hospitalisation.

As if that wasn't gloriously gory enough, earlier in the film the creature captures two girl scouts and bashes them together repeatedly until dead (neither girl relinquishes the knife they are holding, adding to the flesh-rending mayhem). A woodcutter is chopped in the shoulder and the camera seems unable to pull free of the blood-pumping wound. Blood... pumping... endlessly...

In a sequence that has passed into (video nasty) legend, Nugent relates the tale of a motorcyclist who had his penis torn off by the monster. Cut to the motorcyclist travelling from a long way away, down a mountainside road. He (eventually) pulls over for a rest and decides to urinate. Suddenly, from the bushes springs the Bigfoot who grabs the man's penis and lifts him off the ground, leaving him to stumble with a blood-oozing groin stump back to his motorcycle, where he squirts a few drops of crimson urine on the chrome before dropping dead.

There is evidence that the filmmakers have some grasp of technique. Cutaways and dissolves are plentiful, and feature in all the right places (unlike that other woodland nasty, *Don't Go in the Woods*). The camera is far from static, and the cheesy dialogue rarely descends to out-and-out stupidity. (Although there is a good laugh to be had when members of the team disrupt the ritual and inadvertently cause a fire. Nugent tells one concerned student: "We're not equipped to handle it. Let them take care of it – they live in the woods.")

Night of the Demon was released uncut on the IFS label, and a warning identical to that of *Night of the Bloody Apes* appeared on the video sleeve. As the gory madness is all part of the film's strange appeal, there would be little point in releasing a bowdlerised version. *Night of the Demon* typifies the complete obscurity that would never have seen the light of day in Britain if not for the momentary leeway afforded it by pre-certified videocassettes.

NIGHTMARE MAKER

title on print: Butcher, Baker, Nightmare Maker
aka: Night Warning; Thrilled To Death
USA 1981
cast: Jimmy McNichol, Susan Tyrrell, Bo Svenson, Marcia Lewis, Julia Duffy, Steve Eastin, Caskey Swaim, Britt Leach
story: Alan Jay Glueckman & Boon Collins
producer: Stephen Breimer
director: WILLIAM ASHER

Believed orphaned as a child, Billy lives with his overly protective aunt Cheryl. She thwarts his opportunity to attend college, resorting to tantrums and murder.

THE OUTSPOKEN SUSAN Tyrrell (who plays Aunt Cheryl) said of this film in an interview for *Psychotronic Video*: "I liked it because it gave me a chance to go berserk. I always like that, but I don't need a piece of shit movie to make me go berserk... It looks like it was written on the spot, it was a mess... I was trying to make it funny." [1]

Indeed, Tyrrell's performance as Aunt Cheryl is one of the more endearing aspects of *Nightmare Maker*. Her demeanour and facial expressions following the murder of a TV repairman and the final bloody assault are show-stopping. They could be called "funny" but not in the context that springs immediately to mind. Tyrrell takes her performance into a realm of ultra-acting, as if she is attempting to express multi-personalities in the same body, at the same time. In these scenes of transmutation, Tyrrell is recreating characters from another movie – hip to the fact that director William Asher is attempting to emulate Brian de Palma's *Carrie*. Tyrrell stands motionless, drenched in blood, arms in a mannequin-lock, her face in ecstatic delirium – or a state of catatonia. Is she Sissy Spacek or Piper Laurie? No, she is both, at the same time. One can understand where Tyrell is coming from: It transpires that Cheryl is not Billy's aunt, but his biological mother, while at the movie's end she wants to be his "girlfriend".

As with *Carrie*, a mother's puritanical protectiveness toward her offspring lies at the heart of *Nightmare Maker*. Also like *Carrie*, Cheryl's house is adorned with religious iconography,[2] but Asher seems at a loss to make anything of it, short of sharing Lieutenant Carlson's vehement homophobia and making proclamations like "Do you know that homosexuals are very, very sick?"

"I was trying to make it funny." Susan Tyrrell goes berserk in *Nightmare Maker*.

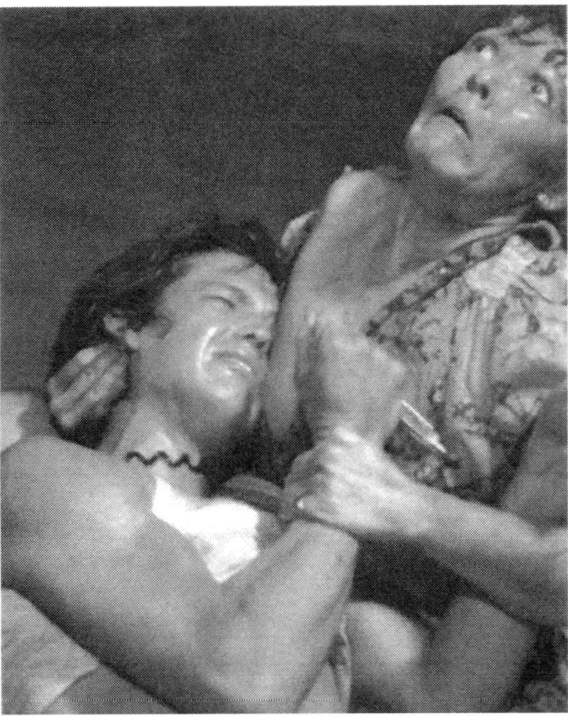

Which brings us to Lieutenant Carlson (Bo Svenson), a bewildering character. He turns up after the murder of a TV repairman, whom Cheryl claims to have stabbed in self-defence after he tried to rape her. (In truth, she got mad when he rejected her advances.) Carlson chastises Billy throughout, claiming he is a "fag". How did Carlson ever manage to solve a case if his only detection constitutes whether a "fag" might be involved, ignoring any real evidence that comes to light? At one point he interrogates a suspect with a gun pointing at their head.

William Asher is a competent enough director, having worked for many years on TV's *I Love Lucy* and created the hugely successful Beach Party cycle of movies for American International Pictures (AIP) in the sixties.[3] But *Nightmare Maker* was a unique departure into horror for him. Not surprising, that while it has some unorthodox and unpleasant elements, it carries all the hallmarks of a TV Movie of the Week – even starring some familiar faces from TV.[4]

Nightmare Maker is a concerted effort to break out of type for Asher, an attempt to draw a cloud over "the longest summer on record," which is how he once described his Beach Party movies. Interestingly, an essential ingredient in the winning Beach Party formula was that they presented the youth market with an idealised, carefree vision of itself, without the authoritarian shadow of parents looming over it; in effect, a direct reversal of *Nightmare Maker*.

It was announced in 1985 that *Nightmare Maker* was among a further four titles to be dropped by the DPP from the nasties list. It came too late for Atlantis, however, the label that had distributed the film. They had gone bust.

Nightmare Maker remains a banned title. Despite the DPP having dropped it, when Film View Video submitted it to the BBFC in 1987 under the title *The Evil Protégé* (a title that makes no sense at all in the context of the movie), it was refused a certificate and rejected outright.[5]

So where does the contention lie? Outside of the opening car accident, the one that kills Billy's parents, and the spectacular shot of a head being knocked off its shoulders (repeated in flashback), the film gets no more graphic than a hand being hacked off with an axe and several stabbings through clothing. Also, Tyrrell does get drenched in blood while dressed in a low-cut top, possibly treading too close to the BBFC's concern about blood on breasts. But it's unlikely that any of these scenes in themselves posed a problem (they could, after all, be cut). Perhaps these factors together with *Nightmare Maker*'s theme of incest and anti-gay crusading proved problematic?

A quick word on Atlantis: They had one of the great, cheesy logos of the video boom. The word 'Atlantis' ripples up from the bottom of the screen, comes to rest in the middle and dematerialises by spinning slowly in fabulous, state of the art, eighties pop promo fashion. And, in case you should miss it, the copyright warning on *Nightmare Maker* pops up twice before the main feature starts,[6] and once again after it has ended.

NIGHTMARES IN A DAMAGED BRAIN

title on print: Scavolini's Nightmares In A Damaged Brain
aka: Nightmare; Dark Games (working title)
USA 1981
cast: Baird Stafford, Sharon Smith, and introducing:
C J Cooke, Mik Cribben, Danny Ronan, John Watkins
producer: John L Watkins
director: ROMANO SCAVOLINI

George Tatum's homicidal tendencies seem to stem back to a day in childhood when he witnessed his parents having kinky sex. Doctors think he is cured. They are wrong.

The DPP39

'SCENES OF EXTREME AND EXPLICIT VIOLENCE'

SOME NOTORIETY SURROUNDS this film on both sides of the Atlantic, stemming in each case from the special makeup effects. Though grisly by any definition, in Britain these effects were responsible for getting the film banned, while in the US the protest was of a more discriminating nature. Under its US title of – simply – *Nightmare*, the film accredited the makeup effects to Tom Savini, whose imaginatively gory work had made him something of a star and box office draw in his own right. (See *The Burning* for further information.) To this day, however, he denies having anything but the most superficial association with *Nightmare* and rejects outright the credit for its makeup effects.

When the film was first released, Savini's was the most prominent name in the advertising. He threatened to sue on the grounds that his only involvement was to offer advice for a decapitation sequence and nothing more. With this, his name was masked from posters with black tape and removed from the credits of the film playing across New York. (It reappeared later.)

Romano Scavolini, the film's director, recollects that Savini was called in to supervise the prosthetics of effects man Lester Lorraine, but had featured in a much greater capacity once shooting got underway. He says Savini was very active in the film, in actual fact crucial to it, but can understand – and even admire – Savini's resentment at the apparent exploitation of his name over that of a fellow technician.[1]

Alas, Scavolini has some exaggerated notions on the quality and influence of his own film, claiming in an interview in *Spaghetti Nightmares* that it remains "one of America's biggest cult movies" and that it's the only work by Savini that has been "a total success." Such declarations are not shared by Savini, who thought the film "came and went" (which is a lot nearer the truth). In an interview elsewhere in *Spaghetti Nightmares*, Savini reflects:

> They never hired me to do the film. So when I was in New York, I met Lester Lorraine and chatted with him about some of the effects and stuff, but I never actually worked on the film. Apart from that I'd only had a brief chat on the phone in the early days of the project when it was known as *Dark Games*.

However laudable Savini's reasons are for disassociating himself from *Nightmare*, he clearly did visit the set – as evidenced in a photograph reproduced in the book, in which the makeup maestro demonstratively holds the axe that chops a woman's head off in a recurring flashback scene.

The dream you can't
escape ALIVE!
NIGHTMARE
IF YOU WERE TERRIFIED BY
"DAWN OF THE DEAD"
& "FRIDAY THE 13th"
YOU MUST SEE NIGHTMARE!
DAVID JONES Presents A GOLDMINE PRODUCTION
Starring SHARON SMITH • BAIRD STAFFORD and introducing C.J. COOKE
Also Starring MIK CRIBBEN • KATHLEEN FERGUSON Produced by JOHN L. WATKINS
Written & Directed by ROMANO SCAVOLINI Music by JACK ERIC WILLIAMS
Executive Producer DAVID JONES
© COPYRIGHT MCMLXXXI ALL RIGHTS RESERVED, GOLDMINE PRODUCTIONS, LTD.

In Britain, the video of *Nightmares in a Damaged Brain* closely followed a theatrical run of the film, which had played with forty-eight seconds of cuts. Press screenings of the movie were shrouded in secrecy and came with a complementary vomit bag, a tired novelty that failed to win over critics. Even the title of the movie was kept secret until the press screenings were underway.

Scavolini makes no pretence that the film is anything but an exercise to shock the audience with gore.[2] He also claims that its theme, which involves secret experiments on the mentally ill, was a delicate issue and an embarrassment to the American government. (George is monitored by a group of doctors, who consider their treatment of schizophrenia, amnesia and seizures a success.) This, Scavolini believes, is the real reason for the hostile reaction to the film.

The British video distributor continued the film's tacky theatrical promotion with a stunt that ultimately backfired. At a video trade show held in Manchester in May 1982, World of Video 2000 launched *Nightmares in a Damaged Brain* with a dealer competition. On their stand was a brain,[3] said to be that of the film's lead character, in a pickling jar. Correctly guessing its weight was awarded with a cash prize of £50. The gimmick was also incorporated in the video sleeve design – a visual montage that implies actor Baird Stafford (George) is in a jar with a brain as blood oozes from his eyes. Whether the police that raided the roadshow and confiscated the exhibit were also a part of the gimmick is not known, but the tasteless prank reached the press and served to aggravate the increasing dissent that horror videos were facing.

World of Video 2000 pulled the same stunt for reporters outside a hospital in Surrey. Again the campaign concluded with police intervention. Such promotional antics brought *Nightmares* to the attention of the DPP, who successfully prosecuted and helped to secure the film a place as one of the most notorious of the 'video nasties'. Following police raids, in which videocassettes of the film were seized, three men and their parent company April Electronics, were charged with possessing obscene articles for publication and gain. They entered the special defence that *Nightmares* was "in the public good." Alas it took the jury five-and-a-half hours to decide on the contrary. (Perhaps, having watched the film themselves, the nine men and three women of the jury left the courtroom suitably depraved and corrupted by the experience?)

April Electronics went into liquidation. Company secretary David Hamilton-Grant received an eighteen-month prison sentence of which twelve months were suspended.[4] Two colleagues, Malcolm Fancey and Roger Morley, received a suspended sentence and fines. (See also CLAMPDOWN.) One issue raised in the trial was that the video print was "left unedited," unlike the theatrical print which had undergone cuts by the BBFC for an X-certificate. Compulsory video certification was still a couple of years away when the tapes were confiscated in October 1982, so while the 'X' that also adorned the video sleeve may not have been wholly accurate, it wasn't a legal requirement to display it at all. The forty-eight seconds difference between theatrical and video prints – which included a close-up shot of an ice-pick being buried in a woman's back – evidently helped to sway the jury. In hindsight, it serves to illustrate the ambiguity that allowed the law to be wielded at a whim, and the minefield that lay in wait for British video.

Scavolini made many short films for Italian TV in the sixties before embarking on his first feature *A Mosca Cieca*, a controversial movie focusing on violence and the human condition. Today, Scavolini claims the government allows him only to show it "privately to an audience of no more than fifteen people."[5] After travelling extensively as a journalist and war photographer, Scavolini made several more movies and documentaries in Italy before settling in the US in 1976. Six years after *Nightmares*, he made *Dogtags*, a grisly war film set in the Vietnam conflict. This utilises the same framing device of *Nightmares*, with titles dividing the story into days ("The First Day," etc). He denies that *Nightmares* was influenced by John Carpenter's *Halloween*, but it could be that Scavolini did derive some inspiration from Ulli Lommel's *The Bogey Man* from the previous year. Both movies feature grisly deaths precipitated by flashbacks, and a young boy who murders a parent figure engaged in kinky sex.

There are rumours that early in his career Scavolini had a hand in making hardcore porn movies. We have been unable to verify this information, and one Italian source told us, "Nobody knows anything about this. I think if Scavolini did make some porn movies, he made them when he was working in the USA... It's not so easy to hide your name making porn here." It is likely these rumours have their origins in Scavolini's convincingly sleazy peepshow sequences at the beginning of *Nightmares*, courtesy of some over-excited critics.

Nightmares in a Damaged Brain has a musical theme that sounds like an outtake from Pink Floyd's *Dark Side of the Moon*. Scavolini claims to have shot six different endings, each offering a different take on the relationship between George and the family to which he is linked throughout the movie.

Forty years after making *Nightmares in a Damaged Brain* he claimed to have been working on a follow-up: *Nightmare – The Wandering Soul*.

VTC released *Possession* with two different video sleeves. The more common one (below) appeared to be printed back-to-front, the reverse blurb as the cover.

POSSESSION

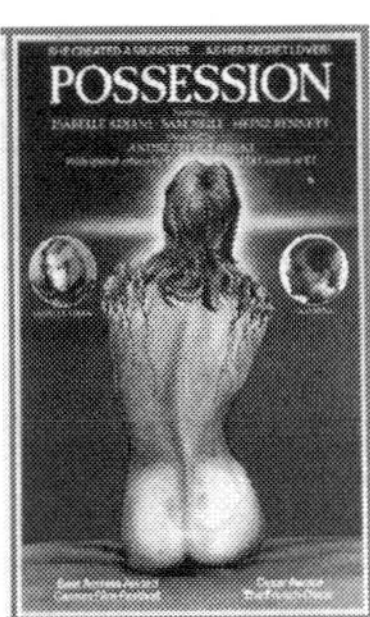

aka: Night the Screaming Stops

France/West Germany 1981

cast: Isabelle Adjani, Sam Neill, Margit Carstensen, Heinz Bennent

story: Andrzej Zulawski

producer: Marie-Laure Reyre

director: ANDRZEJ ZULAWSKI

Anna is acting strangely. Husband Marc assumes she's having an affair. The relationship degenerates until it is revealed that Anna has a Marc-replicant lover.

POSSESSION WAS NEVER meant for the DPP list, an opinion shared by jurors who ruled that a scene where Anna makes love to a tentacled creature – "octopus sex" as it came to be known in the press – was unlikely to deprave

and corrupt. Viewed as a 'video nasty', the film is relatively blood-free and disconcertingly well-acted. Viewed on its own terms, without the ridiculous stigma that arose from its association with the DPP, *Possession* has a subversive quality more potent and unsettling than any scene of prosthetic carnage.

The film doesn't have a linear narrative. Approaching it in a linear frame of mind will spoil the pickings to be had. For its British theatrical release in 1982, *Continental Film and Video Review* devoted considerable space to deciphering the film's mystical and symbolic references,[1] noting the original poster art closely paralleled *The Idol of Perversity*, a painting by Belgian Symbolist Jean Delville. (Arguably another of Delville's paintings, *The Treasures of Satan*, is the inspiration for the film's evolving tentacle-creature.) But reading it as a kind of manifesto is as detrimental as not reading anything into the film at all. It isn't necessary to decipher *Possession* – it works best as a fever dream. Although director Andrzej Zulawski isn't averse to symbolism and subtext, they are just as likely to be the antithesis of what critics believe the film is saying. There appears to be some catechismal significance to the unfolding events – with Anna (Isabelle Adjani) visiting a church, later declaring that God is in her and so forth – but it comes to nothing. Or, flipped on its head, it's a kind of cosmic joke, as when the spiritually enlightened Heinrich, the man with whom Anna might be having an affair, is led dick-first to his death in a public toilet "in a flood of shit." Heinrich is a sinister, touchy-feely character, but also a perversely comedic one.

The more one tries to read the film, the more infuriating it becomes because, while there are clearly symbolic and psychological properties in play, nothing is really being said; for all its colourful and labyrinthine facets, *Possession* is a love story at heart. In an interview that appeared in *Eyeball*,[2] Zulawski stated that "cinema is eyes" and claimed it wasn't important for a director to impart a message. He declared that *Possession* was "essentially a very true-to-life autobiographical story," with much of its dialogue transcribed from experience.[3] However, the creature – the aspect of the film that viewers find most problematic – isn't drawn from real events but provides a fairy tale element to the story.

Said Zulawski in *Eyeball*:

> When I wrote *Possession* as a script I gave it to a dear friend who is a Polish critic... and said "tell me what you think." And he said to me "You should never show the monster, you should always guess," you know, a shadow or something, she goes in, you never see it because it is impossible... All right, but this is the reason I'm making the film! Because otherwise, write or tell it but don't film... Because this is cinema, and I will never hide, a door will never close at the right moment, a light will never go out. If you invent it, think it, then find a way to show it... otherwise do something else.[4]

Viewing the film as a fairy tale spares us from having to assemble it into a coherent whole; better to accept that some pieces simply cannot be made to lock together. What, for instance, is to be made of the air raid sound at the film's end, which commences when Helen, a schoolteacher who looks identical to Anna, is unwittingly about to open the door to a squirming doppelgänger of Marc (Sam Neill), Anna's husband? Has war broken out (on account of Marc refusing to return to the job whose precise nature is never revealed, but seems to involve political subterfuge)? Or is the very fabric of the film coming apart now that anti-Marc is at the door of Helen, the anti-Anna? If we opt for the latter, we get a tidy inversion of the film's opening sequence, where the real Marc – "Coming up from the wars," as he puts it – returns home to the real Anna. (Home is Berlin, a city Zulawski chose because he considered it an anonymous city, a nowhere place.) This cyclic Yin-Yang element is at the heart of *Possession*: as Marc becomes progressively more 'balanced' over the course of the film, his wife degenerates. They die together and are reborn.

It is impossible to imagine *Possession* with anyone but Sam Neill in the role of the vexed Marc, and the same can be said of Heinz Bennent as the cod-mystic Heinrich. They fall into their parts seamlessly. But unquestionably Isabelle Adjani as Anna is the star of the film. She has an innocent, pre-Raphaelite look, with beautiful dark eyes that seem forever in search of something completely removed from this world. When a detective arrives at her flat on the heels of a missing colleague, we can understand why he should be frightened of this outwardly delicate creature going about her chores. In one scene of high emotional drama, she thinks nothing of deliberately pacing in front of a moving truck and causing it to crash (there is never any question that it might knock her over). Anna carries traits of both Marc and Heinrich, the rage of one and the mysticism of the other, producing an amorality of her own. In a flashback, which shows her tutoring a class of young ballerina hopefuls, Anna is fixated by the shortcoming of one particular student and demands more from her, insisting she lifts her leg higher. It isn't good enough – higher, higher! But it can never be good enough and it becomes apparent that the girl is merely an excuse for Anna's own failings. "That's why I'm with you," she tells the camera, "Because you say 'I' for me."

The interpolation of a woman openly venting her sexual frustrations while systematically reducing a little girl to tears is certainly not a comfortable one, but Adjani goes even further physically and emotionally in a later scene...

It is *Possession*'s best remembered scene: Anna is travelling to her flat with groceries when suddenly she breaks into laughter. As she makes her way through an underpass, the laughter switches to anguish and before long Anna is in the throes of a violent fit, hurling herself against the walls. After several minutes in this volatile state she collapses to her knees, dry heaves until she is purple, and 'miscarries'. The ferocity and conviction of her performance is gut-wrenching, and it's satisfying to know that *Possession* landed Adjani with the award for Best Actress at the Cannes Film Festival. Zulawski has stated he gives his actors trance exercises, little programmes that last several days. And it was because she was in one such trance, claims the director, that Adjani was able to give such an intense performance, taking physical knocks without feeling pain. He claims that upon seeing the film for the first time, she locked herself in a bathroom and tried to commit suicide.

> But it's Adjani, it's not real. She committed suicide with a Gillette G2, you know, you can cut zero-zero-one millimetre of your skin with that, these twin blades... It was only to show she was suffering so much having seen herself and she said to me this memorable sentence. "You don't have the right to put the camera in this way because it looks inside one's soul" – and her soul is dark, I think, and she knows it.[5]

Possession exists in a variety of forms. The film was shot in English but there is a French language version (with Adjani dubbing her own part)[6] and numerous other prints of varying lengths. The original pre-certificate video version from VTC – which landed on the DPP list – is complete at 118 minutes. Later it was issued again on video by Visual Corporation Ltd, under a masthead proclaiming it to be "The Director's Cut". In the US, audiences got to see only a hideously truncated version when Limelight removed almost forty minutes from the film. Little wonder the reviewer for *Cinefantastique* was so scathing, not to mention presumptuous, in writing that some of the cut material consisted of "shockingly explicit sex scenes." This is the kind of misinformed statement that breeds apocryphal tales, and one such legend has grown around the sequence in the underpass where Anna throws a fit: several sources erroneously claim that even at five minutes the sequence is truncated and that it originally ran for ten minutes.

Limelight did no favours cutting the film for a stateside release, but it fared even worse when Rugged Films picked it up in 1985. In order to utilise posters left over from Amando de Ossorio's *When the Screaming Stops*,[7] an earlier film the company had distributed, Rugged Films pasted the word 'Night' over 'When' on the posters and promoted *Possession* as *Night the Screaming Stops*. It mattered not a jot that the campaign bore no relation to the film itself. Rugged Films didn't even bother to remove the promise of a free vomit bag, a gimmick that had accompanied de Ossorio's modest chiller.

PRANKS

aka: The Dorm that Dripped Blood; Death Dorm
USA 1981
cast: Laurie Lapinski, Stephen Sachs, David Snow, Pamela Holland, Dennis Ely, Woody Roll
story: Stephen Carpenter, Jeffrey Obrow & Stacey Giachino
producer: Jeffrey Obrow
directors: JEFF OBROW & STEPHEN CARPENTER

A college is soon to be converted into apartments. The four students and a caretaker assigned with clearing the building fall victim to a homicidal maniac.

A headful of steam – *Pranks*.

PRANKS WAS CONCEIVED by college pals not enamoured of having to look for real work. They came up with a three-minute showreel they hoped would generate financial backing for a full-length feature and launch a movie career. Although for Obrow and Carpenter the show reel was a success, there appears to have been little to no additional work in converting it to a fully-fledged production: *Pranks* is very much a vague idea padded to feature length (although it supposedly took three months to write). The tedium belies the film's humble origins. It is over long, filled with uninteresting characters, and is constructed around a dreary, clichéd plot.

"Why don't we split up and look for him?" is the kind of dialogue that would have seemed contrived back in the 1940s but finds a place here. However, co-director Jeff Obrow told *Fangoria* that *Pranks* was "the type of film where the audience is constantly putting themselves in the place of the characters, wondering what they will do next."[1]

The students who stay behind to clear the college building at the end of term are vacuous, and everyone around them sinister or dubious in some fashion. All males are red herrings, and, until the end, the killer is only depicted via prowling point-of-view camera angles – hardly groundbreaking or taxing. And the big denouement? Craig's unrequited love for Joanne has pushed him over the edge into an indiscriminate killing spree.

The persistent music is an uninspired model of the *Psycho* theme – because it's the title theme here, too, things appear desperate before the film has begun.

Although Diana and her father are murdered in a singularly unpleasant fashion – she has her head run over by a car and he is struck by a spiked baseball bat – these are either off-screen or presented in a blink-and-it's-over manner. The only scenes that could be considered remotely 'nasty' are those that show a hand being split open with a knife (an unexplained pre-credit sequence that takes place during a party but is never referred to again), and another where the caretaker has his head drilled. Although the latter shows the drill bit penetrating the skull, it is again very brief, cutting quickly away without detail.[2] *Pranks* was eventually re-released with this scene removed. By contrast, the film's ending – in which Joanne is stuffed into an incinerator – is unexpectedly downbeat and out of character with the rest of the film, as it is the stalk-and-slash genre as a whole. The directorial team of Obrow and Carpenter went on next to direct the markedly better *The Kindred*.

PRISONER OF THE CANNIBAL GOD

aka: Mountain of the Cannibal God; Slave of the Cannibal God; La Montagna del dio Cannibale (original title); The Mountain in the Jungle; El dios de los Canibales

Italy 1979

cast: Ursula Andress, Stacy Keach, Claudio Cassinelli, Antonio Marsina, Franco Fantasia, Lanfranco Spinola, Carlo Longhi, Luigina Rocchi, Akushia Sellajaah, Dudley Wanaguru, T M Munna, M Suki

story: Cesare Frugoni & Sergio Martino

producer: Luciano Martino

director: SERGIO MARTINO

When her husband fails to return from an expedition to an inhospitable region of New Guinea, Susan Stevenson sets off to find him. Her team is slowly decimated by the habitat and by cannibals.

EVEN THE PRESENCE of Ursula Andress and Stacy Keach can't raise *Prisoner of the Cannibal God* above the status of mediocre adventure film. With the interminable edits of stock footage and borrowed scenes previously seen in other cannibal films, the whole thing is a thoroughly dull viewing experience. As with most films of this type, the plot revolves around the greed of the 'civilised' Caucasian invading and conflicting with a 'primitive' culture. The journey to the mountain of the title – located in the Maraba region of New Guinea, said to be cursed and/or sacred – is ponderous and its ascent via waterfall seems to last forever. The slow progress of the film is interrupted with brief moments of violence in which either a wild animal is killed, or a member of the exploration team dies violently. Susan Stevenson (Andress), on her journey to find her husband, is assisted by brother-in-law Arthur, and American anthropologist Edward Foster (Keach). "It's hard enough for a man but for a woman it would be nearly impossible," Foster warns of the journey ahead. When Foster kills a tarantula that threatens Susan, their native helpers quickly determine a sacrifice is required to redress the balance. They cut up a small lizard, skin it and eat it. As they chomp on offal, Foster reminds the disgusted onlookers that "It's part of their religion".

Asaro, one of the helpers, constantly eyes Susan. "Why does he look at me that strange way?" she asks. "Don't worry, he's shy," explains Foster. The journey to the mountain progresses in this fashion. The helpers are systematically diminished, either by crocodile attack, flights of panic, animal traps, or simply go missing, as in the case of Asaro. The remaining members of the team encounter a mission run by Father Moses who warns them of the Puka, a tribe of cannibals. The end takes place in a cave. The Puka slowly disembowel Arthur's corpse, protracting the horrible image by removing his intestines slowly and deliberately, in the manner of a magician drawing a string of silk scarves from a hat.

Although the film's excesses aren't as intense or frequent as those in, say, *Cannibal Holocaust* – showing instead "the (relatively) lighter side of Italian cannibal picture," as noted in the *Delirium* guidebook – *Prisoner of the Cannibal God* remains typical of the genre. The killings follow a contrived evolutionary-racist trajectory: first an insect is killed, then a reptile; next a crocodile kills a black man; black men die at the hands of black men; white man kills black man in self-defence; white man dies from white man's negligence, and finally the 'ultimate' taboo, white man is killed and devoured by black men.

Director Sergio Martino is typical of a jobbing Italian director, having worked in many genres. He credits *Prisoner of the Cannibal God* as one of his most successful films in the foreign markets and followed it with the jungle-themed *Island of Mutations* and *The Great Alligator*. The concept of a jungle adventure yarn with two 'name' stars – pre-dating the big-budget adventure of Michael Douglas

Ursula Andress is a *Prisoner of the Cannibal God*.

and Kathleen Turner in *Romancing the Stone* – succeeded in drawing crowds that otherwise may not have cared for entrails and animal slaughter. *Screen International* was surprised that an actor of Stacy Keach's stature would partake in such a gruesome venture, but determined the rest of the cast toiled just as hard, including Ursula Andress,

> who leaps about on rocks, slogs up the mountain foothills, swims in the river, and strips down to the skin, as if *Dr No* had been filmed no more than a couple of years ago.

Hokushin released *Prisoner of the Cannibal God* on video carrying the BBFC X-certificate granted the film on its 1979 theatrical run (when it was well received by the *Monthly Film Bulletin*, saying it was "executed with spirited authenticity"). The video boxes were the older cardboard slipcase variety, and a sticker – 'Video Movies' – obscured the wording 'Entertainment in Video with Hokushin,' presumably because Entertainment in Video was a company in its own right.

As the plane bringing Susan to New Guinea screeches along the runway at the beginning of the picture, the film freezes abruptly for a written introduction:

> New Guinea is perhaps the last region on Earth which still contains immense unexplored areas shrouded in mystery, where life has remained at its primordial level...

As if an afterthought, the text promptly disappears again, and the plane continues with its noisy landing.

REVENGE OF THE BOGEY MAN

title on print: Revenge of the Boogeyman
USA 1982
cast: Suzanna Love, Shannah Hall, Sholto von Douglas, John Carradine
story: [not credited]
exec producers: David Dubay & Jochem Breitenstein
director: [not credited: ULLI LOMMEL]

In the Hollywood Hills, a film director is at loggerheads with his producer about their next movie. A spate of deaths in the area seems to be connected to a supernatural entity.

SO MUCH EXTRANEOUS dialogue is spent on filmmakers and film-making, one gets the impression that *Revenge of the Bogeyman* (aka *Revenge of the Boogeyman*) has a forgotten subtext within its lame splatter façade. A follow-up to *The Bogey Man*, it opens with film-maker Mickey shooting topless scenes because his producer, Bernie, wants to turn his proposed arthouse movie into one that'll make money. He also wants to change the title from *Natalie and the Age of Diminishing Expectations* to the more commercial *Kiss and Tell*. "In America exploitation is a genre," Bernie impresses upon the "artsy fartsy" European director. The two have much the same argument later in the picture, after Lacey shows up, a character from the previous film. She recounts a story about murders in her hometown and a killer yet to be apprehended. Bernie sees potential in the story and believes it could lead to a new kind of horror film. "*Halloween* and stuff like that is old hat," Bernie tells Mickey.

This latent anti-Hollywood stance takes on a deeper significance given that "arty fartsy" Mickey is played by director Ulli Lommel – who, moping around in a leather jacket, is neither likeable nor a rebel, just a bit pathetic. Lommel directed the original *Bogey Man* but isn't credited as director on this follow-up – most sources bestow that dubious honour on one 'Bruce Starr'. In the British print,[1] Starr is credited only as Line Producer and there is no credit for director, although a title card proclaims *Revenge of the Bogeyman* to be "An Ulli Lommel Film."

Lommel is often regarded as a 'serious' German film-maker thanks to an early association with Fassbinder and a powerful directorial debut in *Tenderness of the Wolves*. Commercial success with *The Bogey Man* obviously weighed heavily on the director's artistic sensitivities, however, manifesting itself in the strange Mickey character for this follow-up, through which Lommel denigrates the very genre to which he is contributing. Whoever Bruce Starr might be,[2] Lommel can't shirk all responsibility for *Revenge of the Bogeyman*. Footage from his original film constitutes an inordinately large amount of running time, while much of the new material bears his idiosyncratic hallmarks, such as the inventive deaths that take place at a party for "low-budget Hollywood types." Also, Suzanna Love, Lommel's wife until 1987, once again appears in the starring role.

Trauma to the mouth is common to both films, while the preposterous death by electric toothbrush in *Revenge* – sadly, the film's highlight – is also replicated in Lommel's thriller the subsequent year, *Double Jeopardy* (prompting one critic to ruminate whether the director has "an oral hygiene fetish").[3]

Perhaps most disappointing is the apathy displayed in *Revenge of the Bogeyman*. Despite its evident resources and talent, no effort has been made and it looks every bit like the filmmakers had their sights firmly on their bank balance. That half its running time is filled with footage from the earlier movie is indefensible, but *Revenge of the Bogeyman* also denigrates other films time and time again to propel itself to a position of superiority. Midway through, a guest encourages Mickey to take on Lacey's story as a project, reasoning that "Brian de Palma spent $18 million on that bomb of his, *Blow Out*. You could make fifty movies for that."[4] The same guest then confesses to never personally watching horror films. Whatever significance the dialogue concerning de Palma may hold,[5] it is turned on its head in the penultimate scene – a hand reaching out from a grave being a direct lift from de Palma's *Carrie*.[6]

A close-up on Mickey's face during *Revenge*'s farcical closing moments reveals not an expression of horror, shock or incredulity, but barely concealed boredom. It'd be reassuring to interpret these passages and dialogues as indicative of the tired state of exploitation in general, but more likely Lommel really is bored. Jokes are delivered with aplomb; battery operated toys jump suddenly to life for no better reason than such scenes were effective in *Close Encounters of the Third Kind*; eerie lighting lends desperately needed 'mood' to periods of absolute static; and the fanfare that comes with the unmasking of the killer overlooks the many red herrings, such as white-gloved hands belonging to a manservant evident every time a murder is committed. Or the Native American arrowhead that Lacey keeps in a box, supposedly given to her by a medicine man of the "Chinkatink" tribe. Must we go on?

Its association with the original *Bogey Man* is the only reason this travesty landed on the DPP list. However, unlike that first film, *Revenge* is completely bereft of gore, and even the gore in the plentiful flashbacks has been removed.[7] The two films were released independently by different video companies, at a time when certification was yet to be made compulsory. Presumably, VTC – distributors of *Revenge of the Bogeyman* – were either sensitive to the rising backlash against violent videos and cut the film themselves or acquired a heavily butchered US print.

SHOGUN ASSASSIN

USA 1980
cast: Tomisaburo Wakayama, Kayo Matsuo, Minoru Ohki, Shoji Kohayashi, Shin Kishida
screenplay: Kazuo Koike, Robert Houston & David Weisman
producer: David Weisman
director: ROBERT HOUSTON
[Shogun Assassin is a composite of two episodes in the Japanese 'Baby Cart' series of films directed by KENJI MISUMI in the early seventies.]

The paranoid Shogun wants his chief executioner, Lone Wolf, killed. A series of ninjas fail in the task and so Lone Wolf and his infant son, Daigoro, wander the land, assassins for hire.

SHOGUN ASSASSIN OPENS with the voiceover narration of Lone Wolf's infant child, Daigoro: "When I was little, my father was famous. He was the greatest samurai in the Empire."

With these innocently delivered words there begins an extraordinary bloodbath of eighty-five minutes that rarely lets up.

"He was the Shogun's decapitator," Daigoro continues. "He cut off the heads of 131 Lords for the Shogun."

Awash in blood – *Shogun Assassin*.

The renegade Lone Wolf speaks little. Following the murder of his wife and the subsequent double-dealing of the decrepit, evil Shogun, he becomes something of a demon spirit wandering the highways of sixteenth-century Japan with his infant. "He became an assassin who walks the road of vengeance," narrates the boy, "and he took me with him." Lone Wolf easily demolishes those who stand in his way with a few deft strokes of his powerful sword (so deft and powerful in fact that when he chops at a foe, he cuts them clean in two, along with anything else that happens to be in the way). Lone Wolf plunges his sword through necks, breaks the swords of others in battle, and even manages to hurl his sword into opponents.

The bloodletting is stylish to the point of beauty. Decapitations and limb-hackings are followed by a momentary stillness, where both victor and victim stand motionless – until a crimson gush from the horrific wound engages the action once again and the victim collapses to the ground. It is as if Lone Wolf's retribution is so swift that his victims need time to contemplate and recognise their own demise, mind and automatic reflexes momentarily frozen (space and time, too). In his battle with the Masters of Death, bodyguards of the Shogun, Lone Wolf swings his sword into the head of one opponent so deftly that the logic and law of physics seems to have been caught unaware. The victim stands bolt

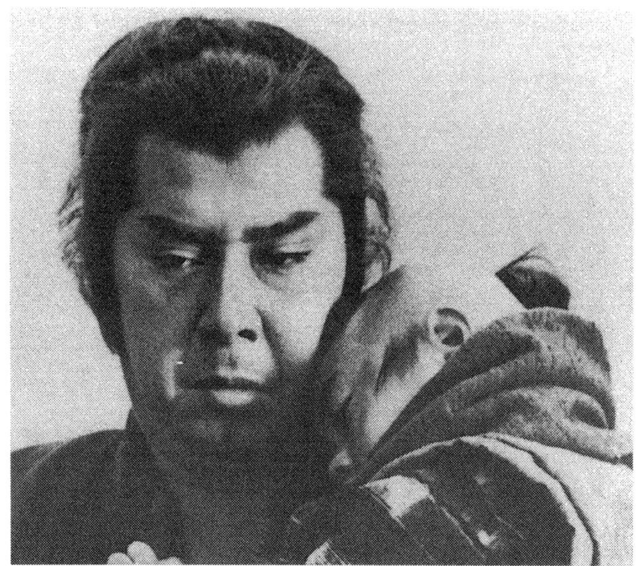
Lone Wolf and Daigoro. *Shogun Assassin*.

upright, and long moments pass before eventually his straw hat falls away, split in half, and his head slowly, unnaturally, splits asunder. A fountain of blood flies into the air for several feet for a finishing touch.

In another memorable sequence, a group of female ninjas prove their mettle in a tournament against the best fighter their male counterparts can offer. In what is a very lopsided exercise (several against one), the male opponent is immobilised and mercilessly hacked to pieces. His face is sliced away, then his limbs, leaving a raw bloody stump.

Not only does *Shogun Assassin* have episodes of wild exaggerated violence, it also has poignant moments – notably the sequence where Daigoro tries to carry water to his father who has fallen ill. Each trip to the river yields nothing as the water soon spills from the infant's cupped hands. Finally he brings the water in his mouth and dribbles it onto his father's lips. Another scene may have caused offence for the more brittle-minded. Following the sinking of a ship on which they're travelling, Daigoro keeps warm between his naked father and "the Supreme ninja", one of the female ninjas whose life his father has spared. The boy playfully brushes one of her nipples with his hand, causing it to become erect.

The film is augmented by the voiceover narration of the infant (in fact the voice of comedienne/actress Sandra Bernhard – a remarkable performance that has fooled fans and critics alike into thinking a genuine non-actor child was utilised). Stumbling over words, the childish observations are a touching counterpoint to the mayhem. A fairy tale quality is established in the opening moments when Daigoro tells of the senile Shogun, who his father once worked for. The Shogun is said to have locked himself away because he believed his people were conspiring against him. "People said he had a lot of enemies," relates Daigoro, "but he killed more people than that." The boy even has a few fighting tricks of his own, and the wooden pram in which he travels – pushed along by his father – conceals a multitude of deadly blades.[1]

The idea of a young child in the company of a professional assassin, exposed to violence and death, was later explored in Jean Luc Besson's *Léon*, which, in some respects, could be considered a remake of *Shogun Assassin*. John Carpenter took the Masters of Death – assassins who, respectively, utilise a spiked club, a studded glove and a claw – and recreated them as the Three Storms in his own *Big Trouble in Little China*.

Shogun Assassin is constructed from two episodes of the cult Japanese 'Baby Cart' series of films (of which there were six) – namely *Sword of Vengeance* and *Baby Cart at the River Styx*.[2] It works well as a seamless composite, and indeed surpasses the source material in some respects. For a start, it removes much expositional dialogue and concentrates almost exclusively on an action narrative (the English language dialogue was written specifically to match the lips of the characters onscreen). The original films do not have Daigoro's voiceovers.[3] Much of the bloodletting in the two source films made the transition to *Shogun Assassin* (a title, incidentally, intended to cash-in on the *Shogun* TV miniseries). Conspicuous in its absence, however, is a shot of Lone Wolf slicing through the breasts and nipple of an attacking female ninja assassin.

Shogun Assassin is so awash in blood that no single scene can be responsible for its banned status. However this welter of spectacularly choreographed violence was soon dropped from the DPP list and the film re-released. (The two source films from which *Shogun Assassin* was constructed have also been made available in Britain.)

THE SLAYER

aka: Nightmare Island (working title)
USA 1981
cast: Sarah Kendall, Frederick Flynn, Carol Kottenbrook, Alam McRae, Michael Holmes
story: J S Cardone & William R Ewing
producer: William R Ewing
director: J S CARDONE

Failing to fully exploit its potential. *The Slayer*.

Two couples are on vacation at a resort on a secluded island. There is much to remind Kay of her nightmares. She cannot shake the sense of impending doom.

A DREAM WORLD that infringes on reality, with a murderer who can transgress the boundaries of sleep – this is the fascinating concept of J S Cardone's *The Slayer*. Wes Craven adopted it as his own *A Nightmare on Elm Street* two years later. Unlike Cardone's film, however, *A Nightmare on Elm Street* proved to be a huge success.

The dream sequence that opens *The Slayer* is subtle and effective, with Kay's pallid face peering, wide-eyed, from a black backdrop. Cutting between open doorways and a swinging pendulum, the whole sequence is reminiscent of German Expressionist cinema and, unfortunately, hints at a quality of production that the film struggles vainly to maintain. Cardone fails to fully exploit the potential of *The Slayer* and instead relegates the idea of a deadly dream state to the backburner. The film plays more as a stalk-and-slash movie tinged with an element of the supernatural, while adhering to obvious clichés and scare tactics (with an inordinate number of doors creaking and shutters banging throughout the duration). It also features the usual stock of tired characters who insist on the group 'splitting up' so that they may go searching for missing companions on their own (gone, it seems, for days at a time). *The Slayer* doesn't really bother to explore the more interesting avenues promised by Kay's predicament until the very end of the picture, by which time it's late enough to qualify as a twist ending. Kay waking up as a little girl, only to discover that her dream is a reality yet to happen, is a pretty good twist, nonetheless.

The characters in *The Slayer* – like the stalk-and-slash sub-genre in general – serve only to be slaughtered in a variety of graphic and disagreeable ways. The first character to be murdered, a fisherman on a beach who gets an oar smashed across his head, has no bearing whatsoever on the story. No one is aware of his presence. No one finds the body. The guy just sits on the beach – of a supposedly deserted island[1] – gutting fishes. The entirety of his screen time comprises the moment of his effectively rendered death. His gutting of fish plies the scene with an expectation of a demise far worse than a 'mere' oar across the head. If nothing else, his brief presence lends the film and subsequent murders a lopsided attitude.

The simplicity of the fisherman's death is amply made up for in the orchestrated deaths that follow. The demise of David, Kay's husband, is particularly contrived. After an eternity of following a noise around the house, David finds himself in the cellar, standing under a trapdoor that leads to an elevator shaft. A pair of stepladders enables him to access the shaft, whereupon David gets his head caught, loses balance on the stepladders and unwittingly hangs himself.

But it is Kay's sister-in-law Brooke who has the most salacious and explicit murder,[2] the one sequence cut on the film's re-release by Vipco in the nineties.[3] Searching a boathouse for her husband (and appearing to find something significant in the name of a boat she sees there), Brooke is frightened by an unseen assailant. She attempts to escape through a boarded window but is impaled on a pitchfork. The scene culminates with the fork prongs jutting out from the woman's bosom, her nipples clearly visible through her blood-soaked frock, treading an area of sexual violence abhorred by the BBFC.

Following *The Slayer*, Cardone went on to direct other films with themes concerning dream states and shifting realities (*Shadowzone* and *Shadow Hunter*). A downside to this of course is that dream realities also provide the perfect opportunity to squander the plot on red herrings, and a lazy storyline that never needs to fully be resolved.

The Slayer was released by Continental video in the US on a double bill with Fred Olen Ray's *Scalps*. Canadian author L A Morse in his book *Video Trash & Treasures* recalls that Cardone's name had been removed from some video versions of *The Slayer*.

Ridiculous but something of a relief, the end of *Snuff*.

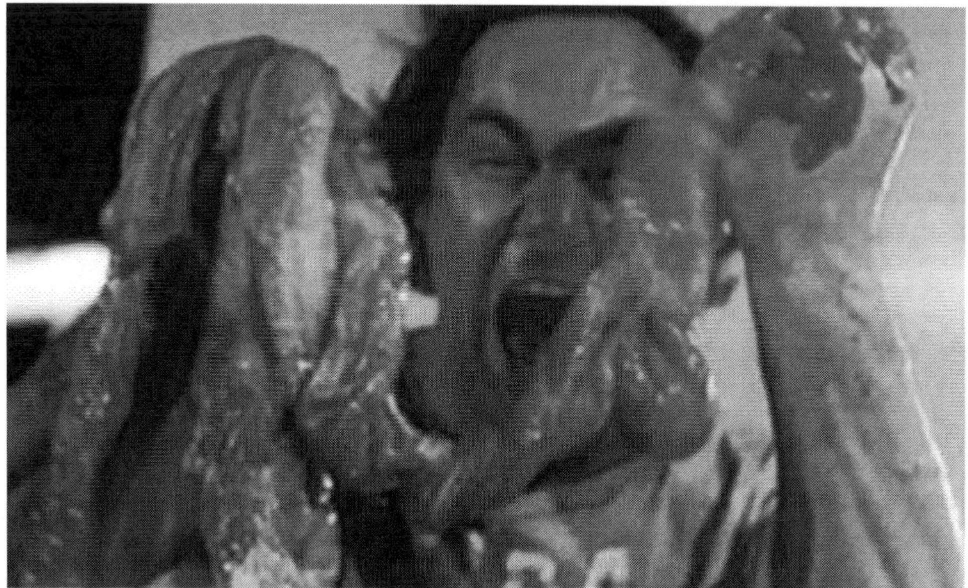

SNUFF

aka: Slaughter (original title); American Cannibale
Argentina/USA 1971/76
cast: [not credited]
story: [not credited]
producers: [not credited: Michael Findlay & Jack Frost]
director: [not credited: MICHAEL FINDLAY & CARTER STEVENS]

A movie loosely inspired by the murder of Sharon Tate by the Manson Family. The final act supposedly features an authentic murder.

"THE ORIGINAL NASTY" is how the *Sunday Times* described *Snuff* in November 1982. The ending of the film motivates viewers into believing they are privy to a great conspiratorial secret; that the last five minutes are a fleeting glimpse of something so abhorrent it can only be referred to in breathless, hushed tones.

Jerky, *cinéma-vérité* camerawork is a technique often used to create a sense of urgency and 'heightened reality' from staged scenes. Mondo documentary filmmakers,[1] and indeed the makers of *Snuff*, used it to fool viewers into thinking they were witnessing a factual document. In this case, an authentic murder taking place on camera.

At the turn of the century, pulp horror writers like H P Lovecraft often presented stories in the form of a forgotten manuscript or diary that had fallen into the hands of the narrator. As these stories unfolded, the incredulous narrator slowly came to terms with the lurking horror that the script spoke of – until, too late, the evil is at their own door. The stories were presented as a 'warning' to the rest of mankind. In this instance 'snuff films' are the 'lurking horror' – human sacrifices perpetrated for the benefit of a film camera, supposedly circulated as entertainment to those people said to be jaded by conventional pornography.[2] These films were said to be distributed via underground networks and difficult, nigh on impossible, to locate. *Snuff* purported to be a rare insight into this hitherto hidden cinema. It 'clued' the public in with ambiguous advertising that promised:

> The film that could only be made in South America... Where Life is *CHEAP!*
> The *Bloodiest* thing that *ever* happened in front of a camera!

However, no one who sat through the ridiculous 'snuff' footage was liable to be fooled into thinking it was anything but a combination of cheap prosthetic effects and animal innards. Still, having endured seventy interminable minutes of plodding direction and a dull story, this impromptu ending came as a relief, signalling the end of the film if nothing else.

Snuff started out as a cash-in on the media furore surrounding the Tate/LaBianca slayings for which Charles Manson and some of his hippie followers were being charged. It was filmed in 1971 in Argentina under the title of *Slaughter*, by husband and wife team, Michael and Roberta Findlay.[3] In Argentina, the Findlays were able to hire a film crew for just $60 a week, and complete the film in four weeks at a total cost of $30,000.[4] (Not for the reason insinuated in the film's advertising, the film really was made where life is cheap.) Sound was dubbed later, partly because many of the players spoke no English – which is why some conversations and reactions in the film seem stilted. The Findlays weren't particularly concerned about coming up with an original story and so shot *Slaughter* as a virtual reconstruction of the most sensational aspect of the Manson Family case – the attack on the home of Roman Polanski and the murder of Polanski's actress wife, Sharon Tate. The heavily pregnant Tate was stabbed sixteen times and left to die. Several guests were also murdered.

Although it was one of the first films to exploit hippie cult hysteria,[5] *Slaughter* never got released. It was simply too awful a film for distributors to risk an investment.[6] Allan Shackleton of the Monarch Releasing Corporation eventually picked it up, and kept it shelved until 1976.[7] The original film didn't include the cutaway that supposedly featured the on-camera murder of a crew member; this was something Shackleton dreamed up.

Roberta Findlay recollected in an interview in *CCVL*,[8] that in the mid seventies rumours of so-called snuff films began to circulate. "I don't know that they ever existed," Findlay said. "Maybe they did, maybe they didn't. Shackleton was reading the paper and said, 'Hey, that's a great idea, that's what I'll call the film.' And that's what he did."

However, there is a strong likelihood that newspaper reports in the *New York Post* dated October 2, 1975, and the *Daily News* the following day, originated from Shackleton himself. Both speak of a film rumoured to have been made in Argentina in which a woman is stabbed. A New York detective quoted in both newspapers stated that 'snuff' films were the ultimate obscenity and available through underworld sources, although later he admitted to the FBI that he had never heard of 'snuff' films before the *New York Post* got in touch.

The story can be traced back to the *National Decency Reporter*, a newsletter issued by an anti-pornography organisation, Citizens for Decency through Law, Inc. The edition dated November-December 1974 contained an article entitled 'Perversion for Profit', which lamented how young people were on a slippery slope. "Just as the liquor industry depends on alcoholics," stated the anonymous writer, "the sexual pervert constitutes pornography's major market." Moreover, as many as twenty-five 'snuff' films were said to be in current circulation and urged citizens "to demand strict enforcement of obscenity laws."[9]

Shackleton changed the title of his film from *Slaughter* to *Snuff*, removed all credits, and hired Simon Nuchtern to shoot the now notorious coda. Nuchtern ran a company in New York that provided production and post-production services. He shot the footage in the apartment studio of porn director Carter Stevens.[10] This new material was brief but provided Shackleton with the angle he needed to spring his exploitation film into a competitive marketplace. With an advertising campaign that made no mention of Manson or killer hippies – but which insinuated that the carnage on screen was genuine, and that a life was being taken for purposes of entertainment – Shackleton foisted *Snuff* onto a public very much familiar with the recent news reports. Not only that, but he also organised pickets to stand outside theatres that showed the film and planted 'high-profile' FBI agents among the crowds. He also contacted feminist organisations – outraged by *Deep Throat* – and 'tipped them off.' They in turn picketed theatres and handed out leaflets which called on "women and other persons of conscience" to demonstrate against the film. Naturally, such acts served to fuel more publicity, and soon *Snuff* – and demonstrations against it – were making primetime news.

The genuine FBI had already begun to investigate Shackleton and his film.

The Freedom of Information and Privacy Acts has made numerous FBI files available, no less those pertaining to supposed 'snuff' films – or 'snuffers'. These files reveal how Shackleton's *Snuff* was under observation following announcements of its imminent release in the trade papers. When it premiered at the Uptown Theatre in Indianapolis on January 16, 1976, FBI agents and an MD-Pathologist attended the screening. They determined that no hardcore pornography was involved and the closing murder "was a staged theatrical production". Special Agents who viewed the film in other parts of the country arrived at the same conclusion.

So great was the furore that had built up around *Snuff* that Robert M Morgenthau, district attorney for Manhattan, was pressed to announce publicly that the murder of a woman in the film was a hoax – the actress having been traced and found to be alive and well. But attacks on *Snuff* didn't stop once it was 'officially' revealed to be a scam, albeit a tasteless one. Organisations simply changed tack and protested the *idea* of a film like *Snuff*. "Whether or not the death depicted in the current film *Snuff* is real or simulated is not the issue," stated one flyer distributed by feminist groups.

Although many years have passed since the film was released and 'debunked,' *Snuff* is still largely perceived as a genuine snuff film by the ignorant. Perversely, many who do acknowledge *Snuff* as a 'fake' believe it represents proof that genuine snuff films do exist. In an episode of the BBC fly-on-the-wall documentary series, *Fraud Squad* (aired towards the end of 1998), Trading Standards officers descended on a car boot sale to confront a trader suspected of selling illegal video cassettes. Amongst the tapes in the man's possession was a copy of *Snuff*, which prompted one officer to remark to the camera that the film featured a real death. (The trader took the opportunity to run away.)

Reporting from a press conference organised by the BVA in April 1983, Liam T Sanford of the *Video Viewer* noted the hostile, knee-jerk reaction to the subject of 'video nasties'. To counter the growing backlash, the BVA wanted to propose plans for a certification scheme for movies on video (this prior to the VRA). Following a Q&A session, where he claims to have been snubbed by the panel for lack of outright condemnation of the 'nasties', Sanford interviewed Norman Abbott, chief executive of the BVA. One question concerned the media's unchecked allegations that *Snuff* was a genuine 'snuff' film, and Abbott was asked why the BVA hadn't stepped forward on the matter. Abbott's curious reply: "It probably is not illegal to make a film of a real murder. It's probably not contrary to the Obscene Publications Act."

Sanford countered that *Snuff* didn't feature a real murder. Abbott continued:

> Every bulletin from Northern Ireland and Falklands war newsreel, could be held to be obscene because they're showing real killing. If it depraves and corrupts, it doesn't matter if what is depicted is real or simulated under the strict terms of the Act. It's quite another question if you put someone to death. That is *murder* and therefore a crime that should be punished. As far as the Obscene Publications Act is concerned, I don't think the filming of a murder has much relevance on the subject.[11]

The availability of *Snuff* on video in Britain is veiled in some mystery. It could be found languishing on video shelves across the country in the days before certification, and – like many other films – promptly disappeared soon after the Video Recordings Act was introduced. But who exactly was distributing it isn't clear. Astra picked the film up and scheduled it for release in May 1982 but, following hostile press, supposedly retracted this decision. No copies had been released, Astra told a *Sunday Times* reporter on May 29, in spite of large orders. Copies did make it into circulation, however, which either suggests that Astra – despite claims to the contrary – continued to handle the film, or that parties unknown issued copies. The *Sunday Times* dated January 16, 1983, noted that

> Thousands of people in Britain who have bought what is considered to be the granddaddy of all 'video nasties,' a noxious movie called *Snuff*, appear to have been conned by black-market pirates.
>
> The pirates have been doing a brisk trade at £15 a copy with a cassette labelled *Snuff*, advertised as 'the original legendary atrocity'...

How people could be "conned" into buying a pirate of a film supposedly not in general release doesn't make a lot of sense. *Snuff* (replete with professional packaging) was most definitely available prior to the clampdown of the Video Recordings Act 1984, even though it never had an official release in Britain. In keeping with Shackleton's original promotional gimmick, British copies lacked cast and credit details – the deception extended to keeping the identity of the British distributor a secret; no company name appeared on either the video box or cassette label.[12] In a trade catalogue published by Land of Video Victoria in the eighties, *Snuff* was one of the titles for which the supplier was listed as "unknown."

SS EXPERIMENT CAMP

aka: SS Experiment; SS Experiment Love Camp; Horreur Nazis; Kastrat Commandatur Satirlagher 23; Le Camp des Filles Perdeues; SS Vrouwenkamp

Italy 1976

cast: Mircha Carven, Paola Corazzi, Giorgio Cerioni, Giovanna Mainardi, Serafino Profumo, Attilio Dottesio, Patrizia Melega

story: Sergio Chiusi

dir of production: Mario Caporali

director: SERGIO GARRONE

Female prisoners and their male guards are subjected to sex experiments in a Nazi prison camp during WWII.

SERGIO GARRONE HAS close on two dozen movies to his credit, reflecting the typically eclectic mix of themes and trends found in Italian exploitation. He shot two horror movies starring Klaus Kinski back-to-back in 1974,[1] a cut-rate endeavour that encouraged Garrone to follow suit a couple of years later with *SS Experiment Camp* and the reputedly nastier *SS Camp 5 Women's Hell* (never officially released in Britain). From here Garrone made only a few more films – the last of which had women-in-prison themes – before retiring from the business.[2] According to an article in *Shock Xpress*,[3] Garrone made his two Nazi camp films for foreign exploitation markets only, claiming that the Nazi theme was a means of getting screen violence past the censors intact.

Garrone rides a bandwagon with these films. But the claim that he "intended neither of them in any way for denunciation" is seemingly supported in *SS Experiment Camp*, which takes pains to avoid identifying the Nazi prisoners as Jewish.[4] Then again, the whole film seems to be taking place in an alternative dimension, where the trappings are those of WWII, but details are twisted or erased. Here, prisoners are more concerned with good-looking Nazi soldiers than they are the torment and indignities of life in a concentration camp, passing comments like, "There's a beautiful man. He'll be able to cure our insomnia." One prisoner, following a tryst with a lesbian doctor, turns to her friends and tells them, "It's incredible – you'll see!" When Helmut and Mirelle – a kind-hearted soldier and a restless prisoner – manage to steal time together, she confides in him, "All this happiness is frightening." ("You're in no position to be in love with someone – especially a Kraut," says a friend, trying to return the lovesick Mirelle to earth.) The prisoners have clearly visible tan-lines and each look the picture of good health. The sole exception are two women in the pre-credit sequence, tortured with electricity – they have sunken eyes and sallow complexions – but the camera manages to steal a wily look at their naked breasts. The clandestine sharing of a cigarette adds to the summer camp atmosphere, as do beefcake soldiers who lounge around their barracks in shorts, pondering the nature of the experiment soon to take place. "With all those beautiful women arriving," says one soldier, "I hope it's a secret mission of a sexual nature."

The goal of the experiment in question is the "proliferation of the German empire," and soldiers are paired off with prisoners. One couple has sexual intercourse partially submerged in a vat of liquid, others are on beds. Fortuitously, Helmut is paired with Mirelle, the girl to whom he gave his cigarettes. She has been sedated, but tells him, "For this there was no need to drug me."

Overseeing the camp is the Colonel, interested in the transplantation of sex organs. One nurse assists with a uterus transplant by rubbing the patient's thigh in a neat circular motion. Elsewhere, the Colonel blackmails one doctor under his command when he discovers he is a famous Jewish surgeon in disguise. It's a wonder Dr Steiner's identity wasn't discovered sooner, given that he spends his evenings in Orthodox Jewish clothing. The Colonel orders Steiner to replace the testicles bitten off by one prisoner. The unwitting donor is Helmut, whose testicles are the size of chicken eggs. But the Colonel gets his comeuppance in the end. Helmut, armed with a machine gun, confronts the Colonel in the final scenes. "How have you been doing with my balls?" he asks before the Colonel is overpowered and killed by the now-free prisoners.

There are other odd, unintentionally humorous, or downright surreal, moments. Guards spy a naked girl making a break for it and ask themselves, "Look at that. Where the hell does she think she's going?" We see the crematorium at work but the scene is constructed in a fashion that looks as if Garrone is interpreting the horror via experimental dance: naked women jerk their limbs in a syncopated fashion as superimposed flames lap over them. The film doesn't so much end as *stop*: there is a gun battle in which Helmut is shot, the sound goes dead, and he falls to the floor with the words 'The End' appearing onscreen.

SS Experiment Camp is one of the most notorious films on the DPP list. This is less to do with the content, mainly softcore sex and lame gore, and more to do with its title and notorious ad campaign for the video release. (See CLAMPDOWN.)

TENEBRAE

aka: Tenebre (original title); Unsane
Italy 1982
cast: Anthony Franciosa, John Saxon, Christian Borromeo, Mirella D'Angelo, Daria Nicolodi
story: Dario Argento
producer: Claudio Argento
director: DARIO ARGENTO

Best-selling crime author Peter Neal visits Rome on a promotional tour for his latest book. Sadistic murders follow, mirroring those described in the book.

FULL OF ENERGY and confidence – lacking in Dario Argento's later work – *Tenebrae* bristles with arresting imagery and a cracking musical score from ex-members of Goblin.[1] It also makes a beautiful spectacle of celluloid murder, with glamorous semi-naked women falling victim to an anonymous, black-gloved killer. Death is painted against a backdrop of pure white (underwear) and splashes of impossibly red blood in brightly lit surroundings – like noir in reverse.

Argento subverts the sexism argument that dogged horror films of the late seventies and eighties by incorporating and questioning it, courtesy of the eponymous novel, 'Tenebrae,' that author, Peter Neal (Anthony Franciosa), is promoting. Tilde, a journalist, accuses Neal of writing sexist novels that contain violence against women. For a while it looks as if Argento might trounce the argument and posit it in a long line of red herrings. Ultimately, he seems to support the argument levelled at Neal (and by extension at himself), killing Tilde in brutal fashion. Like all the victims in *Tenebrae*, she ends up like one of the ciphers that Neal is accused of incorporating in his work. An intelligent, feminist journalist who happens to be a lesbian, she is dispatched as an object – her face and identity obscured at the moment the killer strikes, pulling a shirt over her head at the time of death.

The twist in the end is that the homicidal murderer tailing Neal is, in fact, Neal. He is the killer. The film's coda, a falling metal sculpture that impales and kills Neal, is indicative of Argento's own stand on the sexist/misogynist debate: he shows

Tenebrae – noir in reverse.

murder because it looks good and is engaging. Alive, his girls look like models; dead they still look like models. As per the ugly metal sculpture, he seems to say that it is art. "Art as killing, killing as art," stated one critic of *Tenebrae*.[2] Argento doesn't address the issue of sexism earnestly because he doesn't believe in it. To him, "The fact that Peter Neal turns out to be a murderer is just a game, it shows how foolish people can be."[3] When *Halls of Horror* asked, in 1978, why his movies were so gory, Argento replied: "Because I make violent movies, and because the blood is an inseparable part of them."[4]

After the supernatural-themed horror of *Suspiria* and *Inferno*, *Tenebrae* marked the director's return to the giallo thriller of his early career.[5] (It was supposedly inspired by a true-life incident in which a fan obsessed with *Suspiria* had threatened to kill him.) Its original title was *Tenebre*, Italian for 'darkness,' but became *Tenebrae* when released in Britain.[6] Argento originally conceived the role of Peter Neal should be played by Christopher Walken, and for reasons unknown has claimed the film is set five years in the future.

Tenebrae was passed by the BBFC for theatrical release in 1983, with a few seconds cut from a sequence in which an axe chops off an arm at the film's end. It was this version that Videomedia released on video, and which was determined by the DPP to be a 'nasty'. Further cuts were made to this same sequence when

Tenebrae was submitted to the BBFC and classified 18 for video release in 1999. (See also SEX & WRECKS.) The panning shot that traverses a house in a single take – a spectacular achievement in the eighties and one of the film's cinematic highlights – now, conversely, appears unnecessary and clumsy.

TERROR EYES

aka: Night School
USA 1980
cast: Leonard Mann, Rachel Ward, Drew Snyder, Joseph R Sicari
story: Ruth Avergon
producers: Larry Babb & Ruth Avergon
director: KENNETH HUGHES

A mystery figure in a motorcycle helmet is responsible for a spate of decapitations. Suspicion falls on Prof Millett, teaching anthropology at a night school.

THIS LAME ENTRY in the stalk-and-slash cycle of films is far from representative of the director's earlier work, which includes *The Trials of Oscar Wilde*, *Arriverderci, Baby*, *Casino Royale* (co-director), and *Chitty Chitty Bang Bang*. Given his association with stars like Peter Sellers, Orson Welles, Richard Harris, Alec Guinness, Peter Finch, and even an aged Mae West (in her last "sin-sational" movie, *Sextette*), it is ironic, but fitting, that the best Hughes could muster for *Terror Eyes* is Rachel Ward. She is described on the video box as "Burt Reynolds' beautiful leading lady in *Sharkey's Machine*."

Made in the same year as *Friday the 13th*, Hughes' film completely lacks the grisly set-pieces that became essential to the slasher genre. This goes some way in explaining the film's slim profile and complete absence from several genre-related books. Nothing about it rings true: Why is the night school at the centre of the film exclusive to girls? What manner of detective is the curiously named Taj, who volunteers nothing but wisecracks when faced with a fresh victim? Taj also pulls a lame stunt at the film's end that would have gotten his head blown off in an ideal world. Not that Hughes passes an opportunity to slip into cliché:

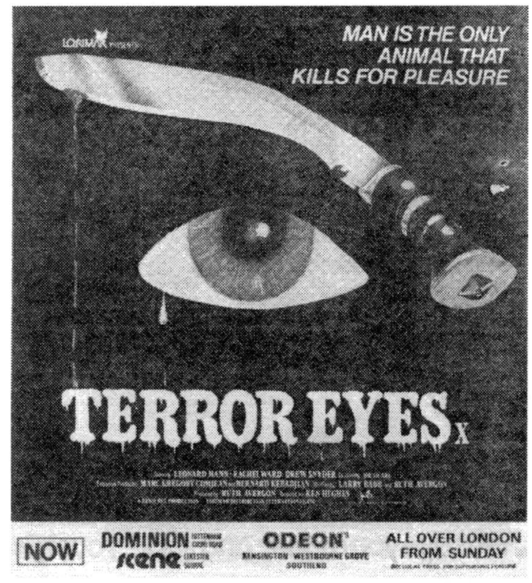

Judd Austin is introduced as a workaholic police lieutenant, who, to the chagrin of his girlfriend, gets called into work on his day off. We never see or hear any more of their relationship, so this set-up is completely irrelevant to the film that follows. There is also a shower scene that threatens to become a bloodbath, but a menacing silhouette turns out to be one of many red herrings. Nonetheless, the director is obligated to pursue the tired *Psycho* reference, except that this shower ends not with blood circling down a drain, as per Hitchcock, but red jam. That's right – a pot of jam is brought into the shower, ostensibly for some messy foreplay.[1]

The motorcycle-helmeted killer is revealed to be a woman, a reversal of Brian de Palma's own Hitchcock riff, *Dressed To Kill* (made the same year, it features Michael Caine as a killer in drag). The only other suspects are blatant red herrings, so most viewers will have figured the twist long ago. Despite its relatively gore-free approach, it is likely that the protracted knife threats and relentless hacking at girls who are pleading for their lives steered *Terror Eyes* onto the DPP list.

THE TOOLBOX MURDERS

aka: Der Killer mit der Bohr-Maschine

USA 1978

cast: Cameron Mitchell, Pamelyn Ferdin, Wesley Eure, Nicholas Beauvy, Tim Donnelly, Aneta Corsaut, Faith McSwain, Marcie Drake

story: Neva Friedenn, Robert Easter & Ann Kindberg

producer: Tony Didio

director: DENNIS DONNELLY

Inspired by true incidents. *The Toolbox Murders*.

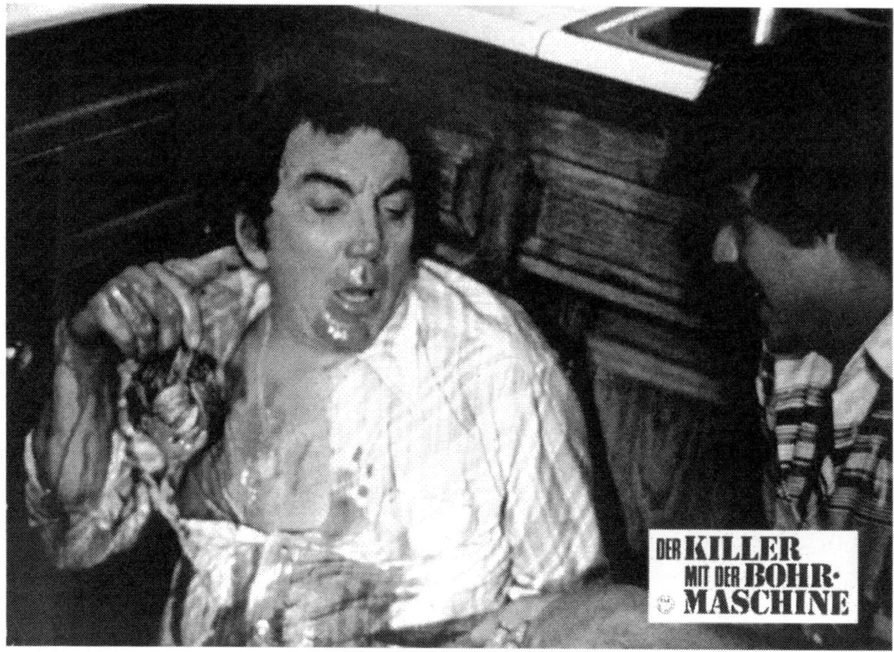

A handyman deploys the contents of his toolbox to kill the 'sinful' female inhabitants of the apartment block where he works.

A CAPTION INFORMS viewers that incidents in *The Toolbox Murders* occurred in 1967. But it seems the film's inspiration is derived exclusively from Tobe Hooper's *The Texas Chain Saw Massacre*: tools are used as murder implements; killers are family; deceased family members are venerated; and a woman is held captive, tortured, humiliated but ultimately escapes, dazed and bloodstained.

The deaths in the first part of the film are offensive, even in the version released on video in Britain, which was heavily cut. Censorial tampering has shifted the focus of the first murder to a record player sitting on a cabinet, albeit with brief flashes of a bloody drill bit.[1] Other scenes are also excised, often obscuring handyman Vance Kingsley's slim motivation for killing. A sequence in which one female tenant is shown masturbating in a bath has been removed completely. Only later, when Vance confesses, do we learn that he killed her because of the "unnatural things" she did to herself.

Even with its hard violence removed, *The Toolbox Murders* remains an unpleasant movie. Cameron Mitchell's portrayal of Vance is unduly nauseating.

He whistles, hums, grunts and sings during the murders, and during the lengthy monologues with Laurie, the tenant he kidnaps. However, Mitchell holds the film together and his death, when it comes, equals that of his victims.

Mitchell was a regular on the long-running TV western *The High Chaparral*, and in the forties and fifties appeared in movies like *How To Marry a Millionaire* and *Carousel*. In 1964, he played the lead in Mario Bava's seminal giallo thriller *Blood and Black Lace*. By the seventies, the only parts offered to him were in low-budget sci-fi and horror, such as *Frankenstein Island* and *Cataclysm*, and later direct-to-video fodder. Although Mitchell claimed to have no interest in gore pictures – "I make 'em, but I don't have to look at 'em!" he told Tom Weaver in *Attack of the Monster Movie Makers* – he seemed proud of his work in *The Toolbox Murders*. He told Weaver:

> The scene where I sing to the girl I'm holding prisoner was my idea; I thought that actress was quite good, Pamelyn Ferdin. The lollipop I carry around, anything weird like that was my idea! A lot of the odd touches that were any good were mine [laughs]! The human touches – 'cause even a killer is human, you know.

In the month before he passed, frail and barely able to raise his voice above a whisper, Mitchell managed to delight fans with an impromptu rendition of 'Sometimes I Feel Like A Motherless Child,' the song he sings in *The Toolbox Murders*.[2] Pamelyn Ferdin, who plays Laurie, for whom Mitchell sings his song, was for many years a popular TV and movie actress but quit showbusiness after *The Toolbox Murders* for Barbie doll commercials. More than Vance, it is his nephew Kent (Wesley Eure) who comes over as the most reprehensible character in the movie, pretending to be Laurie's saviour only to rape her. "You can't remain a little girl for the rest of your life," he tries to reason during her abuse.

To date *The Toolbox Murders* appears to be the only theatrical feature directed by Dennis Donnelly, usually associated with TV work, having directed popular shows like *Airwolf*, *The A-Team*, *Falcon Crest*, *Hart to Hart*, *Dallas*, *Hawaii Five-O* and *Charlie's Angels*. Given the opportunity to break out of his TV confines, one assumes Donnelly wanted to go well and truly overboard with *The Toolbox Murders*. "Disgusting and erotic," was a comment from one viewer.[3] But its hackneyed plot belies a certain TV influence, and the film comes over as little more than a particularly twisted episode of any given generic action show. The actors have little to play with (although, as we have seen, Mitchell brings something of his own to his role) and the whole thing is unnecessarily long and gory.

The Toolbox Murders played theatrically in the early eighties, supporting Fulci's *Zombie Flesh Eaters*. The sequence featuring the nail gun murder of Dee Ann (Marianne Walter, said to be porno actress 'Kelly Nichols') was shorn of three minutes and it was this BBFC X-certificate version that Hokushin released on video. Despite cuts, the film found itself for a time on the DPP list. Militant feminists, disturbed by the trend for stalk-and-slash movies, were particularly outraged by the bathtub masturbation and nail gun killing; it is worth noting that the film's release in Britain came at the tail end of the Yorkshire Ripper's true-life 'toolbox' killings. Jane Caputi, in *The Age of Sex Crime*, described the film as amongst those offering

> A veritable *Kama Sutra* of possible gynocidal [*sic*] styles and techniques: different tools, different settings, different victims, and different fetishes to appeal to the imaginations of as many viewers as possible.

Cameron Mitchell said that a *Toolbox Murders* sequel was in the pipeline – indeed in conversation with Tom Weaver he suggested that it had been "done" – but there has not been a legitimate follow-up: *Toolbox Murders 2*, in 2013, starred Bruce Dern as Vance Henrickson but was a retitle for *Coffin Baby* and otherwise unrelated. Few people admit to liking *The Toolbox Murders* – although Stephen King is supposedly a fan.

UNHINGED

aka: Stark Raving Mad [?]
USA 1982
cast: Laurel Munson, J E Penner, Sara Ansley, Virginia Settle, John Morrison, Barbara Lusch, Bill Simmonds
story: Don Gronquist & Reagan Ramsey
producer: Don Gronquist
director: DON GRONQUIST

The DPP39

'SCENES OF EXTREME AND EXPLICIT VIOLENCE'

Three young women find refuge in an isolated mansion after their car careens off the road. Their predicament proves not to be an accident.

AN EARLY CLUE to the film's twist ending comes with Norman Barnes, handyman to mansion-owners Marion Penrose and her wheelchair-bound mother, Edith – his name is clearly analogous to *Psycho*'s Norman Bates.[1] There are plenty of other parallels with Hitchcock's gender-reversal classic, including a reference to the mansion once having bustled with (paying) guests, the domineering mother, women who are spied on while in the shower, and a denouement that takes place in an attic (as opposed to a cellar). Even the title – *Unhinged* – doesn't stray too far from the proverbial ballpark.[2] But one gets the impression this is a homage rather than a rip-off, and the result is a mindless, mercifully short, piece of schlock entertainment.

Unhinged opens with Terry taking a shower – a sequence designed to wallow in as much flesh as possible short of revealing pubis, which would mean a stronger rating in America. She then chats briefly with her mother on the phone who warns her about the company she keeps and "gallivanting around the country." It's a seemingly throwaway dialogue that proves to have resonance when the end of the picture comes.[3] Travelling with her friends, Nancy and Gloria, to a "music festival", the wail of rock guitars on the car radio is interrupted by a local news report about the disappearance of two girls, just as a rainstorm starts and the car careens off the road. Thus the girls find themselves at a mansion inhabited by Marion Penrose and her wheelchair-bound mother, Edith.

Mrs Penrose carries out a lunatic ritual at mealtimes (she appears to be throttling a pepper pot). This serves no purpose, other than to pad out the running time and give the other diners the opportunity to stare blankly and throw meaningless glances at one another.

Sequences are separated by empty black film that lingers just a little too long (creating the uncomfortable impression the film has a fault and has stopped). More time is wasted with extensive aerial shots of the girls' car travelling along empty roads in the opening scenes. However, these are the only aerial shots in the film and establish a sense that the budget is larger – and the film more 'upmarket' – than it is.

The Penroses also have a habit of reiterating everything they say.

Thankfully, nothing too demanding is asked of the cast of five, given that the few outbursts from the elderly Penrose come over as ridiculous and contrived.

The girls sit around looking pretty, and having prepared for their rock concert by bringing along a full wardrobe and plenty of makeup. Terry and Nancy don't seem unduly bothered by their car accident, while their friend, Gloria, remains in bed and out of sight for the most part because of injuries sustained in the accident.

It's a traditional old dark house mystery, with a mysterious prowler and the gradual disappearance of the guests. At one point, Terry is woken in the night. She tells Nancy that the heavy breathing she heard sounded like a man "doing himself," at which point the girls decide they need to leave. The implication of a masturbating voyeur-killer is hardly enough to get the film banned. *Unhinged*'s most visceral sequence takes place in a shed when Terry stumbles upon a collection of corpses, past victims. But even here the bloody carcasses are presented in an abstract fashion (or incompetently, depending on the slack you are prepared to give the film) and the camera doesn't hang around the gore for too long. Similarly, the demise of each of the three girls comes spattered with blood aplenty but precious little is actually shown. The intensity with which Terry is dispatched at the end of the film, however, is brutal and holds one of the few surprises in the film: 'Marion Penrose' is the killer, a man in drag, as evidenced when the dress he is wearing is torn away to reveal a hairy chest. The pleading Terry is stabbed repeatedly with a hunting knife (out of shot) as the killer enunciates each strike with a vitriolic outburst of expositional dialogue. Even when Terry's screaming has tapered to nothing and a cutaway shows her dead eyes, Marion continues to plunge the knife down several more times.

Unhinged received a theatrical release in Britain in 1983.

Michael Ironside's façade of normality begins to crumble… *Visiting Hours.*

VISITING HOURS

Canada 1981

cast: Lee Grant, William Shatner, Michael Ironside, Lenore Zann, Harvey Atkin, Helen Hughes, Michael J Reynolds, Linda Purl

story: Brian Taggert

producer: Claude Heroux

director: JEAN CLAUDE LORD

Reporter Deborah Ballin becomes the target of a psychopath. Following one attack she ends up in hospital where a deadly game of cat and mouse ensues.

VISITING HOURS IS an unexceptional psycho-on-the-loose tale that places its action in the confines of a hospital – as do *Halloween II* and *X-Ray*, made around the same time.[1] With a TV movie quality, it looks out of place on the DPP list and, unsurprisingly, was dropped before long and certified 18 without further cuts (the video remains the same as the theatrical print, which was cut by one minute).

Michael Ironside's performance is a highlight. Playing the psychotic Colt Hawker, obsessively squeezing a rubber ball, he projects a façade of normality that threatens to collapse at any moment. In a scene where he smashes his own arm in broken glass to be admitted to the hospital, Ironside's demented performance is worthy of an award – popping pills, rolling his eyes back into his head, heaving his chest. However, there appear to have been some problems translating Hawker from script to screen. Several important aspects of his character come to light in the film, only to disappear almost immediately without any further ado.[2] For instance, a golden keepsake he wears around his neck – a little bell – is established as being something of an Achilles heel. TV journalist Deborah Ballin (Lee Grant) recognises the sound it makes prior to going into surgery, and panics that the killer is in the operating room with her.[3] But that's the only time she hears it. Elsewhere, Hawker's criminal actions are established as politically, as well as psychologically, motivated, but beyond the framed hate letters on his wall and a conversation with a girl from a diner, there is no further elaboration.

Beyond Ironside's eye-rolling performance, the only other noteworthy moment comes when Nurse Munroe (Linda Purl) is attacked and stabbed in her home. After searching the house from top to bottom for an intruder and finding none, Munroe – and the audience – relaxes, feeling that the danger has passed. When the knife is stabbed into her belly it comes as a genuine shock, particularly given that the film is in its final stretch and the likeable Munroe plays a pivotal role. Alas, the filmmakers don't have the nerve to let her die (which would have been an even bigger shock), but bring her back for one last pointless appearance – lying unconscious in the X-ray room at the film's end.[4]

The stabbing of Munroe might be one reason *Visiting Hours* landed on the DPP list. No more graphic than a blade jutting out of her dress, the attack is still brutally executed. Another reason could be the killer's penchant for observing his victims in their death throes, and taking snapshots.[5]

William Shatner also turns up. Despite second billing to Lee Grant, his appearance is nothing more than a glorified cameo. Playing TV producer Gary Baylor, Shatner arrives at the hospital to inform Deborah he cannot air her show. He also tells her she has "triggered a psychopath", delivering some of the dumbest lines in the movie with the conviction of a man yet to read the entirety of the script.

Jean Claude Lord went on to direct *The Vindicator* and *Mindfield*, which also starred Michael Ironside.

THE WEREWOLF AND THE YETI

aka: Night of the Howling Beast; La hombre lobo en la yeti; La Maldición de la Bestia (original title); Hall of the Mountain King; Werewolf Vs. Yeti

Spain 1975

cast: Paul Naschy [Jacinto Molina], Grace Mills, Castillo Escalona, Silvia Solar, Gil Vidal, Luis Induni

story: Jacinto Molina

producer: Modesto Perez Redondo

director: M I BONNS [Miguel Iglesias Bonns]

In the footsteps of an earlier ill-fated expedition, scientists head to Tibet in search of the Yeti. Anthropologist Waldemar is bitten by a werewolf, making the journey even more hazardous.

BILLED AS SPAIN'S greatest horror export, Paul Naschy's early film career was subject to the same censorship problems and restraints as that of Eloy de la Iglesia, director of *The Cannibal Man* (and indeed Jesús Franco, who left the country after making his first films). However, where the work of de la Iglesia was politically subversive and motivated, Naschy wanted to emulate the Hollywood monsters. When Naschy made his first horror films in the late sixties, he also thought he might buck the system and perhaps elevate the Spanish film industry out of what he considered its worse period. Naschy was considered mad for "making movies about werewolves, vampires and zombies."[1] It is ironic then, that the liberalisation following General Franco's death in 1975 effectively sounded the death knell for the Spanish horror boom that Naschy had helped to create. The genre took a dive once Spanish filmmakers could show material that had hitherto been considered taboo, such as nudity and gore, and so turned to "cheaper, quicker (and suddenly quite legal and popular) erotic films."[2] Only Naschy steadfastly refused to give up on Spanish horror, continuing to act and direct in a genre whose audience was quickly dwindling.

> I have always respected the old Universal films from Hollywood and admire the [Lon Chaney Jr] portrayal of the wolfman, because his acting is so profound, so

A complete surprise – *The Werewolf and the Yeti*.

sympathetic, you relate [to] the character and feel for him, so much so you forget the film you are seeing is a made up fantasy, not reality... In my role as the wolfman, I also tried to evoke that same sense of tragedy, that same sense of fate, and that same sympathy...
—Interview with Paul Naschy, *Draculina* No 10

A former competitive weightlifter, Paul Naschy (real name: Jacinto Molina Alvarez) showed a particular fondness for playing werewolves, returning several times to the role of the lycanthropy-afflicted Waldemar Daninsky. Some of these films were released on video in the UK, including *Shadow of the Werewolf* and *Curse of the Devil*. However, only *Werewolf and the Yeti* was ascribed to the DPP list, despite the fact they were all equally – though not especially – gory. Indeed, other Naschy films seemed more likely candidates for the 'banned' list. *The Blue Eyes of the Broken Doll*, for instance, contains several bloody murders, and even paraded highlights of some of these on the video sleeve.

Naschy's movies are entertaining with a Hammer-esque grisliness and sinister atmosphere (Hammer is another Naschy favourite and this film echoes Val Guest's *The Abominable Snowman*). But *The Werewolf and the Yeti* is unequivocally tedious, mainly because of M I Bonns' flaccid and uninspired direction. The result is a far cry from the work of Naschy's favoured directors, such as Carlos Aured and Leon Klimovsky, who had an ability to wring atmosphere from any given situation.

The Naschy werewolf has never been too convincing, even less so than Lon Chaney Jr's portrayal of the afflicted Larry Talbot some thirty years prior. In *Werewolf and the Yeti*, the clumsy-looking yeti with whom the werewolf tangles is even worse. Unlike the classic Universal horror films, where monsters generally lumber around, causing mayhem right up to the obligatory climactic confrontation, the yeti appears only momentarily at the end of the film and is quickly dispatched. Neither creature looks like anything but a man dressed in a furry suit. The title of the film, in effect, refers only to the closing moments. The original title, *La Maldición de la Bestia* (*The Curse of the Beast*), relates to Waldemar's plight and so, consequently, is a lot more accurate.

There is a flaying sequence, which isn't particularly strong, and brief shots of a knife leaving a bloody trail on flesh, a medium shot of flesh being peeled away and held aloft, followed by a glimpse of full-frontal nudity.[3] This, in the context of torture and rape, may have given rise to the film's 'nasty' status. Otherwise *The Werewolf and the Yeti* features nothing more horrific than the transformed Waldemar lunging at his foes with his teeth bared, growling and grappling. "With just TEN SECONDS of cuts," noted *Absurd*, "you could safely show this at a Saturday morning kids' matinee – the kids would lap it up."[4]

Video Programme Distributors Ltd (VPD) only became aware that one of their titles was liable for prosecution under the Obscene Publications Act when they opened the trade papers and saw it included on the DPP list. "Frankly it came as a complete surprise," a spokesperson for the company told the press in the eighties. "As far as any of us know here, *The Werewolf and the Yeti* has never been cited in any prosecution... it does seem a curious situation."

Playing safe, VPD withdrew the title and it has remained unavailable since.

THE WITCH WHO CAME FROM THE SEA

USA 1975 [76?]
cast: Millie Perkins, Lonny Chapman, Vanessa Brown, Peggy Feury, Jean Pierre Camps, Mark Livingston
story: Robert Thom
producer: Matt Cimber
director: MATT CIMBER [Matteo Ottaviano]

Molly is a spinster with a troubled recollection of her sea-faring father, missing for fifteen years. Repressed memories cause her to kill the men she meets.

MATT CIMBER IS probably best known for the widely panned *Butterfly*, which starred Stacy Keach and was projected as a star-making vehicle for the young

Molly gets a tattoo of a mermaid because her father was a sailor. *The Witch Who Came from the Sea.*

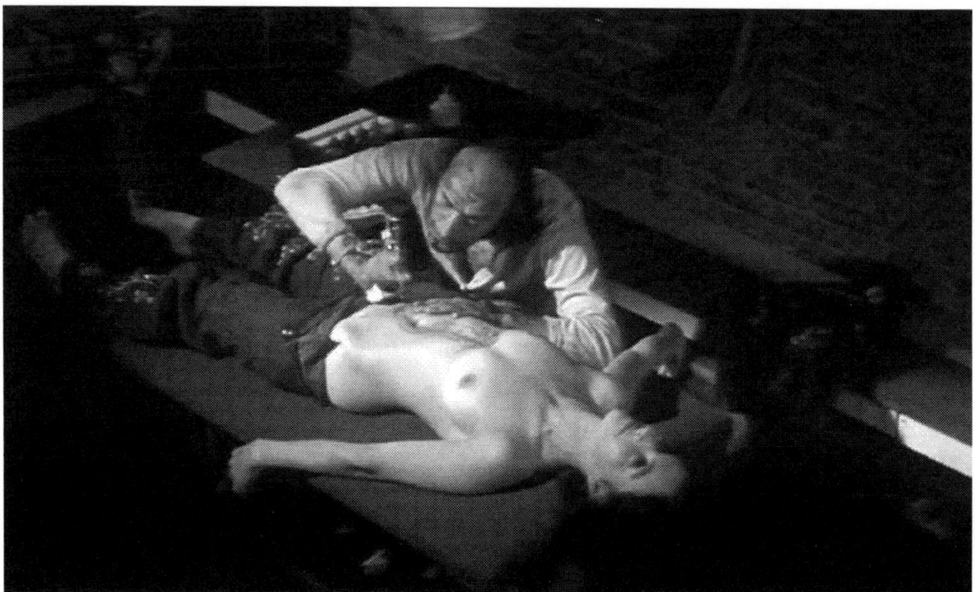

Pia Zadora, real-life bride of multimillionaire Meshulam Riklis.[1] But his life on and off the screen is colourful. He was the last husband of blonde bombshell Jayne Mansfield, becoming her publicist and trying to revitalise her flagging career (*Single Room Furnished* was a 'serious' role for Mansfield but the film would remain without distribution until after her death). The rest of his filmography runs the gamut from blaxploitation – *The Black Six* and *The Candy Tangerine Man* – to Indiana Jones-inspired high adventure – *Hundra* and *Yellow Hair and the Fortress of Gold*. At the beginning of the seventies, prior to *Deep Throat* and the hardcore explosion, Cimber was one of the first film-makers to turn his hand to 'white coaters,' films that violated obscenity laws but avoided prosecution in presenting sexually explicit material in an 'educational' context. *Man and Wife* was Cimber's initial foray into this field, a sort of live action *Kama Sutra*. At a cost of around $86,000 Cimber claimed it made more than $2.5 million at the box office and quickly followed it with *He and She*, which covered much the same ground (while also demonstrating foreplay and masturbation).

Cimber was involved with at least two other sex-ed films – directing *The Sensually Liberated Female* (released through the Institute for Adult Education) and producing *Black is Beautiful*, which "despite its pseudo-anthropology" was a success "in the ghetto theatres of cities with substantial black populations."[2]

There's evidence of his background in *The Witch Who Came from the Sea*, which has more than its fair share of sexual encounters (albeit not explicit) while all are singularly unappealing. Molly, when not eulogising her missing sailor father, shamelessly ogles men and beds them at every given opportunity. At one point she shares her bed with two football players (a stray "Ooh, yeah" is heard in this scene, which also utilises heavy reverb throughout for some reason). She ends up castrating and killing them. Later she is upset, not because of her actions but because her two nephews –teenage boys called Tadd and Tripoli – have lost their sporting heroes, the football players. Molly seems unable to differentiate fact from fiction, and laments at one point, "You don't know if it's true or not unless it's on television."

Molly's father wasn't the hero she makes him out to be. A final flashback reveals the shocking truth: Molly as a little girl is lying perfectly still as her father rapes her. He suffers a fatal heart attack during the rape. Brief as the scene is, it may stand as the most gratuitous and confrontational depiction of paedophile rape ever to grace a motion picture (infant legs are spread between pummelling adult thighs). It isn't difficult to understand why *Witch* was relegated to the DPP list. The scene that follows would undoubtedly have caused further problems with its use of minors: Tadd and Tripoli help their broken aunt Molly to die, with close-ups of them dropping pills into her mouth and holding liquor to her lips.

The Witch Who Came from the Sea is no landmark work and is perhaps too bizarre to be considered pure exploitation. It's a horror film with arthouse pretensions. It draws obvious inspiration from Lewis John Carlino's *The Sailor Who Fell from Grace with the Sea*,[3] described by *MFB* as having "a virtually eventless psychological narrative." Beyond the analogous titles, the two films share some kink and sexcapades – as well as notions concerning the corruption of youth, and the ideology that a sailor's commitment to the sea somehow keeps him pure. Carlino's production even concludes on a sequence in which drugs are used to bring about salvation and a 'return' to innocence for a central character.

Millie Perkins is exemplary in her role as the psychotic Molly (it would be six years before she took another part) and some of her scenes are loaded with a lyrical and tender quality. Curiously, Tadd and Tripoli feeding their aunt a lethal cocktail of drugs and booze is one such moment.

Lina Romay, one of a handful of the *Women Behind Bars*.

WOMEN BEHIND BARS

France/Belgium 1977
cast: Lina Romay, Martine Steed, Nathalie Chapell, Roger Darton, Ronald Weiss, Denis Torre
story: R Marceignac
dir of production: Pierre Querut
director: RICK DECONNINK [Jesús Franco]

A diamond heist... A double-cross... Shirley Fields ends up in a sadistic all-woman prison, where the inmates are always naked. Eventually she escapes.

WOMEN BEHIND BARS[1] belongs to a genre of exploitation film known as women-in-prison movies (WIP for short), counterpoint to the macho, male-only environs of Hollywood prison movies made popular in the 1930s and remaining so today.[2] Initially, the fascination with prison movies was that they offered an insider view of a world alien to most audiences. While this aspect of their appeal has diminished somewhat, the prison film remains a tantalising draw, thanks to the regimen of motifs: confinement, strict rules, constant surveillance, gruelling day-to-day existence and the underlying threat of violence. The result is a cocktail of machismo action and constant threat, but the same tropes can be transposed to an all-female environment for a more overtly sexualised picture, without losing too much threat or even machismo. While adopting these clichés, WIP films have also developed a few of their own.[3]

Female penitentiaries have been a focus for movie storylines for as long as their male counterparts, but it wasn't until John Cromwell's *Caged* in 1950 that they veered away from social melodrama to portray a grittier, more damning, reality. Directors like Jack Hill and Gerry De León, with their respective *The Big Doll House* and *Women in Cages* (both 1971), took things a step further by injecting a liberal dose of torture, rape and nude shower scenes. Before long, the genre was stagnant, with directors concentrating less on story and character, and more on the sexploitative elements. Budgets, which had never been high to begin with, were cut further when the prisons in these films were relocated to isolated settings, like the jungle. The introduction of a slave-trafficking theme also provided a legitimate excuse to downsize the cast and props. Cirio H Santiago's *Hell Hole* (1978) centred on a mere handful of prisoners, incarcerated together in a single cell that looked like any other room in the film. Thanks to the glut of productions lensed in Europe and the Philippines throughout the seventies, the WIP film soon became a blur of interchangeable story lines, with only the increasingly brutal acts of punishment and degradation showing any imagination at all. Jesús Franco's *Women Behind Bars* is no different. It has a convoluting plot full of double-bluffs (both inside and outside the prison) but nothing that stands out more than its two prison-set torture scenes. In Franco's cinematic mud bath, they offer a few minutes of voyeuristic assiduity.[4]

At the whim of the male warden, a prisoner called Maria is subjected to twenty-four lashes, shown in real time, courtesy of a crash zoom each time the whip connects with bare flesh. Elsewhere, Shirley (Lina Romay) is tortured so that she might reveal the content of a hidden note. Electrodes are connected to her crotch, and her bare breasts bounce with each shock. It's little surprise, given these two scenes, that *Women Behind Bars* would find itself on the DPP list. The torture of Shirley is particularly gratuitous, although it has some bearing on the plot, which cannot be said of Maria's flogging – a sequence that also shows blood on breasts, a point of contention with the BBFC in itself.

The movie is filled with ineffectual dialogue. This exchange is between the warden and the guard during Maria's flogging:

> "Harder! More! Just a second – I think she's fainted!"
> "No, not yet."

Women Behind Bars was released the same year as three other WIP-themed films from Franco. Indeed, the director's first foray into the genre in 1968 – *99 Women* – could be described as the template for the decidedly more aggressive WIP features of the seventies. (Despite the title, it rarely featured more than a handful of women onscreen at any given time.) Franco followed the success of *99 Women* with *Lovers of Devil's Island, Caged Women, Wanda The Wicked Warden, Women For Cellblock Nine, Love Camp*, and *Sadomania*.[5]

Curious details: The opening shot of *Women Behind Bars* is a panoramic view of a harbour town and railway station that seems like old stock footage. But as some of the cast find themselves at the railway station at the end of the film, presumably it isn't. The hold-up at the beginning of the film is said to take place on a Chinese junk, but it doesn't – indeed, there doesn't appear to be a junk in the harbour.

Unrelated to Franco's film was a successful Off-Broadway play called *Women Behind Bars*; its campiness and high melodramatics helped reinvent the WIP genre in the eighties. The WIP trope would seem perfectly suited to the adult market, although surprisingly there are few hardcore WIP offshoots. Ted Roter's *Prison Babies* is one, Michel Ricaud's *Women In Prison* another. Osvaldo de Oliveira's *Bare Behind Bars* gallantly tried to make the best of both worlds by featuring sex of a softcore nature for most of its duration, but threw in a couple of brief hardcore encounters for good measure.

XTRO

aka: Monstromo; Monstro; The Judas Goat (working titles)
UK 1982
cast: Philip Sayer, Bernice Stegers, Danny Bainin, Maryam d'Abo, Simon Nash
original story: Michel Parry & Harry Bromley Davenport
producer: Mark Forstater
director: HARRY BROMLEY DAVENPORT

Sam Phillips returns to his family after a mysterious three-year absence. However, despite appearances, this is not Sam but an alien.

THE ALIEN CREATURE is briefly seen roaming the countryside in the film's early moments and remains an unnerving aberration – even if it's clearly a man in a rubber suit. The unnatural limb shape is achieved by the strange posture of the man inside the suit, upside down in a crab position. Movement is restricted in this position and thankfully it is only through tight close-ups and point-of-view shots that the filmmakers imply the creature's progress through the woods.

Most of the visual effects in *Xtro* rely on inventive flourishes, more than they do a sizeable budget, but are no less effective because of it. The alien spacecraft is implied, not with intricate model work but with blinding lights, a wind machine, and the occasional animated cut-out. But what do such concessions matter when the arrival of the thing causes inexplicable, spectacular 'pop art' explosions?!

When invention runs dry, the film falls back on some unpleasant prosthetics, such as the tumescent impregnation scene (replete with bubbling flesh and distended veins) and the adult-birth (in which, fleetingly, we see a full-grown head exit a vagina). A distraction of a more pleasant kind is Maryam D'Abo as Analise the au pair, who looks like a young Nastassja Kinski. She has two completely gratuitous nude scenes.

At the centre of the film is the Phillips family. When Sam goes missing, abducted by a bright light in the sky, no one believes the only witness, Sam's young son Tony. According to *Fangoria*,[1] director Harry Bromley Davenport's "strategy" was to go for fresh talent in the cast as opposed to name stars

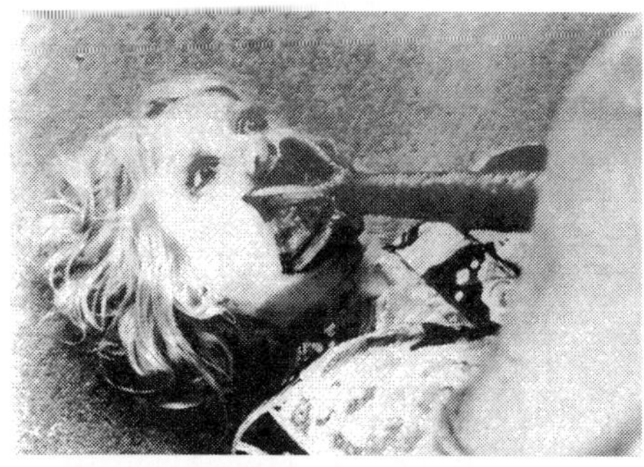

and that way spend more on the film's 'extensive special effects.' The résumés of the technicians employed on *Xtro* suggests an extravaganza on a par with the blockbusters the film so clearly tries to emulate:[2] *An American Werewolf in London* and *Close Encounters of the Third Kind*. But the result has more the look of Norman J. Warren's *Inseminoid*, another low-budget British sci-fi horror picture. Set on a distant planet, this film also incorporates scenes of extraterrestrial rape.

The notion that *Xtro* was destined to be a special effects extravaganza diminished as production progressed. Executive producer and American distributor Robert Shaye had felt *Xtro* should be reliant on special effects to the point that "the plot takes some strange right-angle turns in order to include some of the sequences devised."[3] Realistically, the effects were unlikely to be anything other than modest, rather hit-and-miss, affairs.

"On this picture," Shaye said,

> we learned that effects are *more* expensive than we'd thought... And then, not everything that is built, at whatever expense, works. In fact, a good deal of the effects were done and redone after the principal filming was completed, because we really didn't feel we had what we wanted... There are effects in the film that turned out far better than we'd hoped, and some that turned out worse. And there were some that were far worse, where we had to say "no way".

This latter may account for why several characters credited in the original cinema release of *Xtro* don't appear in any print of the film.[4] (Such as 'Consulting

Gynaecologist,' 'Van Driver' and 'Petrol Pump Attendant.' If any of these missing characters were assigned an unnatural death, one can but wonder in what form it befell the 'Lavatory Attendant'!) But *Xtro* is not the incoherent mess that many critics accuse it of being. At times it does appear to be deliberately obtuse, with clowns and panthers suddenly materialising. The filmmakers conveniently pass off such things as somehow connected to Tony's telekinetic abilities – a conceit that can be applied to just about every indiscretion in the film. That said, there is no excuse for the dull and protracted live Action Man sequence, which is little more than a showcase for 'human robotics,' a fad in the early eighties. Indeed, the commando here is played by Tok, who was a minor celebrity thanks to his convincing robotic performances on British light entertainment programmes. His robot partner, Tik, plays the alien creature at the beginning of *Xtro*.

Unnatural limb shapes – *Xtro*.

One sequence that does fall outside of Tony's telekinetic construct comes at the film's end, when Rachel returns to her London apartment and finds eggs laid by au pair Analise after being impregnated by aliens. The brilliant white, featureless environment gives the sequence a surreal, dream-like look, an unnecessary quality that serves only to befuddle. *Xtro*'s original ending differed from the one on the video release. The theatrical print showed Rachel returning to the apartment to find "lots of Tony-lookalikes, all murmuring 'Mummy.'"[5] This less graphic alternative is reported to be more disturbing than the blood-spattered, face-hugging finale that features in the video release. As to why the switch was made, Nigel Burrell in *Flesh & Blood*[6] believes it was because of negative feedback generated by the original ending.

A review in *Starburst* offers the tantalising suggestion there is even more footage to be mined from *Xtro*, notably stronger scenes of Sam's adult-birth intended for the Japanese market.[7] However, in a rare interview, director Bromley Davenport told *The Dark Side*[8] that while a more explicit model for this scene had been made, ultimately they couldn't use it "as the Japanese market would never have allowed it in the final cut – it had pubic hair..."

Bromley Davenport has to date made two sequels to *Xtro*. Dealing with a creature from a parallel dimension (*Xtro II: The Second Encounter,* 1991) and an alien roaming an island owned by the government (*Xtro III: Watch the Skies,* 1995). These films are related to the first in name only. A 1968 stinker by James A Sullivan, originally titled *Night Fright*, was released in Britain as *The Extra Terrestrial Nastie* (the emphasis being on the 'x' in *Extra*) in an attempt to cash-in on the success of *ET* and notoriety of *Xtro*.

Removed from its sci-fi trappings, *Xtro* might be read as a metaphor for an incestuous relationship. This is most vivid in the scenes where Sam 'interferes' with his son and tells him to keep the matter their secret.

ZOMBIE CREEPING FLESH

aka: Night of the Zombies; Virus (original title); Hell of the Living Dead; Apocalipsis Canibal
Italy/Spain 1981
cast: Margit Evelyn Newton, Frank Garfeeld, Selan Karay, Robert O'Neal, Gaby Renom, Luis Fonoll
story: Claudio Fragasso & J M Cunilles
producer: Sergio Cortona
director: VINCENT DAWN [Bruno Mattei]

A radioactive leak at a research facility in New Guinea turns the local people into flesh-eating zombies. A crack team of commandos tries to contain the threat.

THERE WAS A glut of zombie movies in the late seventies and early eighties triggered by the success of George Romero's downbeat *Dawn of the Dead*. Most imitations were poor,[1] with only Lucio Fulci's *Zombie Flesh Eaters* managing to achieve any credible identity of its own. Falling into the former camp, imitating rather than innovating, is Bruno Mattei's *Zombie Creeping Flesh*.

Like Romero, Mattei puts the cause of zombification down to a scientific

The dead go walkabout in *Zombie Creeping Flesh*.

experiment. Instead of a space probe bringing an unknown virus back to Earth, however,[2] the cause of reanimation in *Zombie Creeping Flesh* is more cynical: a manufactured virus spread deliberately in developing countries. Both films feature central characters working in television, and Mattei closes his movie with a news broadcast reporting on the reanimation of a limbless corpse – inferring that the zombie plague has spread to the US, an attempt by Mattei to lead audiences into thinking that *Zombie Creeping Flesh* is a prologue of sorts to Romero's film (as opposed to simple plagiarism), as *Dawn of the Dead* opens on such a news broadcast.

The connection between the two films is even more clear in a prologue absent from the UK print of *Zombie Creeping Flesh*. The sequence shows a SWAT team storming an embassy under the control of terrorists, derivative of the opening scenes of Romero's *Dawn*. Both films feature a musical soundtrack by Goblin; indeed Mattei acquired the rights to use passages of music created specifically for Romero's film.

Zombie Creeping Flesh offers nothing new or original, and the masses of stock footage (much of it lifted from Akira Ide's 1974 Mondo film *Guinea Ama*) highlights the hastiness and laziness of its production. Any time that a character looks up or out in any direction, grainy wildlife documentary footage is inserted to give the illusion of an exotic location, here New Guinea. The film is full of silly, overstated dialogue and puerile set-pieces: Leah, a member of the news team investigating the unexplained deaths and stories of cannibalism, strips naked and wanders at length through the jungle daubed in paint, having decided this is what it takes to be accepted by the natives.

Bruno Mattei adopted the pseudonym Vincent Dawn, perhaps after Romero's *Dawn of the Dead*.[3] It takes him on average three to four months to complete a movie, "from writing the screenplay to the end product," as he told *European Trash Cinema*.[4] In the same interview Mattei confided he hadn't yet made a film he was happy with, and described the type of cinema he was involved in as "a routine." He has no qualms about changing direction partway through a production to capitalise on fluctuating cinematic trends.[5]

Like many gore movies, *Zombie Creeping Flesh* attempts to hide its insignificant plot behind gruesome special effects. Unfortunately, most of these were removed for its release in the UK, thus rendering the film even more meaningless. As well as the SWAT prologue, several scenes – including documentary footage of real corpses and primitive funerary rites – had been excised from *Zombie Creeping Flesh* for its cinema release in 1982.[6] (In total there were fifteen minutes' worth of cuts.) It was this same version that Merlin released on video, which contained nothing particularly offensive or overtly violent. The film's title and the fact that it had a few fleeting scenes of cannibalism were enough to bring it to the attention of the DPP.

ZOMBIE FLESH EATERS

title on print: Zombie Flesh-Eaters
aka: Zombi 2; Zombie
Italy 1979
cast: Tisa Farrow, Ian McCulloch, Richard Johnson, Al Cliver, Auretta Gay
story: Walter Patricarca
producers: Ugo Tucci & Fabrizio de Angelis
director: LUCIO FULCI

A boat adrift in New York harbour contains a zombie. A small team heads to the Caribbean Island of Matul, where a strange disease is bringing the dead to life.

ZOMBIE FLESH EATERS has a satisfying symmetry to it. It begins with a boat floating in New York harbour and concludes much the same. There is the timeless mystery evoked by crewless vessels adrift. While at sea, the sanctuary of home for Ann Bowles (Tisa Farrow) and Peter West (Ian McCulloch) is no more; they have set out to a Caribbean Island to unearth the fate of the crew of the original

Making a run for it in *Zombie Flesh Eaters*.

vessel, and now that they have the answer, they must also face the same terrible fate; New York is overrun with the living dead.

One outstanding aquatic scene features a battle between two very different man-eaters: the sight of a corpse walking on the seabed and fighting a shark is arresting and marred only by some clumsy editing that breaks the continuity. No doubt the sequence was influenced by the box office draw of *Jaws* and possibly even stuntman Evel Knievel's much heralded, but cancelled, motorcycle leap across a pool of sharks. The shark here is pretty decrepit, but Fulci creates an exciting, dangerous-looking battle (in which the zombie tears a chunk of flesh from the fish before losing its own arm). It remains a jaw-dropping set-piece.[1]

The Caribbean Island setting of Matul is rich in atmosphere. The isolated Dr Menard (Richard Johnson) is a man with a constantly sweating brow, and one gets a true sense that he is way out of his depth. The whole film has a vibrancy, whether it is the camera circling one of the living dead as it wanders through a deserted village, or the rich crimson shock of a horrific throat wound. Courtesy of a perpetual sandstorm, rolling tumbleweeds, distant pounding of tribal drums, and superstitious villagers, Fulci perfectly attunes cliché and stereotype to capture a stifling sense of decay and timeless death in an island setting. The dialogue harkens back to early B-movie chillers and an exchange like this wouldn't be out of place in, say, the 1932 film, *White Zombie* (profanity notwithstanding):

> "Drums!"
> "Getting closer!"
> "I hate it! You bastards! I can't take it!"
> "Playing a little voodoo on us. It's a sound all of its own."

Menard doesn't believe in voodoo, but the dead returning to life is a phenomenon that defies logical explanation. "I've tried to apply the disciplines of bacteriology, virology, even of radiology," he says. "We've performed tests for epilepsy and for catalepsy – nothing fits!" The doctor ascertains that he doesn't believe a curse has been placed on the island, but concedes he hasn't a clue what is happening. Curiously, there is much talk of an evil witchdoctor said to inhabit the island, who the natives believe is responsible for the reanimation of the dead, but he is never actually shown.

Trauma to the eye seemed to be a preoccupation with certain films – i.e. 'nasties' – around this time. A sequence where Menard's wife has her eye skewered on a wooden splinter was regarded as the most contentious moment in the movie (certainly the most talked about) and the scene was removed by the BBFC when they passed *Zombie Flesh Eaters* for video in later years.[2] (Nine other films that featured on the DPP list also had images of violence upon eyeballs.)[3]

> When I was in Atlanta I saw something very funny. I observed three kids playing videogames in the theatre's lobby during a screening of [*Zombie Flesh Eaters*]. When the aforementioned scene was about to be shown, a fourth kid called his friends so that they wouldn't miss this highlight. This was great to see!
>
> –Lucio Fulci[4]

Inspired by Romero's *Dawn of the Dead* (aka *Zombi*), and originally released as *Zombi 2* in an attempt to pass itself off as a bona fide sequel, some critics believe that Fulci's remodel surpasses the original. Among those who don't is Randall Larson. He said, "It's films like this that give the horror genre it's [*sic*] bad name."[5] The half-decayed corpses lumbering about are certainly uglier than Romero's, with maggots that issue from every available orifice the moment the camera moves in close. In comparison to Romero's *Dawn*, the gore is also more outrageous and over the top. For instance, when West cuts down a zombie in the cemetery with a blow to the head, it doesn't merely fall to the floor, it falls to the floor in a bloody mess that expels the aged contents of its skull into a swelling miasma.

Fulci claimed that *Zombie Flesh Eaters* was "based on sensations, hinges on fear, and, of course, horror."[6] This was an approach the director would adopt to varying degrees of success in later films, notably *House by the Cemetery*, *The Beyond* and *A Cat in the Brain*. Not only has the latter the unfortunate distinction of being one of the director's final films and a terrible one at that, but it was initially rejected by the BBFC, due in part to "many sequences involving gross violence committed against women, often in a context with clear sexual overtones."[7]

A highly anticipated sequel to *Zombie Flesh Eaters* arrived in 1988. Titled *Zombi 3* (in keeping with the misappropriated chronology that began with Romero's film) it had plenty of bloody gore effects but not much else to match the flair, impact or atmosphere of its predecessor. Directorial credit went to Fulci, but in truth he was unwell during the troubled production and much of what appeared on screen was handled by Bruno Mattei. *Zombi 3*'s storyline has the dead being reanimated by a chemical virus, which was the case with Mattei's own *Zombie Creeping Flesh*.

Appendix

Appendix

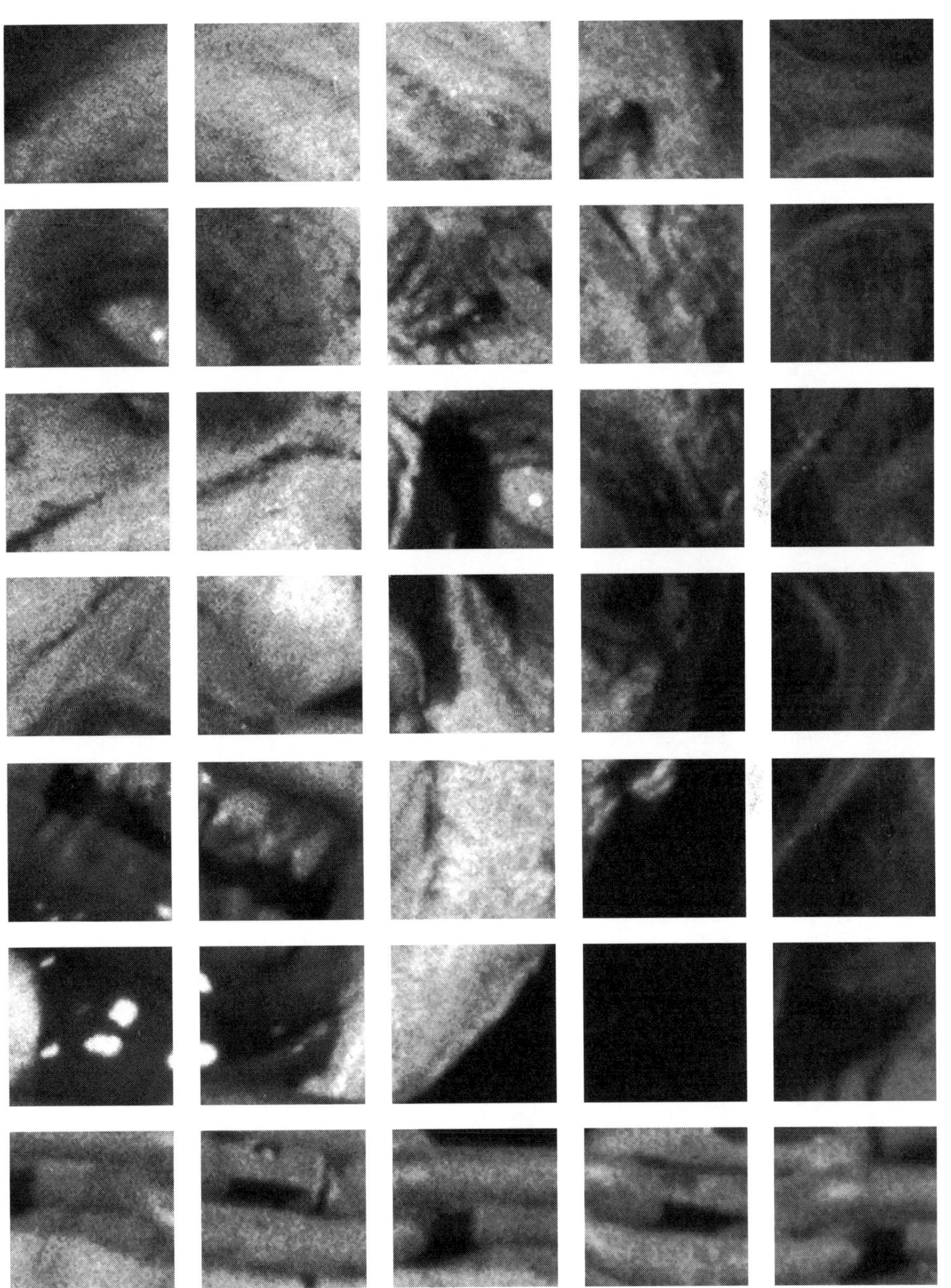

A MISCELLANY OF REJECTED VIDEO WORKS, 1990–PRESENT

THIS IS A selection of works on video submitted to the BBFC post the Video Recordings Act 1984, but denied classification outright. It doesn't include the 'video nasties', covered elsewhere (THE DPP39 and WHERE ARE THEY NOW?), but each represents a different set of circumstances for works having been rejected.

BARE FIST: THE SPORT THAT WOULDN'T DIE

dir: David Monaghan
Rejected by the BBFC on June 21, 1999

DOES THIS WORK have the potential for anti-social influence? That's one question BBFC examiners must ask themselves whenever a film comes before them. (See SEX & WRECKS.) The Board certainly considered the potential audience for *Bare Fist: The Sport That Wouldn't Die* a dubious one, that society was therefore at risk, and duly banned it.

David Monaghan's film focuses upon the outlawed age-old sport of bare knuckle fighting and argues that its practice poses less health risks than more acceptable gloved boxing. The Board claim not to have a problem with the promotion of this belief. However, they regarded the lengthy sequences of illegal fighting as unacceptable, as well as some scenes "giving instruction in achieving lethal effects," for example when a bandaged fist is laced with glass fragments. "These have the effect of promoting gross violence and selling its pleasures," the Board decided. "The extent of the use of the illegal fighting sequences also far outstrips any reasonable justification based on the need to make a case for legalisation."

As well as wanting Monaghan to "re-angle" the film so as "not to encourage violence," the BBFC recommended four cuts. These included the shortening of the "illegal fight footage," removal of part of a knife scene, removal of shots of bandaged hands being laced with glass, and the removal of the words "good shot" heard when a nose was broken. Monaghan said he would comply with making the cuts but regarded them as vague and requested more information in writing. On October 8, 1998, Monaghan visited the BBFC office and was allowed to hear the reports of three examiners concerning his film. However, he wasn't allowed to look at the reports himself or take any notes, and consequently had to deal with the concerns of the Board from memory.

The list of cuts requested by Monaghan to gain a certificate for *Bare Fist* weren't forthcoming, and in June 1999 the film was rejected. Monaghan subsequently gained access to the examiners' secret reports and claimed not only did they contain "personal insults" against him but also "dishonest claims of pornographic content" about his film. Regarding the last claim, it is worth noting that Robin Duval, director of the BBFC, had suggested to a journalist for the *Sunday Times* that R18 rated films – of which he is most certainly not fond – contained "sadistic sex." Which they don't, by law.

(There is another film on the BBFC rejected list with the title *Bare Fist: The Sport That Wouldn't Die*. This was refused a certificate on December 23, 1996, also on the grounds that it sold and demonstrated "the pleasures of gross violence." However, the stated director, production company and running time of this work do not correspond with the documentary above.)

BOY MEETS GIRL

dir: Ray Brady
Rejected by the BBFC on September 13, 1995

BOY MEETS GIRL was passed uncut for cinema release on February 27, 1995, but refused a certificate for video – the Board's reason being that in the home "scenes of torture and mutilation could lend themselves to viewing out of context by sensation seekers old and young."

Following a pickup in a nightclub, a man returns to the apartment of a young woman. The promise of a "quickie" is curtailed when the man passes out, his drink having been spiked. He awakens to find himself strapped into a dentist's chair in a darkened basement. The rest of the film is played out in this location, the man at the mercy of his "one night stand," plus a shadowy (female) filmmaker. To atone for his sins (i.e. infidelity to his wife and homophobia) as well as the savagery of the world in general, the man is tortured before he is murdered.

A low-budget independent production, *Boy Meets Girl* was intended by the filmmakers to draw the viewer into the complex issue of "violence and the portrayal of violence" as well as to highlight inconsistencies within BBFC attitudes to violence. The usual roles of aggressor and victim are reversed, along with what is perceived to be gender etiquette. For instance, in the opening scenes at the woman's apartment, the man is thrilled that his latest pickup should offer to play him some porno, but at the same time he's a little uncomfortable that she should openly do so. "Can you identify with the attitudes the male character stands for?" ask the filmmakers. Are you guilty as he is? He is used and abused by his two dominant female captors, held up as an example of the worst kind of tabloid mentality; he is made to pay for (accepted) social attitudes and behaviour that his captors (and the film makers) believe are wrong.

The man is sodomised with a dildo, cut with a knife, infected with AIDS, refused toilet facilities, and fed excrement. In *Violence and the Censors*, a Channel 4 documentary, a BBFC examiner was heard to say the Board couldn't cut or tone down *Boy Meets Girl* because the film was about "torture and captivity and the horror of being in somebody else's power in a sadistic way." Another examiner was less pragmatic and pondered "whether something can be terminally boring and obscene at the same time" – but then pondered why they should pass Steven Seagal movies and not this one.

Argue the filmmakers: this for once is a film which "has a totally violent subject matter but does not glamorise it."

INTERNATIONAL GUERILLAS

dir: Jaan Mohammed
Rejected by the BBFC on July 22, 1990 | Passed 18 uncut on August 29, 1990

"IF WE WERE to pass this film," a BBFC examiner said of *International Guerillas*, "and Rushdie were killed, how would we ever forgive ourselves?"

Made in Pakistan, this 167-minute film depicted Muslim revenge on the author Salman Rushdie, and showed him torturing Muslims by playing tapes of his 'blasphemous' book, *The Satanic Verses*, before being struck by lightning. In July 1990, the BBFC rejected *International Guerillas* on the grounds that it presented a case of criminal libel on a British citizen, Salman Rushdie, and exposed him to public hatred. (Some argued why ban the film for criminal libel as opposed to, say, incitement to murder – criminal libel remains, to quote Media Law, "an ancient offence that is now unlikely to be invoked against the media by prosecuting authorities: the Law commission has recommended its abolition.") The Board regarded it as one of the most difficult decisions they have had to make. One consideration in refusing a certificate was that other films might follow that urged retribution on specific members of society. The Muslim community argued that double standards were at work because they considered Rushdie's book inflammatory and that it should be banned. In August, the Video Appeals Committee upheld an appeal against the Board's decision to reject *International Guerillas* and the ban was lifted – no less because Rushdie himself was of the opinion the film should be in the public domain. In a statement he said that

> in spite of the film's clearly abusive content, I do not wish to seek the dubious protection of censorship. Censorship is usually counter-productive, and can actually exacerbate the risks which it seeks to reduce.

La Blue Girl

dir: Raizo Kitakawa

Urotsukidoji IV Part One: The Secret Garden

dir: [not known]
Both films rejected by the BBFC on December 30, 1996

JAPANESE CARTOONS – Anime or Manga cartoons being the preferred terms – have been around for many years but it is only relatively recently that the West has come to regard them as anything other than a medium for children. With the huge success of *Akira* and *Urotsukidoji: Legend of the Overfiend* in the early nineties, English-speaking audiences gradually began to unearth a wealth of hitherto unknown Anime material. Some of this dealt with adult themes and contained brutal imagery – a favourite being monsters that capture and literally fuck their female victims to death. Other Anime elements – sadism, incest, a predilection for doe-eyed, young-looking characters – drew from a culture that was impenetrable to most Westerners. British tabloids labelled all Anime as "snuff cartoons", while a perplexed BBFC (in their Annual Report for 1996-97) said of the most virulent examples:

> It is difficult to fathom where such attitudes come from. Male chauvinism is far too mild a term to describe the film-makers' psychology, since many of these cartoons drag misogyny down to the level of atrocity.

The previous year, acknowledging the technical brilliance of Anime, the BBFC suggested a likeness with the fascistic fantasies of the Nazis, which sought to destroy "the female principle" and "'filthy softness' of female bodies."

The Board cut eight Manga cartoons in 1996-97 and rejected two more outright – *La Blue Girl* and *Urotsukidoji IV Part One: The Secret Garden* – because of their "pornographic treatment of sexual violence." The Board were concerned with many scenes, but primarily those that demonstrated "the art of gang rape as a marital technique," the abuse and physical mutilation of women at the hands of children, monsters with penile tentacles that "subject female captives to multiple penetration," and victims who respond, "lasciviously under the influence of an aphrodisiac." The Board considered the overwhelming message was that "rape is the ultimate source of sexual pleasure." Although some critics – such as Helen McCarthy and Jonathan Clements in *The Erotic Anime Movie Guide* – prefer to read this material as "a homage to several popular motifs from Japanese legend, such as the power of the female genitals to subjugate beastly males."

The BBFC makes a "genre allowance" for the fact these films are animation. However, when the content comprises sexual violence or sexualised violence, they make no distinction between animation and live action. As examiner Imtiaz Karim pointed out when discussing cuts made to the film *Overfiend 4* (in an interview in *Manga Mania* No 30):

> When you show somebody a scene like this [sustained anal and oral rape, mutilation and much worse in which the woman is crying repeatedly for the demons to stop] there is often very little argument whether we should censor it or not. There may well be an audience which is mature enough to watch this and appreciate and understand the scene in the way the filmmakers intended. But our concern is that this is presented in a very titillating manner which is not appropriate for an audience in their mid-teens. There is no sense of horror or disgust at what the woman is going through; the way it is shot and designed invites the audience to take pleasure from the scene...

SIXTEEN SPECIAL

dir: [not known]
Rejected by the BBFC on November 9, 1990

THIS PORN TAPE begins with an actress dressed as a schoolgirl and clutching a teddy bear, trying to fight off the amorous advances of a middle-aged man. Several minutes later she disrobes and discards her uniform. The problem with *Sixteen Special* resided in this opening section. The actress was evidently older than sixteen (apparently, she was twenty-one) and therefore the film contained no actual indecent photographs of a child under sixteen, prosecutable under the Protection of Children Act 1978. However, it was the attempt to "glamorise and eroticise the seduction of a schoolgirl" that led the BBFC to believe *Sixteen Special* had a clear tendency to deprave and corrupt. The distributor (BPC) agreed that the film served no purpose other than to turn men onto the idea of seducing schoolgirls, but interpreted the root of the problem to be the title of the film and put forward suggestions for several alternatives – *School Uniform Love*, *Miss Bennison's Older Lover* and *Dirty Ian Gets His Way* – none of which the BBFC "considered an improvement." The Board wanted the opening sequence removed or replaced, suggesting that the film company provide the actress with clothes other than a school uniform. They declined.

"Given the increasing concern in Britain about paedophilia and child sexual abuse," the BBFC said of the film in their Annual Report for 1990, "the Board has accepted the need to exercise the greatest caution in this area."

After *Sixteen Special*, the Board drew up restrictive guidelines concerning the depiction of schoolgirl attire in sex videos. The problem of uniforms was raised again several years later when another film – *Schoolgirl Fantasy* – was submitted and suffered the same fate (rejected on October 5, 1995). In this instance, the story featured two young women "dressed convincingly as schoolgirls" and whose consent to sex is eroded over the course of much of the film. The Board concluded that there

> was no doubt in the minds of anyone who saw the video that it would encourage men to fantasise about seducing unwilling, and probably under-age schoolgirls... For viewers, the link between innocent schoolgirls and sexual excitation would almost certainly be reinforced.

The fact that *Schoolgirl Fantasy* was a camcorder sex video also weighed against the film. Camcorder sex – a growing trend in 'reality porn,' filmed in real time with few edits or cutaways – was perceived by the BBFC to be "less honest and more sexist than frank hardcore porn," in that it tended to bring "porno values into what purports to be the viewer's own neighbourhood." (The comparison here with "frank hardcore porn" is strange, as the Board would certainly not give a certificate to such material.)

The sexualisation of children arose again in the form of Adrian Lyne's movie adaptation of Vladimir Nabokov's *Lolita*. It was passed uncut after the Board sought professional advice (see SEX & WRECKS). However, on March 27, 2000, the Board rejected two outtakes intended as bonus material for the DVD release of the film. 'The Comic Book' (2m 27s) and 'The Lake Point Cottages' (3m 41s) were both said to be "highly sexually charged," showing "images of sexual nudity and behaviour which were not present in the feature version and which are made even more problematic when presented in isolation or out of context as here." Had either scene been present in *Lolita*, the film would not have been passed.

VISIONS OF ECSTASY

dir: Nigel Wingrove
Rejected by the BBFC September 18, 1989

INCORPORATING SELF-INFLICTED WOUNDS, lesbian encounters, and a climb up the cross to wrap herself around the figure of Christ, the rapture experienced by St Teresa of Avila, a sixteenth-century Carmelite nun, is interpreted in this film literally. St Teresa spends the film's eighteen minutes duration in sexual longing for the physical, crucified body of Christ. After seeking legal advice, the BBFC rejected *Visions of Ecstasy* in September 1989 on the grounds that it was "contemptuous of the divinity of Christ" – in other words, they considered it liable to prosecution for blasphemy (which well it could be: after publishing a poem in 1976 recounting a Roman's imagined homosexual acts on the crucified Christ, *Gay News* and its editor were successfully prosecuted for producing a blasphemous libel). The director of *Visions of Ecstasy*, Nigel Wingrove, argued that his film was not intended as a depiction of St Teresa partaking in any actual "overt sexual act," but was instead a fantasy projection of the nun's mind.

Martin Scorsese's *The Last Temptation of Christ* was also drawn into this argument as it had been passed for video release the previous year. This film also featured a fantasy sequence that many Christians regarded as blasphemous. The Board was of the opinion, however, that Scorsese made it very clear "that the illusion was subjective" (Christ leaves the cross but nobody watching notices).

Wingrove in *Visions of Ecstasy* on the other hand, didn't indicate that the human figure of Christ on the cross was a fantasy on the part of St Teresa – the fantasy in this case was the total film, and since this was a sex fantasy, and treated as such, it was bound to risk causing offence if the sexual elements were too blatant.

No doubt influential in the matter was the fact that James Ferman held Scorsese in the highest regard. When the matter of blasphemy was raised at a censorship debate at the ICA in November 1998, Ferman said that *Visions of Ecstasy* was "not on the same plane" as *Last Temptation of Christ*, and when someone remarked that Scorsese was a "decent" film-maker, Ferman snapped back with uncharacteristic ire, "Decent?! He's a great director!"

Wingrove took *Visions of Ecstasy* to the Video Appeals Committee, who upheld the ban. He then went to the European Court of Human Rights – the first time in the BBFC's eighty-four-year history that anyone had challenged a decision of theirs in the courts. However, when finally the Strasbourg court returned its verdict in November 1996 it was in support of the BBFC and the ban was upheld, effectively sounding the death knell for the film in Britain.

Wingrove got the inspiration for *Visions of Ecstasy* in an ecstatic swoon when he stood before Bernini's statue of St Teresa in Rome. "The celestial orgasm is a matter of fact, not fiction," he said.

Even the tabloids seemed divided on the dredging up of a law as archaic as blasphemy. In an article entitled "Blasphemy or freedom?" The *Mail on Sunday* offered some rather half-hearted outrage, directed as much at Euro-judges as the film itself. On the other hand, while he did not mock the religious beliefs of others, Chris Peachment of the *Express* suggested that

> if your religious belief happens to be made weaker by the viewing of a rather silly video, then I would suggest that your personal faith is shaky. Rather than ban the film, would it not be better to examine your faith in the light of an argument against it...?

Wingrove may well be the man most rejected by the BBFC! As well as *Visions of Ecstasy*, cult movies submitted through his company, Salvation Films, have also been ensnared by the Board. These include Osvaldo de Oliveira's *Bare Behind Bars* (rejected September 20, 1994) and Jess Franco's *Demoniac* and *Sadomania* (rejected August 10 and September 21, 1994, respectively).

Despite more leniency in the past few years, the BBFC still rejects works it considers unlawful or liable to encourage lawbreaking. Some films are rejected for reasons echoed in the above selection of titles, but recently several 'how-to' guides have been rejected under the Misuse of Drugs Act 1971. From Devlin Films, these include *Mushroom Growing Made Easy*, *High Yield Hydroponic Systems* and *Introduction to Indoor Growing* (all rejected 2005). A five-minute extra intended for the DVD release of the US comedy series *Weeds* season 2 was rejected in 2007 for its potential to promote and encourage the use of illegal drugs.

TWO INTERVIEWS WITH INDEPENDENT VIDEO DISTRIBUTORS

SCREEN EDGE: INTERVIEW WITH RICHARD KING, CO-FOUNDER & COMPANY DIRECTOR

SCREEN EDGE WAS an offshoot of the Lytham St Annes-based music label, Jettisoundz, created to distribute films and whose catalogue introduced many contemporary low-budget independent films to Britain, as well as encouraging homegrown work, including *Addicted To Murder* (d: Kevin Lindenmuth), *The Dead Next Door* (d: J R Bookwalter), *Der Todesking* (d: Jörg Buttgereit), *Pervirella* (d: Alex Chandon & Josh Collins), *Shatter Dead* (d: Scooter McCrae) and *Transgression* (d: Michael Dipaolo). The following interview was conducted in November 1998, a time when the certification of the horror film, *Original Sins* (d: Howard Berger & Matthew Howe), was raising one problem after another for Screen Edge.

What effect do you think the recent shake-up at the BBFC will have on Screen Edge?

RICHARD KING: I can't see it getting any better, really. Especially since they are aware that their role is getting more and more ludicrous, with the advent of digital television and communications technology in general. What role can they actually play? Basically, it's one of the biggest and most successful scams of the last hundred years, isn't it?

You've had a lot of problems with* Original Sins*. When did you first submit that?

It was two and a half years ago – getting on for three years now.

And they came back to you with a list of initial objections...

Yeah, we did cut some scenes... We sent the cuts list to [co-director] Howard Berger and he told us what he didn't mind doing and what he wanted us to try and save. So we made cuts and sent it back to the BBFC. But even then, they said the cuts hadn't been done at one stage, because we'd put black bands across some images as opposed to taking them out altogether – obscuring blood-on-breasts which they had objected to – and so we had to re-cut it again to satisfy them that we'd done the cuts.

The version that eventually does come out, will that be missing the black bands?

Who knows? Hopefully, we can keep the black bands in. We don't know the new cuts. I daresay it won't make any sense at all by the time we release it – it's a shame, you know. One of the scenes has a guy spewing up his own spine. We had to cut that down by a considerable amount. And there's a scene where the devil emerges from a papier-mâché vagina – we had to cut that out. It's obviously a papier-mâché model, and the devil's got his arse painted bright red for Christ's sake! They didn't even know it was comedy. Because none of them found it funny they didn't consider it a comedy. They couldn't understand it at all.

Did you have any trouble with the sleeve to* Original Sins*?

The BBFC haven't even looked at that yet – that's the next hurdle!

You mentioned that one of the issues brought up with regard to* Original Sins *was the fact that, quite out of the blue, the BBFC decided the girls in it were underage.

Yeah. That was one of the main reasons – underage girls. But nowhere is it suggested in the whole film that they're underage. The BBFC came back to us with that claim after they'd had the film for a number of months... and after we'd made cuts to it at their request.

So, do you think they were trying to railroad you into not releasing it?

It was during all the debate with *Crash*, with David Alton, and the moral majority, when all that sort of thing was going on. And I think there was a lot of hysteria, so James Ferman thought the best thing was to sit on it. He phoned me and explained all this, and I wrote a letter of appeal, but it never got any further. So I got the impression that he was waiting till all the furore over *Crash* and various things had subsided.

And of course it's all expense to you, isn't it?

Yes. We have to pay the initial submission fee. Then there are various other charges on top of that, such as the black title card that they give you – it's £27 for a piece of black cardboard. That's gone up actually. If you put a film in that has been released previously, you have to pay for it to be watched again – to make sure it's the certified cut.

And if the BBFC does request cuts...?

We have to pay somebody to do them. Basically the BBFC gives you the timecode reference, and we have to pay someone to make the cuts. Which is another big expense.

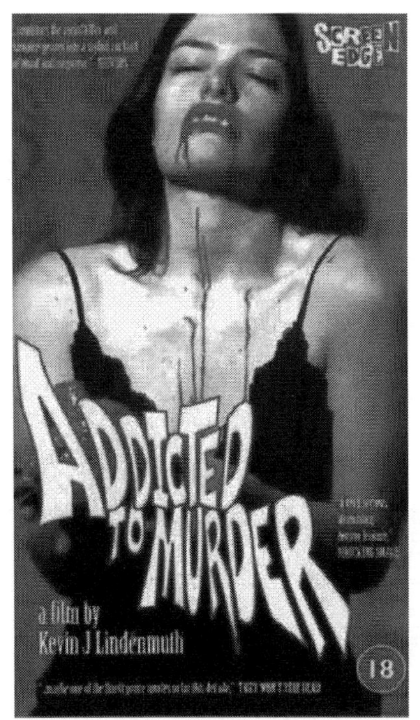

Do you ever predetermine what the BBFC might think is offensive?

We try, but it's impossible to tell really. I mean, we never cut anything before we submit it, because if we'd done that with say, *Addicted to Murder*, we'd have cut out the chainsaw scene – yet that got through completely uncut. Same with *Dead Next Door* – we'd have cut certain things from that if we'd been trying to pre-empt the BBFC. It's basically a good day/bad day scenario with them, I think.

How do you think the BBFC perceives Screen Edge?

Probably find us amusing, patronising us with a pat on the back... Relatively speaking we've had a good relationship. We get on with them because we know that it's something we have to deal with, and we can't afford to kick up a fuss. The BBFC have not actually rejected anything we've put to them. But we've had to go with the flow. In the case of *Transgression* we actually ended up with two completely different versions of the film. It was re-cut following the BBFC's initial examination and list of cuts required. We did it here in the Screen Edge office. Michael Dipaolo, the director, sent us extra footage from his cutting room floor, which we inserted over the offending scenes. He looked at the cuts list, did a re-cut in the States, and then sent us all the extra footage so we could re-cut it according to his directions.

Ironically, when he sent the Beta master with all the inserts that we had to replace, Customs seized it and refused to let us have it. The Customs guy who phoned us up was called Officer Dibble! We had to get James Ferman to phone him back and explain the situation. Half an hour later, Customs let it through. Ferman actually phoned up Customs to say we were re-cutting the film. When we finally resubmitted *Transgression* he said, "Well done, it's a much better film."

***You also had Customs trouble with* Shatter Dead.**

With *Shatter Dead*, Customs seized the tape and destroyed it, along with all literature that was with it, such as biographies and stuff. Customs said I could travel to London and watch the tape under controlled circumstances – padded cell or Mogadon, perhaps? But by this time, another copy was already on its way, so I passed on that little pleasure. Customs weren't interested in the slightest that I was running a legitimate company. But for a while thereafter, I managed to get stuff through via a sympathetic officer who trusted me to have the films on the condition that I sent them back when I'd finished, and showed them to no one else, not even copy them... I guaranteed this in writing. After a few months however, all of this was stopped. I was told that the officer had no right to make such an arrangement in the first place – and they were pretty pissed off with me, too! After that everything coming through Customs got opened.

Strangest of all for me, though, was that Customs were more concerned with the 'shotgun abortion' sequence in *Shatter Dead* than with the 'gun fuck' sequence – which was ultimately cut by the BBFC. Customs seemed to regard the latter as far more offensive, and strictly against their secret little rules. In other words, they were upset by a plastic baby doll and some raspberry syrup – which is what the scene comprises of – as opposed to the use of a deadly weapon as a sex toy!

Like many other people, I spent a lot of time writing letters to various places about the ludicrous inconsistencies between Customs and the BBFC. I was told by Customs that I was virtually breaking the law by even submitting uncut films to the BBFC, as this was tantamount to distribution of obscene material! I wrote to the Home Office but got no reply.

NOTE: *Original Sins* was passed 18 in February 1999 with 6m 14s of cuts. Following this interview Richard King left the video business with, he said, "no real desire to ever [work in it] again." He passed in 2019. Screen Edge now operate primarily as an independent music outlet.

EXPLOITED: INTERVIEW WITH CARL DAFT, COMPANY DIRECTOR

A RELATIVELY NEW FORCE in independent video distribution, Exploited have released some notable cult titles, including *Dead of Night* (d: Bob Clark), *Deranged* (d: Alan Ormsby & Jeff Gillen), *Hated: GG Allin and the Murder Junkies* (d: Todd Phillips) and *Axe* (d: Frederick R Friedel). Many of their tapes include bonus documentary material. One recent release has been an exclusive documentary entitled *The Texas Chain Saw Massacre: The Shocking Truth* (d: David Gregory). To date the company has had two films rejected by the BBFC: *Maniac* (d: William Lustig) and *Deadbeat at Dawn* (d: Jim Van Bebber).

The following interview was conducted in May 2000.

You used to submit your video sleeves for the Video Packaging Review Committee (VPRC) seal of approval. You've stopped doing that, now. Why?

CARL DAFT: Essentially the VPRC are supposed to be independent from the BBFC, and they look at packaging to deem whether it's suitable to be out there on the video shelves. In actual fact they're not separate from the BBFC at all. When we write out the cheques, it is to the "BBFC (VPRC)". But unlike the BBFC classification service itself, the service of the VPRC is voluntary and after the problems we'd had with them over some sleeves we decided that we would elect not to use it anymore and were within our rights to do that.

What benefits are there in submitting packaging to the VPRC in the first place?

When you first start submitting films to the BBFC, they won't release a certificate until the sleeve has been approved by the VPRC. But you're perfectly entitled to write a letter stating that you don't want to use the VPRC, and they will still release the certificate. The majority of people use it. We wouldn't have known at the start that we had a choice, but once we were aware...

If it's in writing that your sleeve won't be going through the VPRC, then your film certificate is released at the time that you get your interim clearance form.

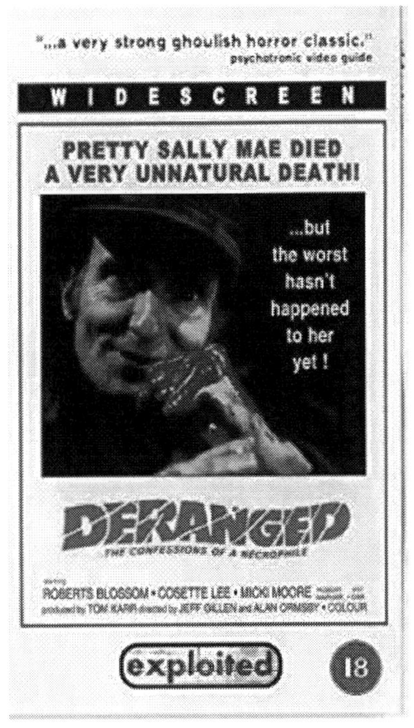

Is the VPRC an expensive process?

It's too expensive, yeah. They charge, I think, £35+VAT just to have a look at the packaging. It must take all of one minute. The reason we stopped comes down to the problem we had with the *Three on a Meathook* sleeve... when we first submitted it, they said we should remove the gory picture of the woman hanging on a meathook on the back. Reluctantly we did so, replaced it with a far less offensive image, and resubmitted it. By the way, you have to pay again when you resubmit material to the VPRC. They looked at the sleeve again and said that the picture on the back was fine, but now they wanted to change the picture on the front – and this was exactly the same picture that was on the front the first time we submitted the sleeve. There was a lack of consistency going on here. We phoned them up and asked how the picture on the front could be OK last week, but not OK this week. Their answer to that was that different examiners sit on different weeks. The BBFC claims to be objective about things! It just shows that it is a subjective thing – who's seeing what and how they feel on the day.

Moving on to* Axe*... Because this particular film had originally been on the DPP list, you had to provide a different version in order to get it released.

Yeah, and this is not actually a law, or a stipulation contained anywhere in the Video Recordings Act – it actually boils down to BBFC guidelines and the codes of practice that they use. It's basically just to cover themselves and show that they're doing the right thing, so they don't get themselves in trouble with the DPP by releasing material that was once liable for prosecution. But

something relatively innocuous like *Axe* gets bundled in with a load of other titles from some obscure prosecution way back in the eighties, and it's just blanketed in the same category as more controversial films like *Cannibal Holocaust* and *Snuff*. Anything that was prosecuted was all tarred with the same brush. So, if there's a record of a film actually having a successful prosecution, I suppose the BBFC have to show they are releasing a version that is different from the version that was originally prosecuted.

So, who suggested the different version? You made nineteen seconds of cuts...

It was suggested by the principal examiner, Mike Bor. As anyone who has seen the film knows, there is very little in it to cause offence. But it had been on the DPP list, and so in spite of the fact that nobody had a problem with the film, it had to now be a different version if we wanted to re-release it. Reluctantly we undertook some cuts, even though the BBFC itself didn't really deem them necessary. In other words they were just following the letter of their code and regulations, rather than what appeared to be practical and sensible.

One scene in* Axe *has been slowed down slightly, which I understand was also to make it a different film to the one that was originally on the DPP list.

We did something similar to that in *Hated* – the [Todd Phillips documentary] about the shock rocker G G Allin – in which the BBFC requested six to eight cuts. What we did to try and get around those and to keep the film as much intact as possible, was just to pan and scan on some of the images. For instance, the scene where Allin squats down on stage and defecates (as the Board so nicely put it in their letter), rather than cut the whole scene as they asked, we panned it, so you don't actually see the offensive slop leave his backside even though it remains patently obvious what he's doing. We did the same thing when he had the prostitute urinating in his mouth for his birthday. We didn't cut the whole scene as they asked, we just panned away. There were no scenes that we actually cut out of that film per se. We got round it the best we could, being rather cheeky with it.

Evidently the Board were happy with that?

Strangely enough, yes. I mean, we took the risk with it, and we got away with it. We tried to do the same with [the Jim Van Bebber short] *My Sweet Satan* when they asked for basically the whole climax to the movie to be cut. Removing it takes away a lot of the impact, a lot of the emphasis and a lot of the point of the film. We tried the same sort of cheap thing on that, panning over a few images instead of making the eighteen seconds of cuts requested. Half we panned and half we cut. We resubmitted *My Sweet Satan* in two different versions and told the BBFC over the phone that one version had the whole eighteen seconds cut out as per their request, while the other version, we believed, removed most of the offensive material without actually making cuts. We'd agreed with the examiners that we'd send these two prints in, but when they received them, they asked why we'd sent in two different copies. Basically they completely ignored the second cut that we'd done and went ahead with the butchered print.

Deadbeat at Dawn – packaging approved by the VPRC and sleeves printed for a release that didn't come.

They don't like being told what to do?

No, they don't. What they say goes. Which is why it's quite a result that we got away with *Hated* in the form that we did. Had we been made to cut everything exactly as their request, it would have greatly lessened the impact of the movie.

Deranged *is a film that has only ever seen a theatrical release in Britain before. Did you have any problems with the video, because again that is quite a strong film?*

The BBFC requested extensive cuts to *Deadbeat at Dawn*... and then rejected it.

BBFC
BRITISH BOARD OF FILM CLASSIFICATION

David Gregory
Exploited
3 Summer Court
27 Mapperley Road
Nottingham
NG3 5AG

3 Soho Square
London W1V 6HD
Telephone 0171 439 7961
Facsimile 0171 287 0141

24/08/98

Dear Mr Gregory

Title: **DEADBEAT AT DAWN** (Video)

I have to inform you that cuts, as detailed below, are required by the Board to the above Video work submitted by you. The proposed category is 18.

Should you desire to discuss the contents of this form, I shall be pleased to make an appointment for this purpose.

The following cuts are required:-

In opening credits (Music) Remove sight of throwing star in ashtray [00.01.30.15. to 00.01.33.07].

At 10 1/2 Mins After mid shot of woman in red dress, remove all sight of chainsticks hanging on wall; remove all sight of man with head scarf taking chainsticks from wall. [00.11.48.07 to 00.11.51.01] Resume on mid shot of man facing door before he removes knife sticking out of door.

At 11 Mins: After sequence in which man with head scarf has been practising martial arts in cemetery, remove all sight of him picking up and wielding chainsticks in practice.[00.12.24.09 to 00.12.52.02]Resume on mid- shot of man walking to right of screen.

At 12 Mins: Remove long shot through railings of man walking towards camera carrying chainsticks.[00.13.09.00 to 00.13.12.06] Resume on shot of man riding motor cycle.

At 12 Mins: As man with head scarf approaches man standing by motor cycle and assaults him, remove all sight of chainsticks.[00.13.32.17. to 00.13.36.13] Resume on man, hands at his waist, about to mount motor cycle.

At 57 Mins: After sequence of man jumping from roof, remove all sight of man holding and throwing combat star, and subsequent shot of star striking and sticking in neck of policeman.[00.58.10.00 to 00.58.13.15] Resume on extreme long shot of man lowering himself on rope against building.

At 59 1/2 Mins: After close up of man picking up magazines, remove all sight of two throwing stars amongst other weapons.[01.01.05.03 to 01.01.06.06] Resume on close up of hand picking up gun.

At 60 Mins: After mid shot of bare-backed man placing a knife in sash, and turning, remove all sight of him picking up throwing star and putting it in his belt. [01.01.24.21 to 01.01.28.02] Resume on close up of back of man in blue jacket.

At 72 1/2 Mins: After mid shot of man on ground with knife near his face, remove all sight of chainsticks being wielded by man in yellow shirt.[01.13.54.02 to 01.13.54.22]. Resume on mid shot of back of man beginning to stand up.

At 72 1/2 Mins: In same fight sequence, remove all sight of chainsticks as man in dark clothes struggles with man in yellow shirt. [01.13.56.04 to 01.13.58.22] Resume on mid shot of man in yellow shirt on ground, arms outstretched.

At 74 Mins: During fight sequence between man in brown jacket and man in black leather jacket, remove all sight of chainsticks being picked up and used in continuing fight. [01.15.22.16 to 01.15.31.24].Resume on close shot of face of man with beard.

At 74 Mins: After close shot of man with red head scarf holding his head, remove all sight of subsequent attack with chainsticks on man in brown jacket - striking him and throttling him; also remove subsequent sequence where man in black leather jacket is carrying chainsticks in fight with three men.[01.15.35.17 to 01.15.48.01] Resume on shot of man's shadow.

At 74 1/2 Mins: After mid shot of man in black leather jacket and beard, remove all sight of him wielding chainsticks. [01.15.53.07 to 01.15.54.08] Resume on long shot of man carrying beam.

At 75 Mins: After long shot of bearded man behind wall, remove all sight of him picking up chainsticks and using them in following fight sequence. [01.16.10.05 to 01.16.29.04] Resume on shot of underside of bridge.

At 75 Mins: In same fight sequence, after mid shot of blond man, remove all sight of man in black leather jacket removing throwing star from shirt and throwing it; also remove subsequent sight of star in man's forehead.[01.16.32.18 to 01.16.36.16]. Resume on long shot of man in black leather jacket sitting on ground.

At 75 1/2 Mins: In fight sequence on roof top, remove all clear sight of throwing star sticking in blond man's head as other man bangs his head against parapet. [01.16.49.20 to 01.16.53.23] Resume on long shot of blond man lying on wall, the other about to push him over edge.

Resubmit.

Signed..............................
Director / Deputy Director / Principal Examiner

It is quite a strong film. I think the BBFC weren't as harsh on that as they could easily have been, probably seeing that it was a well-made film and that it did have artistic points to it. They requested about a half-dozen cuts in the end of only a second here and there.

You had intended to release* Snuff *at one point. I take it that's no longer going ahead?

It's very much on the backburner, shall we say. We did contact the BBFC about the fact we were looking into the idea of picking up *Snuff*. Obviously at this point we were quite upset at [Jim Van Bebber's] *Deadbeat at Dawn* having been rejected – it had cost a lot of money and had basically put the company in a lot of trouble. We'd only been trading for three months, and it was a huge setback for us. We didn't have any releases after that until the following September, so essentially, we lost ten months of trading. *Snuff* was a title we knew we could get the rights for if we wanted, and it was something that we'd looked at. We heard through someone in the BBFC that we know that the very mention of *Snuff* caused a panic there. Robin Duval had a copy fetched up from the vaults especially to watch it, knowing that we were intending to submit it. Anyone who's seen the film knows that it's just a cheap movie that had this ending tagged on – pure exploitation, but not a snuff film. What we wanted to do was put it into a serious context where we could make a documentary about the legend, or the myth if you like, of snuff films. The BBFC are great ones for context; they like to look at everything in context. Hence situations like *Three on a Meathook*, where the film got through completely uncut, but the trailer had to have seven or eight cuts to it, even though it contained nothing that wasn't in the film. That's the context for you. So, we told the BBFC that we'd put *Snuff* into context, that we would take the film seriously and not exploit it, and they wrote back to us saying that whether we put a documentary on the tape or not, it wouldn't alter the fact that *Snuff* was not the sort of film that was suitable for British viewing. I think those were their exact words.

Do you think that the documentaries you include on your releases have helped get some of the more contentious films through the Board?

Exploited contacted the BBFC with regard to the likelihood of *Snuff* getting passed should they submit it. The Board's then new director, Robin Duval, replied (below and bottom).

BBFC
BRITISH BOARD OF FILM CLASSIFICATION

3 Soho Square
London W1V 6HD
Telephone 0171 439 7961
Facsimile 0171 287 0141
http://www.bbfc.co.uk

From: Robin Duval *Director*

23rd September 1999

David Gregory
Exploited

Dear Mr Gregory,

SNUFF

Thank you for your letter of 16th September.

It is not the Board's policy to classify material which has been subject to successful prosecution under the Obscene Publications Act within recent history. Since 1990, I understand that there have been four such actions against **Snuff**, the most recent in 1994. I would recommend that, before you consider submitting the work for classification, you take whatever measures are necessary to remove those elements which are likely to have led to forfeiture and conviction.

You have my assurance that I will give the same advice to any other distributors who approach the Board in similar terms in the next few years.

Yours sincerely,

BBFC
BRITISH BOARD OF FILM CLASSIFICATION

3 Soho Square
London W1V 6HD
Telephone 0171 439 7961
Facsimile 0171 287 0141
http://www.bbfc.co.uk

From: Robin Duval *Director*

27th September 1999

David Gregory
Exploited

Dear Mr Gregory,

SNUFF

I honestly do not believe that preceding **Snuff** with an investigative documentary will make any difference to the acceptability of the main work.

Yours sincerely,

I don't think so. With the market that we're in, obviously we're going to be very borderline on what does get through and what doesn't. That makes it difficult for us to plan ahead. But the special bonus footage that we put on the back of *Deranged* (*The Making of Deranged*) and on *Lemora* (*The Confessions of Lemora*), I don't think helped in any way to get the films themselves through the BBFC net. They do add something extra for the collector, however, and that's what we've always tried to do at Exploited – make things as collectable as possible and give as much value as possible, and that certainly helps in the cases where we unfortunately have to cut the films. Some films are cut so we try to add something on there to make up for that fact.

How do you think that the BBFC view Exploited?

I think they don't like us! I think they are always wary of what we're going to be doing and will keep a special lookout for whatever we send to them. The whole thing boils down to a subjective matter; the BBFC will look at things subjectively and if it is an Exploited title or a Screen Edge title then they will look at it from that point of view. We could talk for days about the subjectivity of the examiners as well. When James Ferman left the BBFC, *The Texas Chain Saw Massacre* and *The Exorcist* were suddenly deemed OK for public viewing when they hadn't been for the past twenty-five years. Is the passing of a great man like Ferman making everyone more morally aware in the country? Plus there are his great quotes as well. At the National Film Theatre at the back end of the screening of *The Texas Chain Saw Massacre* – we actually include this in our documentary *The Shocking Truth* – Ferman says that the film probably won't get a certificate in this country. It was fine playing for middle-class intellectual audiences at the NFT, he said, but imagine the effect it might have on the average car worker in Birmingham. I think that sums it up really. It's the middle-class conservative Christians looking out for the moral good of the country. Surely that's not the way to do it?

NOTE: Exploited no longer exists but Carl Daft, with David Gregory and John Cregan, founded the US based Severin Films in 2006.

TWO INTERVIEWS WITH THE BBFC

INTERVIEW WITH THE BBFC PART I

THE FOLLOWING INTERVIEW was conducted by DAVID KEREKES at the BBFC offices in Soho Square on 8 April 2016. Present were examiner DAVID HYMAN and head of communications, CATHERINE ANDERSON. The questions were supplied in advance with some being forwarded (at the Board's suggestion) to David Austin, who addressed them directly as head of the BBFC by email (see INTERVIEW WITH THE BBFC PART II).

The interview is an attempt to get the Board's perspective on the 'video nasties' era and its impact, absent in the previous edition of this book.

Picture the scene: The BBFC building sits on Soho Square, overlooking Soho Square Garden. This is the doorstep of London's once thriving sex and porn industry, an irony not lost on some BBFC staff. The development work taking place throughout the area signals what I consider another nail in that coffin lid, a sign of a less interesting Soho taking shape, without the edges. The jackhammers stop for lunch. Outside the BBFC, a down-and-out swigs cider from a large plastic bottle as he collides with workmen. In the BBFC reception area is a coffee table on which rests a copy of the latest BBFC Annual Report and a variety of flyers on the topic of the BBFC and younger viewers, aimed at parents and teachers. Refurbishment is taking place here too, in the building, and second-floor staff are temporarily ensconced on the ground floor until the work is completed. Catherine Anderson shows up first, followed by David Hyman, carrying the notes he has had difficulty printing. He apologises: the room with the printer was locked, and he had to go to find the key. The room where the interview will take place is one he says he hasn't visited before, despite having worked here for many years. It turns out to be a small room occupied by a 1990s-type telephone on a big table, the sort of room without much space for chairs. The phone does not ring during the interview but occasionally the sound of hammers and banging is heard from the floor above.

How does the BBFC now view the volatile era of the Video Recordings Act 1984?

DAVID HYMAN: With the VRA 1984, Parliament was responding to understandable public concerns given the fact we had a wholly unregulated environment, which meant children could view material on video that had never been classified by the Board – and obviously, the Board was designated by the VRA to carry out its duties and has done so ever since. The landscape has changed significantly over thirty years. It is regulated; the Board has guidelines which are regularly updated every four to five years, which means that there is a form of contract with the public in that the public effectively tell us what they expect to see in different categories, and we are responding to that. There's a degree of legislation, and within the VRA's own guidelines and policy, we are also aware of the relevant acts of Parliament and interpret those. Prior to this it really was left to individual police forces to decide – certainly in the early days – what was obscene. Then you would get anomalies in different parts of the country. But the main concern, and what Parliament reacted to, was the unregulated environment, which doesn't apply now.

Concern about home viewing was high in the 1980s and 1990s. Is home viewing less of a concern today? For example,* The Exorcist *was initially banned in this respect but is now available for home viewing.

DAVID HYMAN: What's primarily changed is public perceptions as to what it is legitimate to restrict. Because of guidelines research, we get feedback on that. And given the public guidelines there is now more empathy regarding what adults have the freedom to view, than may have been previously the case. [...] You may have seen some of the statements the Board put out when the guidelines were first introduced and one is that adults feel they do not want to be told what they could be offended or shocked by, unless something is harmful or illegal. So, at the time, in the early 1980s, *The Exorcist* was already about ten years old. It was a far more recent film and therefore there was much more interest from children in seeing it. Given those underage viewing concerns at the time,

Reservoir Dogs – scene but not heard.

the Board would have been much more wary – and was much more wary – of classifying. Clearly as the years pass, there is less interest in watching a film that is older (and particularly now that you are talking of a film that is 40 years old). To horror fans, maybe to us, it may still have a lot of the power it once had. But given the advance in effects technology and film-making techniques, it clearly is not a film that has the same power or impact or is likely to affect an underage audience as it might once have done. What's also changed – I mentioned the guidelines earlier – what comes out of research is also the fact that the public has indicated that home viewing is still a significant concern and the vast majority regard a trusted body that provides classification certificates and robust consumer advice as essential and of continued importance when choosing its entertainment. The thing with horror films with special effects in them is that they do date. When *The Exorcist* came out on video it was as recent as a *Saw* movie is now, for example. And, of course, remember it had never been on TV either, at the time. You could only see it at the cinema or on video, and there was more interest in it. Forty years on it's not at the top of the list that younger people choose to watch.

Could you cite a modern equivalent of* The Exorcist *in terms of a film being released theatrically, followed by concern over its video release?

DAVID HYMAN: Modern era? There was the James Ferman era – going back to *Reservoir Dogs* where that and a number of other films were banned around the same time. *Reservoir Dogs* is the most famous one [the release of which in

A new face at the BBFC sees *The Exorcist* granted a release.

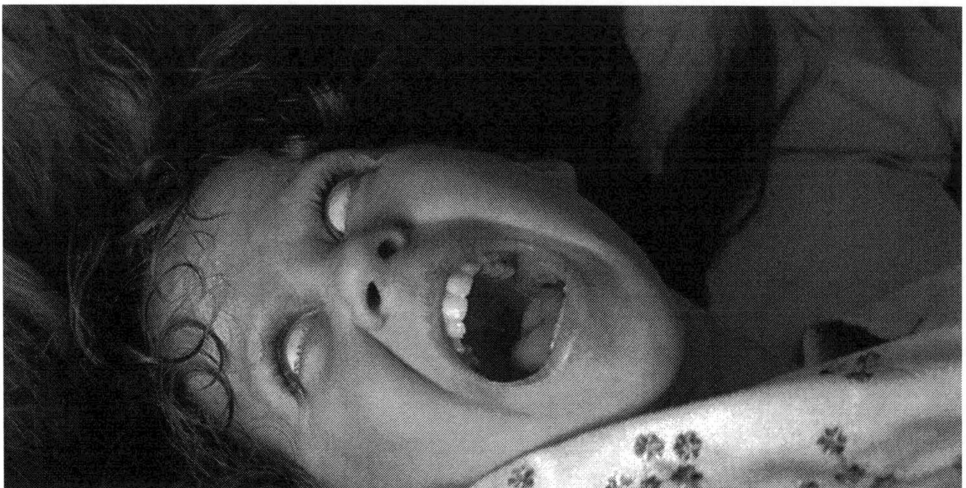

the UK was delayed theatrically because of concerns over violence and banned outright on video, ultimately generating enough interest to see a re-release into cinemas]. It probably made more money than it would have done! But you're really going back to that era – *Reservoir Dogs*, *Bad Lieutenant*, *Man Bites Dog* – the early nineties. That would have been the time of the Alton amendment [to VRA 1984]. Certainly around that time when there were voiced concerns, the time of the James Bulger case. Because of concerns over the comments made at the time of the trial by the judge about violent videos, James Ferman as director of the Board took a view that until those concerns had been worked through, the Board wasn't prepared to just give certificates. What actually happened with those films was that they'd all been classified a year or eighteen months before they'd been released – as often happens or happened more at the time. They'd been released in one throng together, so gave the impression that the cinemas were suddenly awash in extremely violent or troubling films with strong content.

CATHERINE ANDERSON: There is an instance of suicide techniques taken out of theatrical films for the home entertainment release.

DAVID HYMAN: But the actual "hold back" which you're getting at – concerns over something that's been out at the cinema and going into the home – I don't recall anything apart from that period, and that was very much a specific time when there were voiced concerns directed towards these films.

CATHERINE ANDERSON: The Board sat on *The Exorcist* until there was a change from Ferman to [new BBFC president] Robin Duval. Robin Duval used to do broadcast regulation [in his earlier job], and he almost let Sky broadcast *The Exorcist* on TV when it hadn't been given a video release. Until he had a meeting with James Ferman, and James Ferman said that that probably wouldn't be a good idea! But then when Robin got the job here, he started up the consultations and passed *The Exorcist* on video. So, it was a change both in the Board but also moving into public consultation that gave the Board this confidence to pass these works for home entertainment release. Whereas before they'd been very hesitant that the finger would be pointed at them, for having let children have access to this sort of material.

(I am pointed to an episode of BBFC Podcast [episode 50] which, at the time of the interview, had just been completed and is devoted to* The Exorcist *<https://soundcloud.com/bbfc>.)

DAVID HYMAN: Going back to the 1970s, there was quite a lot of hysteria around the initial release of *The Exorcist*, about people being adversely affected – passing out and being taken ill at screenings. The point was that if *that* was transposed to the home viewing it would lead into broader harm concerns. Before *The Exorcist* came out on video, it got a re-release at the cinema – quite a wide re-release for a film from the 1970s – and there was hardly any response at all, which showed how much time had changed. That also enabled the Board to take a view that the initial concerns over the film and its effects had faded over the years.

CATHERINE ANDERSON: By the time *The Exorcist* came out on video it had been parodied and was quite a well-known quantity. It had aged a little bit and all the PR buzz around it had all really died out.

DAVID HYMAN: *Repossessed*, which has actually got Linda Blair in it. So by that time she was sending up her own persona. It does diminish the power of something if people are spending the intervening years laughing at it in various sketch shows and skits. It's to do with power and impact. It can cut the other way. Certain films will retain their power. Horror – particularly from that period – and some of the special effects which were state of the art then, Oscar-winning effects, now look a bit unsophisticated. It's that as well. There's still a strength to *The Exorcist* because it's still an 18 (the same as the X would have been in 73/74) and given its subject matter and content. We haven't been asked to take another look at it for a number of years.

Why might you be asked to take another look at it at this point?

DAVID HYMAN: I don't think we would – unless they discover even more footage! [laughs]

CATHERINE ANDERSON: If it was getting a re-release then the new company would need to submit it.

DAVID HYMAN: As you know there have been some films where they've had however many directors' cuts – *Blade Runner* has had – I've lost track of it – where they suddenly discover another bit of footage somewhere and say, 'we want to put this in as the definitive special edition'. Then obviously the content is different, and we would then have to view it.

Did the Board ever obtain or see a copy of the fabled DPP list of 'banned' films?

DAVID HYMAN: Yes, of course we did, because we were given the list by the DPP because the Board actually needed to know what it could or couldn't classify in its current form, because some films may well have been regarded as obscene. So the short answer is yes. Yes, the Board did for operational reasons.

Do you recall how many titles were mentioned on the list?

DAVID HYMAN: I can't... I think there were titles that were perhaps on an initial list, and then over the years – if there had been a significant number of acquittals – then they would have been less likely to have been put forward to be prosecuted, because they would look at recent precedents in the court. People also cite the DPP 55 or whatever, that may well have been towards the last list. But as with all these things it's all dependent on what's actually happening in the courts. That will obviously dictate whether they regard [these films] as having a likelihood of being found obscene by a jury that's properly directed.

(Catherine volunteers to check the archives for hard copy correspondence between the BBFC and the DPP. She is unable to locate any, but in a follow-up email provides this information:)

> Copies of various DPP lists were sent to the BBFC by the CPS during the early to mid 1980s. This allowed the BBFC to know what types of material was being seized and prosecuted – and therefore what type of material to avoid classifying.
>
> Some of these lists survive within several different BBFC film files (though not as an archive in themselves. This is chiefly because they are not BBFC documents, so we do not archive them in an official way.) Presumably, the CPS would have a full set of all these lists.
>
> What lists we do have in various places would not allow us to say how many titles were on the various DPP lists in total, because the lists changed with time, with certain titles being removed as courts found them Not Guilty (e.g. *The Evil Dead*), whereas other titles were added to later versions of the list as new works came to the attention of the police and were seized. Because of this tendency of the lists to change regularly, the BBFC only kept an eye on the latest lists received, filing outdated iterations if required for future reference. As a general figure, we would estimate that there were around seventy titles on the section 2 list (about half of which were successfully prosecuted), although never all at the same time, and at least eighty on the section 3 list.

CATHERINE ANDERSON: A lot of people get confused about who put the list together and a number of times we have to send corrections to blogs, because they say the BBFC drew up the list of 'video nasties'. And we say, 'no, we didn't!' [laughs]

DAVID HYMAN: When the Board was enjoined by the Home Secretary to seek to avoid classifying material which might fall foul of criminal law, of course the Board then had to have a list of titles that were likely to fall foul of the criminal law given recent legal precedent. Otherwise the Board couldn't actually do its job properly.

I'm presuming then you had a dialogue going on with the DPP, and you didn't simply get one list and that was that?

CATHERINE ANDERSON: I can imagine that was probably a dialogue! [laughs] It normally is in these files.

Many films that were cut for video in the 1980s and 1990s have been re-certified with previously cut scenes reinstated. For some years, according to guidelines, a film that had formerly been rejected or cut could not then be classified and released in its original form. What has changed if anything?

DAVID HYMAN: The Board has always reconsidered previously cut and rejected works, some of which might still require cuts or may well be rejected. The obvious one was *The Trip*, which got rejected on film in, I think, 67, 71 and then 80. And then got rejected on video in 1988 and is now classified on video. If you talk about rejected works you could go right back to when the Board first started operating; a film which was rejected in the thirties or forties would highly unlikely be rejected now. *The Wild One* is the obvious one, which was rejected in 1954 and is actually a PG now on video; thirty-plus years from a rejected film to a PG-rated video. The Board always has looked at films [and has] always taken a view on anything that gets submitted, even if it's previously rejected or cut works.

So, to get this straight:* The Wild One *is available now in exactly the same form as it was submitted in the fifties?

DAVID HYMAN: As far as we know. The thing is, we can't really say it's the same as the version that was submitted in 1954, because none of us were around in 1954, and the files wouldn't reflect that and even the measurement could be slightly different because of logos or whatever. We assume it was but it's difficult to tell. Also, various people have come forward over the years that have said 'I remember a scene in the original film that isn't in the video version'. But this is possibly because there are different versions of films that go to different territories. The Board can only deal with the version submitted to it; it can't demand the same version that's gone out in another territory.

More recently, what about the cut in* Tenebrae*? An arm is chopped off with an axe in the closing scenes.

Tenebrae still had its cuts and chops.

DAVID HYMAN: *Tenebrae* was cut in the eighties. It was a standard horror cut to remove a scene of mutilation – the arm coming off shot. This [cut] was made before the film was placed on the DPP list. When it came in again in 1999 there was a problem, because actually the Board had evidence of recent convictions of *Tenebrae*, so that original cut was sustained and a further cut was made, I think. The spiking that comes after that at the end? However, post-*The Last House on the Left* appeal committee ruling – which stated the Board didn't have to be hamstrung by the fact a tape had been prosecuted as part of a batch and not put before juries, and that the Board could reach a different determination – that played in very strongly when the film was submitted a few years after that, and it was actually passed at 18 uncut. So, the issue about different versions, that kind of does in part explain it. But if the Board is enjoined to seek to avoid classifying material that might fall foul of the criminal law, and the Board was presented with a title which was still successfully getting prosecuted or had very recent successful prosecutions, the Board couldn't put that to one side and say 'well, we are going to take our own view – 18 uncut!' The version that the Board would classify would have to be different, but different in a way that would be evident towards those who would view it. So it wouldn't be a case of taking out one or two frames here or there – which only a horror expert who lined up the versions side by side could spot – it had to actually be something that made it a significantly different work. Obviously, what that was depended on each work itself. It had to be something that would be evident to the layperson, for want of a better word, who could see these were different works. [Thus] those works were made different, so the Board believed this would be unlikely to fall foul of the criminal law. It would be a scene at the heart of what would be considered graphic scenes of mutilation, or violence – 'mischief' is the legal term – the type of material that was perceived as problematic and getting these works prosecuted. So, yes, there were different versions of those [films] created by the Board. The distributors had the rights to the title and needed to exploit them and make money, so if they didn't wish to make the cuts then the work wouldn't be classified.

Is blood on breasts still taboo?

DAVID HYMAN: What has really changed is the fact that now context is central to the question of acceptability of a film or video. When considering this we also take into account the general expectations of the public and the work's audience in particular. Scenes depicting blood-spattered breasts – I think this started to play into people's consciousness because James Ferman used to repeat this regularly at lectures as an image. They weren't ever actually taboo, because the Board did actually pass scenes like that, I think *Angel Heart* for example, which was during Ferman's time here. But the key difference is that the Board applies far more weight now to context than in the past where, say, presumption was viewed as more important. For example, the Board's former weapons policy – chain sticks and flying stars, that sort of thing. And this is also due to changing public perceptions. These are reflected in our regular guidelines reviews and can also be seen in the more nuanced approach taken with regard to sexual violence, which in part stems from the Board's own research and the findings of the Board into sexual violence. In a sense, that's what's really changed, the application of context and the way it's applied to content and the public's perceptions.

Forceful breast exposure was at one time seen as much more of a trigger image. Now it's more nuanced and more context-based than that, and based on public feedback, that is a significant part of the research feedback, which in fact wasn't always reported at the time in that way. People picked up on different things to publicise.

Are there any 'trigger' scenes today that are deemed unsuitable?

DAVID HYMAN: It's context based. Context is key. Something that may be acceptable in one particular context may be less acceptable in another. This is probably not the area you are primarily dealing with, but scenes featuring potentially harmful material or imitable techniques lower down the category scale, which presents these potentially harmful things as safe and fun may well be cut, whereas the actual harm is not evident to the audience. I'm thinking more of U, PG, 12A. But in terms of trigger scenes – no, it's to do with the context.

And that would be what you mentioned before about the suicide technique being an imitable technique?

DAVID HYMAN: This would be the same with a criminal act: If you're teaching somebody a method of breaking into people's houses, disabling alarms or hacking into computers that people would not know... The argument is that you could find this out somewhere else, but the Board is actually obliged to consider likely harm, and if presented with material that is likely to suggest something which could be harmful to society, or by suggesting that something which is potentially lethal or injurious is actually pretty safe and you don't need to worry about it, then... Lower down the category scale, anything to do with children playing with electricity, plastic bags over their heads – I'm trying to think of things where we've actually had discussions over this, where it's all presented as part and parcel of a slapstick comic thing – if it's more outlandish and ridiculous and the characters aren't recognisably human either, which is the difference between a Tom & Jerry type thing and a live action type thing – it's a modality issue.

What's the name of the film with the imitable suicide techniques?

CATHERINE ANDERSON: The one with Dawson from *Dawson's Creek* in it. [James Van Der Beek] Which is why we thought teenagers would seek it out – and it was quite a romanticised suicide. She slits her wrists in the bath?...

DAVID HYMAN: *The Rules of Attraction* [an adaptation of the Bret Easton Ellis novel]. She slits her wrists in the bath with Harry Nilsson's 'Without You' playing...

CATHERINE ANDERSON: It's properly romanticised emotionally...

DAVID HYMAN: Candles burning around her...

CATHERINE ANDERSON: Thirteen- or fourteen-year-old girls' territory. *Dawson's Creek* was massive at the time. He was in it. So, they cut it for video release. But obviously you could see it at the cinema because you would get in if you were under eighteen. But it doesn't happen very often. That film's a real anomaly, where the Board took a decision based on the current climate and the fact that the star was so big, and they just knew teenage girls would seek it out in the home if it was available. They knew teenage girls were going to watch the film, so they took that scene out for home entertainment release.

I happened to watch an old Sydney Pink film last night,* Pyro. *It's about an arsonist and it's got an incredible sequence that depicts step by step how you would set fire to a house in 1964.

CATHERINE ANDERSON: On trigger scenes for sexual and sadistic violence, the research that came out in 2012 has aggravating and mitigating factors. i.e. scenes that make sexual and sadistic violence look appealing, reinforcing the suggestion that victims enjoy rape, invite viewer complicity in rape – so it's all the aggravating factors.

To move onto extras, as in film extras on DVDs and Blu-rays. Are audio commentary tracks exempt from classification?

DAVID HYMAN: No, they're not exempt from classification. In fact, sometimes audio commentary has taken the category *above* the feature category. Particularly when you've got what you might call the *Zoo* [men's lifestyle magazine] format – four or five people in there, encouraging each other to tell stories about it – which often gets as far away from the content of the film as possible. Or, interestingly, we've had instances of the people involved in the making of them have actually explained what they took out of the film in order to get a lower category in the States or over here. They will actually use the language that they couldn't use in the PG13 version of the work. In one case I remember they repeated the word three or four times, either in surprise or emphasis or to make some point. So, the commentary can change a lower category film, especially if they start talking about the sexual undercurrents of a particular scene, theme or even characters.

Can you give me an example of one such film?

CATHERINE ANDERSON: Some of the Monty Python films came in with audio commentary. It also works the other way: sometimes things are quite dark in tone which [might be too much for a 12A in a feature] but are so far removed when they are in an extra because people are talking about them away from the context and it is very, very guided, can therefore be contained at a lower category. Recently, we had to pass the *Rocky Horror Picture Show* at 15 because of strong language in the commentaries, whereas the feature on its own would be a 12.

Are documentary extras reviewed more leniently than feature films?

DAVID HYMAN: As before, context is the key consideration. With an add-on documentary, the documentary feature *may* deconstruct, debrief, decontextualise a scene. You could have interviews overlaying, interspersing, behind-the-scenes footage as well – which, if that's the way in which a scene in the film is presented which might have perhaps got a 15 or 18 – it could if broken up significantly lend the scene a completely different context. So, that could become less stark, shocking, or impactful than the film. Conversely, if you stitch together every single violent scene in the space of thirty seconds or a minute or so, you might end up with something that is more powerful, shocking or stark. *A History of Violence* is interesting – you made a point before about *A History of Violence*. [On the DVD of David Cronenberg's 2005 movie is an extra that features a rapid-fire montage of one particular graphic murder scene and how it differs in different versions of the film.] Different territories have different versions, probably more so in the past – European versions, Japanese versions, especially in the fifties, sixties and seventies, they'd often be stronger versions submitted in other territories. In the case of *A History of Violence*, the Board looked at that in context and that extra also got an 18, so presumably it's still pretty shocking in the extra. I've not seen it, but I remember someone mentioning it at the time. It's the usual thing where people say they saw a different version, different territory – "oh it must have been cut in the UK." Well, it isn't. It was classified 18 uncut.

Today's BBFC assists with trading standards and law enforcement when requested to do so in cases of piracy and bootlegging. Is this a recent development? Did the BBFC work with trading standards and law enforcement in this capacity in the 1980s and 1990s?

DAVID HYMAN: Yes. Back to the enforcement aspect of the VRA, which is administered in the UK by – usually trading standards and the police and Customs & Excise – now predominantly trading standards – and when they present a case to court on somebody who is trafficking in unclassified material, need to have evidence to show the court that it's unclassified. So what the Board would do – and still does – is, if a work had been seized, they would compare it if the Board had a version in the archives to see whether it's the same as the classified version. Or attest that it has never been submitted for classification. This takes the place of witness statements because the court can rely on them on their own as proof the work was or wasn't classified – it's a very simple case in a way: the work either is or isn't classified. So, the Board supplied that since the eighties, and still does, since the VRA started.

I imagine there are fewer cases these days.

DAVID HYMAN: Operations would deal with that, a different department.

CATHERINE ANDERSON: The Board still gets asked to do it. It's only one part of the equation, though, because even a pirated work – all we can do is a technical comparison. We can say we haven't classified the work, it's not on our system, therefore it should definitely not be being retailed in this country – easy, job done. But, if it's a bootleg version of something that *has* been classified and it's the identical length, all we can say is "it's the same as the classified version". Obviously, if it's going out without the distributor knowing – different packaging – then it's copyright theft. That's when people like FACT get involved. And we can't really help at that point.

Has the vogue for so-called torture porn affected the way in which the BBFC considers horror situations?

DAVID HYMAN: Short answer: No. Basically we don't like to refer to them as "torture porn", because that to us evokes a different type of content. They are more torture *themed* horror films. Torture-themed horror is a subgenre that was probably more popular a few years ago, it seems – the cycle seems to have turned again at the moment back toward more supernaturally-oriented films. Those films – torture-themed horror – were viewed within the Board's guidelines. They generally attracted an 18 because they dwelled on the infliction of pain, injury, what you term strongest gory images or strong sadism. Things like the *Saw* movies, *Hostel* got lumped in there as well. We have the guidelines, and these movies haven't affected the way in which we view horror situations, we interpret them in terms of the guidelines. If you read the Annual Reports, you'll usually see there's a bit on the difference between the US and the UK ratings, whereas US PG13 horror films often attract 15 ratings over here, in the last few years things like *Drag Me to Hell*, *The Possession*, and people might look at them and say they are PG13 in the States which should be 12A here. The feedback we get is tone and impact; the way the film makes them feel, which in some cases is more important than the detail, like how many blows to the head somebody takes. And films which have a sort of despairing tone, or worldview, have greater effect and impact on audiences and are more likely to perhaps attract a 15 than a 12A. So, in visual terms with a lot of the films you don't actually see that much blood and guts, or focus on the destruction of the body, torture, that sort of image, which might be more likely to get an 18. But in terms of overall atmosphere, dark tonality and threat, a lot of those films [torture themed] are more likely to get 15.

(At this point there is talk of William Brent Bell's* The Boy *[2016], which had just been classified at the time of the interview.)

DAVID HYMAN: We've classified that 15 and I think it was PG13 in the States. That's a more recent one, but there are quite a lot. Last year the remake of *Poltergeist* was a PG13 in the States and 15 over here. And same with *Krampus*, which was the Christmas one. As with all subgenres, call them what you will, sooner or later someone is going to make a really popular gruesome torture-themed horror film, then you'll get a cycle of films spinning off that until everyone gets tired of them. Recently, certainly theatrically, we haven't had that many 18 rated horror films. So, yeah, the answer is we just apply the guidelines.

CATHERINE ANDERSON: [Looking at the BBFC website] *The Boy* got PG13 for violence and terror and some thematic material, whatever that means, and we gave it a 15 for very strong sustained threat. So, you have, tonally, films treated differently in the States. The public tell us that's how they want us to interpret those kinds of films.

Does the BBFC ever have a direct dialogue with [American ratings board] the MPA?

CATHERINE ANDERSON: Only about once a year, when we catch up at the International Classifiers conference and we speak with them then. But we don't really communicate with them on individual decisions. They are quite a closed organisation. Although we do speak to them at those events and we know them well, we don't really deal with them on a day-to-day basis at all. What they are doing doesn't really come into our sphere of influence. If a very high-profile film comes in, we'll take an interest. But more often than not we are more interested in Europe than America – what the Germans do, what the French do. And then it's more out of interest to see "what did they pass it then?" [laughs] We tend to do it after the fact, after we've rated [a film] and take a look at the other ratings. Mm, ok! Interesting. We'll talk to them about that when we see them again – that kind of thing.

DAVID HYMAN: It may well be that the MPA have possibly seen an earlier cut of the film, or a different cut that is released in their territory. It can be perplexing: *Have I missed something here? Where is all this bad language!* The distributors may well have taken out some of the language in order to secure a 12A rather than a 15, because it's got a PG13 in the States; it may have opened there; the film may have attracted a strong core audience of, I don't know, 11-to-14-year olds. Their marketing might say, "Right, this is the core audience; we need to get a 12A." They submit here with a request, and we say, sorry, it's a 15 because of – as Catherine said with *The Boy* – it's a thematic tonality that runs throughout; it's not a case of saying, "well, if you lost this bit here, or this bit here, or this bit here..." It's the work as a whole. As I say, the Annual Reports over the last few years always mention three or four titles, and they're usually, but not always, horror.

CATHERINE ANDERSON: The second *Woman in Black* film was very much like that. Whereas the first one – yeah, it was scary, but it went up and down and you had moments of relief where everything was fine. The second one was much more – the characters involved were all very young children, and there was no one character that seemed to give off any... *hope*. All throughout the entire film everyone was either a ghost or nuts or trying to kill someone! There was no way that was going to be able to be contained at a 12, even if you cut it, because there was nothing really that you could take out that would give any relief from that sustained sense of everyone's going to die... and there's ghosts everywhere! [laughs]

Sounds quite appealing...

CATHERINE ANDERSON: But maybe not if you're eleven!

INTERVIEW WITH THE BBFC PART II

AS NOTED, SEVERAL questions supplied in advance of my meeting in Soho Square were dealt with at the Board's request by BBFC CEO, David Austin, who responded in an email dated 15 April 2016.

What does the BBFC perceive as the most significant changes in its role as a classification body over the last three decades?

DAVID AUSTIN: In the 1980s Parliament extended the BBFC's statutory classification remit to cover video works under the Video Recordings Act 1984. Under this remit the BBFC is required to have special regard to the likelihood of works being viewed in the home, and to any harm that may be caused to potential viewers or, through their behaviour, to society.

Since 1999 the most significant change in how the BBFC operates has been to derive standards by means of large-scale public consultation. We carry out these consultations every four–five years and supplement them with more specific research, for example into depictions of discrimination, sexual and sadistic violence. As a result we are able to track changes in society's attitudes to the acceptability of certain content at the different age categories and adjust our standards accordingly.

The BBFC has a duty to protect children and empower consumers, particularly parents, in relation to video content. This responsibility does not end simply because a child may be viewing a film or video online. Therefore, in addition to its statutory remit we have developed a number of best practices, voluntary classification services in partnership with industry. Since 2008 the BBFC has been classifying video works distributed over the Internet under a voluntary, self-regulatory service. Online video content the BBFC classifies in 2016 on a voluntary basis includes full-length features, original TV content, music videos and pornography.

Since September 2013, the BBFC has also provided a Classification Framework for commercial and Internet content distributed via the UK's mobile networks provided by O2, Three, EE and Vodafone under another voluntary, self-regulatory service. The Classification Framework defines content that is unsuitable for customers under the age of 18 and is based on the BBFC's Classification Guidelines for film and video. The framework enables commercial content providers to self-classify their mobile commercial content as either suitable or unsuitable for users under 18.

The BBFC is occasionally called upon by distributors to compare existing versions of movies. This suggests the BBFC has copies of every movie/version officially released in the UK. Would that be true? (Including videocassettes?)

Under the terms of the VRA the BBFC may need to provide evidence in a court of law as to whether or not a work is classified on video. To do this we keep copies of all works classified under the VRA. This archive consists of over 250,000 works. In the past, we stored many thousands of VHS tapes in vaults deep underground in the Eisenhower Centre in London. In recent years, however, we digitised this archive, converting over 130,000 files from VHS tape, and it is held on servers in 3 Soho Square.

'Watch & Rate' — streaming video. It's substantially cheaper to submit a film for classification that is to be streamed online than it is for a DVD or theatrical release. Why is that?

Watch & Rate works undergo the same classification process as VRA works, but with fewer formal responsibilities or requirement to produce evidence in court. This lower level of obligation translates to lower operating costs and therefore a lower fee for classification.

The BBFC offers an advisory service to studios and film-makers (script viewing and film viewing). When was this service created and is it used often?

The BBFC has offered advice to film-makers at various stages of production since the 1930s when we first invited film-makers to submit scripts for advice before they went into production as films. Many of the "scenario reports," as they were called, for these scripts and screenplays are held by the BFI. What has changed is the transparency with which the BBFC makes this service known. Today if we see a film or video for advice and the distributor chooses to make cuts to achieve the category it wants, we will publish a summary of this when the final work is classified.

The above is a paid service, so one assumes the advice is more formal than it was in the days of John Trevelyan and James Ferman. What impact in particular has James Ferman had on today's Board, having made some contentious decisions in some rather difficult times?

James Ferman was the first chief executive to expand the BBFC's work beyond its original remit of classifying cinema films on behalf of local authorities. For example, under Ferman the Board moved into the areas of video and video game classification, as well as taking on responsibility for the regulation of pornography offered in licensed sex premises. The BBFC builds upon his work by constantly seeking new areas in which we can use our expertise to protect children and the vulnerable, and empower consumers – for example in the online sphere.

Does an advisory service help avoid 'another Ferman', i.e. a figure that becomes the public face of classification and censorship?

James Ferman and senior members of his staff routinely gave advice on unfinished films, so the advisory service today is no different to how it operated during his tenure. It remains a key part of my role as chief executive to be the public face of the BBFC, as has been the case since at least the late 1940s.

Many previously cut scenes are now being reinstated. Would today's BBFC have handled the era differently?

The BBFC has always agreed to take a fresh look at previously censored material, after a suitable period has elapsed, and arrive at a different decision if standards have changed. James Ferman himself waived many cuts made by his predecessors and John Trevelyan waived many cuts made by his predecessors. It's part of an ongoing process of responding to societal change, rather than any dramatic or sudden change that occurred after Ferman. It is impossible to answer the question of how current members of the BBFC would have approached particular films during James Ferman's time, as circumstances and expectations were different then.

Some would say that the BBFC reacts to outside influence (media/politics/pressure groups), rather than its own rules and guidelines? Is that a fair comment?

No. The only outside influences that inform our decision making are the general public, expert advice, research, and UK law. The BBFC's role is to be consistent and predictable for both the public and the industry. We enjoy strong levels of public trust because our classification standards and decisions reflect public opinion. At the last review of the Guidelines agreement levels with individual decisions were in the 90% range and it's unusual for us to receive more than twenty complaints for a single film classification decision, and the majority of decisions generate virtually no complaints.

When BBFC staff identify a scene that might 'deprave and corrupt' those who view it, how do they remain immune from the assumed corruptive effect? What section of society lacks the same immunity?

The BBFC may not classify content which is in conflict with the criminal law. This includes the Obscene Publications Act 1959. The test under the Obscene Publications Act, which considers whether material might 'deprave and corrupt', is not focused solely on the material, but also on exposure to the material with regard to all relevant circumstances. BBFC staff view material, including challenging material, in a quite specific context which involves the necessary level of engagement coupled with a professional distance where material is not being viewed for entertainment or personal satisfaction, but being judged against the appropriate criteria for the purpose of making a rating recommendation. It is a unique role which tends to provide sufficient personal detachment from what might otherwise be more troubling content.

Nonetheless, BBFC examiners and compliance officers can be exposed to some very challenging material and we do offer a confidential advice service to staff who may want to discuss exposure to any kind of content which they find difficult.

As to which section, or sections, of society may be more vulnerable, the BBFC turns back to the legal test and advice provided by enforcement agencies. In terms of material which might be considered likely to 'deprave and corrupt' the BBFC consults the Crown Prosecution Service, the Metropolitan Police Service, and we use the Crown Prosecution Service's published guidelines. If advised that material is likely to be subject to prosecution, the BBFC deals with the material accordingly.

Occasionally while watching a movie I become conscious of the BBFC. Once this was because of cut scenes; conversely now it tends to be material that gets through. A recent case in point: Babak Najafi's* London Has Fallen *[2016]. My question is two-fold: There is a rather unpleasant knifing in this movie that is inflicted with malice. Did the scene cause any consternation? Arguably it flies in the face of BBFC guidelines involving extended torture.

The film is classified 15 for strong violence, threat, injury detail and strong language. In the scene you mention a knife is twisted in a man's wound; but the scene is dark and injury detail is limited. The scene did not go beyond the Classification Guidelines at 15 where violence may be strong but should not dwell on the infliction of pain or injury. The BBFCinsight for *London Has Fallen* mentions this scene as a key classification issue, allowing potential viewers to be aware of it.

Staying with* London Has Fallen*: This film is very heavy on American gung-ho-ism. How did the BBFC view the film within the current climate and the potential to feed xenophobic attitudes?

The BBFC will keep in mind UK law and whether any special information should be given to the public in relation to how a film may impact on victims of real-world issues. These issues do not generally impact on the classification of the film, but we highlight them in BBFCinsight [information and parental guidance on a film on the BBFC website]. In the case of *London Has Fallen* there is reference to the terrorists threatening the characters in the film, but there is little reference to race, and we did not consider the film likely to encourage xenophobic attitudes.

What, if anything, is different in movie classification post 9/11? Does the portrayal of the 'enemy' in realistic dramas pose a problem, or the potential to do so?

Any film portraying any disaster in a familiar or domestic setting or a real-life disaster, may be potentially problematic to certain audiences. It is unlikely, however, to impact on the classification as a sole issue, though it may cause us to provide an additional warning for viewers in the BBFCinsight for the film. For example, the BBFCinsight for the film *The Impossible* (2013) states: "*The Impossible* is a drama based on the true story of a family who were caught up in the 2004 tsunami. It is rated 12 for natural disaster scenes, moderate injury detail and brief nudity."

A television show like* The Walking Dead *brings gore into the home that is more visceral and realistic than the majority of the so-called 'video nasties' were. What kind of impact has a television show like* The Walking Dead *had on the BBFC? Has it made the Board more lenient on violence?

The Walking Dead is classified in line with the Classification Guidelines. Public opinion impacts on the Guidelines, not any particular film or video. We know from our research that the public accepts realistic gore effects in series like *The Walking Dead* and this is reflected in the Guidelines. We classified episodes of *The Walking Dead* 15 and 18 depending on their content. For example, Season 1, Episode 1 is classified 15 for strong violence and gore, while Season 4, Episodes 1–16 are classified 18 for strong bloody violence, horror, gore.

Video games with pornographic content are classified by the BBFC, but, according to guidelines, 'with a few exceptions, the responsibility for classifying video games falls to the Video Standards Council (VSC), applying the Pan-European Game Information (PEGI) system.' Is this correct? What are the few exceptions and why? How do the criteria for classifying a video game differ if at all to movie classification?

Video games classification in the UK operates in accordance with PEGI standards (www.pegi.info/en/index/). PEGI standards do not result from consultation with the UK public, and they apply on a pan-European basis (excluding Germany). However, the BBFC is responsible for the classification of all video games that feature strong pornographic content (i.e. content that would receive an R18 classification), as well as content and ancillary games attached to a wider and primarily linear submission. In addition, the VSC must send to the BBFC non-integral linear material that may form part of a video game: i.e. content such as 'making of' documentaries or supporting interviews, for example the spoof TV content in *Grand Theft Auto V*, rather than 'cut scenes' which form part of a video game's narrative.

The BBFC classifies video game content according to the same Guidelines used for film, video and online classification.

How does the BBFC address, if at all, unrated streamed movies that are accessible from anywhere in the world?

There is no requirement on the distributors of such content to have these movies classified. However, we have classification expertise that a number of companies that stream movies use. For instance, our voluntary classification system for VoD platforms demonstrates how partnerships with industry can work online in order to empower the public and protect children.

Some would argue that the Internet undermines classification, stating that a classification process defined by borders is redundant. How would you respond to that?

When digital content first emerged this appeared to be a difficult proposition for the BBFC, but the public has made it clear that they expect and want the same consistent guidance for films and videos they watch online as they have when buying a DVD or Blu-ray or going to the cinema. We surveyed the public on this most recently in 2015 and 85% said they consider it important to have consistent classification on and offline. This figure rises to 91% among parents whose youngest child is under ten years old. We also have twenty-four platforms licensed to use BBFC age ratings online, along with four major airlines, which demonstrates again the expectation among consumers, and a desire among many in the home entertainment industry, that film and video should be regulated in a way they recognise and trust.

ANATOMY OF A RAID

INTERVIEW WITH DAVID FLINT

EXPANDING ON MATERIAL in the chapter BLACK MARKET & PIRATES, here follows an interview with author and cultural historian, David Flint. His Stockport, Manchester, home was raided by HM Customs & Excise in 1994 and again by police in 1998, two isolated incidents pertaining to videocassettes.

The interview was conducted by email in February 2021.

Prior to the raid in 1998, you mention an earlier raid in 1994 by HM Customs. What films had been intercepted in this instance and who visited you, customs officers and/or police?

Appendix

ANATOMY OF A RAID

DAVID FLINT: Okay, this is a longish story – I'll try to keep to the basics. In 1994, I went to stay with [filmmaker/artist] Ian Kerkhof in Amsterdam, something I'd done two or three times a year for the last couple of years. I was there a week, did a lot of shopping. Too much, perhaps. Anyway, I brought back around twenty VHS tapes – three of Ian's films, *Mondo Cane 3*, some other horror and around nine classic porn titles – all 1970s/80s movies. The number of tapes meant that I couldn't carry them onto the plane as hand luggage. I knew something was amiss when my bag didn't arrive with the rest of the baggage at Manchester airport; it came alone down the conveyor belt after everyone else had collected their luggage. As soon as I picked it up, there was a customs officer next to me. "Is this your bag, sir?"

What happened next is where it went a little crazy. I sat for a couple of hours as [customs] went through all the tapes – I guess they had to check that the porn films really *were* porn. I watched people walk through checkpoints unchallenged and wondered what they might have been carrying into the country while the customs staff all pored over my copy of *Debbie Does Dallas*. Once satisfied, I was arrested and taken for interview, *sans* lawyer. I was then taken to a cell where I would stay for the next twelve hours. On the basis of what I'd told them in the interview about my publishing activities, they decided that I would have more of this stuff at home, and so organised a house raid. I was still in a Manchester airport cell [while the raid took place and] had to hand over my keys. They took some seventy tapes, twenty-three computer discs and assorted paperwork. There was then another interview (again, no lawyer) in which they tried to get me to concede that the films were obscene, which clearly wasn't going to happen – not only because I knew enough about legal entrapment not to fall down that rabbit hole again, but because I genuinely didn't see vanilla sex films as obscene – and knew that such material was rarely convicted by juries either. At 10:15 PM, I was finally released.

So, the initial seizure included the nine adult movies, Ian Kerkhof's *Return of the Dead Man* and *The Mozart Bird*, and *Mondo Cane 3*. All on the basis of obscenity except *Mondo Cane 3*, which was seized as a 'dog fighting' film, due to one scene. That's how it was described on the paperwork – 'dogfighting film', as though it was some illegal animal abuse video rather than a documentary film with one minute of footage showing – and disapproving of – a dog fight. I wasn't too happy about that.

I told them that I was going to appeal the seizure. Two days later, they sent me a fine – no court case, but they don't need one – based on the 'commercial' value of the films in the UK. It worked out at £50 a title, which seemed a tad ambitious. If I didn't pay up in a week, I would be prosecuted. I asked what would happen to the money if I won the appeal? Guess what? They get to keep it, even if the films are declared not to be obscene.

Anyway, I found a lawyer – Paul Chinnery – who was put onto me by Nigel Wingrove [founder of Salvation Films]. He was also Bob Guccione's lawyer, and later became head of Channel 5's legal department, so he knew a few things. Unfortunately, there wasn't a lot that we could do. He bluntly told me that if it went to court in front of a magistrate, we would lose; if we then went to appeal, we would win. But his legal aid fees wouldn't cover an appeal, and the costs all-round were just too much to bear. So, in the end, we insisted that *The Mozart Bird* was returned, given that it has no hardcore sex in it, just nudity. I think they got a bit excited or porn-blind while viewing it. We set this as an arbitrary line in the sand that we would go to court over (I suggested *Mondo Cane 3* as well, but he rightly pointed out that British people love dogs...). And we insisted that the fine was excessive and wouldn't pay it. In the end, we negotiated down to £200 – at £20 a film. It still stung. I got fifty-four films seized from my house back; I had to go and collect them myself.

My post was being watched for months after this. I know because the postman at the PO Box collection office 'accidentally' gave me the customs notification telling them to hold any international post sent to me (even letters) even though it explicitly said not to let me know.

UK tapes of* I Spit on Your Grave *and* The Image *were also confiscated on this visit. Did the customs officer/police know what to look for? Had they a list?

They were clueless. Absolutely clueless. Certainly, some key titles probably stood out – I imagine their eyes lit up at *I Spit on Your Grave*. But the house raid was telling. I had my 'best' tapes on a shelf, but as you know, there's only so much you can have on display. The rest were boxed up. The boxes were ignored. So they seized *Devil in Miss Jones*, *Nightdreams* and *Sensations* but left *Introducing Kascha* and *Invasion of the Samurai Sluts from Hell*. The films on the shelf were in alphabetical order, but they still seized *Nudie Cuties Vol 2* while leaving *Vol. 1*, which was right next to it. They seized films that clearly had BBFC certificates on the sleeve – not just 18 certificates, either. They seized the PG-rated *Ro.Go.Pa.G.*, presumably because it sounded foreign. I wish I was taking the piss here, but they literally did seize anything with a foreign language title, even if they were Tartan, Connoisseur or Electric Pictures [i.e. British] releases. *Onibaba*, *Deep Red*, *The Honeymoon Killers*, *Der Todesking*, *Swoon*, *Nude on the Moon*, *Teaserama*... I got all that stuff back eventually.

As for *I Spit...* and *The Image*: basically, customs can seize and destroy *any* item found alongside illegally imported material. Anything they wish. It's entirely at their discretion to return anything once you have an item that they declare an illegal import. In the case of these two films, they also made the somewhat dubious claim that because both films are American productions, they still count as 'imports' even though the tapes were UK releases. Obviously, the master copy had been imported. *The Image* was a heavily cut version, to boot – but no matter. It was a crazy logic that barely seemed worth arguing with in the end – Kafkaesque might be an exaggeration, but only a slight one.

Do you think this raid in 1994 had any influence on the one in 1998?

It's hard to tell. I think they were unfortunate coincidences, to be honest, but you never really know how interlinked these things are.

Was there any noticeable domino effect among other collectors because of the raid?

The police raid? Yes, sadly. A colleague in Leeds, who was mad-keen to shoot movies and so was soliciting my assistance, was arrested a few weeks later, based on correspondence found on my Mac. Significantly with that, the fact that we had talked quite clearly about any videos needing BBFC approval or being for export only effectively undercut their claims that we were conspiring to produce obscene material – clearly, we were being careful about following the law. His case was dropped at the same time as mine, but it certainly caused a rift in our friendship for a while; six months under police investigation will do that. There was also someone in Scotland who was arrested after they found a letter from him in my paperwork. He'd sent me a film review on spec and included a little note offering to sell me a few adult tapes. It was so small that I hadn't even seen it in the envelope. But the police did. They informed his local force and he was unfortunate enough

to live in a small town where nothing ever happens. He was taken to court. That's another ludicrous story. I was called as a prosecution witness. This meant spending two nights in [Scottish border town] Jedburgh, because there is only one bus out a day. So my travel (by coach!) and hotel costs probably came to a fair amount. I went to court, full of defiant fury, only to see it all collapse immediately. I was asked one question, his lawyers objected, I was sent out of court while things were discussed and then, after about half an hour, some usher popped his head around the door and cheerfully announced that I could go home. It was all over. They had charged him over committing an offence between two specific dates, and the letter they had asked me to identify was postmarked on a different day; the only piece of evidence deemed inadmissible. They'd had almost a year to find this out.

Anyway, I bumped into the defendant in the street afterwards and we went to the pub. He was none too pleased, but I think the relief at it all being over made him more sociable than he might have otherwise been.

The 1998 raid: Did you get all your tapes back when the case was dropped? Was there any compensation, or apology from the police?

I got all my tapes back, bar one – which they'd 'lost'. I can't remember which one. And a Betamax tape that had been mangled in their player – I don't think they'd used a Beta machine in years. Unlike with customs, the bloke who was in charge of the case brought them back. He managed to [inadvertently] leave one box on the pavement next to his car, as we found when he was just about to leave. There were little kids playing football in the street, and a box of porn movies sat there for the taking.

They had returned my computer after about a month – if I recall correctly. I can thank Nigel Wingrove for that. I was working on something for him, and he did a bit of complaining that holding onto it was a restriction of my ability to make a living and affecting his business. But everything else – tapes, paperwork, VCRs – they kept for six months. No compensation, of course. And the copper was full of "no hard feelings, I don't have any problem with this stuff, it's just my job" platitudes, that frankly didn't convince. We all knew about the evangelical zeal of the Greater Manchester Obscene Publications squad.

Anyway, to this day I have a bunch of 8mm movies that are still in the evidence bag that they were returned with. A souvenir of a very strange and disagreeable experience.

What are your overriding memories of the 1998 raid?

It seemed like the beginning of the end, somehow – a last gasp of the old order. During the raid, one copper picked up the R18 *Batbabe* tape and scoffed "well, we've brought all that to an end", suggesting that the BBFC's tentative experiments with legal hardcore had been crushed and the old rules reinforced. But, of course, the genie was out of the bottle. Their days were numbered.

The press reaction was also telling – I'm not sure that the coverage would have been sympathetic a decade earlier, even for a researcher and writer. The thing that struck me was how out of step the authorities seemed to be – that they had no idea of just how indifferent the public were to this supposed threat.

So, in a weird way, I think that I was part of a cultural shift. It definitely helped that there was the scandal of the police raid on the Birmingham University library to seize a [photographer] Robert Mapplethorpe book shortly before – the two raids definitely seemed like out-of-touch philistines trying to hold back the future. And oddly, it gave me a career boost for a little while – got me media work, gave me some standing in the free speech world (all long forgotten now of course!). And it was the final push to get me out of Stockport. I was very aware that this would never have happened if I was in London.

But the raid itself is still one of the most unpleasant experiences of my life – the sense of helplessness, injustice and terror of what is to come. It leaves you shaken and confused, violated even. But that quickly turns to anger and a determination to fight back. I know that isn't an option for everyone, but I figured I had nothing to lose.

THE 'VIDEO NASTIES' — WHERE ARE THEY NOW?

IN THE FIRST edition of this book, DVD had only just entered the commercial market and Blu-ray was yet to arrive – videocassette was king. Many of the 'video nasties' analysed elsewhere are now widely available in a variety of home entertainment formats. Here, fan and filmmaker DAVID HINDS summarises the relationship of these films with the BBFC following our own investigation (see THE DPP39), and brings their status up to date.

ABSURD

Present UK status: Available uncut on DVD & Blu-ray

Originally released in two versions by Medusa in 1982, one cut and the other uncut. Despite the BBFC granting the film an 18 certificate with 2m 32s of cuts in August 1983, Joe D'Amato's *Absurd* remained on the 'video nasties' list and was successfully prosecuted. *Absurd* is now available uncut in the UK from 88 Films on Blu-ray. It is also uncut in the US on the same format from Severin Films.

ANTHROPOPHAGOUS THE BEAST

Present UK status: Available uncut on DVD & Blu-ray

Video Film Promotions released Joe D'Amato's *Anthropophagous the Beast* uncut in February 1983. By November it was listed as a 'video nasty' and eventually prosecuted. A heavily edited version was released by Videoshack that same year. Presented to the BBFC in a heavily edited R-rated form in 2002, under its alternative title *The Grim Reaper*, no further edits were required. This truly awful edit was released on the budget Hollywood DVD label and could regularly be found in high street stores for as little as £1. All key gore scenes are gone and the film is a slightly different edit with an alternative score. Finally issued with an uncut 18 certificate in 2015 and released on DVD and Blu-ray by 88 Films. Also available uncut in the US from Severin Films in a greatly improved transfer.

AXE

Present UK status: Available uncut on DVD

Although passed with cuts for an X rating by the BBFC for its 1982 theatrical release as *California Axe Massacre*, the film was uncut when released on home video by the Video Releasing Organisation the same year. Frederick R Friedel's film was released in 1999 on the Exploited video label on VHS with nineteen seconds of cuts, and six years later passed uncut for DVD by ILC Prime, and then by 4Digital in 2008. Severin Films have recently released a stunning Blu-ray in the US. The disc also features *Kidnapped Coed* and *Bloody Brothers* (the latter is a re-edit combining *Axe* and *Kidnapped Coed*). Severin announced this package will be offered in the UK, but it remains to be seen.

THE BEAST IN HEAT

Present UK status: BANNED

One of the rarest tapes to emerge in the 'nasties' debacle, *The Beast In Heat* was released uncut by JVI in June 1992. But this insane Nazisploitation effort has yet to receive a certificated UK release: no distributor has presented it to the BBFC to date and the film retains its 'banned' status. It was made available uncut in the US on DVD as a standalone release from Exploitation Video and also from Full Moon in a movie package titled *Nazi Basterds and Bombshells*. Severin Films released a 2K hi-definition transfer from the original uncut camera negative in the US. Highly unlikely to be released in the UK anytime soon after the recent upheld bans of *Gestapo's Last Orgy* and *Love Camp 7*.

THE BEYOND

Present UK status: Available uncut on DVD & Blu-ray

This Lucio Fulci classic was released in cinemas with an X certificate and 1m 39s of cuts. Excised footage included the brutal chain whipping of a warlock in the prologue, eye gouging, a blind woman having her ear torn off and throat ripped open by her guide dog, and a maid having her eyeball forced out with a six-inch nail. Videomedia/Vampix issued the same truncated theatrical version on home video. *The Beyond* was listed as a 'banned' video in November 1983 but dropped in April 1985. Elephant Video re-released the film in 1987 in its approved X cut, as did Vipco in 1992. At this time, Vipco also offered a 'strong uncut version' from Denmark. Vipco finally secured an uncut 18 certificate in 2002. Arrow Video reissued *The Beyond* uncut on DVD and Blu-ray in 2011. Shameless Entertainment re-issued the film on Blu-ray in a slightly improved transfer, and Grindhouse Releasing in the US issued a stunning special edition complete with a CD of Fabio Frizzi's original soundtrack.

BLOOD BATH

Present UK status: Available uncut on DVD & Blu-ray

Mario Bava's stylish splatterfest was rejected outright for cinema release by the BBFC in 1972. Hokushin released the film on video in February 1983 in a full uncut version. After a decade as an outlawed video, *Blood Bath* was granted an 18 certificate after forty-three seconds of cuts were made for Redemption's 1994 home video release, under the title *Bay Of Blood*. Cuts included a machete slashing a throat and smashing into a skull (two seconds), a guy stumbling around with a machete embedded deep in his face (twenty-one seconds), shots of a double impalement by spear (nine seconds), a decapitation and subsequent arterial spray (two seconds) and shots of an impaling with a spear (eleven seconds). In 2010, the BBFC waived all previous cuts and Arrow Video issued an uncut version on DVD and Blu-ray (despite false rumours that it was censored).

Blood Feast

Present UK status: Available uncut on DVD and Blu-ray

Astra released *Blood Feast* in May 1982 uncut. H G Lewis' cheap and unconvincing gore showcase was reissued in 2001 by Tartan Video, a version censored by twenty-three seconds. Cuts were applied to a scene where Ramses whips a woman with a cat o' nine tails. In 2005, *Blood Feast* was resubmitted to the BBFC and passed uncut. Arrow Video have issued the film uncut on Blu-ray in the UK. Their wide release version is unfortunately 1:78:1 ratio, removing the top and bottom of the image, resulting in some overly tight framing. Arrow did release the original fullscreen version as part of their limited edition H G Lewis box set.

Blood Rites

Present UK status: BANNED

Scorpio's uncut videotape was released in March 1983, but has never been submitted to the BBFC and so remains 'banned'. Available uncut under its original title *The Ghastly Ones* in the US: on DVD from Something Weird Video (billed with Milligan's *Seeds Of Sin*), Bayview Entertainment/Widowmaker (with Milligan's *Guru The Mad Monk* and *The Body Beneath*), and in stunning HD Blu-ray from Severin as part of their fourteen-film *The Dungeon Of Andy Milligan* box set. No news about a UK release, but the film would surely pass unscathed if submitted.

Bloody Moon

Present UK status: Available uncut on DVD & Blu-ray

Jesús Franco's *Bloody Moon* received a BBFC approved cinema release in 1982, with 1m 38s of cuts (circular saw decapitation and a knife erupting from a nipple). Interlight issued *Bloody Moon* on home video in two versions; the approved X-rated BBFC edit and an uncensored version. It was resurrected by 'video nasty' darlings Vipco for an attractively packaged but heavily censored VHS release. The BBFC removed 1m 20s of 'offensive' material – an additional eighteen seconds compared to their original treatment of the film in 1982. Of the thirty-nine prosecuted titles, *Bloody Moon* was the only 'nasty' reissued in the 1990s in a version more explicit than its original BBFC X certificate. Vipco's BBFC-approved cut version reduced the opening scissor murder, Eva's stabbing, the decapitation of a real snake, and shots of Eva's bloodied and topless corpse; the circular saw decapitation is reduced to almost nothing (shots of the victim being tied up are also reduced, despite her doing so willingly), and finally there is a slow and unconvincing death by garden shears. Vipco also offered an uncut version which they traded from Denmark and the Netherlands. The packaging was identical, aside from a 'Strong Uncut Version' sticker; the cassette itself bore a completely different label to its UK version however, and no copyright was listed, simply the title of the movie and Vipco catalogue number (VIPO52). Franco's slasher sleaze-cheese was passed uncut in the UK in 2008 for Severin Films DVD. Severin later issued an uncut Blu-ray in 2015 – identical to their stateside release. The BBFC passed the footage of the snake being decapitated, despite their understandably tough stance on animal cruelty.

The Bogey Man

Present UK status: Available uncut on DVD & Blu-ray

Ulli Lommel's *The Bogey Man* was released in cinemas uncut with an X certificate. Vipco issued the same uncut version on home video. The film was listed as a 'banned' video in October 1983 but dropped from the DPP list in July 1985. Vipco re-released the film in 1992 as part of their cult classics range with forty-four seconds of BBFC cuts (shots of a semi-naked woman with scissors forced into her throat, and Lacey's nightmare, in which she is dragged and bound to a bed in her underwear). Vipco also offered a 'strong uncut version' from Denmark but finally secured an uncut 18 certificate in 2000. 88 Films reissued *The Bogey Man* in a stunning uncut transfer on DVD and Blu-ray in 2015. Vinegar Syndrome have now released Lommel's film on 4K UHD, uncut. Viewers should be wary of a so-called 'director's cut' that features a tacked-on camcorder scene, a version cobbled together by Lommel so he could retain rights to the franchise.

THE BURNING

Present UK status: Available uncut on DVD and Blu-ray

With ten seconds of cuts, Tony Maylam's *The Burning* received an X certificate and played UK cinemas in 1981. Thorn EMI released the film uncut on home video and later attempted to recall the tapes and replace them with the censored X version, but it was prosecuted and removed from circulation. Vipco reissued the film after nineteen seconds of cuts in 1992 as part of their cult classic collection. Gone were shots of scissors menacing, a gruesome throat-slashing complete with blood running over bare breasts, and several brief but explicit shots of the raft massacre (specifically shears to the throat, fingers snipped off, forehead slashed open). The uncut version was offered by Vipco on VHS from Denmark. A decade later, Vipco got the film through the BBFC unscathed for a bare bones fullscreen DVD release sourced from their original master VHS tape. It was later issued uncut by Blackhorse in 2008. A remastered uncut special edition Blu-ray and 4K UHD have been released in the US courtesy of Shout! Factory (the packaging suggests the film is rated R, i.e. heavily cut, but it is the unrated version). Arrow Video have issued a Blu-ray in a stunning uncut transfer in the UK.

CAIN'S CUTTHROATS

Present UK status: UNRELEASED/UNAVAILABLE

Released to UK cinemas as *Caine's Way* in 1977 by Alpha Films with four minutes of cuts to obtain an X rating. VTC released the film uncut. It has not been submitted to the BBFC since and is currently unavailable.

CANNIBAL APOCALYPSE

Present UK status: Passed with cuts on DVD

Replay Video issued *Cannibal Apocalypse* uncut on home video in July 1982. After its prosecution, the film was not submitted to the BBFC until 2005 (Cinema Club) when it was passed with only two seconds of cuts (a shot of a rat on fire in a sewer chase). Optimum re-released the film on DVD in 2010 with the cut. Kino Lorber have issued a stunning 4K remaster in the US, and in the UK it has recently received an outstanding transfer on 4K UHD courtesy of 88 Films; fifteen seconds of cuts remain identical to that of the Shameless release.

CANNIBAL FEROX

Present UK status: Passed with cuts on DVD & Blu-ray

One of the nastiest of the 'nasties', Umberto Lenzi's *Cannibal Ferox* was issued by Replay Video in two versions: one uncut and the other edited by 6m 51s. With its frequent and deeply nauseating animal cruelty and obsession with torture and mutilation, it is surprising that *Cannibal Ferox* was passed with an 18 certificate in 2000 when submitted by Vipco (they also offered an uncut version from Denmark on VHS). This approved version was cut by 6m 57s, the extra six seconds of cuts being a shot of a coatimundi hanging from a rope. Other cuts include the coatimundi being killed by a python, a jaguar killing a monkey, an iguana fighting a snake, a turtle slaughtered, a baby pig tortured and killed, a crocodile slashed apart, the terrorisation of a native girl by Mike and Pat, Mike cutting out the eye of a native with a knife, Joe's post-death disembowelment and cannibalisation, Mike's penis being chopped off and devoured, Mike's girlfriend being kicked in the head by a drug dealer, Mike having his hand severed and his brains eaten, and Pat's entire excruciating death scene via hooks through her breasts. This cut version renders the film utterly pointless, albeit remains the version still legally available in the UK today.

Cannibal Ferox has had multiple submissions to the BBFC, the most recent UK release from Shameless being cut by 1m 55s (animal cruelty). Shameless have slowed down portions of the film to maintain the integrity of the soundtrack and running time. The uncut version can be found on DVD in France, Holland and the US. The recent US Blu-ray from Grindhouse Releasing contains the longest version of the film to date and features extra footage (Rudy's death in which he begs to be killed, and a truly repellent extended version of the pig torture scene). You have been warned!

CANNIBAL HOLOCAUST

Present UK status: Passed with cuts on DVD & Blu-ray

The mother of all cannibal movies, Ruggero Deodato's *Cannibal Holocaust* was released by Go Video in February 1982 in a heavily pre-cut form. Regardless, the film became one of the most notorious titles on the 'video nasty' list. It was submitted to the BBFC by Vipco in 2001 and passed 18 with 5m 44s of cuts. The killing of a coatimundi, a turtle, a tethered pig and a monkey have been removed, the sexualised assault with wooden dildo and spiked mudball genital mutilation of an adulteress is heavily reduced, a native being raped on the riverbank during a tribal massacre is absent, the gang rape of another native is heavily cut, and the brutal gang rape and murder of Faye is drastically shortened to remove nudity and tone down the sexual violence. In 2011, Shameless Video resubmitted the uncut version to the Board and it was passed with fifteen seconds of cuts (the killing of a coatimundi). Shameless also submitted an alternative edit, prepared by Deodato himself, designed to reduce the animal cruelty, specifically fifteen seconds of the killing of the coatimundi and cuts to the entrail-riddled turtle killing. The top of a monkey's head being sliced off was digitally altered and masked with a film tear. This new edit was passed uncut by the BBFC. All violence perpetrated on humans is intact in both Shameless versions, including the rape scenes and authentic death footage from the 'Last Road To Hell' segment, the film-within-a-film. *Cannibal Holocaust* has been made available in several versions and this particular sequence differs in many prints (not necessarily censored). Deodato's film is available 'uncut' in Denmark from Another World on Blu-ray and DVD, from Italy on Blu-ray on the CineKult label and from Grindhouse Releasing in the US. The latter offers a truly stunning transfer (not to mention bonus soundtrack CD). Here, the 'Last Road To Hell' sequence is shorter but an extended version of the sequence is included as an extra feature.

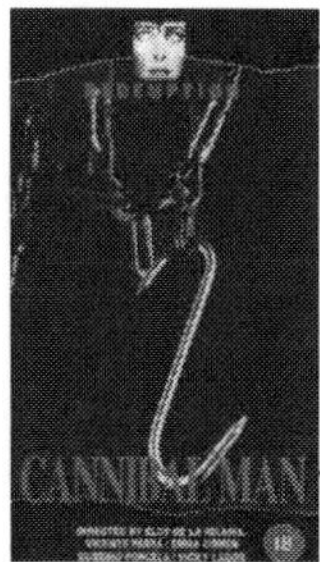

THE CANNIBAL MAN

Present UK status: Passed with cuts for VHS.
CURRENTLY UNAVAILABLE

Intervision released Eloy de la Iglesia's *Cannibal Man* uncut on video in November 1981. After its prosecution as an obscene article, the film didn't surface again until 1993 when Redemption got it passed by the BBFC with three seconds of cuts (a scene in which Marcos slashes Carmen's throat seen in medium shot). *Cannibal Man* has yet to be resubmitted or receive an official UK release but it's unlikely it would cause the censors any headache today. The uncut version is available from Blue Underground on DVD in the US as a standalone item and also packaged with Jess Franco's *Cannibals*, and on Blu-ray from Code Red. In 2021 Severin Films issued a beautifully remastered edition in the US, offering two versions of the film, the commonly seen international version and an extended Spanish version (both uncensored).

CANNIBAL TERROR

Present UK status: Available uncut on DVD & Blu-ray

Modern Films issued Allan W Steeve's *Cannibal Terror* uncut on video in October 1981. It was banned in July 1983 but removed from the 'video nasty' list in September 1985. Passed uncut with an 18 certificate on DVD via International Trading/Film 2000. 88 Films have since released the film uncut on Blu-ray.

CONTAMINATION

Present UK status: Available uncut on DVD & Blu-ray

VIP issued Lewis Coates' *Contamination* uncut in 1982. It was 'banned' in October 1983 but dropped from the list in January 1985. European Creative Films reissued the film with 2m 40s of pre-cuts to the numerous chest-bursting scenes. No further cuts were requested by the BBFC for an 18 certificate. Anchor Bay resubmitted the film uncut for classification in 2004 and obtained a 15 rating. Arrow Films later released an excellent uncut Blu-ray in 2015, also rated 15.

DEAD & BURIED

Present UK status: Available uncut on DVD

Released to UK cinemas uncut with an X rating, Gary A Sherman's *Dead & Buried* later appeared on home video courtesy of Thorn EMI in its uncensored form. It was listed as 'banned' in November 1983 but dropped in January 1985. In 1990, it was reissued with an 18 certificate by Video Collection with thirty seconds of BBFC cuts: a murder of a photographer (shots of him hit with a crowbar), a drunk impaled with a pitchfork and face slashed open, the sound of a hitchhiker's face squished under a brick, a hypodermic needle penetrating an eyeball, and the mutilation of a man's face by acid. Polygram issued the film uncut in 1999 with an 18 rating. It has been released uncut in the UK several times since. Blue Underground released the film uncut in the US on Blu-ray and 4k UHD.

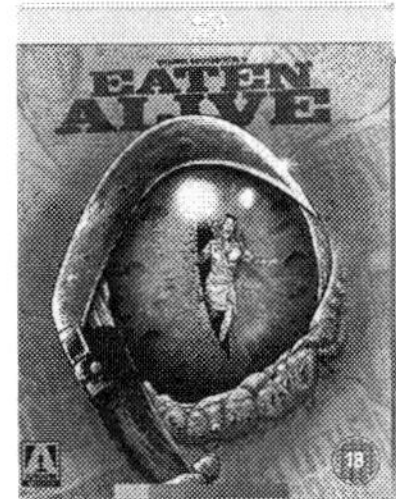

DEATH TRAP

Present UK status: Available uncut on DVD & Blu-ray

Tobe Hooper's *Death Trap* was released in UK cinemas in 1978 with BBFC cuts. In 1980, VCL released the same X version on video. Vipco released a fully uncut version in July 1982. By July 1983 it was listed as 'banned' but dropped in December 1985. Vipco acquired an 18 certificate in 1992 with twenty-five seconds of BBFC cuts. The cut footage includes Judd beating a woman in front of her young child, a scythe to the throat, and several shots of a prostitute hacked with a rake. Vipco got the film past the censor unscathed in 2000 for VHS and DVD. Arrow Video released it uncut on Blu-ray in 2015 in a stunning transfer.

DEEP RIVER SAVAGES

Present UK status: Passed with cuts on DVD & Blu-ray

Umberto Lenzi's original cannibal film was rejected by the BBFC for cinema release in 1975 under the title *Man From Deep River*. The uncut version appeared on home video courtesy of Derann in November 1982. By March 1984 it was listed as 'banned' but dropped in September 1985. International Trading/Screen Entertainment released the film with an 18 certificate and 3m 45s of cuts to scenes of animal cruelty. 88 Films released the same version on DVD and Blu-ray in 2016 in remastered form. The uncut version is available from Shriek Show in the US and Shock Video in the Netherlands (both under the title *Man From Deep River*).

DELIRIUM

Present UK status: Available uncut on Blu-ray

Peter Maris' *Delirium* hit UK video shelves uncut in July 1982, from VTC. It was listed as 'banned' in November 1983 and dropped in May 1985. Two years later it was released by Global Sales Video as *Psycho Puppet*, and earned an 18 certificate with sixteen seconds of cuts to a scene where a topless woman is impaled on a spear. Resubmitted to the BBFC in 2022 by 88 Films and passed uncut.

The Devil Hunter

Present UK status: Available uncut on DVD & Blu-ray

The precertification tape released in the UK by Cinehollywood was heavily pre-cut but still wound up as one of the dreaded thirty-nine. Aside from *The Beast in Heat* and *Snuff*, it remains one of the rarest 'nasties' and commands high collectable prices. In 2008, Severin Films released the film uncut on DVD in the UK and US. The same version was packaged with *Cannibal Terror* for a double header US Blu-ray release in 2015. 88 Films have since issued the film uncut on Blu-ray in the UK in its true director's cut in a stunning transfer.

Don't go in the House

Present UK status: Available uncut on Blu-ray

Joseph Ellison's *Don't Go In The House* was given an X certificate for its theatrical release in 1980, with extensive cuts to a scene of a naked woman being burned alive. This same censored version was released on home video in May 1982 by Arcade/Videospace. The distributor then issued the full uncut version and it was listed as a 'video nasty' in July 1983, but dropped in March 1984. Apex re-released the film on UK home video in 1987 but not before the BBFC excised 3m 7s – all cuts were made to the notorious immolation scene. Arrow Video were granted an uncut 18 certificate for DVD in 2012. Scorpion Releasing have released the film twice in the US on Blu-ray: both are uncut but the latest release includes an extra ten minutes of (non-violent) footage and is considered to be the director's cut. In 2022 Arrow Video released a fantastic collector's edition package on Blu-ray. It offered three different versions of the film: the UK theatrical version (labelled the 'video nasty' version and presented in fullscreen, providing more nudity), the extended edit, and the US theatrical cut. All three versions are uncut in terms of violence and nudity.

DON'T GO IN THE WOODS... ALONE!

Present UK status: Available uncut on DVD & Blu-ray

Video Releasing Organisation's uncertified videotape was uncut when released in March 1982. The BBFC not only passed James Bryan's rag-tag slasher uncut, but they gave it a 15 certificate – not bad for a film once considered too extreme for the UK public. There have been two official releases in the UK, the first by Film 2000 and more recently 88 Films for a surprisingly attractive restored Blu-ray. Both versions carried an 18 certificate on the packaging, despite the BBFC granting a 15 in both instances. One can assume the distributors preferred to play up the film's 'nasty' reputation for promotional purposes.

DON'T GO NEAR THE PARK

Present UK status: Available uncut on DVD

Released uncut on video by Intervision, Lawrence D Foldes' *Don't Go Near The Park* found itself on the 'nasties' list in November 1983 and removed in July 1985. Anchor Bay obtained an uncut 18 certificate when resubmitted to the Board in 2006 and released as part of their *Box Of The Banned Vol. 2* collection. No Blu-ray release is available at present.

DON'T LOOK IN THE BASEMENT

Present UK status: Available uncut on DVD

The BBFC passed S F Brownrigg's asylum shocker with a few trims for its theatrical release in 1977. Derann released a heavily pre-cut version on their Crystal Video label, which made the 'nasties' list in August 1984 but was removed the following December. *Don't Look in the Basement* was passed uncut in 2005 for a budget DVD release by Stax. Code Red have issued the movie uncut on Blu-ray in the US.

The Driller Killer

Present UK status: Available uncut on DVD & Blu-ray

Possibly the most infamous 'video nasty' in its day, thanks to its gloriously blood-soaked packaging, Abel Ferrara's *The Driller Killer* was issued by Vipco in February 1982. This version was uncut in terms of violence and sex but missing ten minutes of footage that showed Reno and girlfriends preparing to go out to a club. Visual Entertainment approached James Ferman at the BBFC in 1999 to discuss the possibility of an 18 certificate but were advised to pre-cut their submission and reduce the tone of the violence. *The Driller Killer* was passed by the BBFC with fifty-four seconds of cuts applied by Visual Entertainment. The material excised included all close-ups of Reno power-drilling various men. Three years later, ILC Prime resubmitted *The Driller Killer* in a full director's cut for an uncut 18 rating. It has since been re-released uncut in the UK by Anchor Bay and 4Digital. Arrow Films now own the UK distribution rights and have issued an excellent Blu-ray featuring the director's cut and the shorter UK video version.

The Evil Dead

Present UK status: Available uncut on DVD & Blu-ray

Sam Raimi's black rainbow of horror was cut by forty-nine seconds for its X-rated 1983 theatrical release. The same version was issued on home video by Palace. It attracted the attention of the DPP and was added to the list in October 1983 but dropped in September 1985. Palace resubmitted the film for home video release in 1990 and the BBFC removed a further 1m 6s, in addition to an existing forty-nine seconds of cuts. This version removes all extreme bloodletting and the tree rape in its entirety. *The Evil Dead* finally acquired an uncut 18 certificate in 2001. Since then all releases have been uncut, albeit all HD releases have been digitally tampered with, smoothing over some of the home-grown effects, i.e. a full moon above the cabin, including the 4K UHD from Sony Pictures in the UK.

EVILSPEAK

Present UK status: Available uncut on DVD & Blu-ray

Videospace released two versions of Eric Weston's *Evilspeak*. The first was uncut and quickly drew the attention of the authorities. Videospace replaced this version with a heavily censored R-rated cut (3m 50s) but both versions were seized and 'banned'. Apex Video resubmitted *Evilspeak* to the BBFC in 1987 and the film earned an 18 certificate for their Horror Classics imprint – but not before 3m 34s were cut (a sacrificial decapitation in the opening credits; Sarge having his head twisted around and his neck broken; boars attacking and tearing intestines from a secretary; a priest receiving a crucifixion nail to the forehead; the Principal having his head smashed apart; boars attacking and feasting on school bullies; a blood-soaked decapitation; an explicit heart removal). Anchor Bay resubmitted *Evilspeak* to the BBFC in 2004 in two versions – an eighty-one-minute version (cut for pacing rather than violent content) and the complete director's cut at 100 minutes. Both were passed uncut with an 18 certificate. 88 Films released the film uncut in the UK on Blu-ray in 2016. Shout! Factory have also released the film uncut on Blu-ray in the US.

EXPOSÉ

Present UK status: Passed with cuts – Available on DVD

James Kenelm Clarke's *Exposé* has had a troubled history in the UK, even prior to its status as a 'video nasty'. When submitted for a cinema release in 1975, the film was pre-cut by 1m 21s by the distributor and cut a further 1m 39s by the

BBFC. All violent scenes were toned down and the sex reduced. It was released as both *Exposé* and *The House on Straw Hill* in the same censored version. In 1980, Intervision released the uncut version on home video. Rumour had it that this version was missing a shot of blood streaming down Fiona Richmond's legs during her knife murder, but it was present in the Intervision tape this author saw. *Exposé* was granted an 18 certificate for VHS in 1997 after fifty-one seconds of cuts to Fiona Richmond's bathroom murder, and a forced sex scene with Linda Hayden and two farm boys. This same version was reissued on DVD by Odyssey (2002) and Village (2006). The film remains unavailable in its uncut form in the UK but is available on Blu-ray from Severin in the US as *The House on Straw Hill*.

FACES OF DEATH

Present UK status: Passed with cuts – Available on DVD

Atlantis Video Productions released *Faces of Death* in the UK in September 1982 in a pre-cut version missing a whopping 32m 36s. Truncated to seventy-eight minutes, this pseudo-documentary was still destined for 'nasty' status. International Trading/Screen Entertainment submitted the uncut 104-minute version to the BBFC in 2003, who passed it 18 after 2m 19s of animal cruelty were removed (notably a monkey hit with hammers and a dog fight). The film remains cut in the UK. Gorgon Video offer an uncut DVD in the US as part of their *Faces of Death* box set, and also issued a thirtieth anniversary Blu-ray and DVD (a fake execution on death row is absent but features as a deleted scene in the extras). The most complete version of *Faces of Death* is the Dutch VHS which contains all footage without any genital fogging, per the Japanese VHS.

FIGHT FOR YOUR LIFE

Present UK status: BANNED

Robert A. Endelson's inflammatory home invasion shocker was rejected outright by the BBFC for theatrical release in 1981. Three years later, Vision

On Video's uncut tape was condemned as a 'nasty' and remains banned in the UK. No distributor has presented *Fight For Your Life* to the BBFC since. Blue Underground released an uncut remastered edition on DVD in the US in 2004. There is no Blu-ray release announced to date, and with racial tensions in the US, this exploitation gem is unlikely to see distribution any time soon.

Forest of Fear

Present UK status: BANNED

Charles McCrann's film was released uncensored by Monte Video in November 1982, although it excised the (pointless) epilogue. It has never been reissued in the UK and remains 'banned' but without doubt would pass uncut if submitted – possibly even with a BBFC 15. An uncut DVD was made available in the US on the Telavista label, an extremely poor transfer that looks like it was sourced from VHS. It does however contain the epilogue missing from the Monte VHS release. In 2021, Massacre Video in the US released the film in an excellent 4K remaster, offering both the US theatrical cut and the extended version with the epilogue.

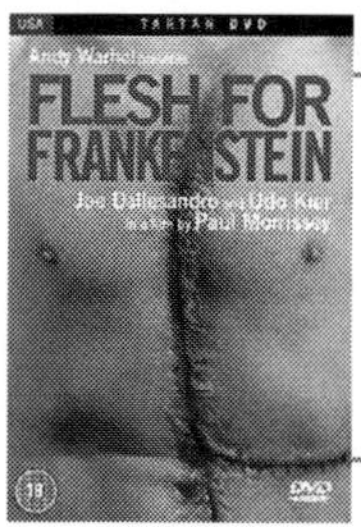

Frankenstein (Andy Warhol's)

Present UK status: Available uncut on DVD

Cut by approximately eight minutes for its cinema release in 1975, Paul Morrissey's *Flesh For Frankenstein* appeared on the home video market in the UK in two versions: a Vipco version cut by 2m 8s, matching the 1982 BBFC X-certificated theatrical re-release, and a Video Gems uncut version. Both were outlawed when the film was successfully prosecuted. First Independent reissued *Flesh For Frankenstein* in 1996 on VHS with fifty-six seconds of BBFC cuts (to a scene where the Baron caresses a corpse in a sexualised manner, smearing blood over its breasts). Tartan Video finally achieved an uncut release of the film in 2006 (and released Morrissey's companion piece, *Blood For Dracula*, at the same time in its uncut form). A German Blu-ray features the uncut version, but the finest edition is Vinegar Syndrome's beautiful 4K remaster in the US.

FROZEN SCREAM

Present UK status: UNAVAILABLE

Intervision issued *Frozen Scream* uncut and uncertified on home video in 1983. By August 1984 it was on the 'video nasties' list but dropped in October 1984. It has never been released in the UK since but would almost certainly pass uncut if submitted to the BBFC now. Vinegar Syndrome have released the film uncut in the US on DVD. No Blu-ray release has been announced.

THE FUNHOUSE

Present UK status: Available uncut on DVD & Blu-ray

Tobe Hooper's *Funhouse* was released uncut to UK cinemas in 1981 with an X certificate. CIC issued the film on home video in June 1983 in a slightly shorter version; none of the violence was excised but rather the film was cut for pacing. It was added to the 'nasties' list in September 1984 but was dropped by June 1985. CIC re-released the same shortened version on UK video in 1987. Arrow Video issued the full uncut version on DVD in 2007 and Blu-ray in 2011.

GESTAPO'S LAST ORGY

Present UK status: BANNED

Two distributors, VFP and Videoshack, issued *Gestapo's Last Orgy* in 1983 and 1984 respectively, both missing a 10m 48s sequence featuring an Aryan cannibal feast in which a Jewish baby is cooked and devoured. The film remains banned in the UK. If *Love Camp 7* is unable to obtain a certificate, it's unlikely this 'nasty' will see the light of day in the UK. A heavily censored R-rated version was released in the US in 2004 by EI and in 2011 by Desert Island. The full uncut version was released in the US on DVD by Intervision in 2011. 88 Films submitted the uncut version of *Gestapo's Last Orgy* to the BBFC in 2021 and the film was refused classification and the 'ban' upheld. 88 Films released the film in the US in an unrated and uncut form shortly after. The transfer is stunning.

THE HOUSE BY THE CEMETERY

Present UK status: Available uncut on DVD & Blu-ray

Lucio Fulci's gothic gorefest was granted an X certificate by the BBFC in 1982 for a cinema release, with cuts totalling 1m 26s. This version was released on home video by Videomedia/Vampix and subsequently 'banned'. In 1988, Elephant Video released an 18 certificated version with 5m 37s of cuts (the opening murder in which the blade of a knife penetrates a skull and exits the mouth, and Dr Freudstein dragging the female victim away; the death of an estate agent by fire poker; the destruction of a very fake looking bat; lingering shots of corpses and mutilated bodies; a throat slashing). In 1992, Vipco issued a version pre-cut by 6m 19s, removing all violence and gory details, rendering some scenes incomprehensible. (The BBFC erroneously states this version was cut by 7m 27s.) Vipco offered an uncut version from Denmark that proudly bore their 'Strong Uncut Version' sticker. They tried again in 2001 for an uncut 18 rating but the BBFC insisted on thirty-three seconds of cuts to the poker murder and the throat slashing. In 2009, Arrow Video acquired an uncut 18 certificate and have issued the film on DVD and Blu-ray. Blue Underground have restored the film in 4K in the US with a healthy extras package.

HOUSE ON THE EDGE OF THE PARK

Present UK status: Uncut release announced on Blu-ray

The BBFC rejected Ruggero Deodato's home invasion rape film for a cinema release in 1981. Skyline released an uncensored videotape in October 1982 that was on the 'nasties' list by July 1983. Vipco applied for a certificate in 2002 and the film was passed 18 with 11m 43s of cuts (reducing all scenes of sexual violence, and removing shots of a razor slashing and a face smashed into a poker table). Shameless resubmitted *House On The Edge of the Park* in 2011, and questioned the Board's request for 1m 20s of cuts. The appeal was partially successful and the Board settled for forty-three seconds of cuts – all applied to the razor slashing of Cindy. For many years, the uncut version could only be found on Dutch and American releases. Code Red issued the film uncut on Blu-ray as a standalone title and as part of a two-pack with *The Last House on Massacre Street* in the US; the transfer was poor. Severin Films came to the film's rescue in 2021 with a beautiful, uncut 4K remaster, with the original soundtrack as a bonus disc. 88 Films submitted this version to the BBFC in April 2022 and it was passed completely uncut for Blu-ray and 4K UHD. The decision is nothing short of a milestone in terms of the BBFC's threshold for sexual violence and exploitation films.

Human Experiments

Present UK status: UNAVAILABLE

Gregory Goodell's mild women-in-prison flick was passed uncut by the BBFC in 1979 for an X-rated theatrical release. The same version appeared on home video courtesy of WOV2000/Jaguar in 1981. *Human Experiments* was added to the 'nasties' list in July 1983 but dropped in March the following year. It has never been re-released in the UK but would undoubtedly pass uncut if submitted today. Scorpion Releasing have released it uncut on Blu-ray in the US.

I Miss You Hugs & Kisses

Present UK status: Passed with cuts for VHS – CURRENTLY UNAVAILABLE

Intercity's uncertified home video of Murray Markowitz's *I Miss You Hugs & Kisses* was uncensored. It made the 'nasties' list in August 1984 but was dropped by October the same year. Heron reissued the film under the title *Drop Dead Dearest* in 1986 with 1m 6s of cuts – most notable are the trims applied to a brief scene of necrophilia. It would likely pass without cuts if submitted today. Severin Films acquired the rights for the North American market in 2022 and released an uncut version of the film on Blu-ray.

I Spit on Your Grave

Present UK status: Passed with cuts – Available on DVD and Blu-ray

Meir Zarchi's infamous rape-revenge film hit UK shelves in January 1982 uncut on the Wizard label. Wizard later rebranded as Astra and continued issuing the uncensored version on home video until it was prosecuted and 'banned'. Vipco released an uncut VHS in the early 2000s from Denmark. International Trading/Screen Entertainment received an 18 rating from the BBFC in 2001 after 7m 2s of cuts to the rape scenes (the violent revenge content was left intact). Anchor Bay later released this heavily truncated edit in their *Box Of The Banned* collection. International Trading/Screen Entertainment had another round with the BBFC, resubmitting a pre-cut and reframed version for reclassification in 2006. In addition to the pre-cuts and reframing, forty-one seconds were excised. 101 Films submitted an uncut version in 2010 but the film was still heavily censored by the BBFC – albeit not nearly as excessively as their treatment nine years earlier. The current UK edition is cut by a total of 2m 54s – again, all cuts applied to rape scenes, most notably Jennifer Hill's violation over a rock. The full uncut version is available from the US on DVD and Blu-ray. The Dutch Blu-ray is also uncensored. Ronin Flix have released the film in the US in incredible 4K.

Inferno

Present UK status: Available uncut on DVD & Blu-ray

Dario Argento's *Inferno* was trimmed for an X-rated theatrical release. 20th Century Fox issued the full uncut version on home video, which was listed as a 'nasty' in August 1984 and removed from the list in September 1985. The 18 certified 1987 home video release was trimmed by twenty-eight seconds. When resubmitted in 1993, the cuts were reduced to twenty seconds (specifically Sacha Pitoeff beating a cat against a chair and shots of a cat devouring a mouse). Arrow Video acquired an uncut 18 certificate for their 2010 DVD and Blu-ray.

ISLAND OF DEATH

Present UK status: Available uncut on DVD & Blu-ray

Nico Mastorakis' objectionable exercise was released in UK cinemas in 1976 under the title, *A Craving For Lust*, with thirteen minutes of cuts. AVI released it uncut as *Island Of Death* on video in November 1982, and the tape was successfully prosecuted. In 1987, Hologram Video tried to sneak the film through the BBFC as *Psychic Killer 2*, with approximately thirteen minutes of cuts. This was likely the heavily edited UK cinema version with an alternative title card. It was rejected and the 'ban' remained. Vipco tried their luck in 2003 and obtained an 18 certificate with 4m 9s of cuts. (The objectionable footage included shots of Christopher urinating on Patricia and banging her head on the floor; the rape of Jane by two hippies; Christopher burning Lesley with a flaming spray can; Christopher sexually assaulting a woman in a shower and stabbing her with a sickle; the shepherd raping Jane and Chris in the barn.) Arrow Video acquired an uncut certificate for the film in 2010 and have issued it on DVD and Blu-ray.

KILLER NUN

Present UK status: Available uncut on DVD

Techno Film/Fletcher Video issued Giulio Berruti's *Killer Nun* uncut and uncertified in April 1981. In August 1984, it was added to the 'nasties' list but was dropped by July 1985. Redemption acquired an 18 certificate after thirteen seconds of cuts in 1993. (Trims to the torture and murder of an old woman, specifically a needle forced into an eye and scalpel slashing.) Shameless released the film uncut with an 18 certificate on DVD in 2006. Arrow Video have released it uncut on Blu-ray in the US. No UK Blu-ray release has been announced to date.

THE LAST HOUSE ON THE LEFT

Present UK status: Available uncut on DVD & Blu-ray

Wes Craven's seminal horror film has suffered a long, difficult history in the UK. The BBFC rejected it outright for cinema release in 1974. When distributors applied for limited, London only screenings, the Greater London Council also rejected it. The film surfaced on home video in June 1982 via Replay in a seventy-eight minute version that contained all violent footage but was missing a couple of minutes of skittish 'comedy' in which two cops try to hitch a ride on a truck containing chickens. Replay's video became one of the more prominent 'video nasties' and was successfully prosecuted. *The Last House on the Left* was submitted to the BBFC in 2000 for a cinema release but rejected again, although it did manage some screenings on the cinema club circuit. Blue Underground applied for home video certification in 2001 and the film was rejected yet again. In 2002, they resubmitted the uncut version and the BBFC offered an 18 certificate with sixteen seconds of cuts. Blue Underground appealed the decision, but the Video Appeals Committee added a further fifteen seconds of cuts on top of the BBFC's initial demands. Blue Underground released the film on DVD with thirty-one seconds of cuts (applied to the forced urination of Phyllis, her stabbing and entrail removal, and shots of Krug carving his name in Mari's chest). In 2003, Anchor Bay submitted the film and suffered a further thirteen seconds of cuts (now totalling forty-four seconds). Anchor Bay also submitted an additional, alternative edit under the title *Krug and Company*. Slightly shorter, this version has a few editorial differences and some new footage while also missing shots evident in other versions. It required twenty-eight seconds of cuts to ensure that it was censored the same way as the original approved cut. Thirty-six years after its original release, Craven's film was finally granted an uncut 18 certificate by the BBFC in 2008 for Second Sight's DVD. Metrodome issued a special three-disc DVD edition in 2009, containing the full uncut *The Last House on the Left* and the alternate *Krug and Company* version. Arrow Video have since released a stunning UK special edition Blu-ray in its uncut form, including the original soundtrack. Also included in this release is the US R-rated version and the *Krug and Company* edit. (A bootleg fan-edit can be found online that features explicit footage of Sadie performing oral sex on Mari as Phyllis looks on, horrified, and a more extreme version of Phyllis' death with a longer shot of entrails being removed. These shots appear to have been sourced from the fake documentary, *Confessions Of A Blue Movie Star,* and are inserted seamlessly.)

LATE NIGHT TRAINS

Present UK status: Available uncut on DVD & Blu-ray

The BBFC rejected Aldo Lado's *Late Night Trains* for a cinema release in 1976. It later appeared on two labels on home video in 1981. Video Warehouse's version is missing approximately three minutes (one minute of violent content and two minutes of non-contentious footage). Cinehollywood issued the film uncut, under the title *Night Train Murders*. In either case, *Late Night Trains* found itself on the 'nasties' list in July 1983, where it stayed until March the following year. Shameless got the film through the BBFC without cuts for an 18 rated DVD in 2008. 88 Films have since issued the film uncut on DVD and Blu-ray.

THE LIVING DEAD

Present UK status: Available uncut on DVD

With 1m 27s of cuts, Jorge Grau's eco-zombie classic appeared in cinemas with an X rating in 1975 as *The Living Dead at Manchester Morgue*. Two versions surfaced on home video in the UK: a heavily cut R-rated version, *Don't Open The Window*, from LVC, and an uncut version titled *The Living Dead* from VIP. Listed as a 'nasty' in October 1983, the film was dropped for prosecution in April 1985. Later that year, the BBFC approved a heavily truncated version for home video with an 18 certificate. An additional twenty-six seconds of cuts were made on top of original cuts of 1m 27s (a policeman mutilated by zombies, shots of zombies on fire, a zombie spiked in the neck, an axe murder, and a nurse having a breast torn off and entrails removed). Anchor Bay acquired an uncut 18 certificate in 2002; subsequent DVD releases have all been uncut. The Blu-ray from Blue Underground in the US is a stunning transfer that showcases the scenic locations. Synapse Films released an uncut 4k restoration on Blu-ray in the US in September 2020.

Love Camp 7

Present UK status: BANNED

Never submitted for a UK cinema release. Uncut on home video in 1983 from Market Video, R L Frost's *Love Camp 7* quickly caught the attention of the DPP and was successfully prosecuted. In 2002, Film 2000 submitted the film to the BBFC for the first time and it was 'banned' outright. The Board argued that "the whole purpose of the work is to invite male viewers to relish the spectacle of naked women being humiliated for their titillation [...] The possibility of cuts was considered. However, because the sexual violence runs throughout the work cutting was not considered to be a viable option." Redemption issued an uncut VHS from Denmark and Something Weird Video a DVD-r bootleg and a downloadable version via its website. It has since been reissued in a stunning 2K scan for Blu-ray in the US. *Love Camp 7* was resubmitted to the BBFC in 2020 but, as with the similarly themed *Gestapo's Last Orgy*, the ban was upheld.

Madhouse

Present UK status: Available uncut on DVD & Blu-ray

Ovidio G Assonitis' *Madhouse* was released by Medusa in January 1983 for UK home video in its uncut form. As the 'video nasty' furore intensified, Medusa released a cut version later that year, missing 1m 15s of violence (a dog biting a man's hand off and tearing his throat; Helen being attacked by the dog; the dog drilled through the head; several cuts to the climactic axe attack). *Madhouse* was 'banned' regardless. Film 2000 obtained an uncut 18 certificate in 2004 for a DVD release. Dark Sky Films offered an uncut DVD from the US. These were superseded by the excellent Arrow Video UK Blu-ray release.

MARDI GRAS MASSACRE

Present UK status: Available uncut on Blu-ray

Released uncut on home video in 1982 by Goldstar/Derann and then later by Market Video. Since its successful prosecution, Jack Weis' *Mardi Gras Massacre* remained, until recently, 'banned'. Code Red offered an uncut DVD in the US, sourced from a video master, as the negative was believed lost. When a print was unearthed, the label released a 2K scan on Blu-ray. In 2022, 88 Films submitted the film to the BBFC and acquired an uncut 18 certificate for a Blu-ray release.

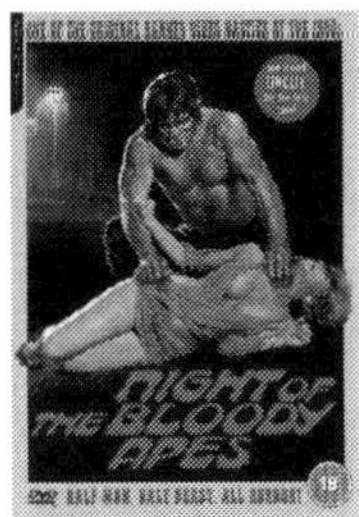

NIGHT OF THE BLOODY APES

Present UK status: Available uncut on DVD

This low-grade Mexican offering played UK cinemas in 1974 with approximately one minute cut (a rape and murder, plus a close-up stabbing). Iver Film Services issued René Cardona's film uncut but their tape was missing approximately 1m 10s of non-violent footage due to print damage; this version was 'banned'. Vipco briefly issued the film uncut on July 26, 1993, on their cult classics label but the tape was withdrawn within days of release. A time-coded sample tape was briefly circulated but this was heavily cut. Vipco never issued the cut version and the title was withdrawn from their catalogue – this is one of the rarest UK videocassettes, and it is easier to track down a copy of the 'banned' Iver Film Services precertification tape than it is Vipco's mysterious release. In 1999,

Satanica Video released Vipco's heavily edited version (Vipco's logo is still present at the beginning of the tape). Pre-cuts totalling 2m 50s were made to this release (edits to heart transplant scenes; a rape and murder; throat slashing; stabbing; eyes gouged out; a head torn off; scalping; a face being crushed). *Night of the Bloody Apes* was finally passed uncut with an 18 certificate in 2012 for Nucleus Films DVD. It is available uncut on Blu-ray from VCI in the US (doubled with *Doctor Of Doom*) and Scanbox in Denmark.

Night of the Demon

Present UK status: Available uncut on Blu-ray

Iver Film Services issued James C Wasson's *Night of the Demon* uncut in June 1982. Following its 'ban', Vipco obtained an 18 certificate with 1m 41s of cuts for their 1993 Cult Classic VHS release. The label later issued this heavily censored version on DVD. (Censored footage includes a man having his arm torn off, a cyclist having his penis ripped off, the demon biting into a neck, the gory aftermath of an axe attack, two women accidentally slashing each other with knives as they are bashed together by the demon, a disembowelling, a woman stabbed with a pitchfork, and a face burned on a stove.) *Night of the Demon* has played uncut on TV on the Zone Horror channel. Code Red offered the film from the US on DVD from a video master featuring a VCI watermark. In 2021, Severin Films resurrected the film in stunning HD in its uncut form in the US. This same version was passed uncut by the BBFC in 2022 for 88 Films.

Nightmare Maker

Present UK status: BANNED

Atlantis released William Asher's *Nightmare Maker* uncut for the UK home video market in April 1983. By November it was listed as a 'nasty' but removed from the DPP list in December 1985. However, when submitted to the BBFC in a pre-cut form for home video classification in 1987, as *The Evil Protégé*, it was rejected.

Nightmare Maker remains 'banned' in the UK but would certainly pass without cuts if resubmitted. Available uncut on DVD and Blu-ray from Code Red in the US.

NIGHTMARES IN A DAMAGED BRAIN

Present UK status: Uncut on DVD & Blu-ray

The BBFC made cuts and gave an X rating to Roman Scavolini's splatter fest for its 1982 cinema release. The same year, World Of Video 2000 released the film on home video in a version that restored approximately one minute of footage but was far from uncut. Aside from violent content, around ten minutes of other material was absent. The film was prosecuted, and distributor David Hamilton-Grant jailed for eighteen months. International Trading/Screen Entertainment submitted *Nightmares in a Damaged Brain* to the BBFC in 2002 with 3m 4s of pre-cuts (matching the US R-rated version). Edits were made to all violent scenes, severely diluting the film's scuzzy tone. The BBFC apparently viewed this version several times before agreeing to certify the film. The same truncated version appeared on Anchor Bay's *Box of The Banned*. 88 Films released it uncut on Blu-ray in November 2015, but this was withdrawn due to confusion over whether the film had been certified. It had. The 88 Films Blu-ray is uncut in terms of sex and violence but missing a few 'insignificant' shots. Code Red released the film unrated on DVD in the US, a version missing approximately 1m 13s of non-violent footage. In 2023, Severin released *Nightmares in a Damaged Brain* uncensored in its true full length version, including missing non-violent footage, on Blu-ray and 4K UHD. The limited edition packaging is a grisly sight!

POSSESSION

Present UK status: Available uncut on DVD & Blu-ray

The 1981 BBFC X-rated cinema verion of Andrzej Zulawski's *Possession* was uncut. This same uncut version was issued on video by VTC in September 1982.

A year later it was on the 'nasty' list. *Possession* was cleared of obscenity charges in September 1984. Visual Entertainment reissued the film on VHS in 1999 in its complete version. Second Sight have since issued an uncut DVD and Blu-ray.

PRANKS

Present UK status: Passed with cuts on DVD

Canon Video released Jeff Obrow and Stephen Carpenter's *Pranks* in its pre-cut R-rated version for home video in 1982, with most of the gore trimmed. VPD re-issued the film in 1992 with ten seconds of cuts (to the drilling of a janitor). *Pranks* was later released by Vipco and Cornerstone in the same censored version. The film has not been resubmitted but it is unlikely that an uncut *Pranks* would have any trouble with the Board today. The director's cut, which contains several more seconds of explicit violence missing from the unrated version, is available on Blu-ray from Synapse Films as *The Dorm That Dripped Blood* (the print bears the original title *Death Dorm*).

PRISONER OF THE CANNIBAL GOD

Present UK status: Passed with cuts on DVD & Blu-ray

The BBFC passed Sergio Martino's *Prisoner of the Cannibal God* with just over two minutes of cuts (to scenes of animal cruelty) for a 1978 theatrical release. Hokushin issued the same BBFC X-rated version on home video in 1981. It was added to the 'nasty' list in November 1983 and dropped in May 1985. Vipco submitted the film to the BBFC under the title *Mountain of the Cannibal God* in 2001 and it passed 18 with 2m 6s of cuts (again removing scenes of animal cruelty). It has been released on DVD several times since in the same censored version. Shameless have released the film on Blu-ray in the UK with extensive cuts to animal cruelty but all other violent scenes intact. In 2007, Blue Underground made an extended director's cut available on DVD in the US. This version is uncut and contains an extra four minutes of extreme material (including simulated bestiality, a girl pleasuring herself, and a more gruesome castration scene). This same 'extreme' version has also been released on Blu-ray in the US by Code Red.

REVENGE OF THE BOGEY MAN

Present UK status: Passed in an alternate version on DVD
Original version technically still BANNED

The sequel to Ulli Lommel's own *The Bogey Man* was released in a pre-cut form by VTC in 1983. Cuts were made to the flashback murder scenes recycled from the first film. It was on the 'nasties' list in September 1984 but dropped in July 1985. In 2003, the budget Hollywood DVD label released *Boogeyman 2* – supposedly a 'redux' version but otherwise unrelated. Although no uncut Blu-ray has been announced anywhere in the world as of writing, a handsome limited hardbox edition DVD is available from Retrofilm in Germany – presented in English, it contains both the original uncut version and the re-edited 'redux' cut.

SHOGUN ASSASSIN

Present UK status: Available uncut on DVD & Blu-ray

Vipco released *Shogun Assassin* uncut on home video in 1981. Despite falling foul of the authorities, the film was never officially prosecuted and was removed from the 'nasties' list. Vipco reissued the film in 1992 with two seconds of cuts, matching the X-rated cinema version (the cut was made to an eye gouging; also missing is a small part of a scene where the infant Daigoro blinds Kurando with a mirror, but as this isn't a BBFC cut presumably the footage is missing due to print damage). Vipco later acquired an uncut fullscreen and widescreen and released them to DVD in 1999. The title has been reissued many times since in the UK without cuts. Criterion have issued the movie uncut on Blu-ray in the UK as part of their *Lone Wolf and Cub* box set.

The Slayer

Present UK status: Available uncut on DVD & Blu-ray

J S Cardone's *The Slayer* was released uncut and uncertified by Vipco. It made the 'nasties' list in October 1983 but was removed by April 1985. It resurfaced on UK home video in 1992 with fourteen seconds of cuts (to the pitchfork murder). Vipco successfully got the film through the BBFC unscathed in 2001 for a DVD release (mastered from their precertification VHS source). Arrow Video have since released this atmospheric slasher uncut in the UK on Blu-ray in a beautiful transfer in its correct aspect ratio.

Snuff

Present UK status: Passed uncut but never released

Astra were scheduled to issue *Snuff* on home video in May 1982 but cancelled the release. However, bootleg copies still circulated and the film became one of the most notorious 'video nasties'. Blue Underground submitted *Snuff* to the BBFC in 2003 and acquired an uncut 18 certificate but the title has yet to be released in the UK. Blue Underground have issued the film in the US in a 2K scan on Blu-ray, highlighting the lame special effects.

SS Experiment Camp

Present UK status: Available uncut on DVD & Blu-ray

When Go Video released Sergio Garrone's *SS Experiment Camp* (uncut) on video in 1982, its lurid cover helped to escalate 'video nasty' hysteria and it became one of the notorious DPP39. All told, it's a mild and dull Nazisploitation feature that was passed uncut by the BBFC in 2005 for Blackhorse DVD, on the understanding it would receive minimal press advertising. It was available to buy on the high street by April 2006. 88 Films released an uncut Blu-ray in the UK in 2015.

TENEBRAE

Present UK status: Available uncut on DVD & Blu-ray

Cut by four seconds for its 1983 cinema release, Dario Argento's *Tenebrae* found its way onto home video in the same truncated version on the Videomedia label and was later 'banned'. Nouveaux obtained an 18 certificate from the BBFC in 2000 with five seconds of cuts – four seconds of which mirrored the original cuts made to the film (the scene where Jane's arm is chopped off with an axe and subsequent arterial spray). The additional one second (Peter being impaled on a metal spike) was a formality by the BBFC – the Board couldn't approve a version identical to one considered obscene in the past. Anchor Bay acquired an uncut certificate in 2003, although some footage was missing due to print damage. The 2015 Arrow Video Blu-ray/DVD releases are uncut. Arrow have released an uncut 4K UHD in the UK.

TERROR EYES

Present UK status: Passed with cuts for VHS – CURRENTLY UNAVAILABLE

Kenneth Hughes's *Terror Eyes* played UK cinemas in 1981 with BBFC cuts. Guild released the film uncut on video in February 1983, and it made the 'nasties' list in March the following year, remaining there until June 1985. Guild reissued the film on UK home video in 1987 with 1m 16s cut (scenes of women being terrorised at knifepoint, specifically a changing room attack and café murder). It has never been resubmitted to the BBFC for reclassification but would certainly pass with no issue today. Warner Brothers released the film uncut on DVD as part of their Archive Collection in 2011, and subsequently on a no-frills Blu-ray.

THE TOOLBOX MURDERS

Present UK status: Available uncut on DVD & Blu-ray

Dennis Donnelly's sleazy slash-fest acquired an X rating with extensive cuts for its theatrical release (it played double-bill with Lucio Fulci's *Zombie Flesh Eaters*). Hokushin issued *The Toolbox Murders* on home video in the same X-rated version, missing around six minutes. Heavy edits were made to early murder scenes: Kelly Nichol's bathtub masturbation and her murder by nail gun. Vipco released *The Toolbox Murders* in 2000 with 1m 46s of BBFC cuts to the nail gun death. Vipco also issued an uncut tape from Denmark and Holland. 88 Films have reissued the film in the UK uncut on Blu-ray in a stunning 4K remaster.

UNHINGED

Present UK status: Available uncut on DVD

The BBFC passed *Unhinged* uncut for a limited cinema release in 1983. The same uncut version appeared on video courtesy of Avatar. Don Gronquist's film found itself on the 'video nasties' list in November 1983, but dropped in May 1985. It was passed by the BBFC uncut in 2004 for Platinum DVD and for 88 Films in 2014. Because of damage to the original negative, this is likely to remain out of the Blu-ray spotlight for some time.

VISITING HOURS

Present UK status: Available uncut on DVD & Blu-ray

With 1m 6s of cuts, Jean Claude Lord's *Visiting Hours* played UK cinemas with a BBFC X rating. (Cuts included the stripping and sexual humiliation of a young woman and the stabbing of a nurse.) This version was released by CBS Fox on home video. *Visiting Hours* briefly joined the 'nasties' list in September 1984 but was dropped by November. ITV broadcast the full uncut version in 1989 but the film remained unavailable in the UK until Final Cut issued it uncut on Blu-ray. An uncut Blu-ray is also available from Shout! Factory in the US.

The Werewolf and the Yeti

Present UK status: BANNED

Canon issued *The Werewolf and the Yeti* uncut on home video in October 1982. It has yet to be classified and therefore 'banned', but would surely pass with no censorial issues if submitted to the BBFC. It is available uncut in a beautiful 2K transfer from Shout! Factory in the US. No UK release has been announced at the time of writing.

The Witch who Came From the Sea

Present UK status: Available uncut on DVD & Blu-ray

VTC released Matt Cimber's *The Witch Who Came From The Sea* on home video in its uncut form and it was added to the 'video nasties' list in August 1984. It was removed in June 1985. Anchor Bay submitted the film to the BBFC in 2006 and acquired an uncut 18 certificate. The film became part of their *Box Of The Banned Vol.2* collection. Arrow Video have since released a stunning, uncut Blu-ray release in the UK.

Women Behind Bars

Present UK status: Available uncut on DVD

Go Video distributed Jesús Franco's sweaty women-in-prison film in an uncertified, pre-cut version on home video. It was added to the 'nasties' list in August 1984, where it remained for two months before being dropped. Maison Rouge have released the film uncut with an 18 certificate in the UK. Blue Underground also offer the uncut version on DVD (region 0) in the US.

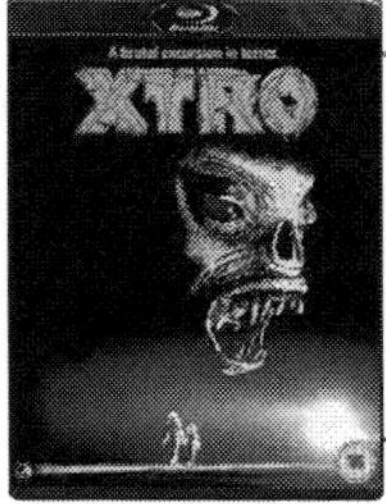

XTRO

Present UK status: Available uncut on DVD & Blu-ray

Harry Bromley Davenport's *Xtro* was passed uncut for theatrical release in 1982. The pre-cert video from Spectrum was released uncut but later seized by police as a potential 'nasty'. It never made the 'official' DPP list because the BBFC alerted authorities to the fact it had hitherto passed the film uncut – albeit not for video release and not the same version; there is a different ending (one upbeat, and the other sad). An uncensored video version was released by Polygram in 1987 with an 18 certificate. Film 2000 acquired an uncut 15 certificate when they resubmitted *Xtro* to the BBFC in 2007. Optimum later released it uncut, rated 15. Seemingly arbitrarily, releases of *Xtro* contain either of the two endings, but in 2018, Second Sight released a special edition Blu-ray in the UK contaiining both.

ZOMBIE CREEPING FLESH

Present UK status: Available uncut on DVD & Blu-ray

Vincent Dawn's *Zombie Creeping Flesh* hit UK video shelves courtesy of Merlin in October 1982. This was a heavily pre-cut version, totalling cuts of 14m 32s of cuts: gore was reduced and the SWAT raid at the beginning of the film was removed in its entirety. This 'light' version made the 'nasties' list in July 1983 but was dropped in July 1985. Video Gems applied for a home video certificate in 1993 but James Ferman advised the distributor not to submit the film because the James Bulger case was high-profile and the film would be rejected. Vipco submitted the film in its full uncut version in 2002. The same version has been reissued on the Cornerstone label. 88 Films have since brought the movie to UK Blu-ray and 4K UHD in its uncut form. The 4K UHD release has faced some criticism for its over-zealous colour grade which presents the blood as purple rather than red.

ZOMBIE FLESH EATERS

Present UK status: Available uncut on DVD & Blu-ray

The BBFC passed Lucio Fulci's *Zombie Flesh Eaters* for theatrical release in 1979 with 1m 46s of cuts. This X-rated cut version appeared on home video from Vipco in 1980. Most of the cuts were for graphic violence and bloodletting, but also absent was a prologue showing Dr Menard shooting a zombie wrapped in a shroud; Vipco's version began with the opening credits. The label released a 'strong uncut version' in 1981, which attracted the attention of the authorities and was 'banned'. They resubmitted *Zombie Flesh Eaters* to the BBFC in 1992, presenting the pre-cut X version, which was passed without further cuts. Vipco misleadingly touted this as an 'uncut version'. They also issued a widescreen version with the same cuts applied. Meanwhile, the film was released uncensored by Vipco in Denmark, in both fullscreen and widescreen formats. In 1999, the label resubmitted the uncut version to the BBFC and the cuts were reduced to twenty-three seconds. This was released as an 'extreme version' (still missing were Mrs Menard's splinter through the eye and footage of her being devoured by zombies). Anchor Bay issued Fulci's classic uncut as part of their *Box Of The Banned* collection. In 2012, Arrow Video released the film uncut on Blu-ray and DVD. Blue Underground have released a 4K special edition on Blu-ray with extra features and the original soundtrack CD.

"YOU CAN'T RUN ALL THESE MACHINES OFF THE STANDARD MAINS"

INTERVIEW WITH STEVE WEBBER

STEVE WEBBER WAS the Marketing Director for VCL Video Services. Here he looks back at the 1970s and early 1980s, the Wild West days of commercial video in the UK. Interview conducted by JULIAN UPTON on 3 March 2012.

STEVE WEBBER: I was there pretty much at the beginning, working with Carl Fischer. I had come out of the music business, playing in a band and working for a music publisher, and I joined a company called London Town Discotheques who ran discotheques for hotel chains around the world. I used to get the music trade mags and I was fascinated by this thing they talked about called the videodisc. They weren't available, but this was something that was said to be coming up. This was the early 1970s. Anyway that was in the back of mind. One of my jobs at the disco company was to ring up entertainment agents, because in those days the law said you had to have a live band in a discotheque in order to get a license. I'm on the phone ringing up agents and I get this girl on the phone and she says we've got this video company, we put videos into discotheques. So I said, whereabouts are you? They were about 100 yards away. The company was called Trans Vision Leasing, run by Carl Fischer, and we got on like a house on fire. So I quit my job and went to work for him because I knew where all the discotheques were.

The whole idea was you sold the whole thing to the discotheque – the TV set, the video player (U-matic at that time) and then you leased them the tapes. They got a new video tape every month. The musician's union hated us. But there were no rules. The tapes were pop promos that we put together to make one hour programmes. The record company sent us master tapes, quad tapes. The only other company doing this was Intervision. We all went out to the discos and we were competing. That effectively was the business. We were charging hundreds of pounds and it wasn't easy.

We were sitting in the office one day and we thought, what if we don't tie people into contracts and just sell the videotapes. No commitment. You don't have to buy the hardware. We had all Intervision's customers so we rang all them up. So, I'd go down to one of their clubs and sell them tapes for £80 or so. Intervision *hated* us. I actually got threatened one night. Now bear in mind that all the tapes had to be duplicated, and we had to go down to Rank for that. The stock cost us a fortune, and we never had stock. We were duplicating only five or ten [tapes] at the time but then it cost a fortune. We believed that the future of video would be music videos, why would people want to watch films more than once? But we did think that maybe we should get into films a little. Anyway in the office we had U-matic and Philips machines. We met a few people in the film business and we licensed a couple of films – rubbish Italian spaghetti westerns that kind of thing – this must have been about 1975, 76. We knew nothing about what we were doing and it never occurred to us not to license stuff for the world, so we licensed things for as many territories as we could. The customers at this time were well-off VCR owners. We also did a deal with Thames TV. We had *The Sweeney* and one or two other series, which was really unusual at that time, on U-matic, and slowly a customer base started to appear and it was mainly wealthy Arabs. We also licensed [1948–54 US TV series] *Greatest Fights of the Century*, all the boxing, and that was unbelievably popular. And we began to see some export business growing. It wasn't much of a catalogue but at the same time we were building up the music. We had half a dozen Arab movies as well, I had no idea where they came from, the rights must have been a bit dodgy. Occasionally an Arab customer would ask for some porn. We were pretty much legit, we didn't pirate, although we were accused of it. Anyway for this porn we bought this Nordmen machine which was like a mini telecine – you put an 8mm film in and transferred it to video, but it was the biggest pile of shit you could imagine. It jammed continually. But around about that time we had an enormous breakthrough. We bought this second U-matic machine and at the back of it it said 'Video In Video Out' and the other one's the same and it suddenly occurred to us that we can record from one U-matic to the other! So we tried it and they were fine! Overnight the business was transformed, because overnight we had stock! It had cost us a fortune to go to Rank to get tapes duplicated. So the business was literally transformed with two U-matics and a Philips.

Then we bought a Philips editing suite and the business started to build. We then had to get someone in who knew a little bit about how the machines worked. We found some guy who'd worked on radar once, so we thought that was good enough. We were then duplicating through the night, one tape at a time, taking it in turns working sixty-hour shifts at a time.

Anyway, before long we heard about VHS. We got the first VHS machine and we thought, this business is changed. We bought five VHS and five Beta and suddenly we had a little duplicating suite, mastering off U-matic. I then went out to shops – this is where I literally had to invent the business, I don't mind blowing my own trumpet, I bloody invented it. Nobody had done it before. Intervision had some titles though, but they didn't sell, they rented. We had some old westerns, and a couple of other odd bits and pieces. The bookshops didn't want to know, so we went to the big record wholesalers and that's when things began to motor. And soon it started growing faster than we could cope with, so we had to go on the hunt for a financier and we found one, Alan Judd, who came in and chucked money at us.

We moved to a Covent Garden premises and there we actually built a studio, to produce our own music shows, which was another way to sort the music rights out. We also had a big duplicating facility there, in the basement. But then Alan fell out with Carl and Carl left. I stayed on. But we were all upping our game. The next technical step was we bought a 1" Ampex machine. We were then duplicating for other distributors, mainly adult labels. The thing to remember about the adult film labels at that time is that they were in effect respectable because they all had to abide by the Obscene Publications Act.

We had banks of machines in this Covent Garden basement and our engineer loved going around saying you can't run all these machines off the standard mains. But we ignored him. It was this really cold winter and eventually we blew the mains box which was under the pavement outside. We blew up the pavement outside! But one of the main problems of this time was just getting hold of enough blank cassettes. There was a massive shortage.

The movies we were putting out were beginning to get better. There were a lot of independent films in those days, so it wasn't too difficult to get rights to things, rights were all over the place. One independent was Hemdale, we had a deal with them. The first 'banner' movie we bought was *Just a Gigolo*, a Hemdale movie starring David Bowie. This was the first time we took out an ad just for one movie. Crappest movie you could ever watch in your whole life! The funny thing was that the packaging for our movies at that time looked a lot like the packaging for EMI movies. So the shops would put ours in the same section, much to EMI's disgust.

Around this time, given that we had been buying international rights where we could, but whether we had the rights or not, using the European Free Trade

Agreement, we started to export mainly to Scandinavia, which was great because they didn't mind English language films or music. That began to build and build. They began to ask for films with subtitles, which of course we didn't know how to do, but we eventually did, and eventually built a big duplicating plant in Norway, where we also did the subtitling.

The first really decent package of movies we bought included *Breaking Glass*, *Scum* (which was a big seller), *The Wanderers*, *Phantasm*, and *Elvis–The Movie*. That was the point where the business really started; we were the top video distributor in Europe, if not the world, at that point. But we were still seen by the film industry as the Devil incarnate, we were going to destroy the business. So a lot of what else was available in terms of rights was exploitation. But we would go to festivals in Cannes twice a year. And we couldn't get the contracts out fast enough. There were people queuing on the stands to do business with us, wanting to sell us movies.

Obviously the business had tipped towards films rather than music at this point. We still did the odd music videogram. We had this great idea to create all these different labels: VCL, TVX, for adults, a family label, etc.

Then we started having run-ins with censorship. We had to go and get the films certified. Things like *Red Nights of the Gestapo* never got through. But at this time the biggest selling videos were the [adult] *Electric Blues* – they used to win industry awards such as the *Video Trade Weekly* awards.

Cost of the Tina Turner special (released 1980)?

We paid her bugger all, she had no contract. The videogram would have cost about £25–£30k to make in those days. It was a big deal for us, a big seller. This was also the point where we needed somebody who knew about music publishing because we had begun to run into rights problems. The thing was, we used to put stuff out without the rights and sort the rights out afterwards, that was the way you could do things then.

Your volume of releases started to go down around 1981, 82...

Once the majors came in and big movies started coming out, that was a game changer. The business was increasing. Tons of people putting stuff out. It became very difficult to compete when you had exploitation stuff, which had been our bread and butter. So the business started to crash. It never went bust, it just wound down.

UPDATE NO 17

PICTURE QUALITY

(A)

SUSPIRIA (UNCUT,WIDESCREEN,OFF LASERDISC)	4½
HOUSE BY THE CEMETARY (UNCUT,WIDESCREEN,OFF LASERDISC,NEW COPY)	4½
NAZZAU-PRISONER IN PARADISE(UNCUT,JOHN HOLMES)	4½
NIGHTDREAMS (UNCUT)	4½
~~THE BURNING (UNCUT,LONGER VERSION,WITH EXTRAS)~~ *	4½
TOM SAVINI F-X (FANGORIA SCREAM GREATS)	4
EXPLOITATION TRAILORS VOLUME 1	4½
BRUCE LEE VERSUS SUPERMAN (LASERDISC TRANSFER)	4½
MARK OF THE DEVIL 2 (UNCUT)	3
RAPE SQUAD (UNCUT)	4
LUNATIC (UNCUT)	4½
ROTTWEILRE DOGS FROM HELL (UNCUT)	4½
THEY STILL CALL ME TRINITY (UNCUT,TERENCE HILL,BUD SPENCER)	4½
MY NAME IS NOBODY (UNCUT," ")	4½
VIOLENT NAPLES (UNCUT,DANISH ENGLISH LANGUAGE)	5
ZOMBIE 2- AKA ZOMBIE FLESH EATERS (UNCUT,WIDESCREEN,OFF DISC)	4½
ILSA-TIGRESS OF SIBERIA (UNCUT,ORIGINAL)	5
SAVAGE WEEKEND (UNCUT)	4
LADY STAY DEAD (UNCUT)	4½
CANNIBAL FEROX (UNCUT,LASERDISC,PLUS COMMENTARY BY UMBERTO LENZI AND JOHN MORGHEN,VERY RECENT RELEASE £10,RUNNING TIME 3HRS)	4½
TENEBRAE (JAPANESE LASERDISC NEW COY) UNCUT	4½
LAST HOUSE ON THE LEFT (UNCUT LASERDISC NEW COPY)	4½

** CHEERS********

XXXX

THANKS TO ALL WHO HAVE ORDERED OVER THE PAST FEW MONTHS,ALL THE BEST

BLACK MARKET MAILING LIST

Fan and collector, DAVID HINDS recalls having acquired this video list from a dealer in the West Midlands circa 1995–96. Fairly typical of trading lists, this was around twenty pages, featured copies of films for sale, with notes, picture quality rating, and was illustrated with photocopy scans of movie posters etc. Says David: "I could only find one solitary page, used as a bookmark, no less!"

SOURCES

BIBLIOGRAPHY

Barker, Martin (ed). *The Video Nasties: Freedom and Censorship in the Media*. Pluto Press, 1984.

Barlow, Geoffrey and Hill, Alison. *Video Violence and Children*. Hodder and Stoughton, 1985.

Bertrock, Alan. *The I Was A Teenage Juvenile Delinquent Rock'n'Roll Horror Beach Party Movie Book!* Plexus, 1986.

British Videogram Association. *A Trade Guide to the Video Recordings Act*. HMSO, 1985.

Brottman, Mikita. *Offensive Films: Towards an Anthropology of Cinéma Vomitif*. Greenwood Press, 1997.

Buchanan, Larry. *It Came From Hunger! Tales of a Cinema Schlockmeister*. McFarland, 1996.

Burrell, Nigel J. *Knights of Terror: The Blind Dead Films of Amando de Ossorio*. Midnight Media, 1995.

——. *Let Sleeping Corpses Lie: The Living Dead at the Manchester Morgue – A Critical Dissection*. Midnight Media, 1996.

Caputi, Jane. *The Age of Sex Crime*. The Women's Press, 1988.

Chester, Graham. *Berserk! Motiveless Random Massacres*. Michael O'Mara Books, 1993.

Clover, Carol J. *Men, Women, and Chainsaws: Gender in the Modern Horror Film*. BFI, 1992.

Cohen, Stanley. *Folk Devils & Moral Panics*. Blackwell, 1987.

Curtis, Tony. *Lyle Price Guide: Film & Rock'n'Roll Collectables*. Lyle, 1994.

Davies, Tom. *The Man of Lawlessness*. Hodder & Stoughton, 1989.

Dhavan, Rajeev & Davies, Christie. *Censorship and Obscenity*. Martin Robertson & Co., 1978.

Elliot, John. *Elliot's Guide to Films on Video*. Boxtree, 1990.

Ernst, Morris L. & Seagle, William. *To the Pure... A Study of Obscenity and the Censor*. Jonathan Cape, 1929.

Fenton, Harvey; Grainger, Julian & Castoldi, Gian Luca. *Cannibal Holocaust and the Savage Cinema of Ruggero Deodato*. FAB Press, 1999.

Ferguson, Michael. *Little Joe Superstar: The Films of Joe Dallesandro*. Companion Press, 1998.

French, Karl (ed). *Screen Violence*. Bloomsbury, 1996.

Fountain, Nigel. *Underground: The London Alternative Press 1966–74*. Routledge, 1988.

Green, Jonathon. *The Encyclopedia of Censorship*. Facts on File, 1990.

Hagell, Ann & Newburn, Tim. *Young Offenders and the Media*. PSI, 1994.

Hardy, Phil (ed). *The Aurum Film Encyclopedia: Horror*. Aurum, 1985.

——. *The Encyclopedia of Science Fiction Movies*. Octopus, 1986.

Hebditch, David & Anning, Nick. *Porn Gold: Inside the Pornography Business*. Faber & Faber, 1988.

Hoberman, J. & Rosenbaum, Jonathan. *Midnight Movies*. Harper & Row, 1983.

Jaworzyn, Stefan (ed). *Shock Xpress 2: The Essential Guide to Exploitation Cinema*. Titan, 1994.

Josephs, Jeremy. *Hungerford: One Man's Massacre*. Smith Gryphon, 1993.

Jouis, Pierre (ed). *Directed By Dario Argento*. Fantasy Film Memory, 1991.

Kelland, Gilbert. *Crime In London*. HarperCollins, 1993.

Kerekes, David & Slater, David. *Killing for Culture: An Illustrated History of Death*

Film from Mondo to Snuff. Creation, 1995.
Killick, Mark. *The Sultan of Sleaze: The Story of David Sullivan's Sex and Media Empire*. Penguin, 1994.
Kinnard, Roy & Davis, Tim. *Divine Images: A History of Jesus on the Screen*. Citadel Press, 1992.
Koch, Stephen. *Stargazer: The Life, World & Films of Andy Warhol, Revised and updated*. Marion Boyars, 1991.
Konow, David. *Schlock-O-Rama: The Films of Al Adamson*. Lone Eagle, 1998.
Lee, Walt. *Reference Guide to Fantastic Films: Science Fiction, Fantasy & Horror, Vols 1, 2 & 3*. Chelsea-Lee Books, 1975
Longford Committee Investigating Pornography, The. *Pornography: The Longford Report*. Coronet, 1972.
Luther-Smith, Adrian (ed). *Delirium: A Guide To Italian Exploitation Cinema 1975–1979*. Media Publications, 1979.
McCarty, John. *The Sleaze Merchants: Adventures in Exploitation Filmmaking*. St Martin's Griffin, 1995.
McCarty, Helen & Clements, Jonathan. *The Erotic Anime Movie Guide*. Titan, 1998.
Mathews, Tom Dewe. *Censored: What They Didn't Allow You To See and Why—The Story of Film Censorship in Britain*. Chatto, 1994.
Medved, Michael. *Hollywood vs. America: Popular Culture and the War on Traditional Values*. HarperCollins, 1992.
Michael, Richard (ed). *The ABZ of Pornography*. Granada, 1972.
Michel, Jean-Claude. *Lucio Fulci: Italy's Gore Master*. Fantasy Film Memory, 1990.
Muller, Eddie & Faris, Daniel. *That's Sexploitation!!: The Forbidden World of "Adults Only" Cinema*. Titan, 1997.
Newman, Kim. *Nightmare Movies: A Critical History of the Horror Film, 1968–88*. Bloomsbury, 1988.
O'Toole, Laurence. *Pornocopia: Porn, Sex, Technology & Desire*. Serpent's Tale, 1998.
Opie, Iona & Moira Tatem (ed). *A Dictionary of Superstitions*. OUP, 1993.
Palmerini, Luca M. & Mistretta, Gaetano. *Spaghetti Nightmares: Italian Fantasy–Horrors as Seen Through the Eyes of Their Protagonists*. Fantasma, 1996.
Parish, James Robert. *Prison Pictures from Hollywood*. McFarland, 1991.
Phelps, Guy. *Film Censorship*. Victor Gollancz, 1975.
Pirie, David. *The Vampire Cinema*. Hamlyn, 1977.
Puchalski, Steven. *Slimetime: A Guide to Sleazy, Mindless, Movie Entertainment*. Headpress/Critical Vision, 1996.
Ray, Fred Olen. *The New Poverty Row: Independent Filmmakers as Distributors*. McFarland, 1991.
Riley, Patrick. *The X-Rated Videotape Star Index*. Prometheus, 1994.
Rimmer, Patrick H. *The X-Rated Videotape Guide I*. Prometheus, 1993.
Robertson, Geoffrey. *Obscenity: An Account of Censorship Laws and their Enforcement in England and Wales*. Weidenfeld & Nicolson, 1979.
——& Andrew Nicol. *Media Law*. Penguin, 1992.
Robertson, James C. *The Hidden Cinema: British Film Censorship in Action, 1913–1972*. Routledge, 1989.
Ross, Jonathan. *The Incredibly Strange Film Book*. Simon & Schuster, 1993.
Shepard, Jewel. *Invasion of the B-Girls*. Eclipse, 1992.
Smith, Tim. *The Complete Video Guide*. Virgin, 1981.
Springhall, John. *Youth, Popular Culture and Moral Panics*. Macmillan, 1998.
Stanley, John. *Creature Features: The Science Fiction, Fantasy, and Horror Movie Guide*. Boulevard, 1997.
Stern, Chester. *Dr Iain West's Casebook*. Little Brown, 1996.
Stevenson, Jack (ed). *Fleshpot: Cinema's Sexual Myth Makers & Taboo Breakers*. Headpress/Critical Vision, 2000.
Sutherland, John. *Offensive Literature: Decensorship in Britain, 1960–1982*. Junction Books, 1982.
Szulkin, David A. *Wes Craven's Last House*

on the Left: The Making of a Cult Classic. FAB Press, 1997.
Taylor, Laurie & Mullan, Bob. *Uninvited Guests: The Intimate Secrets of Television & Radio*. Chatto & Windus, 1986.
Thomas, Mark. *Every Mother's Nightmare: The Killing of James Bulger*. Pan, 1993.
Thompson, Bill. *Soft Core: Moral Crusades Against Pornography in Britain and America*. Cassell, 1994.
Thompson, David & Christie, Ian (ed). *Scorsese on Scorsese*. Faber, 1989.
Thrower, Stephen. *Beyond Terror: The Films of Lucio Fulci*. FAB Press, 1999.
Trevelyan, John. *What the Censor Saw*. Michael Joseph, 1973.
Tribe, David. *Questions of Censorship*. George Allen & Unwin, 1973.
Turan, Kenneth & Zito, Stephen F. *Sinema: American Pornographic Films and the People Who Make Them*. Praeger, 1974.
Vogel, Amos. *Film as a Subversive Art*. London: Weidenfeld and Nicolson, 1974.
Weaver, Tom. *Attack of the Monster Movie Makers*. McFarland, 1994.
Weldon, Michael J. *The Psychotronic Encyclopedia of Film*. Ballantine, 1983.
——. *The Psychotronic Video Guide*. St Martin's Press, 1996.
Whitehouse, Mary. *"Who Does She Think She Is?"* New English Library, 1971.
——. *Whatever Happened To Sex?* Wayland, 1977.
——. *A Most Dangerous Woman?* Lion, 1982.
Williams, Bernard (ed). *Obscenity and Film Censorship: An Abridgement of The Williams Report*. University Press, 1981.
Wingrove, Nigel & Morris, Marc. *The Art of the Nasty*. Salvation Films, 1998.
Yallop, David. *Deliver Us From Evil*. Corgi, 1993.
Zalcock, Bev. *Renegade Sisters: Girl Gangs on Film*. Creation, 1998.

PERIODICALS

Absurd (UK); *Asian Trash Cinema* (US), *BBFC Annual Report* (UK); *Broadcast* (UK); *Castle of Frankenstein* (US); *CineFan* (US); *Continental Film & Video Review* (UK); *Dark Side, The* (UK); *Deep Red* (US); *Delirium* (UK); *Demonique* (US); *Diabolik* (UK); *Draculina* (US); *Dreadful Pleasures* (US); *European Trash Cinema* (US); *Empire* (UK); *Eyeball* (UK); *Fangoria* (US); *Film Extremes* (UK); *Film Threat* (US); *Filmfax* (US); *Flesh & Blood* (UK); *Gore Gazette* (US); *Headpress* (UK); *Hi-Tech Terror* (US); *House of Hammer/ Halls of Horror* (UK); *Imaginator* (UK); *Is it... Uncut?* (UK); *Killbaby* (Can); *Killing Moon* (UK); *Magick Theatre* (US); *Manga Mania* (UK); *Master Detective* (UK); *Men Only* (UK); *Midnight Marquee* (US); *Monster! International* (US); *Monster Times, The* (US); *Monthly Film Bulletin* (UK); *Nocturno* (It); *Nostalgia* (Fr); *Outré* (US); *Panicos!!* (Can); *Photoplay* (UK); *Psychotronic Video* (US); *Samhain* (UK); *Scapegoat* (UK); *Screen International* (UK); *Shock Cinema* (US); *Shock Xpress* (UK); *Sight & Sound* (UK); *Sleazoid Express* (US); *Splatter Times, The* (US); *Sub Human* (US); *Video–The Magazine* (UK); *Video Watchdog* (US); *Video Viewer* (UK); *Videooze* (US); *World of Horror* (UK)

WEBSITES

APBnews (no longer exists)
BBFC | bbfc.co.uk
DVD Nightmare (no longer exists)
IMDb | imdb.com
Melon Farmers' Video Hits | melonfarmers.co.uk
Pre-Cert Video | pre-cert.co.uk
Total Rewind (no longer exists)

NOTES

BEGINNINGS

1 The attempt to absorb rising production costs resulted in b&w prints of films costing the same as colour prints in Britain.

2 Although 600-foot reels were obtainable, choice in this format was limited and expensive, and the accepted standard length tended to be 200-foot and 400-foot, the latter providing approximately eighteen minutes of viewing time. A complete unabridged feature film on Super-8 could run to four or five reels, each of which would require manual changeover and feeding into a projector.

3 The royal wedding left retailers unable to meet the demand for blank videocassettes and hardware.

4 Narrated by Robert Lacey, author of the best-selling book of the same name.

5 The *Electric Blue* series ran to at least twenty-six volumes.

6 The sport section of volume one was film of the 1976 Indy 500 in which more than thirty people died, while volume two featured a compilation of motor racing pileups identified in the *Electric Blue* catalogue only as "carnage for the connoisseur!" Volume seven had skiing accidents.

7 *Continental Film and Video Review* June 1982.

8 Although 3-D movies had been screened on Scottish TV and Philips even demonstrated a prototype 3-D television set at around about the time of the release of *Electric Blue* volume eight, the concept of home 3-D – constantly in development – remains a gimmick.

9 *Aerobicise* producer/director was fashion photographer Ron Harris, who had worked on high-fashion magazines like *Vogue*, *Cosmopolitan* and *Harper's Bazaar*.

10 Trailers for movies could already be found on pre-recorded feature film tapes.

11 Ironically, as pre-recorded tapes were given space for advertising, a device known as the Commercial Cutter came on the market. This was an electronic box that coupled to the VCR and detected advertising breaks. It would automatically activate the pause mode during the commercials. The device was often heard about but very rarely seen.

12 Interview with Steve Webber, formerly Trans Vision Leasing, and Marketing Director of VCL Video Services, by Julian Upton, 3 March, 2012. Full interview on page 526.

13 According to the Department of Trade, cinema attendance in Britain has suffered something of a downslide for many years prior to video. In 1973, 142 million people went to the cinema, compared with

the 107 million who went in 1976. The following year saw the figure rise. The year after that it fell again.

14 Interview with Iain Muspratt, former Managing Director of Guild Home Video by Julian Upton. April 3, 2012.

15 Steve Ellison, interview with the authors, 24 April 1999.

16 RCA's prototype video recorder Selectavision, although never making it to the marketing stage, was heralded by the manufacturer as "the most significant development since the invention of colour television." David Johnson, chief executive of the 400-strong Rumbelows chain of electronics shops, told the *Sunday Times* in July 1981 that "Video is the biggest household spending spree since the colour television boom of the early seventies."

17 Part of the reason for the dominance of VHS over Betamax lies with the giant Thorn EMI group, who owned many high street TV and video rental chains through which they marketed their own Ferguson brand VHS recorder.

18 Steve Ellison, interview with the authors, 24 April 1999.

19 Interview with Iain Muspratt, formerly Managing Director, Guild Home Video, by Julian Upton, 3 April, 2012.

20 Far greater sales were achieved on blank cassettes, however. Time-shift recording – the recording of television programmes for later viewing – remains to this day the most popular use for the VCR.

21 A twelve-month membership cost £85 and came with a full-length feature film which could be exchanged for anything in the Video Club catalogue direct by post. Postage not included.

22 WEA Records handled Warner Home Video, EMI Records handled Thorn EMI, PRT Records handled ITC/Precision, and CBS Records handled CIC Video and MGM.

23 Christopher Glazebrook, interview by mail with the authors, circa mid 1999.

24 Steve Ellison, interview with the authors, 24 April 1999.

25 The majority of mail order companies offered adult titles, and it was this type of product that kept mail order alive when video moved into the high street. The more daring consumer of porn tapes could try the Private chain of shops which, for a while, offered a preview-before-buying option. Customers after hardcore would have been disappointed as such material was illegal and not sold in the Private shops. Customers almost certainly would have been convinced otherwise by the aggressive salesmanship employed in such places, however.

26 Steve Ellison, interview with the authors, 24 April 1999.

27 The voice of Patrick Allen could also be heard on releases from Hokushin, reciting the 'copyright proprietor/home use' warning typically found on videocassettes. He is best known on British television as the once public face (and voice) of the Barrett Homes advertisements.

28 Steve Ellison, interview with the authors, 24 April 1999.

29 The BVA was the brainchild of the British Phonograph Industry (BPI), whose members had become a sizeable force in the distribution of videos for home entertainment. After some negotiation, and in a sense of fair play, it drew on representatives not only from the record industry, but also from film, publishing and the BBC. The head of Thorn EMI was elected the chairman.

30 A 'spoiler signal' that could interfere with recordings made from TV was one consideration, but dismissed because of 'anti-spoiler signal' devices that were sure to surface.

CANNIBAL ERROR

31 In January 1984, the US Supreme Court ruled that using a VCR to record programmes for home use was not a violation. The decision ended a near two-year battle that Walt Disney Productions and Universal Studios had fought against Sony, that the manufacturer of the Betamax video recorder be held accountable under copyright law for time-shift recordings made by consumers.

32 Interview with Iain Muspratt, formerly Managing Director, Guild Home Video, by Julian Upton, 3 April, 2012.

33 Steve Ellison, interview with the authors, 24 April 1999.

34 Steve Webber interview by Julian Upton, 3 March, 2012.

UNEASE

1 The modus operandi of one successful video theft as related to the authors.

2 We are unable to substantiate claims that in April 1985 the Pope warned of video dependence.

3 Go Video, distributors of *SS Experiment Camp* and *Cannibal Holocaust*, had a penchant for outrageous ads. *The Demons* incorporated similarly outrageous imagery.

4 The organisation is also referred to as National VALA – the acronym pronounced Valour.

5 At the time of writing, Whitehouse remained within the NVLA, though frailty has considerably diminished her fervent pro-activity. She finally handed over the position of presidency to Revd Graham Stevens, herself being honoured with President Emeritus.

6 *"Who Does She Think She Is?"*, Mary Whitehouse.

7 When the BBC aired Quentin Tarantino's *Pulp Fiction*, 3.8 million viewers watched the film. Afterwards a mere forty-five complaints were received, yet the NVLA declared that it offended "good taste and decency" and should not have been shown.

8 Commander of the Order of the British Empire.

9 To give some insight into what they consider to be a breach of their moral criterion, here are a few films the association believe should never have been broadcast, on the grounds they contain "unacceptable violence": *The Color Purple*, *The Commitments*, *Four Weddings And A Funeral*, *Pretty Woman*, *Dirty Dancing*, *Great Balls Of Fire!*, *Legal Eagles*, *Stakeout*, *Last Of The Mohicans*, *Planes, Trains And Automobiles*...

10 The degree of restraint is exemplified in the NVLA's guideline for nudity on television, which deems that "the state of undress that we accept in the street is what is appropriate on our screens."

11 See *A Most Dangerous Woman?*, one of Whitehouse's several autobiographies, for the full story.

12 *Outsiders: Studies in the Sociology of Deviance*, Howard Becker, 1963.

13 Some reports put the figure as high as 35,000.

14 The British Humanist Association described Mary Whitehouse and the NFOL as "at the best, a music hall act, at the worst, as a well organised attempt to destroy the basis of individual freedom". The real moral pollution they argued was unemployment figures of one million, schools that had been condemned thirty years ago, the mental hospitals, inner city slums and the poverty of old age pensioners.

15 An observation made by David Tribe in his book *Questions of Censorship*.

Notes

16 Longford was the first to admit that "none of the other subjects in the House of Lords debates ever roused one-tenth of the interest" as did his debate on pornography.

17 *Questions of Censorship*, David Tribe.

18 See Gilbert Kelland's *Crime in London* for a detailed insider's account of the investigation into corrupt detectives and pornographers.

19 Some women's groups wanted men to carry licenses proving they had legitimate business being out at night, while others called for a curfew on all men. Some simply resorted to verbal and physical abuse.

20 *Midnight Marquee* No 31, Fall 1982.

21 The tally of pornographic videocassettes seized by police rose from 125 tapes in 1979, to over 5,000 in the first three months of 1982 alone.

22 The *Times*, April 14, 1983.

23 "Rape Of Our Children's Minds," *Daily Mail*, June 30, 1983.

24 The irony of gauging someone's reaction to a film in which aversion therapy is key is not recorded. What unnerving influence must the Ludovico treatment sequence in *A Clockwork Orange* have had on Dr Carruthers' volunteers, which shows the film's main character being forced to view increasingly violent and sexual imagery?

25 Often the title of a movie would be enough to incite protest, as per *Violation of the Bitch*, a plodding piece of Spanish erotica that had even less titillation value following BBFC cuts totalling fifteen minutes.

26 "Obscenity" for such protestors, according to John Sutherland, author of *Offensive Literature*, "was redefined in sectarian terms as "containing violence or condoning violence against women."

27 As described by the *Sunday Times*, June 13, 1982.

28 Curiously, in the case of *The Driller Killer*, *Death Trap* and *I Spit on Your Grave*, the courts were told that Scotland Yard had originally pressed for the more serious Section Two ruling. But Stephen Wooller, for the DPP, said that the legal papers had been marked in error. "There had been a breakdown of communication between the director's office and the court because, following consultations with the Metropolitan Police, the clear decision was that this matter would be dealt with under Section Three."

29 As described by Andrew Sims and Graham Melville-Thomas in their "Psychiatrist's Survey" chapter of the book, *Video Violence and Children*.

30 The *Sunday Times*, September 5, 1982.

CLAMPDOWN

1 In the article entitled "How High Street Horror is Invading the Home," see also previous chapter.

2 That isn't tainted with libel or racial offensiveness.

3 A 'clean up' campaign in Manchester during the mid seventies resulted in the removal of many books and magazines that were readily obtainable in any other city. Amongst them relatively innocuous fare such as *The Sun Book of Page 3 Girls*. While in Portsmouth, anything outside of child porn, bestiality and torture was tolerated by police.

4 On February 3, 1970.

5 Noted by John Trevelyan, director of the BBFC, who was quick to lodge a public complaint following the police action. See Trevelyan's book, *What*

The Censor Saw.

6 The *Times* described how one cinema in New York reacted to the news by allowing anyone with a British passport in to see the film for nothing, while the *Sun* parodied the raid in a cartoon that showed a cinema full of pop-eyed policemen distracted from their duties by the film playing.

7 At the suggestion of John Trevelyan.

8 Editor Richard Neville's credo was "the weapons of revolution are obscenity, blasphemy and drugs." The editorship of *Oz* 28, the offending issue, had been given over to schoolchildren, who made some appropriately rude contributions.

9 It should be noted that search and seizure of private collections is not authorised by the Act.

10 "Repulsive... filthy... loathsome... indecent... lewd..."

11 Sir Cyril Black, a lay preacher and member of the Public Morality Council. More than one of the prosecution witnesses against *Last Exit to Brooklyn* admitted in court that by reading the book they had been depraved and corrupted.
In February 1998, in court for having tried to import sexually explicit material and several 'video nasties' into Britain, Mark Wright used the defence that he was unlikely to be corrupted by such items because he was an "experienced viewer." He was found guilty, with the two judges ruling that the law was obliged "not only to protect the innocent – but also the less innocent from further corruption."

12 Calder & Boyars refused to cease publication of *Last Exit*, forcing the DPP to proceed with Section Two proceedings. This meant that the firm stood to lose a lot more than forfeiture of goods, but granted them the right to trial by jury – who found the book guilty. This decision was overturned on appeal, because the judge had not instructed the jury sufficiently regarding the Obscene Publications Act.

13 The Act had been extended to cover the public screening of feature films in 1977.

14 "The 1959 Obscene Publications Act, as amended by the 1977 Criminal Law Act, exempts from liability 'anything done in the course of television or sound broadcasting,'" noted Robertson in his book *Obscenity*, "Video cassettes may be fed along short cables to standard television sets, tuned to standard channels, which then decode and depict obscene images, and sometimes emit obscene sounds, for the patrons of Soho's more technologically-advanced clubs. If this process amounts to 'television' or to 'sound broadcasting', such publications would fall outside the Obscene Publications Act..."

15 The pressure was certainly great. Hetherington's stock response to publishers in the seventies who came to him for assistance was: "I regret that I am unable to give you the type of advice you seek regarding the operation of the Obscene Publications Acts. I am unable to do so because of the generally recognised uncertainty in the operation of law in this field."

16 The films had been seized from Leonard Matthews' shop in Highgate over two years prior, a place in which, agreed the police, most of the video cassettes were "perfectly proper." Matthews claimed to have already removed from stock three of the titles because of the bad publicity they had received in the press, and while *Cannibal Apocalypse* had still been for hire, he did not suspect anything wrong with it. After viewing the films in their entirety, it took the jury just one

Notes

hour to acquit Matthews of having obscene articles for publication and gain.

17 Steve Ellison, interview with the authors, 24 April 1999.

18 Christopher Glazebrook, interview by mail with the authors, circa mid 1999.

19 In compiling a list of 'banned' video titles for *Video Violence and Children*, researchers tellingly had to do so without access to a copy of the DPP blacklist and relied instead on 'conversations with officers at Scotland Yard... and off the Obscene Publications department of provincial forces.'

20 Ironically for Hamilton-Grant, the case brought as much publicity to him and his film as had the tasteless promotional gimmick he had created for its video release several years earlier. (See THE DPP39.)

21 Also victorious in the case against *Inside Linda Lovelace* and, much later, the Savoy novel *Lord Horror*.

22 Malcolm was also called to give evidence for *The Story of O*. "One of the most boring softcore sex films I've ever had to sit through," he would concede, although it was well photographed by Just Jaecklin. "Well photographed? Really?" queried the presiding magistrate. "I could do better myself."

23 Christopher Glazebrook, interview by mail with the authors, circa mid 1999.

24 The *Times*, May 31, 1983.

25 Including outlets based in laundrettes, dry cleaners, garages and the like, the total number of video dealers in Britain was anything up to 10,000.

26 Alas, at the beginning of the article, the reporter admits that the same audience who couldn't stomach the film were "feeling slightly sick from a surfeit of British wine the previous evening."

27 On the subject of context, a major grievance with politicians is that they are frequently quoted out of it – an irony evidently lost on Bright when presenting his cut-and-paste showreel.

28 The Annual Assembly of the Methodist Church fell on the same day as the meeting and thus prevented its leaders from attending. They were represented instead by a lecturer from Oxford Polytechnic.

29 It was Hill who instigated the first meeting, having been inspired by various members of the Vice Squad he had spoken to regarding these "horrific" and "dreadful" videos.

30 According to Hill, the secrecy that surrounded the compiling of the Report and the source of its data, was in part due to the threat of "underworld forces" on his life. A mafia-type underworld controlling the video industry was one of the concerns aired at the launch of the enquiry.

31 *Illusions*, a film designed to warn schoolchildren of the perils of sniffing glue, was prevented from being shown in schools by the Department of Health in September 1983.

32 The Report stated that thirty-seven per cent of children aged under-seven had seen a 'video nasty', but a member of Brown's staff could only recall forty-six questionnaires for this age group, in which most children had never watched a video at all. Hill's national average appeared to have been drawn from a total of three children, who had claimed to have watched some seventeen 'video nasties' each.

33 In an experiment replicating the Video Enquiry, psychologist Dr Guy Cumberbatch found that most children readily admitted to watching films that didn't exist. Indeed, *Zombie Terror*, a film cited in the report as being one of the children's 'top ten video nasties', doesn't exist.

34 Palace Video MD, Nik Powell.

35 Steve Ellison, interview with the authors, 24 April 1999.

36 Wrongly presented in the showreel as authentic, the scene was fabricated utilising a rubber monkey head stuffed with red-dyed cauliflower. A similar scene was passed without comment in *Indiana Jones and the Temple of Doom*.

37 David Mellor MP.

38 There were some companies who volunteered works for video classification, however. These included World of Video 2000, who sought to protect their new French Label erotica line by securing a BBFC certificate and ensuring that the content and packaging didn't contravene the Obscene Publications Act.

39 Part (a) of the 'model licensing conditions' drafted by the Home Office states that "no film, other than a current newsreel, shall be exhibited unless it has received a certificate of the British Board of Film Classification or is the subject of the licensing authority's permission."

40 This at a time when the Home Secretary was sensitive to the opinion that a "recent increase in juvenile delinquency is, to a considerable extent, due to demoralising cinematographic films."

41 It isn't often that local authority will overrule a BBFC decision, although it did happen in the case of the Robin Williams comedy *Mrs Doubtfire*. The film was passed with a 12 certificate (because of some American colloquialisms it featured). Parents complained that they couldn't take their children to see the film and as a result some local authorities changed the category to a PG.

42 Under this Act, the Board amended the existing, unsatisfactory category system, as it would again in 1970 and 1983 in keeping with the changing times and attitudes.

43 The Cinematograph Acts 1909, 1952 and 1982 were consolidated into the Cinemas Act 1985.

44 The Report was started amidst the repercussions of several high-profile obscenity cases (involving *Gay News*, *Inside Linda Lovelace* and *Libertine*), the "sickening glut of blood and guts films" invading British cinemas (as highlighted by the *Sun* newspaper et al), and the investigation into police corruption within Scotland Yard's Vice Squad.

45 The *Times* urged "that the knowledge and instinct of the public in this matter is more important than that of the skill of a handful of committee sitters using their intellectual agility to verbalise a social problem out of existence." But in truth, the 'instinct' of an estimated four million members of the public was to read one or more pornographic magazines every month, according to research by the Williams Committee.

46 The fact that many local authorities refuse to licence sex shops or adult cinemas – thus considerably limiting the market for R18 – is one of the troubles facing films in this category. At the time of writing, there were only an estimated eighty licensed sex shops in Britain

47 Although 'Censors' has been replaced with 'Classification' the Board reject or cut (i.e. censor) about seven per cent of submitted material. The title change is more a political ploy than practical reality. The Board is offended by the notion they might be censors. When Tom Dewe Mathews' book *Censored: The Story of Film Censorship* was published, James Ferman responded with a damning article in the *Sunday Times* (July 24, 1994). At a BBFC roadshow in Manchester in March 2000, during a question-and-answer session, the

authors witnessed the new director of the Board, Robin Duval, coldly dismiss the allegation that he might be a censor, snub the question and quickly moved on.

48 Unlike the Obscene Publications Act, the Video Recordings Act made no provision for imprisonment.

49 BBFC Annual Report 1985.

50 In 1977, the BBFC were to discuss the "questionable taste" of a feature film based on a true-life British murder case. Although Ian Merrick's *The Black Panther* made no attempt to glamorise or dwell on the crime or criminal (Donald Neilson), nor stray from facts as they were known, the BBFC felt the film deserved an X-rating. In a bulletin, the Board gave the reason for their decision: "The idea of teenagers seeing a film about the maltreatment of a real girl of seventeen who died less than two years ago seemed sufficiently distasteful for us to prefer to restrict the film to an adult audience."
Asked how the BBFC assessed public taste, its director James Ferman told a Video Consultative Council meeting in September 1985, that it was a continuing process which the Board had been trying to maintain throughout the last seventy years; one which he hoped they had got about right.

51 The BBFC's treatment of rape has often had an adverse effect, and in trimming the portrayal of the crime the Board has often been accused of sanitising it. Ironically, Sam Peckinpah's 1971 *Straw Dogs* remains unavailable in this country (as of writing; it is now) because of BBFC intervention regarding the treatment of rape. The turning point in this tale of petty-mindedness and desperation comes with the rape of the Susan George character, Amy, by two men. John Trevelyan – director of the Board at the time the film was being made – consulted with the film-maker and advised how the scene should be shot, in order that there should be less of a problem during the examination process. Consequently, the editing and cutaways in this scene effectively 'banned' the film in this country for many years, following its initial theatrical run and video release pre-VRA.
Submitted to the BBFC in 1999, *Straw Dogs* was refused a video certificate. The Board outlined several reasons for its decision in a press release: "The first is the fact that the rapes are clearly effected by violence and the threat of violence. The second is the extent of the erotic content, notably Amy's forcible stripping and nudity. The third element of concern is the clear indication that Amy comes to enjoy being raped. It is Board policy not to condone material which endorses the well-known male rape myth that "women like it really.'"

52 This is a list compiled by the Department of Trade and Industry.

53 For instance, as pointed out in the booklet, film distributors whose catalogues had been examined by the BBFC were required "to publish lists of the categories granted to their titles under the Act. In such lists they should indicate instances where the certificate awarded under the Act differs in category from a certificate which may have been granted to that title for the purposes of cinema exhibition. Similarly, such lists should indicate titles where the film and video categories are the same but where the certificated video version has been cut more extensively by the censor than was the certificated film version. Videos of the less cut film version already in circulation must not be labelled with the classification category awarded after additional

cuts to the new video version."

54 Interview with Iain Muspratt, formerly Managing Director, Guild Home Video, by Julian Upton, 3 April, 2012.

55 Neither was it an offence under the Act to supply video records of events like weddings and anniversaries to those who took part in them or their acquaintances (so long, of course, as those events didn't depict sex or acts of violence).

56 Other criteria which prevented video works from qualifying as exempt were added a decade later, courtesy of the Criminal Justice and Public Order Bill 1994. (See SEX & WRECKS.)

57 Non English language work was also entitled to a lower tariff, as were works made by charity or non-profit-making organisations. In the case of video titles voluntarily submitted for classification prior to the VRA, the BBFC were obliged to assess free-of-charge whether their certificates could be confirmed under the Act.

58 Anderton's campaign resulted in Greater Manchester joining Nottinghamshire, Devon and Cornwall in forming a local video traders' association. Between them they were set to create news bulletins and present their members and police with a blacklist of video titles. Members of the association faced expulsion if they continued to hire out films that had been blacklisted – a deterrent that certainly didn't hold much sway with Anderton, who wasn't dissuaded from raiding any video stockist under his jurisdiction as he saw fit.

59 Steve Ellison, interview with the authors, 24 April 1999.

60 Tim Brinton, a Tory MP, went on record in July 1984 as saying that the Bill wouldn't stop the flow of 'nasties' and that the upsurge in a black market was inevitable.

SIEGE

1 Steve Ellison, interview with the authors, 24 April 1999.

2 Interview with James Ferman by David Kenny.

3 Another title released by LVC was *Tiger Love*, a curious Chinese production in which a woman gets intimate with a tiger after she urinates on it. The synopsis on the sleeve ran: "Warning – Some scenes in this film actually happened."

4 Evidently the distributors were unable to obtain original publicity materials for the films and resorted to producing their own artwork – *but who painted those terrible sleeves*?!

5 The slipcases were very fragile and quite often rental outlets cut them apart and placed them inside sturdier plastic cases. Original, intact boxes are collector items in themselves.

6 Palace released all John Waters' early movies. The titles included the Divine-free and "XXX rated" *Desperate Living*, and, as part of "The Divine Collection," *Mondo Trasho* (doubled with *Sex Madness*), *Female Trouble* and *Pink Flamingos*. Arcade Video released Waters' *Polyester* and included a scratch-and-sniff card so that viewers could partake in the 'Odorama' gimmick.

7 This tedious movie about a witch resurrected from a shipwreck was filmed in the Philippines. The opening credits are still popping up almost fifteen minutes into the film.

8 As of writing, it would have cost £1005.57 to get a video certificate for an eighty-minute English language film. With manufacturing costs and duplication fees on top of this, few

obscure low-budget features could hope to make much of a profit.

9 It was submitted yet again in 1999 with a longer running time of 84m 59s and passed without cuts.

10 James Ferman during a debate on Film Censorship and British Social History, at the Institute of Contemporary Arts, November 20, 1998.

BLACK MARKET & PIRATES

1 From an article by Andrew Allard at DVD Nightmare. In 2006, following the first edition of this book, Andrew Allard contacted the authors to say he happened to A—, the 'nasties' dealer in Hull, mentioned on page 103. As a result of the bust in 1990, he was forced to give up a teaching course, but was back on it again after about five years and teaching at the time of writing. "Those days are gone. But my love of films is still there."

2 *News of the World*, March 5, 2000.

3 There has been a serious decline in the apprehension of true criminals. Police in general are hitting soft targets. In this case, with hope they would find evidence of illegal activity.

4 Almost everybody who was interviewed or contributed to this chapter wished to remain anonymous or supplied the authors with an assumed name.

5 Sandwiched between a section on apparel as worn by the cast of *Star Trek*, and lobby cards from the thirties and forties, *Film & Rock'n'Roll Collectables* offers a price guide to a random selection of video titles. For the most part these are pre-certificated video tapes and regarded as "banned" (though some are clearly foreign imports). Not only is the guide occasionally erroneous and the monetary values misleading, but the whole concept of the video section is lawfully suspect, i.e an auction house cannot evaluate an illegal item in terms of collectability.

6 Nowadays, pre-VRA copies of any kind of film are considered collectable and can command high prices.

7 Invariably the dealer was male; during their research, the authors heard of no females dealing in illicit tapes back in the eighties.

8 The Scala had been the location for an anti-Video Recordings Act festival on March 10, 1984. Ten films cited by the DPP as 'video nasties' (but passed for cinema release) were screened: *Don't Go in the House*, *The Beyond*, *The Burning*, *The Evil Dead*, *Zombie Creeping Flesh*, *Zombie Flesh Eaters*, *House by the Cemetery*, *The Living Dead at the Manchester Morgue*, *The Toolbox Murders* and *Dead & Buried*.

9 The police hadn't yet seen the film, as the article concluded with a police spokesperson requesting that the tape be handed over for investigation. And while the newspaper didn't allow the law to get in the way of a good story, they did elicit knee-jerk copy from David Alton MP: he dreaded to think what the psychological effects of viewing the film might be on children.

10 Reprinted from *Fandamania: It's Only a Movie!* No 1, with permission.

11 Another tactic that Trading Standards hoped would help bust video crime was announced in March 1994. Officers in the northwest town of Bury intended to send children into video shops to hire 18-certificate films. These "baby-faced snoopers" – in the words of the *Journal* newspaper – were an attempt to weed out

dealers who broke the law, supplying adult material indiscriminately. A similar scheme had proven successful in helping to prevent newsagents from selling cigarettes and fireworks to those underage. Video dealers who swallowed the bait were said to face a £5,000 fine.

12 Figures vary. Some press reports claimed that "more than 3,500 videos" had been seized, with thirty people held for questioning.

13 Not improbable. Police and Customs were already doing it in their search for porn and fraudsters. According to an article in the *Observer* (April 29, 1990), "disguised as a Jones or a Smith," they peruse the likes of *Video World*, "looking in particular at the classified ads, where a two-line entry may lead them to a trader in bizarre material."

14 This and other quotes attributed to David Flint in this chapter are taken from *Busted!*, Flint's record of the case on the *Melon Farmers' Video Hits* website. For the authors' own interview with Flint, see ANATOMY OF A RAID.

15 Not dissimilar to the furore that surrounded a raid a few days earlier, in which Midlands police took from a student's flat a book by photographer Robert Mapplethorpe on the grounds that it was obscene. Containing images of homosexuality and bondage, the book belonged to the University of Central England and was being used for a thesis on 'Fine Art versus Pornography.' In this instance, police were alerted by a chemist to whom the student had taken photos from the book to be developed.

16 They describe themselves as "a frontline organisation responsible for protecting society against the growing threat of illicit drugs, firearms and paedophile material."

17 *Obscenity*, Geoffrey Robertson.

18 Right alongside other items such as unlicensed drugs (such as heroin, morphine, cocaine, cannabis, amphetamines, barbiturates and LSD), offensive weapons (such as flick knives, swordsticks, knuckle-dusters and some martial arts equipment), indecent and obscene material featuring children (such as books, magazines, films, videotapes, laser discs and software), and counterfeit and pirated goods and goods that infringe patents (such as watches, clocks and CDs and any goods with false marks of their origin).

19 The plan to release the film was abandoned due to its explicitly violent content and potential difficulties with the BBFC.

20 *Cannibal* was available in a cut version in the UK. It was never 'banned' but disappeared from shelves due to its association with other 'banned' cannibal titles. *Primitifs* was released in the UK as *Savage Terror*. *Night of the Devils* never came out officially on video in Britain, but did have a cinema release in the seventies.

21 Official Secrets Act 1989 and Protection of Children Act 1978.

22 'Squish' is the name given to a brand of fetishism that focuses on women – often in high heels – trampling (in its extreme form) insects and small animals. A man in Shropshire was fined £2,000 in 1998 for the importation of squish films, following a joint RSPCA and Customs & Excise investigation. A man from Edinburgh was fined £1,000 in 1999 after Customs intercepted films with titles like *Debased Dolly* and *Pain 32* which, according to the *Scotsman* newspaper, "portrayed horrific sex scenes, including footage of women being raped."

23 Customs Officer Mark Thompson. *Sight & Sound*, May 1998.

24 It isn't accurate to state that the

Notes

VRA was also responsible for creating a black market in hardcore pornography. Despite claims made by some journalists, there has always been a trade in under-the-counter porn in Britain. Indeed, it was porn that helped to galvanise interest and shape video in the first place – as it tends to do with any new technology. A Home Video Show sponsored by the *Daily Mirror* in the early eighties was raided by police who removed videocassettes on the Swedish Erotica label. And while films like *Debbie Does Dallas*, *A Dirty Western* and *Deep Throat* were being released legitimately by companies in Britain in specially trimmed formats – albeit in a form stronger than would be tolerated by the BBFC at the time – full uncut versions of the same titles were always available to those who sought them out.

25 The *ET* anti-piracy task force was in operation a full six months before the film made it onto video. Anti-piracy screenings of *ET* were held for team personnel; master tapes were coded, and their transportation closely supervised and logged as they made their way into the eight major territories.

26 In the first months of 1980, many of the 10,000 owners of VCRs in Israel were watching illegal copies of new films like *The Deer Hunter* and *Kramer Vs. Kramer*. Israeli police sourced them back to London.

27 *The Home Video Revolution in Western Europe*, Economist Intelligence Unit, London, 1983.

28 Another source recalls that many of the pirated Disney films in circulation had Arabic subtitles.

29 Nowadays Southeast Asia is largely considered the piracy epicentre, with illicit copies of films being sold quite openly mere days after they have opened theatrically in the US. Some shops deal exclusively in pirated product. To try and combat the problem, major films have occasionally played in Malaysia and Singapore ahead of their US dates.

30 Macrovision worked by confusing the automatic gain control in the copying recorder. The process was the result of research started in 1983. Embassy Home Entertainment, involved in its development, launched Macrovision with their massively hyped, commercial flop *The Cotton Club*.

31 The ad, shown on TV and in cinemas, starts with the parent of a small boy buying a pirate tape. Instead of watching an innocent cartoon, the child is subjected to a terrifying onslaught of brutally horrific and violent sexual imagery.

32 The claims were made prior to the IRA ceasefire, when acts of terrorism on mainland Britain were still a serious threat.

33 In *Film 95* (September 25), following a report concerning pirate copies of Disney's *The Lion King*, critic Barry Norman advised viewers that "Each pirate video you buy could contribute to your child shooting up in the school lavatory." Two years later, in *Film 97* (September 29), Norman offered viewers another salutary warning: "If you're tempted to buy a pirate copy of – I dunno – *Titanic* at the local car boot sale, do remember that the money you hand over may well be laundered back into the drug trade."

34 The threat of child pornography is a common tactic used to generate support for any campaign. Indeed, most people would be happy to help stamp out the production and distribution of such material. (What's the alternative? To be seen not endorsing a campaign that claims to be fighting child porn?) Take the NVLA – although child pornography has never been legal in the UK, the

CANNIBAL ERROR

NVLA claims to act for "Securing effective legislation to *outlaw child pornography*, 'video nasties' and indecent displays," [our emphasis] and to curtail "media obscenity pervading our country and endangering our children."
The same scare tactic is being used by European Leisure Software Publishers Association (ELSPA) in their crackdown on software piracy. They claim that eighty per cent of organised piracy rings are also involved in drugs, prostitution and funding paramilitary organisations in Northern Ireland.

THE BIG INFLUENCE

1 One of the authors of this book assisted, late one Sunday night, in a local search for a missing child. As people were drawn by the sight of flashlights, sounds of commotion, and a helicopter overhead giving information and direction via loudspeaker, the search party grew. Fortunately, the child turned out not to be lost, but was with his father, who had collected him earlier that day. In a report in the local paper, the mother later expressed her relief the child had not been abducted, and dreaded to think what might have happened if he had. This speculation, of course, side-stepped the real issue: lack of parental communication and even negligence.

2 Influencing has since evolved into a lucrative social media profession, whereby popular personalities directly encourage their followers to behave in a particular manner or purchase sponsored products.

3 A television series depicting footage of accidents and disasters entitled *The World's Most Amazing Videos* opens with the statement that what the viewer will see is "so startling, so awesome, so unbelievable, you might think you're watching a movie." Incongruously, footage of a sinking ship was prefaced with the remark "like a real-life *Titanic*," as though the viewer might believe that *Titanic* is simply the title of a movie and not an historical event.

4 *A Clockwork Orange* was "put on the 'black list' by the Festival of Light although one of the festival's most prominent members stated that it was the best film he had ever seen" – John Trevelyan, *What the Censor Saw*.

5 *In Darkest England and The Way Out* by General Booth, pub: The Salvation Army, 1890.

6 Reminiscing in the pages of *Sight and Sound*, a journalist recalled trying to rent a 16mm copy of *A Clockwork Orange* as part of a film course, in the days when its ban in the UK was less widely publicised. Although it featured in the Columbia-Warner-EMI 16mm catalogue, the journalist was informed that rental of the film was restricted to "prisons, hospitals and borstals." Following Kubrick's death *A Clockwork Orange* was re-released to British cinemas and certified for video.

7 The *Daily News* (philly.com) reported on February 15, 2000, that a man who exposed himself to staff at a McDonald's drive-through restaurant, masturbated and hurled his semen at them, may have been committing the acts for publicity. Psychologist Dr James Pedigo said "the publicity may be encouraging the man."

8 *Breaking Points*, Hodder & Stoughton 1985.

9 Because of the furore and bogus accusations, the BBC would never air the film again, despite having paid for multiple showings. Channel 5 picked

up the film and aired it several times. No violent incidents followed the broadcasts.

10 Davies wrote in a *Sunday Telegraph* article (September 18, 1988) that he "wept and felt a little less lonely" on hearing Prince Charles condemn the television, film and video industry for their menu of violence. Earlier in the same article he mentions the Clint Eastwood western *The Outlaw Josey Wales*, and how the world is "heading for a bitter and dead harvest" – which, without any explanation, he claims is already evident "in the valleys of South Wales, where I went to live recently for two years with the miners." Josey Wales... South Wales...?

11 A claim supposedly related to Davies by a "local teenager" but disputed by everyone else.

12 Untrue. Ryan attempted to murder a cashier; *Rambo* set fire to petrol pumps.

13 In 1999, the European Court of Human Rights declared the two killers had been given an unfair trial.

14 The tabloid editors were on familiar territory, using misinformation and propaganda to worry the nation. Several years earlier, they spread the bogus satanic child abuse scares across the country. That campaign resulted in the break-up of families, the arrest of innocent people, burning of homes, and worst of all, the sexual abuse of children by those claiming to be examining them for signs of abuse: one method used to assess whether a child had been sexually abused was to insert a finger into the child's anus. The reaction of the sphincter muscle determined whether penetration had occurred prior to that moment. At least that is what the examiners claimed.

15 See *Independent on Sunday*, April 17, 1994.

16 The press often reported that James Bulger had part of his face mutilated during his attack. In what appears to be twisted black humour on the part of the *Daily Star*, some of the page describing the Bulger killing was given over to an ad for the film *The Man Without a Face* in which Mel Gibson plays a man with half his face mutilated. See *Daily Star* November 26, 1993, p5.

17 Had either of these contrivances succeeded, what film might the press have then chosen to indict as causative? No such scenes were played out in *Child's Play 3*.

18 A metal fixing of about two-foot long, used to bolt lengths of rail track together.

19 Some would attempt to link the insertion of the batteries to *Child's Play 3* suggesting that dolls often contain batteries. This is a further futile, straw-grasping claim. Even at ten-years-of-age the two killers were fully aware of the fact that humans are not battery operated.

20 "Why Sick Videos Must Be Banned," the *Star*, November 26, 1993.

21 Representing the DPP and instructing counsel for the Crown, Brian Blacklock attended Mary Bell's trial in 1968. In an article published in *Mensa Magazine* in August 1998, he recalls that facts in the case "were simple, and all the more horrific for being so, but clearly not horrific enough for [today's tastes]." Referencing Gitta Sereny's controversial book, *Cries Unheard: The Story of Mary Bell*, he states that a new demonised Mary Bell has been created, thanks to witnesses adding fanciful details over the years, and writers misinterpreting the facts of the case. "How soon," he asks, "before Ms Sereny and others register "Mary Bell plc"? There are, after all, marketing opportunities..."

22 *Young Offenders and the Media*, Hagell & Newburn.

23 It is curious that Alton fails to mention the Bulger case at this point as it was the foundation of his campaign. It is possible that he realised, or was told, that he was over-exploiting the toddler's death.

24 Ireland may have targeted homosexuals to fit with the newspaper's homophobic stance. The *Sun* reached the nadir of its homophobia when reporting on a so-called "gay-mafia" running the British government in November 1998.

25 See *Scapegoat* No 1.

26 Similarly, some tabloids are in the habit of doctoring photos of murderers, making the sometimes-innocuous looking perpetrators appear as sinister and wicked as their actions. This happened with Hamilton's familiar visage in at least one instance, and it also happened with Fred West.

27 A week after the massacre, the *News of the World* turned its attention to the Internet and launched a campaign to "Fight The Filth." The article claimed that Hamilton "could have been tipped over the edge by the stream of paedophile filth available on his computer." By way of illustration, a picture of a child in a bikini with her face blanked out was utilised, dwarfing that of mugshots of Hamilton himself and Sir Cliff Richard, who had sent a heartfelt prayer to the victims of Dunblane. In an unrelated feature the previous December, the *News of the World* ran a double-page story concerning two schoolgirl sisters who aspired to be models. Following the publication of a topless photo of them in a rival ("sleazy") newspaper, the report stated the girls had been "hounded by perverts." Not only did the *News of the World* reproduce the "sleazy" shot (albeit with the word "censored" obscuring their breasts) but ran their own 'tasteful' stocking-tops picture of the two schoolgirl sisters in uniform beside it.

28. 'Shedding Light on Port Arthur Massacre,' *The Age* website. March 26, 2006.

29 Use of the numbers 666 indicate an element of biblical influence. Indeed, more crimes against humanity can be attributed to the Bible than any other single publication, and those who act under the book's influence strongly believe it to be a factual record.

30 Grisham predicted that victory in such a case would "come from the heartland, far away from Southern California, in some small courtroom with no cameras."

31 Take the castration of John Wayne Bobbitt by his wife, Lorena, in 1993. Far from being viewed as a terrible crime, the case was often handled by the media in a light and humorous way. Lorena had suffered escalating abuse at the hand of her husband. Not only did this lead her to seek bloody revenge, but brought sympathetic votes from women world-wide, who regarded Lorena as an innocent victim.

32 In their attempt to lay the blame for criminal activity on video, the press will often play down the felon's criminal record, presenting house-breaking and burglary as slight, inoffensive activities that have little bearing on the bigger picture.

33 Directed by Tim McCoy starring porn actor Harry Reems and released on video by Cal Vista.

34 How differently would the press have reacted to Edward Paisnel, the "Beast of Jersey" – he donned a hideous mask and ghoulish apparel to commit sex offences against children – had his reign of terror not taken place in the 1960s, but post-*Texas Chain Saw Massacre*?

Notes

35 From Minutes of Evidence taken before the Home Affairs Committee, Wednesday, June 22, 1994.

36 Some schools took Heston's advice and did just that. The coats were described by officials as intimidating and inappropriate and could be used to hide weapons. Susan Carlson, spokesperson for schools in Adams County, said that wearing such coats was "alarming enough to others that it disrupts the educational environment..."

37 Far from being the unique, sign-of-the-times monster the press makes him out to be, Marilyn Manson is a contemporary 'shock rocker' Alice Cooper. Like Cooper, Manson is androgynous in name and appearance, sings rebellious songs, and has a provocative stage show. Food for thought: it's not hard to imagine the press implicating Cooper's 1972 hit single 'School's Out' – its final line "school's been blown to pieces..." – as the inspiration for the Columbine massacre.

38 Results taken from an ongoing poll at apbonline.com on May 11, 1999.

39 In spring 2000, there was curious news that one of the emergency services responding to the Columbine High School massacre had subsequently added music to video footage of the devastated classrooms and were selling copies. The report was unclear on the details of the video or who might benefit from its sale.

Time Warner gained access to the security camera footage of the killings and published stills, much to the fury of relatives of the dead, who themselves had been denied the opportunity to view the film.

An independent no-budget satire of the massacre, titled *Duck! The Carbine High Massacre*, resulted in the film-makers being arrested for having carried guns onto school property (the school happened to be closed at the time).

SEX & WRECKS

1 Although amendments had already been made to the 1984 Act in the form of the Criminal Justice Act 1988 and Video Recordings Act 1993, these comprised only minor tweaks and clarifications. The Criminal Justice and Public Order Act 1994 remains the only significant update as of writing.

2 The films rejected in this period are as follows: *Angel of Vengeance* (a woman studying survivalist techniques is abducted by a group of men in the wilderness but uses her skills to escape and kill them all; this film was effectively remade as *Savage Instinct* which was passed 18 for video); *Caligula: The Untold Story* (Italian cash-in that was denied a certificate in spite of the removal of a hardcore sex scene involving a horse); *Chained; Class of 1984* (high school punks take over the classrooms, before a teacher decides to stand up and fight); *A Coming of Angels; Curfew; The Evil Protégé* (aka *Nightmare Maker*, which had initially formed part of the DPP banned list but was dropped); *Game of Survival* (hoodlums take over a tenement block before the residents mete out their revenge); *Head Girl at St Winifreds; Hidden Rage* (AIDS victim seeks retribution by transmitting the disease to as many women as he can rape); *Hotline; House of Hookers;*

Possession (Until Death Do You Part); *Precious Jewels*; *Psychic Killer II*; *Savage Streets* (rape-revenge movie starring Linda Blair armed with a crossbow; an abridged version was later classified 18 with some thirteen-and-a-half minutes missing), *Silent Night Deadly Night Part 2* (serial killer dressed as Santa Claus); *Sixth Form at St Winifreds*; *Slumber Party Massacre II*; *Story of O Part 2*; *Target Massacre*; *The Trip*; *Violators*; *War Victims*; *Warden's End*; and *Wild Riders* (biker movie with a cinematic first: death by cello).

3 BBFC Annual Report 1993.

4 "The Board is conscious that a particular genre that has always been identified as entirely unacceptable is that of so-called 'snuff movies'. Their main identifying feature is that at least one of the participants is actually killed. *Banned from Television* is only different in that, instead of a death being created for the work, actual death and injury is collated from a wide range of pre-existing sources to create the work..." The urban myth of 'snuff' films being one justification the BBFC submitted for having rejected this mondo compilation.

5 This was a pet phrase of Ferman's and used to somehow rationalise the role of the censor – Bond movies, for instance, were said to be "not a work of art [but] a work of commerce." When one of the authors of this book contacted the BBFC in 1988 with relation to 'banned' films and censorship, the response from Guy Phelps – then principal examiner – contained the statement: "I would be most surprised to find many films likely to be of interest to a *serious* collector that have been changed in any way by us." [Our emphasis.]

6 BBFC Annual Report 1996-97.

7 BBFC Annual Report 1985.

8 BBFC Annual Report 1995-96.

9 *The Last Days of the Board*, d: Claire Lasko, Channel 4.

10 BBFC Annual Report 1993.

11 So great was the concern of parents that the BBFC drew up a form letter to respond to all the complaints (allaying fears by offering statistics and quoting from the glowing review given the film by the *Daily Mail*). The follow-up to *Jurassic Park*, *The Lost World*, was the first theatrical release to carry consumer advice. Regarded by the BBFC as a "major initiative", this advice comprised the following: "Passed PG (Parental Guidance) for scary scenes of violence that may be unsuitable for sensitive children or those under 8."

12 BBFC press statement, dated March 20, 1998.

13 *Maniac* was available on video in Britain prior to the Video Recordings Act 1984, in a cut form on the Intervision label.

14 *Samhain* No 69.

15 *A Clockwork Orange* was denied a certificate because its director Stanley Kubrick withdrew the film in 1972. However, it is debatable whether Ferman would have allowed the film to pass intact if it had gone before him: *A Clockwork Orange* is undoubtedly one of the films to which he was referring when lamenting the tirade of movies from the seventies that featured unacceptable scenes of rape.

16 The video sleeve of *Tenebrae* is also notably different. The trickle of blood on a victim's throat is now transformed into a red ribbon and bow.

17 "Sinful Days in Soho" by Maggie Mills, the *Sunday Times*, courtesy Melon Farmers' Video Hits website.

18 James Ferman interviewed by David Kenny.

19 Before it was granted a certificate and the likelihood that it would ever see

Notes

a British release was still debatable, *Natural Born Killers* played the 1994 London Film Festival to a packed house of 850 people. Tickets were exchanging hands for £100 each outside the theatre. One ticket holder told a reporter for the *Daily Telegraph*: "If something is going to be kept from our eyes, and this is our one and only chance to see it, I'm not going to miss out."

20 "Confessions of a Censor," Ros Hodgkiss, the *Guardian*, November 20, 1998.

21 Absent from the biographical notes in *Hollywood vs. America* – and indeed the book as a whole – is Medved's former life as a champion of grade-Z horror fare like *Plan 9 From Outer Space* and *The Thing with Two Heads*. Through his *Golden Turkey* books and television show, Medved made a career out of bringing obscure schlock to a new audience. During a screening of *Blood Feast* in London, he ran up and down the aisle howling with demented glee at the gore displayed on screen. To paraphrase one of the chapters in *Hollywood vs. America*: 'What went wrong?'

22 *Daily Express*, November 26, 1993.

23 The *Times*, April 13, 1994.

24 It was eventually passed with seventeen seconds of cuts on November 8, 1994. The full version was submitted in January 1995 and passed without cuts.

25 Although it wasn't mentioned in the reports, political correctness probably played its part in robbing kids of their innocence. In 1987, the "golliwogs" of Enid Blyton's original *Noddy* books were considered inappropriate and were changed to gnomes.

26 Amiel is the director of *Copycat*, a film in which a serial killer utilises the modus operandi of several infamous murderers. In an episode of *Film 96* (transmitted January 1), Amiel said that the films "most likely to create copycat violence are the ones in which our heroes – the Bruce Willises and Sylvester Stallones and Jean-Claude Van Dammes of this world – go out and, during the course of the movie, waste a good twenty to fifty bad guys on the basis they're so bad they deserve everything they get."

27 Almost a year to the day after calling for Ferman to be sacked, the *Mail* travelled a tired full circle and on December 14, 1997, pledged "It's time to censor the Censor."

28 The depressing plight of tearaway American teenagers, *Kids* was called child porn by the tabloids because of simulated sex scenes (but with actors over the age of consent).

29 In the case of David Cronenberg's *Crash*, the idea of a 'car crash sex film' was enough to stir the tabloids into near orgasmic frenzy at the end of 1996. Barely a day seemed to go by when the film wasn't the focus of an outraged reporter, critic, or letter-writer. The *Daily Mail* – who spearheaded the campaign to try to ban the film – went so far as to 'doorstep' BBFC examiners and pry into their personal lives. The newspaper requested that readers boycott the film (even though it was not yet on general release) and attacked the managing director of distributor Columbia Tristar UK, for being "single, 40, Belgian... and bringing 'depravity' to Britain." Several days prior, the *Mail* film critic expressed disgust that *Crash* included people having sex with "cripples." When asked what film stood out most in his twenty-three years at the BBFC, James Ferman without hesitation cited *Crash*.

30 The story of a female necrophile, loosely based on the real-life case of Karen Greenlee.

31 For more on *Executions*, see *Killing for Culture*, Kerekes & Slater.

32 Via secret filming, *Hookers: Sex for Sale* sees Australian model Peter Benedict visiting prostitutes and awarding them marks out of ten. The film-makers claimed it made a valid point in exposing the world of prostitution. *Everyday...Operations* featured close-ups of common surgical procedures performed in British hospitals. In a press release, the BBFC stated the film was given an 18 certificate because it demystified remedial practices and demonstrated "the skills of the surgeons involved." But in the same statement is an apologia: "When this tape was submitted for classification, the BBFC considered that the material was presented in a factual and informative way with no attempt to sensationalise or exploit"... It could be that the BBFC, having passed the film, got wise to the fact that *Everyday... Operations* came from the same team as *Police Stop!* and *Caught in the Act*, the latter masquerading as a serious look at surveillance but found to contain fabricated footage.

33 Bruce Gyngell, forerunner for BBFC president, writing in the *Mail on Sunday*, December 14, 1997.

34 BBFC Annual Report 1997-98.

35 "More Sex Please, We're British," Laurence O'Toole writing in the *New Statesman*, August 30, 1999.

36 Consequently, the BBFC refused to pass uncut *Makin' Whoopee*, which contained material no more pornographic than either *The Pyramid* or *BatBabe*. Its distributor went to the Video Appeals Committee (VAC), who conceded unanimously that the film was not obscene within the terms of the Obscene Publications Act and should be granted an R18 certificate. Regarding this as a benchmark, seven other videos the Board had also denied R18 certificates, were also taken before the VAC and found not obscene: *Horny Catbabe*, *Nympho Nurse Nancy*, *TV Sex*, *Office Tart*, a trailer for *Carnival* (International Version), *Wet Nurses 2* (Continental Version) and *Miss Nude International* (Continental Version). The Board announced it would be seeking a Judicial Review. In May 2000, the High Court ruled that the videos could be legally sold in Britain.

37 The film's distributor, Alliance, left the forty second scene in but blurred it to remove the offensive detail. They wanted the viewer to be aware that censorship had been imposed.

38 Interview with David Gregory of Exploited films, by Simon Collins, *Headpress* 20.

39 Following the Dunblane massacre, there was a move to ban all handguns above single shot types. The bill met strong criticism from gun enthusiasts and many politicians. One Tory MP went so far as to say that the family of those killed at Dunblane were reacting "emotively." Gun owners were portrayed as victims and, when their weapons had to be handed in, were financially compensated with public money. The emphasis switched from guns, back to film and TV violence.

40 *Today* and *Daily Mirror*, April 13, 1994.

41 BBFC Annual Report 1993.

42 Equally, it could be argued that television gameshows and the National Lottery have encouraged a something-for-nothing generation.

43 Members of the NVLA spend their viewing time specifically watching violence – over an unspecified duration they collated 107 incidents of arson and bomb attacks, 340 stabbings, and forty-four scenes depicting illegal drugs.

44 Ferman interviewed by David Kenny.

45 "The vice hunter declares that most adults are mentally deficient and need

protection..." A statement made in 1929 by Morris L Ernst and William Seagle in their book, *To The Pure*....

46 Vipco, a distributor in the early 1980s, revitalised itself in the 1990s by exhuming former 'nasties'. Although BBFC certified and cut, each re-release carried a bold disclaimer on the box notifying the consumer of the film's former 'banned' status. Similarly, a reissue of *Axe* was, for Exploited, a "commercial decision, because it had been a video nasty."

47 "The Street's video nasty" (in which Granada television were said to face a heavy fine for airing a special episode of the soap *Coronation Street* hitherto marketed as exclusive to video); "Tintin takes on the video nasties" (Herge's famous cartoon creation set to make a comeback); "Video shock for parents" (Scarborough police propose to tackle hooliganism with security cameras and "asking parents to watch video 'nasties' starring their own children"); Writing in *Mail Online (*December 1, 2023), Andrew Neil responded to an online video published by *Guardian* journalist Owen Jones. Neil implied that Jones was downplaying the atrocities committed by Hamas militants when they invaded Israel on October 7 and murdered over 1,000 civilians. Their acts were recorded on GoPro cameras and the Israel Defence Force had compiled footage found on the camera to present to journalists. Neil described Jones' opinionated video as a "video nasty"; In 2023, the BBC quiz show *Only Connect* presented a group of contestants bearing the team name 'Video Nasties'; *Mail Online* (November 13, 2023) concedes that *Faces of Death* is a "legendary cult horror ... controversial but commercially successful" in an article that takes a playful look at "some of the most notorious 'video nasties'".

48 Ferman interviewed by David Kenny.

THE DPP39

1 But compiled for posterity as a Headpress eBook: *Last Orgy by the Cemetery: A 'Video Nasties' Synopsis, Film By Shocking Film!*

Absurd

1 Massaccesi says he plucked the name Joe D'Amato off a calendar, at a time when Italian-American sounding directors were in vogue. At least one other name in *Absurd*'s technical credits is also Massaccesi: Richard Haller (photography). "That's for legal reasons," he told *European Trash Cinema* (No 12). "You can't have too many jobs on one project because of the unions."

2 In *Anthopophagous*, Eastman wore lumpy makeup. Here he wears nothing more sinister than a beard, yet a nurse still refers to him as "strange" looking.

3 *The Dark Side* April 1992.

4 *Filmfax* No 8.

5 Suggested by Lucas Balbo in *Shock Xpress* (Vol 2 No 1), but often reiterated, despite other directors equally 'boring' – Jesús Franco, for example, whose *Bloody Moon*, *Devil Hunter* and *Women Behind Bars* can also be found on the DPP list.

6 As Massaccessi reported in *European Trash Cinema* (No 12), although earlier in the same interview he claims, "every film is like a son to me."

7 If you include cutaway shots of Katya

in traction and Willie elsewhere in the house, Emily's death seems to go on much longer.

8 *Flesh & Blood* No 7.

Anthropophagous The Beast

1 *The Anthropophagous Beast* would make more sense. The wording, as it appears on screen, is ambiguous.

2 D'Amato claims that of all his films, *Anthropophagous* is a favourite. "*Anthropophagous* for horror," he told *Flesh & Blood* (No 7), "and *11 Days, 11 Nights* for softcore, erotic movie."

3 The foetus of a sheep still encased in its amnion was supposedly used for the scene.

Axe

1 It also sounds remarkably similar to a keyboard solo in The Blues Project's 1967 garage favourite, 'No Time Like The Right Time.'

2 A review of the US print of the film that appeared in *The House of Hammer* (No 18), back in 1978, also stated that Lisa's age is thirteen.

3 *Sleazoid Express* Vol 3 No 1.

4 *Date with a Kidnapper* was the British video title. The original title was *The Kidnapper* aka *House of Terror* aka *Kidnapped Coed*.

5 A company called Lynx distributed *Date with a Kidnapper*.

6 More people are credited for the 'Radio and Television Shows' that play in the background than there are people in the movie itself.

7 The limited acting capability of the woman playing the cashier elevates the sequence to a plane in excess of the sum of its parts.

The Beast in Heat

1 This scream and parts of the electronic score – along with a soundbite from Lee Frost's *Love Camp 7* – were utilised in Jörg Buttgereit's *Der Todesking*, in a sequence that was a pastiche of Nazi camp exploitation films.

2 One suspects a more substantial credits list was conceived, but failed to materialise or was cut short for this print. A French release on the Assault label omitted the opening swastika, but retitled the film *Holocauste Nazi...*

3 *Ilsa, She-Wolf of the SS* (d: Don Edmonds), *Ilsa, Harem-Keeper of the Oil Shieks* (d: Don Edmonds), *Ilsa, Tigress of Siberia* (d: Jean Lafleur).

4 The original title is *Kaput Lager: Gli Ultimi Giorni Delle SS*, whose translation bears a confusing similarity to *Horrifing [sic] Experiments of S.S.Last Days:* 'Kaput Camp: The Last Days of the SS.'

5 This still managed to be "boring and insipid" according to the Italian journal *Nocturno*. It starred Gordon Mitchell and was again comprised of excerpts from at least one other film.

6 Gianni Vernuccio's *Frankenstein's Castle of Freaks* among them.

The Beyond

1 The idea of a blind person watching over the gates of Hell is used in Michael Winner's *The Sentinel*. The blind girl's dog being suddenly possessed and tearing out her throat is derivative of a scene in Dario Argento's *Suspiria*. The concept of houses constructed over doorways to Hell is the basis of Argento's *Inferno*.

Blood Feast

1 *Fangoria* No 17.

2 All but a handful of the titles on the DPP list – notably *Blood Feast*, *Blood Rites*, *Cain's Cutthroats* and *Night of the Bloody Apes* – are films from the seventies or the eighties.

3 *The Monster Times* No 24.
4 *Nostalgia* No 4.
5 Producer David Friedman parted ways with Lewis on completing *Color Me Blood Red* after arguing about the quality of their product. Friedman compared their own work with other low-budget film-makers (like Lee Frost and Bob Cresse), telling the director that audiences were getting more sophisticated. Hershell didn't make comparisons and didn't think the pictures had to improve.

Blood Rites

1 Having appeared in fifteen of Milligan's movies, Hal Borske, the actor who played Colin in *Blood Rites*, told *Video Watchdog* No 54 that "an Andy Milligan credit list should read: 'Everything by Andy Milligan.' Period."
2 *Video Watchdog* No 52.
3 *Castle of Frankenstein* No 16.
4 *Demonique* No 4.
5 *Blood*, which was less than an hour long, was released in the UK on the Iver Film Services label.
6 The three films Milligan made for J.E.R. were *Depraved!*, *The Degenerates* and *Blood Rites*.

Bloody Moon

1 Craig Ledbetter in *Hi-Tech Terror* No 25.

The Bogey Man

1 For instance, the painting out of mirrors and Willy being startled by his own reflection (he happens to be possessed by the bogeyman at the time and is strangling a girl) draws on folklore, i.e. it is unlucky for a sick person to see their own reflection; mirrors have to be turned to the wall when death enters the room; death is able to steal one's soul through one's reflection, etc.
2 Interview with Ulli Lommel by Stephen Thrower, *Eyeball* No 5.
3 Many critics believed that Fassbinder would restore German cinema to the status it had enjoyed before the war. Fassbinder worked with a closely knit unit of actors and technicians, of which Lommel was a part.
4 Lommel's other genre films as director include *Brainwaves*, *The Devonsville Terror*, and *Vampire Club*. His 1983 *Strangers in Paradise* is a sci-fi musical in which Lommel plays Hitler and a band called Moonlight Drive provide the music. This same band also released an eponymously titled mini album featuring covers of songs made famous by The Doors (Agara Records).

The Burning

1 *Monthly Film Bulletin*.
2 Although Jason Alexander has little to work on in *The Burning*, he established for himself a varied career in film and television, later to appear in *Brighton Beach Memoirs*, *Pretty Woman*, *Jacob's Ladder*, *North*, and *Love! Valor! Compassion!* Holly Hunter went on to win an Oscar in *The Piano*.

Cain's Cutthroats

1 Neither version, however, has cutaways to "a modern day biker gang," as stated in reviews of *Cain's Way* that appeared in *The Dark Side* (No 40) and *The Psychotronic Encyclopedia of Film*.

Cannibal Apocalypse

1 And made the same year as *Cannibal Apocalypse* was Dawson's *The Last Hunter*, a fully-fledged copy of *Apocalypse Now*.

2 The actress, Cinzia de Carolis, also played a vampire child in Giorgio Ferroni's *Night of the Devils*, where she tore open the blouse of her mother and clawed into her naked breast.
3 *Uncut* No 8.
4 *Video Watchdog* (No 8) accuses the bland direction for "killing the fun and the potent metaphor inherent in the screenplay."
5 In which an albino outlaw by the name of Bad Bob is shot in the back. The gaping hole, the size of a football, frames the assassin in the distance.

Cannibal Ferox

1 *Ferox* is Latin, but like the film's title, its usage here is a bastardisation and its meaning ambiguous. In a good sense *ferox* is courageous, high-spirited, warlike, brave; in a bad sense, it is wild, unbridled, arrogant.
2 "We did everything we could at that time to bring people into the cinemas," Lenzi told *European Trash Cinema*. "Life for directors was very hard and we had to eat, you know."
3 Maybe this is a joke: One cannibal holds Gloria's American Express card up to the camera. Accepted all over the world, as the advertising campaign says, but the card is meaningless here in the jungle.
4 Although it should be noted that at least one animal was spared – the small pig trapped with Gloria in a hole. Actor John Morghen refused to stab it and the scene had to be implied via edits and special effects. Just like a real movie.
5 Large bugs are also used to elicit horror and disgust, reaching absurd proportions when cannibals are about to castrate Mike and another character screams at the sight of a giant leech.
6 *Fangoria* No 53... But not an opinion shared by everyone. When *Cannibal Ferox* opened on New York's 42nd Street, it played directly opposite a theatre showing another Lenzi movie, *Nightmare City*. Wrote Tim Ferrante in *The Splatter Times* (No 4): "What a luxury to have a choice between two shockers by this occasionally brilliant director."
7 This was the boast by Continental Inc, the US company who released Lenzi's third and final cannibal picture as *Doomed To Die!* 'The Most Violent Human Sacrifices You'll Ever See!' promised the poster.

Cannibal Holocaust

1 Typically, the ad for a screening of *Cannibal Holocaust* at Detroit's Adams Theater declared: "SAVAGE! TERRIFYING! TRUE! THOSE WHO FILMED IT WERE ACTUALLY DEVOURED BY CANNIBALS!"
2 Critics of *Cannibal Holocaust* often paraphrase the closing words of the film, Professor Monroe's lament after watching footage of the atrocities in 'The Green Hell': "I wonder who the real cannibals are?" Critics then throw this back at Deodato, calling him a hypocrite for having shown us the footage in the first place.
3 In *Spaghetti Nightmares*, Deodato claims that all through filming *Cannibal Holocaust* he had the Animal Protection League "breathing down my neck," which seems unlikely, and defends the animal slaughter on screen as simply a document of the natives hunting and killing for food in their natural habitat.
4 *Photo* January 1981.
5 "... eaten alive!" Jean-Paul Lacmant, *Fantasy Film Memory* No 1.
6 The *Independent*, April 6, 1993.
7 *Spaghetti Nightmares*, Palmerini & Mistretta.
8 ibid.
9 *European Trash Cinema* Vol 2 No 7.

Notes

The Cannibal Man

1 A title that translates as 'Week of the Killer' and throws up a blackly humorous slant on the subject matter: Marcos commits six murders over the course of a week and on the seventh gives himself up. If this idea was presented blatantly, it could have been perceived as blasphemous by the Spanish authorities and spell trouble for de la Iglesia.

2 Vincent Aranda's *The Blood-Spattered Bride*, Javier Aquirre's *Count Dracula's Great Love*, and Amando de Ossorio's *The Night of the Sorcerors*, to name but a few of the other Spanish films that appeared alongside *The Cannibal Man*, mixing a dash of sex with their horror.

3 Following an evening swim together, Marcos sets off for work the following morning a new man: he wears a brand-new colourful shirt, we discover his promotion, and there's a skip in his step.

4 The lengthy sex scene with Paola is particularly unerotic with some bizarre close-ups and the frisson of loud extraneous noises throughout. When it's over, the post-coital cigarette that Marcos offers to Paola looks like a joke.

5 An effeminate storekeeper later furnishes the film with some tired comic relief, advising Marcos, after he has asked for ten bottles of strong perfume (to mask the odour in his home), "You know, that's enough to supply a whole navy."

6 TV ads and consumerism are elements that reappear in de la Iglesia's peculiar science fiction movie, *Murder in a Blue World*.

Cannibal Terror

1 *Hi-Tech Terror* No 40.

2 *Cannibal Terror* runs a gamut of musical styles, from what sounds like something by The Nice to a virtual reprise of 'La Bamba' at the film's end, when Florence is reunited with her mother. Between are tribal drums, pan pipes, and perhaps a mellotron.

3 But Franco's *Cannibals* is deserving the accolade of 'single most terrible dubbing scene ever committed to celluloid'. Having lost his arm to cannibals, actor Al Cliver lies in a delirious fever in a hospital bed. Tossing and turning, he mutters things like "Get away... foul creatures..." in a tone that suggests somebody at the dubbing plant isn't taking their job seriously.

Contamination

1 Rather than see an unrealised film script go to waste, Cozzi turned them into novels. The unmade sequel(s) to *Starcrash* became *Star Riders*, a book he co-wrote with A E Van Vogt.

2 In the US, *Contamination* was titled *Alien Contamination*.

3 Alas, spectacular is not a word one can use to describe the Cyclops creature that appears later in the film. Despite a special screen credit for its makers, the papier mâché creature is lame, even in half-shadow and supposedly took an exasperated Cozzi "over ninety-six cuts and countless shifts in camera position" to get it looking this good. *Spaghetti Nightmares*.

4 Interview with Luigi Cozzi, *Delirium* No 4.

5 ibid.

6 *The Dark Side* No 66.

7 *Contamination* was shot in the US, Italy and South America. The week's worth of exteriors shot in New York are an attempt to lend the film a certain credibility overseas (as was Cozzi's anglicised pseudonym 'Lewis

Coates'), while the South American location – Columbia to be precise – was worked into the story for cost-cutting reasons and also the fact that one of the film's investors was South American. Interiors were filmed in Italy.

8 Ian McCulloch interview, *Fangoria* No 52.

9 "The original script," says McCulloch of *Zombie Holocaust*, "was called *Queen of the Cannibals*, which I didn't like because everyone thought it referred to me!" *Fangoria* No 52.

Dead & Buried

1 Directed by Christian Marnham. At the time of writing, the only reference to it was found in the *Monthly Film Bulletin*, February 1982.

Death Trap

1 Donald Farmer, *The Splatter Times* No 3.

Deep River Savages

1 One of the few such scenes in *Deep River Savages* – that depicting the cannibalisation of a woman – was edited into Lenzi's later cannibal picture, *Eaten Alive*. Again it was a revolted civilised Caucasian who watched the act from a distance.

2 *European Trash Cinema* Vol 2 No 3.

3 Interview with Umberto Lenzi, *Necronomicon* No 5.

Delirium

1 Some of it recognisable from British television. For instance, a tinkling refrain from cop shows like *The Sweeney*, traditionally used in a dramatic capacity but here accompanying Charlie as he swaggers across open fields. The pompous musical piece that plays over the clandestine meetings and end credits is equally ill-fitting, and forever associated with the long-running quiz show, *Mastermind*.

The Devil Hunter

1 *Tombs of the Blind Dead*, *Return of the Evil Dead*, *Horror of the Zombies*, and *Night of the Seagulls*.

2 Franco, originally a jazz trumpet player, has suggested in interviews that he is "a jazz musician that makes films." There can be little coincidence that Clifford Brown, the pseudonym he uses for *The Devil Hunter*, was also the name of a jazz trumpeter (1930–1956).

3 Some samples:
Reporter: "Can you give me your opinion of men in this country?"
Miss Crawford: "I have no opinion of men – I just love them."
Reporter (deadpan): "Oh, I see."
~~~
Maquillaje (twirling a flower): "Back in my country, we have these flowers and we used to offer them to the virgins."
Chris: "Flowers – Shit! Damn it! Damn it! Damn it! Damn it!"
~~~
Jack: "What was that?"
Weston: "A girl."
Jack: "What happened?"
Weston: "She started screaming. I had to knock her out – what else could I do?" (She wasn't screaming but did pull a gun.)
Jack: "I hope the others didn't hear her scream." (Jack was directly behind Peter and he didn't hear a scream.)
~~~
Also, character names used in the film don't correspond with the names in the end credits.
~~~

Notes

4 "Of about 150 films or so that I have made," Franco told Gerard Alexander in an unpublished interview (as of writing), "I'd say sixty were done using sync sound and the rest were shot without sound."
5 *Ungawa* No 1.
6 Franco also states that the alien creature's point of view in Predator adopts the same bizarre colours as the monster in *Devil Hunter*. This isn't true (and if it was, it's a cheap and familiar cinematic device anyway): the monster in *Devil Hunter* sees the world with a little blurring round the edge of the screen.

Don't go in the House

1 *Eyeball* No 5.
2 *Fangoria* No 27.

Don't Go in the Woods... Alone!

1 *Don't Go in the Woods* had "a budget apparently culled from the refunds on bottles found beside the road during filming," writes L A Morse in his book *Video Trash & Treasures*.
2 Incredibly this might not be the case! A director bearing the name James Bryan is also responsible, it seems, for *Hellriders, I Love You, I Love You Not* and *The Dirtiest Game*. Watching *Don't Go in the Woods*, however, it's nigh impossible to accept that it's made by someone with three pictures already under his belt and with at least thirteen years directorial experience!
3 *Don't Go in the Woods* was released in most areas of the US in 1980 and became a second-feature at drive-ins everywhere else the following year. In 1983 it was re-released in the New York area.
4 *The Splatter Times* No 2.
5 One 'near miss' is nicely done: a girl is locked in a sleeping bag as a prank. She cuts a hole in it, only to spy the wildman approaching. The scene has a parallel in another, earlier low-budget horror yarn, Michael Findlay's *Shriek of the Mutilated*, in which observers watch the approach – from a great distance – of a killer abominable snowman.
6 Suspended and powerless is evidently a pet fear for Bryan, as it happens more than once in the film. "Everyone has nightmares about the ugliest way to die," is the by-line on the video box. Could the film be an exorcising of demons for Bryan?
7 According to *Halls of Horror* (No 30), the original title of the movie was *Don't Go Into the Woods* [our emphasis], until its re-release in 1983 when it became *Don't Go in the Woods*. We have been unable to verify this information.

Don't Go Near the Park

1 Linnea Quigley interviewed by Jewel Shepard, *Invasion of the B-Girls*.
2 A veteran of respected movies like *The Naked and the Dead, We're No Angels* and *The Green Berets*, Aldo Ray was driven out of the Hollywood mainstream due to his heavy drinking. In later years, up until his death in 1991, the only parts being offered to him were courtesy of low-budget film-makers, who liked the idea of a former name star in their humble productions. Volume one of *The X-Rated Videotape Guide* recognises Ray as "the first regular Hollywood actor to appear in a porno film" – a pants-on appearance in Anne Perry's *Sweet Savage*, an explicit western.

Don't Look in the Basement

1 If this is the case, it would be the film's only twist on Roy Ward Baker's similarly themed *Asylum* the previous year. Legend has it that the working

title for *Don't Look in the Basement* was *Asylum*.

2 Outside of her thoroughly unprofessional look of disgust and horror on first meeting the old lady in the corridor.

3 *Draculina* No 13.

4 *Demonique* magazine, reviewing *Don't Look in the Basement* in their first issue, claimed that Brownrigg wasn't the first choice of director. "It is rumoured," wrote Barry Kaufman, "the first director who worked on *Don't Look in the Basement* died."

5 Writing in *Shock Xpress* (Vol 3 No 1), Stephen Thrower suggests that Gene Ross, who plays the Judge in *Basement*, could well be the elusive Brownrigg under a pseudonym. Ross appears in each of Brownrigg's four movies, playing a judge again in his 1979 picture, *Don't Open the Door*.

6 Hallmark also acquired Jorge Grau's *Living Dead at Manchester Morgue* and released it as *Don't Open the Window*.

7 *Demonique* No 2.

8 Some of the material excised from the British release (and found in VCI's 1999 DVD release) includes Allyson, the nymphomaniac, showing her breasts to the Judge and later to Danny. Much exposition is also gone with these passages. The night-time attack on Mrs Callingham reveals, via close-up, that the old woman has had her tongue cut out. Nurse Charlotte screams in affirmation, "Your tongue has been cut out!" The closing scenes of carnage are also considerably protracted in their original form. The pummelling of Dr Masters by the other patients comes with plenty of flesh-rending, as axe, knives and even Harriett's doll (!) are brought down on the screaming woman. There is more bloodshed when Sam enters the scene and kills the Judge before turning the axe on everybody else. Some of the cuts in these final scenes show up in the end credits of the British print.
A review of *Basement* which appeared in *Demonique* (No 1) refers to offal being thrown onto walls in the closing massacre, but this seems unlikely. As does the idea of a sequence where the body of a woman, dead seven months, is exhumed for the bereaved husband, said to result in "a three-minute scene of husband and mutilated corpse making love."

9 Like *Basement*, this film also has a pre-credit axe murder.

10 According to Kim Newman in *Nightmare Movies*, all these films bear out Brownrigg's "auteur status by concentrating on heroines driven insane by exposure to grottily staged violence."

11 McCormick – who also interviewed Brownrigg for *Draculina* – is the director of many straight-to-video movies, like *The Abomination*, *Macon County War* (shot with Brownrigg's "old 16mm Éclair"), and *Fatal Justice*. His inspiration as a director appears to be Brownrigg's *Don't Look in the Basement*.

The Driller Killer

1 Reviewing the film for *The Splatter Times* No 1, Donald Farmer warned "For those hoping for plenty of gross-out effects, the 'driller-killer' of the title doesn't begin unleasing [*sic*] pandemonium until about halfway through the picture..."

2 Abel Ferrara interviewed by Kim Newman, *Shock Xpress* No 1.

3 ibid.

The Evil Dead

1 The wonky camera angles of Ashley with the shotgun are similar to those in Damiano Damiani's *Amityville II: The Possession* – released a few months

Notes

prior to *The Evil Dead* – wherein another young man (wonkily) clutches a shotgun.

2 To bring things full circle – and beyond – when Craven made *A Nightmare on Elm Street*, he showed a clip of *The Evil Dead* playing on a TV set. When Raimi made *Evil Dead II* he supposedly incorporated a Freddy Krueger glove.

3 Fans of *The Evil Dead* were up in arms when Raimi saw to it that a new cut for an American distributor was missing the shot of lightning striking a tree. He considered the poor effect to cheapen the movie.

4 *Starburst* No 57.

5 *The Evil Dead* also inspired a successful Commodore 64 video game and a 7-inch single – 'Another Half Hour Till Sunrise' by The Tall Boys.

6 Guy Phelps interviewed by Alex J Low, *Killing Moon* No 2.

7 Bruce Campbell explained in an interview in *Video–The Magazine* (September 1987) that it was the 'video nasties' furore surrounding *The Evil Dead* that led the film-makers to play part *II* more for laughs.

Evilspeak

1 *Psychotronic* No 23.

Exposé

1 Which suggests that Intervision acquired a US print of the film for video release in Britain; *The House on Straw Hill* has always been known by that, its original title, Stateside.

2 "Linda [Hayden] was hired purely on her strength as a very good young actress," claimed producer Brian Smedley-Aston in an interview with *Gore Creatures* (No 25). Acting abilities to one side, having already appeared in *Baby Love*, *The Blood on Satan's Claw* and *Confessions of a Window Cleaner*, Linda's name on a film almost certainly guaranteed sexual titillation and a flash of bare flesh.

3 "They wanted a punchy, one-word title with vaguely sexual connotations," producer Brian Smedley-Aston told Tim Greaves in *Flesh & Blood* No 8.

4 If only in the local bully boys, who attempt to rape the beautiful outsider. They are described in the end credits as 'Big Youth' and 'Small Youth.' Small Youth is wearing a T-shirt inscribed with 'I am a vampire,' a nod to the previous year's *Vampyres*, a film on which Clarke – and several of the *Exposé* crew – also worked.

5 There is also a paranormal aspect that remains unexplored: lamps flicker, and the telephone makes a strange noise when Paul picks it up – strange enough for him to look quizzically at the receiver, anyway.

6 Clarke would produce Paul Raymond's *Erotica* in 1980, a feature film in which the publishing magnate was able to air his philosophies on life. It was directed by Brian Smedley-Aston.

7 See 'Jolly Hockey Sticks!' by David Kerekes (in Jack Stevenson's book *Fleshpot*) for more on Taboo.

8 Some are labelled 'Mary Millington Classics.' These include *Come Play with Me*, *The Playbirds*, *Confessions from the David Galaxy Affair*, *Queen of the Blues*, and the biopic Mary Millington's *True Blue Confessions*. These films are awful and – given the restrictions of the BBFC – sexless, but managed to turn a tidy profit thanks to the fervent ad campaigning of producer and adult publishing magnate, David Sullivan. He ran reviews and photospreads that promised much more than the films delivered. Eventually the hyperbole

landed him in bother with the Trading Standards Office, and Sullivan pulled out of making films.

9 *Psychotronic* No 8.

10 Tim Greaves, *Flesh & Blood* No 8.

Faces of Death

1 The missing footage includes film of various state executions, all evidently bogus. In the first of these clips, the coughs of a man dying in a gas chamber can be clearly heard emanating from the air-tight room. Next is the death by electrocution of one Larry DeSilva. A mournful harmonica plays as the condemned man is escorted from his cell, but once strapped in the chair the music takes on a merry, slapstick timbre. As the electricity surges, blood leaks from under the tape covering DeSilva's eyes and foam rolls from his mouth. A third execution is said to have been secretly shot by a tourist in the Middle East (which fails to explain the variety of camera angles and close-ups): a man is led from a tent, forced to kneel at a chopping block and beheaded with the single stroke of a sword. The headless body topples to the sand and refuses to bleed, such is the shabbiness of the economical effect.
A satanic cult performing a cannibalistic ritual is next. Said to be "on the outskirts of San Francisco," with a leader who resembles Charles Manson, the cult feast on organs sliced effortlessly from a fresh cadaver. Gröss claims to have gained the trust of the cult's leader and thus was allowed to film the ritual, which culminates in a bloody orgy.
No deaths occur in film of serpent handlers in a Kentucky church.
Newsreel footage of a woman throwing herself to her death from an apartment block is real, but again the choice of music is desperately insensitive. The intro to the Dixieland jazz piece ("One, two, ah-one, two, three, four...") is timed to coincide with the woman's leap. After a brief look at cryogenic suspension, the same musical insensitivity accompanies the bloated, washed-up victim of a drowning.
Concocted footage resumes with a supposedly randomly shot tourist film set in a national park, in which a man exits his car to feed a grizzly bear and is promptly killed. The final shot has the bear ambling into the woods with a rubbery severed limb hanging from its jaws.
An anti-nuclear protestor douses himself in petrol and sets himself on fire to the horror of his fellow campaigners. This bogus set-piece marks the end of the footage excised from the British print of *Faces of Death*.

2 In their review of the film, *Magick Theatre* (No 7) state that "wildlife film-maker Bill Burryd" is amongst the *Faces of Death* crew, but that's not a name that appears anywhere in the credits.

3 Dr Gröss is actor Michael Carr, a name revealed in the end credits. One source has claimed that Carr made guest appearances on TV shows like *Hunter* and *Alias Smith and Jones*, but we are unable to confirm this.
Some of the dialogue spoken by Gröss was sampled by New Mind for 'Life In Hell,' a track on the band's 1993 CD *Fractured*.

4 In these sequels, the spelling of Frances Gröss' name was gender-corrected to Francis.

5 Flellis first appeared in Gorgon Video's compilation *Worst of Faces of Death*, where he admitted to being a surgeon and that Gröss had died under his knife undergoing a simple

Notes

operation. He seems to be playing his role for laughs, fidgeting, staring wide-eyed into the camera, and even offering the viewers of *Part IV* one of his own compositions as a musical backdrop to a scene of unconvincing carnage.

6 Schier's *Faces of Death 5*, for example, takes much of its atrocity footage from Nick Bougas' 1989 film, *Death Scenes*. While *Faces of Death 6* incorporates Fred Warshofsky's 1980 *Days of Fury* – a mondo film with Vincent Price as the host – almost in its entirety. For more on Mondo films, see Kerekes and Slater's book, *Killing for Culture*.

7 Tellingly, the film concludes with the admonition: "Exiguous scenes within this motion picture have been reconstructed to document and further clarify their factual origin."
Perhaps this applies to a scene that shows a movie set and a stunt said to have gone horribly wrong, resulting in a stuntman losing their life. A clapperboard identifies the movie as *Hell Raisin'* or *Hell Raisers*, directed by one Emile Scott. Gröss claims it was released shortly after the stunt was filmed, but no record of a movie or director by those names can be traced.

8 The sequence is probably influenced by a scene in Umberto Lenzi's *Deep River Savages*, where native tribesmen hack the top off a monkey's head and dine on the exposed brain.

Fight For Your Life

1 Directed by Jackson St Louis, it features a prison break that results in three cons taking refuge in a house shared by four beautiful women. "Bet you fucked a lot of assholes in prison," one of the hostages says to Joey Silvera. "Bet you really know how to do it." In no time at all everybody is enjoying sex.

2 Which featured a cancer-ravaged Humphrey Bogart in his last gangster role. He would die two years later.

3 One of its alternative titles – *I Hate Your Guts* – even borrows from Roger Corman's 1962 film, *The Intruder*, which deals with racism in a Mississippi town and which became *I Hate Your Guts!* on its re-release some years later.

4 Kane is played by William Sanderson, whose penchant for cinematic villains prompted him to remark in *Empire* magazine, "I'd rather be typecast than not cast at all." Sanderson also appears in *Coal Miner's Daughter*, *Blade Runner*, *Last Man Standing*, amongst others.

5 The ad with this by-line also makes use of the familiar *Fight for Your Life* artwork, which depicts Kane and Turner, face-to-face, locked in mortal combat. However, it rotates the image slightly in Turner's favour, making it look as if he's got the upper hand, bearing down on the white trash.

6 Told in soft focus flashback, it transpires that the Turners' eldest son had a thing going with Karen, a white girl, and was killed in a car crash. Mrs Turner holds Karen responsible for his death – an insignificant revelation in an otherwise clear-cut script.

7 *Shock Cinema* No 6.

8 Ten minutes of film was cut by the distributors prior to submission to the BBFC, who removed a further thirty-one sections totalling a half-hour.

9 As *Uncle Tom* was an imported film, charges could not have been brought against the film-makers anyway, but only the distributor or exhibitor.

10 The release of *Uncle Tom* saw no race riots erupt in or around theatres. In fact, not much controversy of any

kind, apart from a solitary protest from Mrs Mary Whitehouse.

11 More than one source has erroneously stated that *Fight for Your Life* received a theatrical release in Britain.

12 In removing this final reel, the BBFC also deprived black audiences of the 'joy of total revenge,' and effectively stacked the film in the white man's favour. Making *Uncle Tom* 'more racist' in other words.

13 Here is a flavour of the language used: "Nigger." "Spade." "Turd." "Uncle Remus." "Coon." "Black Ass Coon." "Booger." "Monkey Face." "Chink." "Spic." "Boy." "Poor White Trash." "Brown Dirtball." "Darky." "Jive Ass Coon." "Martin Luther Coon." "Jungle Bunny." "Pink Pig." "Honky." "White Trash Faggot."

14 As noted in the BBFC Annual Report 1993.

15 Mid to late eighties, the location a (now closed) cinema in Manchester city centre, showing a late-night Romero double bill. The character of Peter in *Dawn of the Dead* – wearing full military garb and gasmask – is portrayed first as a hero and then revealed to be black. The other film on the bill that night had been *Night of the Living Dead*, whose central character is also a black man.

16 Cinema licenses in London, however, do carry a condition that prohibits the screening of a film that may stir up hatred "on grounds of colour, race or ethnic or national origins."

17 *Film Censorship and British Social History*, Institute of Contemporary Arts, November 20, 1998.

Forest of Fear

1 *Forest of Fear* was also shot in Pennsylvania, Romero's home state.

2 Indeed most of the cast are murdered off-screen, including the crop pilot and his wife, the two hippies who drink from the stream, the hermit, the pickup truck driver...

Frankenstein (Andy Warhol's)

1 No one is addressed or referred to as Frankenstein in the picture.

2 *Castle of Frankenstein* (No 20) announced in the news column of their Summer 1973 issue that "Andy Warhol is adapting *Frankenstein* in Rome, with Udo Kier..."

3 Given the highly publicised case in which police seized a print of *Flesh* being shown in London (see CLAMPDOWN), it can be no coincidence that the first of Morrissey's two horror pictures is called *<u>Flesh</u> for Frankenstein*.

4 *Dark Side* No 48.

5 "I shot a lot of the special effects scenes with the blood and intestines bursting in the direction of the audience," Margheriti told *Video Watchdog* (No 28). "Of course," he added, "it has to be seen in 3-D, otherwise it is just vulgar and dirty."

6 Vipco's packaging in Britain sported the titles *Andy Warhol's Frankenstein* and *Andy Warhol's Dracula*.

7 Keir's physical appearance changed when he lost ten pounds during the weekend break between filming *Flesh for Frankenstein* and *Blood for Dracula*. "That's why in *Dracula* I had to sit in a wheelchair," Kier told *San Francisco Bay Guardian* in 1998. "I had no more power. I was sweating all over because I had to wear that fur coat, and it was so heavy and I was so weak that I could hardly walk."

8 *The Aurum Encyclopedia of Horror* states that this famous remark is often misquoted... and then goes on to misquote it. However, *Aurum* was one of the first sources to attribute *Flesh for Frankenstein* to Antonio Margheriti. The print under review is

evidently Italian and *Aurum*'s woefully po-faced interpretation of the film suggests that much of the humour in Morrissey's original has been lost in the translation.

9 In the gloriously eccentric tradition of supporting features, the other short film was *Our Cissy*, the tale of a Northern lass moving down to London and finding misery.

10 Directed by Georgie Miller in 1972, this satirical piece runs for only thirteen minutes. *Violence in the Cinema Part 1* is presented as a lecture whose topic is illustrated with violent actions meted out first on the speaker himself and later to a female victim in a torture chamber. These comprise shotgun blasts, a bottle being smashed in a face, immolation, falling from a window, being struck by a car, and disembowelment. *Monthly Film Bulletin* described it as 'unusually detailed stunts and effects, floating like sadistic daydreams in a slough of triviality.' The doctor-lecturing-the-viewer hook was utilised in another Australian film, Richard Franklin's 1976 *Fantasm*. The topic in this instance was sex.

11 *Psychotronic Video* No 6.

Frozen Scream

1 You can spot the legitimate reanimated dead because they have a reflective cat's eye stuck on their neck.

2 The hooded figures look to be modelled on Ray Dennis Steckler's Cash Flagg persona in *The Incredibly Strange Creatures who Stopped Living and Became Mixed-Up Zombies!!?*

The Funhouse

1 With a good old-fashioned, pasty-faced monster, courtesy of a not-very-convincing makeup design from the usually resilient Rick Baker.

2 Most of these references are to films released by Universal, the company also behind *The Funhouse*.

3 In Larry Block's originally screenplay, the barker and owner of the funhouse does have a name: 'Conrad Straker.' Another facet which failed to make the transition to the screen is that Amy's mother – a non-entity in the movie – is strictly religious.

4 Tellingly, she is the only girl in the film whose breasts are exposed for the audience – twice.

5 After a day's shooting, actors must not be back on set until a period of twelve hours has elapsed. Going overtime on one day may mean you lose several hours the next day.

6 The director's chair on *Venom* was given over to Piers Haggard, a film whose cast is described by Leonard Maltin as appearing to be drunk or looking as though it wishes it were in equal measures.

7 Although disappointed with *The Funhouse*, Hooper was evidently impressed enough by the spooky attributes of a carnival-after-dark to feature one at the core of his eagerly awaited *The Texas Chainsaw Massacre 2*.

8 The film has its fans. One set-piece – the carny barker run through with a sword – would resurface in John Dahl's 1993 film, *Red Rock West*.

Gestapo's Last Orgy

1 "When the superman wishes to amuse himself he must do so even at the cost of the life of others."

2 To be fair he doesn't call them rats, but that is obviously the implication. Unless of course the Nazis formulated a strain of gerbil excited by blood or interested in eating flesh as opposed

to feeding on seeds, grasses and roots. Rat substitutes can also be found in *Beast in Heat* and probably other cheap Italian exploitation.

3 The scene appears to have been shot in a functioning industrial brick kiln.

The House by the Cemetery

1 Possibly inspired by Kubrick's *The Shining* with a dash of Stuart Rosenberg's *The Amityville Horror*.

2 Ann's decapitation is foreseen by May, a little girl who may be a ghost. May sees a mannequin in a store window that resembles the babysitter, and watches its face fall apart, inferring the two share a supernatural link.

3 Stephen Thrower, in his book *Beyond Terror*, observes that, after the attack, as the estate agent is dragged away, "we get a glimpse of further injuries to the head that seem to have been omitted... As it turns out, they are all that is left of an effects sequence that was filmed but failed to meet with Fulci's requirements."

4 Stories of the print receiving a police escort out of the country are true, David Hyman, a BBFC principal officer, told the authors. Principal officer Craig Lapper, speaking in the Jake West documentary, *Video Nasties: Draconian Days* (2014), claims the story is an urban myth.

House on the Edge of the Park

1 Riz Ortolani wrote the sickly main theme, one verse of which goes: "Sweetly, oh sweetly / Summertime is coming / Happy and carefree / Waiting just for you." One can only assume Riz had yet to view the film when he penned those lines.

2 The theme of rape is relatively common in 1970s porn. In *Expensive Tastes*, a man brings his dates home, only to orchestrate their rape at the hands of friends in ski-masks.

3 *Gore Gazette* No 73.

4 Sullivan was the first to say, in print, that this elusive version of *House on the Edge of the Park* exists.

I Miss you Hugs & Kisses

1 The video box claims it is based on the "notorious recent Canadian murder trial of one, Peter Demeter."

2 During the rape, he keeps manoeuvring her skirt so that the viewer can see a lot of flesh, albeit not enough to be technically 'indecent.'

I Spit on Your Grave

1 Noted film critic Ebert has also written screenplays for exploitation films, notably Russ Meyer's hit, *Beyond the Valley of the Dolls*.

2 *Los Angeles Times*, March 21, 1982.

3 According to an interview with director Meir Zarchi in *Fangoria* (No 39), he made these cuts himself.

4 *Sleazoid Express* Vol 2 No 3.

5 Camille Keaton – Buster's grand-niece – married director Zarchi shortly after completing *I Spit on Your Grave*, her first American film. Prior, she worked in Italy and appeared in Massimo Dallamano's *What Have They Done To Solange?*, Mino Guerrini's *Decameron II* and Elo Pannaccio's *Sex of the Witch*. Christian Kessler in *ETC* (No 16) suggests she went on to appear in "sex movies."

6 *Draculina* No 7.

7 In *Elliot's Guide to Films on Video*, there are no details listed under 'Wizard,' but a cross-reference to Video Programme Distributors Ltd, based in Middlesex. Could VPD, or some other UK company, have used the US distributor's name/brand for an unofficial release of the film?

8 It's an image that Zarchi said he "duplicated exactly" in the film:

Notes

Jennifer, after being sodomised over a rock, stands before the summerhouse in a daze. It's also a scene that channels a key image of the Vietnam war, that Phan Thi Kim Phuc, the 'napalm girl' running from her village.

9 *Fangoria* No 39.

10 *No Time For Pranksters* and *No Love on the River* were two potential titles Zarchi considered for *I Spit on Your Grave*.

11 "The idea that a rape victim would seduce her attackers to lure them to their deaths," deliberated Michael Gingold in *Fangoria* No 179, "is almost more offensive than the rapes themselves."

12 *Demonique* No 4.

13 'Sola Perduta Abandonatto' from Puccini's *Manon Lescaut* (rough translation: 'Alone Lost Abandoned').

14 Incidentally, the harmonica provides the film with its very own 'Duelling Banjos' – another nod to *Deliverance*.

15 According to Zarchi, he is also responsible for producing the film.

16 He has a co-writer credit on Shlomo Suriano's *Nini*.

17 *Fangoria* No 179.

18 Although the title *The Rape and Revenge of Jennifer Hill* appears to predate this.

19 In his article for *Is it... Uncut?* (No 3), Nigel Burrell states the missing dialogue comes from an early scene in which the gang discuss how women are full of shit and that California is the place to get laid. Talk has also been removed from a scene where the men consider why no one has yet discovered Jennifer's body. The cuts appear to have been made to bring the running time down from an initial 101 minutes.

20 Apparently, some of the material eventually surfaced in the guise of Farmer's *Snuff All Bitches/Ms. Maniac*.

Inferno

1 Lorenzo Battagua is credited with the "Underwater Sequence," although the ageing Mario Bava had a considerable part to play. Bava's son, Lamberto, is credited as assistant director on *Inferno*.

2 *Psychotronic Video* No 18

3 There is a sequence in *Inferno* that looks like it belongs to the murder-mystery setting of *Tenebrae*: black-gloved hands cutting the heads off paper figures.

The Last House on the Left

1 The realistic, throwaway banter between the gang members also brings to the film an almost documentary quality.

2 Wes Craven's *Last House on the Left*, David A Szulkin.

3 The original draft for the story was apparently even more extreme, in terms of both sex and violence.

4 Wes Craven interviewed by Kim Newman, *Shock Xpress* Vol 2 No 4.

5 Craven's next film *The Hills Have Eyes* would similarly focus on middle class characters seeking cartoon-like revenge on the degenerates who have wronged them.

6 Music in the film was by David Hess (and an uncredited Steve Chapin). Hess, a former A&R man at Mercury Records in New York, had completed two albums prior to *Last House*, as well as having written songs that became hits for Elvis Presley, Pat Boone and Andy Williams.

7 A remnant of the sequence can be seen at the end of the Replay Video print, in the flashback moments that one supposes should have credits running over the top. The film has no end credits.

8 The intestine shot as it appears in *Last House* lasts only a few brief seconds.

Late Night Trains

1 Extra footage centred on the switchblade attack could be found in the Dutch Best Video release of the film.

The Living Dead

1 The clumsy grammar can't be attributed to a poor or literal translation of the original Spanish title – *No Profanar el Sueño de los Muertos* – as the two bear no relation whatsoever. (A literal translation would be 'Don't Disturb the Sleep of the Dead.') One US retitle of the film – *Breakfast at Manchester Morgue* – also suffers from being similarly clipped.

2 The way having been paved by Jonas Cornell's *Hugs and Kisses* and Lindsay Anderson's *If*..... Both films showed pubic hair and were passed without cuts. With this, the maxim that "the difference between art and pornography is bodily hair" to which the BBFC had always adhered, was finally laid to rest.

3 Alberto de Martino's *The Tempter*, Ovidio G Assonitis' *Beyond the Door*, Juan Bosch's *Exorcismo*, and Amando de Ossorio's *Demon Witch Child*.

4 The posters and other illustrations in *Monster Mag* were for the most part scenes lifted from Hammer films. Relatively innocuous fare like *Dracula A.D. 1972* and *The Reptile*, which might only have had a split-second of onscreen viscera, looked like complete bloodbaths courtesy of *Monster Mag*'s choice selection. Hammer 'full-gloss gore' later found its way into the lacklustre and short-lived poster-magazine, *Legend Horror Classics*.

5 Romero's own follow-up to *Night of the Living Dead*, the more 'upbeat' *Dawn of the Dead*, would exert an incredible influence on the Italian horror film. See *Zombie Creeping Flesh* and *Zombie Flesh Eaters*.

6 A machine from the Department of Agriculture is pivotal to the story; it is being tested on a farm, and said to be an "ultrasonic radiation" device that attacks primitive nervous systems. But this, George believes, extends to the reanimation of the dead, and later we learn possibly the reason that new-born babies are acting aggressively. There's another affected group: In a sequence handled with some insensitivity, a young person with Downs Syndrome reaches menacingly for a piece of broken glass as the soundtrack plays a foreboding refrain.

7 The British print of *The Living Dead* opens with Guthrie's face popping up in a painting in George's antique shop, suggesting that his part in the film might have been designed as a greater one. The curious mish-mash

8 The X-certificated theatrical print of *The Living Dead at the Manchester Morgue* is missing much of the footage of the zombies devouring the policeman in the churchyard, and the entirety of the sequence where zombies tear apart the telephone receptionist. Here it cuts from them closing in on the receptionist, to them munching on something and then to the bloody aftermath.

9 *Don't Open the Window* was a heavily truncated US version of *The Living Dead*, also made available in Britain in the days before the VRA. This version wasn't classed as a nasty.

10 *The Living Dead at the Manchester Morgue* was the first major work for de Rossi, who went on to handle effects on Fellini's *Casanova*, and countless Italian horror films through the rest of the seventies and eighties.

11 It's unclear what business George has in Windermere. According to his various conversations, he has a weekend retreat there, is working on a house with some people he

knows, and/or has an appointment to sell some antiques to a dealer. Whatever the reason, a phone call he later makes, notifying an anonymous friend/associate of his delay, takes on a sinister, desperate edge.

12 Look to José Larraz' *Vampyres* for a similar sense of the English countryside being an alien landscape, and a film with even fewer characters than *The Living Dead*. The two films also have a curious link in that one of closes with a murder set in a hotel bedroom, and the other opens with a murder set in a hotel bedroom.

13 About location: A local man says to George, accusingly, "Up from London then?" George neither agrees nor disagrees. But then, the film makes no mention of the busy urban sprawl in the opening credits being the city of Manchester (David Pirie, in *The Vampire Cinema*, assumes it's London); it's just a major city from which George must travel. And the Lakes – where "Saturday to Monday I can hear the grass grow," George tells Edna – is simply a place removed from it. It's this lack of definition that helps create the ethereal, other-worldly quality of the film. The only mention of Manchester comes from a doctor at the hospital in Southgate, who explains that Manchester is where they ship bodies for pathological tests.

14 The name of the hotel is inscribed on a glass pane on a door. We only get to see it from its reverse side, but astute viewers may notice a spelling error (perhaps a set-designer's prank?): From the correct side the inscription would actually read: 'THE OLD **OLW** HOTEL.'

15 Music composed, arranged and conducted by Giuliano Sorgini. The soundtrack album was originally released on the Manchester-based Eurobeat label in 1974. Other tracks include 'Mysterious Country' and 'Drowned Guthrie.'

16 *Fandom's Film Gallery* July 1978. Quoted in *Let Sleeping Corpses Lie*, by Nigel Burrell.

Love Camp 7

1 However, there is a fleeting glimpse of pubis near the beginning of the film, but this seems almost an accident, or a crafty insinuation that the film is going to deliver a lot more than it does. To paraphrase Turan and Zito in their book, *Sinema*: although filmmakers like Frost and Cresse would not show the viewer what he wanted to see, the audience kept coming back.

2 The lesbian orgy is filmed in the same way, with women wrestling against the pawing of fellow prisoners.

3 The tale purports to be derived from "one who lived it," stated in the opening title. Though there is no way of knowing whether the story is fact or not, the film-makers pin the unfolding events down with plenty of unnecessarily accurate references to time, as if this alone authenticates matters.

4 His gun was his undoing: Brandishing his revolver and rushing to aid a woman he believed was in distress, Cresse was shot twice in the belly by – the story goes – two police officers, who then opened fire on Cresse's dog.

5 According to Muller & Faris in their book *That's Sexploitation!!*

6 And whilst on the subject... there can be no doubting that the ridiculous nom de plume, Captain Calais, belongs to a French man.

7 Including what is probably the first US nudie documentary, *Hollywood's World of Flesh*.

8 Jack Starrett took his place.

9 *That's Sexploitation!!*, Muller & Faris.

10 The relationship between Frost and Cresse hadn't been helped by the fact Friedman called on Frost to direct one of his films, *The Defilers*, which became a smash hit. The rivalry deepened when Cresse invested more time and money than usual in promoting a western called *Hot Spur*, only to have Friedman ride his coattails and pip him at the post with *Brand of Shame*, a western of his own.

11 It would be many years before Friedman came clean and admitted his involvement in the picture.

Mardi Gras Massacre

1 Dr Lewis is probably a tip of the hat to H G Lewis, director of *Blood Feast*.

2 'Perception and presentation of Mesoamerican groups by the film industry,' a talk by Dr Richard Shupp, Lafayette College, to The Pre-Columbian Society on February 14, 1998. Among the other films excerpted or discussed in the lecture were Larry Cohen's Q, Tobe Hooper's *I'm Dangerous Tonight* and numerous Aztec Mummy films from Mexico.

3 *Psychotronic Video* No 28.

4 *Video Watchdog Special Edition* No 2.

Night of the Bloody Apes

1 Played by José Elias Moreno, "South of the Border's answer to George Kennedy" according to a review in *Dreadful Pleasures* No 3.

2 But the fun doesn't stop there. Later, the same elderly woman runs into a cop and explains, "There around the corner is a man and he's dead!"

3 *Monster Mag* No 13.

4 Some sources suggest a more sexually explicit version of *Bloody Apes* was released under the title *Horror y Sexo*. Although 'Horror and Sex' is possibly the finest title ever to grace an exploitation film, it is highly unlikely that it would have contained additional Cardona footage not present in the IFS version.

Night of the Demon

1 Patterson was a onetime rodeo rider, inventor and promoter, who spent what free time he had roaming the Pacific Northwest woods with a 16mm camera, shooting footage which he hoped to turn into a documentary on the mystery of the Bigfoot. On October 20, 1967, whilst travelling the woods with a companion, Patterson caught on twenty-eight feet of film what is arguably a female Bigfoot.

Nightmare Maker

1 *Psychotronic Video* No 6.

2 The camera makes an issue of religious upbringing only once, in the latter part of the film, when it lingers over a familiar sketch of Jesus Christ that looks to have its eyes both open and closed at the same time.

3 Asher directed all five of AIP's dedicated beach movies: *Beach Party*, *Muscle Beach Party*, *Bikini Beach*, *Beach Blanket Bingo*, and *How To Stuff a Wild Bikini*. AIP's *Pajama Party* and *Ski Party*, not set on a beach, and not directed by Asher, are banded as beach movies nonetheless.

4 Bo Svenson (Lieutenant Carlson) played no-nonsense Tennessee sheriff Buford Pusser in an NBC-TV series in 1981, a reprise of the role he had in two of the *Walking Tall* hit movies of the Seventies. He played cops in a lot of other movies, too. Julia Duffy, who plays Billy's girlfriend Julie, was a regular on the Newhart TV show.

Notes

5 Which begs the question that if the DPP doesn't consider a film to be obscene or liable to be prosecuted, how can the Board justify their decision to reject it?
6 Between which is a peculiar trailer for Tom McLoughlin's *One Dark Night* that has no narration, virtually no dialogue, and looks unfinished.

Nightmares in a Damaged Brain

1 Lester Lorraine committed suicide a year or so after *Nightmares* was released. His name is nowhere in evidence on the British print of the film.
2 Although he does, in his *Spaghetti Nightmares* interview, appropriate some cringe-inducing significance on CJ's pranks and, because they were encouraged to improvise their dialogue, says that the actors spoke "sincerely" and from the "inside."
3 Made of plastic, according to a reporter for the *Sunday Times*.
4 Reporting on the trial, the *Daily Telegraph* recorded that Hamilton-Grant had a previous conviction for indecently exposing himself in a sex cinema.
5 *Spaghetti Nightmares*, Palmerini & Mistretta.

Possession

1 *Continental Film and Video Review* Vol 29 No 4. The unaccredited article is systematic of the eclectic mix that constituted *Continental Film and Video Review*. The high-brow analysis of *Possession* is followed by a variety of photospreads: Michael Winner's *Death Wish 2*, something from Jay Jay Film Distributors that appears to be called *Swedish Erotic Sexations*, and an advertisement for *Bog* starring Aldo Ray.
2 *Eyeball* No 5.
3 Zulawski points to the scene in the kitchen as an example. Indeed, the exchange that takes place here between Marc and Anna – she is deflecting each of his pleas and questions with a pointed "Excuse Me!" – is so skewered that it has no place in the realm of fiction; it could only have been drawn from reality.
4 Interview with Zulawski, *Eyeball* No 5.
5 ibid.
6 This being the result of a French law at the time of *Possession*'s release, which meant that the screening of a foreign-language picture had to be met with the screening of a French language print on another screen, elsewhere in the country.
7 Also known as *The Lorelei's Grasp*.

Pranks

1 *Fangoria* No 17.
2 It does seem as if the film-makers originally intended a lot of gore in *Pranks*. "The effects are almost the most important part of this film," Obrow told *Fangoria*. When New Image Releasing picked up the film for distribution in the US, they did so on the understanding that cuts may be necessary, "because the effects are so very strong, and because it's so very realistic." Of course, Obrow may have simply been trying to generate interest prior to the release of the film.

Revenge of the Bogey Man

1 The British print looks to contain the original credits, being written in dripping 'blood' on a series of title cards (modified credits of this era usually appear over a freeze-frame or on a plain background insert). Fingertips holding the cards fall into shot with alarming regularity. In America, the film was also known as *Boogeyman II*.

2 It's a name that crops up in other Lommel films. *The Devonsville Terror*, a film Lommel directed the same year as *Revenge of the Bogeyman* (and quite possibly back-to-back with it) is sometimes credited to Starr.

3 Review of *Double Jeopardy* (under its US title, *A Taste of Sin*), Donald Farmer, *The Splatter Times* No 4.

4 Some sources credit *Revenge of the Bogeyman* as being made in 1980. However, the reference to de Palma's *Blow Out* – a film made in 1981 – contradicts this.

5 None according to the critic in *Fangoria* (No 31), who claims that the dialogue in *Revenge of the Bogeyman* "is so off-the-beam that the actors seem like they are reciting words learned phonetically without any knowledge of what they mean."

6 The blurb on the video jacket even states as much: "There's black humour all the way to the graveyard ending which is strongly reminiscent of de Palma's *Carrie*."

7 The girl who stabs herself in the bathroom is shown lifting the scissors to her throat. But the point of entry is removed and the next we see, she is falling over, the scissors sticking out of her neck. A sequence where a man gets a knife driven out his mouth while in a car is similarly truncated.

Shogun Assassin

1 The third film in the *Baby Cart* series (*Lightning Swords of Death*) sees Lone Wolf face an entire army and reveals the cart to be fitted with primitive machine guns. It's a ridiculous moment.

2 The films exist under a multitude of different titles, thanks to reference works citing anglicised translations of the original Japanese titles.

3 For more information concerning *Shogun Assassin*, the original Japanese film series and the manga comic that inspired it, see *Asian Trash Cinema* Vol 1 No 2, No 5 and No 6.

The Slayer

1 Actually Tybee Island, off the coast of Georgia.

2 Not to mention one of the more poetic – Brooke makes it to a window and dies in its frame, with the rain falling.

3 In the cut version, all visual references to the woman being stabbed with the fork are gone. As Brooke struggles to exit the boarded window, the pitchfork is seen looming closer. With a close-up of Brooke's hand on the window frame, bleeding from the broken glass, the scene cuts to the pitchfork. Cut back to hand, relaxing in death. Cut to Brooke's face, blood coming out of her mouth (and a very noticeable jump in the musical soundtrack). Cut to the following day.

Snuff

1 Antonio Climati and Mario Morra's *Savage Man... Savage Beast*, a big hit in Times Square and pre-dating *Snuff* by several months, was a Mondo film that featured dubious home cine footage of a man being eaten alive by lions in a safari park. Scenarios like this were incorporated into Mondo films spanning two decades, and surreptitiously passed off as actual fatalities.

2 See Kerekes & Slater's *Killing For Culture* for the full story.

3 The Findlays were no strangers to exploitation. Prior to *Slaughter*, they had made low-budget efforts like *Body of a Female*, *The Sin Syndicate*, and *Ultimate Degenerate*.

4 These figures have been contradicted several times by Findlay herself. She

Notes

told *Fangoria* (No 52) in 1986 that the shoot lasted three months and the budget was $50,000 (even though she didn't get paid and they were able to hire a bus and driver to carry their "large crew" for "about 30¢ a day"). Given the look of the film, and – by Roberta's admission – the gung-ho approach when making it, it's impossible to believe it might have taken three straight months to shoot.

5 Others included Frank Howard's *The Other Side of Madness*, David Durston's *I Drink your Blood*, Lee Madden's *The Night God Screamed*, and Ray Danton's *The Deathmaster*. Al Adamson's *Angels Wild Women* features a cult and a girl-biker gang, and has the distinction of being the last film to be shot at the Spahn ranch – the home of the Family at the time of Manson's arrest. It also had actual Family members as extras. There were also Family inspired porn loops. For more, see *Killing For Culture*.

6 Roberta Findlay, in conversation with the French magazine *Mad Movies* (issue number unknown), defended the film by calling it an "impressionist" movie. In another interview, she dismissed it as making no sense.

7 Shackleton, previously employed as a research engineer and consultant to the Department of Defence, started The Monarch Releasing Corp in 1969 (under the name of A L Shackleton Films). His catalogue generally comprised of watered-down X-rated sex films, but in the mid seventies he experimented with other genres, acquiring the rock concert film *Get Down, Grand Funk*, Arch Oboler's 3-D sci-fi movie *Fantastic Invasion of Planet Earth*, and the Findlays' *Slaughter*.

8 *CCVL* No 2.

9 The FBI launched an investigation following the allegation made by the National Decency Reporter but were unable to uncover any further information pertaining to the films mentioned in the piece.

10 Shackleton was involved with another porn director, Chuck Vincent. He supposedly produced Vincent's first adult picture in 1973 (*Blue Summer*) and announced that Vincent was set to direct for Monarch in 1975 a film called *Vanilla Odyssey* – "a sexy sci-fi comedy about a lovable visitor from outer space."

11 Liam T Sanford, *Video Viewer*, July 1983.

12 "Everywhere had a copy of *Snuff*," recalls Steve Ellison. When pressed who might have been distributing the film, he replied "It was on the Astra label... I'm not sure who was the head honcho at Astra [Mike Behr, by all accounts] – that was always kept a little bit secret. But some of the big players in the early days were incredible characters, and if you could get hold of some of them now... if they're not at the bottom of a river or whatever..."

SS Experiment Camp

1 *Le Amanti del mostro* and *La Mano che nutre la morte*.

2 Sources say became either the owner of a pizzeria or a jeweller.

3 *Shock Xpress* Vol 2 No 3.

4 At least this is the case with the English language print.

Tenebrae

1 Goblin's slapstick zombie tune from Romero's *Dawn of the Dead* makes an appearance here in *Tenebrae*, the muzak playing in a store at the beginning of the film.

2 Ronny Svensson in Fantasy Film Memory's *Directed By Dario Argento*.

3 Dario Argento interview, *Spaghetti Nightmares*, Palmerini & Mistretta.

4 *Halls of Horror* No 23.
5 These early films being *The Bird with the Crystal Plumage*, *Cat O'Nine Tails* and *Four Flies on Grey Velvet*.
6 The title can also be interpreted as a reference to the matins and lauds of Holy Week in which candles are extinguished.

Terror Eyes

1 Prof Millett looks ill at ease spreading the preserve over his lover's body, particularly as the further down he goes the more it begins to look like heavy menstrual discharge.

The Toolbox Murders

1 Cheesy easy listening music plays throughout the film's first half-hour, courtesy of a radio in the room of each victim, or, in one case, a record player. A nice touch is when the record player, left unchecked, begins to start playing over again as the killer leaves.
2 An anecdote told by David Konow in his book *Schlock-O-Rama*.
3 Courtesy of the Pamelyn Ferdin Web Page Fan Mail.

Unhinged

1 Barnes' presence flagrantly contradicts Edith's statement that no man is allowed in the house.
2 *Unhinged* beat *Psycho II* into the cinemas by a few months, which may have been fortuitous or a bid to jump on the bandwagon.
3 Like the heavy breathing she later encounters, the location of the muted radio playing during these opening minutes isn't clear. It appears to be emanating from Terry's apartment – even when she has left it. When her friends arrive to collect her in their car it appears to be emanating from this, too.

Visiting Hours

1 A brief cycle of films influenced by Michael Crichton's *Coma*.
2 Another thing that disappears: Reporter Deborah Ballin is a key character who owes her life to a man seen early in the film, but he is never referred to and his identity remains a mystery.
3 A Nurse Sheila has the curious habit of directly addressing the camera in several dialogues with Deborah. No other character in the film does this.
4 Where would a hospital drama be without a few curtains being ripped off their rails? *Visiting Hours* keeps them all until the end.
5 Snapshots of homicide victims featured in another 'nasty' made the same year, Gary Sherman's *Dead & Buried* – which happens to have a scene where a nurse kills a patient in a hospital.

The Werewolf and the Yeti

1 Paul Naschy, interviewed by José Luis González and Michael Secula, *Videooze* No 6/7.
2 Michael Secula, *Videooze* No 6/7.
3 As stated, Naschy's films often turned up on the export market with specially shot, gorier scenes – material that couldn't be shown in his homeland. The US zine *Demonique* (No 1) ran a review of *The Werewolf and the Yeti* in 1980 and said of the climactic battle: "Until now, the violence and gore was well-handled and restrained, so it is both good and bad that some explicit, bloody scenes take place at this point in the narrative." Should this be true, it would suggest that the print released in Britain was the tamer version intended for the Spanish market as it contains nothing approximating "explicit, bloody scenes."
4 *Absurd* No 3.

Notes

The Witch who Came From the Sea

1 Zadora returned for a starring role in Cimber's next picture, *Fake-Out*, a remake of his own *Lady Cocoa*.
2 Turan & Zito, *Sinema*.
3 If it isn't influenced by Carlino's movie, then Cimber chose to do an unofficial adaptation of the same book (by Yukio Mishima) on which Carlino's movie was based.

Women Behind Bars

1 According to *Video Watchdog* (No 1), the original title is *Un Secondina in un carcere femminila* (trans. 'Wardeness at a Women's Prison'). *Visa pour mourir* – the French release title – is said to not only feature extra footage of the robbers, but also a "slightly different Daniel White score."
2 *Condemned*, *The Big House*, *The Criminal Code*, *I Am a Fugitive From a Chain Gang*, *Escape From Devil's Island*, *Jailbreak*, *Alcatraz Island*, and *Convicted* are just some of the prison films released by major studios at the dawn of the Talkies era. Some recent entries include *Penitentiary III*, *Lock Up*, *Against the Wall* and *Dead Man Walking*. James Robert Parish, in his book *Prison Pictures from Hollywood*, lists close on 300 American movies alone in which prison plays an integral part.
3 A hierarchy of stereotyped characters which, Jim Morton points out in his essay for *RE/Search #10: Incredibly Strange Films*, consists of "The Queen Bee: dominant female prisoner who lords it over the others. The New Fish: usually the lead actress, in jail for the first time. The Sadistic Warden: more often than not the one who proves to be the root of all evil and unrest in prison. The Hooker with the Heart of Gold: a street-smart dame who knows the ropes and befriends the New Fish, for better or worse. The Dyke Guard: sometimes named 'Ruby'..."
4 One scene that does make something of a 'subliminal' impact is the curiously framed head and breast shot. Completely forced and unnatural, it looks almost like one of Ingres' nudes. A similarly staged shot is utilised in another of Franco's WIP film, *Women For Cellblock Nine*. Graf Haufen, in his review for *Film Extremes* (No 1), says of the sequence (in which a prisoner on the run has a bullet removed with some grass!): "There is an unintentionally funny moment during the operation, where a single breast is dangling in the picture, right next to the face of the wounded girl. Is there a hidden message in this poetic moment?"
5 Each film is known by several alternate titles. To make matters more confusing, *Women For Cellblock Nine* has a character called Milton and another called Maria (who, crying for water, is forced to perform cunnilingus on the female warden, then given salted champagne to drink).

Xtro

1 *Fangoria* No 19.
2 Two working titles for *Xtro* were *Monstromo* and *Monstro*, which have a certain resonance with the name of the mother ship in *Alien* – *Nostromo*.
3 *Fangoria* No 24.
4 The PolyGram Video release of *Xtro* also carries a couple of names for characters who don't appear in the film.
5 *Monthly Film Bulletin*.
6 *Flesh & Blood* No 7.
7 *Starburst* No 57 – a review that carries a publicity still which some *Starburst* office wag has doctored: what should be Sam sucking on his son's distended

shoulder has been altered to show Sam sucking on what looks uncannily like an erect penis.

8 *The Dark Side* No 81.

Zombie Creeping Flesh

1 The living dead oeuvre reached bottom with Umberto Lenzi's *Nightmare City*, A M Frank's *Oasis of the Zombies* and Jean Rollin's *Zombie Lake*.

2 Established in the precursor to *Dawn of the Dead* and the first of Romero's *Dead* trilogy: *Night of the Living Dead*.

3 Mattei used various pseudonyms in his career, such as Jordan B Matthews, Jimmy Matheus and Stefan Oblowsky. Although he would credit himself as Vincent Dawn on several productions, *Zombie Creeping Flesh* was the first instance in which he utilised this particular name.

4 *European Trash Cinema* Vol 2 No 5.

5 Other films by Bruno Mattei released in Britain include *SS Girls* (Naziploitation), *The Other Hell* (nunsploitation), *Rats: Night of Terror* (horror), *Strike Commando* (action) and *The Seven Magnificent Gladiators* (sword-and-sorcery).

7 As was common in the days before the multiplex, cinemas in some smaller towns didn't always have official posters to promote the films they were screening and, as a rough-and-ready alternative, often made their own. Sometimes the impromptu posters comprised only plain text – say, a black marker pen on a brightly coloured sheet of paper; other times a member of staff with an artistic bent might include a picture of a zombie with fangs – as happened with *Zombie Creeping Flesh* on its run at one long-gone cinema in the north.

Zombie Flesh Eaters

1 In his review for *Imaginator* No 6, Ken Miller pondered whether the shark bitten by the zombie would "become an undead shark?"

2 Sometime in the early nineties, the scene was broadcast uncut on British cable TV as part of Ken Dixon's undead compilation movie, *Zombiethon*.

3 *Absurd*, *Blood Feast*, *Blood Rites*, *The Bogey Man*, *Cannibal Ferox*, *Dead & Buried*, *Forest of Fear*, *Frozen Scream* and *Night of the Bloody Apes*.

4 *European Trash Cinema* Vol 2 No 4.

5 Randall Larson, *CineFan* No 3.

6 Interview with Lucio Fulci by Robert Schlockoff, *Starburst* No 48.

7 BBFC press statement.

Index

INDEX

Index

Index

Index

Index

Index